FRONTIERS OF FINANCIAL MANAGEMENT

Frontiers of Financial Management

SELECTED READINGS

WILLIAM J. SERRAINO
Chairman, Department of Finance
Miami University
Oxford, Ohio

SURENDRA S. SINGHVI
Financial Planning and Analysis
Armco Steel Corporation
and
Adjunct Associate Professor of Finance
Miami University
Oxford, Ohio

ROBERT M. SOLDOFSKY
Professor of Finance
University of Iowa
Iowa City, Iowa

Published by

F25 **SOUTH-WESTERN PUBLISHING CO.**

Cincinnati   Chicago   Dallas   New Rochelle, N.Y.   Burlingame, Calif.   Brighton, England

Standard Book Number: 0-538-06250-9

Library of Congress Catalog Card Number: 79-129060

1 2 3 4 5 K 5 4 3 2 1

Printed in the United States of America

PREFACE

In this collection of 34 articles on financial management, the authors set up three major criteria to be used in article selection. These prerequisite criteria were a managerial point of view, a concern for real and relevant problems that continue to face financial and other top-level executives, and the judicious introduction of newer approaches to the subject, including new models or techniques that are very likely to come into greater use during the 1970's and beyond. Even though many of the selected articles are at the "frontiers of financial management," none includes mathematical or statistical techniques above the level of training received in undergraduate business schools or by first year graduate students in business.

A fourth criterion was balance in the topics selected so that one or two articles could be assigned each week, along with regular textbook material. The 34 articles are grouped under ten different headings. The first part, Perspectives in Financial Management, sets the general tone for this collection. The history and outlook of financial management as an academic discipline and as a central business activity are discussed. The next six parts, from Capital Budgeting through Financial Side of Mergers and Acquisitions, were included in financial management textbooks written in the 1960's.

Part VIII includes three of the newer approaches or developments in financial management. Some financial management texts give more coverage to accounting problems than others, but the three items in Part IX, Financial Impact of Accounting Practices, Principles, and Disclosure will serve as useful, dramatic supplements to any textbook. The three articles in Part X should serve as a broad introduction to international financial management, a topic of increasing importance to American business.

The articles may be categorized in terms of the position or experience of their authors; the use of models, surveys, or relevant experience; and the number of sources from which they are drawn. Many of the articles or their authors do not fall neatly into these groupings. Eleven of the items were prepared by authors whose primary employment was not academic. Three articles were prepared by five men working for consulting firms; another three articles were prepared by officers at leading commercial banks, and two were prepared by staff researchers of business magazines. Other authors worked for the Federal Reserve Bank of New York, Haskins and Sells (certified public accountants), and International Minerals and Chemical Corporation.

Eight of the articles introduce models or equations of varying degrees of complexity. These include simulation and decision trees for capital budgeting, the Markowitz approach to portfolio planning, a normative equation for dividend policy, a control limit model for cash management, a probalistic model for credit sales, utility curves, and probalistic applications of breakeven charts. Seven articles report and utilize surveys and personal interviews in their development of a topic. Some of the academicians and professional financial economists discuss topics that they have studied carefully in a theoretical and/or practical setting. In one article academicians and financial executives discuss face-to-face the meaning of uncertainty implicit in discount rates. The 34 articles are drawn from 20 different sources. Only the *Financial Executive, Journal of Finance, Harvard Business Review*, and *Accounting Review* are represented more than once.

Some of the areas or topics covered, in addition to the growing use of models, simulations, and other quantitative techniques, will be of great importance for years to come. During the late 1960's, bonds were issued at historically high interest rates for the United States. Decisions to refund bonds (Article 15) will be faced more frequently in coming years. Inflation and its effects on financing are omitted for almost all finance textbooks but are major considerations for businesses of all sizes (Article 21). As multinational business becomes more widespread overseas, reinvestment decisions will have to be made by more people (Article 33). Substantive information such as that needed to bargain with lenders about the terms of direct placements (Article 17), to design a convertible preferred stock (Article 18), or to prepare financial releases will be of continuing use to financial managers themselves.

The number of articles included in this collection is limited for obvious and realistic reasons. We hope that the collection will help to enrich, widen, and deepen undergraduate courses in financial administration. This volume should be especially useful at the graduate level because of its coverage and decision-making orientation.

W. J. S.

S. S. S.

R. M. S.

TABLE OF CONTENTS

PART V.   LONG-TERM FINANCING

Article   **Page**

PART VI.   WORKING CAPITAL MANAGEMENT

PART VII.   FINANCIAL SIDE OF MERGERS AND ACQUISITIONS

PART VIII.   NEW APPROACHES TO FINANCIAL ANALYSIS

PART IX. FINANCIAL IMPACT OF ACCOUNTING PRACTICES, PRINCIPLES, AND DISCLOSURE

Article **Page**

PART X. INTERNATIONAL FINANCIAL MANAGEMENT

ABOUT THE AUTHORS*

Robert W. Ackerman—Harbridge House, Inc., an international consulting firm, Boston, Massachusetts.

Robert N. Anthony—Professor of Business Administration, Harvard University.

Elliott L. Atamian—Professor of Business Administration, Boston University.

Harold Bierman, Jr.—Professor of Accounting and Managerial Economics, Cornell University.

Ernest Bloch—formerly, Federal Reserve Bank of New York; presently, Charles W. Gertenberg Professor of Finance, New York University School of Commerce.

Oswald D. Bowlin—Professor of Finance, Texas Technological College.

Harold Burson—President of Burson Marsteller Associates, director and executive committee member of Marsteller, Inc., and president of Marsteller International S. A., New York City.

John F. Childs—Vice President, Irving Trust Company.

P. Michael Davis—Assistant Professor of Accounting at the University of Southern Mississippi.

Gordon Donaldson—Professor of Business Administration, Graduate School of Business, Harvard University.

Lionel L. Fray—A principal in the General Management Group at Harbridge House, Inc., an international consulting firm, Boston, Massachusetts.

David B. Hertz—Director, McKinsey and Company.

Robert K. Jaedicke—Professor of Accounting, Graduate School of Business, Stanford University.

Roderic C. Lancey—Corporate Planner, International Minerals and Chemical Corporation, Skokie, Illinois.

Carol J. Loomis—Research Analyst, *Fortune*.

Robert M. Mautz—Professor of Accounting, Graduate School of Business, University of Illinois.

---

*The position of some of the authors has changed since the date of their articles. The present position is given where it is known to the editors.

Anthony H. Meyer—Vice President in charge of Counseling Department, Irving Trust Company.

Merton H. Miller—Edward Eagle Brown Professor of Finance and Economics, University of Chicago.

Robert D. Niemeyer—Manager, Management Advisory Services, Haskins and Sells, Certified Public Accountants.

Daniel Orr—Professor of Economics, University of California at La Jolla.

Alexander A. Robichek—Professor of Business Administration, Graduate School of Business, Stanford University.

Surendra S. Singhvi—Associate Professor of Finance, School of Business Administration, Miami University, Oxford, Ohio.

Donald J. Smalter—Corporate Director of Strategic Planning, International Minerals and Chemical Corporation, Skokie, Illinois.

Robert M. Soldofsky—Professor of Finance, University of Iowa.

Ezra Solomon—Dean Witter Professor of Finance, Graduate School of Business, Stanford University.

Stephen H. Sosnick—Professor of Agricultural Economics, University of California—Davis.

Richard A. Stevenson—Associate Professor of Finance, University of Iowa.

William G. Stott—Executive Vice President, Morgan Guaranty Trust Company of New York.

Ralph O. Swalm—Professor of Industrial Engineering at Syracuse University; also Director of the Engineering Economy Division of the American Institute of Industrial Engineers.

James C. Van Horne—Associate Professor of Finance, Graduate School of Business, Stanford University.

James E. Walter—Professor of Finance at the University of Pennsylvania.

Merwin H. Waterman—Professor of Finance, Graduate School of Business Administration, University of Michigan.

F. K. Wright—Department of Commerce, University of Adelaide, South Australia.

David B. Zenoff—Assistant Professor of International Business, Graduate School of Business, Columbia University.

PART I. PERSPECTIVES IN FINANCIAL MANAGEMENT

Since its appearance as a separate branch of institutional economics around the turn of the century, the finance function has changed in both its academic definition and in its practical application. Historically, it has been preoccupied with the procurement of funds, but there has been an evolutionary change toward a broader definition emphasizing the effective utilization of funds. The problems that were emphasized in each era reflected the political, economic, and social preoccupations of the period. For example, the interest in bankruptcy and reorganization in the 1930's and 1940's reflected the Great Depression and its aftermath. The present development and increasing use of statistical and mathematical analysis in many areas of business, government, science, and human concern are the results of such profound movements as the growth in educational levels, new theoretical developments, increases in population and wealth, and the impact of computer technology. The articles in this section provide a proper perspective in financial management.

Professor Gordon Donaldson examines various facets of corporate financial management in an affluent society. Financial management should be viewed in light of a gradual decline in the relative importance of financial resources as a factor in management decisions. The trend toward this gradual decline can be exemplified by unused financial resources that are only partially indicated on accounting statements, by the shift in emphasis from the raising of funds for corporate use to the management of corporate funds available, and by the investment of short-term funds, which tends to reduce the importance of bank relations. Other recent movements in financial management, caused by the declining rates of growth in the domestic market, are diversification of the firm's activities and investment in world markets.

Donaldson suggests five aspects of financial management to be considered in view of these recent trends. These aspects are: (1) research by institutions and schools of business administration into the character and evolution of financial management in the affluent corporation; (2) training and recruitment of potential financial managers with emphasis on a broader background; (3) education for a financial career, including on-the-job experience; (4) development of professional expertise in the new techniques of handling scarce resources within the firm; and (5) reexamination by top management of the role of the financial viewpoint at the board level.

1

Professor Ezra Solomon's paper discusses recent trends and developments in academic and professional thinking on the subject of financial management. He observes that a growing analytical content that started to develop in the 1950's is displacing the traditional descriptive treatment as the center of emphasis in the field of business finance. He traces the evolution of the finance field from the turn of the century to the present time and discusses the implications of this evolution. Solomon distinguishes very lucidly between the traditional approach, which still dominates the field in a numerical sense, and the analytical approach, which is taking over. The traditional approach to finance represents a body of descriptive knowledge and a branch of institutional economics, and it is largely concerned with the process of raising funds and with the liability side of the balance sheet. The newer approach is more a way of thinking and an extension of the micro-economic theory of the firm; it is largely concerned with the optimal usage of funds and with the asset side of the balance sheet. In brief, the old question in finance was, How should a firm raise funds? The new question in finance is, How should a firm make decisions to commit funds for specific purposes and set standards against which it can assay the use of funds? The rapid changes in the field of finance have tremendous significance for investment, money and banking, and international business finance. Therefore, the student of finance must be prepared to enter a discipline which is increasingly analytical and international and which is rapidly changing in scope.

The recent developments in financial management, especially the change in the emphasis from the raising of funds to a broader objective of optimal usage of funds, is demonstrated by both Donaldson and Solomon. They also agree about the trends involving international considerations for investments and the belief that standards and defensible methods should be established for financial decisions. However, Donaldson and Solomon disagree concerning the relative importance of financial resources as a factor in management decisions. Donaldson emphasizes that the necessity of obtaining outside financial resources is declining. Solomon stresses the importance of efficiency measurements in the management of funds. The key points made in these articles are that the finance function is changing and a student of business must understand these changes.

1. FINANCIAL MANAGEMENT IN AN AFFLUENT SOCIETY*

GORDON DONALDSON†

If one could observe a direction of movement in financial affairs—a gradual evolution having apparent characteristics—what would that movement be? And if there is such movement, what is its significance for financial management today?

My answer to these questions is this: corporations in the United States are beginning to experience a long-term decline in the relative importance of financial resources as a factor in management decisions and a consequent decline in the importance attached to the financial viewpoint in top management circles. If this is true, it will have profound significance for the professional financial manager before this century is over.

It is generally acknowledged that the pressure to increase the output of tangible goods produced by private enterprise declines as an economy matures. Even though the production of material goods requiring heavy capital investment has not reached the saturation point, a shift is apparent: there is increasing demand for services rather than goods; there is increasing government expenditure for war and welfare; there is increasing substitution of leisure for income-generating work. A slowing of the growth rate in material output is apparent. The label which I used in my title—the "affluent society"—is appropriate. It indicates how our resources are being allocated.

This country has not had a major economic depression in the past 25 years. Consequently, the growth rate is a measure of what we can produce and consume during a period of sustained high employment and productivity. Economists generally agree that a recurrence of the decline of the Thirties is highly unlikely. Therefore, in the absence of a major war, it is unlikely that we will have a significant pause in the pressure of production on consumption.

These conditions are becoming apparent in the experience of individual corporations. An increasing number of businesses are finding difficulty in achieving the growth rates of the past within traditional markets and product lines. Target rates of return on investments have come under increasing pressure, and profitability, while growing in absolute terms, looks increasingly unattractive when compared with growth industries or growth economies. In some industries the heightened competition for growth has led to mergers, but an increasingly hostile federal regulatory system has placed serious limits on the capacity to grow at a competitor's expense.

---

*From *Financial Executive* (April, 1967), pp. 52-60. Reprinted by permission.
†Professor of Business Administration, Graduate School of Business, Harvard University.

IMPACT ON FINANCIAL MANAGEMENT

Looking more specifically at trends in financial management, we can observe the phenomenon of the mature corporation whose growth can be comfortably handled for years by its own sources with only occasional assistance from a lending institution. Unused capital is only partially indicated by rising cash balances and marketable securities portfolios. Undisclosed on the financial statement are the unused external sources: unused short- and long-term debt capacity, unused leasing opportunities, unused equity money. How many corporate treasurers spend many hours each year politely turning away the representatives of commercial and investment bankers seeking outlets for their funds?

If these comments sound out of place when everyone is talking of tight money, let me remind you that I speak of long-term trends and not of year-to-year events. Even if a trend is apparent, actual conditions will fluctuate around that trend and the short-run experience may not provide supporting evidence.

Further evidence of changing conditions can be observed in the nature of the problems which have concerned financial managers in the last decade or two. My reading of the professional and academic literature and, more significantly, my observation of the content of various professional meetings lead me to conclude that there is a major shift in emphasis from the raising of funds for corporate use to the management of corporate funds already available. In other words, attention has shifted from the right-hand side of the balance sheet to the left-hand side.

If one were to select that topic of finance which has shown the greatest advance in management technique, the answer would surely have to be capital budgeting. A great change has taken place in the methods by which we approach the ranking of investment alternatives. Finding no great problem in getting adequate funds, the financial manager is free to work for greater efficiency in selecting and exploiting his investment opportunities. Significantly, the companies which have applied sophisticated capital budgeting techniques to the greatest extent are the large, mature corporations.

Another topic which has had more than its share of attention at professional meetings in the post World War II period is the management of cash balances. Increasing corporate affluence means money in the bank; treasurers have suddenly found themselves managers of substantial short-term portfolios. The opportunity to make 4 or 5 percent on otherwise idle funds has turned attention to ways of minimizing bank balances. As a result, commercial banks have been confronted with a substantial shrinkage of the corporate balances which form an important part of their investment base. Evidence of the seriousness of this phenomenon is seen in the appearance of the certificate of deposit by which banks have sought to redirect corporate funds back into the banking system. The aggressiveness with which some companies have squeezed bank balances is indicative of decreased reliance on banks as a potential source of short-term capital.

Some experts in the field say this is a temporary phenomenon, and the current evidence of high corporate liquidity will not last indefinitely. Maybe so. I do not pretend to know the future, but I am convinced that for some major businesses the phenomenon of a capital supply which exceeds realizable investment opportunities will be part of their experience as long as they remain efficient and make profits. Theorists have always rejected this possibility, arguing that the basic scarcity of resources and the unlimited supply of investment opportunities would prevent it. I am convinced, however, that the practical limits on investment opportunity for any given business entity over any given planning period are much more severe than theory ever imagined. I do not have the space to elaborate on this point.

EFFORTS TO RESTORE GROWTH TRENDS

Faced with declining rates of growth, aggressively managed companies have not stood idle. I have already mentioned the acquisition route, a path which many have followed within their own industry. Depending on existing size, share of the market, foresight, and so forth, some companies have gone a long way by this means. Sooner or later, however, the company's natural desire to grow is confronted with government's concept of reasonable competition and each new percentage point increase in share of the market becomes more difficult to achieve.

These obstacles to growth may then be outflanked by diversification into different industries through mergers and acquisitions. There are an increasing number of corporate conglomerates, some of which are more and more difficult to distinguish from an investment fund. Diversification may be an end in itself, but it may also be a second-best alternative to expansion in the company's own industry. We have not yet faced up to the effect on our economy of this by-product of anti-trust action.

Many companies have turned to other countries for an opportunity to expand. Growth potential and profit opportunities in emerging world markets have been so promising that the high risks associated with operation abroad have been taken on with enthusiasm. It is only natural for industry in an established economy to turn outward toward the obvious need for industry in less mature economies. This has been the historical pattern. It is also an historical fact, however, that when business crosses national boundaries the road can become rocky indeed. Many companies have already found that to follow such a road successfully requires much more than a hunger for growth and an appetite for higher profits. Often, I am afraid, diversification at home and investment abroad are prompted by a desire to escape the problems and frustrations of the principal domestic operation. The results are sometimes less than what is expected.

Whether the continuing trend of nationalism in the world will permit the mature Western economies to break into major, new, long-term growth opportunities remains to be seen. This growth will not come suddenly and unimpeded and will inevitably be uneven in its effects on the segments of our economy to be released from domestic market limitations.

DECLINE OF TREASURY FUNCTION

So I conclude that although our economy may be able to create renewed pressures on our capital resources, there is the distinct possibility that for the indefinite future we may be faced with an increasing number of affluent corporations with more financial resources than opportunities for their employment. Whether you accept my view of the affluent corporation as real or regard it as imaginary, I ask you to think through with me what the long-term consequences of this would be for the financial management of such a business.

One of the consequences is the effect on the organization of the financial function. A gradual decline of the treasury function in many corporations is already apparent. Considering that the traditional role of treasury was to maintain contact with external sources of funds, the reduction or elimination of need for that contact would naturally lead to decreased involvement of the treasury representatives in top management decisions. A secondary treasury function, the role of custodian of liquid resources, even though increasing in importance, does not require continuous top level review.

To illustrate what I refer to as the decline of the treasury function in management, I picked at random a company which I knew had been in business for many years and checked the composition of its officer group at intervals of 20 years. In 1925, the company had four officers: the chairman of the board, the president, the vice-president and treasurer, and the secretary. Twenty years later it had ten officers: in addition to the officers named in the earlier study, five vice-presidents and a controller had emerged. Twenty years later (in 1965), a new layer had emerged, separating the treasury function from the president with the addition of an executive vice-president, a senior vice-president, five new vice-presidents, and a general counsel.

Obviously, growth had much to do with the increase in the size of the officer group. But also apparent is a substantial dilution of financial influence with many more contending viewpoints, including a second financial viewpoint in the form of the controller. This is consistent with a decline in the critical importance of financial resources and a concurrent increase in the critical importance of other resources to which I will refer later.

The position of financial management in organizational structure has developed in three stages:

1. In the first stage the offices of president and treasurer were essentially one. It was a New England tradition to call the chief executive officer president and treasurer. This made sense when scarcity of capital was so critical it dominated every major decision.

2. The second stage existed (and still exists for many companies) when the treasurer was on a par with several vice-presidents representing other resource viewpoints on policy matters.
3. The third stage, which seems to be emerging now, is apparent in the position of vice-president-finance, who has under him the functions of controller and treasurer.

RISE OF THE CONTROLLER

Another major organizational trend is the rise of the controller in management councils. This is undoubtedly due in part to the enormous amount of information, communication, and control needed in large-scale enterprises. More importantly, it reflects the shift of emphasis from effectiveness in getting funds to efficiency in using funds, with all the problems of information flow and analysis which that entails. In this area the controller is the man with the information and, presumably, the capacity to interpret it.

Some would argue that the rising importance of management of internal funds assures a permanent role for the financial viewpoint in top management even though the getting of funds may be less important now. The question is how permanent is this condition? I wonder whether the attention given to information and control is due more to its complexity than to its importance in top policy decisions. It seems to me possible that, in time (and I won't try to predict how long), the determination of criteria of financial performance and the evaluation of the data related to these criteria will improve, and, with the aid of sophisticated data processing techniques, the present justification for a major input of top management time may be greatly reduced. In other words, when the capacity to measure financial performance catches up with the growth of complex business organizations, there will be less need for the chief executive to have a financial expert constantly at his elbow.

With increasing abundance of financial resources in corporations, the pressure to watch every dollar and measure its performance with the greatest care is reduced. It would be heresy to suggest that business will one day cease to be concerned about profits. The obligation to shareholders and to property values will continue to urge management to use financial resources efficiently. But, significantly, economic theory nowadays talks about optimizing profit rather than maximizing profit, implying some trade-off with non-profit corporate objectives.

In this context I suggest to you a major problem shaping up for the controllers and treasurers of the future. The problem already exists for some companies today. It is this: *how to maintain the effectiveness of performance criteria based on a concept of scarcity when that scarcity no longer exists and how to get management to play the game by rules of artificial scarcity rather than real scarcity.* For example, companies continue to adhere to targets of, say, a 15 percent growth rate when experience records 10 percent or less. Companies continue to set 20 percent ROI hurdles for investment decisions when a realistic appraisal of performance shows 12 or 10 percent. Does management really perform against these targets or does it go through a budgetary masquerade for the sake of corporate self-esteem?

REEVALUATING RESOURCE PRIORITIES

What some companies are going through is a reevaluation of resource priorities. In a linear programming sense, the constraints on management action are several, not just one, and other resource constraints appear to be taking over the priority position long held by capital. Other key resources— organizational and managerial capacity, manpower, and technology—may well be the controlling resources in the future. If this happens, what will the organizational chart look like 25 years from now? It will tend, I think, to reflect in these other areas of management responsibility the same emphasis on acquisition and efficient use of the resource that has character- ized financial resources up to this point. It will tend to change management priorities. It may even mean that the financial officer will ultimately disappear at the executive level next to the president, being succeeded by those responsible for manpower or technology.

These trends also have implications for the composition of boards of directors.

It has been a tradition in many boards to include in their membership a commercial banker and/or an investment banker. While businesses were heavily and continuously involved in the money markets, this made sense from both the external and the internal viewpoint. I question whether this will continue in the future for the reasons I have already emphasized.

I suspect that the boards of the future will have fewer representatives of commercial and investment bankers unless the role they have played in the past changes radically—which is possible, for change is occurring there, too. But as of now, it becomes less and less necessary that the financial viewpoint on the board be that of the suppliers of external funds.

CHANGING ASPECTS OF FINANCIAL MANAGEMENT

Now let me retreat somewhat from my more extreme predictions and come closer to reality by suggesting what long-range trends may have to say about the practice of financial management in the present decade. If there is a gradual decline in the importance of capital relative to other resources, I suggest five aspects of financial management which should be examined in the light of this possibility:

1. My first suggestion is for research by institutes and schools of business administration on the character and evolution of finan- cial management in the affluent corporation. By the "affluent

corporation" I mean the business which has for all practical purposes ceased to use the capital markets for new equity funds, which uses debt capacity only spasmodically and not to the limit of availability, and which has ample liquid reserves on hand. We need information on how abundance affects the criteria which were founded on the concept of scarcity and on which decisions are based. I have already cited the example of investment standards out of line with real opportunities. We need information on what this does to the role of the financial officer in the organization vis-a-vis other resource centers. We need information on possible changes in organizational structure.

2. My second suggestion has to do with the training and recruitment of potential financial managers. I believe the financial manager of the future must be a much broader person, in a professional sense, than he has had to be in the past. The avenue to positions of importance in the past has been via professional education and training in accounting, banking, investment banking, and corporate finance. The language of the ledger may not be sufficient in the future to communicate and operate across the borders of finance and other resource areas. While in the past the controller or financial manager could live out his career within the familiar confines of his narrow specialty, he will find it more difficult in the future affluent corporation. If I were advising my son on preparation for a career in finance, I would recommend that he be bilingual right from the start and combine an education in finance with an education in, say, engineering or law. A finance man is likely to have to be more than a finance man to reach top management levels in the future.

3. A suggestion related to my comments on education for a financial career concerns on-the-job experience. I find more and more that my financial friends in business corporations are being rotated through non-financial operating positions as they move up in the organization. This is in line with my observations on trends in finance. I think that it makes good sense to get exposure to problems of general management. Such experience should greatly improve the financial manager's ability to deal with what modern jargon would call the "interface" between finance and other areas of management. Some of these men may be lost to finance as they show their skill in operations, but some will return to controllership or treasury, and they will be better members of the top management team because of their experience.

4. As limitations of the new areas of resources—manpower, technology, research, organization—emerge, whatever benefit that can be derived from the financial manager's expertise in the handling of scarce resources is needed. Is transfer possible here? What financial skills are being used by financial men who move off into nonfinancial management positions? One area where such transfer is taking place is the capital budgeting area which brings finance, accounting, production, and technology together for the joint solution of a key problem. Perhaps some thinking about how control systems developed for financial purposes might be adapted to other resources would be useful.

5. Finally, to come back to the board of directors, I suggest that top management should reexamine the role of the financial viewpoint at board level and reconsider who should be expressing that viewpoint. As I have already indicated, the time may be past when a close contact with the capital markets through a commercial or investment banker, or both, is essential to the policy decisions of the company. Such men may, of course, be still making a valuable contribution to board decisions in the affluent corporation, but if they are it does not stem from their control over external capital sources. Today the resource they control is different, e.g., information about acquisition opportunities. In any case, the point here is not to get bankers off boards but to recognize that times are changing and organizations should anticipate that change.

EFFECTS ON THE STOCKHOLDER

If many of our large, widely held corporations continue to insulate their financial needs from the external capital markets, I have serious concerns about how the ownership viewpoint in management will be expressed and carried forward. For some mature companies the stockholder is no longer needed. He represents a drain on company finances, not an input to those finances; he is no longer a resource to be expanded but a problem to be minimized.

I recognize, of course, that there are strong legal traditions which bind the corporation to its stockholders, that there are powerful incentives which can be employed to encourage professional management to identify with the objectives of the owners, and that governmental regulation has the stockholder very much in mind. But few relationships endure unless there are real and tangible benefits to be derived on both sides. As in the case of a philosophy of scarcity in an era of abundance, artificial means can be used to perpetuate old behavior. Sooner or later pressure for change builds up, however. When the corporation loses its need for the stockholder in a basic economic sense, the legal and organizational relationships are likely to feel the force of change. I would not attempt to predict what that change might be. I only see this as one of the phenomena of growing economic and financial abundance.

If the concept of an affluent society is anything more than a neat political catchword, then we will probably find the affluent corporation emerging in increasing numbers. In such a business environment, the primacy of the financial viewpoint and the concepts of economic scarcity which characterize finance today will be increasingly out of harmony with the facts. It is not too soon to be looking for some answers.

2. RECENT TRENDS AND DEVELOPMENTS IN ACADEMIC AND PROFESSIONAL THINKING ON THE SUBJECT OF FINANCIAL MANAGEMENT*

EZRA SOLOMON†

The subject matter of financial management is in the process of very rapid change. What appears to be happening is that a growing analytical content virtually nonexistent ten years ago is displacing the traditional descriptive treatment as the center of emphasis in the field. This change is taking place rapidly, both in the academic world and in the professional world, and is taking place both in the United States and abroad.

My talk today falls into two unequal parts: first, I am going to try to outline the nature of the changes that are taking place in the field of financial management; toward the end I shall discuss the implications of these changes for academic courses in finance and perhaps for academic courses in other related fields.

Finance is probably the oldest of the functional fields. Financial management, or corporation finance, as it was then more generally called, emerged as a separate branch of economics around the turn of the century. This was the age of institutional economics in this country. It was also the age in which our giant national corporations were being formed out of financial mergers and consolidations.

In this context, the original purpose of corporation finance as a separate subject was to describe and document the rapidly evolving complex of institutions, instruments, and practices in the capital market. As one of the earlier texts written soon after the turn of the century said: "Corporation finance aims to explain and illustrate the methods employed in the promotion, capitalization, financial management, consolidation and reorganization of business corporations."

By and large, the field continued to use this basic structure and content for nearly 50 years. It might be interesting to determine why. I think there were three factors involved. When academic work in business administration and, of course, in finance developed on a large scale in the 1920's, it simply adopted the early definition of the scope and method of the subject that I have outlined.

Secondly, the wide growth in security ownership after World War I increased public interest in corporations, in corporate securities, and in the network of institutional arrangements through which corporations obtained their funds from the public.

The third factor at work was the publication in 1920 of Arthur Stone Dewing's celebrated book, *The Financial Policy of Corporations*. This great book established the then-existing pattern of treatment firmly by

*From the *AACSB Bulletin* (October, 1965), pp. 1-8. Reprinted by permission.
†Dean Witter Professor of Finance, Graduate School of Business, Stanford University.

providing a definitive and scholarly text and a definitive and scholarly basis for academic courses in the field. The book itself dominated academic work in the field for at least 30 years.

I am not suggesting that this traditional treatment—I think we were all brought up on it—went unchallenged, but almost all of the challenges posed against it concerned matters of emphasis or matters of treatment. Several of these challenges are worth noting.

In the 1930's we had a huge upsurge of legislation and social controls, so we added large segments to the field of finance dealing with social control and legislative and regulatory aspects of finance. Also, in the '30's we had a large wave of reorganizations and bankruptcies, so quite naturally this topic was added. Thus at the end of fairly familiar chapter headings came a large section on bankruptcy and reorganization.

In the early years after World War II, a switch from external financing to internal financing combined with the freeing of interest rates and some degree of tightening in the money market made the whole question of working capital management more important. Consequently, there was a switch in emphasis from the question of long-term financing to working capital financing and working capital management. At the same time, there began a broadening of the subject away from corporation finance as such to business finance. When you deal with stocks and bonds and convertible debentures, you are dealing explicitly with corporations. When you talk about working capital management, you can be talking about noncorporate businesses.

A fourth kind of challenge to the content of the field emerged largely through the case method of instruction. The traditional textbook treatment was too much, as Pearson Hunt put it, "from the outside looking in." This investment banker point of view naturally involved heavy emphasis on a description of markets and institutions. When cases began to deal with decisions from the inside looking out, you got away somewhat from the descriptive body of treatment to the more typically case type decision situations.

In summary, throughout its 50 years of dominance, the traditional treatment of the field was criticized as being too descriptive, too much like an encyclopedia, and not sufficiently analytical.

Students complained about it and teachers complained about it. But very little change took place in spite of these complaints. This was because the basic assumption of the traditional approach was not questioned. This basic assumption was that the central emphasis of finance is on the procurement of funds and, hence, on the instruments, institutions, and practices through which funds are obtained in the marketplace and, by extension, on the legal and accounting relationships between a company on the one hand and its sources of funds on the other.

During the past ten years, and particularly the past five years, we have seen one more challenge to the traditional approach, but, unlike the previous challenges, this hits right at the basic assumption of the traditional approach —the basic assumption regarding the proper content of finance. The traditional assumption that the proper content of finance has to do with the procurement of funds has been questioned and rejected.

In its place we now have a much broader view. This view is that financial management is an integral part of overall management rather than a staff specialty concerned with fund-raising operations. In this new view, the central issue is the wise usage of funds. The central process involved is some sort of rational matching of the advantages of potential fund uses on the one hand against the cost of funds on the other; more properly speaking, against the cost of alternative potential sources of funds.

To state it another way, the present scope of the subject goes much further than the original question. The old basic question was: How should a company raise funds? The new questions are much broader. How should a company make decisions to commit funds for certain purposes? In other words, it is a discussion of the investment decision as such, which in turn involves the question of how we measure the profitability of committing funds in this direction versus another direction. How should a company set standards against which it can assay the use of funds? In other words, what is the minimum yardstick by which a company decides whether this usage is appropriate or not appropriate? And this body of analysis is being applied not only to normal profit-seeking companies but to other enterprises as well. I think you all saw a recent issue of *Time* magazine which reported that the planners in the Soviet Union are now grappling with this question of what minimum financial standards to set for the usage of funds by one state enterprise versus another state enterprise.

Thus, finance is involved not only with measuring profitability but with setting standards, minimum standards for profitability, and hence with the whole question of measuring the cost of capital for any given society or any given industry. This issue in turn leads to the third major question: How does the cost of capital vary with the financing mix which is used? Finally, and only in this context, can one ask the old traditional question: Given the foregoing set of theories or facts or inferences, how should a company go about its task of raising funds at any time in any given capital market?

You might ask whence these new questions have been borrowed. Has finance simply adopted as its subject matter questions that are properly in someone else's domain? The answer, surprisingly enough, is that these questions have not heretofore been studied systematically. It is not that businessmen have not been making these decisions; they have. Decisions to invest funds, decisions about the minimum standard required have been made for thousands of years, but they have been made way at the top, and how they have been made has neither been written down nor discussed. I suppose they were made by judgment of some kind or other. The academic version of finance itself never pondered these questions.

Academic and professional people in finance are now definitely asking these questions and pondering their appropriate solutions. You cannot walk within 20 feet of any finance classroom these days in the United States, or in Britain for that matter, and not hear the words, "the cost of capital." In contrast, look at anything written prior to 1955, and you will not find the phrase mentioned, let alone discussed. One might also ask: Since part of the new and broader view of finance has to do with the older question, how should a company raise funds, is there not a major overlap between the traditional and the new? Again the answer is no.

Taken in isolation, the narrow question, how should a company raise funds, had to devolve into a descriptive treatment of markets and institutions and practices. Taken in the broader context of the new definition of finance, it can be far more analytical. The turning point here came in the now celebrated article by Modigliani and Miller, published, I think, in 1958, which for the first time seriously and analytically tackled the question of optimal fund mixture.

One might also ask why 50 years went by before the scope and method of the subject of finance were redefined. I do not know the answer to this. All one can do is point out the many reasons that existed in the late '50's and in the early '60's for an emphasis on the kinds of questions implied by the new content of finance.

In one sense the developments I have been discussing represent a logical extension of the general scientific management movement into a field which previously had been reserved for judgment at the top. Although the most vigorously decentralized corporations have tended to keep financial decisions at the top, it was natural that scientific management, which began first at the factory level, should extend its way of thinking and its approach to the top itself. I also think that the move from implicit to explicit reasoning has been hastened by the computer. Computers do not take answers like, "Well, you use a little judgment." Computers like numbers, and so we have to find and use these numbers!

I think the implications of these changes in finance are very big, not only for top management but in many other matters. One important area other than top management is the field of utility regulation. Here, while the questions I am discussing have not been asked, the answers have been assumed. Utility regulators have measured the cost of capital without defining it. The other significant area or implication is for government investment of various kinds. I am talking now on a universal basis; in so many countries where state-owned enterprises are trying to maximize human welfare in some way, the older habit simply of engaging in pet projects is giving way now to the questions of engaging in economically feasible and desirable projects. The old capitalistic trick of maximizing wealth is being invoked within socialist economies or within socialist sectors of capitalistic economies, and this depends very much on answers to the financial questions involved.

Let me summarize the differences between what I call the older and the traditional approach, which still dominates the field in a numerical sense, and the new approach, which is taking over. The old approach was a body of knowledge. The new approach is more a way of thinking.

The older approach was concerned with the process of raising funds. The new approach is concerned with the optimal usage of funds—optimal with respect to volume, composition, and timing of both sources and uses.

The old approach was concerned very largely with the liability side of the balance sheet; it was concerned with the asset side of the balance sheet only where it involved cash and securities. The new approach is concerned with a balance between the assets and liabilities sides of the balance sheet.

The old approach was heavily descriptive. The new approach is largely analytical—more an exercise in inference than an exercise in description.

In the older approach, specialized description of corporation law and corporate accounting as they related to specific financing episodes, such as promotion, merger, consolidation, and reorganization, was a very big part of the subject. In the new approach, these episodic phenomena are treated as special aspects of a unifying basic problem, and this basic problem is simply the question of financial evaluation in an uncertain world.

Finally, the older approach represented a branch of institutional economics. The new approach represents much more an extension of the micro-economic theory of the firm; whereas the theory of the firm, price theory as we know it, is concerned largely with the relationship of profits to the level of output with level of capital taken as given, financial theory is concerned with the relationship between profits and a changing level of capital input.

Let me turn to the possible impact of this newer framework, this newer definition of the scope and method of finance. Apart from changing the subject itself, what are its implications? One important one is that it seems to have made the subject a lot more exciting, both to students and to teachers. There is a feeling of excitement within the field now.

Twenty years ago there was almost nothing being done in the way of doctoral dissertations in this field. This was true even ten years ago and five years ago. In other words, in a typical doctoral seminar, given the choice, students would write on then jazzier subjects like monetary theory, international finance, the balance of payments, and so on; very few of them selected topics within corporate financial management proper. This is no longer the case. At Stanford this last year I have had a group of about 15 doctoral students, each one reading and writing on a self-selected topic for the seminar. Only one subject has been outside the field of corporation finance. This was on the balance of payments issue. The other 14 have been within the subject of financial management proper. This is a big switch.

The development of subject matter is taking place at an extremely rapid pace. The young people now working in the field remind me of an incident in the Navy I should like to relate. After getting out of Burma the wrong way—across the mountains on foot—I was tired of land and joined the British Navy and was assigned to a ship run by an old fogey, a sort of universal Queeg. We used to refer to him as "the old woman" because he always seemed to be bothered about little things. About three years later, at the ripe age of 24, I had command of a ship myself, and I was standing up on the deck feeling the usual loneliness of the man at the top when through the speaker tube I heard two midshipmen talking about me; they were referring to me as that "old woman."

I feel that way about finance today. Just a few years ago I was a young Turk trying to overthrow the past. When I hear these young students discussing some of their ideas, I already feel a little out of date. I think in five years I am going to have to quit teaching finance.

In spite of very rapid change and a great deal of controversy, brought on in part by the rapid new quantitative methods and computer technology, the mainstream of the new finance is now reaching that degree of certainty and lucidity which I think makes it quite suitable for undergraduate courses in the field. I also feel that if undergraduate courses in the field of finance were to adopt the new approach, everybody would be better off.

In the first place, the questions it addresses are more universal. It is not confined to particular problems or a particular form of business called a corporation but rather deals with any form of enterprise. Furthermore, it deals with ongoing problems, rather than episodic problems. In short, it is less specialized; more general.

Secondly, it is more analytical and thus challenges and exercises the brain more. It is less a question of memory and learning facts; more a question of inference and thinking and logic.

Finally, I think the new look in finance ties in much better with the other parts of the curriculum in business administration. It ties in beautifully with production, problems of inventory control, and operations research. It ties in very well with business economics. It ties in with management accounting and with business policy.

For all these reasons it does provide a better basis of instruction at the undergraduate level. So while the subject will remain full of controversy and noise and argument for many years to come, there is already sufficient at the core for the new approach to be adopted as the basis for the curriculum in the field.

As far as implications for other subjects are concerned, time does not allow me to go into that in any detail. I do think that two implications are worth noting. I think what has happened in the field of corporation finance or financial management proper has tremendous significance for the field of investment. This highly respected field is one which has not changed very much in 30 years and about which there is a lot of deep discontent at the practitioner level today. Financial analysts feel that the academician has not done his stuff, that he is giving them recipes and not theories, and they want theory, better theory. I think there is a revolution coming in the field of investment. If there are any young faculty interested in working in this field, they should be given free rein. Let them have their heads. Let them experiment, get away from the present format of the field.

I also think that the new emphasis in financial management has some implications for the courses in money and banking which are taught in business schools. This is that they should have somewhat less emphasis on money and banking in the traditional sense and somewhat more emphasis on money in the capital markets in the broader sense; that we need to discuss more than the rate of interest on money—we need to discuss the whole structure of rates in the entire capital markets. This trend has been in existence for a long time, but it is going to be accelerated by developments in financial management.

Finally, there is the new field of international business. With multinational operations increasing rapidly, business schools have been concerned about this new dimension that should be added to the business curriculum. If finance had not changed in the directions I have indicated, very clearly there should be a field of international business finance, for the simple reason that the older style domestic corporation finance dealt almost solely with Americana. Obviously it does little good to talk about convertible debenture bond issues in Malaya or any other country which does not have a capital market. Insofar as the older content of finance was heavily larded with Americana, it was hardly suitable training for people engaging in business overseas.

But this statement is no longer true with the new finance. The content is far more universal, far more abstracted from instruments and practices in a particular market, and definitely more theoretical and analytical. The fact that domestic financial courses now have developed this analytical core means that they are also suitable for students who wish to practice business overseas or in multinational corporations. The need for separate courses in international business finance or multinational business finance is far less than it would have been.

It is true that the different environments in different parts of the world do require somewhat different emphasis in terms of context. For example, at home we face a single type of capital rationing problem. We ration dollars among different projects, whereas in many countries abroad which have exchange control, they have a dual rationing problem. They are rationing domestic savings, and they are also rationing scarce foreign exchange among different projects. In many ways it is a far more difficult problem. On the other hand, because it is a difficult analytical dual rationing problem, it ought to be a part of our domestic curriculum.

Another kind of major difference that is worth noting between conditions here and abroad is that, in many countries abroad, inflation, or the pace of inflation, is a far more serious issue. It, therefore, has to be taken into account explicitly in financial analysis and financial evaluation.

But, by the same token, this is an interesting thing for us to do here anyway, because we too have some rate of inflation, and there may come a time when we have a faster rate of inflation. We ought to be thinking in terms of financial analysis within an inflationary economy.

What I am trying to say is that we can have one integrated course that serves the purposes of both the domestic student and the student who has a multinational interest, and this has been made possible by the fact that finance itself has changed in content and scope and emphasis. A financial management course which is ideal for persons interested in multinational operations comes pretty close to a financial management course which is ideal for people who never intend to leave the United States.

PART II. CAPITAL BUDGETING

Capital budgeting, a critical area of financial management, has received considerable attention in recent years. Decisions concerning long-term capital expenditures are of paramount importance to the long-run welfare of the firm. These decisions involve large sums of money, and mistakes cannot be rectified easily. Efficient and effective capital expenditures require a comprehensive program readily understood by personnel at all levels of management.

The articles in this section are designed to expose the reader to some areas generally not covered in the classroom. In the first article, Professor Robert M. Soldofsky cuts through the formalism of the "what" of capital budgeting so that capital budgeting might be used as a vital tool. The article is based on an interview study of small manufacturing companies in Iowa. The author is not concerned with the problems which fascinate academicians but rather focuses on those misunderstandings which exist in practice. The author concludes that neither the return on investment nor the cost of capital is calculated by small businesses or by most large businesses on a regular basis. A workable statement of capital budgeting is presented with a detailed exposition of the shortcomings found in practice at the time of the interviews.

Professor Robert N. Anthony discusses the methodology of capital budgeting while exposing some of the fallacies in computing the return on investment and conceding the value of utilizing discounted return on investment. He presents five fallacies which are encountered: (1) income taxes are sometimes ignored, (2) present value is too complicated, (3) the higher the return, the better the project, (4) leasing is always advantageous, and (5) the payback never gives a useful answer.

David B. Hertz explains how management is able to utilize computer simulation in examining the risk consequences of various investment policies for individual investments. He concludes that a good investment policy should include the determination of risk profiles for all investments, the use of discounting measures (either discounted internal rate of return or an equivalent net present value) for assessing the merits of an investment proposal, the establishment of alternative screening rules for an investment proposal, and the determination of risk boundaries for the alternative policies.

After reviewing the conventional means of dealing with uncertainty, he presents a discussion of a method called risk analysis. This method involves the identification of leverage factors which will influence key variables determining future costs and revenues. The method involves the development of *uncertainty profiles* for each key variable and the use of computer simulation. A detailed outline of a 7-step simulation and the results of a simulation are presented.

Professor James Van Horne proposes a method of evaluating *combinations* of investments when cash flows are not known with certainty. Matters considered include: (1) the use of a joint and conditional probability concept similar to that used in security-portfolio analysis, (2) the evaluation of combinations with regard to their expected present value and covariance rather than variance alone, and (3) the selection of the best combination which is dependent upon both the *efficiency frontier* and the *risk-return preference function* of the firm.

He points out that in computing variance, existing investment projects must be taken into consideration because investment proposals must be judged in relation to their impact on the total risk of the firm. Due to covariance, the combination of investment proposals providing the lowest total variance may not provide the lowest total variance when combined with existing projects. The selection of the combination of investments deemed most desirable will be dependent upon the utility preference of the firm.

Professor Van Horne very neatly and uniquely applies the advances in the theory of portfolio selection developed in 1952 by Harry Markowitz to the portfolio of investment in real assets. For about 15 years Markowitz's contribution had only been applied to the selection of common stocks.

Professor F. K. Wright examines the limiting factors in the project evaluation process. He contends " . . . that for a large and important class of firms neither funds nor opportunities are the critical factor limiting expansion." He reviews the notion of funds and maintains that they need not be the critical factor. The managerial problem in the capital expenditure program is emphasized. He feels that the managerial limit may well be the critical factor limiting expansion. He explains how the firm's expansion may be limited by the ". . . ability of a few key individuals to accept additional responsibility rather than the number of managers available." Professor Wright presents an interesting discussion of some psychological or behavioral dimensions of the capital expenditure decision-making process.

3. THE WHAT, WHY, AND HOW OF CAPITAL BUDGETING FOR SMALLER BUSINESSES*

ROBERT M. SOLDOFSKY †

INTRODUCTION

Capital budgeting is the process of allocating the financial resources of a business to investment in current and fixed assets in order to maximize the value of the business. Capital budgeting is concerned also with achieving the structures of liabilities and net worth which minimize the cost of funds.

The major purpose of this article is to cut through the apparently forbidding formalism of the "What" of capital budgeting and to help the owners of small businesses use capital budgeting as a vital tool to improve their financial results. In this article, present practices will be probed and constructively criticized. The methods of computing the rate of return on investment, the (rate of) cost of funds or money-capital, and the integration of these two rates in the capital budgeting process comprise the major topics presented.

One of the motivations for this article was the response to an interview study of the capital budgeting practices of small manufacturing companies in Iowa conducted in the summer of 1961 under the auspices of the Small Business Administration.[1] Beginning with the work of Joel Dean in 1951, there has been a steady and increasing outpouring of books and articles about capital budgeting.[2] The academic treatment of capital budgeting has become increasingly refined,[3] and the topic is found frequently in university-sponsored management seminars for business leaders.

Only a few studies of capital budgeting practices have been made, and most of these have concentrated on the large- and giant-sized businesses in the country. The field experience of the author indicates that after a decade of discussion the capital budgeting practices of smaller businesses vary between poor and nonexistent. Table 3-1 shows the number and employment sizes of businesses at which interviews were held. Even though all

---

*From the *Iowa Business Digest* (January, 1966), pp. 3-17. Reprinted by permission.
†Professor of Finance, University of Iowa.

[1]For the detailed report of this study, see Robert M. Soldofsky, "Capital Budgeting Practices in Small Manufacturing Companies," *Studies in the Factor Markets for Small Business Firms*, edited by Dudley G. Luckett and Karl A. Fox (Ames, Iowa: Iowa State University Press, 1964), pp. 46-94. The research reported will be utilized in the remainder of this article with further citation.

[2]Joel Dean, *Capital Budgeting* (New York: Columbia University Press, 1951).

[3]Examples of such recent work are: E. M. Lerner and W. T. Carleton, "Capital Budgeting and Stock Valuation," *American Economic Review* (September, 1964), pp. 683-702; Paul L. Cheng and John P. Shelton, "A Contribution to the Theory of Capital Budgeting—The Multi-Investment Case," *Journal of Finance* (December, 1963). The latter article brought forth a comment by Professor Eli Schwartz and a reply by Professors Cheng and Shelton, both of which appeared in the *Journal of Finance* (December, 1964), pp. 668-670 and pp. 671-672, respectively.

TABLE 3-1

IOWA MANUFACTURING COMPANIES INTERVIEWED

Employment size	Number of interviews completed
20-49	21
50-99	28
100-249	29
250-499	23
500-999	11
1,000 or more	11
	123

Source: See Footnote 1.

these interviews were held in Iowa, there are no convincing reasons to believe that the results would have been different had they been carried out elsewhere.

The author believes that capital budgeting in its main outlines is rather easy to understand. Although very difficult and even bizarre problems fascinate academicians, such problems are not the concern of this article. However, one of the concerns of this article is to point out a number of issues on which misunderstanding exists in practice. Many of these misunderstandings can be clarified readily; somewhat different questions can be raised in place of those now being asked, and the elements of capital budgeting can be brought into clear and correct focus. First, a brief statement of the essence of capital budgeting and its functions will be given.

RATE OF RETURN APPROACH TO CAPITAL BUDGETING

The capital budgeting model is pictured in Figure 3-1. Assume that a firm has $2,000,000 of assets and is considering next year's expenditures for fixed assets. The following rate of return schedule for additional investment has been determined (as described later):

Rate of return (percent)	Investment in r/r class (in dollars)	Cumulative investment (in dollars)
25% up	15,000	15,000
20-24.9	20,000	35,000
15-19.9	25,000	60,000
10-14.9	40,000	100,000
5-9.9	50,000	150,000
0-4.9	100,000	250,000

The weighted average cost of money-capital or finance is approximately 10 percent, and the optimum investment is in the vicinity of $100,000 (Figure 3-1). The method of determining this (rate of) cost for funds is described later. The intersection of the cost of finance curve, k_o, and the rate of return curve, r, in Figure 3-1 determine the equilibrium amount of investment and annual rate of growth. The added investment indicated is $100,000, and the rate of growth is 5 percent, or the initial $2,000,000 in assets divided by the $100,000 increase in fixed assets.[4]

FIGURE 3-1
CAPITAL BUDGETING FRAMEWORK

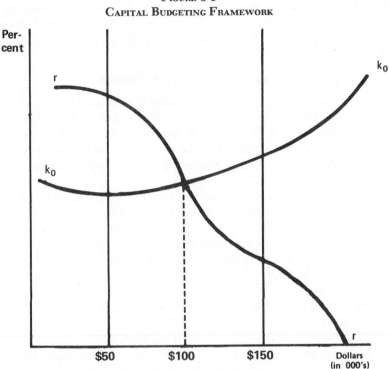

The equilibrium investment is determined by equating the marginal rate of return on added investment with the marginal cost of added finance. If less than $100,000 investment were added, r would lay above k_o; that is, net present worth could be increased by expanding to the equilibrium point.[5] Similarly, any investment greater than $100,000 is larger than the desirable amount in terms of the rate of return equilibrium and maximizing net present worth. It should be clear that under these conditions the net present worth or value of the enterprise is maximized by $100,000 of added investment.

The rate of growth is determined by a similar procedure each year—or more often if necessary. If r and k_o intersect at zero (net) investment, the

---

[4]In this simplification, annual rather than continuous conversion is used. The question of whether or not $2,000,000 is correct may also be raised. Throughout this article these niceties will generally be overlooked. The purpose of this article is to help communicate with owners of small businesses.

[5]Readers who want a brief discussion of the term "net present worth" might see Ezra Solomon, *The Theory of Financial Management* (New York: Columbia University Press, 1963), pp. 17-25, or William Beranek, *Analysis For Financial Decisions* (Homewood, Ill.: Richard D. Irwin, Inc., 1963), pp. 124-127.

firm has reached its optimum size in terms of its present products and policies.

The capital budgeting process indicates not only *how much* to buy and to hold but also *what* to buy. Each of the many individual proposals that comprise the rate of return schedule, such as the one illustrated above, call for the purchase of specific buildings, machinery, equipment, inventory, and so forth.

RATE OF RETURN PRACTICES

The apparently straightforward capital budgeting framework just set forth was not followed by any of the 123 companies interviewed, irrespective of size. One of the larger corporations was starting to use a return on investment (ROI) method that is somewhat similar to that method widely advocated since 1950. Where are the misunderstandings? Where does communication fail?

Only very few of the firms interviewed computed a rate of return on investment or even the rate of return on net worth. When rates of return were computed annually, they were often compared with one another in order to state whether the firm was doing better or worse. Such comparisons do not provide any information about what can be done to improve the rate of return. The rates computed were historical rather than prospective; hence they cannot be used directly in the capital budgeting process. Furthermore, the rates were simple ratios of net income to assets rather than being time-adjusted rates (as explained later). A few firms even confused the rate of profit on sales with the rate of return on assets!

The comparison of r and k_o could not be carried out either, because k_o, the cost of finance, was not computed. Most of the firms interviewed were likely to think of the cost of funds (finance) as the number of dollars that would have to be paid. The general belief of the owners of smaller businesses is that equity funds have no cost because dividends do not have to be paid. The serious misunderstandings which prevail in this area will be developed in more detail in a later section. The emphasis upon cash rather than upon rates implied above introduces a fundamental misunderstanding.

Two of the major themes in capital budgeting practices are cash throw-off (or available cash) and the payback (or payoff) period. In terms of cash throwoff or available cash, firms have a strong tendency to limit their outlays for fixed assets to either net income or retained net income plus depreciation. Owner-managers are willing to borrow only in the face of pressing needs for equipment or machinery. When present equipment is not working well, when newer equipment would result in very great and obvious savings, or when the immediate sales prospects are likely to continue above present capacity, borrowing is considered. Even so, the shorter the term of the loan the better—if the firm believes that it can meet the payment schedule.

In this cash-rationing framework there is little hint of rate of return thinking on the part of the owners or others who participate in the investment decisions. In terms of Figure 3-1, $50,000, $100,000, or $150,000 might be invested in fixed assets. The amount invested depends upon the amount of cash available in the company and, in some circumstances, upon the amount of cash that could be borrowed. As long as cash rationing prevails, there is no assurance that all investments that have high prospective rates of return will be undertaken or that those with low prospective rates of return will be rejected. In most cases, no clear or developed notion of rate of return is used.

TABLE 3-2
CRITERIA USED FOR DETERMINING
MACHINERY AND EQUIPMENT OUTLAYS

Employment size	Number of companies interviewed	Payout period	Rate of return on investment	No formal criterion
20-49	21°	7°	—	14
50-99	28	13†	—	15
100-249	29	11	—	19
250-499	23	20	2††	1
500-1,000	11	10	1††	1
1,000 or more	11	10	2††	1
Total	123	71	5	51

°Two of these respondents were very vague.
†One of these respondents was very vague.
††Also use payout criterion.
Source: See Footnote 1.

Among the firms that use any formal screening device, the payout period is most prevalent, as shown in Table 3-2.[6] The payout-period criterion has many limitations—in terms of both its conceptual basis and its preparation in practice. The major conceptual limitation is that the payout period is a cash-flow concept and not a rate of return concept. The payout period is defined as that period required to recover an amount equal to the original outlay. This cash recovery is the sum of the added income (or net operating savings) plus depreciation. For example, assume that the payout period adopted by a small business is four years. Assume further that the firm is considering the purchase of a $10,000 machine. If the company anticipates that it will recover the $10,000 outlay in less than four years, the purchase will be made; if the anticipated cash recovery period is more than four years, the purchase will not be made. Some adjustments or modifications to this position will be mentioned later. When projecting the cash flow, the smaller business (and almost all larger ones, also) assumes equal annual amounts. Assume that a proposed machine has a payout period of exactly four years and that it is expected to disintegrate or become obsolete at the end of the fourth year. If this machine were purchased, its rate of return would be zero. The amount recovered or paid back would be depreciation. Only in the event that the projected life were more than four years would there be any projected positive rate of return.

---

[6]For a resume of other studies of capital budgeting practices, see Robert M. Soldofsky, *Lectures in Financial Management* (4th ed.; Columbia, Missouri: Lucas Press, 1964), pp. 329-330 and 352-354.

To proceed with the correct formulation, the cash flow may be viewed as an annuity expressed as:

$$V = \frac{R_1}{(1+i)^1} + \frac{R_2}{(1+i)^2} + \frac{R_3}{(1+i)^3} \cdots \cdots \frac{R_n}{(1+i)^n}$$

where V = the present value of the annuity
     R = the annual expected receipt
     i = the discount rate or rate of return.

For the purpose of this article, k_o, the firm's cost of money-capital or finance, will be the same as i, the rate of return. Alternative expressions for the annuity formula that are seen often are:

$$V = R_1 (1+i)^{-1} + R_2 (1+i)^{-2} + \cdots \cdots R_n (1+i)^{-n}$$

and

$$\sum_{t=1}^{n} \frac{R}{(1+i)^n}$$

In the 4-year payout example given above, the $2,500 recovery each year was entirely depreciation. If the projected cash flow is to last for five years (as shown in Table 3-3), the expected sum of receipts is $12,500. Ten thousand dollars of this amount is depreciation, and the balance, $2,500, is a return over cost. The question, what is the rate of return if the expected useful life of the machine is five years, may now be asked.

TABLE 3-3
CONVERSION OF PAYOUT PERIOD
TO RATE OF RETURN°

Year	Cash flow Annual	Cash flow Cumulative	Five-year cash flow discounted at 7.9% Discount factor†	Five-year cash flow discounted at 7.9% Discounted value	Six-year cash flow discounted at 13% Discount factor†	Six-year cash flow discounted at 13% Discounted value
1	$2,500	$2,500	.93	$2,325	.89	$2,225
2	2,500	5,000	.86	2,150	.78	1,950
3	2,500	7,500	.79	1,975	.69.	1,725
4	2,500	10,000	.73	1,825	.62	1,550
5	2,500	12,500	.69	1,725	.54	1,350
6	2,500	15,000			.48	1,200
Sum of discount factors			4.00		4.00	
Present worth of annuity				$10,000		$10,000

°Based upon a $10,000 outlay and a 4-year payout period. Equal annual cash flows assumed.
†Factors rounded to two decimal places for convenience. Each factor is the present worth of $1 for the indicated period and interest rate.

The rate of discount which equates the present value of the annuity payments with the original outlay *is* the rate of return; the rate of return is 7.9 percent in this instance, as shown in Table 3-3. If the expected life had been six years, the rate of return would have been 13.0 percent, as illustrated in the last two columns of Table 3-3.

Several points may now be made about the implications of Table 3-3 and the general table of the payout period and rate of return relationships shown in Table 3-4. Then a number of misunderstandings that businessmen have can be pointed out readily as a necessary prior condition for improved practices. In both the 5-year and 6-year columns of Table 3-3, the sum of the discount factors is 4. When the payout period is four years, the figure 4 represents the ratio of the original outlay (investment) to the annual cash flow or $10,000 : $2,500. No matter how long the machine is expected to last, the rate of return can be determined by finding the discount rate for the annuity which reduces the present value of that annuity to four times the annual cash flow or receipts. Table 3-4 includes the results of this procedure for periods through ten years. The expected useful life of machinery and equipment is more than ten years in relatively few cases. Furthermore, the rates of return associated with the most frequently used payout periods do not rise much after ten years. Even if a payout period as long as five years is selected, the rate of return on a machine that is expected to last for ten years will be about 15 percent. Continuing cash flow beyond ten years is

TABLE 3-4

PAYOUT PERIOD AND RATE OF RETURN

(Assume the original capital outlay is $10,000)°

	Payout Period						
	1.5 yrs.	2 yrs.	2.5 yrs.	3 yrs.	4 yrs.	5 yrs.	6 yrs.
	Annual cash flow implied by payout period†						
Number of years of cash flow at constant amount per year	$6,667	$5,000	$4,000	$3,333	$2,500	$2,000	$1,667
	Rate of return implied by payout period and expected asset life (percent)						
1.5	0						
2.0	21.5	0					
2.5	††	7.9	0				
3.0	44.6	23.4	9.7	0			
4.0	55.0	34.1	21.9	12.5	0		
5.0	60.0	41.1	28.7	19.9	7.9	0	
6.0	††	44.5	32.7	24.3	13.0	5.5	0
7.0	††	46.6	35.1	26.1	16.3	9.2	4.0
8.0	66.0	47.9	36.7	29.0	18.6	11.8	6.9
9.0	††	48.7	37.7	30.3	20.3	13.7	9.0
10.0	††	49.1	38.5	31.2	21.4	15.1	10.6

°Assuming no scrap value at end of income-earning life.
†The total cash flow over the life of the asset (project) is the annual cash flow multiplied by expected life as indicated by the lefthand column.
††Not calculated because of limitations of available interest tables. The rate of return for the 1.5 year payout period rises toward 66.7 percent as a limit. Annual conversion is used in the above table; a very good argument could be made for the use of continuous conversion.

so uncertain that most decision makers have little confidence in such projections for most investments.

If the payout period is two years, the ratio of investment to cash flow is 2 : 1; if the payout period is three years, the ratio is 3 : 1. Table 3-4 was generated by using the payout period and rate-of-return relationships. This table includes payout periods and the length of projected useful lives that cover almost all situations found in practice.

The clear and very strong impression from the field interviews with firms that used the payout period method was that the stress was on the payout period, not the rate of return as a rule of thumb guideline for decisions. When the respondents were urged to verbalize the rationale of the payout period, most of them said it was customary. The most typical response was that after the payout period everything recovered was "gravy"; during the payout period the original outlay was recovered.

Cash flow concepts are implied in such responses. The fact that any investment should earn some rate of return throughout its life was neglected in favor of uncritically accepted custom. Table 3-3 implies that a part of each year's cash flow is depreciation and that a part is return on investment.[7] On occasion, the interviewer compared the cash flow from a business investment with the level monthly payments on real estate mortgages on houses. The small businessmen and their associates quickly perceived the analogy that a part of each payment in the mortgage case and in the business investment case was interest and that a part was principal.

Some respondents said that the reciprocal of the payment period was the rate of return. If these respondents used a 2- or 3-year payout period, they were expecting rates of return of 50 to 33.3 percent. They should have rushed to banks and to other lenders to borrow funds in order to expand assets and to earn net returns of 20 percent and more on their equity, but no such movement was observed. To repeat the point made earlier, the actions of the small businessmen stressed their focus of attention upon cash flow rather than upon rate of return. If any further support for the cash flow orientation is needed, the point can be made that respondents were asked to state the life expectancy of machinery and equipment being discussed during interviews. Not a single person indicated that he understood the relevance of the question to prospective rates of return. The *time-adjusted* rates of return developed in this section can be used to show the misunderstandings involved.

On some occasions, businessmen will not purchase a piece of equipment if they expect that it may be obsolete within four to five years. If the payback period is two years and the machine is expected to be obsolete after four years, the expected rate of return is 34 percent, as shown in Table 3-4. The purchase clearly should be made under such circumstances. A careful review of Table 3-4 may help those who make investment decisions

---

[7]For a complete statement of these relationships, see Soldofsky, *op. cit.*, pp. 320-324.

to realize the high rates of return possible from even short investment periods.

If a machine, or more likely a building, has a very long life expectancy, the rate of return will approach the reciprocal of the payout period as a limit. One of the reasons that the payout period rule of thumb probably has been so useful is that most business investments do have useful lives of five to ten years, so that the indicated rates of return are achieved despite the type of calculations made. Unfortunately, as pointed out in the preceding paragraph, many high-yielding investments are overlooked.

The time-adjusted or discounting method for determining rates of return is very flexible. This method, which is sometimes called discounted cash flows, can be adjusted for unequal expected annual cash flow, for investment in working capital, for expected recovery of working capital, for expected salvage values, for investments made at different points in time, and for many other circumstances. More detailed treatment can be found in textbooks.[8]

As distressing as the foregoing discussion of nature and extent of the misunderstandings of the relationship between payback periods and rate of return may be, the varieties of inept calculations of the payback period itself are equally disturbing. Interviewees using the payback criterion often inquired about the length of the payback period in general use. What they should have inquired about was the correct procedure to follow when preparing the payback period itself. So far as the author could determine from the interviews, only about 10 percent of the 58 firms from which sample calculations of the payout period were obtained were using the correct procedure. The smaller firms using the payout approach were almost as likely to use the preferred procedure as were the largest firms interviewed. A further limitation is that, even among the firms using formally correct payout calculations, the underlying preparation of the values used was lacking in various ways. No systematic data were gathered on this latter point, but some observations will be made concerning this topic at the end of this section.

The payout or payback period is the period required to recover an amount equal to the original investment. The recovery or cash throwoff is the net operating saving or net added cash flow which is, in turn, the algebraic sum of many factors. During the interviews, replacement problems were encountered more frequently than were any other investment situations; therefore, a replacement case will be the basis of the example used. Assume that a new machine costing $10,000 is being considered to replace the old machine now in use. The expected number of labor hours to be saved is calculated first; the direct labor cost and related fringe benefits are priced separately, as shown in Table 3-5. Other miscellaneous

---

[8]Three of the better treatments are by Soldofsky, *op. cit.*, pp. 324-327; Pearson Hunt, Charles M. Williams, and Gordon Donaldson, *Basic Business Finance* (Homewood, Ill.: Richard D. Irwin, Inc., 1961), pp. 612-632; and J. Fred Weston, *Managerial Finance* (New York: Holt, Rinehart & Winston, Inc., 1962), pp. 118-148.

savings such as variable overhead, property taxes, power consumption, and scrap should also be considered.[9] The sum of these factors is the gross savings or operating advantage. Depreciation is notably missing at this point because the example is tracing projected cash flows directly; depreciation does not affect cash flow directly and is omitted. However, depreciation is a deductible expense for tax purposes. Income taxes do not have to be paid on the entire gross savings of $4,000, as shown in Table 3-5, but only on that amount less $1,000 of depreciation. The added taxable income is only $3,000, and the added income taxes taken at 48 percent are $1,440. The net operating advantage is $2,560, and the payout period is 3.9 years. On a before-tax basis the payout period would be only 2.5 years. (If the income rate is lower, the difference between the before- and after-tax methods is less.) The payout period may be increased to as much as 6.9 years by omitting one or more of the elements in the computation (Table 3-5). All the Table 3-5 variations (and others in addition) were found in use. Field

TABLE 3-5

PAYOUT PERIOD COMPUTATIONS°

	Preferred method	Erroneous methods		
	All components	Depreciation omitted	Fringe benefits and miscellaneous omitted	Labor only
COMPONENT				
Labor savings	$2,800	$2,800	$2,800	$2,800
Fringe benefits†	530	530	———	———
Miscellaneous savings (net)	670	670	———	———
Gross savings or operating advantage	$4,000	$4,000	$2,800	$2,800
Depreciation	1,000	———	1,000	———
Added taxable net income	$3,000	$4,000	$1,800	$2,800
Federal income taxes (48%)	1,440	1,920	864	1,344
Net added income or net operating advantage	$1,560	$2,080	$ 936	$1,456
Cash flow	2,560	2,080	1,936	1,456
PAYOUT PERIODS				
Before income taxes	2.5 years	2.5 years	3.6 years	3.6 years
After income taxes	3.9 years	4.8 years	5.2 years	6.9 years

°Assume that a $10,000 investment is being considered. Straight-line depreciation is being used and scrap value is not considered.
†19 percent of wage rates.

[9]For a detailed check list of such factors, see George Terborgh, *The Discounted Cash-Flow Method of Investment Analysis* (Washington: Machinery and Allied Products Institute, 1963), p. 23. This pamphlet is Number 6 in MAPI's Studies in Business Investment Strategy. This series as well as other MAPI publications are very useful to the understanding and application of investment strategy.

experience is reminiscent of Mark Twain's essay on New England weather. Twain describes the experience of an apocryphal friend who sought specimens of different kinds of weather and was overwhelmed by the bewildering variety and complexity of experience. Academic and business prophets are bedeviled also by an intransigent uncertainty.

If the calculation in column 1, Table 3-5, had been in terms of cash throwoff, the following items would have been added:

Net income	$1,560
Depreciation	$1,000
Cash throwoff	$2,560

The results are the same as those reached by the alternative method.

The explanation of the reason for not including depreciation in determining the gross operating advantage in the preferred method shown in Table 3-5 is more complex and leads into the reason for the irrelevance of sunk costs for investment decisions. Only items that change cash flow are relevant; only such changes affect the net receipts stream. If an old machine is sold, cash flow is not affected directly. The indirect effect through income taxes is readily admitted. Any net gain on the sale of an old machine less removal costs would affect cash flow. Other research studies have shown that removal costs are often greater than salvage values. Again, the ordinary or capital gains taxes upon the sale of fixed assets affect the net receipts stream. All such adjustments can be included in the time-adjusted or discounted-cash flows method of determining rate of return on investment.

Accounting charges for floor space may be used to illustrate another aspect of the sunk cost problem. Assume that the firm in the continuing illustration makes an accounting distribution charge for floor space. A new machine requires only half the floor space used by the old one. The firm has ample floor space to begin with. Floor-space charges to the relevant cost center will be reduced, but this reduction is not relevant to the determination of net operating savings or rate of return. The obvious reason is that no outlays have changed for the company so that cash flow cannot be affected.

Early in this section the point was made that the data put into the payout computation were not prepared with enough care. Frequently the average plant-wide wage rates were used rather than the rates for the specific employees or jobs involved. When fringe benefits were not omitted, the rates used were exceedingly "rough." Employers expected rising wage rates—sometimes already provided for in the existing labor agreements—but these were not reflected in annual changes in the level of projected labor savings. Owners were willing to shade their rule-of-thumb payout period for expected changes in wage rates. Cash affluence or cash stringency, personal optimism or pessimism, and other factors affect the pseudo-precision with which the announced payout period guideline of the firm is used in "go or no go" investment decisions.

This entire section on the rate of return has established the correct relationships between the rate of return and the payout period. The major misunderstandings that have blocked the development of the payout criterion toward the more useful rate of return criterion have been pointed out. Ineptness in preparing the underlying calculations of cash throwoff have limited the usefulness of the payout-period criterion among smaller businesses more than has been suspected. The cash rationing methods that are so widely used in capital budgeting are substantially inferior to the rate of return rationing methods advocated by academicians and utilized by an increasing number of larger businesses.

Rate of return rationing requires both the computation of the rate of return on prospective investment and a (rate of) cost of finance. The final and briefest section of this paper will discuss the latter topic.

COST OF FINANCE

The cost of finance or cost of money-capital is the weighted average cost of all long-term sources of funds. The cost of finance is illustrated in Table 3-6. The principles underlying the illustration will be discussed briefly, and then the misunderstandings about this topic which were uncovered in the interviews with small business executives will be reviewed.

TABLE 3-6

COST OF FINANCE BY THE
PUBLIC UTILITY METHOD

	Capital-ization	Capital-ization structure	Cost of each security After taxes	Before taxes[*]	Weighted average cost
6% Long-term debt	$120	.15	.031	.060	.0090
7% Preferred stock	80	.10	.07	.135	.0135
Common stock	100 ⎫	.75	.09	.173	.1298
Earned surplus	500 ⎭				
Capitalization	$800				
Capitalization structure		1.00			
Weighted average cost of finance					.1523

[*]Income taxes assumed to be 48 percent.

The two major procedures for computing the cost of funds, k_o, are called the economic theory method and the public utility method.[10] Only the latter will be detailed in this article, although the former is strongly preferred on theoretical grounds. The economic theory method computes k_o on a current or opportunity cost basis; the public utility method proceeds primarily upon historical and contractual cost assumptions. The public

---

[10]For the most complete textbook treatment and comparison of these two procedures, see Robert M. Soldofsky, *op. cit.*, "Cost of Funds," pp. 185-237. For a balanced, lucid treatment of the economic theory method only, see Ezra Solomon, *op. cit.*, pp. 27-119. Also see E. M. Lerner and W. T. Carleton, *op. cit.*, for aspects of the cost of common stock controversy.

utility method is so called because it is approximately the procedure used by the courts and commissions in public utility rate cases. The public utility method puts the computed rate "in the ball park" and is, therefore, workable, given the many uncertainties in the set of projections involved in capital budgeting. The statement of the public utility method also provides a basis for pointing out the most glaring misconceptions noted in the practices of small business.

The cost of finance is the weighted average cost of long-term funds expressed as a rate. Table 3-6 is a straightforward computation of k_o. The capitalization is taken directly from the balance sheet; the percentage of debt, preferred stock, and common stockholders' equity to the total capitalization are each calculated. In the public utility method, the cost of long-term debt is the nominal or stated rate. In the economic theory method, the rates used are always the going market rates, and the capitalization values are the market's valuations of the securities. If there is more than one security in each class, each one is considered separately in the computation of k_o, irrespective of the method used.

The most difficult, controversial, and exasperating part of the computation is the determination of the cost of equity funds. As an approximation, the cost of equity may be thought of as the ratio of net income to the balance sheet valuation of owners' equity. The topic will be pursued in somewhat more detail later.

The "Before-taxes" column is used to adjust for the differential treatment of interest and net income (before taxes) required by the Internal Revenue Code. In Table 3-6 the cost of preferred stock and common stock has been stepped up to a before-taxes basis. The reasoning in the preferred stock case runs as follows: $13.50 must be earned before income taxes in order to have $7 left after income taxes to pay out as dividends. Although the stepped-up basis of treating the income tax differential is preferred, the alternative of stepping the interest rate down is more widely used. Care must be taken to exclude income taxes from the rate of return computation when the stepped-up basis is used.[11]

Several aspects of Table 3-6 probably strike the small businessman who sees such a display for the first time as being very strange indeed! Not one of the smaller companies interviewed prepared or considered the combined or overall cost of funds, and only four of the larger companies did so. Numerous differences help to explain the omission of this central calculation for capital budgeting.

First, respondents were almost as likely to view interest as a cash flow as they were to view it as a rate. The focus of attention is upon the obligation to pay dollars, especially after a loan is obtained. Second, about one fifth of the respondents believed that equity funds had no cost. A variety of explanations were offered. Small businessmen said such things as,

---

[11]See Soldofsky, *op. cit.*, pp. 217-220, including further references cited there, for a further discussion of the rationale.

"Dividend payments are optional and, therefore, common stock has no cost." If the firm was earning little or no net income, equity had no cost. A few owners said they had received dividends from their business in excess of their original investment, so their equity in the business now had no cost. About one fifth of those respondents who said that equity had a cost also said that the cost was the dollars paid out in dividends, which is interpreted here as a cash flow. Only 57 of the 123 firms said that the cost of equity should be expressed as a rate. Thirty-two companies defined the equity rate as the ratio of earnings to book value. The only use made of this rate was for year-to-year historical comparisons.

A very strange tendency exists among both college students and businessmen to omit Earned Surplus or Retained Earnings when computing the rate of return on common stock. Two explanations for this omission are suggested: first, Earned Surplus is still naively and incorrectly understood to be cash by many individuals; second, Earned Surplus is viewed as a temporary rather than a permanent investment and omitted from the capitalization structure. The latter position is incorrect because American businesses finance expansion by retaining a part of their net income, and they intend to use this source of funds permanently. Even though dividends can be legally charged against Earned Surplus until that account is exhausted (in most states), the equity funds represented by Earned Surplus function as a permanent investment and must be treated as such.

The obligation to pay both the interest and principal of debts is so insistent, the consequences of late or nonpayment so final, and the focus of attention upon the cash flow so hypnotic that the absence of the rate of return view is not surprising. Dividend payments are also seen as an optional cash flow; they are a drain upon the cash balance.

The owner of a small business views net income as his income rather than as a cost of equity funds from the point of view of the business unit. Interest is a cost paid to someone else, but net income is his—whether it is paid to him or left in the business; interest is contractual and dividends are optional. The motivation for and the purposes of combining the cost of borrowed and equity funds are not perceived. From the position of the business, funds have a cost whether they are borrowed or furnished by owners. Only when the overall or combined rate of cost of debt and equity is computed is any rate available that can be compared rationally with the rate of return on prospective investments in order to determine the optimum investment level and to maximize the value of the business.

Another misunderstanding that works against perceiving the rate of cost of equity as the ratio of net income to book value is that usually little, if any, of the earnings are paid out as dividends. The fascination with the cash flow concept of cost leads to the untenable belief that if there is no cash outlay there is no cost. All modern accrual accounting takes a different position. Time-tested elementary economic principles defined economic cost in terms of what the resources could earn in their alternative uses—that is, in terms of opportunity cost.   Every businessman can quickly suggest an array of alternative uses for his funds, ranging from extremely safe to extremely risky investments.   Investments in government bonds yield about 4 percent; first mortgages may yield 5 to 7 percent; and second mortgages may yield up to 10 percent as they do in Southern California.

Expressing net earnings as a rate is not universal, but, when pressed, businessmen would surely say that whether $1 is earned by an investment of $10, $100, or $1,000 makes a difference. In other words, from the viewpoint of the business the rate of cost for equity is an extremely important datum and is absolutely essential to rate of return rationing in capital budgeting.[12]

The discussion thus far was intended to support the propositions that equity funds have a cost and that this cost is best expressed as a rate. The determination of the appropriate rate of return on equity to use in capital budgeting is extremely difficult, and the rate finally selected by any company must be somewhat arbitrary.

One way of establishing the cost of equity is to ask whether debt or equity is more expensive. Most small business respondents who said equity had no cost also said that borrowed funds were the more expensive. The primary basis for this response is the fact that dividends are optional. Most of the respondents who agreed that equity had a cost had either never considered the question of the relative cost of these two sources of funds or believed that borrowed funds were more expensive than owners' funds. Reasons for the latter position, in addition to the compulsory interest payments as contrasted with optional dividend payments, were the low rate of return on equity and the low dividend payments.   Only 14 of the 123 responding companies said that the cost of equity either was or should be higher than the cost of debt!

The key to the problem is the generally accepted doctrine of opportunity cost. The (rate of) cost of funds reflects the expected risks involved. The yield on long-run government bonds is less than the cost on prime business loans because the chances of loss on the former are less. For the same reason, the cost of FHA guaranteed mortgages is less than that of conventional mortgages, and the cost of equity funds or owners' funds is more than the cost of borrowed funds for the same business. *The greater the risk the greater the prospective rate of return to attract or keep funds* in a given company or industry. Whether or not the owners' funds are earning or have earned their opportunity or alternative cost is not the point. The point is that no new investments should be made, and existing investments should be withdrawn, unless either the going or the target rate of return is earned.

---

[12]For widely held corporations, the best definition of the cost of equity funds is the overall growth yield. This yield is the rate of discount which equates the present value of the rising dividends stream and the present value of the market price of the stock at the terminal point with initial market price of the stock. For a detailed discussion of many of the problems involved, see Soldofsky, *op. cit.*, pp. 190-234.

TABLE 3-7

PROFITABILITY OF MANUFACTURING CORPORATIONS

Rate of return
(percent)

Asset size class ($1,000's)	Assets°,†† Before taxes	After taxes	Net worth†,†† After taxes	Assets°°,§ After taxes
0-25	-13.0	-13.9	-113.9	14.9
25-50	- 0.1	- 1.7	- 6.8	12.8
50-100	3.6	1.6	1.1	12.7
100-250	6.3	3.7	4.9	12.2
250-500	8.0	4.5	6.3	12.2
500-1,000	10.0	5.4	7.5	13.4
1,000-2,500	11.3	5.8	7.8	14.4
2,500-5,000	11.8	6.0	8.1	14.4
5,000-10,000	12.6	6.4	8.5	14.9
10,000-25,000	14.0	7.1	9.5	15.5
25,000-50,000	13.0	6.7	8.9	14.3
50,000-100,000	13.0	6.7	9.1	13.9
100,000-250,000	13.3	6.9	9.7	14.6
250,000 plus	13.1	7.0	9.8	13.4

°Profits before and after taxes divided by assets.
†Profits after taxes divided by net worth.
††Includes both profitable and unprofitable corporations.
°°Profitable firms only.
§Profits after taxes.
Source: H. O. Stekler, *Profitability and Size of Firm* (Berkeley: University of California, 1962), pp. 32, 34, and 70.

Table 3-7 shows the rate of return for all manufacturing corporations, both unprofitable and profitable, by asset size classification for 1955-1957. Table 3-8 is unique in that it shows not only average rate of return for manufacturing corporations but also the standard deviation for each size classification. The arithmetic mean and standard deviation are reported separately both for all manufacturing corporations and for profitable manufacturing corporations only. In another context an extended discussion would be appropriate. In the present context the fact that the average rate of return on assets before taxes for profitable corporations by asset size classification ranged between 10.6 and 14.4 percent is important. Even more important are the surprisingly low standard deviations for profitable firms above the smallest size classifications. Even though comparable rate of return and standard deviation data are not available for other years, a rate of return target of 10 percent on an after-tax basis for manufacturing companies financed by common equity only is appropriate. On a before-tax basis, assuming a 48 percent federal income tax rate, the cost of equity steps up to 19.2 percent. The use of preferred stock and long-term loans will reduce the overall cost of funds as long as the proportion of these other sources of funds conforms to well-known financial practices.

In Table 3-6 an after-tax rate of return of 9 percent was used for equity, and the weighted average cost was approximately 15 percent on a before-tax basis. The lower the average income tax rate, the closer the before- and after-taxes weighted average costs of funds will be. The data in Tables 3-7 and 3-8 may be compared with the cost of common equity in Table 3-6.

Whether the firm is organized as a partnership, a proprietorship, or a corporation, the principles involved are the same: the target or hurdle rate of return should be related to the degree of risk involved and to the alternative returns from the use of funds if they were employed elsewhere in [an] undertaking with the same degree of risk. If 6 percent is a good approximation of the cost level of borrowed funds for small business, the target return for the owners' funds should be considerably higher. The cost of borrowed funds is well above 6 percent for many small firms. The average rate of return on stockholders' equity in manufacturing corporations with assets of less than $1,000,000 has been in the 8 to 10 percent range in recent years. The rate of return for larger manufacturing corporations has been somewhat higher. For most small businesses the target rate of return should be at least 10 percent, and it should be substantially higher for many of them. The overall cost of funds is affected by the proportion of debt in the capitalization structures and the average income tax rate. One obvious way to lower the overall cost of funds and to encourage growth is to use a larger proportion of debt. The overall cost of funds for most businesses of any size, large or small, and for most industries is above 10 percent on a before-tax basis.

Before leaving the problem of determining the level of the cost of funds, a few words comparing the cash flow and rate of return concepts

TABLE 3-8

AVERAGE RATE OF RETURN FOR MANUFACTURING ON ASSETS
AND STANDARDS DEVIATION OF RATE OF RETURN—1955

Asset size class ($1,000's)	All corporations		Corporations with profit only	
	Mean firm profit ratio°	Standard deviation of profit ratios	Mean firm profit ratio°	Standard deviation of firm profit ratios
0-25	-15.1%	66.1%	12.0%	27.4%
25-50	- 1.3	26.4	10.6	13.0
50-100	1.9	19.7	10.8	11.1
100-250	5.1	14.8	10.4	9.0
250-500	7.0	12.7	10.5	8.7
500-1,000	9.1	11.4	12.1	9.4
1,000-2,500	9.9	14.0	12.6	8.9
2,500-5,000	11.5	10.6	13.0	8.4
5,000-10,000	12.1	9.4	13.6	7.7
10,000-25,000	13.5	8.3	14.4	6.7
25,000-50,000	13.3	8.7	14.1	7.5
50,000-100,000	12.6	7.3	12.8	7.0
100,000-250,000	12.9	8.0	13.2	7.2
250,000 or more	14.5	5.3	11.1	5.0

°Profit before taxes divided by assets.
Source: H. O. Stekler, *Profitability and Size of Firm* (Berkeley: University of California, 1962), pp. 91, 92, and 93.

of the cost of funds are needed. Nothing that has been said should be taken to minimize the essential condition that obligations must be paid in cash in order to avoid technical insolvency. However, the stress on cash flows—both cash receipts and cash payments—should no longer obscure the fact that cash rationing is the wrong guide; or at best it should be only a supplemental guide for capital budgeting.

SUMMARY

This article began with a simplified but workable statement of capital budgeting. The optimum annual increment of investment is determined by the intersection of the rate of return on investment, r, and the cost of finance, k_o, as shown in Figure 3-1. Neither of these rates is calculated regularly by small businesses—or by most large businesses, either. None of the small businesses included in those interviewed calculated both these rates. When rates were calculated, they were more likely to be incorrect in some respect than to be correct. Forward-looking comparisons of r and k_o in capital budgeting decisions were nonexistent among the small businesses interviewed.

The complete absence of rate of return rationing is hard to understand, but some of the causes of this situation have been suggested. The traditional emphasis of businessmen themselves, and of their bankers, engineers, suppliers and competitors, has been upon *cash*. The motivation to prepare rate computations requires that several misconceptions be overcome on both the real investment side and on the funds side. Once the reasons for computing rates are understood, once the shortcomings of the methods now used are understood, once the rather simple procedures of the rate of return approach to capital budgeting are understood and accepted, capital budgeting as it is described in this article may be quickly adopted by businesses in order to increase their profitability. Understanding the *what, why,* and *how* of capital budgeting is an essential condition for the continued growth, profitability—and even survival—of smaller businesses during the coming decades.

4. SOME FALLACIES IN FIGURING RETURN ON INVESTMENT*

ROBERT N. ANTHONY†

We have come a long way since 1947 when N.A.A. discussion forum material was illustrated by a replacement cost problem solution in which the annual accounting costs associated with the present machine, including its depreciation, were compared with the annual accounting costs of using the new equipment. Actually, most of the changes have occurred in the past five or six years. I doubt that anyone would argue today that book depreciation on the existing equipment should be taken into account in an investment decision, except as it affects income tax calculations; we would all agree it is the cash associated with the proposition that is the crucial fact. And most of us would now agree that a problem of this type cannot be solved without taking into account the time value of money. But it is almost inevitable that, when a technique gains widespread acceptance over a time as short as five years, problems and misuses creep in. Some of these problems and misuses in current practices in computing return on investment form the subject matter of this article.

BASIC CONCEPT OF RETURN ON INVESTMENT

Let us start with a statement of precisely what is meant by the term, "return on investment," because much of the disagreement as to the best way of analyzing problems arises from implicit differences in the way this term is used or interpreted by various people.

Everyone would agree that, if Company A lends someone $1,000, receives $80 interest a year for five years (or indeed any number of years), and at the end of that time receives back the $1,000, it has earned a return of 8 percent. Each year it has earned 8 percent on the money at risk that year. This can be calculated either by the simple process of dividing $1,000 into $80 or by finding the rate at which the future payments have to be discounted in order to equate their present value to the initial $1,000. This concept—that return on investment is the rate earned on the funds *at risk* each year—is basic and underlies all later calculations.

But in the typical business investment in a new machine or in the assets required to launch a new product, the investment is *not* paid back at the end of a time period; therefore, the stream of annual earnings must be large enough both to provide for profit and to recoup the investment itself. This is so because, unless the investment consists entirely of land or of working

---

*From the *NAA Bulletin* (December, 1960), pp. 5-13. Reprinted by permission.
†Professor of Business Administration, Harvard University.

39

TABLE 4-1

RETURN ON INVESTMENT CALCULATION

Year	Earnings in that year (a)	8% discount factor° (b)	Present value (a × b)
1	$250	0.926	$232
2	250	0.857	214
3	250	0.794	198
4	250	0.735	184
5	250	0.681	170
		Total present value	$998

PROOF:

Year	Total earnings (a)	Return at 8% of investment outstanding (b)	Balance, to apply against investment c =(a — b)	Investment outstanding end of year (d)
0	$...	$...	$...	$1,000
1	250	80	170	830
2	250	66	184	646
3	250	52	198	448
4	250	36	214	234
5	250	19	231	3°

°Due to rounding.

capital, we cannot expect to recover the investment at the end of the project as in the case of a simple loan. Nevertheless, the return on this investment can be calculated by the same technique, since this technique automatically takes into account the recouping of the investment.

Table 4-1 shows such a calculation for an investment of $1,000 and anticipated cash earnings of $250 a year for five years but no residual value. (Income taxes are ignored in the interest of keeping the numbers simple.) By a trial of various discount rates, we discover that the present value of the five $250 payments equals $1,000 when discounted at a rate of 8 percent and that the return is, therefore, 8 percent. The proof of this fact is given as the second part of Table 4-1. There is absolutely no other way of obtaining this return; we *must* take the present value of the future payments into account in order to find the true return or, as it is coming to be known, the time-adjusted return.

In the remainder of this article, some of the fallacies that have grown up around this basic idea will be discussed.

FIRST FALLACY: IGNORING INCOME TAXES

The first fallacy is that of ignoring income taxes. It is sometimes said that, since income taxes take approximately 50 percent of profit, the return after taxes equals 50 percent of the return before taxes. Even the simple illustration which follows shows that this is not so:

Annual earnings before taxes	$250
Depreciation	200
Net income subject to tax	50
Tax at 50%	25
Net income after tax	25
plus depreciation	200
Cash earnings after tax	$225

Depreciation shields the cash earnings from the full impact of the income tax and cuts the earnings—not in half but only by some considerably lesser amount. In this case, the after-tax earnings would figure out to somewhat more than 4 percent. When we realize the necessity of taking into account the effect of accelerated depreciation, of gains or losses on the sale of existing equipment and other tax considerations, we see that there can be no simple relationship between the pre-tax and the after-tax return. The only safe procedure is to figure the effect of taxes in each case. We will leave the matter of income tax with this brief mention. In the interest of simplicity, income tax calculations are ignored in the examples used in illustrating other points.

SECOND FALLACY: PRESENT VALUE IS TOO COMPLICATED

The second fallacy, and a much more important one as a practical matter, is the belief that present value techniques are too complicated to be of use to the businessman. Even some authors still consider it "complex and difficult" or advise the practical businessman to use a more "feasible" method, i.e., the accounting return.

To me, this advice completely disregards the realities of the work involved in various phases of analyzing a proposed investment. The "tough" part of such an analysis is always the collection of the underlying estimates. The analyst must make these estimates whether or not he used present value techniques to put the numbers together at the final stage of the calculation. So the problem of making good estimates is in no way peculiar to the present value approach. However, the present value technique does require a little more time in putting the figures together, perhaps a minute or two in some situations, an hour or two for a very complicated major expansion program. Nevertheless, if by spending a few extra minutes or hours, we can improve considerably the validity of the figures on which an important decision must be based, figures that may have required dozens or hundreds of man-hours to assemble, it seems worth doing.

To emphasize the insignificance of the extra time required, let me illustrate a short cut which can be used in any situation where the stream of earnings is relatively level. Simply take the earnings and divide them into the investment (in our example—$1,000 ÷ $250 = 4). Then, using a present value table, like the one a portion of which is shown in Table 4-2, run along the row of figures according to the period of time the project is expected

TABLE 4-2

PRESENT VALUE OF $1 RECEIVED ANNUALLY FOR N YEARS

Years (N)	1%	2%	4%	6%	8%	10%	12%	14%	15%	16%	18%	20%	22%	24%	
1	0.990	0.980	0.962	0.943	0.926	0.909	0.893	0.877	0.870	0.862	0.847	0.833	0.820	0.806	
2	1.970	1.942	1.886	1.833	1.783	1.736	1.690	1.647	1.626	1.605	1.566	1.528	1.492	1.457	
3	2.941	2.884	2.775	2.673	2.577	2.487	2.402	2.322	2.283	2.246	2.174	2.106	2.042	1.981	
4	3.902	3.808	3.630	3.465	3.312	3.170	3.037	2.914	2.855	2.798	2.690	2.589	2.494	2.404	
→5	4.853	4.713	4.452	4.212	(3.993)	3.791	3.605	3.433	3.352	3.274	3.127	2.991	2.864	2.745	
6	5.795	5.601	5.242	4.917	4.623	4.355	4.111	3.889	3.784	3.685	3.498	3.326	3.167	3.020	2.5
7	6.728	6.472	6.002	5.582	5.206	4.868	4.564	4.288	4.160	4.039	3.812	3.605	3.416	3.242	3.1
8	7.652	7.325	6.733	6.210	5.747	5.335	4.968	4.639	4.487	4.344	4.078	3.837	3.619	3.421	3.3
9	8.566	8.162	7.435	6.802	6.247	5.759	5.328	4.946	4.772	4.607	4.303	4.031	3.786	3.566	3.4
10	9.471	8.983	8.111	7.360	6.710	6.145	5.650	5.216	5.019	4.833	4.494	4.192	3.923	3.682	3
11	10.368	9.787	8.760	7.887	7.139	6.495	5.988	5.453	5.234	5.029	4.656	4.327	4.035	3.776	
12	11.255	10.575	9.385	8.384	7.536	6.814	6.194	5.660	5.421	5.197	4.793	4.439	4.127	3.851	
13	12.134	11.343	9.986	8.853	7.904	7.103	6.424	5.842	5.583	5.342	4.910	4.533	4.203	3.912	
14	13.004	12.106	10.563	9.295	8.244	7.367	6.628	6.002	5.724	5.468	5.008	4.611	4.265	3.962	
15	13.865	12.849	11.118	9.712	8.559	7.606	6.811	6.142	5.847	5.575	5.092	4.675	4.315	4.001	
		13.578	11.652	10 1°				5.954	5.669					4.033	

to last, in this case, five years. Stop at the number closest to 4. The heading of this column indicates the return on the investment, 8 percent.

When flows are uneven, this method will not work, but it only takes a few minutes more, and never more than three trials, to find the true return in such cases, to the nearest percent. There is no point in these problems in coming any closer than the nearest percentage, since the underlying estimates are not exact anyway.

THIRD FALLACY: THE HIGHER THE RETURN, THE BETTER THE PROJECT

The third fallacy is much more subtle. The return computed above is indeed the true return. One might think that the higher this return, the better the project. In most cases this is true, but here are some important exceptions. Let us rule out all the unmeasured factors, the intangibles that must be taken into account as extremely important in choosing investment projects, and focus only on the numbers.

Table 4-3 shows two projects, each requiring an investment of $1,000. Project A will earn $1,200 for one year, and Project B will earn $300 for each of five years. A computation of the time-adjusted return on these two projects would show a return of 20 percent for Project A and 15 percent for Project B. But Project A is not necessarily better than Project B. It all depends on what the company can do with the funds released from Project A at the

TABLE 4-3

THE HIGH RETURN PROJECT IS NOT NECESSARILY BETTER

	A	B
Investment	$1,000	$1,000
Annual earnings	1,200	300
Life	1 year	5 years
Return on investment	20%	15%
Profitability at 10%	$1,091	$1,137
Profitability index	1.09	1.14

end of its life, i.e., at the end of the year. If no very good opportunities for investment will exist at that time, Project *B* may be more desirable because the funds are tied up for a longer time and earn a quite satisfactory return over the whole of the longer period.

There is a simple method for solving the problem. We call it the *profitability method*, because this was the term given to it by Bell Telephone Company engineers several years ago. It involves discounting the stream of earnings at the rate the company can reasonably expect to earn on future investments. Assuming this expected earnings rate to be 10 percent, the present values turn out to be $1,091 in Project *A* and $1,137 in Project *B*. The profitability index is found by dividing the present value of the earnings by the investment, $1,000. The result shows that, despite its lower return on investment, Project *B*, with an index of 1.14, is better than Project *A*, with an index of 1.09. This is a valid conclusion.

The problem illustrated above arises whenever two projects with different lives, or with the same lives but different patterns of earnings, are being compared with each other. These situations cannot be safely judged on the basis of return on investment. In all except a few highly unusual circumstances, the profitability index method will accurately signal which of them is better. However it should always be remembered that we are talking about only those aspects of the problem that are reduced to measurable terms. Of course, the problem does not arise at all if the two projects are not competing with each other; if the company can do both projects and if it expects to earn 10 percent on the average, it should do both.

FOURTH FALLACY: LEASING IS ALWAYS ADVANTAGEOUS

Let us now consider some common statements about leasing:

> Leasing frees working capital for other uses.
> Leasing keeps available an unused line of borrowing power.
> Leasing has tax advantages.
> Leasing protects you from the risk of obsolescence.
> We are in the (particular) business, not the real estate (or data processing, or automobile operating) business.
> Leasing is more expensive than debt.
> A lease has junior status in reorganizations.

Each of these statements contains a fallacy or, at best, a half truth. Rather than discuss them one at a time, we shall try to put these and other arguments into the proper frame of reference.

First of all, it is absolutely impossible to talk about leasing in general. There are at least three types of lease arrangements, each so different from the others that quite different kinds of thinking are required. There is, first, the agreement that is intended primarily to provide service which, as a practical matter, the lessee cannot obtain in any other way. The person who rents an automobile for a few hours is not faced with a buy-or-rent decision, nor ordinarily is the company which rents office space in a downtown office building.   These situations are not investment problems at all; the only question is whether the service provided is worth what it costs.

The second main type of lease is the short-term lease cancellable at the lessee's option on relatively short notice and with relatively small penalty. Office and data processing equipment leases are examples. In these situations the user does have to decide whether he is better off to buy the equipment or to rent it.

In our book, *Office Equipment: Buy or Rent?*[1] we have tried to show how this problem can be analyzed. The example used is office equipment, but the same technique is applicable to all short-term cancellable leases. The procedure is to estimate the costs associated with leasing and the costs associated with purchasing.   Since the purchase alternative involves an immediate outlay and the leasing alternative will involve a stream of outlays in the future, the two must be compared by the use of the present value techniques discussed earlier.   Each case depends on its own merits, and the solution is to figure it out, not to rely on some broad generalization whether put out by someone who is for or by someone who is against leasing.

About the only generalization which safely can be made is that these cancellable leases are essentially devices for shifting the risk of ownership. If you own the equipment, you bear the risk that it will not last as long as you anticipated.   If it becomes obsolete sooner or if for some other reason you no longer have a need for it, it is you who suffer the loss.   If you let the manufacturer own the equipment and lease it to you, he is the one who takes the risk.   Since he knows he bears the risk, he sets his lease rates taking this fact into account.   Since all lessees pay the same rate, he must set the rates with regard to the average situation.   So the question is whether you are above or below average—average with respect to what money is worth to you, average with respect to the intensity and length of time you will use the equipment, average with respect to income and capital gains taxes, and so on.   Thus, only calculations geared to your own particular situation can show whether *you* should buy or rent; general rules do not necessarily apply to *your* situation.

The third type of lease is the financial lease, a long-term lease which is either noncancellable or, if cancellable, involves a termination payment equal to the remaining book value of the asset. This lease is strictly a way of raising money. The lease obligation is debt, and, although it does not appear on the balance sheet as such, many well-informed lenders will include this obligation as debt when they are appraising the company's borrowing capacity. The problem, therefore, is whether to finance a transaction by borrowing or by leasing. It is a straight financial problem, to be solved by usual financial methods. The actual numerical solution is a little more complicated than in ordinary financial problems because of the different tax treatments of owned and leased assets, but, in essence, the problem is the same.   The

[1]R. N. Anthony and S. Schwartz, *Office Equipment: Buy or Rent?*,   Management Analysis Center, 1957.

relevant discount rate is low, much lower than in the case of the cancellable lease, because in the financial lease the user bears, in fact, the risk of ownership.

The statement that leasing frees working capital is particularly intriguing and erroneous. Its advocates divide net profit by the working capital to show that the company is earning perhaps 30 percent on its working capital and then dangle before the prospect the possibility of making this return on the working capital freed by leasing. The fact is, of course, that it is not working capital alone that is earning the company's profit; it is all the capital.

Let me make just one comment on the common argument that leasing has tax advantages. Now, throwing money down a "rat hole" has tax advantages; you get a 52 cents tax benefit for every dollar you throw down. In general, the higher your expenses are, the greater the tax deduction, but this is not a sound reason for willingly wasting money. The catch is that you do not make a profit by saving the 52 percent; you make a profit only out of the 48 percent. While it is true that the leasing of land has a tax advantage difficult to obtain in any other way, the leasing of depreciable property may or may not have a tax advantage. It all depends on the facts in a particular case, and the tax aspect is only one aspect of the proposition. The solution is not to generalize but, rather, to do some calculating as to where the net advantage lies in each instance.

FIFTH FALLACY: PAYBACK NEVER GIVES A USEFUL ANSWER

As to the final fallacy, let us go back to the beginning and show how one of the implications that might be read into my initial demonstration is also fallacious, i.e., that any method other than discounted cash flow must be wrong. We should not generalize, for example, that the payback method of computation is obsolete.

As Professor Myron Gordon has demonstrated,[2] although the reciprocal of the payback does indeed overstate the true rate of return, the error is not very important under certain conditions. As a rough rule, most companies will find that, if earnings are expected to be level and if the expected life of the project is somewhat more than twice the payback period, the payback method gives reasonably accurate results.

Table 4-2 can also be used backwards to arrive at a good payback rule. If, for example, a company finds that its ordinary production equipment has a life of ten years and if it demands a return of 15 percent after taxes, the figure of 5.019 in the 10-year row and 15 percent columns shows that the company will be safe in accepting projects with a payback of not more than five years, after taxes. The foremen can be told to use a 5-year after-tax payback in evaluating such projects without any necessity for educating them in present value concepts. With slightly more effort and assuming a

---

[2]Ezra Solomon (ed.), *The Management of Corporate Capital* (New York: The Free Press, 1959).

depreciation pattern for tax purposes, one can convert this calculation to a before-tax payback. This figure can be used safely, however, only if earnings are level from year to year and only if the project involves depreciable assets with negligible residual values.

SUMMING UP

My purpose in exploring these five fallacies has not been to criticize but, rather, to call added attention to certain concepts that are now pretty well established: The only exact way of figuring return on investment is to use present value techniques. The work involved in doing this is only slightly greater than that required by the so-called simple methods. However, the time-adjusted return on investment does not always signal the right decision to the problem, and the newer profitability-index method does. Present value techniques are a rational way of solving buy-or-lease and borrow-or-lease problems, which tend otherwise to get solved on the basis of propaganda and folklore. And, finally, once present value techniques are understood, there are acceptable short cuts that come to the correct result for many common problems.

5. INVESTMENT POLICIES THAT PAY OFF*

DAVID B. HERTZ †

In the next 12 months, U.S. businessmen, acting for the most part on the basis of painstaking staff analyses, will commit an estimated $65 billion to promising new capital investment projects. Two or three years later, when the long-term financial results of those investments are beginning to take shape, a good many of these same businessmen will be suffering the pangs of the big loser at Las Vegas. For, despite all the high-priced staff time and the board-level soul-searching that go into them, most capital investment decisions remain an incongruous blend of the slide rule and the roulette wheel. Consider some recent evidence:

The president of a big international corporation told me recently, "I can't understand why our investment policy hasn't worked the way we expected." Some years ago, he explained, the executive committee had decided that every capital investment, to be acceptable, would have to show an estimated before-tax average annual return on capital of 20 percent. The rule had been scrupulously followed; yet actual results had averaged 14 percent. "And we've got some of the best analysts in the business," added the frustrated president.

In another large and sophisticated company engaged in diversified manufacturing operations, barely half of the new investments during the past ten years are now expected to reach the break-even point, and less than half of those will reach or exceed their predicted return on investment. (On the other hand, some of the winners will be much larger than anticipated.)

The executive committee of a major chemical company is facing a real dilemma. It currently requires each proposed capital project to show an expected return of at least 12 percent after taxes (16 percent for high-risk investments). Applying this policy, the executive committee has not turned down a single capital investment proposal for the past two years. Results from recent investments, however, have been alarmingly uneven. To provide a better screen for future proposals and hopefully to improve investment results, a new policy requiring a three-year payback period plus a discounted cash flow return of 8 percent has been recommended to the committee. The members of the committee do not know what to do.

Capital investment decisions, it would seem, are still more art than science—and often more gamble than art. The reasons, moreover, are fairly obvious.

Any investment decision is (or should be) concerned with a choice among the available alternatives, and it is always subject to an unknown

*Reprinted from *The Harvard Business Review* (January-February, 1968) pp. 96-108: © 1968 by the President and Fellows of Harvard College; all rights reserved.

†Director, McKinsey and Company.

future environment. Actual future costs, markets, and prices will inevitably differ from any single set of assumptions used as a framework for weighing proposals. Moreover, a variety of criteria—payback, average annual return, net present value, internal ROI—may be used as yardsticks for proposals. And, despite much theoretical discussion, it has been hard for management to guess what difference, if any, the choice of a particular yardstick would make in actual long-term dollars-and-cents results. In short, lacking any way to test out the ultimate financial impact of a given investment policy, management literally has had no way of knowing whether it might have done better.

Research results recently obtained by McKinsey & Company through analysis and computer simulation of the investment process indicate that there is a practical way for most companies to make sure that the policies they do choose have the greatest chance of meeting their objectives. Specifically, management can answer these questions with confidence:

Historically, has our investment policy given us the highest possible return, consistent with the risks we have accepted?

How much risk have we been accepting in our investment decisions? Is this consistent with the risks that top management really wants to accept?

Have we been using the best criteria for investment selection, considering long-term corporate objectives? Have we been taking adequate account of uncertainty?

Given the investment alternatives that are available to us and the risks we are willing to accept, what *investment policy* will maximize the earnings-per-share performance of our investments over the long run?

To understand how these questions can be answered and to clarify the methods and results of our research, it will be useful to compare some current approaches to risk and then to explore the concept of an effective investment policy.

RISK AND THE FUTURE

The exact course of future events is unknown when investment choices are made, and uncertainty creates risk. There are two conventional ways of dealing with risk and uncertainty and one less conventional method that is gaining acceptance.

Best-guess Estimates

A simple, widely used conventional approach is to express one's assumptions about the key variables affecting future costs, revenues, and investment requirements in terms of single-point estimates based on the best information available to management at the time the forecast is made. The calculated outcome of the investment, based on these "best guesses," is judged acceptable if it exceeds a specified criterion of return or payback. If the project is considered particularly risky, the hurdle may be raised—in effect, requiring a *risk premium*, an idea carried over from the early days of insurance.

Exhibit 5-1 shows how difficult it is to determine an acceptable risk premium, even in a simple case. Using very reasonable ranges for each of the variables involved (e.g., a best guess of 200,000 units for sales volume, with a range from 175,000 to 225,000 units), it demonstrates that the outcome, in terms of average return on investment, may vary anywhere from 0 percent to 56.5 percent. Thus, as Exhibit 5-1 demonstrates, this approach has a fatal weakness: if the actual outcome for any variable is significantly different from the estimate, the actual results of the investment may be *very* much different from those projected; simply raising the hurdle may not help much.

EXHIBIT 5-1

DRAWBACKS OF SINGLE-POINT ESTIMATES

$$ROI = \frac{(Price \times Unit\ sales) - (Costs)}{(Investment)}$$

Best-guess estimates:
Price = $5.00
Costs = $800,000
ROI = 20%
Sales = 200,000 units
Investment = $1,000,000

Likely ranges:
Price = $5.00 to $5.50
Costs = $700,000 to $875,000
Sales = 175,000 to 225,000 units
Investment = $950,000 to $1,100,000

Worst case: $\dfrac{5.0 \times 175,000 - 875,000}{1,100,000} = \dfrac{0}{1,100,000} = 0\%\ ROI$

Best case: $\dfrac{5.5 \times 225,000 - 700,000}{950,000} = 56.5\%\ ROI$

In an attempt to overcome this weakness, many managements follow the practice of supplementing their best-guess estimates with other values for each variable, e.g., a high (optimistic) and a low (pessimistic) value. By permuting the values for each variable in repeated calculations, it is then possible to see what variations might occur if the best guesses are not all on target—as, in fact, they are highly unlikely to be.

With no information as to the *likelihood* of a given outcome, however, the decision maker has not added much to his assessment of the uncertainty. He has a better idea of what he may be letting the company in for, but he has little real information about what he ought to *expect*. To be sure, managements can and do try out various investment criteria, e.g., payback period, ROI, and net present value, to see whether each seems to yield good results under varying conditions. But they have not really been able to predict the ultimate financial results of using particular criteria.

Forced Fit Forecasts

The second conventional way around the difficulties of an unknown future—a way that seems to have special appeal to marketing-oriented companies—is to acknowledge freely all the uncertainties surrounding the estimated outcome of a new investment and then to wave them away on the grounds that the actual outcome can be forced to fit the estimate. For example, if sales fall short of target, various measures—ranging from heavier advertising to a shake-up of the sales force—can be applied to get the desired results. And since the precise circumstances in which these tactics might be applied cannot be known in advance, there is no point in worrying until the time comes; "something will always turn up."

Of course, this micawberish view completely misses the point. If one can be certain of achieving a particular set of results, the uncertainty disappears and so, in large measure, does the problem of investment policy. If one cannot, the uncertainty and the problem remain. The striking proportion of marketing failures among new products (estimates range from 30 percent to 80 percent, depending on definitions) belies the optimism of the micawbers.

Risk-based Profiles

A third method of dealing with uncertainty, which is less conventional but more sophisticated, has recently been gaining adherents. Some years ago I suggested that the risks inherent in an investment could be directly assessed through computer simulation.[1] In this method, called risk analysis, the first step is to identify the leverage factors that will influence the key variables determining future costs and revenues. For example, capacity will influence sales volume; timing of market entry will influence price; and so forth. The next step is to weigh all of the available information—e.g., historical trends, growth of markets, likely price changes—about each of these leverage factors and then, from this information, to develop the *uncertainty profile* for each key variable.

Estimates of revenues from a proposed new plant, for example, might indicate that there is a two-thirds chance of their falling within ± $40,000 of an *expected*—or average over the long run—$250,000 a year, that there is only one chance in ten of their falling below $180,000, but that there is also one chance in ten that they will exceed $350,000. These estimates are used to define a probability distribution curve for future revenues, which is called the uncertainty profile. These profiles for the elements that enter into an investment project are sometimes determined from historical or other objective data, but they are more likely to be subjective estimates by those most familiar with the various parts of the overall proposal.

Gathering and analyzing the data needed to construct such uncertainty profiles may pose difficult communications problems, it should be noted.

---

[1]See my article "Risk Analysis in Capital Investment," *Harvard Business Review* (January-February, 1964), p. 95.

Exhibit 5-2
Example of Risk-analysis Simulation

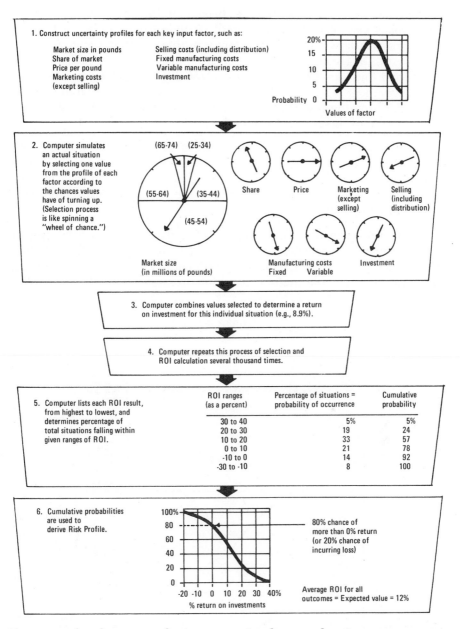

For example, does a marketing executive know what it means to say, "Product A has at least a 90 percent chance of achieving a 15 percent return on investment five years out"? Can he learn to think in these terms? Solving such communications problems is part of the process of developing a rational and effective investment policy. It is not, however, the issue addressed in this article.

Once an "uncertainty profile" has been established for each key investment project variable, we can repeatedly sample from the distributions of these variables shown in their uncertainty profiles. Using a computer, we calculate the financial outcome of the combined variables each time we sample and thus simulate the range of probable outcomes from the proposed investment in terms of the particular investment criterion to be used or tested. From the results of these simulations, a probability distribution or *risk profile* of the criterion can be built up.

Exhibit 5-2 shows the steps employed in simulating the possible outcomes of a given investment and in determining the risk profile. Such profiles can be developed for any criterion that management may wish to use. Exhibit 5-3 shows the payback, average ROI, and discounted ROI profiles of a hypothetical investment.

Of two investments, one is clearly better than the other if it offers a greater probability of achieving any given level of return. In this situation risk analysis permits management to distinguish without question among more and less desirable investments. For example, in Part I of Exhibit

Exhibit 5-3
RISK-ANALYSIS RESULTS USING DIFFERENT CRITERIA

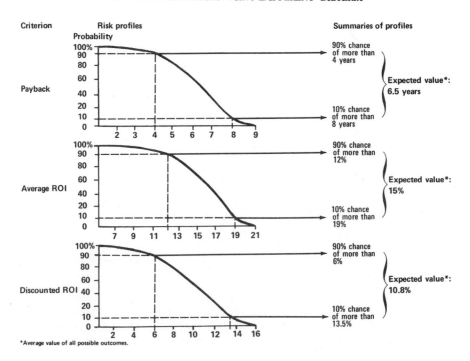

*Average value of all possible outcomes.

5-4, we see that Investment A is a better bet than Investment B at all values of return—that is, it *dominates* Investment B.

But one investment alternative is *not* always dominant. Consider the case of Investments X and Y in Part 2 of Exhibit 5-4. Here, Investment X is more likely than Investment Y to attain at least a 10 percent return on investment but less likely to bring in a 40 percent return. In cases of this kind—and they are numerous—the questions of which investment to select and how to go about establishing a policy to guide the choice have hitherto gone unanswered.

EXHIBIT 5-4
EXAMPLES OF BEST-CHOICE INVESTMENT ALTERNATIVES

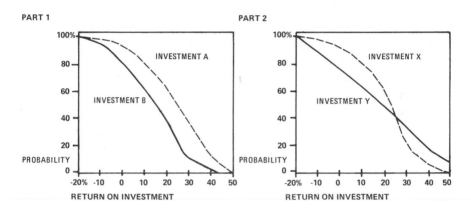

To be sure, in using risk profiles management is availing itself of all, not just part, of the quantitative information that can be put together on the investment possibilities. And more information in the hands of management should mean better decisions. But the question of how to use this information remains. Before it can be answered, we need a clear conception of the nature and function of an investment policy.

NATURE OF POLICY

Any investment policy, if it is to guide management's choices among available investment alternatives, must embody two components: (1) *one or more criteria* by which to measure the relative economic attributes of investment alternatives, and (2) *decision rules*, which may or may not make use of risk analysis or otherwise seek to take uncertainty into account, for selecting "acceptable" investments.

The criteria have been the subject of much analysis and discussion. They include: payback period, which is simply the number of years required for the investment to return its costs; average annual percent return on average funds employed; net present value measures; and internal rates of return, calculated on a discounted cash-flow basis.[2] On the other hand, the rules for making choices, particularly under uncertainty, have been largely left up in the air.[3] Of course, no preestablished policy can take into account all the considerations—human, organizational, strategic, and financial—that typically enter into a major capital investment decision. In this article, however, I am concerned strictly with the question of financial policy, which does lend itself to rigorous formulation.

Dual Role

A consistent and adequate investment policy has a double function. In the short run, it should indicate which investments should be chosen to achieve the financial objectives of the corporation. In the long run, it should serve as a basis for identifying or developing investment alternatives that are likely to match the policies selected. In other words, it serves as a basis for both (a) *acting on* and (b) *communicating about* investment alternatives.

Screening proposals. In the first instance, an investment policy may be regarded as a screen which will pass certain investment proposals and reject others. The screen may be coarse or fine, tight or loose, high risk or low risk, depending on management's knowing or unknowing choice. Through the screen will pass the acceptable investment proposals that will form management's investment set.

Once it is understood that a risk profile attaches, willy-nilly, to all investments and that this profile varies with the criteria chosen even though based on the same estimates of underlying real-world phenomena, it becomes clear that a policy with a determinate, or single-point-based, decision-rule component is a very coarse screen indeed, if it can be called a screen at all. In any case, as we shall see, such a determinate policy is ineffective; it will not guide management to making the best use of its investment funds, no matter what the company's financial objectives may be.

Risk-based policies, on the other hand, may specify how management would prefer to trade off the chances of low return against the chances of high return. For example, would it prefer a virtual certainty of no loss coupled with a virtual ceiling on gains over 20 percent after taxes, or would it accept a one-in-ten chance of significant loss for the sake of a one-in-ten chance of very high gain?

Exhibit 5-5 shows how one specific policy may be defined by the criterion to be used and the rules to be followed in screening investments in

---

[2]For a comprehensive discussion of these measures and their relative merits, see Harold Bierman, Jr. and Seymour Smidt, *The Capital Budgeting Decision* (New York: The Macmillan Company, 1966).

[3]An interesting and provocative discussion of such rules will be found in R. M. Adelson, "Criteria for Capital Investment: An Approach Through Decision Theory," *Operational Research Quarterly*, Vol. 16, No. 1; Adelson approaches the problems suggested in this article and provides, along with a useful list of references, an excellent analytical discussion of the difficulties in presently used methods.

terms of their risk profiles. These rules, which make explicit management's entrepreneurial or risk-taking attitudes, do allow consistent investment choices.[4] The methods described in this article assume that uncertainty—that is, the spread of distribution of potential returns around the expected value, or average of all outcomes—is a useful measure of risk. It is generally accepted that the further the return might exceed the expected value, the further it could also fall short, and lucky indeed is the company to which this principle does not apply.

EXHIBIT 5-5
EXAMPLE OF RISK-BASED INVESTMENT POLICY

1. Criterion to be used as a measure of investment worth: Before-tax return on investment, on a discounted cash flow basis
2. Rules to be used to screen investments based on risk profiles of proposed projects:
Accept proposals that have—
   a. Expected value (average of all outcomes) of 5% or greater
   b. One chance in ten that the ROI will exceed 25%
   c. Nine chances in ten that the ROI will exceed 0%

Communicating alternatives. In the second instance, an investment policy can be a powerful communications tool. It enables top management to make known in advance to those responsible for developing investment proposals what sort of projects the company seeks. The object is to control the selection and development of alternatives so that they reflect the gains the company wants to make and the risks it is willing to undergo to achieve them.

In theory, of course, this function could be served by policy statements such as, "All investments must have an estimated average return on capital employed at 12 percent or more after taxes." But, on the practical level, the complexity of most present-day investment projects and the multitude of future variables to which they are subject rob such statements of most of their usefulness. This is why top management today, confronted with requests for capital, so often finds that the only significant response it can make is to approve the results of all the analyses that have previously taken place at divisional and staff levels.

With a risk-based policy, using one or more criteria and such rules as shown in Exhibit 5-5, management still has no guarantee that all or any of the available investments will pass through the screen. But it does have a better, more specific means for discriminating among proposed investments. And it also has a tool for testing out its own procedures for developing investment proposals and for checking out alternative policies. To analyze its own past investments and requests for capital, a company can estimate the risk profiles of these past investments and determine (a) whether it has been consistent in its past selections and (b) what changes in the mix selected would be indicated by different policy choices.

---

[4]See Ralph O. Swalm, "Utility Theory—Insights Into Risk Taking," *Harvard Business Review* (November-December, 1966), p. 123. [See Article 26 in this book.]

This analysis, however, still will not indicate what is the best overall investment policy, that is, what impact the choice of a particular criterion, such as net present value, payback, or return on investment, has on the likely outcome of specific real-world variables, such as costs and revenues, or what differences there are (again, in terms of real-world financial results) between high-risk and low-risk screens. In this connection I think it is important to note that the criteria are mathematically derived in fairly complicated ways from real-world events, such as sales, price changes, equipment installations, and so on. Since the uncertainty profiles of the events must be used to determine the final risk profile of the criterion, simulation methods are required.

EFFICIENCY CONCEPT

Most managements would like to have investment policies that both maximize financial results over the long run and minimize uncertainty or risk. Seeking additional returns, however, normally entails accepting additional uncertainty, that is, risk. If two policies produce the same average result, e.g., the same average earnings per share over a 5-year period, the one that involves less "variability" (or uncertainty as to the outcome), for the same yield is a more desirable or "efficient" policy. Conversely, of two policies entailing the same variability, the one producing the higher expected return ("expected" meaning the average of all outcomes) is obviously the better policy. Variability is best measured in terms of the probability distribution of the values within which the actual results are likely to fall.

Standard Deviation

The spread or variability of risk profile can be measured by the size of the standard deviation, which represents the spread around the expected value of the criterion encompassing two thirds of all the actual outcomes. Thus, if one can simulate the financial results of investments selected on the basis of a particular policy, the expected return, along with the standard deviation of the financial results obtained with that policy, will indicate the "efficiency" of the investment project set selected under that policy. (With this simulation, the distributions of the uncertainty profiles of revenues, costs, and investments in a specific year are combined. These combinations are linear, and we can expect the results to be normally distributed.)

The expected return and the standard deviation can be plotted on a graph to show the effectiveness of any policy, and a line can then be drawn through the points of greatest yield for a given standard deviation. This line is called the *efficiency frontier* because it represents the best return management can get for a given variance, unless, of course, management either (a) finds a policy that will yield a greater return on investment for no more variance or (b) develops investment proposals with different uncer-

EXHIBIT 5-6
COMPARING INVESTMENT POLICIES

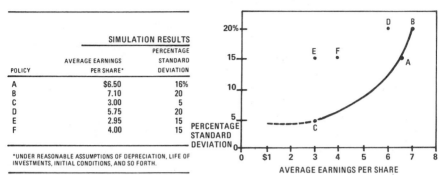

| POLICY | SIMULATION RESULTS | |
	AVERAGE EARNINGS PER SHARE*	PERCENTAGE STANDARD DEVIATION
A	$6.50	16%
B	7.10	20
C	3.00	5
D	5.75	20
E	2.95	15
F	4.00	15

*UNDER REASONABLE ASSUMPTIONS OF DEPRECIATION, LIFE OF INVESTMENTS, INITIAL CONDITIONS, AND SO FORTH.

tainty profiles that provide project choices with less variance for equivalent returns.

Exhibit 5-6 illustrates how the average returns, in this case, earnings per share, are plotted against the standard deviation of those earnings to give an efficiency frontier.[5] Each point on the graph represents the financial results to be expected from a combination of investments selected by passing the same group of proposals through the screen of a particular investment policy. (The results shown in this exhibit were obtained by simulating the operation of a company using this policy for 15 years.)

Policies A, B, and C lie on the efficiency frontier because each produces the maximum earnings per share for a given degree of risk. Policies D, E, and F do not lie on the frontier because none of them produces, for a given standard deviation, as much earnings as management could obtain by using a different policy. Policy F, for example, is better than E because it earns $4.00 against $2.95 for the same risk (15 percent standard deviation), but it is worse than A, which produces earnings of $6.50 at a standard deviation of 16 percent. An efficient policy at 15 percent standard deviation should produce average earnings of approximately $6.25 per share.

Specific policies can, of course, be developed to fill in the entire efficiency frontier curve. For example, the simulation can take into account the capital structure of a real or hypothetical firm, both currently and in the (uncertain) future, thereby dealing effectively with the problem of the marginal cost of capital.

If the objective of an investment policy is to maximize average long-term earnings or yield for a given variation of those earnings or that yield, there is literally no reason why a management that has calculated its own efficiency frontier should use a policy that is not on that frontier. By

[5]In *Portfolio Selection: Effective Diversification of Investments* (New York: John Wiley & Sons, Inc., 1959), Harry M. Markowitz develops a similar concept; the method he describes does not, however, select investments with reference to their risk characteristics; see Michael L. Kirby, "The Current State of Chance-Constrained Programming," *Systems Research Memorandum No. 181.* (Evanston, Ill.: The Technological Institute, Northwestern University Press, August, 1967).

EXHIBIT 5-7
EXAMPLES OF INVESTMENT POLICIES (AFTER TAX)

Criterion	Conservative policy			High-risk policy		
	90% probability of doing better than	Expected value better than	10% probability of doing better than	90% probability of doing better than	Expected value better than	10% probability of doing better than
1. Payback (years to recover investment)	7	5	—	10	4	2
2. Average annual proceeds/investment (percent)	15%	20%	—	− 5%	15%	45%
3. ROI-dcf (percent)	10%	15%	—	−10%	10%	35%
4. NPV-dcf* Discount rate:						
10	1.0					
15		1.0			1.0	
45						1.0

*The indicated values are ratios of NPV of cash flow at the specified discount rates, divided by the present value of the investment.

definition, such a policy entails more variability in investment results and/or a lower expected return than the company is in fact obliged to accept. A management that wants to invest rationally, that is, wants to optimize results, has every reason, therefore, to locate its efficiency frontier and continually strive to improve it.

RESEARCH RESULTS

How practicable is the concept of efficient investment sets (on the efficiency frontier) and effective investment policies that will lead to a choice of such sets? In terms of actual investment results, what light does it throw on the choice of particular investment criteria, such as payback period, average annual return, and the like? To help answer these questions, a computer model was developed that made it possible to simulate the effects of various policies, operating over a period of years, on the financial results of a hypothetical company which selects annually from a wide range of investment proposals. Generally acceptable accounting procedures were used to determine financial results. Straight-line depreciation was used, and a fixed percentage dividend, along with a constant allowable debt ratio, was required to be paid where profits were available. At initial start-up each simulation run had standard conditions of assets, earnings, and so forth.[6]

Seven-step Simulation

As input to the computer simulation model, we developed three sets of 37 hypothetical investments. Each of the hypothetical investments, in turn, was characterized by uncertainty profiles for each of the three key variables for each year of the particular investment: sales, costs, and investment requirements. The computer simulation involved seven steps:

[6]This simulation was programmed for an IBM 7094 computer by my colleague at McKinsey & Company, Joan Morthland Bush.

1. Choose an investment policy by (a) selecting financial criterion or criteria and (b) establishing decision rules. Except in the case of single-point estimates, these rules specified criterion values, along with a minimum expected value, at the 10 percent and 90 percent probability points on the criterion-risk profile (see Exhibit 5-5).
2. From the uncertainty profiles of key variables for each investment given in the available investment set, develop risk profiles for each.
3. Screen investments against policy and accept all those that pass the screen, subject to realistic constraints on size and number of investments to be made in a given year.
4. Simulate the financial performance of the chosen investments over a 15-year period, selecting at random the operating results for each year from the individual uncertainty profiles for the investment project in order to obtain one set of operating results for that investment for each year.
5. Combine the various revenues, costs, and investment requirements for each of the years and then compute the yearly financial results for this investment set.
6. Repeat the entire process until a stable distribution of the financial results for the policy chosen and the investments available has been built up. Determine the average or expected value and the standard deviation of the key financial results.
7. Repeat for other policies and other sets of investment alternatives.

Policies Tested

For each of the three investment sets, investment policies covering conservative, medium-risk, and high-risk screens were tested. The conservative ones required a very high probability of no loss along with moderate expectations, while the high-risk ones accepted significant chances of loss but required good chances of high gains.

Exhibit 5-7 shows the nature of the policies used for the test, illustrating the low-risk and high-risk policies. (Note that single-point determinate policies, not shown on the exhibit, were also included in the tests.) The investments available were varied, ranging from short-term to longer term payouts, with cash investment requirements sometimes extending into later years.[7] The simulation was repeated 500 times for each policy and each set of investments, and the financial results were calculated for each year of a 15-year period. The average of each financial result and its standard deviation was determined for each year and for the combination of the last five years of the runs.

---

[7]On a single-point basis, the investments ranged from 1.9 years to 6.8 years for payback, from 16.9 percent to 47.2 percent average annual return, and from 7.5 percent to 77 percent ROI-dcf.

General Findings

Exhibit 5-8 shows the results of all the runs, plotted on a standard index basis, for the new investments selected. As can be seen, these results permit us to draw at least four general conclusions.

First, there is a wide gap in financial performance between some commonly used investment policies and those policies that lie on the efficiency frontier.

Second, risk-based policies consistently give better results than those using single-point, determinate decision rules. Using determinate decision rules, one cannot compensate for high risk by raising the level-of-return hurdle; single-point estimates produce, at best, half the return for a given degree of risk, no matter how the required return level is raised or lowered.

Third, long-term financial results are highly dependent on the risk accepted for a given return or on the return achieved for a given degree of risk. Thus, on the efficiency frontier, to get a long-term average of $6 per share, management would have to accept fluctuations on the order of 45 percent in two years out of three, whereas it could get only $3 if it decided to accept a probable fluctuation no greater than 10 percent.

EXHIBIT 5-8
INVESTMENT POLICY SIMULATION

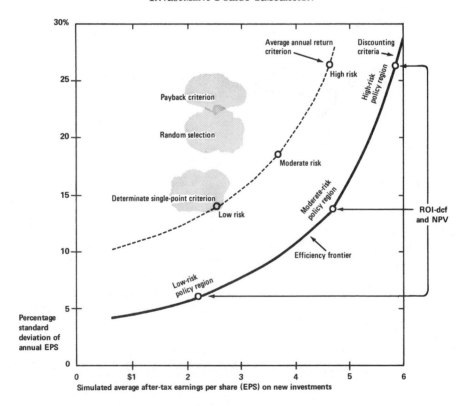

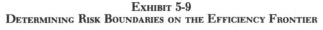

EXHIBIT 5-9
DETERMINING RISK BOUNDARIES ON THE EFFICIENCY FRONTIER

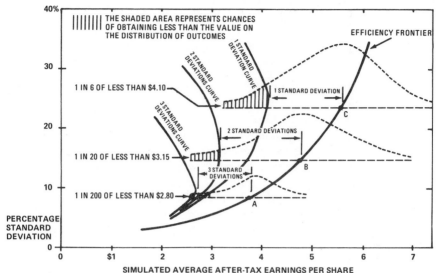

Fourth, some investment criteria are empirically better than others. Whenever growth is a goal, that is, whenever results are measured on an earnings-per-share (EPS) basis, net present value (NPV) and internal discounted cash flow return (ROI-dcf), both of which are based on discounting future returns, are superior to criteria, such as average annual return, which do not take the time value of money into account. At 25 percent annual standard deviation, for example—that is, accepting one chance in three of the results falling outside ± 25 percent of the expected values in any given year—the discounting criterion gives expected EPS of $5.50 while the non-discounted criterion gives $4.10, or 25 percent less.

Policies that produce equivalent financial results for NPV and ROI-dcf can also be developed. That is, by specifying appropriate values for (a) the discount rate and (b) the probability of achieving a particular ratio of the NPV of the cash flow stream to the NPV of the investment, one can obtain exactly the same screen for investments as is provided by specific risk-based values of the ROI-dcf criterion.

Although payback period is still an extremely popular criterion, it turns out to be an extremely crude, inconsistent, and inefficient yardstick from the standpoint of actual financial results. Thus all the investments selected with payback criteria showed higher variances and lower returns than the others.

A more general conclusion to be drawn from this simulation project is that the same approach can profitably be used by management to evaluate its past investments, to determine its efficiency frontier, and to select efficient investment policies that more accurately reflect its risk preferences.

Note that the results shown in Exhibit 5-8 are charted in terms of standard deviation. That is, the vertical coordinate of any point on the chart represents the range of variation that may be expected *two thirds of the time* in the results of a particular policy. If management is unwilling to accept one chance in six of results falling below this range, it will have to accept a lower average return.

How much lower depends, of course, on what odds are acceptable. If, for example, assurance is wanted that results will fall above a given boundary five sixths of the time, *one standard deviation* must be subtracted from average earnings per share for each policy on the efficiency frontier, thereby creating a new curve inside the efficiency frontier as shown in Exhibit 5-9. Or, if management has a still more conservative attitude toward risk and wants a 19-to-1 probability of a given range of results—that is, an assurance that results will fall below the range indicated for a given return only one time in 20—*two standard deviations* may be subtracted, giving still another curve along which the returns offered by particular policies can be located.

Of significance here is the fact that different risk preferences, as exemplified by different risk boundaries, dictate different investment policy choices. Thus, in the situation illustrated by Exhibit 5-9, Policy C provides an expected return of $5.50 with a $\pm$ 25 percent standard deviation. Since these are typical Gaussian or normal distributions, we know that one standard deviation (25% × $5.50) subtracted from the mean will give a value —approximately $4.10 in this case—below which no more than one sixth of the possible future values may be expected to fall. Two standard deviations subtracted would mean no more than a 1-in-20 chance of getting less than $2.70.

In the example a *very* conservative management might wish to accept no more than a 1-in-200 risk. In this case Policy A would offer the best return possible; all others would give less after subtracting three standard deviations. For a management inclined to moderate risk, however, Policy B is the best choice; it offers a 19-in-20 chance of getting $3.15 or better.[8]

Which risk boundary is used determines which investment policy is best; which boundary to select depends on management's willingness to assume risk. Moreover, the risk aversion inherent in any policy can be assessed by determining the risk boundary on which that policy gives better results than all others. The fewer standard deviations one must subtract to define a frontier on which a given policy is best, the greater is the indicated willingness to accept risk.

---

[8]William J. Baumol has suggested a somewhat similar approach to stock portfolio selection in "An Expected Gain-Confidence Limit Criterion for Portfolio Selection," *Management Science* (October, 1963), p. 174.

CONCLUSION

Computer simulation offers corporate management, for the first time, a tool that will enable it to examine the risk consequences of various investment policies. As the research reported in this article shows, the development of a good investment policy involves four requirements:

1. The determination of risk profiles for all investments.
2. The use of a discounting measure (either discounted internal rate of return or an equivalent net present value) for assessing the merit of an investment proposal.
3. The establishment of alternative screening rules for investment proposals.
4. The determination of risk boundaries for the alternative policies.

It should be clear that the same policy will not necessarily show the same risk characteristics (or risk boundaries) when used to screen different classes of investments. In one application, for example, a diversified chemical company found that the projects proposed by various divisions—overseas, heavy chemical, and so on—varied widely in their efficiency frontiers and, therefore, entailed different risks for the same policies. Having decided what level of risk it wished to assume for each of the businesses, management was able to choose its policies accordingly.

Moreover, the company was able to determine the level of investment in each class of projects that would combine with investment levels and risks in other classes to maximize its chances of achieving its long-range growth goals. With the aid of simulation, it was able to establish ceilings and targets in the various investment classes and to describe in detail the screens or policies to be used to make choices in each of them. This enabled division managers and staff personnel to understand management's objectives and to develop more appropriate and promising investment alternatives.

Using the same approach, other companies can now examine in detail the kind of investment opportunities generated by various segments of their businesses and select investment policies that will give them firmer control over their long-term growth. Top executives can analyze their own prejudices and test out the historical effects of inconsistent and irrational choices on their companies' long-term financial results. In short, top management can get back in the driver's seat, in charge of the most important element of the corporate future—effective investment for growth.

6. CAPITAL-BUDGETING DECISIONS INVOLVING COMBINATIONS OF RISKY INVESTMENTS*

JAMES VAN HORNE †

INTRODUCTION

It is becoming recognized that wise capital-budgeting decisions must be based upon more than knowledge of expected returns; indeed, the distribution of cash flows is important.[1] The purpose of this paper is to develop a framework for evaluating combinations of investment proposals when cash flows are not known with certainty.[2] In this regard, we apply certain probability concepts that have been used in security-portfolio analysis.[3] Our concern is with providing information by which a firm, given its utility preferences, can make rational investment decisions in keeping with the total complexion of risk.

THE SINGLE INVESTMENT PROPOSAL

Before we are able to analyze combinations of investment proposals, it is necessary to analyze first the individual proposal. Consider the situation where investments are evaluated according to two parameters—the expected net-present value and the variance. For our purposes, the expected net-present value of a proposal is

$$(1) \qquad \mu_P = \sum_{n=0}^{\infty} \left[\frac{fn}{(1+i)^n} \right],$$

where fn is the expected net-cash flow (cash inflow less cash outflow) during the nth period, and i is a risk-free rate of discount. We assume that this rate is an opportunity cost and represents the most profitable investment of funds in other than the investment proposals under consideration.

How are we able to determine the expected net-cash flow for each future period? One method is by a series of conditional-probability distributions.[4] For example, an investment proposal at time 0 might be expected

---

*From *Management Science* (October, 1966), pp. B84-92. Reprinted by permission.
†Associate Professor of Finance, Graduate School of Business, Stanford University.
[1]See, for example, references, [3] [5] [6], [7] and [14].
[2]Decision situations may be broken down into three types: certainty, risk, and uncertainty. Knight's distinction in reference [10] between risk and uncertainty is that risk involves situations where the probabilities of a particular event occurring are known, whereas with uncertainty, these probabilities are not known. The problem we analyze involves risk situations.
[3]For discussion of the portfolio-selection problem, see references [12] [18] [19] [11].
[4]For exposition on conditional probabilities and Bayesian-decision theory, see Schlaifer, reference [17].

to generate net-cash flows during the first two periods with the following probabilities:

TABLE 6-1

Period 1		Period 2		
Initial probability $P(1)$	Net cash flow	Conditional probability $P(2\|1)$	Net cash flow	Joint probability $P(1,2)$
.25	− $100	.40	− $400	.10
		.40	− $100	.10
		.20	$200	.05
.50	$200	.20	− $100	.10
		.60	$200	.30
		.20	$500	.10
.25	$500	.20	$200	.05
		.40	$500	.10
		.40	$800	.10

Given a cash flow of −$100 in Period 1, the probability is .40 that this negative flow will increase to −$400 in Period 2, .40 that it will remain at −$100, and .20 that it will be $200. Totaling the joint probabilities in the last column, we see that at time 0, our point of reference, there is a .10 probability that the net cash flow in Period 2 will be −$400, .20 that it will be −$100, .40 that it will be $200, .20 that it will be $500, and .10 that it will be $800. The expected net-cash flow for Period 2 is $200. The approach outlined above enables us to estimate net-cash flows in various future periods as being dependent in nature; the probability of cash flows in period n depends upon what happens in period $n − 1$. Thus, we are able to take account of the correlation of cash flows over time.[5]

The expected net-present value for an individual investment proposal is given by equation (1), where f_n is the expected net-cash flow of the initial, or joint, probability distribution for period n. The variance may be determined mathematically for the simple case by

(2)
$$\sigma^2 = \sum_{x=1}^{l} (u_x - u_p)^2 \, P_x \,,$$

where u_x is the net present value for a series of net cash flows, covering all periods, and P_x is the probability of occurrence of that series. For the above example, there are nine possible series of cash flows, the first of which is a net cash flow of −$100 in Period 1, followed by a −$400 net cash flow in Period 2. The probability of occurrence of that series is .10. For complex

---

[5]Hillier in reference [6] developed a model where the net-cash flow for each period is treated as being composed of an independent component and certain other components which are perfectly correlated with corresponding components in other periods.

situations, the mathematical calculation of variance is infeasible. For these situations, we can approximate variance by means of simulation.

The expected net-present value and variance give us considerable information about the individual investment proposal. If the expected net-present value u_p has a normal distribution, we are able to calculate through the use of cumulative distribution functions the probability of a project providing a net-present value of zero or less, or a value greater than a certain amount.[6] A firm then is able to evaluate the probability of adverse events according to its utility preferences. Even when the distribution is not normal, we usually are able to make reasonably strong probability statements by using Chebyshev's inequality.[7] Given two investment proposals, a firm is able to compare their expected net-present values and variances. While the above method of comparing investment proposals is feasible when choosing between two proposals, it does not provide an objective framework for evaluation when there are existing investment projects and/or when more than one new proposal may be selected. It is to this problem that we turn.

COMBINATIONS OF INVESTMENT PROPOSALS

We assume that a firm has existing investment projects generating expected future cash flows and that disinvestment with respect to these projects is not possible. A method is needed by which it can evaluate the expected net-present value and variances of various combinations of existing investment projects and proposals under consideration.[8] A combination includes all existing investment projects and one or more proposals under consideration.[9] Selecting investment proposals based upon the expected net-present value and variance for each proposal ignores the element of covariance. The total variance for a particular combination is not the summation of the individual variances, but

$$(3) \qquad V = \sum_{j=1}^{m} \sum_{k=1}^{m} \sigma_{jk},$$

where σ_{jk} is the variance of expected net-present value (equation (2)) when $j = k$ and the covariance between the expected net-present values of investments j and k when $j \neq k$. The covariance is

$$(4) \qquad \sigma_{jk} = r_{jk} \, \sigma_j \, \sigma_k,$$

where r_{jk} is the expected correlation between the two expected net-present values, σ_j is the standard deviation of the expected net-present value for investment j, and σ_k is the standard deviation for investment k.

---

[6]See, for example, Beranek, reference [2], pp. 149-152.
[7]Kemeny, et al, reference [9].
[8]In the Appendix, we consider the external financing of investment proposals.
[9]Existing projects comprise a subset which is included in all combinations. Proposals under consideration are assumed to represent all future proposals on the investment horizon, regardless of the time of initial outlay.

The standard deviations, σ_j and σ_k, are obtained from equation (2). Deriving the correlation coefficient, r_{jk}, is a more difficult matter. Unlike the security-portfolio case, derivation of these coefficients cannot necessarily be based upon the past variation of two investments. When two investments are similar to projects with which the company has had experience, it may be feasible to compute the correlation coefficient using historical data. For other investments, however, estimates of the correlation coefficients must be based upon an assessment of the future as well as upon relevant past experience.[10]

Management might have reason to expect only slight correlation between a project involving investment in research and development for an electronic transistor and investment in a new consumer product. On the other hand, it might expect high, positive correlation between investments in a milling machine and a turret lathe, if both were used in the production of industrial lift trucks. The profit from a machine to be used in a production line will be highly, if not completely, correlated with the profit for the production line itself.[11] Correlation between net-present values of the various investments may be positive, negative, or zero, depending upon the nature of the association. Estimates of the correlation coefficients must be as objective as possible if the total variance figure obtained in equation (3) is to be realistic. It is not unreasonable to suppose, however, that management is able to make fairly accurate estimates of these coefficients.[12]

We have now a procedure for determining the total net-present value and variance of a combination of existing investment projects and proposals under consideration.[13] The expected net-present value of the combination is the sum of expected net-present values of all projects and proposals making up the combination. In computing variance, it is extremely important that we take account of existing investment projects, for investment proposals must be evaluated in relation to their influence on the total risk of the company. We are able to analyze the latter question only if we consider existing investment projects. Due to covariance, the combination of investment proposals that provides the lowest total variance may not provide the lowest total variance when existing projects are included. A variance figure solely based upon investment proposals under consideration is not a measure of total variance to the firm and, consequently, is inadequate as a basis for judging total risk.

---

[10]Hillier in reference [7], pp. 66-69, discusses the mathematics of estimating correlation coefficients.

[11]See English, reference [4], p. 13.

[12]To the extent that actual correlation differs from expected correlation, future correlation estimates on existing projects should be revised in keeping with the learning process. The learning process applies also to future estimates of correlation between investments that are similar to existing investments.

[13]It would be possible to attach probability distributions to the correlation coefficients. For simplicity, we shall not include this dimension in our analysis but will work with only the expected values of the correlation coefficients.

EVALUATION OF COMBINATIONS

The next step involves evaluation of feasible combinations of existing investment projects and proposals under consideration.[14] While the difficulty of calculating the total expected net present value and variance for each feasible combination should not be minimized, procedures can be employed to streamline the task.[15] An example of a total set is illustrated by the shaded area in Figure 6-1, where the horizontal axis represents expected net-present value and the vertical axis, total variance for a combination.

This set corresponds to Markowitz's set of attainable combinations of securities. The dark line at the bottom of the set is the line of efficient combinations, or the investment-opportunity curve.[16]

According to the Markowitz mean-variance maxim, management should seek a combination of investments that lies on the efficient-combination line. A combination is not efficient if there is another combination with either a higher u_P and a lower V, a higher u_P and the same V, or the same u_P but a lower V. The efficient-combination line tells us the additional variance that must be accepted for an increase in net-present value.[17] The mean-variance maxim implies diversification of investments to reduce the total amount of variance.[18] However, diversification must be with respect to proposals not having high degrees of covariance among themselves or with existing projects. Thus, an investment proposal having only a moderate expected net-present value but very low covariance with other projects and proposals may be preferred to a proposal having a higher expected net-present value but also a high degree of covariance with other projects and proposals. The reason for this preference is that the proposal with low covariance may result in a total variance that is sufficiently lower

---

[14]Where two or more proposals are mutually exclusive, such that the acceptance of one precludes acceptance of the other(s), these proposals cannot appear in the same combination. If two or more proposals are contingent, so that the acceptance of one is dependent upon the acceptance of one or more other proposals, a combination containing a dependent project also must contain the proposal(s) on which it is dependent.

[15]The total net-present value and variance for existing investment projects is the same for all combinations. The problem reduces to calculating the incremental net-present value and variance for the addition of one or more proposals under consideration to existing investment projects.

[16]Markowitz, reference [12], Chapters VII and VIII. The slope of the efficient-combination line will depend upon the degree of correlation among combinations along the line. If we assume nondivisibility of investment proposals, this lower line may be somewhat jagged.

[17]Baumol recently has proposed a modification of Markowitz's efficiency criterion for evaluating expected value and variance. This criterion involves the use of a lower confidence limit represented by $E\text{-}K_\sigma$, where E is expected value, σ is standard deviation from expected value, and K is a confidence coefficient. K is specified in terms of the number of standard deviations from expected value and represents the lowest plausible outcome from the standpoint of the investor. Given a lower confidence limit, an investor is able to determine how much risk he must assume in order to obtain a certain expected value. According to Baumol, only when $E\text{-}K_\sigma$ decreases as portfolios with greater expected value are considered would there be a sacrifice of safety. Baumol's efficient-combination line is represented by the downward-sloping portion of the $E\text{-}K_\sigma$ curve and is a subset of that of Markowitz. As K increases, Baumol's efficient set approaches the Markowitz efficient set as a limit. See Baumol, reference [1] It would be possible to incorporate Baumol's efficiency criterion into the above analysis.

[18]See Markowitz, reference [12], pp. 112-115 and 207.

FIGURE 6-1

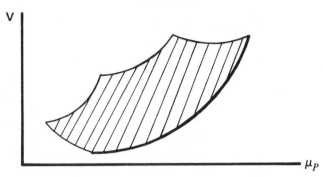

from the standpoint of the company to offset the difference in expected net-present values of the two proposals. It is important to recognize, however, that the objective of diversification is not to reduce variance per se but to obtain the best combination of expected net-present value and variance.

SELECTION OF BEST COMBINATION

The selection of the most desirable combination of investments will depend upon the utility preferences of a company with respect to expected net-present value and variance, assuming, of course, that a preference function indeed does exist.[19] If the company is risk averse and associates risk with the variance of net present value, its utility function may be a monotonic increasing-concave one, indicating diminishing marginal rates of substitution between variance and expected net-present value. An example of this type of function is shown by the indifference curves in Figure 6-2.

FIGURE 6-2

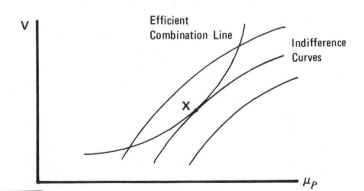

[19]The utility preferences of the company, as set forth by management, may differ from those of its shareholders.

A firm would choose that combination of investments placing it on the highest indifference curve because this curve represents the greatest utility. The combination is determined by the point of tangency between the efficient combination line and an indifference curve, point X in the example. This point describes the most desirable combination of expected net-present value and risk.

The exact shape of the utility function does not have to be constant; indeed, it is likely to change over time with the states of nature. There are a number of ways of integrating the utility preferences of a firm into our analysis.[20] The example shown in this section illustrates but one way a company might select a combination of investment proposals; our principal concern has been with perfecting a framework for evaluating combinations of risky investments, given the utility preferences of a company.

CONCLUSIONS

In this paper, we develop a framework by which combinations of risky investments may be evaluated for capital-budgeting purposes through the use of probability distributions. The method allows cash flows for various future periods generated from an individual investment to be treated as being dependent in nature. Of particular importance is the recognition of covariance among investments and the fact that total variance must take account of existing investment projects as well as proposals under consideration. Risk cannot be analyzed in isolation; rather, the interrelation of risk among all investments must be assessed. Through proper diversification of investments, a firm is able to obtain the most desirable combination of expected net-present value and risk. The framework proposed in this paper enables management to appraise realistically these factors in its effort to make sound capital-budgeting decisions.

APPENDIX
External Financing of Investment Proposals

In this paper we have abstracted from the effect that external financing of investment proposals may have on the net-present value of a firm. It will be recalled that expected net-cash flows are discounted by a risk-free rate to determine their net-present value; and this rate is assumed to represent the most profitable investment of funds in other than the investment proposals under consideration. Implicitly implied in our analysis is that the cost of funds is this opportunity cost. If a firm has excess cash and liquid investments—at the risk-free rate—in excess of the maximum outlay required for all proposals under consideration, this cost is not unrealistic. However, if any of the combinations needs to be financed externally, either partially or wholly, an adjustment of the net present-value figure may be in order.

---

[20]For discussion of risk aversion and utility, see references [4] [8] [15] [21].

Consider first the situation where a firm has existing debt and intends to finance the investment proposals with the same proportion of debt and equity as already exists. One approach to the problem might be to deduct from the net-present value of each combination the net-present value of contractual payments of principal and interest on both existing debt and debt to be incurred. The discount factor would be the risk-free rate; and the adjusted net present-value figure for each combination then would be used when evaluating the combinations to determine which is most desirable. In keeping with this approach, if the firm has no existing debt and intends to finance new investments with equity, no adjustment is necessary.[21]

If, however, the firm intends to finance new investments with greater or lesser proportions of debt than already exist, an additional problem is introduced. As before, the net-present value of contractual payments should be deducted. However, the firm also must take account of the effect, if any, that the change in the proportion of debt and equity has, *ceteris paribus,* on the way investors value shares of the firm.[22] While the above discussion has been only cursory, it does suggest ways that we may take account of the financing decision.

---

[21]Expectations of investors about the investment proposals may affect the price that they are willing to pay for new shares of stock. If the stock issued is not on a preemptive rights basis, the benefit of the investment decision to existing shareholders in some measure will depend upon this price. See reference [2], pp. 201-209.

[22]For discussion of the controversial question of leverage and the valuation of a company's shares, see references [13] [20] [16].

REFERENCES

1. Baumol, William J. "An Expected Gain—Confidence Limit Criterion for Portfolio Selection." *Management Science*, X (October, 1963), pp. 174-182.
2. Beranek, William. *Analysis for Financial Decisions.* Homewood, Ill.: Richard D. Irwin, Inc., 1963.
3. Cord, Joel. "A Method for Allocating Funds to Investment Projects When Returns Are Subject to Uncertainty." *Management Science*, X (January, 1964), pp. 335-341.
4. English, J. M. "Economic Comparison of Projects Incorporating a Utility Criterion in the Rate of Return." *The Engineering Economist*, X (Winter, 1965), pp. 1-14.
5. Hertz, David B. "Risk Analysis in Capital Investment." *Harvard Business Review*, XLII (January-February, 1964), pp. 95-106.
6. Hillier, Frederick S. "The Derivation of Probabilistic Information for the Evaluation of Risky Investments." *Management Science*, IX (April, 1963), pp. 443-457.
7. _____. *The Evaluation of Risky Interrelated Investments*, Technical Report No. 73. Stanford, Calif.: Stanford University Department of Statistics, 1964.
8. Hirshleifer, Jack. "Efficient Allocation of Capital in an Uncertain World." *American Economic Review* (May, 1964), pp. 77-85.
9. Kemeny, John G., *et al. Finite Mathematical Structures.* Englewood Cliffs, N. J.: Prentice-Hall, Inc., 1959, pp. 172-178.

10. Knight, Frank H. *Risk, Uncertainty and Profit*. Boston: Houghton Mifflin Company, 1921.
11. Lintner, John. "Security Prices, Risk, and Maximal Gains from Diversification." *Journal of Finance*, XX (December, 1965), pp. 587-615.
12. Markowitz, Harry M. *Portfolio Selection: Efficient Diversification of Investments*. New York: John Wiley & Sons, Inc., 1959.
13. Modigliani, F., and M. H. Miller. "The Cost of Capital, Corporation Finance, and the Theory of Investment." *American Economic Review*, XLVIII (June, 1958), pp. 261-297.
14. Paine, Neil R. "Uncertainty and Capital Budgeting." *Accounting Review*, XXXIX (April, 1964), pp. 330-332.
15. Pratt, John W. "Risk Aversion in the Small and in the Large." *Econometrica*, XXXII (April, 1964), pp. 122-136.
16. Robichek, Alexander A., and Stewart C. Myers. *Optimal Financing Decisions*. Englewood Cliffs, N.J.: Prentice-Hall, Inc., 1965, Chapter 3.
17. Schlaifer, Robert. *Probability and Statistics for Business Decisions*. New York: McGraw-Hill Book Company, 1959.
18. Sharpe, William F. "Capital Asset Prices: A Theory of Market Equilibrium Under Conditions of Risk." *Journal of Finance*, XIX (September, 1964), pp. 425-442.
19. _____. "A Simplified Model for Portfolio Analysis." *Management Science*, IX (January, 1963), pp. 277-293.
20. Solomon, Ezra. *The Theory of Financial Management*. New York: Columbia University Press, 1963, Chapters 6-9.
21. Tobin, James. "Liquidity Preference as Behavior Towards Risk." *Review of Economic Studies*, XXV (February, 1958), pp. 65-86.

7. PROJECT EVALUATION AND THE MANAGERIAL LIMIT*

F. K. WRIGHT†

A great deal has been written, especially since the publication of Joel Dean's pioneering work in 1951,[1] on the criteria which should govern the selection of investment projects for implementation if the objective is maximization of profits or maximization of share prices. Dean's recommendation that projects should be ranked according to their prospective rates of return has been strongly attacked, and alternative criteria have been put forward, based on the present value of expected cash flows discounted at a rate equal to the cost of capital or to the opportunity cost of funds.

But all these criteria have this in common: they depend for their rationality upon the assumption that the volume of projects which can be undertaken is limited either by the amount of funds available or by shortage of investment opportunities. In this paper it will be suggested that for a large and important class of firms neither funds nor opportunities are the critical factor limiting expansion and that for those firms the ranking of projects according to simple financial criteria will not lead to an optimal investment policy.

MAXIMIZATION WITH RESPECT TO A LIMITING FACTOR

Whenever we speak of maximizing a variable, we imply the existence of a constraint which sets an upper bound to the value of the maximand; in the absence of such a constraint, maximization would have no meaning. In economics, this constraint frequently takes the form of a scarce factor which is used up in the process of increasing the maximand.

We may use this conceptual framework to generalize the capital-budgeting problem in its simplest form.[2] Suppose that all the business opportunities open to a particular firm, at a particular point of time, can be characterized by pairs of variables (x_i, y_i), where y_i is a measure of the contribution which the ith project would make to some maximand Y, and x_i is the quantity of some scarce factor X which the ith project would absorb or consume.

Then, if the supply of X limits the volume of projects that can be undertaken, the ratio y_i/x_i will represent the *index of merit* of the ith project; Y will be maximized with respect to the limiting factor X if projects are chosen

*Reprinted from *The Journal of Business* (April, 1964), pp. 179-185, by permission of the University of Chicago Press. Copyright 1964 by the University of Chicago. All rights reserved.
†Department of Commerce, University of Adelaide, South Australia.
[1] Joel Dean, *Capital Budgeting* (New York: Columbia University Press, 1951).
[2] Initially, independence of projects will be assumed

for implementation in the order indicated by this ratio, until the supply of X is exhausted.

The opportunity cost of the factor X, expressed in units of the maximand Y per unit of X, will be given by the index of merit of that project which just fails to qualify for inclusion in the capital budget. Knowledge of this opportunity cost will be helpful to management in deciding what efforts should be made to increase the supply of factor X; it may also assist in the evaluation of mutually exclusive projects, as we shall see later.

THE CONCEPT OF THE CRITICAL FACTOR

In any particular situation, over a given period of time, there is almost invariably *one* factor which effectively limits the value of a given maximand. For instance, if the output of a factory during a particular month is to be maximized, it might be found that this output is limited by the amount of labor which can be hired, or by the supply of materials, or by the number of machines installed, or by the area of floor space available.[3] Any one of these *could* limit the output of the factory, but in a given situation, at a given time, there will almost certainly be one factor which *effectively* limits output. If the supply of that factor could be increased, another factor might become the effective limit, and so on. We shall use the term "critical" to describe that factor which is effective, for the time being, in limiting the growth of the maximand.

For a given set of projects and a given maximand, different limiting factors will usually give rise to different optimal subsets. A given subset of projects will be optimal with respect to several limiting factors only if the quantities of the various factors consumed by each project are highly correlated.

In order to make a rational choice of projects for implementation, therefore, it is necessary to know not only how much each project would contribute to the maximand but also what is the critical factor in the situation and how much of that critical factor each project would absorb.

MUTUALLY EXCLUSIVE PROJECTS

Among the opportunities open to a firm, there may be some which are mutually exclusive, that is, a subset of projects out of which, for practical reasons, only one can be implemented. Such a subset might consist, for instance, of various proposals for developing a given site.

The mutually exclusive character of the projects in such a subset results from the operation of a special limiting factor peculiar to this subset, such as the area of the site to be developed. Optimal choice from within the subset must somehow take into account both the special limiting factor for the subset and the critical factor in the overall situation.

---

[3]It is assumed that factors cannot be substituted for each other, at least in the short run.

The general solution of such a problem, involving two independent constraints, calls for some form of mathematical programming. With the aid of simplifying assumptions, however, we may be able to arrive at a useful approximation.

One simplifying assumption which might be made is that the opportunity cost of the critical factor will not be affected by the choice from within the subset. We can then define a subset maximand Z such that

$$Z = Y - mX,$$

where m is the opportunity cost (in units of Y) of the critical factor X. Choice from within the subset may then be based upon an index of merit z_i/s_i, where z_i is the contribution which the ith project makes to the maximand Z, and s_i is the quantity of the special limiting factor for the subset which the ith project would absorb.

In practice, mutually exclusive proposals are usually framed in such a way that each utilizes the whole supply of the special limiting factors. In that case all the s_i's are equal, and the index of merit is simply z_i, the project's contribution to the subset maximand. The project with the highest z_i will then be the optimal choice from the subset.

This project then becomes the representative of the subset for further evaluation in competition with the general run of projects. If its inclusion in the capital budget should change the value of m, successive approximation may lead to an optimal solution.

FUNDS AS THE CRITICAL FACTOR

There are two main ways in which the supply of funds may play the role of critical factor: (1) there may be some absolute limitation upon the supply of funds available for investment by a particular firm; or (2) the cost of funds to the firm may rise steeply beyond a certain point, making it uneconomic for that firm to raise more than a certain amount. It seems likely that, in one or another of these senses, the supply of funds will always be a potential limiting factor; but it need not always be this factor which effectively restricts the growth of the enterprise.

When supply of funds is in fact critical, in either of these ways, the opportunity cost of funds to the enterprise will be determined by the intersection of the long-run demand and supply curves for investment funds. The present value of a project, discounted at the opportunity-cost rate, will represent the contribution of the project to the net present worth of the enterprise, and the present value of the cash outflows associated with the project, also discounted at the opportunity-cost rate, will represent the project's requirement of the critical factor, investment funds. If maximization of net present worth is the objective, the index of merit of the project will, therefore, be the ratio of these two present values.[4]

---

[4]In the Lutzes' symbols, this corresponds to maximization of $(V - C/C)$, which is, of course, equivalent to maximizing V/C (see F. and V. Lutz, *The Theory of Investment of the Firm* [Princeton, N.J.: Princeton University Press, 1951]). It might be asked why there is any (cont.)

FUNDS NEED NOT BE CRITICAL

It is, of course, well known that the supply of funds is not always the critical factor. Dean, for instance, has pointed out that "large, established firms may be unaware of the rising phase of their supply curve."[5] It seems highly unlikely that the growth of such firms would be critically limited by the supply of funds.

Usually it is assumed that such firms are limited in their growth by shortage of opportunities for profitable investment in the geographical area or area of specialization in which they operate. This is no doubt true in many instances. Where this limit applies, capital-budgeting becomes simply a matter of adopting all projects which show positive present values at the firm's cost of capital.

But we should not be too ready to accept this explanation at its face value in every case in which it is offered. Frequently it may be worth inquiring whether the opportunities are in fact as limited as they are perceived to be by the management of the firm and, in particular, whether the firm is confined to its area of specialization by choice or by inability to operate profitably outside it.

Dean also states: "In some companies, capital expenditures are confined completely to the amount that can be obtained internally . . . many companies . . . have no intention of ever using outside funds. For many firms it is a source of pride that they never go to the market for financing a new opportunity, no matter how profitable it appears."[6] Where exclusive reliance on internal funds is a matter of choice and not of necessity, it would be difficult to justify the assumption that the supply of funds is the critical factor limiting the growth of that firm. Here again, shortage of opportunities may be a possible explanation but only if the firm is in fact accepting all investment opportunities which would be profitable at the rate at which external funds could be raised. If any potentially profitable investment opportunities are being rejected, one must conclude either that the firm is not interested in maximizing profits or that its growth is limited by some other, possibly unrecognized, critical factor.

Let us now try to see what factors might prevent a well established corporation, with an excellent profit record and aggressive management, from expanding to the fullest extent permitted by the capital market. Edith T. Penrose has considered this question carefully and has reached the following conclusions:

> External barriers to expansion can be ruled out if we make two basic assumptions: First, that the supply to the firm of capital, labour, or man-

---

need for such an index of merit in a situation where every project showing a positive present value at the opportunity cost of funds can and should be undertaken. The answer is that the opportunity cost might have been estimated for a longer period than that covered by the current capital budget, so that funds may not be immediately available for every project which would be profitable at the opportunity-cost rate of discount.

[5]Dean, *op. cit.,* p. 52.

[6]*Ibid.,* pp. 37, 53, and 54.

agement is not absolutely fixed . . . ; second, that there are opportunities for profitable investment open somewhere in the economy . . . These assumptions are, in general, fairly reasonable for many firms.

. . . further expansion [may become] unprofitable in particular locations and in particular products. But a firm is not confined to particular products or locations . . . the fundamental limit to the productive opportunity of the firm cannot be found in external supply and demand conditions; we must look within the firm itself.[7]

THE MANAGERIAL LIMIT

Mrs. Penrose then goes on to argue that the size of the management team must set a limit to the amount of project work that the company is able to carry out. The nature of the training process for executives in turn sets a limit to the rate at which the management team can grow; hence the rate of physical expansion is ultimately limited by the rate at which the company can expand its management team. Her reasoning is summarized in the following passage:

> First, the services available from the existing managerial group limit the amount of expansion that can be planned at any time because all plans for expansion absorb some of the services available from this group, and the larger and more complex the plans the more services will be required to digest and approve them on behalf of the firm. . . . Secondly, the amount of activity that can be planned at a given time limits the amount of new personnel that can be profitably absorbed in the "next period."[8]

It seems clear that the rate at which the managerial group can be expanded is potentially a limiting factor in any growing firm and that it may well be the critical factor for a particular firm over a given period of time. But it is doubtful whether a company can continue to expand at the maximum rate set by this factor for very long. Given an appropriate staff-development program, I do not believe that the difficulty of training executives to become useful members of the managerial group is great enough to act as a brake on the long-term growth of a successful company.

It is my belief that in many firms expansion is ultimately limited not by the *number* of managers at any particular level but rather by the *ability of a few individuals in key positions to accept additional responsibility.* In the typical corporation, these key people would be the president and those who report directly to him, the group usually referred to as the top management team. It is the load that expansion imposes upon these people which is likely to prove critical in the long run.

As the firm expands, its management structure will change to meet the new conditions created by the expansion; it is well recognized that "growth requires the constant internal reorganization of the firm."[9] New positions will be created, and functions formerly carried out by one person may be

---

[7]Edith T. Penrose, *The Theory of the Growth of the Firm* (Oxford: Basil Blackwell, 1959), pp. 43 and 44.

[8]*Ibid.*, p. 49.

[9]Tibor Barna, *Investment and Growth Policies in British Industrial Firms* (Cambridge, England: Cambridge University Press, 1962), p. 42.

split up among several people. But the responsibility of top management for the overall direction and control of the enterprise cannot be split in this way. Assistants may be appointed and staff positions created to free the top men of detail, but no one can free them of the increased responsibility that comes with growth.

TIME SPAN AS A MEASURE OF RESPONSIBILITY

Elliott Jaques, of the Tavistock Institute, has discussed this problem in his book on the measurement of responsibility.[10] He believes that the burden of responsibility is closely related to the length of the interval which elapses between the time when a decision is made and the time when the consequences of that decision become apparent. During that interval, not only must the executive bear the uncertainty of not knowing how one particular decision will turn out, but he must, of course, go on making other decisions without knowing the outcome of those he has already made. The total burden of uncertainty is, therefore, represented by all the decisions whose outcome is unknown to him at any particular time, and this will be closely related to the length of the interval between a decision and the knowledge of its outcome.

P. F. Drucker has pointed out that growth is associated with a lengthening of that interval: "As the business gets larger, the job of top management acquires a different time dimension; the larger the business, the farther ahead in the future top management operates."[11] This must have the effect of increasing the burden of uncertainty on top management.

Individuals differ widely in their ability to tolerate such burdens of uncertainty; Jaques calls this ability their "time-span capacity." In those whose potential time-span capacity is high, actual capacity grows rapidly during their thirties and forties but grows more slowly or ceases to grow in their fifties and sixties. From his studies, Jaques concludes: "Whether or not changes occur in the size of business of a particular firm will depend directly upon whether the time-span capacity of the individuals in charge is consistent with the level of work being done. If their time-span capacity is growing beyond the level of work in the firm, they will grow [sic] the firm."[12]

Note, however, that it is the capacity of the *individuals in charge* of the firm that determines its growth. The emergence of excess managerial capacity lower down in the hierarchy does not have the same effect. Mrs. Penrose has observed this herself: "That promotion does not fully take care of the increase in [managerial] services . . . is the common experience of many firms in periods when growth is slow. Pressure from younger executives for advancement sometimes even creates for the firm a problem of maintaining the morale of personnel.[13] Jaques would interpret this observation by saying

---

[10]Elliott Jaques, *Measurement of Responsibility: A Study of Work, Payment, and Individual Capacity* (London: Tavistock Institute, 1956).
[11]P. F. Drucker, *The Practice of Management* (London: Heinemann, 1955), p. 219.
[12]Jaques, *op. cit.*, p. 104.
[13]Penrose, *op. cit.*, p. 54.

that the time-span capacity of the younger executives was increasing more rapidly than that of the (presumably older) top management group.

To sum up this argument, it seems that the critical factor which limits the expansion of a successful, diversified corporation must be sought within the corporation itself. Over particular periods, that factor may be the availability of managerial services within the corporation; in the long run, however, the critical factor is more likely to be the time-span capacity of top management.

IMPLICATIONS FOR PROJECT EVALUATION

If we now try to apply these theories to the problem of project evaluation, we are confronted by the difficulty of measuring the relevant critical factors.

Where a managerial limit of the Penrose type is encountered, we must first identify the particular group of skills whose scarcity is likely to be critical over the period under consideration; we must then estimate, for each project, the number of man-days or man-years of people possessing these skills which the project would absorb. The index of merit of a project (if net present worth is to be maximized) will be its present value when discounted at the firm's cost of capital, divided by the quantity of critical managerial services which the project would consume.[14]

Where the managerial limit appears to be of the Jaques type, however, the prospects of successful measurement seem poor. It would be extremely difficult to quantify the increase in top management responsibility to which a particular project might give rise. But unless we are able to measure the critical factor, we cannot hope to calculate a numerical index of merit for each project. All we can do is to make qualitative statements to the effect that, other things being equal, projects adding little to top management responsibility are to be preferred to those which are managerially more demanding. Even this vague guide rule can, however, lead to significantly better decisions than the application of a common cutoff rate to every project, in a situation where funds are not the critical factor.

In general, it seems likely that cost-reduction projects will add less to the top management burden than other types of projects. A change in layout or manufacturing method, or the replacement of obsolete machinery with modern equipment, will do little if anything to raise the level of responsibility at which top management is working. At the other extreme are such revenue-increasing projects as the development of new products or entry into new sales territories; these might be expected to strain the time-span capacity of top management more heavily than other projects (and, incidentally, to place heavy demands on managerial time at lower levels also). An intermediate position would probably be occupied by revenue-maintaining

---

[14]Another approach, suggested to me by Dr. Maureen Brunt, would be to determine the opportunity cost of the critical service and impute to each project an appropriately high charge for the quantity consumed.

projects, such as those designed to prevent a loss of revenue which would otherwise occur as the result of changes in the market or activities of competitors.

In firms where time-span capacity is critical, therefore, cost-reduction projects should be undertaken whenever they appear profitable at the firm's cost of capital, since they will add to profits without adding appreciably to the strain on the critical factor. Other projects may be required to show substantially higher earnings. As between revenue-maintaining and revenue-increasing projects, preference should be given to revenue-maintaining projects where the earning rates are similar.

CONCLUSION

In 1951, Joel Dean argued that "replacement investments can and should be forced to compete for money with alternative proposals on the basis of their prospective rate of return, and that . . . there is no particular reason for favoring replacement outlays over other investments that promise higher rates of return."[15] This view seems to have been shared, at least implicitly, by practically every writer on the subject during the following decade.

As recently as 1961, however, Tibor Barna reported after a survey of 74 British companies: "The classification of investment projects is material because expansion projects tend to be judged by different standards from replacement projects. It is generally easier to obtain approval for 'replacement' investment."[16]

If the arguments advanced in this paper have any merit, it would appear that the businessmen interviewed by Barna have not necessarily been wrong in rejecting the proffered advice and that there may be, in many cases, a sound theoretical basis for such discrimination. Our aim should be to make this basis explicit and to substitute, wherever possible, measurement and index-of-merit ranking for the hunches on which businessmen have hitherto had to rely.

---

[15]Dean, *op. cit.*, p. 89.
[16]Barna, *op. cit.*, p. 31.

PART III. CAPITAL STRUCTURE AND COST OF CAPITAL

The effect of capital structure on the cost of capital has been closely studied since Modigliani and Miller's provocative work in 1958. Since then questions relating to leverage and the cost of capital for the firm have been expounded by both acadamecians and practitioners. The question of how the risk factor should be considered when computing the cost of capital has been discussed widely but is still far from being settled. The articles included in this section attempt to answer some of these questions.

Mr. John F. Childs deals with the question of ". . . what profit goals should be used for expansion purposes?" The importance of capital expansion decisions to the economy as well as to the individual firm dictates the need for informed decision making on the part of management. The author sees the analysis of an expansion program divided into three parts: 1) a forecast of sales, expenses, and capital outlays; 2) a profitability calculation based on the forecast; and 3) the subject under consideration in this article—establishing a profit goal.

The author reviews goals he deems unsound, including profit as a percentage of sales and experienced return on capital. He concludes that ". . .to be successful a company must earn enough to cover all costs, including capital costs." A company should earn at least something above the bare minimum rate which investors require to induce them to provide all the capital, that is, the cost of capital. He discusses three rates: (1) cost of capital, (2) return on capital target, and (3) expansion profit goal. Attention is given to calculating cost of capital, with emphasis on the composite rate of all the company's capital. The determination of the cost of common equity is thoroughly and realistically investigated by the use of empirical data. Mr. Childs' discussion of unsound goals and his emphasis on realistic situations reflect his experience as a financial consultant and as an expert witness in public utility rate cases.

Professor Ezra Solomon is concerned with ". . .the effect that a change in financial leverage has, or can be assumed to have, on a company's cost of capital." The author takes issue with Modigliani and Miller's position. A review of the traditional versus the Modigliani-Miller position clearly states each position. A diagram is presented which indicates that the marginal cost of borrowing can be higher than the average cost of capital and thereby refutes the Modigliani and Miller thesis that the overall cost of capital will not rise regardless of the proportion of leverage. The article not only presents a clear discourse on the traditional view of the effect of financial leverage on the cost of capital, but it also helps the reader to understand the fundamental difference in the two approaches.

Professor Harold J. Bierman, several other professors, and two treasurers from industry discuss whether the risk factor should be included in the cost of capital or whether it should be considered as a separate factor. There are some who feel that the discount factor should be adjusted to compensate for riskier undertakings; Professor Bierman does not feel that this is an adequate solution. While the results of the discussion are inconclusive, the reader has an opportunity to sit in on a conference of leaders in the field of finance. The comments portray the practical problems confronting the business executive.

8. PROFIT GOALS FOR MANAGEMENT*

JOHN F. CHILDS†

The success of a company today depends to a great extent on correct decisions on major capital expenditures. The principal question is a difficult one: What should be the goal in deciding on whether to give a project the green light? Profits are the catalyst in our free enterprise system and management's guide in expansion. Therefore, management needs answers to the question: What profit goals should be used for expansion purposes?

This article will deal primarily with the application of profit goals to plant expansion and with that type of plant expansion which is relatively independent of the rest of the company's operations. However, the ideas discussed are the foundation for thinking in the many other areas: acquisitions, plant abandonment, parts of financial policy such as capital structure determination, etc.

THE IMPACT OF EXPANSION

If a company makes a mistake in this area, how serious is it? When a company expands, management directs the flow of the savings of our nation into means of production. Uncalled-for expansion has serious consequences:

Investors are hurt because of the effect on profits!

All companies in an industry suffer because overexpansion by one company will depress prices in the entire industry and restrict profits!

Our entire economy is blighted because capital directed where it is not needed means production of the wrong goods and a reduction in usable goods and, consequently, our standard of living. Furthermore, if excessive expansion occurs in a prosperous period, it will accentuate the business cycle and the unemployment problem!

Thus, a smooth flow of capital into production, where it is needed, is essential to our economy. And yet, this is one of management's most difficult areas. It requires the best possible judgment with regard to the profit element.

THREE PARTS TO PROFIT DETERMINATION IN EXPANSION

The analysis of an expansion program includes three parts:

1. A *forecast* of sales, expenses, and capital outlays.
2. A *profitability calculation based on the forecast.* In other words, what rate of return will the forecast produce? Allowance must be made for the time value of money. This can only be done

*From *The Financial Executive* (February, 1964), pp. 13-23. Reprinted by permission.
†Vice-President, Irving Trust Company.

by such methods as "discounted cash flow" or "present value." Such methods as payback, return on original investment, and return on average investment are inadequate.
3. *Establishing a profit goal.* Before the final decision can be made, it is necessary to establish a profit goal as a cutoff rate of return on capital. This is the rate with which the project's profitability can be compared, in order to determine whether there is sufficient profit to justify the project.

Part 3, profit goal, is our present subject. In order to simplify the explanation, some ABC types of examples will be used. Since all top management should understand the subject, the article is written so that those only casually acquainted with finance can grasp it. However, the subject is truly a part of finance, and the greater a person's financial knowledge the more readily the subject can be understood.

What we are seeking is a rate of return on capital which can be used as a goal to determine whether the forecast profit rate on capital to be invested in an expansion project is sufficient to justify a project.

UNSOUND GOALS

If you ask managements what goal they use for expansion decisions, you will find that each has some goal, but you may be surprised at their rationale. In order to start our thinking on the subject, we will review some of the goals that managements feel have value. Some of them are obviously wrong. Others may seem reasonable, and their errors only become apparent after the complete discussion of the subject.

Profit as a Percent of Sales

It leaves out the amount of capital required to produce the sales. The rate must always be related to the investment required to produce the profit.

Interest Rate on Long-Term Debt

What about the common stockholders if the company just earned its interest or slightly over its interest? Interest is a part of the cost of capital, but only a part because it overlooks the rate that should be earned on the money the common stockholders provide.

Interest on Long-Term Debt and Dividends on Common

If two identical companies had different dividend policies, their goals would be different. And suppose a company had no debt and paid no dividends—what then, a zero goal? Of course, the real reason that dividends alone are no measure is the fact that it ignores the importance of earnings per share to the stockholders.

Company's Experienced Return on Capital

Experienced return on capital can be expressed by dividing total income (interest plus net earnings after taxes before dividends) by total long-term capital (long-term debt, preferred stock, and common equity). If this were used as a goal, a company with poor earnings would tend to perpetuate its failure; a company with high earnings might think it should forego profitable investments unless the past rate were achieved. Neither is the rate that other companies in the industry have earned any good as a goal. All these rates leave unsolved what is correct as a minimum goal.

Improving Common Stock Earnings Per Share

This is one goal which some executives and financial analysts consider sound. I do not dispute the fact that managements should attempt to increase earnings per share, but it is not just that simple as far as new investment is concerned. Suppose an industrial company is earning an inadequate return of 6 percent on its total capital, which results in earnings per share on its common stock of $1, and the company is considering an expansion program which will increase earnings per share to $1.25. The question immediately arises whether this is sufficient to justify the project. There must be adequate earnings per share, but what is adequate? The ultimate test must be based on a proper profit goal as a percent return on new investment. I will explain more fully why I object to earnings per share as a goal at the end of the article, after I have developed the tools with which to work.

WHERE CAN MANAGEMENT LOOK FOR AN ANSWER?

There is a competitive market for capital in our system of private capital just as there is a competitive market for other types of goods and services. Furthermore, capital has a cost, and to be successful a company must earn enough to cover all costs, including capital costs. Very briefly, a company should earn at least something above the bare minimum rate which investors require to induce them to provide all the capital, that is the cost of capital. We are really interested in three rates:

Cost of Capital—that is the cost to attract capital.

Return on Capital Target—the rate a company should earn on its capital, which should be at least somewhat above the cost of capital.

Expansion Profit Goal—well above the cost of capital to take care of risk elements in expansion.

Broadly speaking, cost of capital includes two elements. One element is the amount necessary to induce people to invest and save their money rather than hold it idle or spend it. The other element is the amount necessary to compensate investors for the risk they take. Therefore, it is the nature of the company and its risk which determines the cost of capital. We will define cost of capital at this point and hope that the explanation which follows will make its meaning clear.

Cost of capital is the overall composite percent net cost rate, after allowing for underwriter's compensation and expenses of financing, which investors require to induce them to provide all forms of long-term capital, in a competitive market, on an average over a period of years.

FRAMEWORK FOR REASONING

In order to have a base for our thinking, we will start with a look at how capital flows into a corporation and how it is put to use. This may seem elementary, but it is often lost sight of. A look at a balance sheet will give us the best picture. Assume that you start a new industrial company with the simplified balance sheet shown below; practically any balance sheet can be summarized in a similar manner.

When determining cost of capital, we will be looking to the right-hand side of the balance sheet and dealing with the total capital of $100. It comes from investors through the sale of long-term securities—debt $20 and common equity $80. All common equity, whether it be the stated or par value, capital surplus or earned surplus, should be treated alike for cost of capital purposes. There is no distinction so far as the common stockholders are concerned. It all represents part of their ownership. Surplus arising from retained earnings is equivalent to raising new common equity. In fact, as earnings are plowed back, a company regularly raises new common equity. If management made a distinction as regards the rate to be earned on earned surplus, stockholders would be well advised to have the company pay out all its earnings in dividends and then raise new equity money by sale of stock to stockholders. If you question this statement, consider a private company with one stockholder. Would he accept a lower return on money he leaves in versus money he put in? Stockholders of a publicly owned company should not be treated differently by management.

Assets		Liabilities		
Current assets	$100	Current liabilities		$ 50
Plant	50	Long-term capital		
		Debt	$20	
		Common equity	80	100
Total	$150	Total		$150

When applying a profit goal we will be working with assets on the left-hand side. It is necessary to visualize the relationship between the two sides of the balance sheet so that the rate obtained on the right-hand side will be correctly associated with the assets on the left. Therefore, we must note that the $100 of long-term securities provide the money for $50 of plant and $50 of working capital. (Current assets $100 less current liabilities $50.) The working capital is required to earn the same rate as the plant.

In order to cover the entire subject of cost of capital, we should discuss capital structure and the cost of debt, but to save space we will skip them. A further point we will omit is the question of costs associated with current liabilities. Generally, such costs are so small as not to be important; in any event, they can be handled fairly readily.

Cost of capital would actually be easy to understand and calculate if all capital consisted of debt since its cost is the interest rate. The problem becomes difficult because of the common equity part of our capital structure. Does it have a cost and how can it be calculated? We will concentrate on trying to answer this question.

AN ALL-DEBT CAPITAL STRUCTURE TO ASSIST IN EXPLANATION

Before we try to answer the question of the common cost rate, let's take another view of the capital structure in the simplified balance sheet shown, that is, the $20 of debt and $80 of common equity. For the moment, let's reason in terms of debt securities since we can probably agree that debt has a cost.

If we assign an interest rate of 5 percent to the $20 of debt, the picture would be as shown below. Forget about the tax savings that interest produces; we are now only talking about the rates that investors require, and they do not pay the corporate tax. We will cover the effect of interest on taxes later on.

	Amount	Rate	Cost
Debt	$20	5%	$1.00
Common	80		

Now let's change the composition of our capital structure and first substitute a layer of $30 of junior debt for $30 of the common equity. Since the added debt would be junior and in a more risky position, it would require a higher rate. For illustrative purposes let's use 6 percent. For an industrial company, we have already added much more debt than would be wise from the point of view of sound financial policy, but, purely for the purpose of illustrating the idea of cost of capital, let's go one step further and substitute a third layer of $49 more junior, junior debt for $49 of common. Certainly, no ordinary investor would purchase such debt, and any rate we assign to it would be a pure guess. But, if we did try to sell it to anyone, the type of person who might be interested would be a so-called money lender. If you have ever heard about the rates they charge, you are aware of their magnitudes. At least, it is not inconceivable that with 99 percent total debt that the rate on the third layer might be between 10 percent and 20 percent; let's use 15 percent. The picture would be as follows:

	Amount	Rate	Cost
Debt	$20	5%	$ 1.00
Jr. Debt	30	6	1.80
Jr., Jr. Debit	49	15	7.35
Common	1		
	$100		$10.15

Thus, leaving out the cost for the remaining $1 of common and just using the debt costs as above, the overall cost for 99 percent of our capital is about 10 percent.

We used this approach as a first step in explaining cost of capital to show that:

1. All capital has a cost, whether it be debt or equity. Merely substituting debt for equity or vice versa does not change the fact that there is a cost to all capital.
2. Capital is not cheap. As the debt becomes more junior, the interest rate must rise because of the added risk. The common stock has all the risk with no junior security protecting it, and, in fact, it must provide protection for the senior securities. Therefore, the common should justifiably receive a substantially higher rate.
3. The rate we are trying to seek for a cost of capital is the overall composite cost of all the capital. It is the composite rate which must be used as a basis for the goal in deciding how much should be earned on assets when an expansion program is being weighed.

Sometimes managements are attracted to the idea of applying the increment cost rate to a particular project. This mistake is most often made in connection with lease financing,[1] which is a form of debt financing. This is wrong. If a company sold debt securities and used the proceeds to build a factory, the goal should still be based on a composite rate of all the company's capital. It could not sell the debt unless it had some common equity. Visualize the situation which would arise if a company did use the rate on the type of security sold to raise money for a particular project. The goal would shift depending on whether it used debt or equity even for the same type of project.

With this background, we can attack the difficult task—the cost of the common equity. As stated above, common stock does not have a cost in the sense that debt has a cost, but common stock has an economic cost. Some people prefer such a term as "required earnings rate."

In essence, when a person buys a stock he looks forward to receiving two benefits: dividends as they are paid in the future and capital appreciation. It is future prospects of these two elements that induce stockholders to pay a price for common stock. But, both dividends and market appreciation come from future earnings per share. Many things affect the price of a stock, but the principal factor which includes all the returns that accrue to the common stock is the earnings per share. The price is affected by both the amount and quality of earnings.

The measurement of the common cost rate on the basis of this concept is not easy to explain. First, let's look at an old guidepost for pricing a com-

---

[1]These remarks are not to be confused with the necessity of comparing the cost for one type of security with the cost rate for the other similar types of securities, when deciding on how to finance. For example, the rate on one type of debt obligation such as a lease should be compared with the rate on the other types of debt and not with equity or with a composite figure.

mon stock. The old rule of thumb for the price-earnings ratio of a stock, without prospects of growth, was ten times. This means that a stock earning $10 per share would sell for $100 as long as it had prospects of earning the $10. Since a company would have to earn the $10 in order for it to maintain the common stock at a price of $100, then the percentage earnings rate would be 10 percent. This, in essence, is what is meant by a cost rate for the common, but unfortunately, it is not that simple.

The important point is that the cost rate for common is the relationship of price to *future* prospects of earnings rather than to current earnings per share. Current earnings are over the dam once a stock is purchased; all gains to the stockholders come from future earnings. Past earnings may well be a guide to future earnings, but they are not what benefit the common stock-holders. This is particularly important to keep in mind for growth stocks which sell at high price-earnings ratios.

There is another more subtle point with regard to the common cost, to which we have alluded but not explained. There are actually three earnings per share from which we have to choose. This can be illustrated by the simple figures below:

a. Price of stock	$100
b. Current earnings per share	5
c. Estimated potential earnings per share by company	8
d. Expected potential earnings per share by investors	10

These simple examples of estimated and expected earnings per share and those that follow are supposed to reflect the full future potential earning power including all growth prospects.

Now then, what is it that makes investors pay $100 per share for the stock—$5, $8, or $10? It is the *investors' expectations* of $10! Thus, the cost rate for common, or in other words, the rate that induces investors to buy the stock, has to be based on the price investors pay for a stock related to the prospects of earnings that *they expect* to receive. The rate is:

$$\text{Common Cost Rate: } \frac{d}{a} = \frac{\$10}{\$100} = 10\%$$

Eventually, if the company's estimate of $8 proved to be correct rather than the $10 the investors expected and this became known to investors, the price of the stock would fall to $80 per share. Then, the common cost rate would still be 10 percent, that is, the same expectancy rate by investors. Actually, as noted above, no future single earnings per share figure can represent investors' full expectations if there are prospects for continuous growth.

We have to add one further point with regard to common cost. To simplify the picture, we have left out financing costs. If a company's common stock sells for $100 per share in the market, and it sold some new stock, the net amount it would receive per share would be less than the $100 because of financing costs. A company should be able to sell stock through rights if it is required to do so for its stockholders' benefit. As a rough rule of thumb, a figure of 10 percent is a reasonable allowance for financing costs

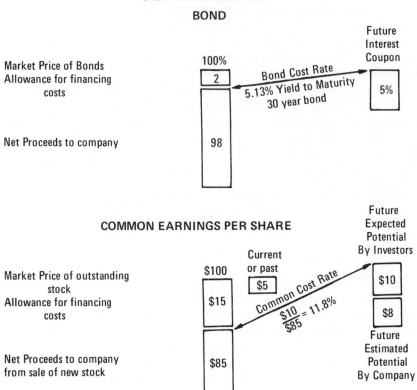

Figure 8-1
Cost Rate Illustration

and rights value, for cost of capital purposes, for a large, relatively stable company like an electric utility. For a large, well-situated industrial company a slightly higher figure of 15 percent may be used. There may be variations from these percentages depending on the circumstances surrounding a particular common offering, but they are sufficiently within the range of reasonableness for our purposes. Therefore, our illustration for the common cost rate would have to be modified by allowing 15 percent for financing costs.[2] The common cost rate would be $10 ÷ $85, giving a rate of 11.8 percent. The figures, which we have used to describe the common cost rate, are shown in Figure 8-1. For illustrative purposes, the bond cost rate is also included.

Our explanation has admittedly compounded the problem of actually

---

[2]There is one possible small difference between funds raised through the sale of stock and retained earnings. A stock sale involves financing costs, but none is associated with retained earnings. Therefore, it may be contended that a slightly lower rate can be applied to earned surplus to the extent of financing costs. There is a good argument against any difference: a company should earn enough on its equity in order to be able to pay out all its earnings in dividends if it chooses to do so and still cover its cost of capital. This article treats all equity the same.

figuring the common cost rate. Investors' expectations at times may be above, below, or the same as is actually realized by the company in the future. In the long run, as their errors become apparent, the market should eventually correct itself to conform to reality. However, either excessive optimism or pessimism may persist for a long time, and failure to take it into account can lead to meaningless results in the common cost rate. We will see how to try to handle the idea of expected earnings when we get to actual common cost rate calculations. At this point we can, at least, define the common cost rate. The common cost rate is obtained by dividing the net amount a company would receive from the sale of common stock, after all financing costs, on an average over a period of years, including both favorable and unfavorable market conditions, into all future benefits the stockholders expected to receive when they bought the stock.

COMMON COST: SOME ACTUAL FIGURES

To turn to some actual figures, let's look at a company which, aside from some ups and downs, has exhibited a relatively stable earnings picture in recent years. With such a situation, on an average over a period of years, the relationship of current earnings to price should give some indication of the common cost rate. A discussion with some qualified security analysts confirmed the fact that investors generally viewed the stock as lacking any marked growth prospects during the period. Without revealing the company's name, figures for the common stock for the past ten years are shown in Table 8-1.

On this basis, the common cost rate would be 11 percent. There are reasons to suggest that this figure is too low: First, the figures indicate that common stockholders might at least have had some expectation of growth. Secondly, the stock market was at a relatively high level during recent years. Thus it would seem to be justified to increase this figure somewhat on the basis of judgment. As an approximation we might use 12 percent as

TABLE 8-1

Years	Earnings per share	Dividends per share	Book value per share	Average market price	Average market price discounted 15%	Earnings divided by market price discounted 15%
1962	$10.83	$6.00	$120.33	$123.93	$105.33	10.3%
1961	7.71	6.00	115.50	126.18	107.25	7.2
1960	9.03	6.00	113.97	120.18	102.24	8.8
1959	13.08	6.00	111.33	129.39	109.98	11.9
1958	7.02	6.00	104.46	97.14	82.56	8.5
1957	11.43	7.20	103.47	107.82	91.65	12.5
1956	12.03	6.90	97.53	134.07	113.97	10.6
1955	15.51	5.79	90.15	124.50	105.81	14.7
1954	9.81	5.01	81.09	112.14	95.31	10.3
1953	9.78	5.01	76.77	75.36	64.07	15.3
Average						11.0%

a cost for common. The capital structure, during this 10-year period, included 6 percent of senior securities and 94 percent common equity. Therefore, the overall cost of capital would be only slightly less than the common rate, or about 11.5 percent. The nature of this company's business in terms of risk was such during the 10-year period that one would expect the cost of capital to be above that for the average for industrial companies.

A word of caution should be noted here: Merely because a company's earnings have been level does not necessarily mean that investors expected them to be level. If investors had hopes of increased earnings and were willing to pay high prices for the stock on such hopes, then the technique used of relating earnings per share to adjusted market price would give too low a common cost rate. Figures for cost of capital purposes can only be used properly after a review has been made of the investors' attitude towards the company. As an example, one of the large companies in the chemical industry showed a ratio of earnings per share to price, adjusted for financing costs, on an average over the past ten years of 5.1 percent. There was some increase in earnings but certainly not enough to justify such a low rate. The low price-earnings ratio was accounted for by the fact that the company was in a business which was considered to have great prospects. Furthermore, this particular company had large expenditures for research, which made investors feel that the future earnings prospects would be very favorable. If they are not realized, a price adjustment is inevitable.

Now turning to the question of the significance of price-earnings ratios for growth stocks, it is interesting to note the following remark (*New York Times,* June 17, 1962) made by Secretary of the Treasury Douglas Dillon about stock prices before a Senate Finance Committee:

> . . . many investment advisors believe that a stock selling at a price 15 times earnings was probably on a pretty sound basis. . . .

It has been suggested that some managements may have taken the reciprocal, or price-earnings ratio of 6.7 percent, as a clue to the common cost rate. If investors did not expect growth in earnings, would they be willing to buy stocks on such a price-earnings basis? Obviously not! Cost of capital measurement must take into consideration expectations of investors. This can be illustrated by taking a look at a typical picture of increasing earnings. We will use as an example, Moody's Common Stock Average for 125 industrials. As a matter of fact it showed average price-earnings for the past ten years of 15.5 times. The figures are shown in Table 8-2.

The earnings to adjusted price shows an average figure of 8 percent. Obviously, this is too low, because investors must have expected some growth in earnings. Assuming that their expectations were the same as were actually realized by these companies, how do we allow for it in obtaining a common cost rate? There is no easy answer.

The following approach gives some interesting figures: Assume that investors looked one year ahead when they purchased stock and that on the

TABLE 8-2
MOODY'S COMMON STOCK AVERAGE FOR 125 INDUSTRIALS

	Earnings per share	Market price	Price-earnings ratios	Market price discounted 15%	Earnings divided by market price discounted 15%
1962	$11.10	$189.95	17.1	$161.46	6.9%
1961	9.61	199.90	20.8	169.91	5.7
1960	9.62	173.18	18.0	147.20	6.5
1959	9.85	186.26	18.9	158.32	6.2
1958	8.31	149.81	18.0	127.34	6.5
1957	10.27	143.65	14.0	122.10	8.4
1956	10.35	149.41	14.4	127.00	8.1
1955	10.51	130.66	12.4	111.06	9.5
1954	8.38	95.81	11.4	81.44	10.3
1953	7.71	76.05	9.9	64.64	11.9
Average			15.5		8.0%

average their forecasting was correct. This would call for dividing each adjusted price into the next year's earnings. This would give us 8.5 percent. If we did it for two years ahead, it would be 9.3 percent; and for three years ahead, 9.5 percent. These figures are too low because in each case they give no effect to still further growth which investors would be entitled to expect. If investors felt that all growth in earnings would disappear after three years, they would certainly lower their market appraisal drastically.

Since we are trying to interpret how investors viewed the picture, we cannot come up with any exact figure, but at least it would not seem unreasonable to take 11 percent as a rough figure. The companies included in the index had a debt ratio of about 15 percent. Assuming a 5 percent interest rate for the debt and applying 11 percent to the equity would give an approximate composite cost of capital of about 10 percent. This is a reasonable figure for the cost of capital for an industrial company.

No pat rule can be given to determine the common cost rate for a particular company. Space does not permit a discussion of other approaches. All the circumstances surrounding a company must be considered, having in mind the way the investors view it. In some situations it may be impossible to use a company's own securities to determine the rate. Then a company must arrive at a figure based on judgment, having in mind the nature of its risk as compared with the risk for other types of companies for which there are known figures. This problem always exists for a privately owned company since there are no market prices for its securities. True, the owner of a privately owned company can disregard cost of capital and even run his company at a loss if he chooses to do so, since it is his property. However, presumably he will wish to run it so as to make the same profit as though his capital were invested in a similar type of publicly owned company. Thus, a privately owned company should wish to apply the same principles.

The above qualifications on the approximate nature of the common cost rate may make it appear as though the overall cost of capital cannot be determined sufficiently accurately to be of real value. However, it is not really necessary to refine a cost of capital closely for an industrial company; in an expansion program, forecasts of sales expenses and expenditures are bound to contain substantial errors, and the calculated profitability of a project is only an approximate figure. This approach is based on sound principles and an understanding of the idea will assist management in arriving at sound conclusions.

SOME COMPOSITE RATES

To give you an idea of the magnitude of the figures for certain types of business, we will now present a few approximate figures in summary form without proof. We include figures on regulated industries because much work has been done in this field. Furthermore, they give us a good reference point for comparison. Because of the relatively stable nature of their business, they are the lowest rates we can expect to find. The rate for any industrial company should be substantially higher.

The rates shown in Table 8-3 apply to total capital after taxes for investors. We will discuss the treatment of taxes subsequently.

TABLE 8-3

	Cost of capital	Return on capital target	Expansion profit goal
Electric utility		6½ to 7½%	
Telephone		8%	
Department stores	8% ⎫	At least ⎫	
Industrial company, average	10% ⎬	above bare ⎬	up to 20%
Textile	13% ⎭	cost ⎭	

The spread between the three rates depends on many factors. In regulated industries the spread is small. On the other hand, managements of industrial companies may set the expansion goal well in excess of cost of capital for many reasons. How much the spread should be above cost of capital in order to arrive at the expansion profit goal is a matter of judgment. It must take into account the fact that when a company goes into a new venture there is added risk because of the lack of familiarity with the business. Basically, allowance must be made for the fact that if, in each new venture, a company used the cost of capital as its goal, and it failed in some of its ventures, the average return would be below cost of capital. It has been reported[3] that some major companies have used 20 percent after taxes as an expansion goal.

It is interesting to note that the managements of companies which have shown good profits recognize the importance of setting high profit goals. On

---

[3]Variability of Private Investment in Plant and Equipment. Materials submitted to the Joint Economic Committee Congress of the United States (87th Congress, 2d Session), Part II, Some Elements Shaping Investment Decisions, page 14.

the other hand, companies which have shown poor results argue that they cannot find projects which will provide high profits, so they struggle with themselves and in the end usually lower their goals. This can only lead to perpetuation of poor performance with all the unfortunate consequences of misdirecting capital.

If there is a significant variation in risk between products, a company will wish to set different goals. This may have to be handled on the basis of judgment, because it may be impossible to find any evidence in the securities markets. This may appear difficult at first, but once a person has become familiar with the subject, satisfactory figures can be established.

In recent years, more and more companies are turning to investing in foreign countries. The risk will obviously depend on the country. However, on the basis of logic, there must be at least some increase in risk in any foreign investment over a similar type of investment in this country. There are the added risks of foreign exchange problems and political attitudes towards the foreign investment. It seems that some companies today, in their eagerness to enter the foreign market, are underestimating the risk element.

The question sometimes arises whether a company can take on some independent projects below the cost of capital if other projects are sufficiently high so that the average of all projects is satisfactory. No! This is misdirecting capital. This is entirely different from the question of how to handle certain types of investment which contribute no direct income such as recreational facilities for employees, etc. To provide a satisfactory return on all capital, the deficit on such investment must be made up on the income-producing projects.

TAX TREATMENT

We have defined cost of capital as the rate required to induce investors to provide long-term capital, and we refer to it as the "to investor rate." Thus far, we have not been concerned with the effect of corporate income taxes. How to handle it depends on the purpose to which the rate is to be applied. There are various ways to treat taxes; we will discuss three of them:

1. *To Investor Rate.* As already stated, the rate to investors provides the starting point for calculation of cost of capital. It disregards corporate taxes. Investors are not directly concerned with the taxes the corporation pays. This rate which is the target for return on capital can be used to compare with the company's past experienced return to determine whether it has been sufficient.[4]

   The company's experienced return is derived by adding the net income after taxes, before any dividends to the interest

[4]Actually, a company, to be successful, should earn such a return on its capital giving effect to a present value of its assets. Also, in analyzing policies with regard to plant abandonment and making additional capital expenditures in order to save existing investment, current values of existing plant must be used. The cost of capital approach should be applied within the framework of these values. These situations sometimes present some nice complications.

charges on long-term debt, and dividing the total by the total capital structure. This is referred to under the title "Company's Experienced Return on Capital." It is comparable with the "to investor rate."

When using cost of capital for this purpose, the spread above the cost of capital and goal can be much smaller than the spread for an expansion profit goal. To be successful, a company should earn at least something above cost of capital.

2. *To Company, Pre-Tax Rate.* The nature of this rate is obvious; it gives the cost to the company before income taxes.

3. *To Company, After-Tax Equivalent Rate.* A project's profitability is generally figured after the taxes which apply to the income of the particular project. This does not take into account the tax savings that will accrue to the company if it has some interest charges on long-term debt.

Therefore, to make the goal comparable with the profit rate calculated for the project, adjustment is made in the goal for the tax savings if the company has some debt in its capital and thus some interest charges. It is an after-tax rate, adjusted for the tax savings resulting from the interest charges. This is the expansion profit goal rate generally used to compare with the profitability of a project figured on a discounted cash flow basis.

Assuming a 50 percent income tax rate, these three rates can be compared as shown in Table 8-4. Of course, there should be substantial allowance for the amount above the cost of capital when a company sets a profit goal.

EFFECT OF CAPITAL STRUCTURE ON COST OF CAPITAL

One of the controversies about cost of capital revolves around the question of the effect of varying debt ratios on cost of capital. Pure economic theory tells us that cost of capital is dependent on the risk of the enterprise and not the way the capital structure pie is divided between debt and equity. Here we are talking about the "to investor rate" and not considering the effect of interest on tax savings. This idea is based on the principle that, as debt is increased, the common stock becomes more risky and the rate on the common must rise so that the two combined equal the same overall cost. For example, suppose one person owned all the company: could he change the cost of capital by exchanging half of his stock for debt so that his investment would consist of 50 percent debt/50 percent equity? Obviously, it makes no difference to him how the pie is divided; the overall

TABLE 8-4

	Capital structure	Rate	I To investors	II To company, pre-tax	III To company, after-tax Equivalent
Debt	$ 15	5 %	0.75	0.75	0.375
Common	85	10.5	8.925	17.85	8.925
Cost of capital	$100		9.675	18.60	9.300

risk is the same. Now, suppose the two different securities are owned by different investors, would they take lower rates on each or on either one so that overall cost would be lower? Not on the basis of pure theory.

However, as a practical matter, the markets for debt and equity are not entirely overlapping, and debt may be used up to a certain point without substantially increasing the common cost rate so that there will be a decrease in the overall cost. Then within an added range of debt there will be some increase in the cost of debt and equity but not in the overall cost. At some point, as debt is further increased, risk is added to the capital structure so that the rate of debt and equity rise to such an extent as to cause an increase in the overall cost of capital. The amount of debt which each company should carry will depend on all the surrounding circumstances.

There are those who erroneously believe that the cost of capital can be reduced by piling on all the debt the traffic will bear. They contend that debt, with interest deductible for tax purposes, is cheap, and common is expensive; therefore, using all the debt possible will result in a decrease in the overall cost of capital. The proponents of this idea fail to consider the greater risk to the common and the fact that the rate on both debt and common will increase so as to cause an increase in the overall cost. This may be labeled the short-range view. In the short run, during a bull market, when investors are not worrying about the possibility of adverse developments, they

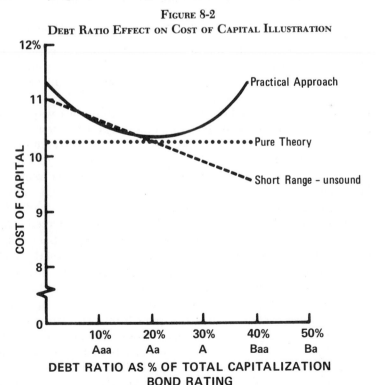

FIGURE 8-2
DEBT RATIO EFFECT ON COST OF CAPITAL ILLUSTRATION

may tend to disregard the danger of too much debt. Of course, they have in the back of their minds that they will sell their stock before the company encounters adversity.

From the long-range point of view of the stockholders, the short-range approach must be assiduously avoided. The company does not have the mobility of a security holder who can sell out if he expects trouble. A company will have to consider the effect on cost of capital when adversity is encountered. During such periods an overly heavy debt burden may jeopardize the stockholders, it may hurt dividend payments, and it may put a company in a difficult position in raising new capital on a reasonable basis. Thus, there are many reasons why it is best for a company in the long run to keep its debt within the high-grade category.

These ideas are shown in Figure 8-2 as they might apply to an industrial company. The figures, bond ratings, etc. are for illustrative purposes only and not supposed to represent their relationship for any specific company.

If you are familiar with the many factors which affect security prices, you will realize that adequate statistical proof is not readily available. It is impossible to isolate the effect of debt ratio from all the other factors which affect security prices so as to determine its effect alone. Those efforts at statistical proof which have been based on an earnings-price ratio are wrong because they do not measure the common cost rate properly.

EARNINGS PER SHARE AS A GOAL — WHY A FALLACY

Management should attempt to increase earnings on existing invest-ment. However, as was mentioned under "Unsound Goals," some manage-ments erroneously hold to the belief that increasing current earnings per share is a sound goal for new expansion or acquisitions. Now we have the tools to show why this is a fallacy. There are numerous ways in which earnings per share can be increased. In all instances if the new investment earns at least something more than the cost of capital, the common stock-holders will benefit. However, if it earns less than the cost of capital, the stockholders will ultimately experience a loss even though current earnings may show some improvement. We will illustrate this point with an example.

Suppose that a company with great prospects has one share of stock outstanding, earning $4 per share, which sells for $100 or a 4 percent earnings-price ratio. It has a chance to acquire a privately owned company which has one share of stock outstanding, earning $6 per share currently and with potential earnings per share of $8 per share. The risk in the business to be acquired, we will assume on the basis of cost of capital, is 10 percent. It acquires the second company by issuing another share and swapping it on a share-for-share basis. Thus, in effect, it pays $100 per share for the new company. After the acquisition, the total current earnings will be $10, and earnings per share will be $5. Thus, the earnings per share of the acquiring company will be increased from $4 to $5. However, since the stock to be acquired is only worth $80 on the assumption that the risk is 10 percent, the acquiring company will be hurt by a capital loss of 20 percent in the new investment when it fails to live up to investors' expectations and earn the 10 percent. Since this loss will be spread over two shares after the acquisition, the average capital loss will be 10 percent.

It is not hard to find examples of companies which have acquired many companies through exchanges of stock, and the results have ultimately been disappointing even though current earnings may show some increase. This is bound to occur if managements follow the theory of basing acquisitions on increasing current earnings per share and pay exorbitant prices in relation to potential profits.

An acquisition with stock must be calculated on the basis that the company has invested an amount of cash equivalent to the market value of common stock. Based on that amount, the acquisition must show a return above the cost of capital. The cost of capital should take into account the risk of the enterprise and any increase in rate if in fact the common stock of the company to be acquired is highly leveraged with debt. The profitability calculation for an acquisition must be figured on a discounted cash flow analysis of forecast profits and capital outlays, etc. The test for an acquisition is no different in principle from expansion through capital investment.

The above comments are not to suggest that management should fail to pay careful attention to the effect of expansion on earnings per share because of the possible immediate effect on the market price of the stock and thus the common stockholders. In other words, projects must first and foremost meet the goal based on cost of capital. Then the effect on earnings per share should be examined.

Actually, correctly interpreted, earnings per share can even be used as a test, but it must conform to idea of cost of capital as previously explained. It is the earnings per share expected by investors which must be achieved. The test thus conforms to the cost of capital approach. All the qualifications observed in that approach must be kept in mind.

A quick comment about some other examples which require a knowledge of the principles we have discussed. Suppose a company is earning 30 percent on its capital, can it expand at a lower rate on new capital without hurting the common stockholders? The answer is yes, as long as the company achieves at least something above the cost of capital on the new investment. What about the case of a company having excess funds invested in government bonds earning 4 percent? In order to increase earnings per share, it wants to go into a project which will earn 8 percent but has a risk equivalent to a 10 percent cost of capital. This would be a mistake on the basis of the principles we have discussed.

In conclusion, an understanding of cost of capital will assist managements in making many types of decisions on a sound basis. Profits are the key to our free enterprise system. Our economy, including the consumers, employees, and savers, is directly dependent for its continued progress on management decisions based on a correct understanding of this vital key.

9. LEVERAGE AND THE COST OF CAPITAL*

EZRA SOLOMON †

The proper use of debt financing is one of the major decision areas of corporate financial management. My paper confines itself to just one facet of the many considerations which jointly determine the optimal use of debt —namely, the effect that a change in financial leverage has, or can be assumed to have, on a company's cost of capital. In particular, it addresses itself to the thesis put forward by Modigliani and Miller that, apart from a tax effect, a company's cost of capital is independent of the degree of leverage in its financial structure.[1]

I

To isolate the effect of leverage alone from the many other factors that may be involved in using debt wisely, it is useful to conduct the analysis in terms of the following simplified model:

Let X be a company which holds or acquires only one kind of asset. Each dollar invested in these assets generates a flow of operating earnings, before taxes, which provides a rate of return of k per annum of a given quality with respect to the certainty or uncertainty with which it can be expected to occur. We will assume that this company may use any mixture of only two kinds of financing—pure, externally derived: equity, on the one hand, and pure debt, on the other. Third, we assume that the structure of market capitalization rates is given and that this *structure* does not change over time.

The following notation will be used:

Total market value of company's securities	V
Market value of bonds	B
Market value of stock	S
Leverage	$L = B/S$
Operating earnings (before taxes or interest)	O
Debt charges	F
Residual earnings on equity (before taxes)	$E = O - F$
Rate of return on investment	k
Pretax overall capitalization rate (cost of capital)	$k_0 = O/V$
Pretax equity capitalization rate (cost of equity capital)	$k_e = E/S$
Pretax debt capitalization rate (cost of debt capital)	$k_i = F/B$
Pretax marginal cost of borrowing	$m = \triangle F / \triangle B$

For the all-equity case we have $k_e = k_0 = k$. When debt is used, we have $k_e > k_0$. Specifically, regardless of the valuation theory one embraces, the

*From the *Journal of Finance* (May, 1963), pp. 273-279. Reprinted by permission.
†Dean Witter Professor of Finance, Graduate School of Business, Stanford University.
[1]Franco Modigliani and Merton H. Miller, "The Cost of Capital, Corporation Finance and the Theory of Investment," *American Economic Review* (June, 1958).

relationship $k_e = k_0 + (k_0 - k_i) B/S$ and $k_0 = (k_e S + k_i B)/(B+S)$ must hold.[2] The heart of the leverage question can now be stated as follows: What happens to V and k_0 as we increase the degree of leverage (other things remaining unchanged) from $L = O$ to $L \to \infty$?

For the purpose of analysis, there are two ways in which leverage can be altered in the model. We can assume that Company X *substitutes* debt for equity in its capital structure, i.e., it issues debt and uses the proceeds to redeem outstanding stock. This model has the virtue that it keeps the asset structure constant as leverage changes and, therefore, permits a direct comparison of V at one level of leverage with V at other levels. But it does not allow for the easy identification of the marginal cost of debt as this is generally measured. As we shall see, this variable is an important key to the entire leverage question.

An alternative model for analyzing changes in leverage is to permit Company X to expand, i.e., to issue more and more debt, using the proceeds to acquire additional assets. This permits an easy identification of the marginal cost of each increment of debt. However, in order not to contaminate the leverage effect, it is necessary to assume that each new asset acquired generates operating earnings, before tax, of the same size and quality as those produced by existing assets.

On the whole, the latter model is more convenient for present purposes, and we shall use it. Modigliani and Miller have generally used the former model in their illustrations, but it is relatively easy to restate their conclusions and arguments in terms of the latter.

Introducing positive amounts of debt into the model introduces the problem of corporate income and the complication that interest payments are deductible in computing taxes. However, everybody agrees that the tax-effect factor does tend to lower the overall cost of capital of a more highly levered company relative to a less levered company, and we can conveniently ignore the tax effect in addressing ourselves to the more controversial issues.

II

Ignoring the tax effect, the Modigliani-Miller position is that Company X's overall cost of capital k_0 is constant for all levels of leverage from $L = O$ to $L \to \infty$. If k_0^* is used to represent the overall cost of capital for a more levered company and k_0 to represent the overall cost of capital for a less levered company in the same risk class, their basic thesis is that, except for

---

[2]These two relationships are derived as follows:

(a) Since $k_e = E/S = O - F/S$ and $O = k_0 V = k_0 (B+S)$ and $F = k_i B$, we have
$$k_e = \frac{k_0(B+S) - k_i B}{S},$$
$$= k_0 + (k_0 - k_i)\ B/S.$$

(b) Since $k_0 = O/V = (E+F)/(B+S)$ and $E = k_e S$ and $F = k_i B$, we have
$$k_0 = \frac{k_e S + k_i B}{B+S}.$$

the tax effect, $k_0{}^* = k_0$ for any and all levels of leverage.

It is useful to divide their basic thesis into two component statements. Still ignoring the tax effect, these are (1) an increase in borrowing (and hence in leverage), no matter how moderate or "judicious," can never lower a company's cost of capital; (2) an increase in borrowing (and hence in leverage), no matter how immoderate or "excessive," can never raise a company's cost of capital.

Almost all the analytical controversy generated thus far by the Modigliani-Miller thesis seems to have centered on the first of these two component statements and on the proof put forward on its behalf by its proponents. The proof offered by Modigliani-Miller is that a process akin to arbitrage, in which individual investors engage in "homemade" leverage as a substitute for corporate leverage will keep $k_0{}^*$, the capitalization rate for the more levered situation, equal to k_0, the capitalization rate for the less levered situation.

The traditional position is that, even if the tax effect of leverage is ignored, moderate leverage can lower $k_0{}^*$ relative to k_0.[3] The traditionalists' counterargument to Modigliani and Miller's arbitrage model is that homemade leverage is not a perfect substitute for corporate leverage and that the equilibrating mechanism posited in the arbitrage model may not fully erase the tendency for $k_0{}^*$ to fall below k_0.

While this aspect of the controversy is an interesting one, it is not of great practical consequence for the issue at hand. Whether, in a tax-free world, the traditional view that k_0 does fall is correct or whether the Modigliani-Miller argument that k_0 does not fall is correct, in a world of taxable corporate incomes in which interest payments are tax-deductible, everybody agrees that, up to a certain judicious limit of debt, k_0 declines as leverage is increased.

The really crucial part of the Modigliani-Miller thesis is their second statement, namely, that k_0 will not *rise*, no matter how far the use of leverage is carried. This conclusion might hold if we assume that the rate of interest paid on debt does not rise as leverage is increased. At least it is possible, given this assumption, to invoke the *arbitrage* argument in order to show that it *should* hold if investors behave rationally.

But in practice k_i, the average rate of interest paid on debt, must rise as leverage is increased. For extreme leverage positions, i.e., as the company approaches an all-debt situation, it is clear that k_i will be at least equal to k_0. Given the general attitude of bondholders and bond-rating agencies, it is highly likely that k_i will be *above* k_0 for positions of extreme leverage.

Now as k_i, the average cost of debt, rises, the marginal cost of borrowing, $m = \triangle F / \triangle B$, must be above k_i. Therefore, there is some point of lever-

---

[3]For an explicit statement of the traditional position, see Harry G. Guthmann and Herbert E. Dougall, *Corporate Financial Policy* (3d ed.; Englewood Cliffs, N.J.: Prentice-Hall, Inc., 1955), p. 245.

age at which Company X finds that m, the marginal cost of more debt, is *higher* than its average cost of capital, k_0. Again taking into account the general attitudes of those who supply debt funds, this point is likely to be reached quite rapidly if leverage is increased beyond levels acceptable to the debt markets.

For all practical purposes, the point at which a company finds that $m \geq k_0$ represents the maximum use of leverage, for it can be argued that no rational company will finance with more pure debt if it can do so more cheaply by using a mixture of debt and equity similar to that outstanding in its existing structure. If this fact is accepted, then the argument between Modigliani and Miller and the traditional position vanishes. Both would agree that leverage is clearly excessive if carried beyond the point at which the rising marginal cost-of-debt curve intersects the overall cost of capital at that point.

III

Assuming that the straightforward logic of this argument is accepted, what we are left with is something very similar to the U-shaped k_0 curve envisaged by traditional theory. This is outlined in Figure 9-1. In the early or moderate phases of leverage, k_0 declines, possibly because of market imperfections but at the very least because of the tax-effect factor. As leverage reaches and then exceeds the limits acceptable to the debt markets, m rises rapidly, and the tax advantage of even more leverage is offset by the rising cost of each further increment of debt. When m rises above k_0, any further increase in leverage will bring about a rise in k_0. We thus have a clearly determinate point or range of optimal leverage.

Unfortunately, Modigliani and Miller have not been willing to accept this

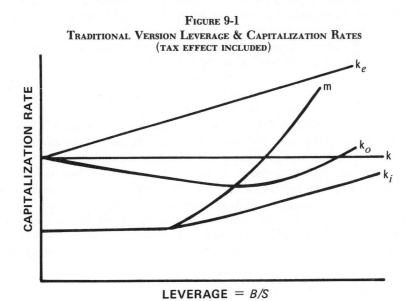

FIGURE 9-1
TRADITIONAL VERSION LEVERAGE & CAPITALIZATION RATES
(TAX EFFECT INCLUDED)

FIGURE 9-2
MODIGLIANI AND MILLER VERSION

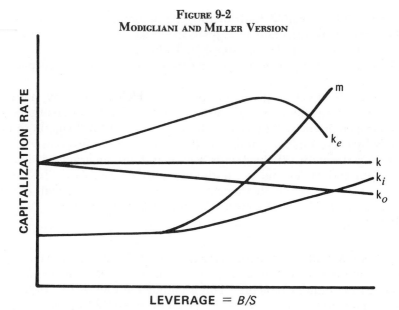

conclusion. Instead, they argue that k_0 remains constant even when leverage is increased beyond the point at which $m > k_e$. According to them what brings about this startling and wholly illogical result is that k_e, the cost of equity capital, *falls* as leverage is increased through the use of increments of debt which cost more than k_0. The behavior of the capitalization rates, as they view it, is outlined in Figure 9-2.

This device of having k_e fall as leverage is increased leads squarely into a second dilemma. We now have to assume that rational investors in the equity markets capitalize a more uncertain stream of residual earnings at a *lower* k_e than they capitalize a less uncertain stream.

It is difficult to reconcile this assumption with Modigliani and Miller's own assumptions about rational investor behavior and reasonably perfect markets. The only explanation they offer in support of a k_e curve that *falls* as leverage is increased is as follows: "Should demand by risk-lovers prove insufficient to keep the market to this peculiar yield-curve, this demand would be reinforced by the action of arbitrage operators."[4]

The introduction of subjective risk preference as a major determinant of equity prices just for this phase of the leverage argument is hardly admissible unless one is also prepared to accept it for other phases of leverage.

As a last line of defense in support of a constant k_0, even under these circumstances, Modigliani and Miller simply assert that arbitrage will see to it that k_e*, the equity-capitalization rate for the overly levered stream of net earnings, is kept sufficiently *below* k_e, the rate for the less-levered stream, so as to maintain an equality between k_0* and k_0. If we examine

---

[4]Modigliani and Miller, *op. cit.*, p. 276.

the relationships between the various capitalization rates for situations in which $m > k_0$, we find that this assertion is not justified. Indeed, the opposite is true. Rational investor behavior, including the equilibrating process envisaged in their arbitrage model, will push k_e^* *above* k_e and k_0^* above k_0.

IV

There is, therefore, no legitimate basis for assuming that k_e will *fall* as leverage is increased and, hence, no basis for assuming that k_0 can remain constant as leverage is increased through the use of debt issues which involve a marginal cost higher than k_0. Given this conclusion, it must follow that the cost of capital k_0 rises with increased leverage whenever $m > k_0$.

In short, the thesis that a company's cost of capital is independent of its financial structure is not valid. As far as the leverage effect *alone* is concerned (and ignoring all the other considerations that might influence the choice between debt and equity), there does exist a clearly definable optimum position—namely, the point at which the marginal cost of more debt is equal to, or greater than, a company's average cost of capital.

10. CAPITAL STRUCTURE AND FINANCIAL DECISIONS*

HAROLD J. BIERMAN †

This discussion followed a paper presented by Professor Harold J. Bierman, Jr., entitled "Capital Structure and Financial Decisions" at the Stanford Graduate School of Business-Finance Conference 1966.[1] This portion of the discussion covered the question of how the risk factor should be taken into consideration. Should it be included in the cost of capital, or should there be a separate discount factor for risk? Participants in the discussion are: Professor Harold J. Bierman of Cornell University, Professor Merton H. Miller of the University of Chicago, Professors Ezra Solomon and Herbert C. Dougall of Stanford University, Professor J. Fred Weston of the University of California at Los Angeles, Professor C. Jackson Grayson, Jr. of Tulane University, Mr. David J. Jones, Treasurer of Standard Oil Company of New Jersey, and Mr. Herbert D. Armstrong, Treasurer of the Standard Oil Company of California.

THE BIERMAN DISCUSSION

Bierman

I would like to discuss what discount rate should be used to evaluate investments.

The investor expects payment from a corporation for two factors: (*a*) the utilization of the funds through time, and (*b*) the risk element associated with the possibility of the corporation failing to repay the investment or the interest on the investment.

The cost of capital combines these two factors into one measure, a percentage. This percentage is then used in a basic discounting formula. It is assumed that one should multiply a future cash flow X_n by $(1+r)^{-n}$ to find the present value of X_n. The validity of this computation can be shown to be correct if r measures the time value of money. It has not been shown to be correct if r is a combination of two factors: a time value factor k and a risk factor j. There are several ways to show that a compounding formula applied to future cash flow fails to take risk effectively into consideration.

Question

You lost me somewhere. I'm not quite sure what you are doing. I do not understand what it is you are complaining about or who you are complaining about.

*From A. A. Robichek, ed., *Financial Research and Management Decisions* (New York: John Wiley & Sons, Inc., 1967), pp. 47-52. Reprinted by permission.
†Professor of Accounting and Managerial Economics, Cornell University.
[1]Alexander A. Robichek, ed., *Financial Research and Management Decisions* (New York: John Wiley & Sons, Inc., 1967), pp. 34-43.

Bierman

I'm complaining about incorporating the j factor into the formula $(1 + k + j)^{-n}$ and compounding j through time; j is an adjustment for risk, and there is no reason to assume that risk increases by a constant percentage each period.

Jones

Is anybody advocating that you do put in a j factor?

Bierman

You do it when you compute the cost of capital. I would venture to say that many firms represented here distinguish between less risky and more risky investment by incorporation of some sort of risk factor in their discount rate. You may be taking risk into account the wrong way by adjusting the rate of discount.

Question

If I understand your premise correctly, you're saying that you don't put a risk factor into your discount rate?

Bierman

I suggest the use of a default-free interest rate to accomplish the discounting for time. That is, the possibility of default is being excluded from the discount factor.

Question

If we take three different projects, we might expect a return on investment of 10 percent on the first one, 15 percent on the second one, and 20 percent on the third one. They are all expected to last the same length of time. Taking into account risk inherent in the particular project, we may decide that different minimum rates of return factors are appropriate. In one case we may use 12 percent, in the other 15 percent. Have we not taken risk into account at the time we make that decision? Or am I off the beam?

Bierman

You're saying that you have taken risk into account. I certainly can't argue with that. You have taken the risk factor into account by making the required return higher. No quarrel with that! Now whether you have done it correctly or not is open to question.

Question

Well, do you mean we have to postaudit?

Bierman

No, I don't mean the postaudit. I mean that, if you reject some investments that promise a 20 percent return and accept others which return the same rate, I would not know how to handle the problem of risk by varying the cutoff rate.

Miller

Let me try to see if I can throw any light on this thing. It appears to me that what you're really saying is that there is not yet any rigorously worked out theory of the optimal way to make investment decisions under uncertainty. We have been doing research along this line, but we haven't gotton the answer yet. In the meantime, however, as a practical matter, it seems to me to make sense to put these risk handicaps on. We can't prove that it is correct. You are certainly right there. Still, unless it can be shown to be wrong, it seems sensible to continue using it in practice. On the basis of some preliminary investigation, my hunch is that use of something close to a discount rate adjusted for risk will ultimately turn out to be proven optimal. Our use of risk-adjusted discount rates will be regarded as having been a good guess on everybody's part and an acceptable approximation. The discount rates we use are not exact, but in general when we discount a low-risk investment at a lower discount rate than a high-risk investment, we are likely to be moving closer to the real optimum even though we can't precisely quantify how much.

Bierman

Yes, any procedure I would recommend would move in that direction. That is, the more risky investments would have an expected yield that would be higher than the yield of less risky investments.

Miller

Then, what you're objecting to is that you can't prove the optimality of the procedure which uses a risk-adjusted discount rate. Well, that's life.

Solomon

Harold [Bierman], aren't you really objecting to discounting of the risk factor over time?

Bierman

Yes, I'm not in favor of assuming that risk is compounded through time.

Solomon

Harold, you're mixing up two things. Everybody would agree that you might use two different cutoff rates for two investments that are different. Nobody's quarreling about this. Researchers as well as practitioners are quarreling about the technicality of adjusting for risk. You can do it two ways. You can adjust the expected returns and compare them to the interest rates. Or, you can adjust the discount rate. You're saying the latter is wrong. You think it's wrong because of the way you define the premium you call *j*. But the fact of the matter is this premium is not a premium for risk; it is a premium for bearing uncertainty, and you bear uncertainty each year during the life of the investment.

Bierman

But not necessarily compounded through time.

Solomon

Why not do it on a year-by-year basis? You bear it every year. Consider a 10 percent bond, which returns 5 percent more than a 5 percent government bond. The bond holder is bearing uncertainty every year of that bond's existence.

Dougall

Yes, though you could argue that as time proceeds toward the maturity of a bond, or toward the end of the life of a project, that the rate of uncertainty changes.

Solomon

We can do that if you want, but there is some uncertainty with each moment of time, and, therefore, you count something for each moment of time. It's the bearing of uncertainty which has a time dimension, and the use of a risk-adjusted discount rate is still feasible.

Weston

Well, Harold, there's another aspect adding on to what Ezra [Solomon] says. It is a matter of what you can read out of a system of market relationships. Consider an investment which, over your appropriate time horizon, yields 3 percent more than another one. There's no argument involved. What you're saying is, "I don't believe the market; the market shouldn't have a 3 percent differential."

Bierman

I didn't say that! My comments were not directed to the appropriate historical returns on investment.

Weston

You have no right to argue about the market. Well, what you're saying is, "I don't like that j factor in there included over the entire time horizon."

Bierman

No, that isn't what I'm saying at all. I'm saying that you can obtain the rate of discount which equates future dividends to the price but that this rate cannot be used to evaluate investments being considered by the firm.

Grayson

Harold, may I say something for your side?

Bierman

Thank you. I need it!

Grayson

I think Harold is right. You have been saying that intuitively a higher discount rate sounds reasonable. But there are a lot of assumptions in the discounting procedures that are not fully understood. If you checked out all the assumptions and looked at an application to a particular project, they may not match. There is a danger of making a wrong investment decision by merely assuming that the built-in assumptions of the risk-adjusted discounting procedure hold.

Jones

I like that answer very much.

Solomon

So do I! Surely this applies for a rather long time over which you are doing the discounting.

Bierman

That's rather important, yes. I do not suggest that you accept every investment with a yield greater than the default-free rate; I suggest that this investment is eligible for consideration. When you get done adding in your risk consideration, it could come out to be exactly the set of investments which you would have gotten by consulting your ouija board or using the cost of capital. It probably will be highly similar, but there also might be differences. Look, we've got some fifty-odd top-level executives here and a dozen academicians, and we're talking about the current and future state of the art of making investment decisions. In the recent past nearly everybody was in agreement that under uncertainty you use the present value method and you use the cost of capital as the discount rate. Now, it's not that obvious that you use the cost of capital as a discount rate. Now, I may be wrong and Mert [Miller] may be right. Still, there is a difference of opinion here.

Miller

I still don't see what you're shooting at. No one has suggested that you use our concept of the cost of capital to discount nonstandard items or additions to assets that will change the nature of your asset-mix. If an asset is really a good deal less risky than the present asset mix, then you should use a lower rate for that kind of asset. If it's a good deal more risky, it's a simple sensible approximation to try using a higher hurdle rate. If what you're saying is, "don't do this mechanically," fine.

Armstrong

I think that you're talking about two different things here. On the one hand, we have the cost of capital which is the kind of thing that the investor in your shares is very much interested in. On the other hand, what you're talking about at this point seems to be an entirely different cost. It is a return factor that is used by management in selecting alternative utilizations of the capital.

Miller

Well, I'd prefer to say that the single cost of capital figure that I have been writing about should be thought of as a sort of average cost of capital that applies to the investment budget considered as a whole. In practice some projects will be more risky than the average and some, less so. The cost of capital we would want to use for setting our overall investment budget is not to be applied blindly to each and every project in the budget. It will, however, apply on the average and to standard items, but for the nonstandard ones you have to use your common sense and adjust the rate up or down according to the risk.

Question

It seems to me that one of the real problems is to determine just what is risk with regard to a project? What would you suggest now? Probability distributions of return?

Bierman

I would suggest using probability distributions, risk attitudes incorporated in some systematic way, and then as Mert has said, use your judgment. Basically, I question the dogmatic use of cost of capital as the rate of discount. I have no objection to its use as a practical rule of thumb. We have to get off home base someway; we can't have a situation where we're incapable of making business decisions because academic types don't know how to handle uncertainty. That would be a horrible thought. Okay, it is a complex world with no easy answers. If I have at least raised a question in your mind about the possibility of not rejecting investments that yield less than your cost of capital, my mission is accomplished. I am certainly not offering an ironclad rule instead. I'm not saying you should accept investments with yields greater than the default-free rate.

That is not what I'm saying. I'm saying, to take the time value of money into account, use a rate that does not include an adjustment for the possibility of default. I have a point of view that's not universally held. If you take the time value of money into account using a default-free rate, it does not mean that you then accept all investments with a present value greater than zero. It is more complex than that. This is where the use of the cost of capital as a guide is a useful rule.

Miller

I remind you of the first edition of a certain textbook on capital budgeting which used the cost of capital rate to discount all of the expected funds flows even for the no-risk cases like bond refunding.

Bierman

In Chapter 3 or so, we made a statement that knocked taking uncertainty into account by using a higher rate of discount. In Chapters 7, 8, and 9, however, we skipped to the use of cost of capital. So, I'll have to admit that Mert is correct.

PART IV.   DIVIDEND POLICY AND VALUATION

Dividend policy determines what portion of earnings will be retained in the business and what portion of earnings will be paid out to stockholders. Valuation of a firm's common stock may well be affected by the dividend policy formulated. The formulation of a dividend policy poses many problems. On the one hand, theory would seem to dictate that the firm should retain all funds which can be employed at a rate higher than the capitalization rate; on the other hand, stockholders' preference must also be considered. The articles in this section deal with both the theoretical and the practical problems of dividend policy and valuation.

Professor James E. Walter has developed a theoretical model which shows the relationship between dividend policies and common stock prices. The basic premise underlying the formulation is that stock prices reflect the present value of expected dividends in the long run. Accordingly, stock prices are influenced by retained earnings through their effect on future dividends. The model operates on the objective of maximizing common stockholders' wealth. In general, if a firm is able to earn a higher return on earnings retained than the stockholder is able to earn on a like investment, then it would appear to be beneficial to retain these earnings, all other things being equal. Professor Walter enriches the discussion with his detailed analysis of growth stocks, intermediate stocks, and creditor stocks. He presents a meaningful model for classifying common stocks.

Professor Stephen H. Sosnick sets out to show how stock dividends, rather than being advantageous, are often burdens to the recipient. Among these burdens he includes a reduction in the surplus available for future dividends, a substantial expense to the corporation, and a considerable increase in the recipient's transaction costs. He acknowledges that under particular circumstances supposedly these dividends may have favorable effects on the recipient; such circumstances include an increase in cash dividends or in convenience and value from a finer division of units of ownership. Admittedly, these effects might better be affected by the use of stock splits or, in the case of the increase in dividend, a simple increase in the cash rate.

Each burden is thoroughly analyzed. Under the category of "costly to the corporation," he enumerates ten expense items and includes the results of a comprehensive study of actual costs encountered by two companies. A discussion of stock splits is presented, and considerable attention is given to choosing an appropriate split ratio. Included in the appendix is an excellent detailed discourse on corporate costs and recipient costs referred to in the article.

Professor Richard A. Stevenson explores the ethics of corporate stock reacquisitions. In examining the relationships between ethics and law, he concludes that the ". . . law represents the minimum standard for an ethical individual." However, because something is legal does not mean that it is ethical ". . . when viewed within the proper social and economic context." He indicates that the corporate directors should make any decision with the best interests of the stockholders in mind. He feels that the transaction should be adequately disclosed, and no conflict-of-interest situations should arise because of the decision to reacquire the stock. A study, made to determine the extent of press disclosure of stock reacquisitions from 1958-1963, indicated that press coverage was somewhat less than desirable. Professor Stevenson concludes his paper by citing from four actual cases to illustrate possible ethical problems.

Carol J. Loomis makes a case for firms to minimize cash payouts. In a period when money-capital is scarce, it would seem that there would be advantages accruing to the stockholder if the firm would employ these funds in productive investments rather than in paying cash dividends. The tax implications are emphasized together with the disadvantages to the firm when it must rely on the capital markets to raise the funds necessary to pay cash dividends.

An actual case of a firm which proposed to substitute stock dividends for three of its quarterly cash dividends is cited. Although the advantages to the stockholders appear to be substantial, the plan was never implemented because of the adverse reaction to the proposal from individual stockholders as well as institutional holders, particularly bank trust departments. It seems that if there is to be any shift toward lower dividend payments, the stockholders will have to be reeducated. Also, if a major shift does take place, the possibility of a change in tax laws exists. The author concludes by citing actual cases in which various types of securities are used to minimize cash payments.

11. DIVIDEND POLICIES AND COMMON STOCK PRICES*

I

In a recent issue of the *Journal of Finance*, Professor Harkavy presented a statistical analysis of the relationship between retained earnings and common stock prices.[1] His principal conclusion is that, while common stock prices vary directly with dividend payout ratios at any given time, their degree of appreciation over a period of time is associated with the proportion of earnings which are retained. Only brief reference is made to the fact that the crucial consideration is the profitable utilization of investors' funds. Empirical studies of this type should be encouraged and are of definite value provided careful consideration is given, both before and after their preparation, to the underlying theoretical propositions.

Based upon the belief that stock market behavior is susceptible of rationalization, an attempt is made in this paper to fabricate a theoretical model which depicts the relationship between dividend policies and common stock prices. Attention is of necessity restricted to the common stocks of large public corporations because of the imperfect market for the securities of small companies and of the close identification of small firms with their principal shareholders. The fundamental premise upon which the formulation rests is that, over longer periods, stock prices reflect the present values of expected dividends.[2] The phrase "over long periods" is inserted to permit abstraction from the distortions caused by short-run speculative considerations.

Granted this premise, retained earnings influence stock prices principally through their effect upon future dividends. The fact that some stocks may have substantial market value even though little or no dividends are anticipated in the foreseeable future need not contradict this proposition. Undistributed earnings are immediately realizable to the shareholder, at least in part, provided prospective investors can be found who are willing to wait and to assume the required risk.

In analyzing the present worth of future dividends, the concept of capitalization rate is utilized in preference to that of multiplier, which is customarily employed by security analysts. The capitalization rate for any stock is simply the reciprocal of the multiplier. Since capitalization rates are expressed in percentage terms, their use simplifies the presentation and facilitates direct comparisons with rates of return on additional investment.

*From *The Journal of Finance* (March, 1956), pp. 24-41. Reprinted by permission.
†Professor of Finance at the University of Pennsylvania.
[1]Oscar Harkavy, "The Relation Between Retained Earnings and Common Stock Prices for Large, Listed Corporation," *Journal of Finance*, Vol. VIII, No. 3 (September, 1953), 283-297.
[2]See J. B. Williams, *The Theory of Investment Value* (Cambridge, Mass.: Harvard University Press, 1938), p. 6, for a similar position.

Capitalization rates are determined by the underlying yield on safe securities and by the required risk premiums. The yield on safe securities is conditioned by such factors as monetary and debt policy, income distribution, the intensity of present as opposed to future wants, and productivity. The basic risk premium, as measured by the difference between the yield on safe securities and the capitalization rate on high-grade common stocks, is dependent upon the economic climate and government policy. Inter-industry differences in size, capital structure, efficiency, and diversification occasion substantial variations in capitalization rates among corporations.

The level and diversity of capitalization rates influence the succeeding analysis in at least two respects. The higher the level of capitalization rates, both individually and generally, the fewer are the companies whose stocks qualify as growth stocks. The greater the diversity of capitalization rates and the more numerous their determinants, the less feasible it becomes to talk in terms of average or normal capitalization rates. The concept of market capitalization rate must, therefore, be defined arbitrarily in order to exclude irrelevant heterogeneity.

The proposition that all common stocks behave in a reasonably uniform manner does not appear to be warranted by the observed variations in stock prices. As a result, three groups, referred to respectively as growth stock, intermediate, and creditor stock categories, are isolated for consideration. A fourth possibility, the declining stock category, is ignored because of its presumed unimportance in a growing economy.

Diversity of dividend policy is often regarded as one of the principal features which differentiate among these groups. Growth stocks are customarily characterized by low dividend payout ratios; intermediate stocks, by medium to high ratios; and creditor stocks, by fixed dividend rates irrespective of short-run earnings. With the possible exception of creditor stocks, however, the dividend-earnings relationship is neither a necessary nor a sufficient condition for assigning stocks to any given category. The crucial consideration is the rate of return on additional investment. The greater the profitability, the more likely is management—in the interests of rapid expansion—to retain a substantial percentage of earnings.

II

The concept "growth stock" is familiar to investors and is understood to refer, in general terms, to common stocks which possess superior prospects for long-term appreciation. Surface characteristics of growth stocks include low dividend payout ratios, high market multipliers (i.e., low capitalization rates), and prices which increase through time with relative rapidity. Low dividend payout ratios constitute an accepted feature of growth stocks, since shareholders are presumed to benefit more from the retention of earnings than from their employment elsewhere at the going rates.

In qualifying for membership in the growth stock category, marginal profitability is the basic criterion. The rate of return on additional investment determines the magnitude of future dividends obtainable from given amounts of retained earnings or external financing. The anticipated level of future dividends, when discounted at the appropriate capitalization rate, in turn yields the present value for a given stock. If the rate of return on added investment is sufficiently great, it follows that low dividend payout ratios may add to, rather than subtract from, stock values.

For the purpose of demonstrating the potential influence of retained earnings upon stock prices, let us assume that earnings retention is the sole source of additional funds, that both the rate of return on added investment and the market capitalization rate are constants, and that all increments to earnings are immediately distributed to shareholders. The market capitalization rate for any given corporation is defined as the reciprocal of the multiplier which would prevail in the market if the dividend payout ratio were 100 percent.[3] Treating the stream of future earnings as perpetual (or at least of indefinite duration), the present value of any common stocks can then be expressed in mathematical terms as

$$(1) \qquad V_c = \frac{D + \dfrac{R_a}{R_c}(E - D)}{R_c} = \frac{E}{R_c} + \frac{R_a - R_c}{R_c^2}(E - D),$$

where D is cash dividends, E is earnings, R_a is the rate of return on additional investment, and R_c is the market capitalization rate.[4]

Equation (1) reveals the importance of both the dividend payout ratio and the relationship between R_a and R_c. Whenever R_a exceeds R_c, the present worth of future dividends resulting from the retention of earnings is greater than the dollar magnitude of retained earnings. The lower the dividend payout ratio, under such circumstances, the higher is the value of the growth stock.

A currently high rate of return on additional investment for a given corporation need not automatically transform its stock into a growth stock. In the first place, the high rate must persist over a reasonable period of time.

---

[3]This definition is introduced simply to preclude the possibility that capitalization rates will be interpreted to reflect the effect of varying dividend policies. To illustrate, let us assume that companies A and B have identical earnings per share ($10), R_a (20 percent), and R_c (10 percent), but have payout ratios of 75 percent and 50 percent respectively. Substituting in equation (1), we find that A has a V_c of $125 and B, of $150. The ratio of E to V_c, which might be called the unadjusted or composite capitalization rate, is thus 8 percent for A and $6\frac{2}{3}$ percent for B. The difference is attributable to divergent dividend policies.

[4]The second version of equation (1) is presented to show the extent to which V_c will exceed (or fall short of) the ratio of E to R_c. As in the case of most gross simplifications, equation (1) presents difficulties if used without modification. To illustrate the point and to indicate the type of modification which might be made, let us consider time as an endless succession of periods. Based upon equation (1) and its underlying assumptions, the value of the stock in question will rise in each period (without cessation) by an amount equal to R_a $(E - D)/R_c$. Since diminishing returns are an almost inevitable consequence, R_a must be viewed—for practical purposes—as a weighted average of $r_1, r_2, \ldots, r_{n-1}$, where r represents the rate of return on added investment at any given point (period) in time and $r_n = 0$. By weighted is simply meant that r_1, r_2, etc., must, because of the proximity to the present, be assigned greater importance than r_{n-1}, r_{n-2}, etc.

The market's judgment of a common stock is of necessity based primarily upon past experience. The corporation's willingness to invest is also influenced by the anticipated permanence of R_a to the extent that increments to earnings lag behind the retention of earnings. In the second place, high rates of return on added investment must not be offset by correspondingly high market capitalization rates. In so far as new industries are characterized by small, insufficiently capitalized firms and mature industries by large, conservatively financed companies, R_a and R_c may well be directly associated.

As observed in footnote 4, modifications in equation (1), which provide added realism at the expense of simplicity, do not alter the results in any fundamental respect. Anticipated declines in the return on additional investment (R_a) affect stock values and raise serious doubts as to the propriety of permanently low dividend payout ratios. As long as R_a continues to exceed R_c, however, the substantial retention of earnings appears beneficial to shareholders.

The recognition of external sources of new financing enables growth stocks to possess low *composite* capitalization rates even in the presence of high dividend payout ratios.[5] The market in effect endeavors to forecast the willingness and ability to use external sources and discounts future dividends attributable thereto. Despite this consideration, stock prices can still be expected to vary inversely with dividend payout ratios, provided R_a exceeds R_c.

Even without reference to capital gains taxation, the market appears justified in according special treatment to growth stocks in the sense of low composite capitalization rates. The all-pervasiveness of uncertainty may of course occasion conservative interpretations of future earnings and may restrict recognized membership in the growth stock category to a relatively few outstanding corporations. For doubtful cases, retained earnings and dividends may simply be regarded as equivalents. Alternatively, the prices of marginal growth stocks may be adversely affected, provided dividend payout ratios are below what the market believes to be a reasonable compromise.

At least one further factor functions to lessen the present worth of retained earnings relative to current dividends. This consideration concerns the emphasis placed upon balanced portfolios, i.e., diversification by investors. To the extent that the market values of growth stocks appreciate through time more rapidly than those of their asset holdings, investors may be induced to redistribute the increment among all components of their portfolios.[6]

---

[5] The prevailing ratio of earnings to stock prices for a given company at any time can be thought of as a composite rate. The basic component is the market capitalization rate (R_c), as interpreted above. From R_c is deducted (if a growth stock) a percentage equivalent to the relative increase in the present worth of future dividends which is attributable to earnings retention or, as the case may be, to external financing.

[6] The line of reasoning is quite similar to that underlying the "substitution effect" in   (cont.)

   Whenever portfolio readjustment must be achieved through the sale of shares, as opposed to the utilization of cash dividends, certain costs and risks are incurred.[7] Transfer costs, comprising commissions and taxes, have to be met. Market prices are conditioned by short-run influences and need not reflect longer run capitalized values at any given time. In addition, the augmented supply of growth shares on the market—resulting from efforts to diversify—may depress their prices below what they otherwise would have been.

   The consequence is that the appropriate test for growth stocks from the viewpoint of shareholders may not be simply R_a exceeds R_c, but rather R_a exceeds R_c by an amount sufficient to cover the cost of added diversification. That is to say,

(1a)
$$V_c = \frac{D + \dfrac{R_a}{R_c + p}(E - D)}{R_c},$$

where p is the premium associated with the cost of diversification.

   Except for outstanding cases, the isolation of growth stocks for empirical study does not appear to be a simple task. As suggested previously, changes in earnings from period to period are likely to be discontinuous and to be associated with past, rather than current, sources of funds. The reason is simply that the expansion of both facilities and markets takes time. The reported levels of historical earnings, which is the principal basis for estimating future earnings, are dependent upon arbitrary accounting techniques. In addition, price-level changes often provide a misleading illusion of growth. In some instances, these and other factors lead the market astray; in other cases, they lead the analyst to believe that the market's evaluation is incorrect when in actual fact it is not.

III

   Preferential tax treatment of capital gains, as opposed to dividend income, affects growth stocks in at least two respects. It augments the value of retained earnings and hence increases growth stock prices, provided personal income taxes levied upon marginal shareholders exceed zero. It also gives certain superior non-growth stocks the status of growth stocks.

   Wherever rates of return on additional investment are positive, the retention of earnings by corporations raises both the anticipated level and the present worth of future dividends. As the present values of future dividends change through time and are reflected in stock prices, shareholders are able to realize these gains by selling portions of their holdings. Shareholders

---

the theory of consumer choice, For the sake of simplicity, however, it is assumed that the problem of present versus future consumption does not arise.

   [7] As indicated subsequently, these considerations may be partially offset by the preferential tax treatment of capital gains.

benefit from this form of income realization to the extent that the preferential tax treatment of capital gains reduces their total tax. In addition, the realization criterion for the capital gains tax enables shareholders to time security sales so as to minimize further their total tax burden.

The presence of organized security exchanges limits rather substantially the observed impact of capital gains taxation. The more perfect the market in which common stocks are traded, the less is the ability to distinguish between buyers or sellers unless legal or institutional barriers are erected. In the absence of discrimination and of individual bargaining, only the tax savings derived by marginal shareholders from capital gains taxation will be reflected in security prices.

Equation (1) indicates that, given certain simplifying assumptions which do not distort the underlying relationships, a dollar of retained earnings is the equivalent of a dollar of dividends multiplied by the ratio of R_a to R_c. If this equivalence is adjusted for the special tax treatment of capital gains, the equation becomes

(2)
$$s \frac{R_a}{R_c} = t; \quad \text{or} \quad R_a = \frac{t}{s} R_c,$$

where s is one *minus* the tax rate on capital gains and t is one *minus* the marginal tax rate on personal income, both as related to marginal shareholders. If allowance is also made for the existence of dividend tax credits, as provided in the recently passed technical tax relief bill (1954), form (2) is transformed into

(2a)
$$R_a = \frac{t + c}{s} R_c,$$

where c is the dividend tax credit, expressed in percentage terms.

Equations (2) and (2a) demonstrate that superior non-growth stocks may be raised to the status of growth stocks as a result of preferred tax treatment for capital gains. That is to say, the retention of earnings need not be disadvantageous to shareholders even though R_a is somewhat less than R_c.

For illustrative purposes, let us assume that the marginal tax rate on the personal income of marginal shareholders is 50 percent, that the tax rate on capital gain is 25 percent, that the dividend tax credit is 4 percent, and that the market capitalization rate (R_c) is 10 percent. Substituting these figures into equation (2a), R_a is found to be 7.2 percent. At this point it is immaterial to marginal shareholders whether earnings are retained or distributed. In the event that R_a exceeds 7.2 percent, under these conditions the stock in question takes on the characteristics of a growth stock.

Alternative assumptions may produce significantly different results. If, for example, the marginal tax rate on personal income is 20 percent and the rate on capital gains is 10 percent, R_a becomes 9.3 percent. The basic propositions, nonetheless, continue to hold.

IV

A substantial majority of all *listed* industrial common stocks undoubtedly belong to the intermediate stock group. Surface characteristics of this category are dividend payout ratios in excess of 50 percent, multipliers which range in the neighborhood of the average multiplier for all listed corporations, and prices which increase slowly through time. Shareholder pressure is exerted for substantial payout ratios, since stock prices tend to vary directly with the level of dividend payout ratios. Although the retention of earnings leads to appreciation in stock values, shareholders benefit from the receipt of dividends and their investment elsewhere at the going market rate.

In assigning stocks to this category, the underlying consideration is whether the present value of future dividends attributable to retained earnings at the margin is greater or less than the corresponding dollar amount of earnings retention. This question is essentially the same as that raised in connection with growth stocks. Its resolution hinges, in similar fashion, upon the relationship between R_a, adjusted for the preferred tax treatment of capital gains, and R_c. As shown by equation (1) and as modified by equation (2), if adjusted R_a exceeds R_c, the common stock in question is a growth stock; if adjusted R_a is less than R_c but greater than zero, it is an intermediate stock.

The preponderance of the intermediate stock group, particularly where large and mature public corporations are concerned, apparently leads many investment analysts to recommend high dividend payout ratios as a general rule. The best-known advocates, Graham and Dodd, state that the investment value of any industrial common stock equals

$$(3) \qquad\qquad M(D + \tfrac{1}{3}E),$$

where M, the multiplier, is the reciprocal of the *assumed* appropriate capitalization rate, D is expected dividends, and E is expected earnings.[8] Essentially theirs must be regarded as a conservative approach which presumably emphasizes both the uncertainness of future earnings and the inevitable decline, at some point in time, in the rate of return on additional investment even for expanding enterprises.

Since equation (3) stresses the dividend factor, it is reasonably well adapted to the intermediate stock category. In the equation proper, $1 of dividends is presumed to be the equivalent of $4 of retained earnings. In

---

[8]B. Graham and D. L. Dodd, *Security Analysis* (3d ed.; New York: McGraw-Hill Book Company, 1951), p. 410.

terms of equation (1), the ratio of adjusted R_a to R_c is thus fixed at one fourth. Inasmuch as the numerous other possible relationships between R_a and R_c are ignored, the multiplier must be adjusted for differences between the assumed normal relationship and the actual relationship in any given circumstance. For growth stocks, the magnitudes of the adjustments required in M assume such significance that the general application of equation (3) does not appear to be feasible.

Whatever the approach employed to evaluate intermediate stocks, the presumed level of current dividends is important but not all important. Expansion may still be beneficial to shareholders even though R_a is less than R_c, provided the added investment is financed at least in part by borrowed funds.[9] The essential requirements are that the corporation in question be conservatively financed and that the excess of R_a over the interest rate be sufficient to offset the excess of R_c over R_a. If conservatively financed, the augmented use of borrowed funds need not appreciably affect either the multiplier or its reciprocal.

For illustrative purposes, let us assume that the conventional debt-equity ratio is one half, that the market capitalization rate is unaffected as long as this relationship holds, and that added investment is financed by the same proportions of debt and retained earnings as the conventional ratio. If, under such conditions, R_a is 6 percent and the interest rate is 3 percent, the rate of return on retained earnings becomes 7.5 percent. The retention of earnings is thus beneficial to shareholders, provided R_c is less than 7.5 percent.

Even if the use of borrowed funds is ignored, the maximum feasible dividend payout ratio is likely to be something less than 100 percent for intermediate stocks. In some instances, maintenance of relative position within the industry may be essential for profit maintenance. Whatever the relation of R_a to R_c, the affected corporation must then keep pace with the industry and with other firms. Otherwise, the company loses out, and its overall profit rate declines. In other instances, a substantial portion of reported earnings may be attributable to price-level changes. If the real position of a given company is to be maintained, a portion of reported earnings will then have to be retained. In still other instances, cash may simply be unavailable for dividends.

V

A third group, the creditor stock category, may now be isolated for examination. Creditor stocks are so named because they possess many of the attributes of debt instruments. The most important of the similarities is that, in determining the present worth of creditor stocks, almost exclusive

---

[9]Unlike the case of capital gains taxation, benefits derived from the use of borrowed funds do not accrue automatically to shareholders. Their existence depends upon management policy. For this reason, the possibility of utilizing borrowed funds is introduced simply as a qualification to the intermediate stock category.

emphasis is placed upon the prevailing level of dividends. Average yields on creditor stocks are somewhat higher than those on bonds, for shareholders lack legal protection and have no equity cushion upon which to rest. The limited ability of institutional investors to hold any type of equity share, due principally to legislative restrictions and to the nature of their obligations, also contributes to the yield differential between bonds and creditor stocks.[10]

As contrasted with the growth and intermediate stock categories, the retention of earnings occasions little or no appreciation in creditor stock prices over time. The low present value of retained earnings may be attributable to the fact that the rate of return on additional investment approximates zero. It may be attributable to management which elects to retain earnings during prosperous periods and to hold them in liquid form for distribution during depressed periods. It may be attributable to public regulatory commissions which pass the benefits derived from earnings retention on to the public.

In a relevant sense the inclusion of this category modifies, as well as extends beyond, the preceding analysis. Stocks can no longer be said to qualify automatically for membership in the growth and intermediate stock groups depending upon whether adjusted R_a is greater or less than R_c. The ultimate distribution of additional earnings is not a foregone conclusion; retained earnings need not be employed in the most profitable fashion; and economic considerations are not the sole criterion.

The ability of shareholders to influence the policies of either management or regulatory commissions is frequently circumscribed. As a result, stock prices are of necessity conditioned by the expected behavior of management and government in the light of their past actions. If management and/or regulatory commissions regard shareholders as creditors and if the underlying economic conditions permit their treatment as such, it follows that the stocks which are thus affected will assume many of the characteristics of credit instruments.

Common stocks of large, well established public utilities offer excellent possibilities for inclusion in the creditor stock category.[11] Public utilities in general are characterized by an underlying element of stability and by close regulation. Rates tend to be adjusted so as to provide reasonable and stable returns to shareholders. Dividend payout ratios normally range in the neighborhood of 75 percent, and sources of additional funds are largely external.[12]

The acceptance of the idea that shareholders are creditors is reflected in the dividend policy of the largest of all public utilities. For more than three

---

[10]As the pressure to obtain satisfactory yields on investments increases, however, the gradual relaxation of legislative restrictions is likely to occur.

[11]It is not meant to imply that all, or even the great majority, of utility stocks are creditor stocks. Some may actually be growth stocks. The crucial considerations appear to be whether regulatory commissions permit retained earnings to augment the invested capital base and whether the allowable rate of return exceeds or falls short of R_c.

[12]Postwar payout ratios are noticeably below those for the immediate prewar period, perhaps reflecting the impact of substantial price-level changes.

decades American Telephone and Telegraph has annually declared a $9 dividend.

Common stocks of large, mature industrial corporations whose earnings possess a reasonable degree of stability are likely to exhibit at least some features of creditor stocks. Management often elects to stabilize the dollar amount of dividends declared annually, thereby reducing dividend payout ratios during prosperous periods and raising them during depressed periods. To the extent that retained earnings are then held in liquid form, *cash* cushions are created which bear marked similarities to the equity or earning-power cushions provided for senior securities.

Needless to say, the point of delineation between intermediate stocks and creditor stocks is difficult to ascertain.[13] Given the separation of ownership from control for large, public corporations, it may well be that shareholders are generally viewed by the managements of these companies as a form of creditor. In numerous instances, however, the nature of the corporation may be such that this attitude cannot readily be translated into policy.

A further consideration relates to the willingness of the market to recognize and accept creditor stocks. Unless the corporation in question is extremely well known and has a long and stable dividend record, it is doubtful whether the market will accord its stock special treatment. Special treatment, in this instance, refers to lower capitalization rates and to more stable stock prices than would otherwise be the case. If market acceptance is not forthcoming, the stock remains simply an inferior member of the intermediate stock category.

As a final point, the behavior of creditor stock prices can still be expected to resemble in many respects that of common stock prices in general. First, even where common stocks are creditor oriented, dividends ordinarily exhibit some relation to earnings and vary accordingly. This proposition follows from the absence of contractual agreements between management and shareholders. Second, since common stocks have no maturity dates, creditor stock prices are not conditioned by maturity values. This situation is, however, little different from that of bonds possessing remote maturities and no different from that of Consols.

Third, wherever regulatory commissions exist, rate revisions customarily operate with a lag. During the interim, higher earnings attributable to the retention of earnings may permit higher dividends. The converse is, of course, also true. Finally, the possibility is always present that, as management and commissions change, policies may also change.

VI

The basic premise that stock prices, over longer periods, reflect the present values of anticipated future dividends permits derivation of a model which possesses substantial plausibility. In distinguishing between growth and intermediate stocks, the crucial question becomes whether or

---

[13]In other words, R_a —in the sense of most profitable uses of funds—may be less than R_c, but greater than zero, for creditor stocks as well as intermediate stocks.

not the capitalized values of future dividends attributable to the retention of earnings are greater than the dollar magnitudes of retained earnings. Wherever greater, i.e., wherever rates of return on additional investment exceed market capitalization rates, the common stocks in question belong to the growth stock category. In the case of growth stocks, low dividend payout ratios can be expected to enhance stock values.

In certain instances, common stocks may assume the characteristics of growth stocks despite the fact that rates of return on added investment are less than market capitalization rates. The preferred tax treatment of capital gains augments the worth of retained earnings and enables more stocks to qualify as growth stocks. In addition, the combined use of borrowed funds and retained earnings makes it beneficial to retain earnings under special circumstances.

For most large industrials, rates of return on additional investment are presumed to exceed zero but to be less than the corresponding market capitalization rates. This condition leads to the commonly observed, direct relationship between dividend payout ratios and common stock prices. Although earnings retention occasions appreciation in stock prices over time, shareholders benefit from the distribution of the maximum feasible amount of earnings.

Acceptance of the fact that the control over large public corporations is often vested in management and regulatory commissions gives rise to the creditor stock category. For this group, the principal determinant of common stock prices is the prevailing level of dividends, capitalized at appropriate rates. Although retained earnings may augment dividend stability and thereby reduce capitalization rates, they contribute little to the prospects for higher dividends in the future.

Granted the inadequacies and diversity of statistical data, a model of this type has considerable utility as a foundation for empirical analysis. Most important of all, it provides a tentative basis for classifying common stocks. Even in the event that the model is not entirely valid, the heterogeneity of the statistical sample may still be reduced. Secondly, it specifies the necessary information and establishes interesting relationships for empirical verification. Finally, if, as is more than likely, the statistical data are inadequate for thoroughgoing analyses, they may nonetheless be sufficient to confirm or deny the model.

12. STOCK DIVIDENDS ARE LEMONS, NOT MELONS*

STEPHEN H. SOSNICK†

Half the battle over the issuance of ordinary stock dividends by publicly held corporations (common on common, with a debit to surplus) has been fought and won. They are not "melons" in theory or in the eyes of the tax collector. The other half has not yet been joined. Are they actually burdens to the recipients? It is the purpose of this paper to show that they often are.

The argument has two parts. First, ordinary stock dividends carry effects that are unfavorable to the common stockholders. These effects can be summarized by saying that stock dividends (a) reduce the surplus available for future cash dividends, (b) require adjustment of previously reported data, (c) cause the corporation substantial expense, and (d) considerably increase the recipients' transaction costs.

Second, under certain circumstances, such dividends may also carry effects that are favorable to the recipients. These are primarily (a) an increase in cash dividends and (b) a gain in convenience and value from finer division of the units of ownership. But these effects, when relevant, could often better be accomplished by other means—most notably by a stock split.

TAX PROBLEMS

Various aspects of both points are well known. However, they seem always to be mentioned as reasons for rejecting the popular view that stock dividends are gains, rather than brought together as reasons for taking, not a neutral, but a contrary position.[1] Conversely, the neutral position seems invariably to be attacked from the melon viewpoint.

The latter underlay the dissent of Justice Brandeis in the leading case on taxation of stock dividends—*Eisner* v. *Macomber*, 252 U.S. 189 (1920). A few words about Brandeis' argument may clarify some of the issues discussed in the pages that follow.

Brandeis argued that a stock dividend is equivalent to a cash dividend that is applied to a privileged subscription and should be taxed equivalently. The two are indeed parallel, but the moral—if one insists on consistency in substance, not form—is not to tax the stock dividend but to refrain from taxing the cash dividend. This was the conclusion of A. C. Whitaker, who,

*Reprinted from the *California Management Review*, Vol. III, No. 2 (Winter, 1961) pp. 61-70. Copyright 1961 by the Regents of the University of California.
†Professor of Agricultural Economics, University of California—Davis.
[1]One can illustrate from works of the highest quality. For example: "The stock dividend has no real effect on the stockholders." M. Moonitz and C. C. Staehling, *Accounting—An Analysis of Its Problems* (Brooklyn, 1952), II, p. 140. "From the stockholder standpoint the stock 'dividend' transaction is nothing more nor less than a straight split-up." W. A. Paton, Jr., *Corporation Accounts and Statements* (New York, 1955), p. 128.

more than 30 years ago, analyzed the question incisively in *The American Economic Review*.[2]

SHARE VALUES REALLY DECREASE

Whitaker pointed out that the grounds for treating an ordinary stock dividend differently from an ordinary cash dividend are not that the latter increases the stockholders' assets and the former does not; in both cases the value of the previous share holding decreases correspondingly—if not exactly correspondingly, at least with a discrepancy that cannot be measured by the dividend.

Rather, the grounds are that cash dividends (and, less clearly, property and bond dividends) are a convenient criterion of when a stockholder realizes gains, but stock dividends are not. "Funds remaining with your corporation are subject to the claims of its creditors and the risks of its business and the policy of its directors. They are not in your control," Whitaker points out.

It "is upon the occasion of the passing over of the profits to the shareholders that income to the latter arises, which is a way of saying that cash dividends (at least cash dividends from profits) are income to the shareholder despite the fact that they do not increase the shareholders' net worths or net estates." Stock dividends "likewise fail to increase the recipient's net estate . . . for there is only a mock transfer of value to him."[3]

"If appreciation of A's capital interest is income to him, . . . it does not take the gesture of a stock dividend to make it income."[4] But why does the gesture not suffice, he continues, "as marking the point in time at which corporate income is to be recognized by shareholders"?[5] Because, to condense this author's reasoning, (a) there is no real change in any entity's assets, (b) a split is equivalent and would not be so regarded, and (c) the debit to surplus is a poor indicator of the appreciation in value of the stockholding.[6]

Note, however, that in this view cash dividends are either no gain whatever (since the gain has already occurred, to the stockholder, by appreciation of his holding) or else (if cash transfers are used as the criterion of when the gain constitutes "income" to the stockholder) a capital gains transaction, equivalent to sale to the corporation of part of the shares owned plus receipt of the shares back through a stock dividend.

Of course, adopting this view in conjunction with the prevailing method of taxing capital gains would further reduce taxes on property incomes. But the prevailing treatment of stock dividends and cash dividends is explained

---

[2]A. C. Whitaker, "The Stock Dividend Question," *American Economic Review*, Vol. XIX, No. 1 (March, 1929), p. 39.

[3]*Ibid*, pp. 28, 29, 32, and 33.

[4]A. C. Whitaker, "Stock Dividends, Investment Trusts, and the Exchange," *American Economic Review*, Vol. XXI, No. 2 (June, 1931), p. 279.

[5]E. B. Wilcox, dissenting to American Institute of Accountants, "Accounting for Stock Dividends and Stock Split-Ups," *Accounting Research Bulletin No. 11 (Revised)* (New York, 1952), p. 104-A.

[6]Whitaker, "The Stock Dividend Question," *loc. cit.*, p. 34.

by reference to separate entities and realized gains in income accounting, and by a decision not to confer the capital gains tax rates on property income when it is realized in the form of cash dividends.

REDUCTION OF SURPLUS

Any discussion of the unfavorable effects outlined above falls naturally into four principal categories. The first is that stock dividends represent a reduction of surplus. Stock dividends involving a debit to a surplus account that can lawfully be debited for cash dividends will reduce the surplus available for future cash dividends.[7]

Of course, it may turn out that the corporation is never short of chargeable surplus. Surpluses may rebuild; there may always be more than enough to cover the cash dividends that the directors would choose to declare; and there are certain shrewd ways of creating usable surpluses.[8] Nevertheless, the tendency is in this direction. If surplus is not plentiful in the future, the devices to create it are neither costless nor polite, and cash dividends are likely to be cut.

The directors, however, may desire to reduce chargeable surplus. Why? One reason is precisely in order to forestall demands by stockholders for cash dividends. Another reason is to improve credit standing when mere protective provisions would not suffice. A third reason is emphasized by W. A. Paton and W. A. Paton, Jr., who state in their book on corporation accounts and statements that the "situation is clarified if the decision to retain earnings is given legal and accounting sanction."[9]

These reasons, where applicable, should not be viewed as an advantage of stock dividends. At best, they would negate one disadvantage. I say "at best" on two grounds. First, for at least the second purpose just mentioned, a stock dividend would be self-defeating if a positive rate of cash dividends per share is maintained.[10] Second, there are other ways to accomplish a reduction in surplus which are less costly and/or more reversible. These alternatives merit brief comment.

THE RIGHT WAY

By a charter amendment or even a mere resolution, the directors could transfer some earned surplus either to formal capital (by increasing par or stated value) or to capital surplus. "For example, section 1903 of the

---

[7]"The surplus is frozen by the stock dividend so that it cannot later be distributed as a cash or property dividend." N. D. Lattin, *The Law of Corporations* (Brooklyn, 1959), p. 467. "A dividend is basically a distribution of corporate assets, and it is nothing short of ridiculous . . . to label a procedure which ensures the permanent retention . . . of a specified amount of income funds as a 'distribution.'" Paton, *op. cit.*, pp. 95 and 127. Paton and Paton place quotation marks around "dividends" of stock. *Accounting Research Bulletin No. 11 (Revised)* suggests that large or repeated issuance of new shares be called a "split-up" or, less desirably, "a split-up effected in the form of a dividend." Wilcox, *op. cit.*, p. 102-A.

[8]See A. S. Dewing, *Financial Policy of Corporations* (5th ed.; New York, 1953), I, Chpt. 22.

[9]See Note 8, p. 122. This is also called "a strong argument" in R. Wixon (ed.), *Accountants' Handbook* (4th ed.; New York, 1956), pp. 21-43.

[10]This is pointed out by Moonitz and Staehling, *op. cit.*, p. 141.

California Corporations Code states that 'the stated capital of a corporation may be increased from time to time by resolution of the board of directors directing that a portion of the surplus of the corporation be transferred to the stated capital account.' This power to 'capitalize' surplus at will is a more flexible and straightforward means of reflecting 'forced reinvestment' than the more formal stock dividend with its misleading implications and overtones."[11]

There is also the alternative of creating surplus reserves. Paton and Paton scorn this "supplementary and relatively insignificant alternative . . . 'Reserving' earnings as compared with outright capitalization has the advantage of simplicity of procedure and also affords opportunity for revision of policy. . . . On the other hand, actual capitalization is a reasonable and sound procedure where the decision has been made, for the long pull, to build up invested capital through retention of income, and there is probably less danger of misunderstanding with respect to practical dividend possibilities. . . ."

"Subdivision of retained earnings," they continue, ". . . becomes definitely objectionable, moreover, when the purpose is to . . . make possible a resurrection of buried earnings when current conditions are unfavorable and those in control wish to keep up appearances."[12]

Maintaining appearances is one way to put it; another way is to say that if stockholders would later be eliminated in a reorganization or liquidation in any event, they might first have had the consolation of another cash dividend if surplus had merely been reserved instead of transferred.[13]

ADJUSTMENT OF REPORTED DATA

Stock dividends are confusing and will require adjustment of previously reported per-share data that might otherwise not need correction. The adjustment "would vary from one that you can do in your head to one that would necessitate extensive IBM undertakings. Also the job would depend on how far back you want to go."[14] Much of the physical burden here falls on the various reporting services.

That is, much of the cost here is social, not private, whereas in the case, for example, of increased transfer taxes, there is a private but not a social cost. Nevertheless, stockholders as a group probably bear such costs indirectly, in the form of higher prices for their publications and higher commissions for their transactions.

The company's own stockholders bear directly the pain involved in correcting data in their own records and in mentally adjusting per-share

---

[11]Moonitz and Staehling, *op. cit.*, p. 142. Nevertheless, it must be conceded that precisely because of its misleading implications, "the stock dividend may be very helpful in securing the stockholders' acquiescence in this policy of reinvestment of earnings." Whitaker, "Stock Dividends, Investment Trusts, and the Exchange," *loc. cit.*

[12]Paton, *op. cit.*, p. 132.

[13]Dewing remarks, "In making this transfer from surplus to capital stock, the directors should realize that the average stockholder values his ownership in the corporation only as a source of cash dividends." *Op. cit.*, p. 782, fn. ggg.

[14]Letter of February 11, 1960 from Frank E. Glenney, Investment Administrator, Moody's Investors Service.

information that was published before the latest stock dividend was paid—or else in being misinformed.

COSTLY TO CORPORATION

A corporation issuing a stock dividend will incur up to ten kinds of expense. The major ones are (1) use of officers' time, (2) handling of fractional shares, (3) issuing of certificates, (4) revision of the stockholders ledger, (5) mailing costs, (6) miscellaneous supplies, (7) increased franchise taxes, (8) charter amendment, (9) stock issue tax, (10) listing fees.

To express these costs in money terms is a difficult and often arbitrary process but one worth undertaking in order to have an idea of the amount of money at stake. Suppose we estimate costs for a 2 percent increase in the number of shares and for a large, but not outstandingly large, corporation such as the Dow Chemical Company. A conservative estimate of the total is $200,000, or about $2.50 per stockholder, or 0.7 cent per old share. The cost of a 200 percent increase is conservatively estimated at about $1 million for Dow, or about $13 per stockholder, or 4 cents per old share. These and other totals, together with itemization, appear in Table 12-1. The supporting analysis appears in the appendix.

HIGH COST TO RECIPIENTS

Recipients of ordinary stock dividends will incur up to four kinds of expense: (1) nuisance value, (2) increased transfer taxes, (3) increased brokers' commissions, (4) more odd lot differentials.

I have again attempted to obtain some idea of the magnitudes involved. For a 2 percent increase in shares, a conservative estimate of the total is $50,000 for a corporation such as Dow, or about 70 cents per shareholder, or 0.2 cent per old share. For a 200 percent increase, the figures are $1.6 million, or 20 dollars per stockholder, or 6 cents per old share. These and other figures appear in Table 12-1.

Supporting analysis appears in the appendix and includes discussion of the power of different large dividends or splits to round out odd lot holdings.

Suppose we add together the cost to the corporation and to the recipients. As Table 12-1 indicates, a conservative estimate of the amount at issue with a 2 percent dividend is $3 per stockholder, or 1 cent per old share, or a quarter of a million dollars for a corporation such as Dow. With a 200 percent increase in shares, the magnitudes are $30 per stockholder, 10 cents per old share, or for Dow, $2.6 million.

Totals for other corporations might be estimated from the following equation, which approximates the four grand totals in Table 12-1 rather closely: $T = 22 + 2.05H - 0.0062HP + 2.33C + 0.47CP$, where T represents total cost in thousand dollars, H represents the number of shareholders in

TABLE 12-1

CONSERVATIVE ESTIMATE OF THE COST OF STOCK DIVIDENDS

	2 Percent			5 Percent			200 Percent			500 Percent		
	With 26.6 Million Shares and 80,000 Shareholders	Per Old Share	Per Share-holder	With 26.6 Million Shares and 80,000 Shareholders	Per Old Share	Per Share-holder	With 26.6 Million Shares and 80,000 Shareholders	Per Old Share	Per Share-holder	With 26.6 Million Shares and 80,000 Shareholders	Per Old Share	Per Share-holder
1. Officers' time	$ 1,000*	$0.0000	$0.01	$ 1,000*	$0.0000	$0.01	$ 10,000*	$0.0004	$ 0.13	$ 10,000*	$0.0004	$ 0.13
2. Fractional shares	110,000	0.0041	1.38*	107,000	0.0040	1.34*	100,000	0.0038	1.25*	100,000	0.0038	1.25*
3. Certificates	35,000	0.0013	0.44*	35,000	0.0013	0.44*	56,000	0.0021	0.70*	56,000	0.0021	0.70*
4. Ledger revision	19,000	0.0007	0.24*	19,000	0.0007	0.24*	3,000	0.0001	0.04*	3,000	0.0001	0.04*
5. Mailing costs	3,000	0.0001	0.04*	3,000	0.0001	0.04*	25,000	0.0009	0.31*	25,000	0.0009	0.31*
6. Supplies	6,000	0.0002	0.08*	6,000	0.0002	0.08*						
7. Franchise taxes												
8. Amendment	.....	.....	.....	.....	.....	.....	3,000	0.0001	0.04*	3,000	0.0001	0.04*
9. Issue tax	14,000	0.0005*	0.18	34,000	0.0013*	0.43	474,000	0.0178*	5.93	593,000	0.0223*	7.41
10. Listing fees	3,000	0.0001*	0.04	9,000	0.0003*	0.11	340,000	0.0128*	4.25	851,000	0.0320*	10.64
Total Corporation Cost	191,000	0.0070	2.41	214,000	0.0079	2.69	1,011,000	0.0380	12.65	1,641,000	0.0617	20.52
11. Nuisance value	16,000	0.0006	0.20*	16,000	0.0006	0.20*	8,000	0.0003	0.10*	8,000	0.0003	0.10*
12. Transfer taxes	19,000	0.0007*	0.24	48,000	0.0018*	0.60	1,915,000	0.0720*	23.94	4,788,000	0.1800*	59.85
13. Commissions	5,000	0.0002	0.06*	8,000	0.0003	0.10*	160,000	0.0060	2.00*	360,000	0.0135	4.50*
14. Odd lot differentials	15,000	0.0006	0.19*	45,000	0.0017	0.56*	(475,000)	(0.0179)	(5.94)*	(500,000)	(0.0188)	(6.25)*
Total Shareholder Costs	55,000	0.0021	0.69	117,000	0.0044	1.46	1,608,000	0.0604	20.10	4,656,000	0.1750	58.20
Grand Total	250,000	0.009	3.10	330,000	0.012	4.20	2,600,000	0.098	33.00	6,300,000	0.24	79.00

*Primary figure to use in estimating cost to other corporations.

thousands, C represents the number of common shares in millions, and P represents the percentage increase in shares.

The cost burden is not crippling and even appears rather small when expressed per old share. Nevertheless, such cost is hardly negligible, and to it must be added the reduction of surplus and the adjustment of reported data.[15] These considerations should suffice to put a burden of proof on those who claim that a stock dividend would be beneficial.

SUPPOSED BENEFITS

There are two principal ways in which stockholders supposedly benefit from stock dividends—increased cash dividends and greater convenience and value—and several related minor ways, which are mentioned en route. We shall see that there are other ways to confer these benefits and reasons to prefer these other ways.

A small stock dividend is often, because of the well-known practice of stabilizing cash dividends, associated with maintenance of the rate of cash dividends per share and, therefore, starting the following period, with an increase in total cash dividends. Let us consider this contention in its own context—that is, assuming that cash dividends are being paid, that the stock dividend does not substitute for an immediate increase in cash dividends and that the increase in cash dividends is to the advantage of all stockholders.

STABILIZING DIVIDENDS

There is an obvious alternative to maintaining the cash rate per share and increasing the number of shares by some proportion. It is, starting next period, to increase the cash rate by the same proportion.[16] Indeed, this alternative has the advantage of introducing a change in the company's record that remains visible even on a per-share basis.[17]

True, the stock dividend would, in effect, announce the change one period sooner. But this too can be accomplished without a stock dividend if the board indeed wants to commit itself. An announcement would suffice. A scrip dividend might also be considered, or, more permanent, a bond dividend—perhaps subordinated income debentures. Interest paid on either of these would, in general, be deductible.[18] At minimum, there is also the

---

[15]Historically, a fifth burden was sometimes relevant. Until "the middle [nineteen] thirties, stockholders in our national banks were liable for the bank debts up to the par value of their shares." Dewing, *op. cit.,* p. 15.

[16]"There is evidence that many financial managements, sensitive to critical attitudes of employees and others with respect to higher dividends, prefer increasing the number of shares . . . to increasing the amount of cash per share. This is rather silly, as . . . there should be no necessity either for apologizing for or disguising such an increase." Paton, *op. cit.,* p. 128.

[17]Studies have yielded positive correlations between payout ratios and share prices per dollar of current earnings. F. Modigliani and M. H. Miller point out that these correlations may reflect not investors' desire for income or lack of understanding but merely the fact that dividends are regarded as indications of other things, most notably insiders' views as to the firm's long-run earning power. "The Cost of Capital, Corporation Finance, and the Theory of Investment: Reply," *American Economic Review,* XLIX (September, 1959), p. 668. In either event, it pays to have an increase in dividends visible.

[18]Paton, *op. cit.,* p. 115, remarks, "About the only excuse one can think of for (cont.)

alternative of a stock split of equal magnitude instead of the stock dividend; we will compare the two shortly.

GREATER CONVENIENCE AND VALUE

Stock dividends produce a finer division of the units of ownership. Up to some point, this supposedly will tend both to be convenient to stockholders and to increase the value of preexisting holdings.[19]

Greater convenience supposedly results from a lower price per share. Then amounts of money can be raised or invested either more exactly or with less resort to odd lots. In special cases a lower price per share may also facilitate sale of new shares or simplify certain aspects of intercorporate mergers. It has also been said that it is better for public relations to keep per-share profits low—especially in the case of public utilities.

INSIDERS MAY ANTICIPATE EFFECT

The putative increase in value may appear gradually, or it may roughly be reflected immediately as investors anticipate long-run developments. (There is some evidence that the entire increase, if any, occurs prior to the public announcement; this suggests that insiders anticipate any long-run effect.[20])

The long-run increase supposedly occurs because demand for the shares decreases less than proportionately. This occurs because some investors may not be aware of the dilution, because more people will now be able to afford to buy one share or to stretch to a round lot, because there are widespread feelings that high-priced shares decline more rapidly and rise more slowly than low-priced shares and that high-priced shares are suitable only for persons of large means, and because wider ownership of the company may improve its sales.[21]

---

converting retained earnings into bonds is to develop an interest charge for the sake of increasing tax deductions. . . . Even this point has its offset in the fact . . . that the bonds issued are legally income to the recipients, in the amount of their fair market value."

[19]The popular view is that a stock dividend is roughly equivalent to a cash dividend because the recipients could realize cash by selling the additional shares. The obvious answer is that a stockholder could sell part of his proportionate interest in the company whether or not there is an increase in the number of shares into which his interest is divided. Hence, if any benefit is obtained, it must be of the sorts mentioned in the text; that is, either it must become more convenient for stockholders to sell part of their holdings, or their holdings must be increased in value because price per share decreases a smaller proportion than the number of shares increases. It is also without merit to argue that a stock dividend conserves cash, avoids underwriting fees, provides cheap capital, or saves on income taxes; there is no reason why a cash dividend of equal bookkeeping amount would otherwise have to be declared. It is misleading to state that "the alternative to the stock dividend . . . is the disbursement of a cash dividend followed by issue of privileged subscription rights. . . . Such procedure would have been very costly . . . because [of] personal income taxes on dividends and because of the underpricing and underwriters' fees necessary. . . ." Wixon (ed.), *op. cit.*, pp. 21-43. See also Bothwell, cited in footnote 23.

[20]See especially the study of Burrell, cited in footnote 23.

[21]Cf. Dewing, *op. cit.*, II, p. 1188.

It may also occur that the supply of the shares increases less than proportionately. This may occur because, if the number of stockholders will be larger at a lower price and if tenacity will be greater with a larger number of shareholders, less of the equity would be offered per period.[22]

POINT OF NO RETURNS

The point up to which these effects will occur is often said to be reached when price per share has been driven down to about $10—$25. Further reductions supposedly would add little in convenience and in fact affect value adversely, by raising doubts about the investment quality of the shares and by impairing their standing as collateral.

Within such limits, the effects are plausible. That an increase in value will result seems possible, especially when price per share was very high (say above $200), although it has not clearly been confirmed or quantified by statistical analyses.[23] Equally, a gain in convenience seems reasonable, especially with respect to very high prices per share, although the gain is hard to evaluate.[24]

There is considerable appeal in the idea that corporations whose marginal earning power is high (how high, is a separate and complicated question) should retain all their earnings; they could, to quote one observer, then "simply split their stocks into shares of conveniently small value, so that each stockholder could in effect declare his own dividends by selling that portion of his holdings which he chose...."[25]

---

[22]Both parts of this sentence are supported by the studies, cited in footnote 23, of Dolley and of Fogg. Wider distribution of ownership may also be a prerequisite of listing on an exchange. It has also been said that wider distribution of ownership will reduce the chance of capture of control by "pirates," will lessen price fluctuations "because there is less money invested in the average holding which can be shaken out if a market break occurs," and will facilitate raising capital because "the added contribution which is asked of each individual stockholder is smaller." (The quotations are from the article in *Barron's* cited in footnote 23.) Indeed, according to Dolley, wider ownership is, for management, the primary purpose of splits, despite the higher costs attendant on wider ownership.

[23]The evidence, indeed, is contradictory. And even where the results are positive, as in the study of Myers and Bakey, there are some disconcerting notes. Thus, the only attribute that Myers and Bakey found among their 70 stocks that was significantly associated with an increase in value was a low pre-split price (less than $60). Similarly, the article in *Barron's* asserts that "there also appeared to be only a slight relation between the size of the split and the size of the increase in stockholders."

See: *Barron's Magazine*, Vol. 27, No. 37 (September 15, 1947). J. C. Bothwell, Jr., "Periodic Stock Dividends," *Harvard Business Review*, XXVIII (January, 1950), pp. 89-100. O. K. Burrell, "Price Effects of Stock Dividends," *Commercial and Financial Chronicle*, Convention Number (December 2, 1948), pp. 10 and 68-70. J. C. Dolley, "Common Stock Split-Ups—Motives and Effects," *Harvard Business Review*, XII (October, 1933), pp. 70-81. P. S. Fogg, *Stock Split-Ups* (Boston, Mass.: Harvard Graduate School of Business Administration, 1929). S. Livermore, "The Value of Stock Dividends," *American Economic Review*, XX (December, 1930), p. 687. J. H. Myers and A. J. Bakey, "The Influence of Stock Split-Ups on Market Price," *Harvard Business Review*, XXVI (March, 1948), pp. 251-255. S. N. Siegel, "Stock Dividends," *Harvard Business Review*, XI (October, 1932), pp. 76-87.

[24]Lattin comments, "While the shareholder derives no greater property interest by the issue of another piece of paper, he does find it more convenient, in case he desires to sell, to have these share-dividend units to use instead of splitting his larger units. ... The inconvenience does not add up to much." *Op. cit.*, p. 465.

[25]J. T. S. Porterfield, "Dividends, Dilution, and Delusion," *Harvard Business Review*, Vol. 37, No. 6 (November-December, 1959), p. 60.

"GAINS" TAX ADVANTAGE

This policy would be predicated on the idea, advocated by Modigliani and Miller, [26] that the only significance of cash dividend policy to the stockholder is to determine how much of the earnings of the firm will accrue to him in the form of cash and how much in the form of capital gains or losses. If this is the only significance, tax considerations and the cost of reinvestment of cash received would lead many stockholders to prefer greater capital gains instead of cash dividends, and the policy would give them their choice.

On the other hand, there are two opposing ideas. One is that the price of a share reflects the present value of the cash expected to be received on it in the future. The other is that small investors would encounter a 6 percent commission when they wanted to declare their own dividends by selling some shares. In any event, for present purposes it should be observed that the proposal favors, not stock dividends per se, but a low price per share, for convenience.

TIME LAG

Both greater conveniences and greater value, then, may follow. Notice, however, that the supporting reasons imply that the gains increase with the size of the stock dividend up to the specified limit. The argument supplies little reason for increases in the number of shares of the order of 2 percent. There is one exception; investors' unawareness of dilution probably weighs more heavily with small dividends.

Presumably (and it is a presumption) there is a tendency for price per share ultimately to adjust proportionately; small differences in the number of shares should not alter the equilibrium value of a firm. But with lags in awareness, the tendency may take some time to be substantially worked out—perhaps one reporting period if adjusted data are published at that interval.

Thus, it might take a year after a 2 percent dividend before price per share reaches 50/51 of what it otherwise would have been. If so, a semiannual 2 percent increase in the number of shares might cause a permanent increase in value of about 2 percent (perpetually, not per period).

Several things should be noticed about this gain. First, it presupposes that investors will not eventually comprehend the semiannual dilution and adjust previously reported data accordingly. Second, if the semiannual installments were interrupted, perhaps because surplus runs dry, the 2 percent improvement would decay despite all the costs of creating and maintaining it and the fact that later generations of stockholders would have bought while price was inflated.

---

[26]Modigliani and Miller, op. cit., p. 665.

MORTGAGING THE FUTURE

Third, the gain would accrue primarily to the persons who owned shares at the time the policy was initiated. Later generations would bear the cost of semiannual installments but gain only if the extra 2 percent they sold for represented more money than the extra 2 percent they bought at. And not even the original shareholders would directly gain unless they sold out— that is, unless they severed part or all of the very connection that makes their interests a matter of concern to management.

For original stockholders who do not sell out, the semiannual costs would accumulate. Ultimately, unless the value of the corporation rose fairly rapidly, these costs would outweigh the 2 percent gain if it were ever realized. Of course, byproduct gains, such as greater convenience, may occur as the increases in number of shares add up. But these could more cheaply be obtained by occasional large increases in the number of shares— for example, by a 100 percent dividend every, say, seventeenth year.

FOOLING THE PUBLIC

These considerations are not conclusive. Nevertheless, they seem to me sufficient to warrant a categorical rejection of occasional or periodic small stock dividends (or splits) aimed at fooling most of the people all of the time—unless the directors want to benefit a few insiders who plan to sell out.

The third of these considerations would apply also to an occasional large stock dividend (say 100 percent or greater), although with diminished force, since the cost of a given increase in the number of shares would be substantially less, especially if the split ratio is chosen to round out odd lots and to reduce the odd lot differential.

OTHER WAYS TO SPLIT STOCK

But suppose that price per share is very high, that the directors want to benefit those who would sell out or to broaden ownership, and that they believe that an increase in the number of shares would do so. Even so, a stock dividend is not necessarily indicated. There is another way—a stock split of corresponding magnitude.

While a split would be equivalent with respect to its impact on convenience and price, it may offer some definite advantages in four other directions. First, unlike a stock dividend, a split would not increase stated capital and with it, sometimes, franchise taxes.[27] Second, similarly, if the shares have a par value, the split would leave unchanged the aggregate par value associated with a given proportionate interest in the company and

---

[27]For exceptions to this and the next point, see footnote 29 and the text sentence preceding it.

with it the transfer taxes levied by states that base their transfer taxes on the aggregate par value sold.[28]   Third, a split would not reduce surplus and with it potential cash dividends (and the split could be undertaken even when negative surplus or negative profits would prevent a stock dividend).

EXCHANGE REGULATIONS

At least surplus would not be reduced except as required by state law, a regulatory commission, or a stock exchange.[29]   Thus, the New York Stock Exchange will not authorize listing of the additional shares even from a split unless an amount equal to the fair value of the shares is transferred from earned surplus—this qualification applying, however, only if the number of shares is increased less than 25 percent.[30]   Fourth, if preferred stock is outstanding—especially preferred with voting rights or rights to participate in dividends or assets beyond any preference—the question may arise whether the preferred shareholders are legally or morally entitled, because of either preemptive or participation rights, also to receive additional shares.   The answer may be clearer in the case of a stock split.[31]

On the other hand, a split may have two disadvantages compared to a stock dividend. (1) Stockholders usually are sent not only a second stock certificate but also a stamp to affix over the nominal value stated on the old certificates, this procedure involving less trouble and delay than does recalling the old certificates; a similar change is involved for the inventory of unissued certificates, stamping by The American Bank Note Company costing about 2 cents per certificate.

This trouble occurs if the shares have a par value (as do about two thirds of the common issues listed on national exchanges[32]), or if, anomalously, a stated value appears on the certificates for no-par shares. (2) In the case of either par-value shares or no-par shares with a stated value in the

---

[28]See footnote 42.

[29]Another exception to the nonreduction of surplus applies to the splitting of par-value stock whose par value has reached the minimum (often one dollar, but sometimes less), if there is one, specified by the chartering state for shares with par value. Further split-ups would require either charges to a surplus account or a conversion to no-par stock (which is authorized in all states except Nebraska).

[30]The requirement is unfortunate from an accounting viewpoint. "The preferable accounting procedure . . . [for a stock dividend is to use] the *capital* book value per share (either par or stated value or, more logically, average amount received per share from stockholders). . . ." Paton, *op. cit.,* p. 125. See also Moonitz and Staehling, *op. cit.* However, the requirement has the sanction of *Accounting Research Bulletin No. 11 (Revised),* p. 101-A—with dissents. (See footnote 5.).

[31]Dilution of participating preferred stock, as well as dilution of convertible bonds and stocks, and stock warrants and options, should be recognized as an additional way in which a stock dividend may benefit the common stockholders. The benefit depends on the existence of these instruments, on the absence of enforceable protective provisions in their contracts, on the decision not to alter their rights proportionately, and on the preservation of the corporation's reputation. If these conditions are met, however, a stock split could also result in dilution, unless the contracts have a loophole only for stock dividends or the corporation is chartered in Nebraska, which (cf. E. F. Donaldson, *Corporate Finance,* [N.Y., 1957], p. 110, fn. 1) requires that all shares have the same par value. Indeed, as just indicated in the text, dilution by a split can be easier—provided the preferred would not veto the charter amendment, which is required except in the case of "true" no-par shares.

[32]Cf. Donaldson, *op. cit.,* p. 110.

corporation's charter, it would be necessary to amend the charter each time a split is to occur, instead of merely when authorized but unissued shares run low, as is the case with stock dividends. A charter amendment is costly ($3,000—or possibly $20,000—for our example, Dow), and it might be vetoed by the preferred shareholders if they would suffer dilution.

These disadvantages are not conclusive. Neither stamping nor amendment is a major expense. Moreover, amendment would often be needed for a stock dividend too—and even more often should be needed in view of the extra franchise taxes that may be produced by authorized but unissued shares. Most important, neither stamping nor amendment could be a differential burden in the case of true no-par shares.

IMPLICATIONS

In the case of corporations with true no-par shares, there would seem to be no reason for directors who are concerned with the welfare of the stockholders ever to declare a stock dividend. This statement is qualified by the fact that a stock dividend is equivalent—but not preferable—to a stock split in one set of circumstances: where either one would have the same effect on franchise taxes, where either one would have the same problems with dilution of other securities, and where either one would have the same effect on surplus that is chargeable for cash dividends (because either a regulatory institution or the directors themselves insist on reducing surplus).

Given other circumstances, the board should choose not a stock dividend but a stock split if it wants to increase the number of shares, either alone or in conjunction with an increase in total cash dividends.

But a decision to increase the number of shares, even by a stock split, should be made only if the benefits appear likely to outweigh the burdens. The potential benefits are greater convenience and value, and possibly conversion of odd lots, a lower odd lot differential, better public relations, wider ownership, less instability, easier capital-raising, listing on an exchange, less "piracy," and some dilution of other securities. However, it seems unlikely that these various benefits would in fact outweigh the burdens unless price per share is very high—say above $200—and is to be brought into a popular price range. That the benefits would predominate if this condition is met is plausible but a matter of conjecture.

The particular split ratio chosen should attempt to maximize the net benefit. This implies three things. First, it implies choosing a whole number for the split ratio, not a ratio such as 5-for-2. A whole number simplifies calculations, facilitates adjustment of reported data, avoids fractional shares and creating odd lots in existing round lot holdings. Second, it implies choosing a whole number that has the power to round out existing odd lots, not a ratio such as 3-for-1.

Third, it implies choosing a ratio that is large enough to realize side benefits. The power to convert odd lots is greater, the larger the ratio chosen, provided the choice is confined to the basic ratios mentioned in the appendix. With a 100-share unit of trading, they are 2-for-1, 4-for-1, 5-for-1, 10-for-1, 20-for-1, 25-for-1, 50-for-1, and 100-for-1.

CHOOSING PROPER SPLIT RATIO

Furthermore, a ratio large enough to bring price per share below $40 would reduce the odd lot differential, and a ratio large enough to bring price below $20 would reduce the rate of the New York stock transfer tax. On the other hand, certain burdens also increase as the ratio grows. Franchise taxes and listing fees may increase; the New York transfer tax relates to the number of shares; commission charges increase relative to sales proceeds as price per share falls; and there is a feeling that price per share should not be "too low."

While most of these considerations are quantifiable, they cannot in the abstract be weighted to determine an optimum split ratio for shares of given prices. Their importance depends on circumstances such as the state of incorporation, the proportion of odd lot holdings, and the proportion of transactions larger than the minimum shareholding whose commission is affected by different split ratios. It can be said, however, that the basic split ratios provide a sufficiently varied set of alternatives that one of them should fit any particular situation.

On the other hand, splits or stock dividends under 100 percent, whether occasional or periodic, should be avoided (unless stockholders' wishes are given precedence over their welfare, or the goal is to benefit some insiders who want to sell out). Direct benefit from small increases in the number of shares—from investors' unawareness of dilution—will be short-lived if the action is occasional or quite expensive if it is periodic.

Indirect benefits can better be accomplished separately. That is, if merely an increase in total cash payments is desired, an increase in the cash rate per share should be announced or perhaps a scrip or bond dividend declared. If merely retention of earnings or a substitute for a cash dividend is desired, a syrupy letter should be preferred. If merely a reduction in surplus is desired, purely accounting action should be taken. If merely an eventual large increase in the number of shares is desired, an occasional large split should be undertaken.

In the case of a corporation with either par-value shares or no-par shares with a stated value in the charter, the same considerations apply to a desire merely to increase cash payments, or to give the stockholders a substitute for cash, or to reduce surplus; there are less costly ways than by increasing the numbers of shares. Similarly, occasional or periodic small increases in shares are not melons and should be avoided. And here, too, no strong case can be made against substantially reducing a high price per share by a well chosen round number multiplication of the number of shares.

In choosing between the two methods of accomplishing a large increase in the number of shares, however, it is possible that here a stock dividend would be less burdensome than a stock split. If a charter amendment need not be undertaken, the dividend will have in its favor avoidance of the process of amending. The dividend would also, in the case at least of par-value shares, avoid the use of stamps for the old certificates. The split may have in its favor effects on franchise taxes, on earned surplus, on dilution problems, and, in the case of par-value shares, on certain states' transfer taxes. The balance will depend on the firm's circumstances.

APPENDIX

CORPORATION COSTS AND RECIPIENT COSTS

Corporation Costs

For a number of items, I have relied on data that were kindly furnished me by the Dow Chemical Company and by a company that wishes to remain anonymous. The figures for Dow came primarily in a letter of February 15, 1960, from Mr. D. N. LeVert of the company's Treasury Department, the information pertaining to a 2 percent stock dividend and to a 3-for-1 stock split, the latter being equivalent for the present purpose to a 200 percent stock dividend.

Mr. LeVert stated that "the cost of the stock dividend is reasonably accurate for it is based on an actual stock dividend just recently (November, 1959) paid. The stock split costs are only estimates based on today's cost and could be either slightly higher or lower." The figures for Corporation Anonymous came in a letter of March 18, 1960, from the company's treasurer. They indicate, to the dollar, expenses incurred by Anonymous in connection with a recently issued 5 percent dividend.

Officers' Time. A stock dividend requires action by the highest officials of the corporation and, therefore, consumes their time. To assign a figure here is especially arbitrary, and Anonymous made no attempt. Dow lists $1,000 for the 2 percent increase in shares and $10,000 for the 200 percent increase. The difference is plausible; a large increase in shares is likely to be less frequent and more debated than a small increase. Furthermore, the cost probably is substantially independent of the exact size of the small or the large increase—and of the size of the company. Let us simply indicate the magnitude involved with any small increase as $1,000, and with any large increase as $10,000.

Fractional Shares. A stock dividend not in a multiple of 100 percent involves trouble with rights to fractions of a share. Sometimes stockholders are given cash equivalent to the fractions, in which case the corporation bears the expense of calculation and check writing. Sometimes warrants are given, made out to bearer and transferable by delivery, which the corporation or its transfer agent may for several years redeem for cash, accept with cash for a whole share, or maintain a market for—the corporation bearing the expense of calculation, printing, and redemption.

Sometimes the corporation gives stockholders order forms, with envelopes, on which to instruct the corporation or its transfer agent whether to sell the fractions or to buy the complements, any imbalance of orders being balanced by stock market transactions.[33]   Both Dow and Anonymous followed this third route, and both indicate the cost of handling fractional shares as the largest single item in the cost of a small dividend: $110,000 for Dow, $24,456 for Anonymous.

The figures correspond nicely. Anonymous has about one fourth as many stockholders as Dow, which has somewhat more than 80,000.   Furthermore, a 5 percent dividend involves fractional shares for 95 percent of the possible stock holdings, as against 98 percent for a 2 percent dividend. Even the small discrepancy that may remain can be reconciled; it can be attributed to the fact that the cost stated for Anonymous includes only the fee of the transfer agent, not any part of the $8,432 spent for clerical assistance at the company's offices. We may put the rate per stockholder, then—with exaggerated accuracy—at $1.38 for a 2 percent dividend and at $1.34 for a 5 percent dividend, expecting that the cost would vary among corporations about in proportion to the number of stockholders. That is, a corporation such as General Motors, which has about 750,000 common stockholders, would incur a cost about nine times the cost to Dow.

Certificate Cost. A stock dividend uses up stock certificates and requires that names, dates, and signatures be added. Dow puts the cost at $35,000 for the 2 percent increase in shares and at $100,000 for the 200 percent increase, figures which can be reconciled by supposing that only about a third of the stockholders ended up with additional shares after the small dividend. Anonymous lists the cost of 30,000 certificates and of dating at $4,927, or at $5,255 including the fee of The Signature Company. In addition, part of the $8,432 spent for temporary employees represents a cost of preparing the certificates; this part would be $3,500 if the aggregate certificate cost were proportional to Dow's. On this basis, we may put the cost per stockholder at $0.44 for a small dividend and at $1.25 for a large dividend.

Ledger Revision. A stock dividend necessitates revision of the stockholders ledger and preparation of a distribution list. Dow figures the cost at $86,000 for the 2 percent increase in shares and at $250,000 for the 200 percent increase. The cost to Anonymous is included in the $8,432 spent for temporary employees, of which $4,932 remains. For a conservative estimate, let us use this lowest figure. Then the cost per stockholder comes—again with exaggerated accuracy—to $0.24 for a small dividend and to $0.70 for a large dividend.

Mailing Costs. A stock dividend entails mailing costs. Dow lists $8,000 for the 2 percent increase and $10,000 for the 200 percent increase, the difference being attributed to the larger number of certificates and greater

---

[33]Cf. Donaldson, *op. cit.*, p. 630. J. I. Bogen (ed.), *Financial Handbook* (3d ed.; New York, 1948), p. 792.

insured value in the case of the larger increase. Anonymous lists merely $900 for the first class postage. Using the Anonymous figure, the cost per stockholder comes to $0.04.

Miscellaneous Supplies. This category includes "fractional order cards, billing statements, checks for use when fractional orders are sold, extra lists for registrar, phone calls, and numerous other small items." Dow lists the cost of miscellaneous supplies as $6,000 for the 2 percent increase and as $25,000 for the 200 percent increase. Anonymous lists $3,000. Using the implicitly lower Dow figures, the cost per stockholder is $0.08 for a small dividend and $0.31 for a large dividend.

Franchise Taxes. A stock dividend will sometimes produce an increase in the franchise tax levied by the state of incorporation and in corresponding taxes imposed by states in which the corporation transacts business as a qualifying foreign corporation. "In a few states, such as Arizona, Nevada, Indiana, North Dakota, and South Dakota, there is no annual franchise tax;" in "several states, such as California, Connecticut, Iowa, Massachusetts, Minnesota, New York, Utah, and Wisconsin, the state income tax has replaced the franchise tax." In "other states the amount is calculated on a variety of bases, such as authorized capital stock (Oregon), outstanding stock (Florida), capital stock and paid-in surplus (Illinois) . . ."[34] Capital stock is usually valued at par or, in the case of no-par shares, at an arbitrary amount per share ranging from $10 to $100. Tax bases such as these would tend to be increased by a stock dividend. Marginal tax rates vary widely, ranging from a probable low of 0.275 cent per year per additional share authorized (Delaware) to a high of 50 cents per year per additional $100 of capitalization (Pennsylvania).[35]

Both Dow and Anonymous are in fact incorporated in Delaware. At the Delaware rate, a 2 percent increase in the number of shares authorized would correspond to a tax increase of 0.0055 cent per old share; a 5 percent increase would correspond to 0.014 cent per old share; a 200 percent increase would correspond to 0.55 cent per old share. These amounts, however, represent only one year's increase in taxes, whereas the increase is in effect a perpetuity.

For Dow, however, there was no extra franchise tax. Delaware has a maximum tax of $50,000 per year;[36] with 26.6 million common shares already outstanding (and 50 million authorized), Dow was already paying the maximum. Anonymous too lists zero as the franchise tax cost. Here the reason was the availability of unissued shares.

It is unacceptable, however, to make a deduction for utilization of shares already authorized but presently not outstanding. The reason is not that a future increase in the number authorized may then have to occur sooner. More fundamentally, the reason is that a corporation with unissued (or

[34]H. G. Guthmann and H. E. Dougall, *Corporate Financial Policy* (3d ed.; Englewood Cliffs, N.J., 1955), pp. 47 and 48.
[35]Donaldson, *op. cit.*, p. 60.
[36]*Delaware Code Annotated,* Title 8, sec. 503c.

treasury) stock has an alternative that would cause it to save the indicated deduction, yet end up with the same number of unissued shares as it has after the stock dividend. This alternative is to reduce the number of shares authorized by the same amount that the dividend would utilize unissued shares. In view of this alternative, the tax cost of the dividend is, at minimum, the perpetuity above minus the cost of charter amendment. I say "at minimum" because the corporation may originally have obtained authorization for the unissued shares partly in order later to issue them as a dividend. Then it has been paying extra franchise taxes from the time the shares were authorized; that is, we should not merely reject the indicated deduction, but actually increase the tax cost by the present value of the extra taxes already paid. For present purposes, however, let us accept zero as the franchise tax cost.

Charter Amendment. A stock dividend may require amendment of the corporation's charter—immediately if the number of authorized but unissued shares is insufficient for the dividend, at some future date if the dividend consumes unissued shares that would later have covered the sale of additional stock. Neither Dow [nor] Anonymous needed to amend for their small dividends, since the number of shares already authorized substantially exceeded the number outstanding.

As to the cost, Dow estimates $3,000, which amounts to $0.04 per stockholder. This figure seems low. Charter amendment involves preparing, printing, and posting the proposal for approval by the voting stockholders, filing with the appropriate official in at least one state, and paying small filing fees. A less conservative figure might be $20,000.

Stock Issue Tax. The federal stock issue tax is 10 cents for each $100 (or major fraction thereof) of actual value, regardless of par value. "Actual value is a question of fact which may be determined by reference to quoted values in the market, book values or any other information which has a bearing on the question."[37] Declaration of the value is the responsibility of the issuing corporation.

The amount of the original issue tax paid by Anonymous implies a declared value per share equal to an average of the market prices of Anonymous common on the day of payment. Dow paid $46,400 on its 531,092 dividend shares. This implies a declared value per share of 87⅞, which also falls within the trading range of the day of payment. The figures in Table 12-1 assume an "actual value" of merely $26.75 per share before the dividend.

Listing Fees. A stock dividend may increase the charges for listing the issue on securities exchanges. Anonymous common stock is listed on the New York and Pacific Coast stock exchanges, and the dividend shares, plus another 30,000 reserve shares to prevent dilution of stock options, were listed there too.[38] Dow common stock is listed on the New York, Boston,

---

[37]Letter of May 9, 1960 from R. J. Bobb, Chief, Excise Tax Branch, Internal Revenue Service, Washington, D.C.

[38]Letter of April 20, 1960 from R. L. Callanan, Department of Public Information, (cont.)

Cincinnati, Detroit, Midwest, Pacific Coast, and Philadelphia-Baltimore exchanges. The 2 percent dividend resulted in the listing of 531,092 additional shares, plus 120,000 shares for the employees stock purchase plan. Let us calculate the listing fees of merely the two exchanges on which Anonymous is listed.

The New York Stock Exchange charges an initial listing fee and an annual fee payable for 15 years.[39] The initial fee is graduated according to the number of shares originally listed; the annual fee is graduated according to the number outstanding and listed at each anniversary. Both fees apply to listing dividend shares of previously listed stock, the charges being at the marginal rate or rates applicable to the entire issue. The initial fee is $100 per 10,000 shares or fraction thereof for the first 500,000 shares, $50 per 10,000 shares for the next 1.5 million shares, and $25 per 10,000 shares for shares in excess of 2 million, but not less than $2,000 for a corporation having no other stock listed. The annual fee is $100 per 100,000 shares or fraction thereof for the first 2 million shares and $50 per 100,000 shares above 2 million, but not less than $250 per stock issue or $500 per company.

At the lowest of these rates, a 2 percent increase in shares would produce an initial fee of 0.005 cent per old share; it would also produce a 15 year annual fee of 0.001 cent per old share. Discounting the 15 year annuity at 10 percent, the total cost would amount to 0.0126 cent per old share. A 5 percent dividend would correspond to 0.0315 cent per old share; a 200 percent dividend, to 1.26 cents.

The initial fee of the Pacific Coast Stock Exchange is $500 for 500,000 shares or less, or $1,000 for more than 500,000 shares; the annual fee is a flat $100. However, the charge for listing dividend shares of a previously listed stock is $10 per 100,000 shares or fraction thereof, but not less than $100.[40] The $10 rate corresponds to 0.0002 cent per old share for a 2 percent dividend, 0.005 cent for 5 percent, and 0.02 cent for 200 percent.

The total cost per old share, then, comes to 0.0128 cent for 2 percent, 0.0320 cent for 5 percent, and 1.28 cents for 200 percent. With 26.6 million old shares, these rates correspond to $3,400, $8,500, and $340,000, respectively.

These are conservative figures. They include the charges of only two exchanges. They assume the lowest rates of the NYSE and neglect the minimum charges of both exchanges. They neglect that any fraction of 10,000 or 100,000 shares counts for a full unit. They disregard the listing of reserve shares, as occurred with both Anonymous and Dow.[41]

Recipient Costs

Nuisance Value. The trouble imposed on shareholders is at minimum the effort of opening an envelope and filing a certificate. The trouble may

New York Stock Exchange.

[39]New York Stock Exchange, Department of Stock List, *Schedule of Listing Fees* (March 1, 1950).

[40]Telephone conversation.

[41]Thus, the NYSE initial fee for Dow was in fact $1,775, not $1,330 as in our (cont.)

include an entry in the record books and a trip to the safe deposit box. If warrants or order cards are given, the recipient has the trouble of converting to cash or shares—and the possibility of loss or lapse of the warrants. He may also need to read the entirety of a 2-page, closely printed cover letter. Twenty cents per stockholder would seem to be a conservative price tag for a small increase in shares; ten cents for a large one. With 80,000 stockholders these rates correspond to $16,000 and $8,000, respectively.

Transfer Taxes. There are stock transfer taxes in a number of states—most notably in New York. The New York tax rate on shares selling at $20 or more is a flat 4 cents per share, to be paid by the seller.[42] Consider the effect that a stock dividend would have on stockholders who later sell their given proportionate interests in New York. Assuming that the price remains above $20, a 2 percent dividend would increase their transfer taxes by 0.08 cent per old share. Using what seems to be the most reasonable way of obtaining a total (and the way that would be comparable with estimates of the supposed gain in value), this amounts to $21,300 on 26.6 million old shares sold once. A 5 percent dividend would reduce net proceeds by 0.2 cent per old share, or $53,200; a 200 percent dividend would cost 8 cents per old share, or $2,128,000. For our cost estimate, let us conservatively reduce these figures by 10 percent, since New York's two major exchanges account for somewhat less than 95 percent of the dollar value of all stock sold on the country's exchanges.[43] The loss should vary among large corporations about in proportion to the number of additional shares.[44]

Commissions. A stock dividend tends to increase brokers' commissions. This tendency results from the interaction of three practices. First, commission charges on multiples of 100 shares are computed by multiplying the charge for 100 shares times the number of 100-share lots involved. Second, the charge for 100 shares represents a larger proportion of the gross value of 100 shares if the price per share is lower. Third, the commission on any odd lots involved is computed separately.[45] Put together, these practices imply

---

calculations. The annual fee was in fact $300 per year, not $266.

[42]The rate is 1 cent per share on shares sold at less than $5, 2 cents for $5.00-$9.99, and 3 cents for $10.00-$19.99. Rates in several other states are given in *The Fitch Stock Record:*

Per $100 par value, or per share on no-par stock, regardless of selling price...	*Florida*	*South Carolina*	*Texas*
	$0.10	$0.4	$0.033

[43]Donaldson, *op. cit.*, p. 434.

[44]As of January 1, 1959, the federal stock transfer tax became 4 cents for each $100 (or major fraction thereof) of actual value of the total shares transferred but in no case less than 4 cents on the entire transaction or more than 8 cents on each share. The 8 cents maximum implies that stock dividends can also increase the federal tax. This would occur if the price per share of the larger number of shares remained above $200. However, publicly held common stocks usually are kept below $200 for "marketability."

[45]Since April, 1959 the following commission rates have been in effect on the country's major stock exchanges for a transaction of 100 shares or less, except that the commission is $2 less in the case of an odd lot amounting to $100 or more:

Money Value	*Commission*
Under $100	6%
$100 to $399	2% plus $3
$400 to $2,399	1% plus $7
$2,400 to $4,999	1/2% plus $19
$5,000 and above	1/10% plus $39 (cont.)

that when a stock holding of some given gross value is sold, the commission will be greater if a larger number of 100-share units, or the same number but also an odd lot, is involved.

Suppose, for example, that a 2 percent dividend occurs which, because price per share falls from $51 to $50, leaves the gross value of each stockholder's interest unchanged. Consider a stockholder who previously held 100 shares and now has 102. The commission for selling his complete holding would increase from $44.10 to $50. This is an increase of 5.9 cents per old share; in other words, a reduction of 0.12 percent in net sales proceeds.

It is difficult to generalize about the increase in commissions. The increase will vary with the original price, the size of the transaction, the impact of the $6 minimum and the $1.50 and $75 maxima, and the percentage increases in shares. Table 12-2 indicates the effect of four percentage increases under varying circumstances. (Additional commissions for new stockholders would tend to be twice as much, since they would also buy at a higher cost.)

For the proportion of stockholders that would be affected, we may refer to information from Anonymous that approximately 95 percent of its stockholders own less than 100 shares, and less than 1 percent own more than 225 shares—even though Anonymous common is not a high priced stock. Of the 5 percent of shareholders with 100 or more old shares, perhaps two fifths would have holdings without small odd lots and, therefore, incur substantially larger commissions as a result of a 2 to 5 percent dividend. Judging by Table 12-2, it seems conservative to say that these shareholders would lose an average of $3 from a 2 percent dividend or $5 from a 5 percent dividend.

With 200 percent, these 5 percent might average, say, $20, and one fifth of the others, say, $5. With 500 percent, the former might average $40 and one third of the others lose $8.46.

Odd Lot Differentials. Stock dividends not in multiples of 100 percent will create odd lots in existing round lot holdings and additional shares in what remain odd lot holdings. Consider the effect of a 2 percent dividend when, as is usual, the unit of trading is 100 shares and the odd lot differential is 25 cents per share or 12.5 cents for shares selling below $40. Holders of

---

Notwithstanding the above, when the money value is $100 or more, the commission shall not exceed $1.50 per share or $75 per single transaction but in any event shall not be less than $6 per single transaction. In the case of a number of 100-share lots, or of one or more 100-share lots plus an odd lot, each part is regarded as an entirely separate transaction.
These rates imply the following relation between selling price and commission:

Price per Share	Commission on 100 Shares	100-Share Commission Relative to Gross Value of 100 Shares
$400	$75	0.19%
300	69	0.23
200	59	0.30
100	49	0.49
50	44	0.88
30	34	1.13
10	17	1.70
5	12	2.40
1	6	6.00

TABLE 12-2
EFFECT OF STOCK DIVIDENDS ON COMMISSIONS

Increase in Number of Shares	Original Price per Share	Smallest Transaction Affected (old shares)	Increase in Commission on:			
			Smallest Affected Transaction	100 Old Shares	150 Old Shares except 140 for 5%	500 Old Shares
	$408		$6.00	$ 6.00	$ 0.80	$ 15.00
	306		7.71	5.40	0	12.00
	204		7.80	5.60	0	13.00
2%	102	99	7.90	5.80	0	14.00
	51		4.95	5.90	0.40	9.50
	25.50		3.38	2.75	0.25	4.75
	12.75		2.63	1.75	0	4.75
	420		6.00	7.50	2.00	37.50
	315		7.76	6.00	0	30.00
	210		8.84	6.50	0	32.50
5%	105	96	7.20	7.00	2.00	27.00
	52.50		5.52	5.75	2.25	16.25
	26.25		3.40	5.37	0.62	8.10
	13.125		2.65	3.12	0	4.10
	420		7.72	84.00	123.00	420.00
	360		7.76	78.00	117.00	390.00
	240		7.84	78.00	113.00	390.00
200%	180	34	7.88	78.00	109.00	390.00
	90		5.30	54.00	68.50	270.00
	60		4.00	36.00	46.00	180.00
	30		3.00	17.00	24.00	85.00
	420		7.86	201.00	281.00	1005.00
	360		7.88	195.00	275.00	975.00
	240		6.40	171.00	239.00	855.00
500%	180	17	5.30	147.00	203.00	735.00
	90		3.50	84.00	110.50	420.00
	60		3.00	57.00	76.00	285.00
	30		2.50	38.00	54.00	190.00

even multiples of 5,000 old shares will receive round lots. Other share-holders will receive rights to odd lots, amounting to 2 percent of the number of old shares for holders of less than 5,000 old shares, amounting to between zero and 1 percent for holders of 5,001-9,999 old shares, etc. In the net, this may increase odd lots by one share per holding—or by three shares with a 5 percent dividend—costing to sell an average of $0.1875 each.

In contrast, no multiple tends to increase the number of odd shares and certain ratios will unidirectionally convert odd lots into round ones.

Certain multiples, or split ratios, can simultaneously convert existing odd lots into round lots. These are the ratios that divide evenly into the number of shares that constitutes a unit of trading, and also multiples of these ratios. Given the usual 100-share unit of trading, the basic ratios are 2-for-1, 4-for-1, 5-for-1, 10-for-1, 20-for-1, 25-for-1, 50-for-1, and 100-for-1.

But there are also differences among these ratios. There are 99 possible odd lots when the unit of trading is 100 shares. As Table 12-3 indicates, a

TABLE 12-3
POWER OF DIFFERENT SPLIT RATIOS TO ROUND OUT ODD LOTS

Split Ratio	Odd Lots Converted	
	Number Out of 99	Holdings Rounded Out
1, 3, 7, 9, 11, 13, 17, 19, 21, 23, 27, 29, etc..	0	
2, 6, 14, 18, 22, 26, 34, 38, 42, 46, 54, etc. ..	1	50 old shares
4, 8, 12, 16, 24, 28, 32, 36, 44, 48, 52, etc. ..	3	25, 50, 75
5, 15, 35, 45, 55, 65, 75, 85, 95, 105, etc. ...	4	20, 40, 60, 80
10, 30, 60, 70, 90, 110, etc.	9	10, 20, 30, 40, 50, 60, etc.
20, 40, 60, 80, 120, 140, etc.	19	5, 10, 15, 20, 25, 30, etc.
25, 75, 125, 175, etc.....................	24	4, 8, 12, 16, 20, 24, etc.
50, 150, 250, etc........................	49	2, 4, 6, 8, 10, 12, etc.
100, 200, 300, etc.......................	99	1, 2, 3, 4, 5, 6, etc.

100-for-1 ratio, or multiple thereof, would round out all 99; 50-for-1, or multiple thereof, would round out the 49 even numbers; 25-for-1 would round out the 24 multiples of four; 20-for-1 would round out the 19 multiples of five; 10-for-1 would round out the nine multiples of ten; 5-for-1 would round out the four multiples of 20; 4-for-1 would round out 25, 50, and 75; 2-for-1 would round out only 50. Clearly the proportion of odd lot holdings that are rounded out tends to be greater the larger is the split ratio, if it is chosen wisely. If odd lots are to be minimized, therefore, the larger the ratio among those mentioned, the better.

Our 200 percent increase, of course, receives absolutely no credit here. Other ratios would receive a credit varying with the ratio involved, the proportion of holdings that were rounded out, the average number of shares in such holdings, and the odd lot differential. In the case of a 500 percent increase in shares, holdings containing a 50-share odd lot would be rounded out. Suppose that these constitute 5 percent of all holdings. Then the savings, at 12.5 cents per share, come to $0.31 per stockholder. In addition, let us suppose that a credit of $5.94 per stockholder is due for reducing the odd lot differential. This corresponds to 95 percent of stockholders holding 50-share odd lots.

13. CORPORATE STOCK REACQUISITIONS*

RICHARD A. STEVENSON †

Stock reacquisitions have become fairly common corporate transactions in the past few years. This is indicated in a recent article estimating that the distribution of corporate funds for reacquired shares has risen from $273.9 million in 1954 to $1,302.9 million in 1963.[1] This increased interest in corporate stock reacquisition raises ethical problems of concern to both accountants and financial managers. It is the purpose of this article to examine the ethics of corporate stock reacquisition. After a general discussion of ethics and its application to corporate stock reacquisition, several recent stock reacquisitions will be examined with regard to their ethical implications.

ETHICS IN GENERAL

Ethics has been defined as "the recognition of and responsibility for the realities involved in any relationship."[2] As many writers have pointed out, this is an area which is neither completely black nor completely white. This is as true with corporate stock repurchase as with any other business or personal activity. It is not always easy to appreciate the realities of any situation, and the understanding is naturally dependent upon the personality and moral training of the person involved.

Within the area of business ethics, the most important single development is the rise of the professional manager and the decline in the importance of the owner-manager. This separation of ownership from management has created the need for an ethical code to guide management in corporate transactions that directly affect stockholders, including repurchases of common stock.

RELATIONSHIP BETWEEN ETHICS AND THE LAW

The relationship between ethics and the law is an interesting yet somewhat intangible relationship. It is reasonably clear, in most circumstances, that the law represents the minimum standard for an ethical individual. However, something that is legal may very well be unethical when viewed within the proper social and economic context. William L. Cary makes an important distinction between ethics and the law when he writes:

> The law . . . represents the standards currently imposed by governmental or quasi-governmental authority. Ethical action, on the other hand,

---

*From *The Accounting Review* (April, 1966), pp. 312-317. Reprinted by permission.
†Associate Professor of Finance, University of Iowa.
[1]Leo A. Gurthart, "More Companies Are Buying Back Their Stock," *Harvard Business Review* (March-April, 1965), p. 44.
[2]Samuel H. Miller, "The Tangle of Ethics," *Harvard Business Review* (January-February, 1960), p. 60.

is supposedly motivated by a self-imposed standard, rather than compelled by law. Beyond that, however, the wise counselor will assess the need for ethical restraint because he tends to view it as potential legal restraint; it might be described as 'becoming law.'[3]

Corporate directors must make the decision on whether or not to reacquire stock. It is important that this decision be made in the best interests of the stockholders. The two main considerations are: (1) to see that adequate disclosure is made of the transaction and (2) to see that no conflict-of-interest situations result because of the decision to reacquire stock. In many instances, it is impossible to separate these two considerations because adequate disclosure often greatly reduces any possibility of a conflict-of-interest situation.

The anti-fraud provisions of the federal securities laws are founded upon the principle of adequate disclosure and should serve as one of the guides to directors in deciding whether to reacquire stock for the corporate treasury. Rules 10b-5, 10b-6, and 10b-7 constitute the main anti-fraud provisions that are applicable to corporate stock reacquisition. Rule 10b-5 deals with the employment of manipulative and deceptive devices to influence stock prices and requires that all material information be disclosed. Thus, directors may expose themselves to liability if they rely on inside information in the reacquisition of stock.

Rule 10b-6 deals with the magnitude of trading activity and is important when considering such reacquisitions as the Merritt-Chapman & Scott Corporation tender offer to be discussed later. Rule 10b-7 deals with the principles to be followed in the stabilization of the market price of a stock. While this rule is especially important in underwriting new issues, it seems to apply in certain corporate stock reacquisitions.

PRESS DISCLOSURE OF STOCK REACQUISITIONS

In order to reach a conclusion as to the extent of the press disclosure of stock reacquisition, *Wall Street Journal* Indexes for the 1958-1963 period were used to compile Exhibit 13-1. The companies included each year were determined by the following criterion: any New York Stock Exchange industrial company reducing its outstanding common stock by 1 percent or more from one year to the next as revealed by *Moody's Industrial Manuals*. This method has the advantage of including those companies reacquiring stock in amounts large enough to cause a significant reduction in common stock equity. Exhibit 13-1 shows the number and percentage of companies that had any type of press release concerning their reacquisition in the *Wall Street Journal*. It is true that the New York Stock Exchange does publish a list of companies repurchasing stock each quarter, but many investors would not normally see this tabulation. The *Wall Street Journal*, however, is widely read by the financial public and seems a logical place to send a press release

---

[3]William L. Cary, "The Case for Higher Corporate Standards," *Harvard Business Review* (September-October, 1962), p. 53.

Exhibit 13-1

DISCLOSURE OF CORPORATE STOCK REACQUISITIONS IN THE
WALL STREET JOURNAL

	Number of companies	Number and percentage in WSJ	
1958	33	4	12%
1959	14	4	28
1960	27	4	15
1961	28	5	18
1962	54	8	15
1963	61	10	16
Total	217	35	16%

Sources: *Moody's Industrial Manuals (1958-1964)* and *Wall Street Journal Index (1958-1963)*.

concerning the stock reacquisition—especially in view of the criterion used to select the companies in Exhibit 13-1.

Exhibit 13-1 reveals rather poor coverage of these stock reacquisitions in the *Wall Street Journal*. Perhaps the average percentage of disclosure (16 percent) is biased somewhat in a downward direction because companies reacquiring stock in more than one year, using open market purchases, send only one press release to the *Wall Street Journal* prior to the initial repurchase. However, of the 36 companies reacquiring stock for the first time in 1963, only 4 (or 11.1 percent) had a press release in the *Wall Street Journal* during 1963. This does not confirm the suspicion of a bias in Exhibit 13-1.

It is desirable that the situation regarding press disclosure improve since stock reacquisitions are currently achieving wider support among corporate directors. Even if they are adequately disclosed in the annual report, this may, nevertheless, mean an informational time lag of months during which this information may have been useful to the large body of investors. In addition, the magnitude of the transaction is often sufficient to justify a separate press release.

Accountants are aware that adequate disclosure can deter conflict-of-interest situations. Hence, Exhibit 13-1 suggests that there is considerable room for better disclosure in the financial press. A conflict of interest has been defined as existing "where an employee has an outside personal financial interest or any other relationship which has the *potentiality* of being antagonistic to the best interests of his company even though it may result in no loss to it."[4] Corporate stock reacquisitions create many possible conflict-of-interest situations; but public reaction to these situations, assuming prompt and adequate disclosure, could be a deterring factor.

---

[4] "Ethics for Today's Business Society," *Controller* (April, 1961), p. 193. This article contains excerpts from a speech by Thomas C. Higgins, C.P.A. Italics in original.

OPEN MARKET PURCHASE VERSUS TENDER OFFER

There is a question as to whether an open-market purchase or a tender offer is better under circumstances existing at any given time. The ethical and legal implications of this question revolve around the influence on the market price. That method of reacquisition should be used which is least disruptive to the maintenance of an orderly market. This means that the directors must consider the amount of stock to be repurchased in relation to the volume of trading in the stock. Larger repurchases should be made via a tender offer.

With an open market purchase, greater attention must be given to the disclosure problem than with a tender offer. The tender offer almost automatically tells the stockholder much important information, such as the price to be paid and the number of shares to be repurchased. Of course, the tender offer itself does not tell the stockholder whether or not the directors are acting on the basis of information that is not public knowledge. This problem exists with either method of reacquisition.

The events surrounding the recent Texas Gulf Sulphur Company ore discovery at Timmins, Ontario, highlight the importance of insider information. In April, 1965, the Securities and Exchange Commission brought suit against certain officers and directors of Texas Gulf, charging them with a violation of the 1934 Securities and Exchange Act. The SEC alleged that these officials and directors had made purchases of company stock without disclosing material facts relating to the Timmins ore discovery. Specifically, the lawsuit charged that between November 12, 1963 (when Texas Gulf officials first became aware of the extent of the discovery), and April 16, 1964 (when an announcement was promulgated), 13 individuals "purchased on the open market an aggregate of 9,100 Texas Gulf shares, bought 'calls' or options to purchase on 5,200 shares, and received options to purchase 31,200 shares at a price of about $24 a share."[5]

In discussing conflict-of-interest situations recently, the president of the New York Stock Exchange, Keith Funston, suggested that corporate officials consider purchasing shares of their own company periodically instead of sporadically and that they might also confine their purchases to a 30-day period starting a week after the release of the annual report.[6]

The main problem raised by the Texas Gulf case is the timing of the disclosure of material information. Certainly a company planning to reacquire its own stock in the open market is faced with the same type of problem. Shareholders should be informed of the average price paid for shares purchased in the open market and other significant information such as the corporate reasons for the reacquisition. It

---

[5]"Texas Gulf Sulphur Officers Accused by SEC of Profiting by Inside Data," *Wall Street Journal* (April 20, 1965), p. 3.

[6]"Funston Suggests How 'Insiders' Can Avoid Any Conflict of Interest in Stock Dealings," *Wall Street Journal* (October 27, 1965), p. 4.

EXHIBIT 13-2

MERRITT-CHAPMAN & SCOTT CORPORATION (1957-1964)

	Gross Revenue (mil.)	Net Income (mil.)	No. Shares Common (mil.)	Earnings per Share
1957	$354.3	$13.2	5.79	$2.27
1958	382.1	10.2	5.79	1.77
1959	427.5	9.0	5.82	1.55
1960	355.6	(29.7)	5.81	(5.11)
1961	318.2	5.8	5.80	1.01
1962	292.2	6.0	5.40	1.11
1963	269.4	3.9	4.86	.80
1964	177.4	4.7	2.87	1.64°

°Excluding $2.70 nonrecurring credit.
Source: *Moody's Industrial Manual (1965)*.

does not seem necessary that the company inform stockholders of the intended purchase in the open market if the number of shares to be reacquired is relatively small in relation to the number of shares currently outstanding. Even in this case, however, the completed reacquisition should be adequately disclosed to stockholders.

The four examples discussed below are intended to illustrate possible ethical problems resulting from corporate stock repurchase.

Merritt-Chapman & Scott Corporation

Merritt-Chapman & Scott Corporation (MCS) represents a case in which ethical problems may exist because of the large amount of shares repurchased in the open market relative to the volume of trading during the period prior to the repurchase. On November 20, 1964, MCS offered to buy 1.2 to 1.3 million shares of the 3,383,294 common shares outstanding as of November 10. Louis E. Wolfson, chairman of MCS, had indicated that he and his associates might tender up to 400,000 of the shares they owned.

From January 1, 1964, to November 10, 1964, purchases of MCS common stock by MCS and Revday (an 84 percent owned subsidiary of MCS) accounted for 63 percent of the MCS stock traded on the New York Stock Exchange. For the 25 trading days prior to November 10, the corresponding percentage was 94 percent. MCS's tender offer was a $19 package, including $10 in cash, a 5 percent subordinated note, due December 1, 1965, for $4.50, and a similar note due a year later for $4.50. During 1964, MCS stock had gone from a first quarter low of $11.625 to a fourth quarter high of $19.25.

Wolfson decided not to tender any shares on "the advice of tax counsel."[7]

---

[7]"Merritt-Chapman Says Its Holders Tendered About 432,000 Shares," *Wall Street Journal* (December 9, 1964), p. 15.

Other stockholders tendered 415,843 shares, all of which MCS said it would purchase. The fact that Wolfson did not tender any shares did not prevent a lawsuit from developing charging that "the purchases were designed specifically 'to benefit and unjustly enrich Mr. Wolfson and Wolfson interests.' "[8] It was also charged that the purchases tended to create an artificial market in violation of stock exchange regulations. MCS was allowed to buy the shares tendered.

Exhibit 13-2 shows gross revenue, net income, and the number of shares from 1957 to 1964 for MCS. Earnings per share in 1964 rose as one of the results of the decrease in shares outstanding. Sales decreased in 1964 because of the sale of Devoe & Raynolds to the Celanese Corporation for $60 million. Since material changes in earnings per share can result from corporate stock reacquisitions, the public needs better information on potential stock reacquisitions via the financial press as soon as is practicable.

Schenley Industries

Schenley Industries offered to buy up to 1 million of its common shares representing up to 16.7 percent of the shares then outstanding at $32 a share. This offer was made on January 27, 1965, while the common was trading at $27 a share. In announcing the tender offer, Schenley announced that "officers and directors of the corporation wouldn't be permitted to tender their own shares."[9]

A stockholder lawsuit maintained that the tender price was too high relative to the market price and that it was designed to benefit officials of the company. The complaint was dismissed and an injunction prohibiting the reacquisition lifted by a federal court in Chicago. During the preceding year, 1964, trading in Schenley stock on the NYSE accounted for approximately 2 percent monthly of the outstanding common stock. This was undoubtedly a factor in the decision to make a tender offer rather than to reacquire the shares in the open market. In determining a fair price to be paid for the tendered shares, it would have been necessary in this case to consider the alternative average cost of purchasing 1 million shares in the open market.

Union Oil-Pure Oil Merger

D. K. Ludwig, a Union Oil director and the company's largest stockholder, was opposed to the Union Oil-Pure Oil merger. This opposition was apparently a factor in Union Oil's decision to repurchase Mr. Ludwig's stock during early 1965.[10] It amounted to 14 percent

---

[8]"Merritt-Chapman Sued by 2 Holders Opposing Tender-Offer Purchases," *Wall Street Journal* (January 4, 1965), p. 6.
[9]"Schenley Asks to Buy Up to 1,000,000 Shares From Holders at $32," *Wall Street Journal* (January 28, 1965), p. 2.
[10]"Union Oil Acquires Stock of Biggest Holder Amid Word of Offer by it to Buy Pure Oil," *Wall Street Journal* (February 15, 1965), p. 28.

of the outstanding common stock.

With a private purchase such as this, there is always a danger of a conflict-of-interest situation. Adequate disclosure would be especially important in this case. The benefits of the repurchase would include the consummation of the proposed merger. Since the public was generally aware of the pending merger, the disclosure was adequate with regard to the reason for the stock repurchase. Union Oil also disclosed the exact number of shares repurchased and the price paid. The company also stated that the $35.50 per share that was paid to Ludwig was the closing price on the New York Stock Exchange the day the offer was made. The profit made by Ludwig on this transaction was also disclosed. The disclosure of these material facts greatly reduced the danger of a conflict-of-interest situation.

Burroughs Corporation

Should a corporation loan money to its officers so that they might purchase treasury stock from the company? That this is a real problem is indicated by the following quotation:

> Burroughs Corp. lent $745,075 to 14 of its top officers so they could buy Burroughs stock held in the company's treasury . . . The officers . . . gave . . . interest-bearing (4.5 percent) notes payable in ten equal installments beginning one year from the purchase of the stock . . . The company said no discounts from the median market price or any other favors were extended to officers in the stock buying.[11]

Mortimer Feuer discusses the problem of loans of this type. It is not normally a part of the business of a nonfinancial corporation to make this type of loan unless business necessitates. As Feuer states:

> . . . if loans are made to directors or officers to enable them to take advantage of business opportunities for personal gain, an even more serious (than with a loan for business purposes) conflict with ordinary principles applicable to fiduciaries is presented.[12]

Several considerations become important in analyzing these loans. One factor is the size of the loan. Fairly small salary advances can be easily defended. These loans by the Burroughs Corporation were not of this nature and must be defended in a different manner. Another consideration deals with the use of inside information (such as was claimed in the Texas Gulf Sulphur controversy). Since top officers normally have information that is not available to stockholders, a conflict-of-interest situation might easily develop as a result of sizable loans to officers. A third problem exists regarding any profit made by directors as a result

---

[11]"Burroughs Lends $745,075 To 14 of Its Top Officers," *Wall Street Journal* (April 13, 1965), p. 8.

[12]Mortimer Feuer, *Personal Liabilities of Corporate Officers and Directors* (Prentice-Hall, Inc., 1961), p. 131.

of these loans. Should the corporation receive part of this profit and, if so, how much?

There are two leading legal cases that help with the ethical implications of corporate loans to officers. The first case, *Bailey* v. *Jacobs*, reaches the conclusion that if these funds do not serve any purpose for the corporation, the directors have violated the precept of using these funds only for the common good.[13] Using this reasoning, the loans by the Burroughs Corporation would have to be rationalized on the basis of executive compensation and the corporate benefits to be derived from having well qualified, well paid executives manage the corporate affairs.

The second case, *Felsenheld* v. *Block Bros. Tobacco Co.*, reaches a slightly different conclusion.[14] The court held that it was not inherently wrong (legally) for excess funds to be loaned to corporate officials provided that: (1) the funds could not have been safely invested elsewhere at a more substantial yield and (2) the matter was decided by directors not interested in the loan. The loans by Burroughs carried an interest rate of 4.5 percent; but other factors need to be considered. As indicated previously, the rather intangible benefits to the corporation from having satisfied employees should be considered. In addition, the prime interest rate is probably not the most suitable basis for comparison if the company is experiencing growth and acceptable capital investment opportunities are available.

SUMMARY

The growth of stock reacquisitions in the past three or four years has created the need to examine the relevant ethical principles. The law provides certain minimum standards of ethical conduct, but the conscientious executive is interested in doing more than the minimum required by the law.

Adequate accounting disclosure is an important consideration in such financial transactions. Our inquiry indicates that disclosures of corporate stock reacquisitions in the financial press have not been common. Executives should give more consideration to the public relations aspect of such an important activity, if only to quell speculative rumors when a sizable amount of funds is involved. The increase in stock reacquisition indicates a greater awareness of the possible financial consequences. Ethical considerations should receive the same attention. These include not only adequate disclosure but also the avoidance of conflict-of-interest situations, and a careful evaluation of the method of repurchase in relation to the amount of stock to be reacquired.

---

[13]325 Pa. 187, 194; 189 Atl. 320, 325 (1937).
[14]119 W. Va. 167, 175-76; 192 S.E. 545, 549 (1937).

14. A CASE FOR DROPPING DIVIDENDS*

CAROL J. LOOMIS†

Earlier this year, General Public Utilities Corp., No. 11 on *Fortune's* list of the 50 largest utilities, notified its 79,000 stockholders that it was considering adoption of a radically different dividend plan that seemed to offer some large advantages to just about everyone concerned. The company proposed to substitute stock dividends for three of its quarterly cash dividends. Simultaneously it offered to sell the shares (with minimal brokerage costs) for any stockholder who wanted to realize the same cash income he had been getting previously. The advantage to the shareholder—at least to any shareholder paying income taxes—would be a sharp reduction in his tax liability: he would be taxed on his stock dividends only if he decided to sell them and then only on that part of his proceeds that represented profit. Furthermore, any profits would be taxed at capital-gains rates (assuming the stockholder had owned his original stock for at least six months), whereas the cash dividends would, of course, be taxed at the higher rates applying to regular income. All told, it looked as if the plan might result in an immediate tax saving to the shareholders of at least $4 million annually—and probably more.

The advantages to G.P.U. itself looked equally imposing. The company is going to need enormous amounts of money for capital expenditures over the next few years—upwards of $200 million annually—and it needs to hang on to every cent it can. The elimination of three quarterly cash dividends would save the company nearly $30 million annually. Lacking that money and already burdened by a high debt ratio, the company knew it would simply have to raise an equivalent amount by selling new common stock. As it happens, G.P.U. is obligated to sell its stock through rights offerings to its present stockholders. Thus, any sale of stock would have put the company in the position of asking its stockholders, in effect, to reinvest the dollars they had received in dividends—except that those dollars would have been depleted by the payment of income taxes. Considering all that, G.P.U. President William G. Kuhns figured that it made more sense for the company just to hang on to the dividends in the first place.

Unfortunately a lot of the company's stockholders didn't see it that way. Right after G.P.U.'s plan become generally known, the company's stock, which sells in the mid-20's, dropped nearly two points. And then the letters began to come in. Some were approving, but a dismaying number blistered

*Reprinted from the June 15, 1968 issue of *Fortune Magazine*, pp. 81 ff., by special permission; © 1968 Time, Inc.
†Research analyst, *Fortune Magazine*.

the company and its officers for even considering such a move. One stockholder called Kuhns "a hypocritical ass"; another suggested that the president ought to see a psychiatrist. Worse yet, a large number of institutional
holders of the stock—in particular, bank trust departments—put themselves
on record as being so resolutely against the plan that its implementation
would probably impel them to sell their stock. Some of the banks pointed
out that they were committed, in their handling of most trusts, to seek
"income," and that, in their particular states, they were barred by law from
using stock dividends to get it. Other banks had far less substantive objections. In any case, it began to look as if up to 20 percent of G.P.U.'s stock
might hit the market if the company persisted with the plan. Kuhns and the
board of directors decided that neither they nor the stockholders could
stand that. And so the plan was abandoned.

HOW TO BUY EARNINGS PER SHARE

The case for cutting dividend payments at G.P.U. is of a kind that
might be made at many other companies. Under today's tax laws, any
taxpaying stockholder who gets his returns through dividends rather than
capital gains is odds on to come out second best. Furthermore, corporate
demands for capital tend to be extraordinary these days, and for many
companies, money going out in dividends is money they need badly to
finance their growth. In fact, these companies must turn to the capital
markets just to raise the funds they pay out in dividends. Some companies,
like G.P.U., end up getting their money through sales of common stock.
Others take on debt, which is now to be had only at interest rates of around
7 percent. The interest, of course, is tax-deductible, but, even so, the charges
take a big bite out of earnings—a bite that could have been avoided had
those dividends been retained by the company.

Some companies, it is true, are not financially strained—a few are even
cash-rich—and can easily afford to pay dividends. But even for these
fortunate few, it seems likely that dividend payments are a poor way to
benefit the stockholders. The best way would be to employ the funds in
productive investments. After all, it is generally accepted in this era of
"conglomeration" that corporate investment horizons are virtually unlimited, that any lack of opportunities within a company's own industry
need not constrict its growth. It can go into any business it wants; alternatively, it can buy stock in another company. And finally, even if none of
these moves seems right, there is still a better way to reward stockholders
than with dividends. The company can simply buy in its own stock—a
procedure that, by reducing the number of shares outstanding, increases
the earnings on those that remain. Any stockholder wanting to realize income would simply sell some of his stock. He would get a price reflecting
both the new, higher earnings and the presence of his own company in the
market as a heavy buyer.

SKIP THE SURPRISES

The general case, then, is that dividend income received means capital-gains opportunities forgone. Most stockholders will admit the logic of this case and will declare themselves unequivocally on the side of capital gains—in general. Even in particular cases, many investors make it clear by their actions that they attach no real importance to dividends. For example, most of those who keep their stock in *Street name* allow dividends to pile up in their accounts. Ordinarily, they get around at some point to reinvesting the money in stock. About 57 percent of the dividend income received by mutual-fund shareholders is reinvested automatically—even though these shareholders include many relatively small investors whose dependence on dividends is ordinarily assumed to be great. Then, too, as just about everyone knows, most of the attention in the mutual-fund field these days is focused on *performance* funds, whose interest in dividends is almost nonexistent. Among the mutual funds started since the beginning of 1967, less than 10 percent have specified dividend income as one of their objectives.

Yet it is a peculiar fact of life that many stockholders who acknowledge that dividends generally eat into capital gains will vigorously resist any attempt by their own companies to cut their dividends. In other words, they will not concede that what is good for them generally is also good for them specifically. A company's cash dividend, once established, becomes almost sacrosanct, and any talk of reducing it, no matter for what reasons, means that the company's stock is likely to fall. Said a trust officer at a large New York bank recently: "We're not very interested in dividends around here. We're capital-gains oriented. But I'd say this about dividends— we don't want any surprises."

Obviously, then, any sweeping move by corporations toward lower dividend payments would entail some practical difficulties. The move would surely have to be accompanied by a major reeducation program aimed at persuading stockholders that dividend cuts are bullish, not bearish. There is also some danger that any such move might lead to a change in the tax laws, possibly one imposing a higher tax on capital gains. Right now the government realizes more than $5 billion annually from taxes on dividends, and it would clearly not give up this revenue without demanding something in return. Some proponents of lower dividends have argued that greater retention of earnings by corporations would so increase their profits, and thus their tax liabilities, that any related reduction in dividend taxes could be tolerated. The Treasury does not seem to agree.

For the time being, however, the government is holding its peace and not objecting to those (admittedly few) corporate policies against paying cash dividends. Some companies now implement this policy with the help of a brand-new kind of security (so far known only as "special") that looks like a common stock, has the rights of a common stock, and yet exists mainly to allow its holders to get their returns through capital gains rather then dividends. So far there are very few specimens of this stock around but—as we shall see—more seem sure to appear.

Taking the 500 industrials as a whole, the number of companies that, as a matter of policy, pay no cash dividends on their common stocks is still small but growing somewhat. Ten years ago, in the list reporting on 1957, there were only 31 companies not paying a cash dividend, and of these most had been forced into that position by adversity. In all, there were only six companies on the list that seem to have had a clear policy of not paying cash dividends. But on the 1967 list there are 16 companies of that kind (there are 23 others not paying dividends, most having experienced adversity). Many of these 16 have been holdouts against cash dividends throughout their history. In addition, the 1967 list contains a handful of companies that, though they have not been so bold as to cut their dividends altogether, have frozen them at relatively low levels. One of these is Burroughs, which, though its earnings have more than tripled in the last three years (to $4.25 per share in 1967), has kept its annual payout at only $1 per share.

TWO WAYS TO A PAYOFF

The case against cash dividends is plainly supported by those 16 companies on the 1967 list. They would have made a rather interesting stock portfolio over the years. One of the companies is Seagram, which is special in that it has only one stockholder, Distillers Corp.-Seagram. The others: Ampex, Coastal States Gas Producing, Control Data, Crowell Collier & Macmillan, Crown Cork & Seal, Iowa Beef Packers, Eastern Gas & Fuel, General Instrument, Itek, Walter Kidde, Litton, Phillips-Van Heusen, Teledyne, Varian, and Whittaker. These 15 companies recently had a median price-earnings ratio of 30, a number suggesting forcibly that the market regards most of them as growth situations. (The p/e prevailing on Standard & Poor's 425 industrials is 19.)

Economists, however, have long striven to make some broader points concerning the relationship between dividends and stock prices. One main question has been this: What is the relative importance of retained earnings and dividends in determining a stock's p/e? Underlying this question is the proposition that both retained earnings and dividends convey a return to the stockholder. Dividends, of course, are a direct payoff. Retained earnings, on the other hand, increase the book value of the stockholder's business and, more important in today's markets, increase the power of the business to produce additional earnings. As these are capitalized in the market, the value of the stockholder's shares increases. The question, then, is which method of payment do most investors prefer?

Considering the tax laws, one might suppose the answer was retained earnings and the capital gains resulting from them. It has been clear for many years that many shareholders, nevertheless, prefer dividends. Benjamin Graham and D. L. Dodd, in the first (1934) edition of their immensely influential *Security Analysis,* observed that a dollar's worth of dividends had about four times as much effect on market values as did a dollar's worth of retained earnings. Taxes, of course, have risen since then. However, various academicians, notably Myron Gordon of the University of Rochester, have recently done studies that seem to support Graham's and Dodd's general findings, if not their 4-to-1 relationship. Gordon says that for most companies (all but those showing "super" growth) generous dividend payouts tend to lift price-earnings ratios, and niggardly payouts, to depress them. Gordon goes on to suggest that stockholders are right in preferring dividends; he believes that it is rational to prefer the certainty of a dividend payment now to the uncertainty of a possible future return (realized through growth) flowing out of retained earnings.

Putting aside for a moment the question of what most stockholders *should* prefer, we may note that there are intense disagreements about what most of them in fact prefer. Indeed, the whole question of dividends and stock prices has produced a kind of academic sparring match, in which one authority after another has come under attack. One of Gordon's most distinguished critics is Franco Modigliani, of the Massachusetts Institute of Technology. "Gordon's mathematical models are all wrong," says Modigliani. "He builds things into them that say dividends count, and then he goes on to prove that dividends count."

ONE THIRD FOR THE FEDS

Modigliani's own findings, worked out in collaboration with Merton H. Miller of the University of Chicago, are that dividends do not count—i.e., he contends that investors are essentially indifferent to the level of dividends and that, therefore, they have virtually no effect on price-earnings ratios. (Gordon says that Modigliani's and Miller's models are poorly designed and their conclusions invalid.) Still a third view has been propounded by Irwin Friend of the University of Pennsylvania and Marshall Puckett of the Federal Reserve Bank of New York. Studying data for 1956 and 1958, they saw some indication that in nongrowth industries (they included food and steel in this category) investors tended to value dividends somewhat higher than retained earnings. But the opposite, they felt, was true for growth industries—identified as electronics, utilities, and chemicals.

As some of the formulations above suggest, the case against dividends rests very largely on the huge toll that income taxes take out of them. The toll is particularly great because so many dividends go to people in high tax brackets. As [an] illustration, consider the government's figures for 1966 (the latest available), which show that about $15.2 billion in dividend income was reported on individuals' tax returns and that about $13.3 billion of this came down to "adjusted gross income" on taxable returns—i.e., this amount remained after reported income has been reduced by the dividend exclusion (up to $100) that every taxpayer is allowed. Of the $13.3 billion, about $8.7 billion, or 65 percent, showed up on the returns of the relatively few taxpayers reporting income of $20,000 and up. Indeed, no less than $3.1 billion, or 23 percent of the taxable total, belonged to the few thousand tax-payers reporting income of $100,000 or more. Since tax rates at the $100,000 level are 62 percent (for a joint return) and at $200,000 are the maximum 70 percent, close to two thirds of this $3.1 billion can be figured to have gone to the government (the *federal* government, that is; many stockholders, of course, also have state and/or city income taxes to worry about).

Overall, the government took slightly over $5 billion, or 33 percent of that original $15.2 billion of reported dividends. By contrast, the effective rate on long-term capital gains has been estimated by the government to be 21.6 percent. This figure is derived from data showing that upwards of one third of all such gains are taxed at the maximum 25 percent rate, which applies solely to people in a tax bracket of 50 percent or higher—those re-porting $52,000 of taxable income on a joint return. Taxpayers in lower brackets pay capital-gains rates that are, in effect, one half of their regular rates.

Some stockholders, of course, are not "individuals" and, therefore, have different—generally very different—tax considerations to think about. Corporations, for example, receive several billion dollars in dividends annually (typically, about one third the amount going to individuals), and they have a strong reason to prefer this kind of investment payoff—i.e., most are allowed to exclude 85 percent of their dividends from taxable income, while they are taxed fully on capital gains (though only at capital-gains rates). Several more billions in dividends go annually to various kinds of institutional investors that pay no taxes at all, notably foundations, educa-tional institutions, and corporate pension funds. The first two of these tend to want dividends, viewing them as spendable money, which they need; and though some are coming around, many still resist spending their capital gains. Most pension funds, on the other hand, have had considerably more money coming in than has been going out, and so they normally reinvest their dividends, incurring commission costs in the process. Pre-sumably, the pension funds would just as soon have the money retained by the corporations involved.

A COST OF ZERO

But *all* investors have one good reason to forgo dividends insofar as they originate at companies having growth prospects and continuing needs for new capital—which, after all, essentially describes the kinds of companies that most investors look for. New capital acquired from external sources is both expensive and hard to get; new capital acquired through retained earnings is both cheap and readily obtained, and for this reason stockholders should wish to see it used.

The word "cheap" applied to retained earnings is controversial. If you believe, with Professor Gordon, that high retention of earnings generally depresses a stock's p/e ratio and, therefore, levies a "cost" on the stock-holders (and on the company as well, should it desire to sell additional stock) then retention might be viewed as expensive. This issue, as has been noted, is unresolved. But there is nothing at all debatable about the fact that retained earnings are "cheap" in the sense that their use involves neither the payment of interest (as debt does) nor the allocation of earnings to new shares (as the sale of common stock does). They, consequently, produce higher earnings per share than other kinds of capital.

Since retained earnings, in this particular sense, have a cost of zero and since their use does not involve the issuance of additional shares, *anything* made on this capital increases earnings per share. Some economists, acknowledging this general principle, have, nevertheless, argued that cost-free capital may sometimes be undesirable. They contend that it may make managements sloppy in their investment decisions; these economists say, for example, that a management demanding a certain return from new projects to be financed with capital obtained externally will often settle for a more modest return on projects to be financed with retained earnings. Logically, the economists go on, retained earnings should not be committed to the business unless the return expected on them exceeds the stockholders' *opportunity cost*—i.e., the return they could expect to earn on these funds as individuals if they had the funds in hand and could deploy them where-ever the investment opportunities seemed most promising. The difficulty with this approach is that most stockholders can get their hands on these earnings only by paying income taxes, an outlay that leaves them with con-siderably less capital to work with than was originally available to the com-pany and that greatly handicaps them in any contest with the company regarding rate of return.

TAKE IT IN, PAY IT OUT

Take, for example, that odd situation at General Public Utilities. The company's retained earnings in the last few years can be assumed to have been producing an after-tax return of around 11 percent—i.e., the company earns that much on its stockholders' equity and the rate of return has actually been rising, not declining, under the thrust of new capital. Now suppose, to simplify matters drastically, that the company has $1 million in earnings and that its stockholders are all in a low, 20 percent tax bracket (in fact, the average tax rate paid by G.P.U.'s stockholders is probably a lot higher). If G.P.U. retains the $1 million, it may expect to earn 11 percent, or $110,000, on the money. If it pays the $1 million out, its stockholders, after paying their 20 percent income taxes, will be left with $800,000. To earn $110,000 on that money (that is, to come out at least even with G.P.U.), the stock-holders must find an investment yielding 13.75 percent. This higher per-centage return is likely to be available only at great risk.

As this illustration suggests, a stockholder is bound to be a loser if he takes dividends out of a company, pays his taxes, and then puts the money right back into the same company. Yet that is, in effect, what many of G.P.U.'s real-life stockholders have done at one time or another. For example, in the company's last stock offering, in late 1966, over 50 percent of its stockholders exercised their rights to subscribe to new shares. Considering this, the stockholders' resistance to G.P.U.'s proposed change in dividend policy seems particularly irrational.

Corporations also manage to do some pretty odd things with their money, and one of these is to pay dividends out of borrowed money. Most corporations doing this don't like to think of it that way; instead, they would say that dividends are paid out of earnings and that the money they borrow goes for capital expenditures. But it is obvious that if there were no dividends, earnings could go for capital expenditures, and much of the borrowing would become unnecessary (a thought that naturally discomfits commercial and investment bankers, who earn their living by arranging for corporations to borrow). Indeed, Federal Reserve figures for the country's nonfinancial corporations, taken as a whole, show a close relationship between the amount of money raised externally (through loans and sales of securities) and the amount paid out in dividends: over the last ten years these corporations acquired $141 billion in new money from external sources, and they spent $127 billion on dividends.

Since there are some corporations that borrow but do not pay dividends and some that pay dividends but do not borrow, it is plainly not correct to think of all companies covered by the Fed's figures as having, in effect, borrowed to pay dividends. But many individual companies have been doing precisely that. In the last five years Alcoa has added $293 million to its debt and paid $156 million in common dividends, having raised its payout four times during that period. Reynolds Metals' record for the same years is $252 million in new money borrowed, $55 million paid out, and three dividend increases. Just in the last few months, higher dividend rates have been announced by: Standard Oil of Indiana, which in the last two years has been to the bond market twice for a total of $375 million, all of it acquired at an interest cost of more than 6 percent; Chase Manhattan Bank, whose increase came simultaneously with an announcement that it would sell $150 million in convertible notes by means of a rights offering to its stockholders; and Bethlehem Steel, whose dividend increase came after a year in which it had borrowed $150 million in the bond market, experienced a 24 percent decline in earnings, and so drained working capital that it was considering selling commercial paper for the first time.

If the personal income tax did not exist and if it did not take such a whack out of dividends, there would be a lot to be said for companies' borrowing and passing the proceeds along to their stockholders, for corporations can usually borrow at better terms and with greater ease than can their stockholders, and thus corporate debt theoretically represents the best way for stockholders to get leverage—assuming, of course, they're willing to have it. But the tax penalty is so great as to make most dividends uneconomic, with or without leverage.

THE PRICE OF CERTAINTY

For some companies, dividends represent an extravagance that may jeopardize their future—and that may ultimately cause the stockholders to realize that they have paid a very dear price for the "certainty" that, Professor Gordon argues, makes dividends today more attractive than earnings tomorrow. Consider, for instance, American Motors. After its formation in 1954, it recorded three years of big losses and then, in 1958, hit the jackpot with its compact car. Only a few months later it began paying dividends. Many sophisticated investors were shocked; they felt that the company should be using the money to modernize its facilities and prepare otherwise for competition with Detroit's Big Three. By the early 1960's the company was battling to stay even, and by late 1965 the losses were back—and the dividends gone. Right now the company is burdened by debt, its outlook is clouded, and it might be supposed its executives had other things to think about than dividends. But Chairman Roy D. Chapin Jr. recently said he had every intention of making American Motors a "profitable, dividend-paying" company again.

When executives are asked why their companies borrow to pay dividends or why they pay them at all, they often insist that the stockholders want it that way. Most of them seem unaware that this proposition is under fire from some economists. But even aside from the findings of Modigliani and others, it may reasonably be asked why managements, which seldom rely on stockholders for advice about corporate policy, should bend so readily to their wishes in this area.

A few managements have fought dividends in recent years. Eastern Gas & Fuel Associates, a Boston industrial company mainly producing coal, used to be known on Wall Street principally as a payer of good dividends and a substantial holder of Norfolk & Western Railway stock. In 1962 a new management, headed by Eli Goldston, a lawyer who had recently turned businessman, took control of the company and soon after proposed to do away with cash dividends.

That was quite a shock to all those stockholders who had been cherishing Eastern Gas for its reliable dividend. But Goldston had something special in mind for them. Norfolk & Western paid a nice dividend, and so Goldston offered his stockholders a chance to exchange their Eastern Gas shares for the N. & W. shares owned by the company. About 35 percent of Eastern Gas stockholders accepted the exchange offer. (This proportion might have been even lower had it not been for one circumstance unique to the Eastern Gas case: Goldston himself had only a skimpy track record in business, and any stockholders who stayed with him were obviously taking a chance.) The other 65 percent were presumably attracted by Goldston's pledge "to take the cash that went into dividends and run like hell with it."

And that's what he did. He poured money into modernization, went after long-term contracts for the sale of coal, got rid of some unprofitable divisions, and whenever he had money to spare and the price looked right, bought in his own stock. The pared-down company began to show some sparkling earnings gains, and the stock market wasted no time in acknowledging them. By last year earnings were more than four times their 1962 level, and by late last month a share of stock that in early 1963 was worth $7.50 (adjusted for splits and stock dividends) was up to $38. That's an increase of more than 400 percent.

And Norfolk & Western stock? It was 109 when the exchange offer took place in early 1963, and late last month it was 96 (in 1964 it got up to 150). In between, the stockholders have received $33.50 in dividends, which, when offset against the $13 in market depreciation, gives the stockholders who switched a gain of 19 percent (not counting such profits as they might have realized by reinvesting their dividends along the way).

A SMALLER PIECE OF PIE

When he abandoned cash dividends, Goldston replaced them with stock dividends. Stock dividends have some limited uses, but many companies—and Eastern Gas appears to be among them—employ them less for their utility than as a sort of sop to the stockholders, many of whom tend to think they get something of value when stock dividends are handed out. Actually, about all they get is some pieces of paper and some bookkeeping problems. For, in the familiar analogy, a stock dividend does nothing but divide the pie into a greater number of pieces, leaving the stockholder with no more than he had in the first place. Some managements argue that this isn't exactly so—that small stock dividends (3 or 4 percent) enable a stockholder who wants income to realize it by selling them while still getting capital-gains treatment. This argument is invalid as far as most stockholders are concerned, since they could achieve the same end by selling shares out of their original holdings.

Stock dividends have just one real advantage. They furnish, at least in some states, a means for trusts, which normally must be managed to provide income, to hold stocks that do not pay cash dividends. For example, in New York the laws say that, unless the trust instrument specifies otherwise, all stock dividends of less than 6 percent shall be considered income. The situation, however, is different in Massachusetts, whose laws specify that stock dividends may *not* be treated as income. A lot of Boston banks got that point across to General Public Utilities when it was considering its new dividend plan.

Until it was knocked out of the box by this and other objections, G.P.U. was planning to make stock dividends especially attractive to shareholders who planned to sell them. They would have done it through the company, which, by pooling orders, could have sold the stock at the advantageous commission prices applying to round lots.

WHILE THE GOVERNMENT WAS NAPPING

One imaginative effort to minimize cash payouts has been under way for over a decade at Citizens Utilities, a medium-size company ($77 million in assets) that has headquarters in Stamford, Connecticut, and operations in ten states. It also has a Series A common stock that is absolutely unique and that came into being one day when the government was napping. That was in the mid-1950's, when the company's president, Richard Rosenthal, got the idea that his stockholders should be allowed to choose between cash dividends and stock dividends—and that they should all get just what they wanted.

To carry out this plan, he proposed to create two classes of common stock, identical except that the first would pay stock, the second would pay cash, and the first would be convertible into the second on a share-for-share basis. The dividends were to be of equal value—e.g., if the cash dividend during a year amounted to 4 percent of market value, then the stock dividend would also run to 4 percent. But to make sure that the stockholders who chose stock dividends would not be taxed on them at the time of declaration (as the recipients of cash dividends are), Rosenthal needed a ruling from the Internal Revenue Service. When he asked for its approval, something remarkable happened: he got it.

Then, after another favorable ruling on a somewhat similar request made by a small Ohio trucking company, there was a flood of other requests for rulings. But I.R.S. rather belatedly realized that its action put the government in danger of losing large amounts of taxes on dividends. And so it adopted a new position: that securities of the Citizens' Series A type involved an "election" by the stockholders as to the kind of distribution they would receive and that, therefore, their stock dividends were taxable. Following standard procedure, it published a set of proposed regulations that would have made this position official. But many lawyers said from the outset that the I.R.S. position was untenable and that it would lose if it came to court. The I.R.S. apparently began worrying about that, too. At any rate, it never got around to pushing its regulations beyond the "proposed" stage, and after 12 years they still exist only in that form. Nevertheless, with rulings denied, not a single additional company got up the nerve to create its own version of the Citizens Utilities Series A.

But Rosenthal, clutching his ruling, shoved his own recapitalization ahead. As it turned out, about three fourths of the company's shares were exchanged for the Series A, which paid stock, and the remainder for the Series B, which paid cash. There have since, of course, been some conversions of Series A to Series B. But, nevertheless, the Series A holders still have about three fourths of Citizens' stock. For every year, as each Series A shareholder gets his stock dividends, he increases his proportional interest in the company. In the meantime, because the company itself has been exceedingly prosperous (between 1957 and 1967 its earnings quadrupled), both stocks have done tremendously well. The Series A stock, however, being the conduit for capital gains, rates—as it should—a premium in the market. Recently, its price (both stocks trade over-the-counter) was about 26, while the Series B was selling at 23.

FOUR STOCKS THAT ACCUMULATE

Another way of minimizing cash payouts is provided by an intriguing new kind of security called a "special stock," or sometimes an "accumulating stock." The first of these securities was introduced earlier this year by International Utilities Corp., an expanding conglomerate now realizing some $450 million operating revenues annually. There are only three other such stocks around, and all of them are the creations of James J. Ling.

The accumulating stocks are similar in a number of respects to Citizens Utilities' Series A stock: they share voting rights with the common, they are convertible into common, and they are geared to give their holders capital gains instead of cash dividends. But there are a number of sizable differences—enough so, indeed, that the issuing companies feel confident (or at least say they do) that the accumulations connected to the stocks will not, for tax purposes, be treated like dividends. Unlike the Citizens' securities, there is no distribution related directly to the value of the cash dividends paid on the common. Instead, these stocks gain in value by virtue of a conversion ratio that improves, or accumulates, every year. In this respect, these securities are similar to Litton Industries' relatively new participating preference stock, which also offers improving convertibility. (But Litton pays no cash dividends on its common, and if it did, it would also have to pay them on its participating stock; so the situation is basically different.)

A SURPRISING DISCOUNT

Some details about International Utilities' new stock, which it calls Special Series A, will illustrate some of the wrinkles built into these new securities. I.U.'s stock came into being as the result of a deal whereby the company acquired General Waterworks Corp., also a conglomerate. The two companies shared the same top management: both had as chairman Howard Butcher III, also senior partner of the Philadelphia stockbrokerage firm of Butcher & Sherrerd; and as president, John Seabrook. I.U. pays a cash dividend (right now it is at a $1.11 annual rate), but General Waterworks paid none—nor did Butcher and Seabrook want themselves or their stockholders to start getting dividends when they gave up their General Waterworks stock in exchange for I.U. shares. In addition, they wanted I.U. to have a capitalization that had something to offer just about any kind of stockholder, including those who didn't want cash dividends. The solution was the Series A stock, for which all the General Waterworks common was exchanged. It would appear that a stock of this kind represents about the only acceptable way for a company paying cash dividends to acquire one that is by choice not doing so.

Between now and 1970, the Series A stock is convertible into the common on a one-for-one basis, but at that point the conversion ratio changes to 1.0816 shares of common per shares of Series A. After that, the conversion ratio increases annually by 4 percent until 1988, when the maximum ratio of 2.1911 shares of common per Series A share is reached (and automatic conversion takes place). The effect is that of an annual 4 percent stock dividend.

After long negotiations with the New York Stock Exchange, which tends to be leery of new and strange securities, I.U. listed its Series A stock in March, and to nearly everybody's surprise it proceeded to sell at a slight discount to the regular common, which is also listed. The discount was a surprise because by 1970 the Series A stock will *have* to sell at no less than an 8.16 percent premium over the common (because of the 1.0816 conversion ratio). It is possible that this discount may be explained by the fact that 1970 is still some time away or perhaps by the fact that the features of the Series A stock are not widely understood.

GALLOPING CONVERTIBILITY

Jim Ling's three stocks, not surprisingly, add some wrinkles to I.U.'s wrinkles. One of the stocks belongs to Braniff Airways, which may be viewed as a subsidiary once removed of Ling-Temco-Vought's, i.e., L-T-V controls Greatamerica Corp., which in turn controls Braniff. Ling conceived Braniff's stock, which is called a Class A, as a means of saving Braniff money; like most airlines, Braniff is strapped for capital. But it, nevertheless, had been paying dividends, most of them to Greatamerica, which owned over 80 percent of the company's stock. Ling figured that those payments were needless and could be eliminated if Greatamerica exchanged its common for a newly created Class A stock that would pay stock dividends (2 percent to begin with, 3 percent later). The exchange offer was, of course, also made to Braniff's other stockholders, but Ling made no effort to encourage them to accept. The offering material for the new Class A stated that Braniff did not anticipate listing the stock on an exchange—a declaration that was enough to ward off all but a very few stockholders. As of last month, though the Class A stock had been in existence for several weeks, there was no public market in it.

One of Ling's other stocks is a so-called Class A belonging to National Car Rental System, also a subsidiary once removed of L-T-V's. It was offered this spring to National's stockholders (including Greatamerica, which owned about 60 percent of the shares) in exchange for their regular common. Like Braniff's Class A, it is to be traded over-the-counter, but recently it, too, lacked a market there. Ling's third stock, however, seems likely to have a more conspicuous existence. It is a Class AA belonging to Ling-Temco-Vought itself, and it was being offered at the beginning of the month as this article went to press. In this case, the exchange offer was being made to both the company's common shareholders and to those holding one class of its preferred.

L-T-V's Class AA stock is a wonderfully esoteric security and involves arrangements that perhaps only Ling could have conceived. For example, any common stockholder accepting the offer will start off behind: that is, his new shares of Class AA (which he will have got on a one-for-one basis) will initially be convertible only into .75 shares of common. After that, however, he catches up in a gallop, getting not only a very rapid increase in convertibility but also annual stock dividends of 3 percent. A lot of sleep has no doubt been lost by investors trying to decide whether to bite. Also, down at the Big Board, where Ling would like the stock to be traded, they're *really* looking this one over.

Neither Ling's stocks nor International Utilities Series A have lacked for attention elsewhere. A lot of other companies are interested in the idea, and it seems inevitable that more accumulating stocks will appear. For this reason the Internal Revenue Service and the Treasury Department have been looking, too; they know quite well that if this kind of stock takes hold, the government's worries about collecting taxes on dividends are going to become real. It also seems likely that if the stocks are a success, quite a few companies will do something about dividends on their regular common stocks. Well, maybe.

What the 500 Pay Out

Most of the companies in FORTUNE's 500 list follow a "middle course" in their dividend policy: last year about 340 of them paid out between 31 and 70 percent of their earnings per common share in cash dividends. An analysis of the same 500 companies for the previous year, 1966, shows a comparable pattern but with a slight shift to the left—i.e., percentage pay-outs in 1966 were somewhat lower than in 1967. Last year's higher ratios were not the result of any widespread move toward higher dividends but rather of the drop in profits. It is typical of companies to maintain existing dividends even though earnings turn down.

The 39 companies that do not pay cash dividends include some that don't believe in them (e.g., Litton, Teledyne) and some that can't afford them (American Motors, Wheeling Steel). At the other end of the spectrum are companies whose dividends exceeded earnings, either because the earnings were depressed (Ford, Allis-Chalmers) or nonexistent (Fairchild Camera, Admiral). In between these two extremes are a few companies that pay only nominal dividends—say, 5 to 10 percent of earnings—so as to qualify themselves for purchase in ten states having laws prohibiting certain institutions (insurance companies and/or banks) from buying stocks that do not pay cash dividends. The chart does not take into account any stock

FIGURE 14-4

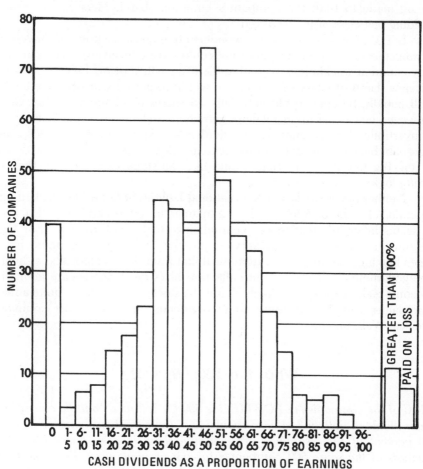

dividends paid by companies; there were 26 that last year paid a combination of cash and stock, and ten paying stock alone.

Similar distribution charts for the various "fifty" lists in this issue would show the merchandisers spread out in a pattern similar to that of the 500: the transportation companies leaning toward lower payouts, with thirty of them below 50 percent; the banks overwhelmingly bunched in the middle; and the utilities just as overwhelmingly bunched somewhat above the middle (31 paid out between 56 and 70 percent of earnings). A similar analysis of the insurance list is not possible because of the large definitional problems in calculating their "earnings" and "dividends."

PART V. LONG-TERM FINANCING

Long-term financing can take many forms. The readings in this section present some of the more timely subjects concerned with long-term financing. The articles provide the reader with an insight into some real-life problems which are faced by financial administrators.

Professor Oswald D. Bowlin is concerned primarily with measuring the interest cost savings through refunding. He treats debt refunding as a special case in capital budgeting akin to lease financing. He recommends that when the present value method is used, ". . . future interest savings from refunding should be discounted at the cost of debt, normally the net yield on the refunding bond." A detailed description of the refunding operation is presented. Basic problems analyzed include those arising when the refunding bonds have a later maturity than the refunded bonds. A review of the various approaches to the measurement of interest savings recommended by several noted authors is presented, and various points of disagreement are analyzed. A case is made for using the cost of debt in discounting future interest savings. The results of an empirical study of returns from refunding by public utilities during 1962-1963 are analyzed.

Mr. Anthony H. Meyer examines, from the corporate financial viewpoint, the major considerations in designing a convertible preferred stock when a firm is in a position to issue or receive them in a merger situation. One of the prime questions to be answered is, What will they (convertible preferred stocks) sell for in the market place and why? This question is important because the price of an acquisition financed with convertible preferred is the market value which the issue will command, and both the issuer and the recipient have to reach an agreement on what that value is likely to be. A discussion of the various items such as investment value and conversion value follows.

Mr. Meyer discusses the features that make convertible preferred popular in acquisitions. The topics covered include: (1) minimizing dilution, (2) tailoring the dividend so as to satisfy the seller's desires without altering the buyer's dividend policy, and (3) the effect on the common stock price. Also, the controversial topics, the changes in financial reporting of convertibles and earnings per share reporting, are discussed in detail. The author presents specific steps to be followed in designing the issue to meet desired objectives. The article vividly portrays the many ramifications in designing a convertible preferred issue.

Professor Elliott L. Atamian focuses on those protective covenants which are referred to in trade jargon as "the negative covenants" and which vitally restrict managerial decisions. The article is based on a sample of mutual life insurance companies selected for a variety of specific reasons. The seven specific covenants discussed are the negative pledge, additional indebtedness, investments, sinking funds, dividends, mergers, and working capital clauses. The author points out that despite the importance of these covenants, many financial managers simply are not familiar with them. The author concludes that, in general, although the lender seeks all the protection he can obtain, the covenants do not appear to be unduly restrictive. In some instances, borrowers are able to bargain for less stringent restrictions, and because of the *trade off* which takes place, it is suggested that the borrower be represented by an able intermediary.

Mr. Ernest Bloch relates the problems of pricing a security issue in competitive underwriting. An actual case is used to illustrate the process. In this particular case, the offering was quite sizable and the decision was made by an underwriting syndicate. The author takes the reader step-by-step from the first informal price meeting through the various other meetings to the post mortems. The discussion concerning the marketing strategy, syndicate tactics, and the final price meeting present the reader with an unusual opportunity to live through the competitive underwriting process.

15. THE REFUNDING DECISION: ANOTHER SPECIAL CASE IN CAPITAL BUDGETING*

OSWALD D. BOWLIN†

INTRODUCTION

Business firms may refund their outstanding debt for a number of reasons, e.g., to extend maturity or to eliminate onerous covenants in the indenture. The principal concern here, however, is with refunding for the purpose of reducing interest costs. Techniques used by business firms to measure the interest savings from refunding debt at lower coupon rates vary widely and give very different results. Teachers and researchers in business finance have made little progress in reducing the confusion surrounding this problem, despite the fact that the monetary benefits from refunding are considerably easier to estimate than those obtained from investments in operating assets. Hopefully, this paper will eliminate some of the confusion.

Refunding debt at a lower coupon rate is an anomaly among investments made by business firms, because of the degree of certainty concerning future monetary benefits. Usually most of the savings in financial expenses obtained through refunding with a lower coupon issue are assured, once the new issue is sold, whereas normally prospective earnings from assets are very uncertain at the time of purchase. This peculiar characteristic of certainty of future savings can and should be taken into account in measuring the net monetary benefits to the firm from refunding. The vehicle that can be employed to accomplish this end should be the rate used to make time adjustments of relevant cash flows.

The objective of this paper is both descriptive and normative. First, the bond refunding operation will be described. Second, some empirical evidence of methods used in measuring interest savings by public utilities that refunded bonds in the 1962-63 period will be presented. Third, several approaches to measuring interest savings in bond refunding recommended in the financial literature will be presented and compared. Next, an attempt will be made to determine the best analytical technique for use in measuring interest savings. The most important question which will have to be answered concerns the rate that should be used in making time adjustment of cash flows resulting from the refunding operation. Last, the profitability of the 1962-63 refundings by public utilities will be determined by use of the analytical technique found to be correct. This part of the study will give some empirical evidence of the extent to which techniques generally used

*From the *Journal of Finance* (March, 1966), pp. 55-68. Reprinted by permission.
†Professor of Finance, Texas Technological College.

by business firms cause managements to make unprofitable refunding decisions. The practicality of generalizing about refunding policies of business firms also will be considered in this section.

THE REFUNDING DECISION

The decision to refund a bond issue for the purpose of reducing interest costs is an investment decision. The refunding operation requires a cash outlay which is followed by interest savings in future years. The net cash investment equals the sum of (1) the call premium on the refunded bonds, (2) duplicate interest payments, (3) issue expenses on the refunding bonds, and (4) any discount on the refunding bonds less (a) any premium on the refunding bonds and (b) any tax saving obtained because of the refunding operation.[1] The tax savings occur because the call premium, duplicate interest, and remaining issue expense and discount on the old bonds are tax deductible immediately. An unamortized premium on the old bonds would reduce immediately the tax deductible expenses.

Normally, the tax savings will not be realized at the exact time the initial investment in the refunding operation is made. Thus, the tax savings will have to be discounted back to the date of the investment. The discount rate should be the same rate used to make time adjustments of all cash flows resulting from the refunding operation. The determination of the correct discount rate is the fundamental issue with which this paper is concerned.

Future net cash benefits from the refunding operation are determined by subtracting the annual net cash outlays required on the refunding bonds from the annual net cash outlays required on the refunded bonds. The net cash outlays in both cases are the after-tax annual interest cost of the bonds less the reduction in taxes resulting from the amortization of the bond issue expenses and any bond discount. The amortization of a bond premium would increase taxes. Computation of the amount of interest charges on both bonds must be based on the total par of the refunded bonds.[2]

Usually a firm extends the maturity of the refunding bonds beyond the maturity of the refunded bonds. Thus, the new issue replaces not only the refunded bonds but also other financing that would have been required at the maturity of the refunded bonds. For example, assume that a firm refunds Bond A, maturing in 20 years, with Bond B, maturing in 25 years. Bond B is a replacement for other financing during the last five years of the life of Bond B. The cost of the other financing that would have been required to replace Bond A after 20 years, if it had not been refunded earlier,

---

[1]Duplicate interest occurs when the bonds which are to be refunded and the refunding bonds are outstanding concurrently. The duplicate interest period is frequently 30 to 60 days because the corporation usually desires to have the refunding cash on hand or assured before the old bonds are called.

[2]This statement assumes that the new bond issue is of sufficient size to refund all of the old bond issue, which is normally the case. If only part of the old bond issue is refunded with the new issue, the interest savings should be based on the total par of the bonds refunded.

will affect the net savings actually realized from refunding with Bond B. The net savings might be increased or decreased, depending upon future financing costs. Since financing costs in the future are highly uncertain, interest savings, as a practicality, are estimated generally only for the period up to the maturity of the earlier maturing bonds, normally the maturity of the refunded bonds.[3] Any error that results from this procedure would be fairly small when the maturities of both bonds are 20 years or longer in the future and the difference in maturities is only a few years, as in the above example. However, the probability of significant errors increases, the earlier the maturity of the refunded bonds and the greater the difference in the maturities.

Another problem in measuring future interest savings from refunding can arise if either the refunded or the refunding bonds, or both, are to be retired partially before maturity, e.g., through a sinking fund. The point was made above that interest charges for both bonds should be based on the total par of the refunded bonds. If the old bonds were to be retired partially before maturity, future interest savings from refunding will be reduced accordingly. If the rate of retirement of the refunding bonds is such that the amount outstanding at some date after refunding is reduced below the amount of the refunded bonds that would have been outstanding in the absence of refunding, additional financing will be required at that time unless the assets of the firm are to be reduced. The cost of the additional financing, theoretically, should be added to the interest charges on the refunding bonds outstanding in determining the net savings. Usually, however, business firms will find this procedure impractical because of the uncertainty of future financing costs and the relatively small difference in the planned rate of retirement of the two issues.

In summary, debt refunding is an investment on the part of the corporation. The cash outlay necessary to effect the refunding is followed by interest savings in future years. The measurement of the monetary benefits must relate the interest savings to the required investment.

THE MEASUREMENT OF INTEREST SAVING BY BUSINESS FIRMS

Little empirical evidence is available concerning procedures business firms actually follow in making refunding decisions. To throw some light on the subject, the author sent a questionnaire to the 33 public utilities that refunded publicly held bonds with new public bond issues carrying lower coupons during the period 1962-1963. A total of 40 bond issues was refunded by these firms during the period.

Thirty firms responded to the questionnaire. These firms included 22 companies engaged primarily in the production and distribution of electricity; five companies engaged primarily in the purchase and distribution

---

[3]This procedure usually is recommended (sometimes implicitly) in the literature. See below.

of natural gas; one large holding company whose subsidiaries are engaged primarily in the production, purchase, and distribution of natural gas; and two telephone companies.[4] Size of the firms ranged from very large companies servicing wide, heavily populated areas to small companies servicing small, sparsely populated areas. Gross revenues ranged from less than $12 million to over $1 billion.

Twenty of the responding firms indicated that the only purpose of their refunding was to reduce interest charges. The ten other respondents listed the reduction of interest charges as the most important reason for refunding. Eight of the ten indicated that the second most important reason for refunding was to lengthen the maturity of outstanding debt. The two other reasons listed as being second in importance were "to remove high interest rate issue from balance sheet" and to refund at a time when additional capital was needed. Only one firm listed as many as three reasons for refunding. The third reason indicated by this firm was to improve the appearance of the company's debt structure.

The firms were asked to state as specifically as possible how the interest savings which they had hoped to obtain by refunding were measured. An answer which could be used here required either a good record of a study of the refunding savings or a degree of technical knowledge on the part of the individual who completed the questionnaire.[5] In addition, a sufficient answer required considerable time and effort. Nineteen responses were sufficiently clear and complete to show conclusively that the firms used a wide variety of methods of measuring interest savings in bond refunding. Five firms used more than one method, and one firm used several. A tabular presentation of the responses is impractical, but a general summary will indicate the lack of certainty of the "best" method.

Seven firms used some form of payback-period calculation either exclusively or in conjunction with other procedures. Eight firms indicated the use of some form of time-adjusted calculations, but usually the procedures were not equivalent. Other methods used preclude specific classification except that they involved measuring interest savings with difference to the time of their realization.

The eight firms that used time-adjusted approaches were in general disagreement as to the rate to use in making the time adjustments. One firm used a rate which was "an indication of what overall money is worth" to the firm. Another firm used the return on equity. A total of three firms used the yield on the refunding bond. A sixth firm used all three of these rates but prefaced its specific explanation with the following statement:

---

[4]The nonresponding firms included two companies engaged primarily in the generation and distribution of electricity and one pipeline company. Gross revenues of these firms ranged from approximately $20 million to a little over $120 million.

[5]The questionnaire was sent to the individual believed to be the chief financial officer of each firm. In at least two cases the responsibility for its completion was delegated to the assistant treasurer. However, in several cases the basis for the answer to this question was a study conducted by an investment bank or a management consulting firm.

Anticipated interest savings were measured in several ways; however, the desirability of refunding was based primarily on establishing a break-even point." This break-even point was calculated by more than one method, as well.... Consequently, precise savings were not projected. Rather, anticipated effective cost of money below the range of break-even points indicated that real savings would be achieved. These break-even points ranged from 4.845 percent to 5.29 percent, depending upon the method used in their calculation.

The rates used by the two other firms that employed time-adjusted techniques were not defined specifically.

Break-even analysis was used frequently in evaluating refunding opportunities. Ordinarily, the net yield on the refunding bonds would have to be well below the "break-even yield" before the firm would seriously consider the possibility of refunding. There was no consistency, however, among the firms that used this type of analysis in the computation of the break-even yield.

In summary, the empirical evidence indicates that neither financial managers of business firms, investment bankers, nor management consultants are certain of the procedure that should be used to measure interest savings in bond refunding. Some form of the payback period calculation is a popular method but can be adequately defended only in cases in which the firm is more interested in liquidity or avoidance of risk than profitability. Time-adjusted techniques are used by some firms but in no consistent manner. Other approaches used by firms have little theoretical justification. Thus, the uncertainty in this area of finance can and does lead to widely differing results.

APPROACHES TO THE MEASUREMENT OF INTEREST SAVINGS RECOMMENDED IN THE LITERATURE

Academic writers have not been in agreement concerning the procedure that should be used in measuring interest savings in bond refunding. Four approaches recommended in the literature will be presented here in order to depict the major points of disagreement. The disagreement in recommended procedures has not resulted in active debate in the literature. Indeed, not one of the authors has stated why his approach is better than the others.

A few writers have recommended the use of the cost of capital in measuring interest savings.[6] Interest savings are determined for the period up to the maturity of the earlier maturing bond. Either the net present value or the rate of return technique is employed.

---

[6]See, for example, Robert W. Johnson, *Financial Management* (2d ed.; Boston: Allyn & Bacon, Inc., 1962), pp. 447-451; Pearson Hunt, Charles M. Williams, and Gordon Donaldson, *Basic Business Finance: Text and Cases* (Rev. ed.; Homewood, Ill.: Richard D. Irwin, Inc., 1961), pp. 560-564; Earl A. Spiller, Jr., "Time-Adjusted Break-Even Rate for Refunding," *Financial Executive* (July, 1963), pp. 32-35. Johnson does not distinguish between the investment opportunity rate and the average cost of future financing when discussing refunding. Hunt, Williams, and Donaldson, and Spiller use the investment opportunity rate.

Net present value is determined in the usual manner, by subtracting the net cash investment in the refunding operation from the present value of the interest savings. Future interest savings are discounted at the firm's cost of capital. If the net present value is positive, the refunding operation would be profitable for the firm. Although the literature is not always clear concerning the results of refunding when net present value is negative, the inference is that refunding would not be profitable.

If the rate of return technique is used, the present value of future interest savings and the refunding investment are equated. The discount rate required to equate the two is the rate of return. The rate of return is compared to the firm's cost of capital to determine whether or not refunding would be beneficial.

The use of the cost of capital in the measurement of interest savings in refunding will be referred to hereafter as the cost of capital approach.

Two other approaches are presented by John F. Childs in his book entitled *Long-Term Financing*.[7] Presumably, the first approach is preferred since it is presented in the text, whereas the second approach appears in a footnote.

Childs' example is a refunding decision facing a company with an issue of $10 million principal amount of bonds outstanding. The bonds carry a coupon of 5 percent, mature in 24 years, and are callable on 30-days notice at 104¾. Interest rates have declined, and the company finds that the bonds can be refunded with a new 25-year bond issue which can be sold at about 100 if the coupon rate is set at 4 percent. After underwriters' compensation and expenses of approximately 1.50, the company will net 98.50 from the sale of the new issue. Applying this information to Bond Value Tables, the cost of new money to the firm is found to be 4.10 percent.

His first approach is explained as follows:

> Now then, we have to decide what to compare the 4.10 percent cost of our new money with in order to determine the savings in terms of yield. In effect, what we are doing is selling new bonds and reinvesting the proceeds in our old bonds at their call price. Thus, we are interested in the rate to call the outstanding bonds. They have a 5 percent interest coupon, a 24-year remaining maturity, and a call price of 104¾ (call premium 4¾). The yield at the call price is 4.67 percent, as shown by referring to Bond Value Tables. On the basis of yield, we would realize a saving of 0.57 percent, which is a result of subtracting the cost rate for the new bonds of 4.10 percent from the cost to call the outstanding bonds of 4.67 percent. This is a gross saving and must be adjusted for the tax effect to get the net savings. Assuming a 50 percent tax rate, there would be a net saving of substantially one half.[8]

The second approach suggested by Childs includes the call premium on the refunded bonds in the computation of the cost of the new money. The procedure is presented as follows:

---

[7]John F. Childs, *Long-Term Financing* (Englewood Cliffs, N.J.: Prentice-Hall, Inc., 1961), pp. 239-241.

[8]*Ibid.*, pp. 239-240.

1. New bonds—4 percent coupon, maturity 25
   yrs., to be sold   100.00%
2. Less compensation and expenses   1.50
3. Net proceeds   98.50%
4. Less premium to call old bonds   4.75
5. Net to company after calling old bonds   93.75%
6. Cost of old bonds: 5 percent coupon—
   price 100 percent   5.00%
7. Cost of new money: 4 percent coupon,
   maturity 25 yrs. Price 93.75 (line 5 above)   4.41
8. Savings before taxes   0.59%

This method produces a slightly greater savings because the call premium is written off at the lower interest rate over a longer period of time.[9]

Both methods suggested by Childs would base a refunding decision on the net interest savings per annum, expressed as a difference in yield, for the period up to the earlier maturity of the two bonds [10] The net cash investment in refunding, other than the call premium under the first approach, is written off on an annuity basis over the longer period of 25 years.[11] In both approaches, the write-off of the net cash investment reduces future interest savings.

The only difference in Childs' two approaches is the way in which the call premium is handled. In both approaches the write-off of the premium affects the computation of a cost, the "yield at the call price" in the first approach and the "cost of new money" in the second approach.

The significant difference in the cost of capital approach and Childs' two approaches is the rate used to adjust cash flows over time.[12] The cost of capital approach utilizes the firm's cost of capital in making time adjustments. In the example used by Childs, net refunding investment included only underwriters' compensation and expenses pertinent to the refunding bonds and the call premium on the refunded bonds. The compensation and expenses were written off on an annuity basis at the "cost of new money." The call premium was written off on an annuity basis in the first approach at the "yield at the call price," and in the second approach at the "cost of new money." In both methods used by Childs, the call premium affected the computed rate at which it was written off. In the cost of capital approach, the cost of capital is not affected by the call premium on the refunded bonds.

The net difference in the result obtained from using either of Childs' two approaches, or the cost of capital approach, depends upon the differ-

---

[9]*Ibid.*, p. 240.

[10]Note that interest is converted semiannually on both bonds.

[11]In the Childs example, the net cash investment includes only the call premium on the refunded bonds and compensation and expenses on the refunding bonds. The other components of the refunding investment are discussed in Childs' book on pages 240-241. However, the rate at which some of these components should be written off is not clear.

[12]The difference in the format used by Childs and the net present value and rate of return formats used above to explain the cost of capital approach is relatively unimportant. The (cont.)

ence in the "yield at the call price," the "cost of new money," and the firm's cost of capital. For most firms, the difference in results obtained will be substantial because of the difference in the net interest cost of new debt financing and the firm's cost of capital. This point will be further considered in the following section.

Another approach has been suggested by J. Fred Weston.[13] The essence of his approach is to reduce the future net cash benefits per year from refunding by (1) the interest cost on the additional bonds that would have to be sold to finance the net cash investment plus (2) the amount of money set aside each year which would accumulate to the par of the additional bonds.[14] The formats of the Weston and Childs approaches are similar except that Weston expresses interest savings in terms of dollars per annum whereas Childs expresses them in terms of differences in yield.

Weston's own example will be presented in order to examine his recommendations in the context in which they were made. Later, his approach will be compared with the Childs approaches.

The problem is a company which refunds a $60 million 6½ percent bond issue, callable at 106, with a new bond issue carrying a coupon of 5 percent and sold to net 96. The maturity date of neither bond is explicit in the example, but the savings are determined for a 20-year period. A total par value of $66,250,000 would have to be sold at 96 to net the firm the required $63,600,000 ($60,000,000 × 106) to refund the old bonds. The savings per annum are determined as follows:

Interest on 6.5 percent bonds	$3,900,000
Interest on 5 percent bonds	3,312,500
Savings per annum	$ 587,500

He points out, however, that the savings per annum should be reduced because an additional $6,250,000 ($66,250,000 — $60,000,000) will have to be paid at the end of the 20-year period. The reduction in savings per annum according to his example is the amount of money which, set aside each year to increase at the compound rate of 5 percent per annum, will accumulate to $6,250,000 in 20 years. This amount is found to be approximately $189,000. Subtracting $189,000 from the annual savings of $587,500 gives a net savings per annum of $398,500.

The use of a 5 percent interest rate in determining the amount which would accumulate to $6,250,000 is a minor error. Perhaps the intent was to use the net yield on the bonds as the interest rate. Since the bonds carried a coupon rate of 5 percent and were sold to net 96, the net yield was approximately 5.32 percent. Using 5.32 percent in place of 5 percent to determine

---

use of different formats will be discussed in the following section.

[13]J. Fred Weston, *Managerial Finance* (New York: Holt, Rinehart & Winston, Inc., 1962), pp. 147-148.

[14]Reducing the future net cash benefits per year by (1) the interest cost of the additional bonds that would have to be sold plus (2) the amount of money set aside each year which would accumulate to the par of the additional bonds is equivalent to writing off the net investment on an annuity basis against the future benefits.

the amount of money which must be set aside each year to accumulate to $6,250,000 results in a difference in amount of about $6,250.

Incorporating the minor correction, the Weston method assumes that the net yield on the additional bonds sold to finance the net cash investment in the refunding operation is the total cost of the funds.

The significant difference in the Weston and Childs approaches is the way in which the call premium on a refunded bond affects the results. The call premium was written off against future cash benefits in Childs' first approach at the "yield at the call price," and in his second approach at the "cost of new money." In both methods the call premium affected the computation of the rate at which it was written off. In the Weston approach the call premium was written off at the net interest cost of the refunding bonds, but the write-off did not affect the computation of the net interest cost.

The difference in the Weston and Childs approaches usually will not affect the results significantly. For example, writing off the call premium in the refunding problem used as an example by Childs at the 4.10 percent interest cost of the new bonds results in savings before taxes of approximately 0.59 percent, which was the savings obtained by Childs in his second approach.

In summary, academic writers have not been in agreement concerning the measurement of interest savings in bond refunding.[15] The significant difference in the approaches that have been presented is the rate used to make time adjustments of cash flows. In the following section, an attempt will be made to determine the rate that should be used.

WHICH PROCEDURE IS BEST IN MEASURING INTEREST SAVING FROM BOND REFUNDING?

The point was made earlier that bond refunding involves an investment of funds which is followed in future time periods by savings in interest charges. If the present value of the future interest savings exceeds the present value of the investment, the refunding operation will be a profitable undertaking for the firm because a net savings has been obtained. The dis-

---

[15]The works of three other authors should be mentioned. See Arleigh P. Hess, Jr. and Willis J. Winn, *The Value of the Call Privilege* (Philadelphia: University of Pennsylvania Press 1962), particularly Chapter II and Appendix A. Appendix A is entitled "A Technical Note on the Value of the Call Privilege" and was written by Jean A. Crockett. See also Willis J. Winn and Arleigh P. Hess, Jr., "The Value of the Call Privilege," *Journal of Finance* (May, 1959), pp. 182-195.

Hess and Winn use the net present value technique in measuring interest saving in bond refunding. However, the two authors do not define the discount rate that should be used in determining the present value of future interest savings. In Appendix A of the book, Jean Crockett uses the current long-term interest rate, even when measuring interest savings from future refunding. She states on page 124, "We assume that the current long-term interest rate ... is the proper rate for discounting ... : but, if desired, some other rate could easily be substituted in the expressions obtained."

The present author feels that the use of the current long-term interest rate in determining the present value of interest savings from future refunding is questionable. However, this problem is beyond the scope of this paper.

count rate to apply to future interest savings should be the total cost (including both explicit and implicit costs) of the funds necessary to make the investment.

According to the net present value technique in capital budgeting theory, the cash benefits from an investment should be discounted at the firm's average cost of capital. The crucial fact here, however, is that the cash benefits from a refunding operation are not equivalent to those of the usual investment by a business firm. An investment in an operating asset involves considerable risk because the future cash benefits from its use are uncertain. Refunding a bond issue with another bond issue is entirely different, because the future cash benefits up to the earlier maturity of the two bonds are the result of contractual interest charges on the refunding bonds being less than those on the refunded bonds. Thus, once the refunding bonds are sold, the interest savings up to the earlier maturity are assured to the company.[16]

In the development of the argument that follows, interest savings will be measured up to the earlier maturity of the refunded and refunding bonds. The problem created by differences in the maturities of the two bonds will be considered later.

If a firm is able to make an investment from which earnings are certain, the financing of the investment involves no financial risk to the firm so long as the earnings are sufficient to meet all financial expenses. For example, the investment can be financed by a fixed debt without risk to the firm.[17] Since no risk is incurred, no implicit cost is associated with the debt financing; the only cost of the funds necessary to make the investment would be the net interest cost of the debt financing. The investment would be profitable to the firm if the future cash earnings discounted back to the present at the net interest cost of the debt are greater than the present value of the investment. Any part of the investment not made immediately should be discounted back to the present at the net interest cost of the debt.

Refunding a bond at a net interest savings results in a net reduction in cash outlays rather than an increase in cash inflows. Nevertheless, the refunding will cause the firm's total profits to increase or its total losses to decrease.

Since the savings are certain, the net cash investment required in the refunding can be financed by debt without necessitating an increase in equity capital to optimize the firm's capital structure. Thus, the net present value

---

[16]The refunding decision involves a risk that interest rates will rise between the date of the decision and the date the refunding bonds are sold (or if the issue is underwritten, the date the contract with the underwriters is consummated). The management of the firm may require that expected interest savings be sufficient to compensate for this risk before a decision to refund is made. The amount of expected interest savings required to compensate for the risk is a judgment problem for management.

[17]If the assumption of certainty of return on investment is extended to the lender, the net interest cost of the funds to the borrowing firm would be the pure rate of interest. However certainty of earnings on the investment by the borrowing firm does not eliminate all of the risk to the lender. The earnings could be dissipated by the borrowing firm before the lender is paid.

of the refunding operation should be determined by discounting the future net cash benefits at the after-tax cost of the source of funds used to finance the refunding investment, presumably the net yield on the refunding bonds. The net cash investment would be subtracted from the present value of the future cash benefits to determine the net present value in the usual manner. The decision to refund when the net present value is positive would be profitable for the firm. Since the interest savings are assured if the new bonds can be sold at the expected rate, the refunding operation will reduce the overall risk of the firm even though the debt to equity ratio increases. On the other hand, a negative net present value would be unprofitable.

The above procedure in measuring net interest savings will be referred to hereafter as the net yield approach. Of the four approaches discussed in the previous section, only the Weston approach, with the minor correction noted earlier, is entirely correct.

Very different results can be obtained by the use of the net yield and cost of capital approaches. As an example, assume that after a decline in interest rates a corporation finds it can refund its $20 million par 4½ percent bonds, due in 20 years, with 4 percent bonds of the same type, quality, and maturity date. Interest on both bonds is paid semiannually. Assume further that all bonds are sold at par and that the annual amortization of issue expenses amounts to $4,000 for each issue. Using a corporate income tax rate of 50 percent, the refunding operation would result in semiannual after-tax savings of $25,000 for 20 years.

If the corporation's cost of capital is 8 percent, the cost of capital approach would result in a present value of the savings stream of 19.7928 × $25,000 = $494,820. Discounting the future savings at 2 percent, the approximate after-tax cost of debt,[18] results in a present value of 32.8347 × $25,000 = $820,868. If the net cash investment required to refund is $600,000, for example, use of the cost of capital as the discount rate would lead to the rejection of the operation because a negative net present value results.

On the other hand, the bonds would be refunded if the after-tax cost of debt is the discount rate used because the net present value is $220,868. The $220,868 net present value is a net gain to the common stockholders. No additional equity capital will have to be raised to counterbalance the additional bonds; the refunding operation has reduced the financial risk of the firm.

The discussion above has been concerned primarily with the concept rather than the format of measuring the profitability of refunding. The principle of discounting future interest saving at the cost of debt can be employed in several ways. For example, either the rate of return or the Weston technique can be employed.

The use of the Childs format requires the computation of a synthetic yield on the refunding bonds. The process would be to write off the net

---

[18]The after-tax cost of the bonds is slightly higher than 2 percent because of the issue expenses.

cash investment on an annuity basis to future interest periods. The rate used to write off the investment should be the net interest cost of the refunding bonds computed in the conventional manner.[19] The write-off of the investment will serve to increase future interest costs. Then, the synthetic yield on the refunding bond is computed by discounting the future interest costs, which include the write-off of the refunding investment, back to equal the par of the refunded bonds. The yield is synthetic because it is affected by the components of the refunding investment which do not affect the conventional computation of the yield cost on bonds.[20] These components include (1) the call premium on the refunded bonds, (2) duplicate interest, and (3) any tax savings obtained because of the refunding operation.[21] If the synthetic yield on the new bonds is less than the coupon rate on the old bonds, refunding would result in a net monetary benefit to the firm.

The net yield approach recommended here can be adapted easily to a breakeven basis. For example, a firm could compute the yield on a new bond at which it would break even from refunding its debt. At lower yields, refunding would be profitable.

Another problem with which the management of a firm is confronted is whether to refund now or at some later time. If the net present value from refunding later is greater than the net present value from refunding now, the firm should delay. The difficulty in determining the net present value from a delayed refunding is in estimating future interest rates. Hess, Winn, and Crockett have proposed a solution to this problem by the use of probability analysis.[22]

This procedure might be adapted also to refunding cases in which the maturities of the refunded and refunding bonds differ. Thus, a probability estimate of the savings in financial costs between the maturities of the two bonds could be added to (or subtracted from, if the estimated savings are negative) the savings up to the earlier maturity. The development of this procedure, however, is beyond the scope of the present paper.

RETURNS FROM REFUNDING BY PUBLIC UTILITIES IN 1962-1963

The conclusion has been reached that debt refunding will be profitable to a firm when the rate of return obtained is greater than the cost of the particular funds required to finance the net cash investment. Normally, the cost of the funds would be the net yield on the refunding bonds. Thus, the

---

[19]Recall that Childs writes off the call premium on the refunded bonds at two different rates, neither of which is the net interest cost of the refunding bonds computed in the conventional manner.

[20]The significance of these components for a refunding decision is that they affect the amount of funds that must be obtained to refund the old issue. However, they should not affect the computation of the cost of the new funds, although they do affect the computation of the synthetic yield as indicated above.

[21]Components of the refunding investment that affect the conventional computation of yield include the issue expenses and any discount or premium on the refunding bonds. The refunding investment was discussed in Section II of the present paper.

[22]Arleigh P. Hess, Jr. and Willis J. Winn, *op. cit.*, Chapter II and Appendix A.

TABLE 15-1

RATES OF RETURN EARNED ON FORTY BOND REFUNDINGS BY PUBLIC UTILITIES
IN 1962 AND 1963
(Percent)

3.6°	9.1	11.5°	14.7°
5.5	9.5	11.9°	14.8
5.7	9.6°	12.3	15.3°
6.5	9.7	12.3	16.1
6.8	9.9	12.8°	16.1
7.1°	10.1	12.8	17.2
7.3	10.4°	13.0	19.7
8.0	10.4	13.1	23.8
8.2	11.2	13.8	26.7°
8.7	11.3	14.6°	43.4

Note: The 40 bonds were refunded by 34 refunding bonds. One new bond was used to refund two old bonds in four cases and three old bonds in one case.

One utility refunded bonds at two different times.

°Denotes that at least one other reason in addition to interest savings was indicated by the respondent to the questionnaire as a factor causing the decision to refund. In all cases, interest savings were indicated as the primary reason for refunding. Ten responding firms indicated more than one reason for refunding; the 9.6 percent and the 14.6 percent rates of return were earned from refunding two old bond issues with one new bond issue.

profitability of the refundings by the public utility firms discussed earlier can be seen by comparing the net yield on the refunding bonds with the rates of return obtained.

The yield on every refunding bond included in the study fell somewhere between 4 and 5 percent. The results of computations by the present author of the rate of return earned by the public utilities in their 1962-63 refundings are shown in Table 15-1.

The procedure followed in the computations of the rates shown in Table 15-1 was to discount net interest savings for each year to the maturity date of the refunded bonds, at a rate which would equate their present value with the net cash investment. The only data necessary for the computations which could not be obtained from Moody's *Public Utility Manual* were issue expenses on both the old and new bonds. These were estimated from the Securities and Exchange Commission's *Cost of Flotation of Corporate Securities, 1951-55*.[23]

Probably the most obvious observation that can be made from a study of the data in the table is the wide range of rates of return obtained by the refundings. Although a little more than 50 percent of the rates fell between 10 and 20 percent, there is no salient concentration.

Since the rates of return shown in the table are on an after-tax basis and the yields before taxes on all of the refunding bonds fell somewhere between 4 and 5 percent, none of the refunding operations appear unprofitable. The reader should note that the rate of return computations probably

---

[23]Securities and Exchange Commission, *Cost of Flotation of Corporate Securities, 1951-55* (Washington 25, D.C., June, 1957), Table 12, p. 51.

involved some errors because issue expenses for all bond issues were estimated from the Securities and Exchange Commission's *Cost of Flotation of Corporate Securities, 1951-55.* While these probable errors would have had a relatively small effect on the results, too much faith should not be put in the *exact* figures obtained.

The rates of return obtained by the refundings were plotted graphically against a long list of quantitative variables depicting financial characteristics of the firms, e.g., sales, assets, rates of profits, rates of growth, and debt to equity ratios. No correlations whatsoever were found. Neither were the rates of return related to the particular type of utility. Furthermore, there was no consistent relationship between the rates of return and the extension of maturity dates by refunding[24] or the procurement of additional capital.[25] Thus, no generalization can be made about the effect of any factors on the rate of return required to entice the firms to refund.

These are several reasons why rates of return will vary considerably in debt refunding. First, opportunities for interest savings vary among firms. For example, firms with high-yield bonds outstanding will often be able to refund at great savings if interest rates decline, particularly if the financial position of the firm has improved. Second, since firms use methods of measuring interest savings which give different results, the same refunding opportunities will be evaluated differently. Thus, the enticement to refund will vary. Third, management expectations of future interest rates will affect refunding decisions. If a substantial decline in interest rates is expected, refunding will probably be deferred. Management expectations of interest rates will vary among firms and for the same firm at different times. Fourth, refunding often has advantages other than interest savings. Ten firms that answered the questionnaire indicated reasons for refunding in addition to interest savings, although the latter was always given as the primary reason. The wide range of rates which have an asterisk beside them in Table 15-1 indicates that no relationship existed between the rates of return obtained and the fact that factors in addition to interest savings led to the refunding decision. Nor was any consistent relationship found between any particular secondary reason for refunding and the rates of return obtained. Fifth, firms differ in respect to policies and aggressiveness. Although this factor is difficult if not impossible to measure, doubtless it was of great importance in the case of the refundings that have been examined in this study.

SUMMARY AND CONCLUSIONS

This study has found that the investment required to refund debt should be analyzed differently from ordinary investments in operating

[24]All of the maturity extensions except one fell within the range of approximately two to six years. The one exception was an extension of a little over 17 years.

[25]A total of 34 refunding bonds was sold to refund the 40 refunded bonds. In 21 of these 34 refunding operations, the firm obtained more capital than was required to call in the old bonds. In 18 cases, the addition was 10 percent or more of the amount of the old bonds outstanding. In several cases, very large amounts of additional capital were (cont.)

assets. Thus, debt refunding should join the leasing of assets as a special case in capital budgeting.

Refunding will be profitable for a business firm whenever the rate of return earned on the net cash investment in the operation is greater than the cost of debt capital to the firm. If the net present value method is used as the analytical tool, future interest savings from refunding should be discounted at the cost of debt, normally the net yield on the refunding bond. Use of this rate is better than the use of the cost of capital because debt financing of the refunding investment does not require future additions to equity capital.

Few firms use the method recommended here in measuring interest savings. The great variety of methods in use depicts the confusion and uncertainty concerning the correct procedure.

Some of the procedures used by public utilities that refunded in 1962-63 would have resulted in losses on a time-adjusted basis if the firms had not followed the practice of deferring refunding until a new bond could be sold to yield well below the computed break-even yield. Other firms employed methods of measuring interest savings which could result in passing up profitable refunding opportunities. For these reasons, it is difficult to generalize about the net effect of the widespread use of theoretically incorrect procedures in measuring interest savings. The effect probably has not been great, because most firms that refund primarily to take advantage of lower interest rates do not base their decisions on precise estimates of profits, although these are generally made. The reasonable assurance of considerable profits seems to be much more important.

---

obtained. Recall, however, that only one firm that answered the questionnaire discussed earlier indicated that the need for additional capital had any effect on the decision to refund.

16. DESIGNING A CONVERTIBLE PREFERRED ISSUE*

ANTHONY H. MEYER †

A convertible preferred stock is a preferred stock which gives the holder the right to exchange his shares for common stock at a stated rate under stated conditions. Because its special features are advantageous in corporate acquisitions, convertible preferred has been used extensively in acquisitions and mergers in recent years. Moody's lists well over 200 publicly traded issues in its monthly survey of convertible preferreds and usually about 50 more which have been designed for mergers not yet completed.[1]

When a company first considers convertible preferred in an acquisition, many important questions arise. What will the market price of the security be? How will it affect the market for the common stock? Does convertible preferred allow the issuer to avoid or postpone dilution of earnings per share? How should the terms be set? Is there some limit to the amount that can or should be issued? Are there any disadvantages? This article will consider the major aspects of convertible preferred from the viewpoint of corporate financial managers whose companies may issue or receive them in a merger.

MARKET PRICE

One of the most intriguing aspects of convertible preferreds is the question of what they will sell for in the marketplace and why. Even though estimating the probable market value of a convertible preferred before it is publicly traded presents some problems, the question cannot be avoided. The price of an acquisition financed with convertible preferred is the market value the issue will command, and both the issuer and the recipient have to reach some sort of agreement on what that value is likely to be.

Conversion Value

As a starting point, the preferred has a value because it is convertible into common stock with a known market price. This value, called conversion value, is calculated simply by multiplying the market price of a share of the issuer's common by the conversion ratio—the number of shares of common into which one share of preferred is convertible. Signal Oil's $2.40 convertible preferred, for instance, has a conversion ratio of 2.0. A recent price for the common was $34. The price of the common ($34) multiplied by the 2.0 conversion ratio produces a $68 conversion value.

---

*From *Financial Executive* (April, 1968), pp. 42-62. Reprinted by permission.
†Vice-President in Charge of Counseling Department, Irving Trust Company.
[1]*Moody's Convertible Preferreds*, a monthly publication of Moody's Investors Service, Inc., 99 Church Street, New York, New York 10007. This survey contains useful data on all outstanding and forthcoming issues and brief comments on issues of special interest.

Confusion sometimes arises over the difference between conversion ratio and conversion price. Conversion price is usually nothing more than the par or stated value of convertible preferred which can be exchanged for one share of common. It is another way of expressing the conversion ratio. To convert a conversion price to a conversion ratio, the par or stated value of the preferred is divided by its conversion price.

For example, Commercial Solvents has a $20 par value convertible preferred. The conversion price of the preferred is $33.50. All this means is that $33.50 in par value of the preferred can be exchanged for one share of common. The same idea is often conveyed by saying the preferred converts at $33.50.

To obtain the conversion ratio:

$$\frac{\$20.00}{\$33.50} = .579$$

One share of preferred can be exchanged for .579 shares of common.

Investment Value

Entirely apart from the convertible preferred's conversion value is its worth as a straight preferred stock. This value is usually called investment value or straight preferred value. For example, a convertible preferred with a $5 dividend would have a $100 investment value if the same preferred could be sold without the conversion feature on a 5 percent yield basis.

Although it cannot be calculated, investment value can be estimated with a fair degree of accuracy by a competent security analyst. Basically, the procedure is to price the issue on the basis of its dividend rate related to its quality. The analyst first judges the quality of the preferred by considering such factors as the issuer's earning power, the risks of the business and the future outlook, the overall capitalization, and the position and terms of the preferred itself. Next he reviews publicly held straight preferreds for issues of similar quality. Finally, he relates the dividend rate on the convertible preferred to the yields of similar straight preferred stocks and derives an estimate of investment value.

Premium

Clearly, a preferred will sell for no less than the floor price established by the higher of its investment or conversion value. Generally, convertible preferreds will sell at some premium, and often a considerable premium, over that floor price.

At this point, something should be said about the word "premium" itself. Premium is often taken to mean premium over conversion value, and the word carries with it the idea that the issuer has achieved something for nothing in terms of market price. However, in many cases where the market price of a preferred is substantially higher than its conversion value, the price may reflect no more than the worth of the stock as a straight preferred. A recent price for Flintkote's $4.50 Series A convertible preferred was $72½, which was 35 percent higher than its $53⅝ conversion value. It would be inaccurate to describe the 35 percent as premium. Estimated investment value of the stock at the time was $69¼, and the preferred was selling for only about 5 percent over that figure.[2] Premium is really the amount by which the market price of a convertible preferred exceeds the higher of its investment or conversion value.

Three major factors and several less important ones affect the size of the premium.

Upside potential of the common is a vital consideration. Suppose that a preferred has an investment value of $100.00 by virtue of a $5.00 dividend, and a conversion value of $80.00 because it is convertible into two shares of common currently trading at $40.00 per share. There is at least some possibility that the common will appreciate enough to give the conversion feature real value. Consequently, the preferred is almost sure to be somewhat more attractive to investors than a straight preferred of similar quality yielding 5 percent. How much more attractive, and therefore how much higher the market value of the convertible will be than its $100.00 investment value floor price, depends largely on how much growth is expected for the common.

Downside risk in the common is an equally important factor affecting premium. Suppose the preferred described above is convertible into three shares of common rather than two. Investment value is still $100.00, but conversion value is now serving as the floor price at $120.00, and the question is how much more than $120.00 the preferred will sell for. If the common were to go down sharply, one could expect the preferred to go down less sharply, and to stop declining entirely at $100.00 because of its investment value.[3] Therefore, the convertible preferred should sell at some premium over its conversion value floor price because it is more protected against downside risk than the common. The size of the premium will be related to the riskiness of the common—the greater the risk, the greater the price investors are likely to pay to be protected from it.

Special market demand is the third major factor which has a significant bearing on the size of the premium. Certain types of investors have important reasons for buying convertible preferreds. Because these stocks offer both capital gains potential and more current income than is ordinarily provided by the dividend on the underlying common, banks and other trustees can reconcile the divergent interests of income beneficiaries and remaindermen of trusts by investing in them. Insurance companies and

---

[2]The investment value estimates made by *Moody's Convertible Preferreds* are used throughout this article.

[3]Investment value itself could change, of course, but only with changes in money market conditions or the investment quality of the preferred, and these factors are characteristically much more stable than common stock prices.

other corporate investors find them attractive because of regulatory and tax considerations. One or another of these factors can cause some convertible preferreds to sell at higher prices than would otherwise seem reasonable.

Other factors affecting premium are call features, yield differential, special conversion features, and marketability.

Call features. If the preferred is callable at a price low enough to force conversion, the convertible will not sell at any appreciable premium over its conversion value. On the other hand, high redemption prices and lengthy call protection contribute to the size of the premium.

Yield differential. The size of the spread between the preferred dividend and the common dividend available through conversion (the cash dividend per common share times the conversion ratio) will affect the premium. Usually this spread narrows over time with increases in the dividend rate on the common.

Special conversion features. Such features generally work against the holder and tend to reduce premiums. Delay before conversion is allowed, termination of the right to convert after a period of years, and reductions in the conversion ratio over time are typical special features.

Marketability. Convertible preferreds issued to acquire closely held companies are usually not marketable initially because SEC registration has not taken place. Further, restrictions against sale or conversion are often built into the terms of the issue. By normal securities valuation standards, this limitation impairs their worth.

Premiums will vary widely, and there is no rule or formula with which to determine in advance what premium the market will pay for a particular preferred stock when it is issued. To reach an estimate, all the factors which influence premium must be judged in the light of the contemporary market for comparable outstanding issues. By way of illustration, consider two preferreds issued several years ago at about the same time. One issuer was a high-technology conglomerate whose common sold at a high price/earnings ratio. The other was a cement company whose common sold at a relatively low multiple of earnings.

The conglomerate's preferred traded initially at about 30 percent more than its conversion value and 43 percent more than its estimated investment value. The cement company's preferred traded for only about 6 percent over its estimated investment value and 21 percent over its conversion value. In the case of the conglomerate, the big factors behind the 30 percent premium over the conversion value floor were probably special institutional demand, yield differential (no cash dividends were paid on the common), and the fact that the investment value of the preferred afforded a degree of protection against downside risk in the common. This protection may well have been considered valuable since stocks having high price/earnings ratios are generally considered more vulnerable to radical price declines than conservatively priced issues. In the case of the cement company, relatively modest upside potential for the common probably contributed importantly to the small premium of the preferred over its investment value floor. The market does not usually expect a great deal of growth from the cement industry.

While premiums differ from stock to stock, the premium for any one stock will generally be best when conversion value and investment value are equal. If investment value is a great deal higher than conversion value, the common has so much ground to cover before the conversion privilege becomes valuable that investors will not pay much for the convertibility feature. If conversion value is a great deal higher than investment value, the common has to decline substantially before investment value begins to support the market price of the preferred; investors will not pay much for such slim protection against downside risk. Only when investment and conversion values are close to each other does each provide maximum support for the other. At that point, investment value affords immediate protection for the preferred if the market drops for the underlying common, and conversion value affords an immediate gain if the common goes up.

The three exhibits which follow illustrate in various ways how convertible preferred premiums behave.

Figure 16-1 is a theoretical model which suggests how premiums will vary with the relationship between investment and conversion values. In Case I, the premium is small because conversion value is so much lower than investment value that the worth of the call on the common is negligible. The convertible sells almost as if it were straight preferred. In Case II, the premium is again small, this time because investment value is so much lower than conversion value that there is little protection against downside risk in the common. The convertible sells almost as if it were common. In Cases IV and V, investment and conversion values are closer to one another, so premiums are bigger. Premium is best in Case III, where conversion and investment values are equal. The convertible will benefit from any upward move in the common and be sheltered from any decline.

Figure 16-2 shows the premiums for a random sample of 50 of the stocks listed in a recent issue of *Moody's Convertible Preferreds*. The premium is measured in each case from the floor price provided by the higher of the investment value estimated by Moody's or the conversion value. Figure 16-2 supports the premise that premiums are best when conversion and investment values are close together and tend to disappear when these values are far apart. It also points up the valuation problem by showing how widely premiums can vary from issue to issue even when the same relationship between investment

FIGURE 16-1

PREMIUM ILLUSTRATION

Preferred pays a $2.50 dividend and is assumed to have an investment value of $50 per share. Common has a current market value of $50 per share.

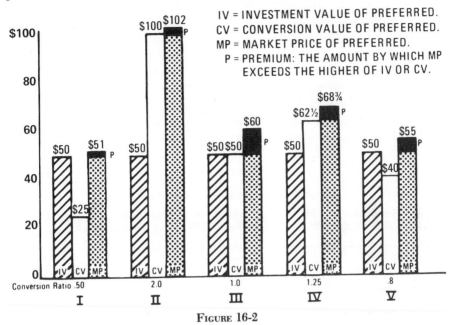

IV = INVESTMENT VALUE OF PREFERRED.
CV = CONVERSION VALUE OF PREFERRED.
MP = MARKET PRICE OF PREFERRED.
P = PREMIUM: THE AMOUNT BY WHICH MP EXCEEDS THE HIGHER OF IV OR CV.

FIGURE 16-2

INFLUENCE OF INVESTMENT/CONVERSION VALUE RELATIONSHIP ON PREMIUM

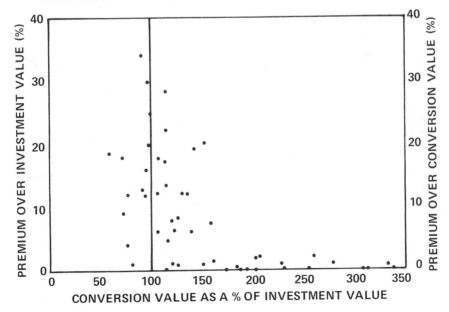

and conversion value exists.

Figure 16-3 charts the market behavior of an actual convertible preferred, the $2.70 Beatrice Foods preference stock issued in 1967 to acquire Melnor Industries. At the end of February, conversion and estimated investment values were nearly identical at $54⅛ and $54½ respectively, and the preferred sold (on a when-issued basis) for $61½, a 13 percent premium over its investment value floor. In subsequent months, the premium began to disappear as conversion value rose with an increase in the price of the common and investment value declined in an increasingly tight money market. By the end of July, with conversion value 46 percent higher than investment value, the premium was virtually gone and the preferred was selling almost entirely on the basis of its conversion value.

Unless the issue is disproportionately large in the issuer's capitalization, the probable market value of a new money convertible preferred can

FIGURE 16-3

BEATRICE FOODS CO. $2.70 PREFERENCE STOCK

Issued in connection with the acquisition of Melnor Industries, Inc., effective 1/31/67, stated value $60, convertible into 1.165 shares common stock.

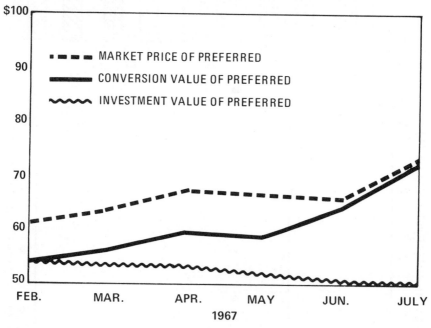

be estimated fairly closely on the basis of the considerations discussed so far. However, the market price of a convertible preferred created to acquire a company may be affected by still another factor—the character of the acquisition itself.

Impact of the Acquisition

When one company acquires another one, the picture changes. The extent of the change will depend on the size, nature, and credit standing of the acquired company, the price of the acquisition, and the manner in which it is financed. The news of a proposed acquisition will prompt investors to consider its consequences, and their conclusions may affect the price of the acquirer's common stock. The new financial structure and altered earnings prospects which result from the acquisition may also affect the quality of the acquirer's senior securities.

The probable impact of an acquisition on the acquirer's securities is obviously important for any number of reasons. In the context of designing a convertible preferred as an acquisition stock, it is important because it might influence the investment value, the conversion value, and the premium on the preferred. The impact will probably be insignificant if the acquirer is big and the seller is small. However, very careful study of the possible market consequences is in order if the use of convertible preferred is considered for a major acquisition.

USE IN ACQUISITIONS

Convertible preferreds have become highly popular acquisition securities because of the special features they offer both seller and buyer.

Taxes are often a paramount consideration for the seller. The seller can avoid a capital gains tax liability at the time of sale by receiving voting stock[4]—straight preferred, convertible preferred, or common. Of these, convertible preferred offers what many sellers consider the most attractive package. It combines most of the protection of a senior security paying a fixed return with most of the growth potential of the underlying common.

Many buyers will not ordinarily favor convertible preferred in an acquisition if the company to be acquired will sell for cash at the same price. However, prospective selling shareholders will often want a nontaxable transaction and a stock with growth potential. If a prospective seller is publicly held, its management will generally presume that this is true when negotiating terms. Moreover, credit considerations will often rule out the possibility that an acquisition can be financed with debt. Consequently, a buyer is frequently limited to the use of convertible preferred or common. With this choice, convertible preferred can offer the issuer several advantages.

Minimization of Dilution

Foremost is the fact that, if convertible preferred designed to sell

---

[4]This need not be the case when the transaction takes the form of a statutory merger.

at a premium over its conversion value is used, rather than common, fewer common shares will ultimately be issued. To illustrate, suppose an acquiring company's stock sells for $50 a share, and the price of the acquisition is $10 million. An acquisition using common would require 200,000 shares. Instead, a convertible preferred could be designed to sell at $100 with a conversion ratio of, perhaps, 1.7—producing a conversion value of $85—and an appropriate dividend. An issue of 100,000 shares would achieve the required $10 million market value and would eventually convert into only 170,000 shares of common. The issuer has still paid $10 million and should make his return-on-investment analysis of the acquisition on this basis. But only part of the price is the current conversion value of the preferred. The balance is represented by his commitment to pay cumulative fixed dividends unless and until conversion takes place.

Tailoring the Dividend

Convertible preferred also permits the buyer to meet the seller's dividend objectives without altering its own dividend policy. For example, a seller may have a high payout policy and the prospective buyer, a low one. A proposed common-for-common exchange acceptable in every other way would be objectionable to the seller if it cut his dividend income. If the buyer does not want to commit his common stock to a dividend rate which suits the seller, convertible preferred offers a solution.

Minimization of Seller's Vote

Another feature of convertible preferred is its potential for minimizing the voting power of a selling company's stockholders. This can be important on occasion, particularly if the seller is closely held. In the example used above to illustrate the minimization of dilution, a common-for-common acquisition would give the selling stockholders 200,000 votes at the outset. A convertible preferred with one vote per share would give the sellers only 100,000 votes before conversion and 170,000 thereafter. The conversion ratio and the initial premium over conversion value are the key factors in this context.

Effect on Price of Common

A final argument in favor of convertible preferred has considerably less to recommend it, although it figures prominently in the thinking of many acquisition-minded companies, many investors, and much of Wall Street. This is the proposition that convertible preferred adds leverage to the common because earnings per common share are computed after deducting only the preferred dividend from net income. Any earnings thrown off by an acquired company in excess of the dividend on the preferred issued to acquire it go toward increasing earnings on the issuer's common.

TABLE 16-1

Year	Equity Capital	Net Income @ 12%	Pre-ferred Divi-dends @ $2	Income Avail-able for Common	Dividends @ 50%	Per Share	Re-tained Earn-ings
				(in thousands)			
1	$10,000	$1,200	$200	$1,000	$500	$1.67	$500
2	10,500	1,260	200	1,060	530	1.77	530
3	11,030	1,324	200	1,124	562	1.87	562
4	11,592	1,391	200	1,191	595	1.98	596
5	12,188	1,463	200	1,263	631	2.10	632
6	12,820	1,538	—	1,538	°	°	°

°No dividend shown because company may wish to revise dividend payout after fifth year.

The dilution in earnings per share which conversion would cause is concealed and postponed until conversion takes place, and the common is entitled to sell at a better price in the meanwhile.

The fact is that the position of the common stockholders of most companies with convertible preferreds outstanding would be improved if these preferreds converted immediately. This is true even though conversion will usually result in a decrease in reported earnings per share.

Consider the following case. A company has preferred and common equity of $10 million and is able to earn at the rate of 12 percent after taxes on this capital and on any earnings it retains for reinvestment in the business. It has outstanding 100,000 shares of $2 preferred, convertible share-for-share into common, and 300,000 shares of common. It plans to pay out to the common stockholders 50 percent of its net income after preferred dividends. If conversion occurs at the beginning of the sixth year, the record will be as shown in Table 16-1.

Suppose instead that conversion occurs at the beginning of the first year. If the company retains earnings to the same extent and maintains the same per-share dividend rate on the increased number of shares, the record will be as shown in Table 16-2.

The position of the common stockholder after conversion is not affected by the timing of the conversion. There are still 400,000 shares

TABLE 16-2

Year	Equity Capital	Net Income @ 12%	Dividends Per Share As Above	Total Dividends	Retained Earnings As Above	Surplus Earnings
			(in thousands)			
1	$10,000	$1,200	$1.67	$667	$500	$33
2	10,500	1,260	1.77	707	530	23
3	11,030	1,324	1.87	749	562	13
4	11,592	1,391	1.98	793	595	3
5	12,188	1,463	2.10	841	631	(9)
6	12,820	1,538	°	°	°	°

°No dividend shown because company may wish to revise dividend payout after fifth year.

outstanding, and assets and earning power are the same.

However, if conversion occurs in the first year, the company can give the stockholder every real benefit he gets if conversion is deferred until the sixth year, and it can give him something extra as well. It can pay him the same dividends per share. It can retain the same amount of income to build his future equity and earning power. Moreover, the company's earnings will provide not just the amount needed to satisfy these dividend and earnings retention requirements. There will be a surplus until the point is reached when the preferred dividend no longer exceeds the dividend on the common into which it is convertible. This surplus is the net benefit the stockholder receives with early conversion, and it can be used either to pay more dividends or to reinvest in the business.

The relationship between the preferred dividend and the common dividend available through conversion is the governing factor. As long as the preferred dividend is higher, the common stockholder benefits if conversion comes early rather than late.

Bearing this in mind, it is hard at first to understand how the common stock of a company with a convertible preferred outstanding could sell at a better price than it would command if the preferred converted. But consider the effect of the convertible on reported earnings per share. The company used as an example above would report the results shown in Table 16-3 if the disposition of the excess earnings generated by early conversion is not taken into account.

With deferred conversion, there is a 5-year period during which the common stockholder *appears* to be better off because reported earnings per share are higher and grow at a slightly faster rate.

It is commonly held that statistics on earnings per share and the growth rate in earnings per share exert a major influence on the price of a common stock. This should really be true only if the past record gives investors a firm basis on which to predict future per-share earning power and dividend paying ability, but it does not always work out that way. Some investors fail to realize that earnings statistics may not always be a reliable indicator of future prospects, especially when convertible securities are outstanding and emphatically when the issuer piles convertible on convertible to create

TABLE 16-3

	Earnings Per Share		Dividends Per Share
Year	Conversion in Year 1	Conversion in Year 6	Conversion in Either Year
1	$3.00	$3.33	$1.67
2	3.15	3.53	1.77
3	3.31	3.75	1.87
4	3.48	3.97	1.98
5	3.66	4.21	2.10
6	3.85	3.85	°

°No dividend shown because company may wish to revise dividend payout after fifth year.

an overblown record of year-to-year growth. Other investors who are far more sophisticated themselves will, nevertheless, buy overpriced stocks if they think they can later get out at a profit before less informed holders decide to sell. Consequently, a company which issues convertible preferred is quite likely to enjoy better prices for its common while the convertible is outstanding and can often issue stock in acquisitions or sell stock for cash on a very favorable basis during this period.

However, there are several points a prospective issuer should consider before concluding that a market advantage which has no rational basis is sure to result. In the first place, competent analysts will consider the future claim on the common stock represented by a convertible security. Their evaluations will generally influence stock prices and may often determine them. Secondly, most convertibles will ultimately convert. The issuing company which believes otherwise is betting against itself. Any overpricing of the common in the meanwhile will be eliminated by conversion if not before. Finally, and probably most important, new developments in earnings-per-share reporting may well focus the attention of the average investor on the potential for dilution represented by convertible securities. These developments are reviewed in detail in the next section of this article.

CONVERTIBLES AND EARNINGS-PER-SHARE REPORTING

Current changes in financial reporting will make it easier for investors to recognize and discount for the effects of potential conversion on the future earnings per share of companies with convertible securities outstanding. An important recent development in this connection was the publication in December, 1966 of *Opinion No. 9* of the Accounting Principles Board of the American Institute of Certified Public Accountants, "Reporting the Results of Operations."

Paragraph 43 of this *Opinion* calls for the reporting of two separate earnings-per-share figures if convertible senior securities are outstanding whose conversion would result in a material dilution of per-share earnings. The first figure to be reported is earnings per outstanding share. The second is a supplementary pro-forma computation reflecting the conversion into common stock of all outstanding convertible senior securities. In cases where convertible preferred is the only convertible senior security present, the conventional pro-forma earnings-per-share computation is a simple one. Net income after dividends on any straight preferred which may be outstanding, but before dividends on the convertible preferred are deducted, is divided by the sum of common shares outstanding plus the new shares which conversion would produce.

Paragraph 33 of *Opinion No. 9* poses other problems for issuers of convertible preferred. This section draws a distinction between senior and residual securities. It defines a residual security as any outstanding security which "has participating dividend rights with the common stock, or . . . derives a major portion of its value from its conversion rights or its common stock characteristics," and calls for the inclusion of residual securities not in a supplementary pro-forma presentation but instead as a factor in the computation of actual earnings per outstanding share. "Appropriate consideration" is to be given to related senior dividend rights and participation provisions.

Presumably a convertible preferred is residual if its conversion value is more than twice its investment value.[5] A preferred may be residual when it is first issued; it may become residual with a rise in the market price of the common into which it can be converted; and it might even move from senior to residual security status and back over the years as its conversion and investment values fluctuate. Any company with a residual preferred in its capitalization will be subject to the earnings-per-share reporting procedures called for in paragraph 33.

"Appropriate consideration" is not further defined either in paragraph 33 itself or elsewhere. However, the Accounting Principles Board and the SEC are currently considering two general approaches to earnings-per-share reporting in cases where a residual security is present. One possibility— call it Approach #1—is to divide net income after preferred and common dividends are paid by the sum of common shares outstanding plus the new common shares which would result from conversion of the preferred. The figure this produces, which could be called retained earnings per pro-forma share, is added to the cash dividend paid per common share to arrive at reported earnings per share. This method is currently favored by the SEC when the residual security involved is a participating preferred.

A second possibility—call it Approach #2—is to use conventionally calculated pro-forma earnings as actual reported earnings per share.

These approaches are similar in part. They both recognize that earnings per share are valuable to the stockholder only to the extent that they are paid to him in dividends or retained for his future benefit. Thus, they both go beyond conventional earnings-per-share reporting, which fails to consider the equity claim represented by convertible securities. However, Approach #1 differs from Approach #2 in one way which could be important on occasion. Approach #1 attempts to come to terms with the permanent loss to the common stockholder of the annual difference between the preferred dividend and the common dividend available through conversion, while Approach #2 ignores the problem. In this respect, Approach #1, although it raises some difficult questions, is certainly the more thoughtful of the two.

To illustrate some of the accounting consequences of *Opinion No. 9,* assume that a company is in this position:

---

[5]See Frank T. Weston, "Increased Emphasis on Reporting Earnings per Share," *Financial Analysts Journal* (July-August, 1967).

Convertible Preferred Stock
    A 250,000 shares outstanding
    B Dividends per share, $2
    C Conversion ratio, 1:1
    D Common shares issuable in full conversion (A x C), 250,000

Common Stock
    E 1,000,000 shares outstanding
    F Dividends per share, $1.00

Net Income	G	$5,000,000
Less Preferred Dividends (A x B)	H	500,000
Income Available for Common	I	4,500,000
Less Common Dividends (E x F)	J	1,000,000
Retained Earnings	K	$3,500,000

If the preferred is not considered residual, paragraph 43 applies. The company will report two earnings-per-share figures, earnings per outstanding share, and a supplementary pro-forma figure showing what earnings would have been if all the preferred had been converted at the beginning of the year. These are the calculations:

Earnings per Outstanding Share =

$$\frac{I}{E} = \$4.50$$

Pro-forma Earnings per Share =

$$\frac{G}{D + E} = \$4.00$$

If the preferred *is* considered residual, paragraph 33 applies. Only one earnings-per-share figure will be reported. With Approach #1, that figure will be computed as follows:

Earnings per Share =

$$\frac{K}{D + E} + F = \$3.80$$

With Approach #2, the figure will be computed by making the conventional pro-forma calculation as shown above:

Pro-forma Earnings per Share =

$$\frac{G}{D + E} = \$4.00$$

Approach #1 will produce a lower earnings-per-share figure when the dividend on the preferred exceeds the dividend on the common into which it is convertible, and a higher figure when the reverse is true.

The effort to develop more meaningful per-share data will certainly be constructive if it produces accounting methods which make it easier for investors to interpret the past and estimate the future of common stock earnings and dividends, taking convertible preferred into account. It may also discourage some issuers from adding to securities valuation problems by designing ever more complex convertibles. There is no way to predict now just what earnings-per-share reporting techniques will eventually find mutual acceptance among the corporate community, the AICPA, and the SEC. The important point is that future earnings reports will have to reflect in one way or another the potential for dilution represented by convertible securities, a fact which may well influence the market prices of the issuers' common stocks.[6]

PARTICIPATING PREFERENCE STOCK

Several convertible preferreds issued in recent years incorporated special features designed to make them sell for an extended time at premiums over their conversion values. The main idea in issuing such stock was to create a security the issuer could use for a series of acquisitions over a period of years without having to change its terms to keep pace with increases in the dividend rate or the market price of the common.

To perpetuate the premium, two basic techniques were used, one involving dividends and the other involving the conversion ratio. International Telephone and Telegraph Corporation's cumulative convertible preference stock illustrates the use of a special dividend feature. Litton Industries' convertible participating preference stock is an example of a special conversion feature.

The ITT stock, which has since been retired in an exchange offer, was convertible share-for-share into common and was entitled to double the dividend on the common with a minimum of $2.40. The Litton stock, which is entitled to cash dividends equal to those paid on the common (none at present), was initially convertible share-for-share into common but has a somewhat complex escalating conversion feature. The net effect of the conversion privilege is to give the holder a compound annual growth rate of about .6 percent in the conversion ratio after taking into account an expected 2½ percent annual stock dividend on the common. The dividend feature of the ITT preference stock was perpetual; escalation in the Litton stock's conversion ratio terminates after 23 years. Both issues were noncallable for ten years.

These securities were issued before APB *Opinion No. 9* was published. The situation changed with the publication of the *Opinion*, since paragraph 33, in its present form, defines participating preferreds as residual securities, with all their associated earnings-per-share reporting problems. Market reception raises further questions, although the data is very

---

[6]In May, 1969, APB *Opinion No. 15, Earnings Per Share*, was issued. Paragraphs 31 through 34 are devoted to convertible securities and should be consulted for changes after Mr. Meyer's article was written. One change from APB *Opinion No. 9* is that now " . . . a convertible security should be considered as a common stock equivalent (residual security) at the time of issuance if, based on its market price, it has a cash yield of less than 66 2/3% of the then current bank prime interest rate."

limited. The market for ITT's issue was too thin and the premium too erratic for any useful conclusions to be drawn. However, the market premiums for Litton's issue have clearly been small in comparison with the extra common the holders eventually will receive as a result of the escalating conversion ratio. In short, participating preference stocks no longer enjoy favorable financial reporting treatment nor can they be relied on to command premiums which fully reflect what their issuers are giving up in dividends or convertibility. It is hard to visualize situations in which they could be used to advantage under existing circumstances.

CONVERSION

There are four principal reasons for convertible preferred stockholders to exchange their shares for common: an opportunity for arbitrage, a dividend differential in favor of the common, a change in conversion rights, or a call.

Arbitrage

When the conversion value of the preferred is so much higher than its investment value that premium has disappeared, imperfections in the market will probably cause the stock to sell from time to time at a slight discount from its conversion value. Whenever this occurs, arbitrageurs will buy it, sell the common short simultaneously, and then convert the preferred to cover their short sales at a profit.

Dividend Differential

A favorable difference between the common dividend available through conversion and the convertible preferred dividend could induce some voluntary conversion. However, there is no single point where all shareholders will convert. They have to weigh not only the relative yields available to them but also the relative risks of the securities. With or without conversion, the convertible preferred holder will benefit from any market appreciation in the common. Therefore, an investor loses only the difference in yields by delaying conversion. If the preferred position of the senior security is worth more to the investor than the difference in yields, he will not convert.

A Change in Conversion Rights

Most convertible preferreds have perpetual conversion rights at a fixed conversion ratio. However, some preferreds lose their conversion rights after a specified date, which results in voluntary conversion as the date approaches if conversion value exceeds investment value. Others are subject to a stepped-down conversion ratio after a specified date, which can also cause some conversion depending on the size of the step-down and the relationship between investment value and the conversion values before and after the change.

Calling the Issue

If the issuer calls a convertible preferred, the holder has the choice of converting his shares or allowing the company to redeem them at the call price. If the conversion value is in excess of the call price, a shareholder would lose money if he did not convert. Thus, the company effectively forces conversion.

A company should wait until the conversion value is well above the call price if it wishes to insure conversion when calling the convertible preferred. Otherwise a drop in the market price of the common might put the conversion value of the preferred below the call price during the notice of redemption period, and the company would be obliged to redeem the preferred for cash. The spread between conversion value and the call price necessary to provide an adequate margin of safety depends largely on general market conditions and the volatility of the common.

Occasionally a company may wish to call an issue when the call price is not far enough below the conversion value to insure conversion. In this situation an investment banker may be willing to underwrite the call for a fee. In an underwritten call the banker agrees to buy at the call price and convert into common all shares presented for redemption.

AUTHORIZATION

Many companies have recently obtained from their stockholders "blank check" authorizations to issue up to a certain amount of preferred stock. The number of issues of preferred which may be created under these authorizations, and the dividend rate, conversion rights, and other features of each issue, are normally left to the discretion of the company's directors. When convertible preferred is chosen as the security to use for an acquisition, an acquirer with a blank check authorization already in hand can close the deal without going to its stockholders if their approval is not required for the acquisition itself.

Of course, stockholder approval of an acquisition may well be required by the acquiring company's charter or bylaws, the statutes of the state in which it is incorporated, or the rules of any stock exchange on which its securities may be listed. Under New York Stock Exchange rules, for example, listed companies are expected to seek stockholder approval of acquisitions involving the issuance of common or securities convertible into common which would increase outstanding shares by approximately 20 percent. The Exchange will also want stockholder approval of an acquisition involving the issuance of a package of securities, or cash and securities, if common or convertibles are included and the fair market value of the package is equal to approximately 20 percent of the market value of the outstanding common. And it will want stockholder approval of any acquisition which is not an arm's length transaction.

When a blank check authorization is being considered, a question often arises on the number of shares the stockholders should be asked to authorize. Management knows that this number is not really important, since the dividend rate and conversion ratio can later be set so as to achieve almost any desired market value per share. However, the possibility that stockholders might react badly to a proposal to authorize a very large number of shares is often a source of concern. Recent experience suggests that the size of the authorization within reasonable limits makes no difference when the company is substantial and reputable. In a sample of 15 companies among the many which obtained blank check preferred authorizations within the last year, the number of preferred shares authorized ranged from a high of 100 percent of the common shares outstanding to a low of 7 percent. The median figure was 16 percent.

TERMS

There are no hard rules for setting the terms of a convertible preferred issue, but there are major features which must be dealt with in one way or another. They tend to follow certain patterns, as follows.

Dividend Rights

Payment dates and dollar amounts of preferred dividends are specified. In a few cases future increases or decreases in the dividend rate are provided for. Dividends are almost always cumulative.

Conversion Rights

The simplest and most frequently used form gives the holder the right to convert his preferred into a specified amount of common at any time. This privilege is perpetual unless the issue is called and will be fully protected against dilution. Most preferreds issued in mergers among public companies follow this pattern. More complex conversion rights are sometimes found, particularly in acquisitions of closely held companies.

Liquidation Rights

The senior claim of the preferred on corporate assets in liquidation is specified. Liquidating value can vary widely. In most cases, involuntary liquidating value is set close to the price at which the issue is designed to sell initially, while voluntary liquidating value will be set somewhat higher— often at the call price. Holders are generally entitled to accumulated dividends in either case.

Voting Rights

Preferred shareholders generally vote with the common, especially when the preferred is an acquisition security designed for a tax-free transaction. The preferred usually has one vote per share, although there are a number of cases of fractional voting rights. In these instances, the fractional vote is usually equal to the fraction of a share of common into which a share of preferred is convertible. The main points to review here are control considerations and the possibility that an absurdly low voting privilege for the preferred relative to its value could affect the tax status of the exchange.

In addition to voting with the common, the preferred generally votes as a class to authorize a prior preferred or a change in the terms of the issue, or to approve a sale of major assets or merger of the company. A two-thirds vote is generally required. The preferred as a class will also be entitled to board representation if dividends are defaulted for a specified number of quarters. To qualify for a NYSE listing, the preferred must have the right to elect at least two directors if dividends are the equivalent of six quarterly payments in arrears.

Par Value

Par value is often avoided in favor of a low stated value. This eliminates certain legal and accounting problems which might otherwise arise. It will not allow the issuer to minimize the significance of the issue on the balance sheet, however. Paragraph 10 of *Opinion No. 10* of the APB, also published in December of 1966, notes that "companies at times issue preferred . . . which has a preference in involuntary liquidation considerably in excess of the par or stated value. . . . The Board recommends that, in these cases, the liquidation preference of the stock be disclosed in the equity section of the balance sheet in the aggregate, either parenthetically or 'in short,' rather than on a per-share basis or by disclosure in notes."

Preemptive Rights

The preferred usually has none.

Limitations on Senior Indebtedness

The holders of the preferred are generally not protected.

Sinking Fund Provisions

A sinking fund is sometimes but not generally provided.

Call Provisions

The recipients usually have call protection for at least five years. In an acquisition, this feature is generally considered desirable to assure tax-free treatment of the transaction. Thereafter, the preferred is typically callable on 30 days' notice. There is a fair amount of variety in call prices. Some convertible preferreds follow a pattern typical of straight preferreds. The initial call price will be the expected market value of the security plus a premium equal to the annual dividend rate; thereafter, the premium will be reduced down to zero in equal annual amounts over a period of five or ten years. Others will carry higher call prices, some of which are reduced over time and others not. The call price can be a significant negotiating point, since a high call price favors the holder and a low one, the issuer.

DESIGNING AN ISSUE

In setting the basic terms of a convertible preferred, the issuer has considerable latitude. Convertible preferreds can be designed to fit almost any situation, and a number of recent issues carry unusual dividend or conversion features.

If maximum premium is the object, two rules should be followed.

1. Establish investment and conversion values which are equal. Frequently this will improve the dividend payout to the acquired company's shareholders to an extent considered unnecessary by the acquirer. However, some loss of premium may be expected if a lower dividend rate is chosen.
2. Keep the terms simple. Complicated conversion and dividend features are likely to hurt the premium more than they help the issuer. Moreover, complex senior securities are a source of confusion, and investors may pay less for the company's common in the long run because of the uncertainties an involved capital structure creates.

One way of equalizing investment and conversion values so as to produce the maximum premium is shown in the following steps:

1. Select a target market price. This is completely arbitrary, although it is common practice to avoid a very low or a very high price.
2. Estimate the premium at which the preferred might sell over conversion and investment values when these two values are equal. This estimate will require expert evaluation.
3. Compute what the investment/conversion value should be based on the target market price and the estimated premium.
4. Estimate what yield would be required to sell the convertible as a straight preferred.
5. Compute the dividend by relating the estimated required straight preferred yield to the desired investment value.
6. Compute the conversion ratio by relating the market price of the common to the desired conversion value.

To illustrate:

A target market price of $60 is chosen for the convertible preferred. It is estimated that the preferred would sell at a 20 percent premium over its investment and conversion values when these two are identical. Investment/conversion value can now be calculated to be $50. It is estimated that the issuer could sell a straight preferred on a 5 percent yield basis. The dividend representing a 5 percent yield on an investment value of $50 is calculated to be $2.50. The common sells for $30. The conversion ratio which would produce a $50 conversion value is calculated to be 1.67.

HOW MUCH TO ISSUE

There are two important factors which bear on the question of how much convertible preferred a company can issue within the limits of sound financial policy. One is dilution, used here to mean the percentage of increase in common stock which would result if the convertible securities in the company's capitalization were all converted. The other is the ranking of the preferred with respect to the common stock.

It is hard to deal with the question of what effect dilution has on the issuer's common. In the past, the conventional view has been that potential dilution from conversion affects the market for the common only when conversion becomes likely. At that point the convertible will overhang and depress the common, which may have difficulty breaking through to a new, higher price level where conversion can be forced with a call. Since the amount of dilution will govern the extent to which the common will be depressed, it is obviously desirable to keep the dilution low.

A case can be made for a different point of view. To the extent that potential dilution is perceived and discounted by investors when it is created, the underlying common should be affected when the convertible is first issued, not when it is about to convert. If stock prices, thereafter, are based on earnings performance adjusted for potential dilution, the common ought to move smoothly into the area where conversion can be forced. It seems likely that this sort of market action will become more typical as larger numbers of investors become aware of the effects of dilution from convertible securities. Thus, the relevant consideration with respect to dilution may really be the immediate impact on earnings per share, adjusted pro-forma for dilution, when the preferred is first issued. Since most convertible preferreds are acquisition securities, the effect of the issue on adjusted earnings has to be evaluated with specific reference to the current and prospective earnings of the company being acquired.

As for ranking, it is worthwhile to recall that the preferred is after all in the driver's seat. If things go poorly, the preferred retains its cumulative senior claim on dividends. If things go well, the preferred can participate by converting. A large amount of a security like this might weaken the underlying common by limiting the issuer's ability to pay common dividends and retain earnings for future growth. A package of convertible preferred and common could represent a better way to finance a really sizable acquisition.

To illustrate with an extreme example, suppose that a company earns $1 million and pays out $500,000 in common dividends. It uses a new convertible preferred with an aggregate market value of $20 million and a 5 percent yield to acquire another company with $1 million in earnings. In other words, the earnings of the acquired company are equal to the dividend on the preferred. If combined net income of $2 million declines by 25 percent to $1.5 million in the following year, earnings will just cover preferred and common dividends. The leverage of the fixed senior dividend charge turns a change in net income into a much larger change in income available for common dividends and retention.

There is no rule-of-thumb answer to the question of how much convertible preferred is too much. Each case has to be weighed on its merits. A prospective issuer should consider very carefully its dividend policy, its current and projected consolidated earnings and earnings variance possibilities, and the likelihood of conversion as these factors would relate to the preferred dividend commitment.

SUMMING UP

Convertible preferred stock is often a useful security for corporate acquisitions. It can provide the basis for a tax-free exchange. It will usually sell at a premium over the market price of the common into which it is convertible. It can allow the issuing company to satisfy the dividend requirements of the acquired company without disturbing its own dividend policy. And it can be used to reduce the voting power of the acquired company's shareholders.

One thing convertible preferred will *not* do is allow the issuer to avoid dilution of common share earnings. The groundwork for dilution is laid when a convertible is first created rather than when conversion actually occurs. Convertible preferred will probably not even allow the issuer to postpone dilution. New financial reporting standards may well prompt an increasing number of investors to discount their estimates of the worth of a company's common share earnings as soon as the company issues a convertible. What convertible preferred *will* do is permit the issuer to reduce dilution somewhat. To the extent that it sells at a premium over its conversion value, an issue of convertible preferred will require fewer common shares in conversion than an issue of common with the same market value. Of course the premium has a cost: the cumulative fixed senior dividend charge is the price the issuer pays for it.

Until converted, convertible preferred has a senior claim on earnings and on assets. Like any senior security, it can be overused. However, it can also be a valuable part of the securities inventory of the corporate financial manager when it is employed with restraint and common sense.

17. NEGOTIATING THE RESTRICTIVE COVENANTS OF LOAN AGREEMENTS ASSOCIATED WITH THE PRIVATE PLACEMENT OF CORPORATE DEBT SECURITIES*

ELLIOTT L. ATAMIAN†

Direct placement of corporate securities is a financial mechanism well known to financial managers.[1] Simply stated, the phrase "direct placements" describes a financial process whereby a corporation (the issuer) negotiates directly with the supplier of funds (the buyer). Principal buyers of privately placed corporate securities are the major life insurance companies.[2]

Before funds are provided, however, the buyer (lender) and issuer (borrower) negotiate an agreement which outlines the terms under which both parties must operate for the life of the loan. The importance of the agreement's covenants cannot be overstated, for they affect managerial prerogatives. Furthermore, they provide the foundation for the borrower-lender relationship which evolves from the private placement. Despite the obvious importance of the terms, many financial managers know relatively little about the covenants included in the loan agreement. The following comments by financial managers illustrate this point:

Financial Manager No. 1, small corporation (assets $5 million):

> I didn't know what to expect; I was at their [negotiators for a life insurance company] mercy.

Financial Manager No. 2, medium-sized corporation (assets $50 million):

> I was determined to make sure that we could continue our long history of uninterrupted dividend payments. On this point we had to have a dividend clause we could live with.

Financial Manager No. 3, large retail chain (sales $200 million):

> What about the noncallability clause? I can't prepay this note even though we have idle cash. Is it normal practice to prevent a borrower from pre-

---

*Reprinted from the October, 1964 issue of *The University of Washington Business Review*, pp. 56-72.

†Professor of Business Administration, Boston University.

[1]Technical and other aspects of direct placements have been comprehensively covered by the following writers: Rogers, "Purchase by Insurance Companies of Securities Privately Offered," *Harvard Law Review, LII* (1939), p. 773; Bell and Fraine, "Legal Framework, Trends and Developments in Investment Practices of Life Insurance Companies," *Law and Contemporary Problems, XVII* (Winter, 1952), p. 45; Mendel, "Institutional Investment Through Private Placements," *Columbia Law Review, LIII* (1953), p. 804; E. Raymond Corey, *Direct Placement of Corporate Securities* (Boston: Division of Research, Graduate School of Business Administration, Harvard University Press, 1951).

[2]Practically all securities offered privately by corporations are debt instruments—notes, bonds, and debentures. Hereafter, the analysis focuses on debt instruments of industrial corporations and the practices of life insurance companies as the principal buyers.

paying?

The comments above trigger the following questions.

(1) What are the terms typically found in note agreements, and what is their underlying rationale?
(2) Are the terms tailor-made, or do they typically follow set patterns of detail?
(3) What are the limits of bargaining associated with these terms?
(4) Do some lenders bargain for more stringent terms than other lenders?

Obviously we are not concerned with those terms which are "boilerplate."[3] Rather, this article centers attention on the other protective covenants which are called, in the jargon of the trade, "the negative covenants." Their drafting is a negotiation which starts at complete prohibition and develops suitable exceptions. The exceptions are intentional, predicated allegedly on the borrower's needs. In other words, these are the provisions which are drafted to fit the circumstances of each case and which lend themselves to bargaining.

THE IMPORTANT PROTECTIVE PROVISIONS

In order to keep this article within manageable proportions,[4] discussion is confined to the protective covenants which appear to be most important in limiting risk for the sample lenders.[5] This point of view has been adopted because these are the clauses for which lenders bargain. These include seven clauses relating to: negative pledge, additional indebtedness, investments, sinking funds, dividends, working capital, and mergers. Conversations with investment officers indicated that they attached crucial importance to these covenants in limiting risk.[6]

---

[3] I refer here particularly to the "affirmative" covenants and various "warranties" made by the borrower. Requiring borrowers to provide periodic financial data illustrates affirmative covenants. The absence of litigations or representations regarding operating statements illustrates warranties.

[4] In the interests of simplicity, the provisions are described to apply to the borrower and not its subsidiaries. In reality, if the covenants applied solely to the borrower, practically every provision could be circumscribed, at least partially, by the creation and use of subsidiaries.

[5] The sample of lenders consisted of five mutual life insurance companies headquartered in New England. They were selected for a variety of reasons. One was chosen because it is the largest in New England in terms of asset size. Another was selected because it was labeled as an oddball outfit by financial finders. Another company was chosen because it was small in asset size. Another was selected as the *depth company* because it agreed to allow the writer to spend several months accumulating data from loan agreements, tabulating modifications to original agreements, interviewing loan officers, etc. Furthermore, it had actively promoted direct placements as an instrument of investment policy since the end of World War II. It had, therefore, considerable experience and background in private deals. On the basis of an understanding of the administration of this company in limiting risk, the study was continued with considerably less detail for other lenders in the sample.

Although no attempt was made to support the assumption that most practices used by New England companies are used by lenders elsewhere, conversations with investment officers and others knowledgeable in the area led the writer to suspect that such is the case.

The focus of the investigation centered on the years 1956-58. There is no reason to feel that current practice is significantly different from that of the 1956-58 period.

[6] A variety of research techniques was used in collecting data. The author analyzed (cont.)

Negative Pledge Clause

The lender limits its risk position by controlling the amount of secured indebtedness which the borrower can incur. The negative pledge limits prior or equal claims by other creditors upon the borrower's assets. The lender is in a position to express a strong voice concerning the selection of new, long-term creditors. In addition, the clause usually is drafted to cover not only real estate and chattel mortgages but also conditional sales, whereby title is retained by the seller. Typically, the negative pledge clause takes the form of an outright prohibition of mortgages[7] or other liens on the borrower's assets.

Loan officers agreed that there is no bargaining relative to the clause's inclusion in the loan agreement. The lender insists upon controlling the secured indebtedness of the borrower and in this manner limits its risk position. One loan officer seemed to reflect the viewpoint of most loan officers when he said, " . . . . . without a pledge we would be giving away our rights. If, for example, we allowed the borrowers to make bank loans and pledge their best assets, receivables, and inventories against them, we would be putting ourselves, obviously, in an inferior position which is, in effect, giving away our rights."

Additional Indebtedness

Whereas the negative pledge clause restricts the lender's risk position by limiting secured liens, the additional indebtedness covenant offers protection by limiting the borrower's ability to incur unsecured debt on a parity with the note. The additional debt covenant includes fixed debt (long-term) and current debt. Purchase-money mortgages[8] and long-term leases are included with long-term debt. Leases are included as long-term debt because loan officers regard leases as fixed, long-term obligations of the lessee. With respect to current debt, attention is confined to bank borrowings.

Funded Debt. Most investment officers in the sample lending institutions stated that the borrowers usually were not allowed to incur funded debt

---

112 industrial private placements purchased by the depth company during 1956-58. The financial provisions included in the agreements were tabulated to quantify many of the observations made throughout this report. Thus, investment officers were interviewed for rationale and procedure with respect to the negative covenants, and the lender's records were checked for supporting data.

Most of the quantitative material received from the other companies in the sample represents the *considered estimates* of responsible loan officers. Therefore, the report does not purport to present exact performances for all of the sample companies as an aggregate.

Personal interviews with eight corporate treasurers in the Boston area were conducted, and a questionnaire which served the same purpose as the interviews was sent to 50 corporate treasurers. There were 30 respondents to the questionnaire.

[7]In agreements studied by the author, purchase-money mortgages were usually allowed according to qualifications which were usually drafted in the covenant limiting additional indebtedness. Accordingly, purchase-money liens are described in connection with that covenant. In addition, there were other exceptions, including liens and pledges involved with the routine administration of a business—i.e., tax liens, pledges under workman's compensation, etc.

[8]Purchase-money mortgages will be treated as a separate part of this clause. Therefore, reference hereafter to funded debt in this section will not include purchase-money mortgages.

in addition to the current placement without prior consent of the lender. The one exception to this finding was the Able Life Insurance Company.[9] Loan officers of this company showed a definite preference for a formula-type covenant which allowed additional funded debt at the option of the borrower, provided the note issuer was able to comply with specified earnings and assets tests. Thus, as the borrower's operations grow, this type of clause automatically allows the borrower to incur additional funded debt in amounts consistent with the company's growth.

The degree of restriction in this covenant was related to the size of the borrower's assets. Companies which were allowed unlimited additional indebtedness were very large and enjoyed financially distinguished, national reputations. The relationship of size and degree of detail is revealed further by the statement of an investment officer: "Of course, with bigger and stronger companies, their bargaining position is such that they insist on formula-type provisions, and thus they are allowed to have additional debt provided they stay within the limits."

When the borrower successfully bargains for a formula-type debt provision, the lender frequently limits its risk position by requiring the borrower to comply with several tests, of which the following are representative but not exhaustive:

(1) a dollar limit;
(2) a specified ratio relating funded debt to net current assets;
(3) a specified ratio relating funded debt to net tangible assets;
(4) a specified ratio relating funded debt to total capitalization;
(5) a specified earnings requirement;
(6) a combination of two or more of the foregoing.

The author observed in all lending institutions, except the Able Life Insurance Company, that the formula-type restriction usually was not drafted unless the borrower specifically requested its inclusion in that particular form. Most lenders asserted that the formula-type provision compelled them to assume greater risks, despite the safeguards provided by the various earnings and assets tests mentioned earlier. Investment officers of these companies expressed a preference for the provision which prohibited additional funded debt without the lender's consent. They took this position because a prohibition of additional debt required borrowers to reveal their planned use for the new funds. In other words, a stringent debt clause enabled lenders to review the loan and have a "look-see" at proposed activities whenever the latter requested permission to obtain additional long-term debt.

Purchase-Money Mortgages. Purchase-money liens usually are confined by this provision to after-acquired properties. The acquisition of these properties is financed in part by the mortgage.[10] The provision is drafted in

---

[9]Fictitious name.

[10]Also, the provision generally allows the acquisition of property, subject to a preexisting mortgage. In addition, the clause usually includes liens on improvements to existing property.

this manner to avoid the replacement of the borrower's unencumbered assets by assets upon which other creditors have prior liens. Limitations on purchase-money mortgages restrict, therefore, the borrower's flexibility to borrow long-term funds as it sees fit from other lenders by weakening the asset support behind the existing note.

The inclusion of this clause in the agreement limits the lender's risk position in several ways. First, as was indicated earlier, existing unencumbered property of the borrower does not come under the lien privileges extended by this clause. Purchase-money mortgages can be incurred only in connection with the acquisition of new property. Second, risk is limited by usually requiring the borrower to provide cash for $33\frac{1}{3}$-40 percent of the new asset's cost or market value. In the event the new facility results in financial adversities, the maximum extent to which the borrower's net worth is affected is approximately 60 percent of the new asset's cost or market value. Third, a 60 percent loss on a new facility probably will not be critical to the borrower because the clause limits mortgage debt in the aggregate to a specified dollar maximum, usually a nominal amount.

Studies showed that the aggregate figure was a combination of two factors: an historical figure representing an amount of purchase-money mortgages which the borrower has been able to handle with ease in the past; and the loan officer's personal judgment concerning the amount needed. Bargaining was possible, however, for when the borrower had a well conceived program calling for a larger amount than its historical experience, the probabilities were very high that the larger figure would be allowed.

The degree of restriction to which borrowers must agree is related to the individual firm's asset size. For example, almost 15 percent of all cases were not allowed any latitude under the covenant. With only one exception, all borrowers in the group agreeing to complete prohibition, without consent of the lender, had total assets under $50 million. Unlimited privileges were bargained for only by very large and nationally distinguished firms.

Long-Term Leases. Provisions dealing with long-term leases, including leaseback transactions, limit the risk position of the lender by further controlling the ability of the borrower to incur financial obligations. All loan officers agreed that long-term leases were fixed charges. Therefore, the earnings flow of the borrower must be adequate not only to meet the note's fixed debt-service charges but also to meet the fixed charges associated with the various leasing arrangements to which the firm is committed.[11]

In addition, as the insurance companies in the sample became more active as landlords in leaseback transactions, they became increasingly aware of the effect which leasebacks would have on their risk position as lenders. Thus, federal laws relating to bankruptcy and reorganization seem to favor

---

[11]Debt service charges include both interest and amortization payments. For analytic purposes, amortization payments are made from earnings after taxes and preferred dividends. Therefore, most analysts compute coverage of debt service charges by relating earnings before taxes to the sum of interest plus the other charges converted into pretax terms.

the landlord at the expense of the other creditors. For example, "under the Federal Bankruptcy Law, a landlord can prove a claim for the equivalent of one year's rental in a Chapter X proceeding.[40]. . . The amount of the claim which can be proved becomes important only if the lease has been rejected by the trustee in bankruptcy and the landlord has received the property back. The bankruptcy of a corporation is usually the means of reorganization, and seldom of liquidation. In such a case, the trustee generally will continue to occupy it, and as long as he does, the rental is a charge against the trustee and, therefore, a preferred claim."[12] For these reasons almost all loan contracts observed by the author prohibited additional sale-leaseback transactions without the lender's prior consent.

However, the reader should not interpret prohibition of additional lease-back arrangements to signify that lenders objected to leases. In many agreements, borrowers were allowed to enter into long-term leases with terms in excess of three years, provided aggregate rentals of the note issuer did not exceed a specified dollar figure.

In order to limit risk by the terms of this provision, investment officers rely heavily on the borrower's historical use of leasing arrangements. Thus, unless a borrower has a history of leases, probability is high that both leases and leaseback will be prohibited in the loan agreement. When the borrower has a background of leases, however, the historical charges will be used as a frame of reference in setting the amount of annual rentals. Increments to historical rental charges can be negotiated, provided the borrower possesses a well developed program calling for increased rentals.

Current debt. The provision pertaining to current debt typically is divided into two subject areas. The first includes current liabilities incurred in the ordinary course of business. These liabilities are usually unlimited, unless they represent indebtedness for borrowed money or guarantees of the obligations of others. The second subject area deals with current borrowings; with respect to these, the clause usually includes a specified dollar limit.

Lenders limit risk by restricting current borrowings to truly current needs. Investment officers frequently draft some of the following elements in the current debt covenant:

(1) a maximum dollar amount;
(2) a period of time—30, 60, or 90 days—during which borrowing must be liquidated (cleaned up) each year;
(3) a period of time when borrowings must be minimized, if complete liquidation is not feasible without jeopardizing the best interests of the business.

Most loan officers considered the liquidation period to be the most restrictive clause in the current debt clause. It is significant that the depth

---

[12]Bell and Fraine, "Legal Framework, Trends and Developments in Investment Practices of Life Insurance Companies," *Law and Contemporary Problems,* XVII (Winter, 1952), p. 63-64; the superscript numeral "40" in the quotation refers to 30 Stat. 562 (1898) as amended, and 52 Stat. 893 (1938), 11 U.S.C. Sections 103, 602, (1946).

company was willing to grant unlimited current borrowings in 47 percent of all cases studied, despite the fact that its loan officers stated a preference for restricted dollar amounts. However, of the 47 loans without dollar limits in the current debt clause, 27, or 57 percent, agreed to a restriction in the form of an extinguishment period or a current ratio.

Empirical data showed that borrowers with substantial assets bargained successfully for greater latitude with respect to current borrowings. Most of the borrowers who bargained for unlimited current borrowings had assets over $25 million. Furthermore, concerns with assets over $100 million were rarely required to extinguish their current debt or restrict their borrowing activities to the limitations of a current ratio. Finally, the nature of the borrower's industry and the competitive pressures it faces has an important bearing on the degree of restriction drafted into this provision.

Investments, Loans, and Advances

The provision with respect to investments, loans, and advances limits the lender's risk position by restricting the borrower's capital investments and advances to subsidiaries. In addition, investments in subsidiaries are almost always confined to domestic subsidiaries, because foreign subsidiaries are subject to expropriation and currency control. Thus, this clause may in some cases restrict the ability of the borrower to invest as it sees fit unless it first gains the consent of the lender.

Most lenders were critical of investment practices which resulted in a minority ownership position for the borrower. One investment officer explained that this attitude stems from a realization that the borrower normally would not have a significant voice in the activities of a subsidiary in which it held only a minority interest. Thus, the borrower would have little or no control over the use of its investments, even though the funds advanced may be the capital borrowed from the insurance companies. It would seem that the lender is interested in exercising some voice over the use of its funds, particularly in its dealings with smaller borrowers. Furthermore, as a minority owner, the borrower's claim against the subsidiary's assets can be weakened by an issuance of senior debt or preferred stocks by the subsidiary's majority owners. For these reasons, loan agreements in most instances impose a dollar limit on investments and advances relating to majority or minority ownership positions in subsidiaries.

Loan officers of the Able Life Insurance Company, however, seemed to disagree with the underlying rationale responsible for the limitations included in this provision. They stated that they preferred to buy the placements of companies with proven managerial talent and depth. Therefore, if the borrower has excess working capital, the lender is satisfied, at least initially, to allow unrestricted latitude to this management concerning domestic investments. In other words, this lender relies on the working capital provision (see below) to limit the borrower's activities in domestic capital investments.

Investments in wholly-owned subsidiaries typically are not restricted dollarwise,[13] whereas investments in less than wholly-owned subsidiaries or loans to individuals are typically limited to a specific dollar amount. Once the decision is made to limit investments to a dollar amount, the specified figure results from a combination of processes. During the selection period,[14] lenders determine the borrower's formulated plans regarding future investments in subsidiaries. To this figure, lenders add the amounts already sunk in existing investments. Lastly, during the selection process loan officers appraise the borrower's procedures for controlling capital expenditures— i.e., is management impetuous or conservative in its approach to capital expenditures? This judgment may be tempered by the borrower's net worth position or the availability of financial cushion from other sources. From these processes, loan officers and borrowers negotiate a mutually acceptable dollar amount.

Fixed Sinking Fund, Prepayment, and Nonrefundability Clauses

Two types of provisions are concerned principally with the mechanics of the debt's repayment. The first type is the fixed schedule of payments which the borrower must make periodically over the life of the loan.[15] This type is referred to as "sinking fund" payments, "fixed" payments, or "amortization" payments. The second type involves prepayments of the loan in advance of the planned schedule of amortization payments. This provision is further divided into two classes: (1) there are prepayments which are contingent on the level of the borrower's earnings; (2) there are prepayments when the borrower exercises the option to call the loan according to the terms of the call or redemption provision. It is to be noted that contingent prepayments are mandatory; the borrower has no choice but to make prepayments according to stipulations of the prepayment covenant in the event that net earnings exceed a certain level. On the other hand, the borrower exercises a choice when it makes prepayments under the "call privilege."[16] Thus, these prepayments are regarded as optional. The re-

---

[13]However, loans or advances from the parent to the subsidiary might be prohibited or limited even though the subsidiary is wholly owned.

[14]For an analysis of the practices and techniques used in the selection period (sometimes called a screening or investigatory period), see Elliott L. Atamian, *Limiting Risk in the Administrative of Direct Placements by Life Insurance Companies Headquartered in New England,"* (Doctoral thesis, Harvard Business School, 1962).

[15]Despite the impressions created by much literature related to direct placement administration, fixed payments do not begin at the end of the note's first year in most cases. Planned deferrals for three to five years are typical and are advantageous to both parties. The borrower may use the deferred payments in the business until the facility financed by the loan generates earnings. The lender profits from the deferral because it raises effectively the overall yield of the loan. Furthermore, the reader should not assume that the note is always amortized completely on the date of maturity. Balloons ranking from 10 percent to 100 percent can be negotiated on some occasions, depending on the borrower's asset size and industry in which it operates.

[16]The call privilege is explained later in this section. The expression was taken from the following article: Willis J. Winn and Arleigh P. Hess, "The Value of the Call Privilege," *Journal of Finance*, XIV (May, 1959).

mainder of this section will be devoted to the optional prepayment provision.

The optional prepayment clause deals with the right of the borrower to call the loan at par or at a premium prior to the expiration of the contract's maturity. Unless its right is restricted, the borrower is potentially in a position to redeem its note because of a variety of reasons, including refunding of the note at a lower rate of interest. The lender, however, does not have comparable rights, and as long as the borrower is unrestricted in the exercise of the call privilege, the lending institution probably will experience both inconvenience and loss of income. These unfavorable results are inevitable because, historically, borrowers usually redeem their bonds only when new funds are available at a lower rate of interest.[17]

The optional prepayment clause contains two elements of interest to this article: the call price (premium) to be paid by the borrower when the clause is exercised; and the restrictions placed on the prepayment privilege.

In dealing with the two elements, this article presents the experiences and comments associated with the depth company in administering this clause. When significant variations among the other sample lenders exist, these differences will be specifically noted and identified as viewpoints or experiences separate from the depth company.

Premiums. When the borrower exercises its option and prepays its loan prior to a prearranged schedule, the loan agreement invariably provides for the payment of a premium. Its purpose is to reimburse the lender for undergoing additional expense and inconvenience when reinvesting the optional prepayments.

In the vast majority of cases, premiums start at the interest rate on the face of the note and decline periodically until the year of maturity, at which time there is no premium. Not infrequently, however, lenders voluntarily waive the prepayment premium for one of the following reasons:

(1) the waived premium is small because the note has only a relatively short time to continue until maturity;

(2) in the opinion of cognizant loan officers, the request is made under favorable borrower-lender relationships;

(3) the interest rate on the called note is low; the prepaid funds can be reinvested promptly at a higher rate of interest.

Restrictions to Optional Prepayments. The attitude of lenders in the sample with respect to restrictions placed on the call privilege varied. All agreed that some protection in the form of nonrefundability clauses was both necessary and just. However, some were more indifferent than others concerning the degree of protection. A senior loan officer in the Dependable Life Insurance Company (fictitious name) stated that his company's experiences seemed to suggest that industrial borrowers are not anxious to refund at lower rates because of their desire to establish long-term relationships with

---

[17]*Ibid.*, p. 183. This article covers the history of the call privilege and, more important, suggests an approach to assessing the privilege's value.

TABLE 17-1

PROTECTION PERIOD° OF NONREFUNDABILITY AND NONCALLABILITY† CLAUSES
IN INDUSTRIAL PLACEMENTS PURCHASED BY DEPTH COMPANY
1956-1958

Year	Numbers of Loans with Protection Period							Number of Loans with No Reference††	Totals
	25%	33%	50%	66%	75%	85%	100%		
1958	—	5	12	5	—	2	4	3	31
1957	2	1	8	4	2	2	8	2	29
1956	—	6	9	—	—	—	4	20	39
Total Loans	2	12	29	9	2	4	16	25	99

°Protection period is defined as the number of years, stated as a percentage of the note's maturity, during which refunding at an equal or lower rate of interest is prohibited. Thus, a protection period of 33 percent is indicated when refunding at an equal or lower rate of interest is prohibited during the first five years of a 15-year maturity.

†Noncall protection was observed in 10 percent of all industrial loans.

††Reference to nonrefundable or noncallability clauses was not included in the write-up of protective covenants.

the lender. Therefore, he continued, his company is willing to forego some of this clause's protective qualities in favor of greater protection in other clauses, i.e., working capital, additional debt, etc. A loan officer in the depth company claimed that the nonrefundability problem with industrial borrowers was largely "academic." He elaborated by stating that most industrial borrowers do not refund debt issues privately placed even though new capital is available at rates cheaper than the existing note. Loan officers in another company, on the other hand, stated that they strove for maximum protection in the optional prepayment clause. Whenever there was (1) a plethora of attractive, alternative investment opportunities and/or (2) superior negotiating skill on the part of the lender, loan officers in this company exploited their increased bargaining position to draft a noncallability clause.[18] The increasing stringency, drafted into nonrefundability clauses during 1957 and 1958, is self-evident in Table 17-1, based on 99 loan agreements.

Limitations on Cash Dividends, Stock Purchases, and Salaries

The dividend clause limits the lender's risk position by controlling the borrower's ability to divert cash to dividends, stock purchases and retirements, and salaries. Before cash distributions can be made, the borrower must subject the distribution to two tests: an earnings test and an assets test.

Earnings Test. Typically, the sample lenders drafted the dividend covenant so that a borrower could distribute in cash a percentage of net profits earned after a cut-off date. Also, typically, the percentage of net earnings

---

[18]A noncallability clause prohibits the borrower from calling the note during a specified period for *any* reason, except those that are specifically exempted from the clause's control. Obviously it is more stringent than a nonrefundability clause. See Table 17-1.

which could be distributed ranged among the sample lenders from 75 percent to 100 percent; and the cutoff date invariably was said to be the last day of the borrower's previous fiscal year.

In order to provide for a continuation of dividends if the borrower experienced adverse conditions immediately following the note's closing, the borrower was allowed in practically every instance to draw down surplus within a specified dollar amount, alleged by loan officers to be the equivalent of one year's normal dividends.[19] Thus, the inflows to aggregate funds available for dividends were determined by two factors: one was a percentage of net earnings after a cutoff date; the other factor involved a draw-down of surplus.

Assets Test.   In fewer cases, approximately 25 percent of the total, the lender completely prohibited cash distributions if the borrower's working capital fell below a specified minimum.   Invariably this minimum was set at a dollar figure higher than the minimum in the provision concerned with the maintenance of working capital.   Thus, there were two working capital minimums in some agreements, and dividends were prohibited if the borrower's working capital level did not exceed the higher of the two.   Also, the assets test always seemed to be included in agreements in which the borrower's prerogative to control the level of dividends was not restricted, irrespective of its earnings preformance.   These were agreements with large corporations.

Lenders include stock purchases and, on some occasions, the salaries of specific members of management in this covenant.   These clauses are included principally as a protection against cash distributions by owner-managers or by closely held corporations, despite a disappointing or unfavorable earnings performance.   It is important to include these restrictions because a stock repurchase can be tantamount to a dividend during periods when earnings do not justify a cash distribution.   Similarly, lenders need protection against spending in the form of increased salaries or bonuses when corporate earnings do not allow a dividend distribution in the form of cash.

Maintenance of Working Capital

All lenders in the sample agreed that the maintenance of working capital provision played an important role in limiting risk while administering the direct placement portfolio.   Most loan officers stated that a working capital clause in the dividend covenant, or additional debt clause, is not sufficient protection for the lender's risk position.   It is true that working capital minimums in these clauses prohibit the borrowing firm's management from making certain cash disbursements or financial commitments once a specified working capital level is not maintained.

The straight maintenance of working capital covenant, however, has

---

[19]The writer's findings show that the allowable draw-down usually exceeded one year but was less than two years.

an additional advantage in limiting risk. It provides the lender with an opportunity to take the steps necessary to remedy a deteriorating situation if the working capital clause is defaulted. The focus of this covenant is therefore positive; the lender can take action once the working capital level drops to a dangerous level.

Lending institutions guard against a deterioration of the borrower's current position because note holders rely on current assets to play a significant role in generating the earnings from which the borrower will repay the loan. In addition, noteholders rely on liquidation of the borrower's net working capital position to repay the loan in the event the borrower encounters serious business difficulties.

A stringent working capital covenant usually includes two elements. First, and more important, the borrower agrees to maintain a minimum net working capital position. Second, the borrower agrees always to maintain a working capital position expressed as a percentage of the loan's outstanding balance. Thus, when both a percentage and dollar amount are included in the provision, the percentage has greater restrictive qualities in the early years of the loan, whereas the dollar requirement is the controlling factor in the later years of the note's operation.

Some investment officers, however, are indifferent to the percentage requirement. These officers point to the obvious fact that a loan may progress within the percentage clause and yet the borrower may be on the verge of insolvency. Thus, practically all of the depth company's agreements required the borrower to maintain only a specific dollar level.

The practices of various lenders in drafting this covenant in direct placements range from complete freedom in some cases to dollar amounts, percentages, formulae, and current ratios in others. Some of these elements are used in combination, depending upon the preference of a lending institution for ratios or percentages.

Unrestricted borrowers, as well as borrowers restricted by a formula arrangement, are invariably large in asset size—over $75 million to $100 million. In addition, these companies operate in industries in which the amount of funded debt frequently exceeds working capital needs—i.e., the transportation or the extractive industries.

The bargaining efforts of some borrowers are more intense than usual when negotiating the restrictive limits of this clause. However, intense bargaining is confined probably to no more than 10 percent of all negotiations. In setting dollar amounts, investment officers analyze the borrower's historical needs and adjust these requirements to reflect the projected sales activities of the issuer. In addition, the borrower can take part in setting the minimum working capital level. The borrower's participation achieves two objectives: first, it tends to reduce the possible dissatisfaction of the borrower with the lender's drafting of the covenant; second, when the borrower operates in an industry new to the lender, the issuer has an opportunity to educate the noteholder about working capital needs.

Limitations of Mergers, Consolidations, and Unrelated Activities[20]

The merger covenant seeks to limit the lender's risk position by fulfilling three functions. First, the clause, in many cases, successfully shields the lending institution from a management which is different from the operating group to whom the loan was granted. Thus, because the new management may be unfamiliar to the lender, the latter may wish to impose additional restrictions, or the lender may feel that the new management's aims and integrity are detrimental to the note's underlying security.

A second function of this clause in limiting risk is to sustain the original borrower's high level of financial stability. When the lender feels that the proposed merger threatens the financial position supporting a note's credit quality, the lender is able to protect its interests by demanding compliance with the merger clause. When compliance is not forthcoming, the lender is in a position to demand payment of the note. The importance of this second function is evident from the following incident involving an ineffective merger clause.

> One of the sample lending institutions was concerned with the financial consequences of a proposed merger involving one of its borrowers with an outside firm. The lender, when it learned of the proposed merger, expressed its displeasure to the borrower. However, by the terms of the covenant, it could not prevent the proposed merger from taking place. The fears of the lender became a reality. The merger caused a significant deterioration of the borrower's financial condition; and as a consequence, the note finally was placed on a "special review" basis reserved for troublesome loans.

A third purpose of the clause is to prevent borrowers from increasing the risk potential of loans by engaging in unrelated activities via the merger route. The unrelated activities clause is particularly important to noteholders whenever they feel that a borrower's management lacks depth.

Most lenders revealed a definite preference for complete prohibition of mergers and consolidations (except with a wholly-owned subsidiary) unless the prior consent of the lending institution is obtained. Unquestionably, the present attitude of most lenders stems from the increased diversification activities of borrowers in recent years, particularly with respect to the acquisition of unrelated activities.

Two lenders, in contrast, indicated that only 20 percent of their industrial placements prohibited mergers completely. These agreements involved corporations characterized by small asset size and thinness of management. These same lenders typically draft the merger provision so that the borrower is allowed to merge without the noteholder's consent, provided the borrower is the surviving corporation. The lender's risk position is still protected by the

---

[20]The clause focusing on unrelated activities is included in the Maintenance of Business covenant, one of the *affirmative covenants.* We deal with the clause at this time because of its relation to the merger covenant. As a reader will learn, borrowers may try to circumvent the restrictive impact of the unrelated activities clause via mergers.

original agreement—that is, the borrower must observe the same debt limits, working capital constraints, restrictions focusing on the acquisition of fixed assets, etc. For example, if the original borrower assumes the debts of the merged firm, the probability is high that it will have violated the debt covenant of its note agreement. Even before the merger takes place, the borrower probably will request the lender to approve appropriate modifications of its loan contract in order to make the consolidations possible within the agreement's terms. The lender, at that time, can voice its pleasure or displeasure with the proposed merger. In the event that the original borrower is not the surviving corporation, the lender's consent must be obtained before the surviving corporation may assume the note obligations of the original borrower.

The merger clauses do not prevent an undesirable management from assuming control of the borrower by stock purchases in the open market. However, attempts of the new management to merge the borrower with another company are still subject to the note's agreements.

Under the terms of the merger provision, an unfriendly management may gain control of the borrower's operations by purchasing the issuer's assets. However, the proceeds of the sale probably would be used to prepay the note. Merger covenants usually contain a clause which prohibits the sale, lease, or disposal of the corporate properties as an entirety unless the proceeds are used to prepay the note.

LIMITS OF BARGAINING AND VARIATIONS IN STRINGENCY

Although some difference exists among lenders concerning the degree of stringency drafted in some covenants, the extent of the differences does not seem to be substantial; similarities are more striking than differences. It was mentioned earlier, however, that the Able Life Insurance Company seemed willing more frequently to extend greater latitude to borrowers than the other lenders, in connection with several terms. In particular, these terms related to additional indebtedness and investments. On the other hand, this company seemed to bargain for greater protection with respect to the optional prepayment clause than some of its competitors.[21] As a contrast, the Dependable Life Company preferred to obtain additional protection in the debt, working capital, and investment clauses. To obtain this incremental protection, the company was willing to "trade off" less protection from the clause limiting optional prepayments by the borrower.

---

[21]Able's different viewpoint stems from its finance committee's particular interest in the nonrefundability, sinking fund, and merger clauses. Loan officers, aware of this interest, tried to draft these covenants within the framework of the committee's stipulations wherever possible. However, the drafting of terms usually is on a competitive basis. If the terms of one lender are more onerous than another, then the referring agent will withdraw the proposal from the former and place it with the latter. To provide balance to the loan agreement—or put it differently, to be competitive—Able's loan officers frequently granted (traded off) greater latitude than its competitors to borrowers in those covenants which were of comparatively little interest to the committee. These covenants include additional indebtedness and investments.

Covenants Not Unduly Restrictive

Despite the apparent tendency of lenders to seek as much protection as they can bargain for successfully, evidence seems to indicate that the covenants are not unduly restrictive. Loan officers insist that the covenants are not intended to hinder smooth operation of the borrower's business. Therefore, they do not seek to prohibit or stringently limit an activity necessary to the business but prefer, upon the presentation of a reasonable explanation, to provide for its inclusion in the loan agreement. For example, it was observed that the investment officer handling an agreement with which the writer was familiar included in the purchase-money mortgage clause a surprisingly large dollar limitation on aggregate mortgage liens. This inclusion was deliberate because the borrower revealed its desire to exercise an option to purchase a plant which it had been leasing. In addition, the lender made certain concessions with respect to both the dividend and current debt provisions. The "trade-off" for these concessions was an additional 25 basis points in the interest rate. The lender, as one may expect, bargained for its *quid pro quo*.

The degree of stringency which a lender negotiates into a contract is affected by factors other than the lending institution's philosophy or the well conceived plans of the borrower. The lender may be anxious, for example, to buy the notes of some borrowers because of the applicants' high credit-worthiness. Therefore, these borrowers probably are able to bargain for less stringent restrictions with respect to the protective covenants in their agreements.

Greater Latitude Negotiated By Large Borrowers

As indicated earlier, greater latitude is negotiated by large borrowers. Investment officers feel that most large firms usually possess managerial depth. Thus, the combination of asset size and managerial depth enabled some borrowers to negotiate greater latitude in the terms relating to the debt provisions, investments, mergers, dividends, balloons, and working capital. However, size and depth had little or no influence on the degree of stringency drafted in the negative pledge clause or the provision relating to optional prepayments.

The industry in which the borrower operated is another corporate characteristic which could influence the degree of latitude effectively bargained for by the borrower. Most balloon privileges in the industrial and miscellaneous placements, for example, involved borrowers with operations generating substantial "cash throwoffs"—working capital or extractive industries. Borrowers operating in industries characterized by unstable earnings might be required to make contingent prepayments. Greater latitude with respect to leases, additional funded debt, or wholly-owned subsidiaries can be bargained for successfully by operators in the retail food business or other retail merchandising activities. Working capital minimums are considered less meaningful to limit risk with borrowers operating in the transportation or extractive industries because of the high ratio of fixed assets to sales. Finally, finance companies, because of their frequent and easy access to the capital markets, may be asked to agree to more stringent optional prepayment clauses.

CONCLUSIONS

The underlying rationale of the restrictive terms is to limit the lenders' risk positions. Investment officers, however, do not wish to hamper borrowers' operations. Therefore, the negotiation of terms for borrowers usually involves the development of appropriate exceptions to complete prohibitions. In this sense, the terms are tailor-made; each covenant *can be* drafted to fit the borrower's particular needs.

Yet the fact remains that the restrictive covenants are more alike than dissimilar. Although some variations in practices exist among lenders, they are minor. Lenders prefer to follow traditional patterns, either because they always have operated in this manner or because of policies enunciated by finance committees. Exceptions or variations can be negotiated, but it is important to realize that borrowers must take the initiative to obtain greater flexibility.

On the other hand, borrowers' requests for latitude must make good sense to lending institutions. Exceptions to basic prohibitions, therefore, are more probable when borrowers carefully present their cases for less stringent protective covenants. The need for careful presentation is particularly important when borrowers do not have operational histories calling for the particular latitude—leases, purchase-money mortgages, etc.

It is clear that a working knowledge of the terms, the reasoning underlying their inclusion, the varying stringency of the terms, etc., requires a specialized background. Furthermore, borrowers, unfamiliar with the lending personality and administration of terms of the sample institutions, probably will experience difficulty in locating the best lenders for their needs. Clearly, the complexity of the various "trade-offs" and negotiations in general strongly suggest the use of an able intermediary to represent the borrower when protective covenants are drafted.[22]

Lastly, borrowing managements must realize at the outset that restrictive terms affect many of their decision-making prerogatives. It is, therefore, very important that top management familiarize itself completely with restrictive terms. If the provisions bind management too severely in view of its plans, then other financial arrangements must be investigated. If the terms are inadvertently violated because of the borrower's unfamiliarity with the agreement's provisions, lender-borrower relationships may be adversely affected, thereby jarring the foundation of the issuer's private placement experience.

---

[22]For a description of the intermediary's role in private placements see Chapter 3 of the doctoral thesis cited in footnote 14.

18. PRICING A CORPORATE BOND ISSUE: A LOOK BEHIND THE SCENES*

ERNEST BLOCH †

Making markets for securities means setting prices. This is a demanding job, for it requires a continuous evaluation of the various factors acting and reacting in the markets. Securities dealers must make day-to-day, hour-to-hour, and sometimes minute-to-minute adjustments, and the dealer who falls asleep, even briefly, may find his snooze a costly one.

Underwriters engaged in competitive bidding for new corporate bonds have a special pricing problem in that each flotation involves the distribution of a relatively large supply of securities in the shortest time feasible. While the market for outstanding securities does provide some guidance to the pricing process, it is a rough guide at best. A new bond issue will be similar to, but rarely identical with, any securities being traded in the secondary market. Furthermore, the relatively large amount involved in many new offerings increases the difficulty of gauging the market. Finally, pricing decisions on new securities are not made at the actual time of sale to the ultimate investors but must be made a short time before the bonds are released for trading, while the distribution itself may stretch over a number of days during which market rates may be in motion. The pricing of a new issue even under the best conditions thus takes place at the edge of the unknown.

The specialized job of buying, selling, and pricing new corporate securities is primarily the province of investment bankers.[1] Not all issues are priced through a competitive bidding process, however, and the pricing of some flotations is negotiated directly between borrower and underwriter. But in all successful flotations, investment bankers function as quick intermediaries for new securities between borrowers and ultimate investors. This involves two distinct, although closely related, objectives. In cases of competitive bidding—formal or informal—the first objective is to "win" the right to offer the security to the public by paying the borrower more for it than any other underwriter. The second is to "reoffer" the security to investors at a price higher than that paid the borrower. If a number of underwriting groups are

---

*From *Essays in Money and Credit* (New York: Federal Reserve Bank of New York, 1964), pp. 72-76. Reprinted by permission.

†Formerly, Federal Reserve Bank of New York; presently, Charles W. Gerstenberg Professor of Finance, New York University School of Commerce.

[1]These firms have traditionally been called "investment bankers" although they are now bankers in name only. As is well known, the Banking Act of 1933 specifically prohibits commercial banks that accept deposits and make loans from underwriting corporate securities. Under the act, commercial banks are permitted to continue some "investment banking"-type activities, such as underwriting direct obligations of the United States and general obligations of states and political subdivisions. At present, underwriters for corporate issues perform none of the basic functions of commercial banks, but the term "investment bankers" continues in use, and this usage will be followed in this article.

competing against each other for an issue, each must strike a balance between (1) pressing hard to win the issue by paying a relatively high price to the borrower and (2) increasing the risk that the issue cannot be sold to the public at a price to yield a profit.[2]

This article is concerned with the pricing problem in a competitive underwriting process, the resolution of which boils down to setting the bid price to the borrower. It illustrates how this price is set by following through the process for an actual issue of corporate bonds. Nonessential details that might serve to identify the borrower or the investment banking houses that underwrote the issue have been slightly altered.

Because the offering discussed below was quite sizable, the pricing problem involved an added dimension. The pricing decision was made not by a single underwriter, but by a large underwriting group acting jointly as a syndicate. The pricing decision thus was to be hammered out among the members of the underwriting group, each of which had been tentatively assigned a share of the new issue. And this pricing decision, if successful, had to better that of the strong rival syndicate.

PREPARATION FOR A LARGE ISSUE

When a corporation plans a large financing, it customarily gives fair warning as a means of preparing the capital market. In line with this practice, the firm to be called Large Company, Inc., had announced its intention to borrow $100 million *several months* before the date of actual issue. The early announcement gave potential investors, such as insurance companies, pension funds, and bank trust accounts, the opportunity to adjust their financial commitments so as to make room, if they wished, for sizable chunks of the Large Company issue. At the same time, other potential corporate borrowers were made aware that the Large Company underwriting would bring special pressures on the market, making it unwise to schedule other sizable flotations around that period.

A light calendar of flotations makes possible a more eager participation in the underwriting by syndicate members because their overall market commitments during the flotation period will be less. And the better the demand for bonds among syndicate members, the stronger their bid will be and the lower the borrowing cost to the borrowing firm. As noted, in the underwriting of the Large Company issue, two competing syndicates were formed. One of the groups, managed by X Investment Bank, consisted of

---

[2]In a negotiated flotation, the problem of reaching an optimum bid between (1) and (2) would appear to be less than it is under the competitive bidding process. And a negotiated deal clearly offers the short-run advantage to the underwriter that he cannot "lose" the issue to another syndicate. A negotiated underwriting will not necessarily carry a higher borrowing cost, however, for many large borrowers have some degree of choice between competitive and negotiated flotations. If borrowing costs in, say, negotiated deals were to rise out of line with costs on competitively priced flotations, the cheaper method of raising funds would be used to a greater extent.

more than 100 investment firms, and the competing syndicate, led by Y Investment Bank, was about as sizable.

Managing such large syndicates has become the business of about a half dozen large investment banking houses. Only the largest among them have the capital, the manpower, and the market contacts necessary to propose the proper price for a large offering. If a given house, acting as syndicate manager, wins what the market considers a fair share of the bidding competitions in which it participates, it gains in a number of ways. Not only is its prestige enhanced—which helps in managing future syndicates—but the house that is continuously proving the high quality of its market judgment may be more successful in attracting *negotiated* financings. This concern for the future tends to intensify present competition among managing underwriters.

But while the half dozen syndicate leaders are rivals, they are also potential allies because a grouping of underwriters exists only for a given flotation, and the next offering on the market will involve a different group. Indeed, during the preparation for the Large Company issue, two of the major firms in the rival syndicate led by Y Investment Bank knew that they would be associated with X Investment Bank in a large secondary stock offering within two weeks. As a consequence of the shifting associations and combinations of firms from syndicate to syndicate, the current associate in an underwriting insists on conserving his own independence of action, and this has an important bearing on the pricing process, as we shall see below.

The first formal "price meeting" on the forthcoming issue took place at X Investment Bank two days before the actual bidding date set for the issue. Fifteen senior officers of X Investment Bank actively engaged in trading and underwriting met at this point to discuss pricing recommendations that would win the issue and at the same time find ready acceptance in the market. The terms of the new issue were discussed in the light of current market factors, and each pricing suggestion was, in effect, an answer to a double-barreled question: first, how attractive was the issue in terms of quality, maturity, call provisions, and other features; and, secondly, how receptive was the market at this time? Among the factors discussed as leading to a lower yield was the new bonds' Aaa rating, while factors leading to a higher yield included the lack of call protection and the large size of the issue.

The preliminary discussion of the offering price then shifted to the "feel of the market." Even the proponents of a relatively high yield recognized that the final bid should be close to current market yields on similar securities, owing to the relatively light calendar of forthcoming new corporate flotations. Another sign pointing to aggressive bidding was a relatively light dealer inventory of corporate securities. The discussion of competitive demands for funds was not confined to the corporate securities market, however, but extended to the markets for municipal and Treasury issues as well. Here the picture was mixed. The light calendar of forthcoming municipal issues was cited by proponents of a lower yield, while those in favor of a higher yield pointed to expectations of a relatively heavy volume of Treasury financing. Finally, the discussion moved on to assess the possibility of changes in significant market rates such as the prime loan rate and Federal Reserve Bank discount rates during the flotation period. It was agreed that the likelihood of such changes during the financing period was small. Each of the officers of X Investment Bank then independently set down his opinion of the proper pricing of the issue (i.e., the combination of coupon rate and price offered the borrower) and the reoffering "spread" (i.e., the difference between the bid price and the reoffering price to the public).

The majority of the 15 members of the group agreed that the new bonds should carry a rate of 4¼ percent to the borrower with the bonds priced at par, and with a reoffering spread of about $7 per $1,000 bond.[3] One member of the group thought that a lower yield might be needed to win the bid, and two or three others indicated yields higher than 4¼ percent. The aggressiveness of X Investment Bank's price ideas can be judged from the fact that newspaper comment on the likely level for the winning bid on the day of this meeting indicated a yield in the neighborhood of 4.30 percent.

MARKETING STRATEGY

Simultaneously, assessments of the market for the purpose of establishing a proper bid for the issue were under way in the offices of the allied syndicate members. The comparison of various opinions of the "best" bid of the syndicate members took place a day later, the day before the actual opening of the bids by the borrower. This was the "preliminary price meeting," to which each firm in the syndicate was invited. At the meeting each participant firm named the price it was willing to pay for the number of bonds tentatively assigned in the underwriting.[4] The poll of the 100-odd allied syndicate members revealed far less aggressiveness (i.e., willingness to accept a low yield) by the smaller firms than was shown by the syndicate manager. Relatively few ideas were at 4¼ percent, while one of the major underwriters (i.e., a firm tentatively assigned $3 million of bonds or more) put his offering yield at 4.35 percent, and a small firm went as high as 4.40 percent.

In this particular underwriting, X Investment Bank seemed quite eager to win the bid, partly because of its optimistic appraisals of the state of the bond market and partly because it is the syndicate manager's responsibility to push for a winning bid and to exercise the proper persuasion to carry his syndicate along. Prestige is peculiarly the concern of the syndicate manager because, rightly or wrongly, the market apparently does not attach nearly so much significance to membership as to leadership in a losing syndicate.

---

[3]It should be noted once again that these rates have been changed from those placed on the actual bond issue.

[4]In this meeting, as in the final price meeting, a number of security measures were taken to prevent a leak of information to the competing syndicate.

This factor explains the paradox that the followers, rather than the manager, may be more responsible for the failure to win a bid for lack of aggressiveness, even though the market tends to place the blame on the manager. But smaller syndicate members may be reluctant participants at lower yields because their commitment of funds for even a relatively small portion of a large underwriting may represent a larger call (or contingent liability) against the small firm's capital than it does for a bigger firm. Even though the larger firm's capital may be as fully employed as that of the smaller firm in its *total* underwriting business, the commitment of a large portion of capital for a single underwriting may make the smaller firm more hesitant to take that particular marketing risk.

In preparing for the final price meeting, the syndicate manager held the first of a number of behind-the-scenes strategy sessions. At these meetings, some basic decisions were made about ways and means of holding the syndicate together. During the final price meeting, any firm believing that the market risk of the proposed group bid was too great (i.e., that the yield was too low to sell well) had the right to drop out of the syndicate. Conversely, if the syndicate member liked the group bid, he could raise the extent of his participation. Of course, if many syndicate members drop out, particularly major underwriters, too much of a burden is placed on the remaining members, and the result is, in effect, to veto the proposed bid. The aggressive manager thus is placed squarely in the middle of a tug-of-war: if his bid is too aggressive, and carries a relatively low yield, the syndicate may refuse to take down the bonds; if the bid is too cautious and carries too high a yield, the syndicate may lose the bidding competition to the rival group. This conflict was resolved at the final price meeting.

SYNDICATE TACTICS

On the morning of the day on which the final bids were made to the borrower, the officers of the syndicate manager held their final conference at which decisions were reached regarding their willingness to raise their own share of the underwriting. In effect, a manager who believes in an aggressive bid puts up or shuts up by expressing his willingness to absorb a greater or a lesser share of the total underwriting as firms drop out of the syndicate at lower yields. A strong offer to take more bonds by the manager may induce a number of potential dropouts to stay at a lower yield, partly because their share of the flotation won't be raised by a given number of dropouts since the manager is picking up the pieces. But beyond the arithmetic effect, a strong offer may have a psychological impact, and some reluctant participants may decide that the manager knows more than they do and that his willingness to raise his share at a given yield is his way of backing the strength of his judgment.

This psychological downward push on yields may be small, but sometimes even a tiny difference between two competing bids can spell the difference between success and failure. For example, in late 1959, the winning syndicate for a $30 million utility issue bid 1/100 of a *cent* more per $1,000 bond than the loser; the borrower received exactly $3 more from the winning syndicate for the $30 million issue than was offered by the loser.[5]

Another important factor in holding the syndicate together is the strength of the "book" for the new issue. The "book" is a compilation of investor interest in the new bonds. This interest may have been solicited or unsolicited and may have gone directly to X Investment Bank from, say, institutional investors or to other members of the syndicate. Thus, the book is a sample of market strength. All the interest in the book is tentative since no lender would commit funds for an issue of unknown yield. Nevertheless, it is impossible to exaggerate the importance of a large book to an aggressive syndicate manager in holding his group together at the lowest possible yield. Because reluctant participants in an underwriting are particularly concerned about the selling risk, the larger the book the more reassured they will feel at any given rate. Put another way, the better the book, the more bonds a firm will take at a given rate, thus absorbing more dropouts. Indeed, the size of the book was considered so important that the final price meeting on the Large Company underwriting was interrupted a number of times by the latest indications of interest in the issue.

THE FINAL PRICE MEETING

As a means of preventing information leaks, representatives of the firms attending the final price meeting were locked in a room. The meeting was opened by a vice-president of X Investment Bank with a brief review of the good state of the "book" — about half the issue had been spoken for, tentatively. He derived further encouragement for an aggressive bid from the healthy state of the bond market. Thus, he proposed to make his bid at the 4¼ percent rate agreed upon at the X Investment Bank preliminary meeting two days earlier.

The immediate reaction to this statement was a chorus of moans. Apparently, the book was not sufficiently broad to carry the doubters along with the first bid, nor did the manager indicate any other action that would have made his proposal more acceptable. When the group was polled, large and small dropouts cut the $100 million underwriting by about a third. The failure to carry the syndicate at the first go-around was later attributed by some X Investment Bank people to the fact that three dropouts occurred among the first set of major underwriters polled (i.e., the eight largest firms, each of which had been tentatively assigned $3 million of bonds). And in the second set ($2 million assigned to each firm), another few had fallen by the wayside.

---

[5]At times, tie bids are received. On September 12, 1961, two underwriters bid identical amounts, down to the last 1/100 of a penny per $1,000 bond, for a $3 million issue of municipal bonds. Such tie bids are as rare as a golfer's hole in one, however.

Thus, a new bid proposal had to be presented to the group. Following another behind-the-scenes consultation of the senior officers of the managing underwriter, a 4⅜ percent coupon was proposed with a bid yield of 4.27 percent. Amid continued grumbling of the majority of the members of the meeting, this was readily accepted by nearly every firm.

Judging that they might have leaned over too far in the direction of their reluctant followers, the officers of the syndicate manager consulted once again and decided to present a somewhat more aggressive bid to the syndicate. In the third proposal, the bid price on the 4⅜ coupon was upped by 20 cents per $1,000 bond. The underwriters, still grumbling, were polled again and, following a few minor dropouts, approved the new price. The final allocation of the bonds differed relatively little from the tentative original allocation except that the manager picked up the allotments of the dropouts by adding about $3 million to his own commitment. By this time only a few minutes were left until the formal opening of the competitive bids by Large Company, Inc. The final coupon and price decisions were telephoned to the syndicate's representative at the bidding, who formally submitted the bid to Large Company.

Promptly at 11:30 A.M. the doors of the price committee meeting were thrown open, and within 30 seconds of that time the news was shouted from the trading room that the X Investment Bank bid had lost. The difference in the bid prices between the two syndicates came to little more than $1 per $1,000 bond.

The bonds were released for trading by the Securities and Exchange Commission at around 4 P.M. and were quickly snapped up by market investors. At X Investment Bank the feeling of gloom hung heavy, particularly since the first bid offered to the price meeting would have won the issue.

Would a better X Investment Bank book have carried the defecting major underwriters along on the first bid? Should the manager have been willing to take more bonds to carry the group along in the first recommendation which would have won the issue? And would market acceptance of that bid have been as good as that accorded the actual winning bid of Y syndicate? These post mortems were bound to be inconclusive, and the unremitting pressures of the underwriting business soon cut them short. Within the next several days a number of other securities were scheduled to come to market. Tomorrow was another day and another price meeting.

PART VI. WORKING CAPITAL MANAGEMENT

Despite the importance of many of the other areas of financial management, a considerable portion of the financial manager's time is spent on current asset management. He must continually strive to utilize the liquid resources of the firm more efficiently. The articles in this section discuss more effective means of managing cash, accounts receivable, and inventory.

Professors Merton H. Miller and Daniel Orr demonstrate how *operations research* or *management science* applies to the field of finance. The authors describe and develop a mathematical model of cash management and apply it to a specific firm. The problem concerns managing a cash balance in conjunction with a portfolio of short-term securities of Union Tank Car. The use of a *control limit* inventory model is illustrated. The authors were fortunate to secure the cooperation of an assistant treasurer who was trying to implement policies which were similar to those of the model. The treasurer's performance was evaluated by use of the model. The results are presented in detail.

Professor P. Michael Davis presents a model which is designed to assist management in implementing a credit policy which will allow maximum sales consistent with some level of bad-debt losses. The model utilizes marginal analysis techniques. The basic premise is that sales may be lost if credit is too tight and yet a credit policy that is too easy might cause high debt losses. The author underlines the importance of two basic costs; namely, the costs of goods sold and the bad-debt expense. First, costs are classified into "escapable" and "inescapable" categories, and each transaction should cover all escapable costs and contribute to the inescapable costs. Secondly, customers are placed in credit risk categories, and the bad-debt probability is determined for each group. With this information, management is able to determine more objectively the amount of merchandise to be sold to customers of various risk classes. The author presents a workable model which can be used by management.

Professor Robert M. Soldofsky offers a timely discussion of the impact of rising prices on net incomes and financing. He presents an illustration of the consequences of *paper profits* (the difference between net income determined on the basis of current or opportunity costs and net income determined on the basis of historical costs) for financing and determining rates of return on investments. The tax rate on real net income is shown to be substantially higher than the indicated marginal rate. He shows that a substantial amount of *conventional net income* is needed simply to maintain the stock of physical assets in a period of inflation. The fiscal policy implication of using accounting and income tax procedures that would recognize net income on a current or market-price basis is discussed. The article provides the reader with an often forgotton problem related to rising prices.

Mr. Robert D. Niemeyer is concerned with inventory control techniques that are directed toward unit control of inventory. He attacks the problem of inventory control by considering the following four items: methods of control, inventory costs, determination of expected inventory usage, and other refinements. Attention is given to the questions of when and in what quantity should an item be replenished. A full explanation of the categories of inventory costs is given. The author emphasizes the practical limitations in determining precisely the acquisition and holding costs. Various means of forecasting expected usage are presented. Under the "other refinements" category, attention is given to two inventory control concepts that have been used in practice. It is the author's purpose to present basic principles which can be applied to the solution of practical problems.

19. MATHEMATICAL MODELS FOR FINANCIAL MANAGEMENT*

MERTON H. MILLER †

and DANIEL ORR ††

One stream of current research in finance involves the extension to the field of finance of the methods and approaches that have come to be called "operations research" or "management science." Researchers working along these lines try to develop mathematical representations or "models" of typical decision-making problems in finance and, where they are given the opportunity to do so, to test and apply these models in actual decision settings. At the moment, this stream of research is still a relatively small one—really only a trickle as compared to the flood of material pouring out on the subjects of capital budgeting or valuation. But it is a stream that can be expected to grow rapidly in the years ahead with the improvement in mathematical and computer technology and especially with the increase in the number of people who are being taught to use the tools effectively and creatively.

Rather than attempting any broad survey of work to date, this paper will present a single example of this type of research, describing both the development of the mathematical model and its application in a specific firm. Such an example can convey more graphically and more convincingly than any amount of preaching many of the important implications for management of this kind of research.

THE CASH BALANCE AS AN INVENTORY

The particular financial problem involved in our example is that of managing a cash balance in conjunction with a portfolio of short-term securities. And the particular mathematical model that will be used is a type of *inventory* model that might be called a "control-limit" model.

It may be a little startling at first to think of your firm's cash balance as just another inventory—an inventory of dollars, so to speak—but is it

---

*From Selected Paper No. 23 (Chicago: University of Chicago Graduate School of Business, 1966). This paper was originally presented at the Conference of Financial Research and its Implications for Management, Stanford University, June, 1966.

†Merton H. Miller, Edward Eagle Brown Professor of Finance and Economics, University of Chicago.

††Daniel Orr, Professor of Economics, the University of California—La Jolla.

really so farfetched? Consider, for example, some raw material item that your company stocks, and ask yourself why you keep so much of it around or why you don't simply order each day's or each hour's requirement on a hand-to-mouth basis. The answer is, of course, that this would be a very wasteful policy. The clerical and other costs involved in placing orders for the material are not trivial; and there would be further costs incurred in the form of production delays or interruptions if materials were slow in arriving or if requirements on any day should happen to be higher than had been anticipated. Why, then, not eliminate these costs once and for all by placing one big order for a mountain of the stuff? Here, of course, the answer would be that there are also costs connected with *holding* inventory. These would include not just the physical costs connected with the storage space and handling but also the cost of deterioration, or of obsolescence, or of adverse price fluctuations, and especially of the earnings foregone on the capital tied up in the inventory. The inventory management problem for any physical commodity is thus one of striking a balance between these different kinds of costs; and the goal is to develop a policy in which orders will be placed on the average at just the right frequency and in just the right amounts so as to produce the smallest *combined* costs of ordering, of holding inventory, and of running out of stock.

Similarly with cash. If you want to add to or subtract from your inventory of cash by making a transfer to or from your portfolio of securities, there is an order cost involved, partly in the form of internal clerical and decision-making costs and partly in the form of brokerage fees, wire transfer costs, and the like. In the other direction, if you try to cut down these in-and-out costs by holding large cash balances, there is a substantial holding cost in the form of the interest loss on the funds tied up in the balance. As for the costs connected with running out of cash, these are perhaps too obvious to require discussion before a group of this kind.

THE CONTROL-LIMIT APPROACH TO CASH MANAGEMENT

Accepting the inventory analogy as valid, what form of inventory management policy would be suitable for cash balances? Here, since the typical cash balance fluctuates up and down and, in part, unpredictably, it seemed to us that the most natural approach for a wide variety of cases might be a control-limit policy.

How one particular kind of control-limit policy might work when applied to a cash balance is illustrated in Figure 19-1. We say "one particular kind" since the control-limit approach is quite flexible and many different variations can be used depending on the circumstances. The one illustrated happens to be an especially simple one and one that can be shown to be appropriate whenever the internal clerical and decision-making costs are the main costs involved in making portfolio transactions. It is also the form of policy actually used in the specific application to be described later.

The wiggly line that starts at the left at m_0 traces out the hypothetical

FIGURE 19-1

path of a cash balance over time. As drawn, it first seems to fluctuate aimlessly until about day t_0, at which point a rising trend appears to set in. During this interval receipts are exceeding expenditures and the cash balance is building up. The buildup is allowed to continue until the day on which the cash balance first reaches or breaks through the *upper control limit* of h dollars. At this point in time—day t_1 on the graph—a portfolio purchase is made in an amount large enough to restore the cash balance to the *return point* z. Once back at z, the cash balance is allowed to wander again. No further purchases or sales are made until the balance either breaks through the upper bound at h again or until it breaks through the *lower control limit* as at day t_2. When the lower control limit is reached, a sale of securities from the portfolio is signalled in an amount such that the balance is once again restored to the return point z.

AN OPTIMAL SOLUTION FOR A SIMPLE SPECIAL CASE

Given that this kind of control policy seems reasonable—and we would argue that it is reasonable not only in dealing with some types of cash management problems but in many other kinds of settings where there is a substantial cost in managerial intervention to restore a "wandering" system to some desired state—the task of the researcher then becomes that of applying mathematical or numerical methods to determine the *optimal* values of the limits. By optimal we mean values that provide the most advantageous trade-off between interest loss on idle cash and the costs involved in transfers of cash to and from the portfolio. As it turns out, there happen to be some simple but important special cases in which these optimal values can be derived in relatively straightforward fashion and where the results can be expressed in the form of a simple, compact formula. In particular, we have been able to obtain such a formula for the optimal values of the limits for cases which meet the following conditions: (1) where it is meaningful to talk about both the cash balance and the portfolio as if they were each single homogeneous assets;[1] (2) where transfers between cash and the portfolio may take place at any time but only at a given "fixed" cost, i.e., a cost that is the same regardless of the amount transferred, the direction of the transfer, or of the time since the previous transfer;[2] (3) where such transfers may be regarded as taking place instantaneously, that is, where the "lead time" involved in portfolio transfers is short enough to be ignored; (4) where the lower limit on the cash balance is determined outside the model, presumably as the result of negotiations between the bank and the firm as to what the firm's required minimum balance is to be; and (5) where the fluctuations in the cash balance are entirely random. There may perhaps be a trend or "drift" as it is called in this kind of analysis; but aside from this kind of simple systematic component, the day-to-day changes in the cash balance are completely unpredictable.

As for the specific formula that constitutes the solution under these assumptions, there is little point in discussing it any length here. The complete derivations and other details can be found in a recently published article.[3] It might, perhaps, just be worth noting here that the solution defines the limits in terms of the fixed transfer cost, the daily rate of interest on the portfolio, and the variability of daily changes in the cash balance (exclusive of changes related to the portfolio). As would be expected, the higher the transfer cost and greater the variability, the wider the spread between the upper and the lower limits; and the higher the rate of interest, the lower the spread. There are, however, some surprises. In particular, for the "no-drift" case, it turns out that despite the fact that the cash balance is equally likely to go up or down and that it's equally costly to buy or to sell securities, the optimal return point z—the point at which the average long-run costs of operating the system are lowest—does not lie midway between the upper and lower limits. Instead, it lies substantially below the midpoint. To be precise, it lies at one third of the way between the lower and upper bounds, and it stays at the one third point regardless of the numerical values that are assigned to the transfer costs or to the daily rate of interest that can be earned on the portfolio. As these values are changed, the whole system expands or contracts, but the relation between the parts remains the same.

---

[1]We have also recently been able to develop approximately optimal solutions for certain special kinds of "three-asset" models, i.e., models in which there are two kinds of securities (e.g., a line of credit and commercial paper) in addition to cash.

[2]Simple solutions also have been developed for the case in which the cost is not fixed but proportional to the amount transferred. More complicated, mixed cases involving both a fixed and a proportional component have been analyzed by our colleagues G. Eppen and E. Fama who have developed a very flexible method of obtaining numerical values for the limits under a wide variety of circumstances.

[3]M. H. Miller and D. Orr, "Model of the Demand for Money by Firms," *Quarterly Journal of Economics*, LXXX (August, 1966), pp. 413-435.

A TEST APPLICATION OF THE SIMPLE MODEL

Your initial reaction is likely to be that this model and the assumptions on which it was based are much too special and restrictive to have any important applicability to real-world problems. In management science, however, as in science generally, it is rash to pass judgment on the range of applicability of a model solely on the basis of assumptions that underlie it. Mathematical models often turn out to be surprisingly robust and insensitive to errors in the assumptions. The only safe way to determine how well or how poorly a model works is to try it out and see.

In obtaining the basis for this kind of test of the model, we were extremely fortunate in having the active collaboration of Mr. D. B. Romans, Assistant Treasurer of the Union Tank Car Company.[4] Mr. Romans had seen an earlier version of our original paper and was struck by the similarity between the model and his own policies in putting his firm's idle cash to work. The systematic investment of idle cash in short term, money market securities was a relatively new program for his company—one that he had instituted only about a year previously. The interest earnings for that year were quite large not only in relation to the costs involved but to the total budget of the treasurer's department. Now that the year's experience had been accumulated, he wanted to go back over the record, to study it in detail and to see whether any changes in practice might be suggested that would make the operation even more profitable. He felt, and we agreed, that the model might be extremely helpful in this kind of evaluation. If the model did seem to behave sensibly when applied to the company's past cash flow, then it might be used to provide an objective standard or "bogey" against which past performance could be measured.

Since mathematical modeling of business decisions is still quite new, and since few people outside the production area have had much direct connection with it, it is perhaps worth emphasizing that at no time was it intended or contemplated that a model should be developed to do the actual on-line decision making. The purpose of the study was to be *evaluation* by the treasurer of his own operation. This is a valuable but unglamorous use of models that tends to be overlooked amidst all the hoopla of the Sunday supplement variety surrounding the subject of automated management. An important point that must be kept in mind about mathematical models is that they are not intended to *replace* management—though, like any other technological improvement, they sometimes have that effect—but that they provide managers with new tools or techniques to be used *in conjunction with* other managerial techniques (including good judgment) for improving overall performance.

---

[4]We have also benefited greatly from discussions of cash management problems and practices with several officers of the Harris Trust and Savings Bank of Chicago. We hope that they will benefit too from this chance to see how the problem looks from the other side of the account.

THE SETTING OF THE OPERATION

Since our objective was to compare the model's decisions over some trial period with those of the Assistant Treasurer, the first step was to examine carefully the setting in which he actually operated and to see how closely or how poorly the circumstances matched the assumptions of the model. As would be expected, the results were mixed. On the one hand, there were some respects in which the assumptions fit quite well. The Assistant Treasurer did behave, for example, as if he were in fact controlling only a single-central cash balance. Note the phrase "as if," because as a matter of fact the firm does have many separate balances in many banks. For purposes of cash management, however, the Assistant Treasurer works with one single balance representing the free funds that he can marshal throughout the system without regard to the particular banks they happen to be in at the moment (or where the funds derived from a portfolio liquidation must ultimately be routed).

It was also clear that there were substantial order costs involved in making portfolio transfers. In the case of a portfolio purchase, for example, some of the main cost components include: (a) making two or more long-distance phone calls plus 15 minutes to a half hour of the Assistant Treasurer's time; (b) typing up and carefully checking an authorization letter with four copies; (c) carrying the original of the letter to be signed by the Treasurer; and (d) carrying the copies to the controller's office where special accounts are opened, the entries are posted, and further checks of the arithmetic made. It is hard to establish a precise dollar figure for these costs, but at least the approximate order of magnitude for a complete round trip is probably somewhere between $20 and $50. That this is not a trivial amount of money in the present context becomes clear when you remember that interest earnings at the then prevailing level of interest rates were running at about $10 per day per $100,000 in the portfolio and that his average size of portfolio purchase during the test period was about $400,000.

Not surprisingly, we also found that there was a considerable amount of randomness or unpredictability in the daily cash flow. In fact, the Assistant Treasurer did not even attempt to forecast or project flows more than a day or two ahead except for certain large recurring outflows such as tax payments, dividend payments, sinking fund deposits, transfers to subsidiaries and the like; and even here the forecasts were made more with a view to deciding the appropriate maturities to hold in the portfolio than as part of the cash balance control *per se*. As for the drift or trend, analysis of the cash flow over the 9-month test period showed no evidence of any significant drift in either direction.

As opposed to these similarities between the assumptions of the model and the reality of the firm's operation, there were very definitely a number of respects in which the fit was much less comfortable. The model assumes, for example, that when the lower bound on cash is hit or breached, there will

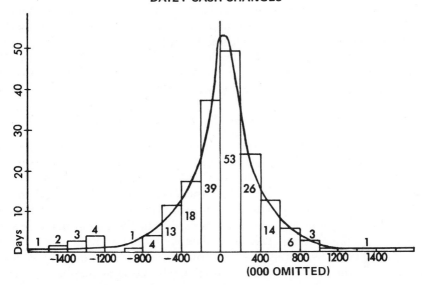

FIGURE 19-2

DAILY CASH CHANGES

be an immediate sale of securities out of the portfolio to make up the cash deficiency. The Assistant Treasurer, however, followed a policy of buying only nonmarketable securities and holding them to maturity primarily because he wanted to try his new cash management program without requiring any change in the company's standard accounting procedures. Hence, if a large net cash drain occurred unexpectedly on a day on which he had no maturing security, he simply let his cash balance drop below his normal minimum which he and his banks regarded as an average minimum rather than as the strict minimum contemplated by the model.

A discrepancy between the model and reality that was more disturbing appeared when we constructed the frequency distribution of daily cash changes by size of change over the 9-month sample period of 189 working days. The distribution of these daily changes is shown in graphic form in Figure 19-2. The logic of the model requires that this distribution be at least approximately of a form that statisticians refer to as "normal" or "Gaussian." A hasty glance at the figure might lead one to conclude that this requirement is met. Closer study reveals, however, that not only is the distribution not normal, but it almost seems to be a member of a particularly ill-behaved class of *fat-tailed* distributions that have come to be called *Paretian distributions.*[5] In these distributions—which may be familiar to

---

[5]We say "almost seems to be" because despite the conspicuously fat tails, the distributions as computed cumulatively month by month remain roughly similar with no tendency for the tails to get fatter and fatter over time as in a true Paretian process. The Paretian-like tails are mainly the reflection of such large but relatively controllable and definitely size-limited items as dividends, taxes, transfers to and from subsidiaries, and the like.

those of you who have been following the debate about random walks in the stock market[6]—large changes occur much more frequently than in the case of the normal distribution. In fact, the frequency of large changes is so much greater that we were quite uncertain as to whether the model would behave in even roughly sensible fashion or whether it would simply find itself being whipsawed to death by the violent swings through the control range. As indicated earlier, however, there is only one way to tell; and that's by trying it out and seeing what happens.

THE TEST OF THE MODEL AGAINST THE DATA

To get a close basis for comparison with the Assistant Treasurer's actual decisions, it was decided to run the model under various alternative assumptions about the true value of the transfer cost. That is, we would start with a conservatively high value of say $90 per transfer, compute the optimal upper limit h and return point z, run the model against the actual data, and tabulate its portfolio purchases and sales. If, as expected, the model made fewer transfers than the Assistant Treasurer, then we would go back, use a lower value for the costs, recompute the new optimal limits, and so on until we had finally forced the model to make approximately the same number of transfers over the sample interval as the Assistant Treasurer himself. Then, assuming the model was behaving sensibly, we could compare and contrast their patterns of portfolio decisions over the interval as well as get at least some rough idea of what figure for the cost of a transfer the Assistant Treasurer was implicitly using in his own operation.

The only difficulty encountered in implementing this straightforward kind of test was in the matter of deciding precisely how many transfers the Assistant Treasurer should be regarded as having made. Because of his policy of holding only nonmarketable issues, his portfolio tended to be of quite short average duration. Hence, there were inevitably days on which he had a maturity that proved to be too early. If he had merely rolled these issues over, there would have been no problem; we would simply have washed that transaction out and not counted either the maturity or the reinvestment as a transfer. But it is clearly not always efficient just to roll over the maturing issue. Given that a purchase must be made anyway on that day, it would be wise to pick up any additional cash that also happened to be lying around, even if the amount involved would not have been large enough by itself to have justified incurring a transfer cost. Accordingly, we decided not to count any transfers on roll-over days unless the Assistant Treasurer indicated that the balance was so large even without the maturing issue that he would almost certainly have bought anyway (in which case he would be charged with the purchase but not the sale). Similarly with the case of net sale days. If there was a larger maturity on a given day than was

---

[6]*Random Walks in Stock-Market Prices,* Selected Paper No. 16 (Chicago: Graduate School of Business, University of Chicago).

actually needed to meet the cash drain and if some small part of the excess proceeds were rolled over, then he was charged with a sale but not a purchase. By this criterion we were able to agree on a figure of 112 total transactions by the Assistant Treasurer during the 189 test days of which 58 were purchases and 54 were sales (maturities).

THE RESULTS OF THE TEST

When we commenced the trial-and-error process of matching the total number of transactions by the model with those of the Assistant Treasurer, our hope was that the model might be able to achieve an average daily cash balance no more than say 20 to 30 percent above the Assistant Treasurer's average. We felt that if we could get that close and if the model did behave sensibly, then there was a very real prospect of being able to use the model as a bogey against which to measure and evaluate actual performance. As it turned out, however, we found that, at 112 transactions, the model not only came close but actually did better—producing an average daily cash balance about 40 percent *lower* than that of the Assistant Treasurer ($160,000 for the model as compared with about $275,000). Or, looking at it from the other side, if we matched the average daily cash holdings at $275,000, the model was able to reach this level with only about 80 transactions or about one third less than the 112 actually required.

It can be argued, of course, that this sort of comparison is unfairly loaded in favor of the model not only because it was applied on a hindsight basis but because the transfer costs would actually have been higher for the model than the simple matching of total numbers of transfers would seem to suggest. The Assistant Treasurer, it will be recalled, never really sold a security; he merely let it run off. Hence, the model would have had to incur additional costs on at least those sales that did not occur on the easily forecastable, large outflow days. Check of the numbers involved showed, however, that the model would still have dominated in terms of net interest minus transfer costs over the sample period even if these extra costs of liquidation were included on every sale. And, of course, that is much too extreme an adjustment. Many of the actual sale days of the model coincided with the large outflow days, and appropriately maturing securities could have been purchased to hit these dates. In fact, the postmortem showed that about half the model's sales took place on days when the Assistant Treasurer also sold, and nearly 80 percent occurred either on the same day or within one day either way of a day on which he scheduled a maturity.

Furthermore, the model too is operating under some handicaps in the comparison. At no time, for example, did the model ever violate the minimum cash balance marked on the Assistant Treasurer's work sheets, whereas no less than 10 percent of his total dollar days invested were represented by the cash deficiencies on the days in which he let his balance dip temporarily below the minimum. In addition, the model did not receive instructions to

FIGURE 19-3a

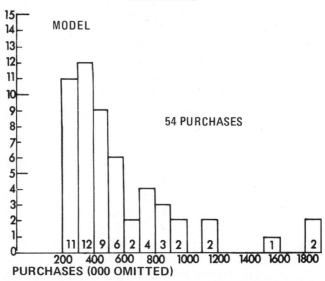

change its policies before weekends and holidays. The Assistant Treasurer, on the other hand, always knew when it was Friday and was thus able to sock away additional amounts on which he could get two extra days' interest.

All in all then the comparison would seem to be basically a fair one; and it is a tribute to the Assistant Treasurer's personal and professional character that he never became ego-involved in the comparison or wasted time alibiing.

FIGURE 19-3b

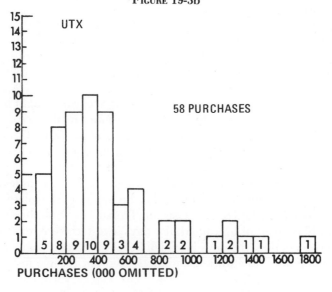

He was concerned about one thing and one thing only: how to do an even better job.

THE COMPARISON OF OPERATING POLICIES

With this question in mind, we then went on to make a detailed comparison of the actual decisions with those called for by the model. The complete record of these comparisons is, of course, too long and too specialized to be spelled out at length here, but there are at least a few simple contrasts that can be presented to illustrate the sorts of things that turned up.

Figures 19-3a and 19-3b, for example, show the frequency distributions of portfolio purchases by size of purchase for the model and for the Assistant Treasurer. Notice that even though we have forced the total number of transfers to match, the model makes somewhat fewer purchases (54 as against 58) and does so in considerably larger average size (about $600,000 as compared with only $440,000). The difference in operating policy is particularly striking at the lower end of the size scale because of the rigid rule built into the model that keeps it from ever buying in units smaller than h—z, which was about $250,000 when the model was set to produce 112 transfers. The Assistant Treasurer, by contrast, made about 13 purchases (or nearly 25 percent of his total purchases) in amounts smaller than that size including five in amounts of $100,000 or less. Even allowing for the fact that some of these small transactions were for weekends, the total impression conveyed is one of an excessive amount of small-lot purchasing activity. This impression was further reinforced both by the very low implicit transfer cost that was necessary to force the model to make 112 transfers as well as by the fact that more than 90 percent of the total interest earnings achieved by the model with 112 transfers could have been attained with only about 50 total transfers. Of these 50, moreover, only some 20 were purchases, and all were of fairly large size.

Even more revealing are Figures 19-4a and 19-4b which show the distribution of the closing cash balance by size on days when no portfolio action was taken in either direction. Notice again that, because of its rigid upper limit, the model never lets the cash balance go above h which in this case is about $400,000. The Assistant Treasurer, however, seems to be much less consistent in this respect, having foregone no less than 23 buying opportunities of this amount or larger including three of over $1 million. When and why so many opportunities were missed is still not entirely clear. Part of the trouble undoubtedly stems from the fact that the Assistant Treasurer has many other responsibilities and cannot always count on being at his desk at the time of day when the decision has to be made. And without actually interrupting to construct his worksheet, there is no way for him to determine whether an interruption of his other work would really be profitable. Hopefully, however, by making his limits more explicit (in the spirit of the model) and by delegating to others much of the purely mechanical task of monitoring these limits, he will be able to achieve in the future a significant reduction in the size and frequency of these lost opportunities.

CONCLUSION

We have tried here to present a concrete example of how mathematical methods can be and are being applied to management problems in the

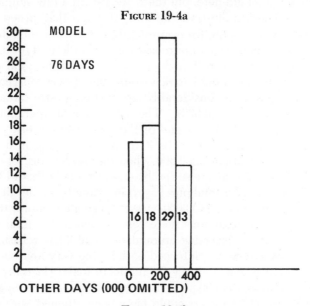

FIGURE 19-4a

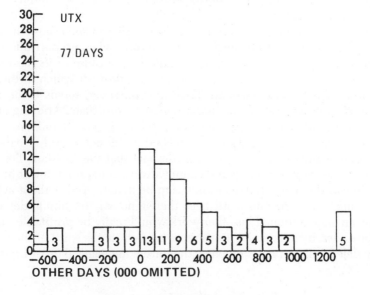

FIGURE 19-4b

field of finance. The example happens to be a particularly simple one. But it does at least serve to illustrate very neatly a number of points about this kind of research that senior financial managers would do well to keep in mind.

First, it is important for financial managers to disabuse themselves of the notion that there is something special or unique about financial problems. In particular, we have seen that what is commonly regarded as a peculiarly financial problem—to wit, managing the cash balance and a portfolio of liquid securities—turns out to be nothing more than an inventory problem.

Second, mathematical models of decision or control problems should not be thought of as something fundamentally different from ordinary management principles or techniques. They are merely more disciplined and systematic ways of exploiting these principles. In particular, control-limit models of the kind we have seen here—and remember that many additional variations are possible—are essentially extensions of the fundamental notion of *management by exception*.

Third, be careful not to prejudge mathematical models solely on the basis of the lack of literal realism in the assumptions underlying them. To develop a workable model, simplifications—sometimes, extreme simplifications—must be made. But if it has been properly conceived, a simple model may still perform extremely well. It is not a matter of getting something for nothing; rather that the gains made by doing a good job on the really essential parts of the problem are often more than large enough to offset the errors introduced by the simplifications (errors, incidentally, that often cancel out).

Finally, remember that there is a trade-off between improving decision procedures and improving the information and forecasts used in arriving at the decisions. In the present instance, for example, we saw a case in which a model that assumed the cash flow to be completely random was still able to do a very successful job of decision making. Nor is this result unique or exceptional. The slogan everywhere today is "more, better, and faster information for management." We suspect, however, that thanks to the computer, many firms may already be in the position of having more, better, and faster information than they can use effectively with present management techniques. There is likely to be as much or more real pay-off in the years ahead in rationalizing and improving decision procedures than there is in simply trying to get an even bigger bang from the information explosion.

20. MARGINAL ANALYSIS OF CREDIT SALES*

P. MICHAEL DAVIS †

Electronic data processing has brought about vast changes in every area of business management, and the credit department is certainly no exception. The credit manager has always had special skills and knowledge which could be of great value to management. Unfortunately, however, his potential has often been dissipated by his forced attendance to the many routine duties of credit management. Now that the computer has taken over much of the customary data processing and analysis of credit information, the credit manager is in a better position to make a worthwhile contribution in the solution of problems facing management.[1]

Moreover, changes in business in general have placed greater emphasis on credit management. The National Association of Credit Management reports that the dollar quantity of receivables is on the rise.[2] With a growing industrial output one would expect receivables to increase. To a certain extent, however, the growth in receivables has been fostered by highly competitive conditions. This suggests that perhaps credit is being used as an instrument by the sales department to generate additional sales volume.

New and more sophisticated quantitative techniques have been developed to assist credit management in assuming a new role in the total management of the firm. One such technique, developed by Haskel Benishay, determines control limits through the use of statistics and provides a criteria to ascertain whether the accounts receivable system is operating under conditions of control.[3] Another technique, developed by R. M. Cyert, H. J. Davidson, and G. L. Thompson, uses Markov chains to determine the allowance for uncollectible accounts.[4] A third technique, developed by Allen Weiss, makes use of aging procedures to assist management in projecting future cash flows for budgetary purposes.[5] Other procedures will surely follow.

On one hand, management is concerned about the possible loss of sales due to a credit policy which is too tight; on the other hand, the concern is with

*From *The Accounting Review* (January, 1966), pp. 121-126. Reprinted by permission.
†Assistant Professor of Accounting, The University of Southern Mississippi.

[1]For an interesting discussion of changes which have taken place in credit management, see Robert W. Johnson, "More Scope for Credit Managers," *Harvard Business Review* (November-December, 1961), pp. 109-120.

[2]National Association of Credit Management, "The Outlook for Credit," *Credit and Financial Management* (February, 1965), p. 23.

[3]Haskel Benishay, "Managerial Control of Accounts Receivable: A Deterministic Approach," *Journal of Accounting Research* (Spring, 1965), pp. 114-132.

[4]R. M. Cyert, H. J. Davidson, and G. L. Thompson, "Estimation of the Allowance for Doubtful Accounts by Markov Chains," *Management Science* (April, 1962), pp. 287-303.

[5]Allen Weiss, "Forecasting Collections of Receivables," *The Journal of Accountancy* (September, 1964), pp. 63-66.

possibly high bad-debt losses caused by an easy credit policy. The purpose of the model to be developed here is to assist management in resolving this conflict.

DEVELOPMENT OF THE MODEL

From microeconomics, let us borrow the basic model for marginal analysis with which everyone is familiar. It is said that a firm interested in maximizing its profit would attempt to expand production until marginal cost is equal to marginal revenue. Once marginal cost exceeds marginal revenue, total profit is reduced. It follows that the optimum level of production is at the point where marginal cost just equals marginal revenue.

The same reasoning can easily be applied to the credit sale decision. Using the above criteria, an acceptable sale is indicated any time the marginal cost of making the sale is less than or just equal to the marginal revenue to be derived from the sale. The problem is to define and locate specific inputs for the model. The marginal revenue input needs no explanation, as it is merely the total revenue to be derived from a potential sale of goods on account. However, the selection of suitable marginal cost inputs is surrounded with a certain difficulty with respect to the costs relevant to the decision to be made. Cost factors to be considered include cost of goods sold, cost of additional capital committed to accounts receivable, additional bookkeeping costs, cost of additional capital committed to inventories by virtue of increased sales volume, and bad-debts expense.

Because the model will be used to evaluate a potential sale on its merits alone, the writer believes the two most important cost inputs to be cost of goods sold and bad-debts expense. Bookkeeping costs do not vary in direct proportion to changes in accounts receivable. These costs are fixed within certain ranges of accounts-receivable activity and would be considered semi-variable if observed over all possible levels of activity. If graphed, bookkeeping costs would have the characteristics of a step function. Moreover, the costs associated with higher inventory levels due to greater sales volume would behave in the same manner as the cost function associated with increased bookkeeping costs. It would be quite difficult, if not meaningless, to associate these costs with specific credit sales being considered.

Before we consider the effect of the cost of additional capital to be tied up in accounts receivable, let us develop the model. Cost of goods sold is stated as a percentage of marginal revenue. The actual bad debt loss cannot be known in advance and, therefore, must be stated in terms of the probability that a receivable created by a sale to a certain class of customer will ultimately become a bad debt.

Thus, the model $MC = MR$ can be restated as

$$R = mR + pR,$$

where R equals the marginal revenue to be derived from the sale; m equals

the cost of goods sold, stated as a percentage of R; and p equals the probability that the account will never be collected.
Then

$$R = (m + p)R.$$

Dividing by R, we have

$$\frac{R}{R} = \frac{(m + p)R}{R}$$

and hence

$$1 = m + p.$$

Marginal cost then becomes equal to marginal revenue at that point where cost of goods sold, stated as a percentage of selling price, plus the probability of uncollectibility become equal to 1.

   The necessary inputs for such a model are available to any firm that has a well developed information system and is willing to take advantage of other sources of information. With respect to cost of goods sold, several variables must be considered. If the firm is a merchandising enterprise, it purchases its goods for resale in an arm's length transaction, and a cost of goods sold figure associated with a particular sale can be readily determined. The percentage required by the model can be ascertained by comparing the cost of goods sold with the selling price of the same goods.

   However, if the firm is a manufacturing enterprise, a true marginal cost of goods is difficult to locate due to the presence of allocated fixed costs and the inability of most present day cost accounting systems to differentiate clearly between fixed and variable costs. Several cost concepts are worth brief consideration at this point: full costs, short-run variable costs, and attributable costs.

   In choosing the cost concept to be used in the model, it is necessary to develop a function that clearly includes all costs relevant to the decision and excludes those that are not. While the short-run variable cost concept is most acceptable to economists, due to the absence of arbitrary allocated fixed costs, the business community is likely to object to any concept that ignores costs that must be recovered in the long run by the successful firm. Businessmen are more comfortable using full costs for decisions even though the use of this concept may cause the firm to refuse business which could be profitable in the short run. Often this fear of marginal concepts is caused by a lack of understanding on the part of many managements. As a practical matter, it would be quite rare for a firm to accept business at the point where $MC = MR$. Marginal cost provides a point at which any reductions in revenue would cause the firm to recover less than out-of-pocket expenses and is thus a good reference point for managerial decisions. An analysis of fixed costs in relation to the present level of operations would show management how much less marginal cost must be than marginal revenue to achieve a recovery of all costs.

Gordon Shillinglaw's attributable cost concept may be applicable to the model. Shillinglaw views fixed costs in terms of traceability and divisibility. If a fixed cost increases or decreases when there are changes in activity within the relevant range of operations, it is said to be divisible. If a fixed cost can be traced logically to a particular segment of the operation without an arbitrary allocation, it is said to be traceable.[6] According to this, our cost of goods sold function should include all applicable variable costs, all divisible and traceable fixed costs, and all indivisible and traceable fixed costs.

It would seem reasonable to submit, to management, functions for each concept of cost, as follows: short-run variable cost, .70; attributable cost, .80; and full cost, .85. Then management would be in a position to select the concept to be used in the model on the basis of existing idle capacity, market conditions, and outlook for the future.

Information concerning bad-debt experience should be accessible from the firm's information system and outside sources, although in most cases reclassification and additional calculations would be necessary.[7] At this point, one must beware of drawing rash conclusions as to the bad-debt probability of a particular potential customer. In order to make valid probability statements, it is necessary to have sufficient credit experience to classify all customers by some objective criteria and then determine bad-debt probabilities for all that fall within each classification. Suitable criteria for such a classification will be discussed later in the paper. If experience demonstrates that 15 percent of the dollar value of all sales within a particular classification will become bad-debt losses, the probability for that classification would be stated as .15.

Let us suppose, then, that the X Company has the following credit risk classifications and associated bad-debt probabilities:[8]

Account Classification	Bad-Debt Probability
A	.02
B	.08
C	.14
D	.23

The firm would be willing to sell merchandise having a cost of goods sold percentage of 85 to customers in classes A, B, and C. It would be unwilling to sell these goods to a customer in class D, because the cost of goods sold plus the associated bad-debt probability is greater than the marginal revenue to be derived from the sale. However, it would be willing to sell a class D

[6]For a complete treatment of this, see Gordon Shillinglaw, "Concept of Attributable Cost," *Journal of Accounting Research* (Spring, 1963), pp. 73-85.

[7]For one method of classifying accounts receivable according to bad-debt loss experience, see Dun & Bradstreet, *How to Control Accounts Receivable for Greater Profits* ((Dun & Bradstreet, 1959), pp. 7-9.

[8]These classifications have no relationship to the rating of estimated financial strength by Dun & Bradstreet, Inc. that will be discussed later.

customer goods with a cost percentage of 75. Goods with a cost of 95 percent would be sold only to customers in class A.

It is appropriate to consider the possibility of including a factor representing a cost of the capital to be committed to accounts receivable if the credit sale is accepted. However, such an inclusion must be consistent with the purpose of the model, which is to assist management in evaluating the profitability of a particular credit sale. The following arguments can be offered for the exclusion of any cost of capital factor from the model.

First, it would be very difficult to associate a cost of capital to a short-term change in the structure of the firm's working capital. Capital released by the reduction of inventory is merely invested in accounts receivable. If the goods had been sold on cash terms, it is quite likely that this change would be represented by an increase in demand deposits. This being the case, the possible cost of capital is a sunk cost and irrelevant to the decision at hand.

Second, the selection of a cost of capital to be used in the model is surrounded with controversy. Should a borrowing rate be selected or should the firm use the minimum rate of return acceptable for investment purposes? As a practical matter, any figure selected would have little effect upon the decision. Using a 12 percent cost of capital and assuming that the collection period is two months, .02 would be added to the cost side of the model. It is unlikely that the omission of a factor this small would cause the firm to make a wrong decision.

The decision to expand business to a higher level of operations, however, must consider many factors, of which a very important one is the cost of additional capital required to sustain this increased activity. But this is a decision of another character that requires its own related tools and decisional premises. One should avoid the notion that a model developed for a particular decision can be used for all decisions of a similar nature merely because some of the inputs would be required for both decisions.

There may be several nonquantitative factors that must also be considered in the credit-sale decision. Two very important factors are the availability of goods and the status of competition. If the supply of goods is limited, they should be sold to customers from the classification with the most favorable bad-debt experience. However, if market conditions are very competitive and goods are readily available from alternative suppliers, the firm would likely make almost any sale that the model indicates as profitable.

Thus, management has a workable model to assist in making certain credit decisions. It must be remembered, however, that models like this one are not panaceas that will solve all problems facing management. While they do assist, by programming the decision and providing a reasonably objective basis upon which to act, the ultimate decision will be made after a review of the facts by an experienced and responsible executive.

ANALYTICAL CRITERIA FOR ACCOUNT CLASSIFICATION

As was stated earlier, a suitable criterion for grouping potential customers into bad-debt classifications is one of the inputs which the model requires. Because of the many variables involved, this can be a rather difficult problem. In many respects it is quite similar to the problem encountered in allocating factory overhead in that a positive correlation should exist between bad-debts experience and some other readily quantifiable indicator.

In order to make valid probability statements about the firm's bad-debt experience, a large quantity of data must be accumulated. It might be possible to draw probability conclusions from internal data available to the firm. However, the conclusions will be better if credit experiences of other firms can also be considered. It is highly unlikely that a firm could internally accumulate sufficient data to make a prediction that all customers of a certain classification should be assigned a probability of .09.

Perhaps a more direct approach to the problem would be to utilize ratings supplied by a national credit investigating and reporting agency as a method of classifying potential customers. The oldest and probably the best known of the national agencies is Dun & Bradstreet, Inc.[9] Subscribers to its reference service receive a book of ratings which classifies the potential customer according to its estimated financial strength and the agency's composite credit estimate of it. The estimate of financial strength is essentially a net worth concept and is indicated in the rating by the letters AA (over $1 million net worth) to L (up to $1,000 net worth). The composite credit appraisal is indicated in the rating by numbers A-1 (high credit appraisal for AA rated subjects) to 5 (limited credit appraisal for L rated subjects). Within each estimate of financial strength are four possible classifications: high, good, fair, and limited. The numbers are assigned relative to the financial strength as the number 2 indicates a limited credit appraisal for an A subject ($500,000-$750,000 net worth) but indicates a high credit appraisal for an E subject ($20,000-$35,000 net worth). Thus, the rating C-2 indicates a subject with a net worth of between $75,000 and $125,000 and a good composite credit appraisal.[10] These credit ratings are the result of an exhaustive search for information pertinent to the subject. The analysis includes an evaluation of financial statements received directly from the subject as well as information received from individuals in the community, such as bankers and attorneys.[11] Although these credit rating procedures are not without criticism on many accounts, their results have been well received by the business community.

---

[9]Theodore M. Beckman, *Credits and Collections: Management and Theory* (New York: McGraw-Hill Book Company, 1962), p. 272.

[10]For a complete discussion of the nature and significance of credit ratings, see *ibid.*, pp. 293-295.

[11]Roy A. Foulke, *The Sinews of American Commerce* (Dun & Bradstreet, 1941), pp. 305-310.

It would appear that sufficient credit experience could be accumulated in order to determine bad-debt probabilities for customers which fall into each of the Dun & Bradstreet ratings. The agency is in a position to accumulate a vast amount of credit experience data and could thus offer more reliable distributions than the firm. Although the agency would have to make a special effort to accumulate the required data and program it within its information system, this could be accomplished by periodically requesting each subscribing firm to supply a list of its credit customers and the associated credit experience. Electronic data processing would make this task relatively simple. Thus, if the credit reporting agency computes a bad-debt probability of .15 for all firms with a credit rating of F-4, the model would indicate an acceptable sale only if the cost of goods sold factor was .85 or less.

AN OVERALL CREDIT POLICY

Clearly, then, the overall credit policy of a firm must usually fall somewhere between a policy of granting no credit and a policy of indiscriminately granting credit to everyone. The model developed here will assist management in implementing a sound credit policy which maximizes sales and minimizes bad-debt losses to the extent that the firm will be led to an optimum position by making as many sales as market conditions justify while denying credit only when it is absolutely necessary. A firm would clearly be hurting its profit position by granting credit to any customer if the bad-debt probability plus the cost of goods sold was greater than the selling price of the goods. Likewise, it would be unwise to refuse credit if the bad-debt probability plus the cost of goods sold was less than selling price of the goods. Under a condition like this, the transaction covers all escapable costs and makes a net contribution to inescapable costs and net income. However, the outlook for the economy and the ability of the granting firm's capital structure and cash position to withstand increased receivables must be considered in the decision as well as alternative uses for the goods in question. In any event, it is clear that the use of such a model will point the firm toward a more objective basis for making credit decisions.

In concluding such a discussion, it is important not to overlook a very important aspect of the overall credit policy which is the firm's attitude toward collection of receivables. No amount of sophistication in the credit-granting decision can compensate for an ineffective collection policy. Statistics show that the older an account is, the greater the probability that it will never be collected.[12] Therefore, a necessary part of the overall credit policy must be a sound collection policy which should include the use of all reasonable methods of collection and thus help to insure that bad-debt losses are kept to a minimum.

---

[12]Robert H. Cole and Robert S. Hancock, *Consumer and Commercial Credit Management* (Homewood, Ill.: Richard D. Irwin, Inc., 1964), p. 294.

21. NET INCOME, FINANCING, AND RISING PRICES*

ROBERT M. SOLDOFSKY †

Prices in the United States have been rising at an average of about 2 percent a year for at least several decades; during shorter periods the rate of increase obviously has been above or below the average. (See Figure 21-1.) In 1967 the rate of increase in consumer prices exceeded 3 percent and is very likely to be greater in 1968. The prospect for a continuation of as much price stability as has been achieved since World War II looks bleak. Our military and economic commitments to orderly worldwide economic and political development, the continuing possibility of the devaluation of the American dollar, the prospect of a monetary system progressively less subject to the discipline of our gold supply, and the intensifying crises in our cities all help to generate this bleak outlook.

Even with prices rising no faster than they have been in the United States, the consequences for the rate of growth of business income, the distortion of reported net income between companies and industries, the maintenance of technologically up-to-date plant and equipment, and financing the added investment related directly to price-level increases have been serious. Congressional and professional studies of this many-sided problem are frequent.[1]

My major concern in this brief article will be with the income statement rather than the balance sheet. The purpose is to explore in some detail the impact of generally rising prices upon the net income and financing of business firms. In order to achieve this objective, the level and meaning of net income against a background of prices rising at a specific rate—6 percent a year—will be sketched. In the next section the impact of conventional, historical-based costs upon net income, income tax payments, and income tax rates will be contrasted with the impact of a price-level-adjusted cost basis upon these critical factors. Although the differences in the net income and income tax implications of these two cost bases are important, the conclusion emerges that price-level-adjusted net income—if that concept became acceptable for accounting practice and income tax purposes—would provide business firms with only a small part of the relief they seek

---

*From *The Quarterly Review of Economics and Business* (Autumn, 1968), pp. 67-74. Reprinted by permission.

†Professor of Finance, the University of Iowa.

[1]For example, Jules Backman and Martin R. Gainsbrugh, *Inflation and Price Indexes* (Washington: U.S. Government Printing Office, 1966), *Reporting the Financial Effects of Price-Level Changes, Accounting Research Study No. 6* (New York: American Institute of Certified Public Accountants, 1963); *A Statement of Basic Accounting Theory* (Evanston: American Accounting Association, 1966).

FIGURE 21-1

A HALF CENTURY OF PRICE CHANGES

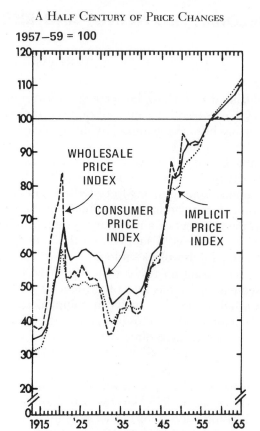

1957–59 = 100

SOURCE: JULES BACKMAN AND MARTIN R. GAINS-
BRUGH, *INFLATION AND THE PRICE INDEXES*
(WASHINGTON: U.S. GOVERNMENT PRINTING OFFICE,
1966), p.3.

from the pressures for outside financing during periods of sharply rising prices.

In the last section the relationship between fiscal policy and the acceptance of price-level-adjusted taxable income is discussed. Income tax regulations that do not accept price-level-adjusted costs are seen as providing an automatic stabilizer against some of those pressures which would push prices higher faster in an overheated economy. The implicit higher corporate income tax rate that develops under conventional accounting and income tax regulations tends to dampen capital investments in the right industries at the right time for fiscal policy purposes.

Under conditions of certainty, economic and financial decisions are made that will maximize net present worth or wealth. Even when prices are constant, new investments will not be made nor new products introduced unless the expected discounted value of the net receipts stream is greater than the initial (or time-adjusted) outlay. When prices are rising at some known rate or amount, new investment will not take place unless the same condition prevails, namely, that there will be an increase in net worth or wealth. To state the same point in a slightly different way, within the capital-budgeting framework of analysis, matching requires the use of the time-adjusted value of money. In conventional accounting the time value of money is not a consideration in the matching process.[2]

Within the decision-making framework for capital budgeting, the analytical procedure is the same whether prices are constant or rising at some given rate. When prices are rising, the data on which the decision will be made will include the expected higher prices dated for each point in time at the appropriate and discounted rate. The latter is expected to increase enough to offset the rise in prices.[3]

One of the many problems that exist in the real world is that the selling price, the quantity sold, and the related costs are not known with a high degree of assurance. The certainty device of economic theory will be used in order to facilitate and to clarify the exposition of the way in which changes in costs flow through the accounting records and the impact of these flows of cost upon the net income and income taxes of the firm.[4]

NET INCOME AND RISING PRICES

First, the accounting process by which generally rising prices impinge on the net income of a firm will be illustrated. The amount of paper profits will be quantified in the case developed. Second, the impact of alternative cost assumptions on income tax amounts and rates will be specified in terms of the illustration.

The terms "paper profits," "fictitious profits," and "capital consumption taxes" are used widely, and their meaning should be carefully defined. Paper profits, which are associated with the rising price level, are the difference between net income determined on the basis of current or opportunity costs and net income determined on the basis of historical or book costs. The term "paper profit" is usually used to refer to this difference on a before-tax

---

[2]For a similar criticism of conventional accounting, see John W. Coughlan, "Industrial Accounting," reprinted in Hector R. Anton and Peter A. Firmin, *Contemporary Issues in Cost Accounting* (Boston: Houghton Mifflin Company, 1960), pp. 50-68. Alexander A. Robichek and Stewart C. Myers, *Optimal Financing Decisions* (Englewood Cliffs, N. J.: Prentice-Hall, Inc., 1965), pp. 11-16, also point out differences between net income based upon the conventional accounting and discounted-present-value approaches.

[3]As an aside, note that the controversy between the advocates of absorption costing and direct costing is undercut by the capital-budgeting or time-adjusted decision framework. Neither absorption costing nor direct costing faces the problem of the dating of costs and revenues squarely. The attempt to approximate the marginal-cost concept of static economic analysis, as discussed in most textbooks on price theory, does not help in deciding within a considerable range whether the decision or policy in question will aid in increasing the net present wealth or worth of the firm. Of course, so far as direct costing results in an income in each accounting period different from absorption costing, the market price of the company's stock may be affected.

[4]Briefly, under conditions of certainty, there is a one-to-one correspondence between anticipated events and their outcomes.

TABLE 21-1
DETERMINATION OF NET INCOME WHEN PRICE LEVEL IS RISING°

Period	Sales	Costs				Taxable net income	Income taxes°°	Net income
		Depreciation†	Material, labor, overhead††	Current	Total			
Conventional (historical) cost								
First year								
January 1-June 30	$350,000	$50,000	$350,000	$100,000	$500,000	$50,000	$20,000	$30,000
July 1-December 31	566,500	50,000	360,500	103,000	513,500	53,000	21,200	31,800
Total						103,000	41,200	61,800
Second year								
January 1-June 30	583,495	50,000	371,315	106,090	527,405	56,090	22,436	33,654
July 1-December 31	601,000	50,000	382,454	109,273	541,727	59,273	23,709	35,564
Total						115,363	46,145	69,218
Third year								
January 1-June 30	619,030	50,000	393,928	112,551	556,479	62,551	25,020	37,531
July 1-December 31	637,601	50,000	405,746	115,927	571,673	65,928	26,371	39,557
Total						128,479	51,391	77,088
Current cost§								
First year								
January 1-June 30	550,000	51,500	360,500	100,000	512,000	38,000	15,200	22,800
July 1-December 31	566,500	53,045	371,315	103,000	527,360	39,140	15,656	23,484
Total						77,140	30,856	46,284
Second year								
January 1-June 30	583,495	54,636	382,454	106,090	543,180	40,315	16,126	24,189
July 1-December 31	601,000	56,275	393,928	109,273	559,476	41,524	16,610	24,914
Total						81,839	32,736	49,103
Third year								
January 1-June 30	619,030	57,964	405,746	112,551	576,261	42,769	17,108	25,661
July 1-December 31	637,601	59,703	417,918	115,927	593,548	44,053	17,621	26,432
Total						86,822	34,729	52,093

°Prices and costs assumed to be rising steadily at 6 percent a year.
†Constant. No purchases made during this 3-year period.
††All costs and expenses for which there is a 6-month lag between date of acquisition or use and date of sale. Depreciation expense excluded.
°°Income tax rate at 40 percent assumed.
§Costs and expenses adjusted to current cost basis as of date of sale.

TABLE 21-2

RELATIVE IMPORTANCE OF DEPRECIATION FOR LEADING CORPORATIONS
IN SELECTED INDUSTRIES
(1965 DATA)

Corporation	Depreciation as a percentage of		
	Receipts	Net income	Assets
American Telephone and Telegraph	14.7	90.4	8.1
International Business Machines	13.9	109.7	14.0
Commonwealth Edison	12.6	57.9	3.7
American Airlines	10.0	175.6	7.5
Du Pont de Nemours	8.0	59.6	9.4
United Air Lines	7.8	194.0	6.3
United States Steel°	7.4	117.8	6.1
Standard Oil (N.J.)°	5.7	63.3	5.0
Pennsylvania Railroad	4.7	89.9	1.8
International Harvester	2.7	61.9	3.4
Coca-Cola	2.7	30.4	4.0
General Motors	2.7	26.2	4.8
Boeing	1.3	32.6	3.3
Sears, Roebuck	1.2	24.1	1.6
McKesson and Robbins	0.2	17.0	0.7

°Includes depletion.
Sources: *Moody's Industrial Manual* and *Moody's Transportation Manual*.

basis. The well known difficulty is that the before-tax paper profits are defined as taxable income for income tax purposes and are taxed as such. The consequences of paper profits for financing and determining rates of return on investment will be made clearer with the aid of an example.

Paper Profits Illustrated

Assume that a firm (the Able Corporation) has a six-month product cycle. Its product costs and other expenses are rising at 6 percent a year, which is very close to the rate at which the general price level is rising. The product and the productivity of Able Corporation do not change during the three-year period being considered. In Table 21-1 costs are shown in separate terms to approximate both conventional (historical cost) accounting and economic (current cost) accounting. The same quantity is sold in each of the six-month periods, and the rising sales dollars reflect the increases in the selling price, which is assumed to be rising at 3 percent every six months. Sales revenues are identical in terms of conventional and economic accounting.[5] In current- or opportunity-cost terms, the period and product costs would be reported as rising to reflect the market conditions exactly. In conventional accounting, depreciation is reported on the basis of the historical prices that are shown on the books of account. For the Able

---

[5]The time-adjusted differences in value between the date of sale and collection are disregarded at this point.

Corporation this condition is indicated by the constant $50,000 depreciation expense. In practice most of this depreciation element would be related to product costs and would be matched with realized revenues. The costs of material and labor reflected in the inventory or product would be incurred on the average approximately six months prior to the time of sale. Hence, in this example there would be a 3 percent lag in the material- and labor-cost components of the product cost on the conventional statement as compared with the statement of economic income. Some costs, primarily period costs, would be reported on (almost) a current basis in both statements. The greatest difference between the economic and accounting versions of taxable net income relates to depreciation of fixed assets.

Notice that for the first six months taxable conventional-accounting net income and taxable net income on a current-cost basis are $50,000 and $38,000 respectively. The difference of $12,000 is the *paper profit*. When the income tax rate is set at 40 percent, the income tax on this $12,000 difference is $4,800, which is the difference between the income taxes in the two panels of Table 21-1. Table 21-2 shows depreciation as a percentage of receipts, net income, and assets for 15 different leading corporations representing a wide variety of industries.

Effect on Real Income Tax Rates

One complaint of companies that use relatively large amounts of fixed assets in their production is that their real income tax rate rises during periods of rising prices. The income tax paid in the circumstances described would be $41,200 for Able Company in the first year under existing accounting conventions and income tax regulations. The real rate of income taxes would be stated as the $41,200 divided by the $77,140 of real net income, or 53.7 percent as compared with the apparent or nominal rate of 40 percent. For the second year the effective income tax on real taxable income would be 56.4 percent. The increase in the second year is related to the method of accounting for depreciation. The increase in the real over the nominal tax rate amounts to about one third of the nominal income tax rate. Using the same illustration and considering the first year only, if the annual rate of price increase is set at 8 percent, the effective income tax rate on real taxable income would advance to about 57 percent.

Another way of viewing this difference in income taxes is to state that it is a levy on the use or consumption of capital goods. If one of the axioms of accounting and business is that capital goods should be conserved, this axiom appears to be violated. The reported rate of return is of interest to managers, investors, and others.[6]

---

[6]The stockholder also is not fully protected against inflation. The point made here is that the real income tax rate on the corporation rises and that corporate net income does not rise in proportion to the rising level price. For a discussion of this point and related problems, see Diran Bodenhorn, "Depreciation, Price Level Changes, and Investment Decisions," *Journal of Business*, Vol. XXXVI, No. 4 (October, 1963), pp. 448-457.

If the asset value of the firm were $1 million according to conventional accounting at the end of the first year, the conventionally computed rate of return would be 6.2 percent and income in current terms would be 4.6 percent when related to the same base. The difficulty with the latter computation is clear: the current-cost-based rate of return should be related to the market value of the assets. Determination of the latter value is more difficult although it is a part of the business of appraisers to make such estimates. Another way to attempt a market-validated rate of return is to relate the earnings per share of a company to the market value of its stock.[7] However, both the management and the stockholders should be at least as much concerned with the decision process for selecting investment opportunities and reviewing their individual results as they are with the aggregate results.

FINANCING AND RISING PRICES

A point that is often overlooked by those who take the position of outside critics of the financial system is the impact of price-level increases on the problem of financing business. Using Table 21-1, for example, during the first year the conventional net income was $61,800. Some $21,000 of this amount must be used to finance the higher cost of goods sold next year and another $6,000 to finance the expected higher expenses. The difficulty has been simplified further in that the inventory valuation problem has been sidestepped, but the maintenance of inventory at the same physical level would also require more funds. The replacement of depreciating assets is also avoided temporarily. Even so, financing the higher expense levels absorbs almost half of the conventionally reported net income. If current cost accounting were used and were acceptable for federal income tax purposes, the outlay for income taxes would be less, but the same amount of funds would be absorbed to finance the higher expense levels. In fact, the amount of funds absorbed at the minimum would be about 60 percent of the correctly computed net income.

The remaining net income in either case would be available for such uses as financing expansion in real terms and for dividend payments or debt repayment. Periods of rising prices are most likely to be those during which firms would prefer to expand because they anticipate rising demand for their products and rising profit margins. Financing such expansion becomes a more difficult problem because part of the internal funds that might be used are absorbed to finance the price-level increases in costs and assets. When many (or most) firms experience such pressure to expand and seek to finance the expansion with borrowed funds, this latter factor alone operates in the direction of increasing the interest rate. Expansion by widely held firms could be financed by equity offerings as well as by borrowing, but many

---

[7]This rough-and-ready procedure has many obvious faults. The reported net income of companies reflects a host of accounting problems. The market price at a particular point in time may not be representative, and the yield for a given year may not be representative of past history or of future prospects.

investigators have pointed out the great reluctance of industrial firms in general to offer new common stock.[8] Large numbers of firms do not know whether they are expanding up to the point (or even into the neighborhood) at which their internal rate of return on added investment is approximately equal to the added cost of funds. Speculation about the impact of added equity financing upon the firm's cost of funds, and the added impact of attempting further expansion upon the price level, would take this discussion too far afield. The concern here is to point out that rising prices intensify the financial problems of the firm. Price-level accounting practices which are widely discussed have numerous advantages, but their adoption would have only a small salutary effect upon the financing problem.

Caution should be exercised in using the illustrative numbers that have been presented; these amounts are intended to be realistic, but the proportions of current, lagged, and slowly responsive costs (such as depreciation) differ widely by company and industry. The illustration is also limited in other directions. Increases in the price level for three years only was illustrated; nothing was stated about how long the price rise had been under way or about how much longer it might be expected to continue before reversing itself. The rate of price change need not and should not be expected to be constant. The price changes for different classes of goods are likely to proceed at rates different from the average rate of increase.[9]

FISCAL POLICY IMPLICATIONS, ALTERNATE NET INCOME BASES, AND RISING PRICES

The use of accounting and income tax procedures that recognize net income computed on a current or market-price basis have important fiscal policy implications. First, the real income tax rates would be lowered, and this decrease would be most favorable for the heavier capital-using companies and industries. Income tax payments would tend to be lower, and the cash flow of corporations higher, during periods of more rapidly rising prices. The higher cash flow would be desirable from the point of view of facilitating corporate investment but would be destabilizing and tend to feed *demand pull* inflation.

Historical-cost depreciation tends to increase real income tax rates faster the greater the rate of price increases, and in that sense it is an automatic stabilizer. The higher real income tax rate impinges more on heavy capital-goods-using industries, but that effect is also in a stabilizing direction.

Many of those who favor price-adjusted depreciation point out that the

---

[8]For example, Gordon Donaldson, *Corporate Debt Capacity* (Boston: Harvard University, 1961), and Walter Heller, "The Anatomy of Investment Decisions," *Harvard Business Review*, Vol. XXIX, No. 2 (March-April, 1951), pp. 95-103.

[9]E. Cary Brown demonstrates a number of similar but more complex situations. He illustrates and discusses the problems of asset-replacement values based upon depreciation, longer periods of time, and patterns of rising, falling, and sporadic changes in prices. *Effects of Taxation: Depreciation Adjustments for Price Level Changes* (Boston: Harvard University, 1952).

revenue loss to the federal government would be small. For example, an executive of American Telephone and Telegraph Company suggested that only $2 billion dollars in revenue would be lost.[10] However, few would doubt that the federal government would maintain its expenditures level by either increasing taxes or borrowing. In the United States and in other nations of the world, historical-cost depreciation is almost universal. Revenue officials almost everywhere appear to be reluctant to condone the erosion of the income tax base and to face the higher explicit income tax rates that might be a likely consequence. Only in Sweden does the corporate income tax policy appear to be substantially modified and integrated into a fiscal policy rationally designed to influence the performance of the economy.[11]

Only when price level increases have been much larger than historically they have been in the United States have any nations enacted replacement or price-level cost depreciation relief, and then it was generally of a temporary nature. If more business costs were permitted on an escalator basis for tax purposes and if personal retirement incomes were also expected to be fully adjusted for price-level changes, the question might be asked, Who will stand up for maintaining a nearly constant price level? Who will stand up against inflation?

---

[10]Statement of Alexander L. Stott, comptroller of American Telephone and Telegraph Company, before the Committee on Ways and Means of the U.S. House of Representatives, quoted by Francis J. Walsh, *Inflation and Corporate Accounting* (New York: National Industrial Conference Board, 1962), p. 9.

[11]Sidney Davidson and John M. Kohlmeier, "A Measure of the Impact of Some Foreign Accounting Principles," *Journal of Accounting Research*, Vol. IV, No. 2 (Autumn, 1966), pp. 183-212.

22. INVENTORY CONTROL*

ROBERT D. NIEMEYER †

Inventory control is concerned with establishing and maintaining desired inventory levels. In keeping with this concept, the inventory control techniques that will be discussed are directed toward unit control of inventory rather than the closely related function of accounting for inventory dollars.

Broadly stated, the basic objective of inventory control is to establish and maintain an adequate inventory level at a minimum inventory cost. Achievement of this objective requires solution to two basic problems:

Determination of desired inventory levels, weighing inventory costs against such inventory benefits as:

Improved customer service that may result in increased sales
Smoother production operations yielding lower production costs

Minimization of total inventory costs for a given inventory level, giving consideration to the interaction between:
Acquisition costs
Holding costs

An approach to the solution of these basic inventory control problems will be discussed in the following sequence:
Methods of control
Inventory costs
Determination of expected inventory usage
Other refinements

There are two primary factors that must be considered in the control of inventories:

How much of an item is replenished at a time
When the item is replenished

These two factors control inventory levels, and through these factors, total inventory costs can be minimized for any given inventory level.

How Much

In discussing this factor, we should first look at the basic sawtooth inventory pattern to visualize the effect of replenishment quantities on inventory levels. This basic pattern is depicted in Charts 22-1 and 22-2.

In these charts we have assumed that the "when" factor is controlled so that a replenishment is received when on-hand balance has reached zero. From Chart 22-1 we can also easily see that the average inventory is 100 and that this amount is also equal to one half of the replenishment quantity. If

---

*From *Management Services* (July-August, 1964), pp. 25-31. Reprinted by permission.
†Manager, Management Advisory Services, Haskins and Sells, Certified Public Accountants.

CHART 22-1
BASIC SAWTOOTH INVENTORY PATTERN I

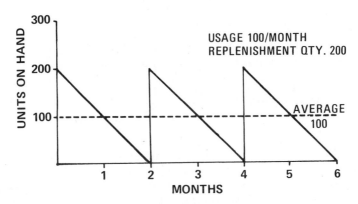

we increase the order quantity to 300 units, we increase the average inventory to 150 units as shown on Chart 22-2.

When

Charts 22-1 and 22-2 demonstrate that "how much" is a definite factor in determining inventory levels. Now consider the "when" factor. On these charts, the "when" factor was controlled so that a replenishment was received when the on-hand balance reached zero. However, some replenishment lead time is normally involved and this factor must be known in solving the "when" problem. Assuming a lead time of one month, we find that on our first chart the items must be ordered at the end of the first month so that replenishment will arrive when on-hand balance reaches zero. This order point

CHART 22-2
BASIC SAWTOOTH INVENTORY PATTERN II

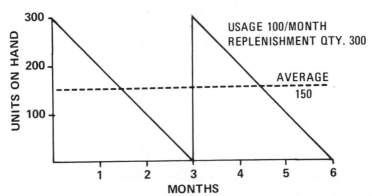

THESE CHARTS ILLUSTRATE THE EFFECT OF REPLENISHMENT QUANTITIES ON INVENTORY LEVELS. STOCK IS REPLENISHED IN QUANTITIES OF 200 (CHART 22-1) AND 300 (CHART 22-2).

CHART 22-3

PRACTICAL INVENTORY PATTERN WITHOUT SAFETY STOCK

could also be expressed in terms of on-hand balance as 100 units, this quantity representing expected usage during the lead-time period. So we see that lead time and expected usage are both required for determining a reorder point expressed in terms of on-hand balance. However we have [not] yet considered just how the "when" factor influences inventory levels. When we do this, we find that the basic sawtooth pattern with usage and other variations would appear as shown on Charts 22-3 and 22-4.

In Chart 22-3 the basic inventory pattern is disrupted by two factors found in practical inventory situations:

Usage variations
Lead-time variations

As this chart indicates, these factors cause stock-outs when inventories are controlled under the premise that a replenishment will be received when on-hand balance reaches zero.

To provide for these inherent variations, an additional amount of stock must be carried. This additional quantity or safety stock thus makes our practical inventory chart appear as it does in Chart 22-4.

This protection is built into our inventory balance by the "when" factor. Under an order-point system the protection is primarily needed during the replenishment (lead-time) period and is obtained by adding the protection

CHART 22-4

PRACTICAL INVENTORY PATTERN WITH SAFETY STOCK

VARIATIONS IN USAGE AND LEAD TIME MAY CAUSE STOCK-OUTS (CHART 22-3) UNLESS A HIGHER INVENTORY LEVEL IS MAINTAINED (CHART 22-4) TO PROVIDE SAFETY STOCK.

CHART 22-5

BASIC SAWTOOTH INVENTORY PATTERN WITH SAFETY STOCK

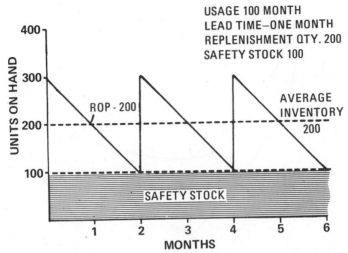

USAGE 100 MONTH
LEAD TIME—ONE MONTH
REPLENISHMENT QTY. 200
SAFETY STOCK 100

THIS CHART SHOWS WHAT HAPPENS TO AVERAGE INVENTORY IF THE REORDER POINT IS
CALCULATED WITH ALLOWANCE FOR BOTH EXPECTED USAGE DURING THE LEAD-TIME
PERIOD AND SAFETY STOCK.

required to the reorder point expressed in terms of on-hand balance. The formula for the reorder point then becomes:

R.O.P. = expected usage during the lead-time period + safety stock

This action can probably best be shown with these new factors superimposed on our first basic chart (see Chart 22-5). In this illustration, we have assumed a desirable safety stock of 100 units and have accordingly increased the reorder point from 100 to 200 units. Under these conditions the average inventory becomes 200 units. It can also be seen that this average inventory is composed of two elements:

One half of replenishment quantity
Safety stock

We have now determined a formula for development of average inventory under an order-point system:

Average inventory = ½ order quantity + safety stock

This same formula holds approximately true under our practical inventory problem previously charted. Safety stock tends to be on the average a constant amount, while working stocks are composed of replenishment quantities, the average of which is approximately one half of the established replenishment quantity.

Before discussing these principles of basic inventory control further, let us summarize the points that have been covered:

Replenishment quantity directly affects average inventory levels.
When to replenish stock can be expressed in terms of on-hand units

CHART 22-6

GRAPHIC PRESENTATION OF INVENTORY COSTS

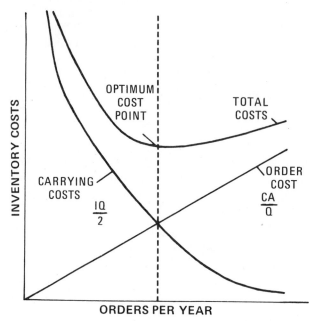

THE ECONOMIC ORDER QUANTITY FORMULA IS BASED ON THE RELATIONSHIP BETWEEN HOLDING
AND ACQUISITION COSTS. TOTAL COST IS LOWEST WHERE THE LINES CROSS.

as reorder point.

Reorder point = expected usage during the lead-time period plus safety stock.

Average inventory = ½ replenishment quantity + safety stock.

These basic rules lead normally then to the question of determining replenishment and safety-stock quantities since these two factors determine average inventory levels.

Replenishment Quantities. Since replenishment (order) quantities affect average inventory levels, they affect the costs associated with having inventory (holding or carrying costs). The size of replenishment quantity also affects the frequency with which an item must be reordered. Therefore, the replenishment quantity also affects order or acquisition costs, and economic order quantity formulas consider both holding and acquisition cost factors in arriving at the best balanced or least-cost order quantity.

This relationship between the two individual cost lines and the total cost line is shown graphically on Chart 22-6. It can be seen that the minimum total cost occurs at the same order quantity at which the two individual lines meet. A basic economic order quantity formula can be developed from the relationships as charted.

Let Q = economic order quantity in dollars
     A = annual usage in dollars
     C = cost of an order in dollars
     I = inventory carrying cost, as a decimal

Then,
$$\text{Order cost line} = \frac{CA}{Q}$$

and
$$\text{Carrying cost line} = \frac{IQ}{2}$$

When these two are equated, we have
$$\frac{CA}{Q} = \frac{IQ}{2}$$

and
$$Q = \sqrt{\frac{2\,CA}{I}}$$

By additional mathematics we can also express order quantity in units as follows:

$$Q\,(\text{units}) = \sqrt{\frac{2 \times C \times \text{annual usage units}}{I \times \text{unit cost}}}$$

For example, if we assume that we annually use 100 units of an item that costs \$4 a unit and that we have an order cost of \$10 and an inventory carrying cost of 20 percent, our formula becomes:

$$\text{Units to order} = \sqrt{\frac{2 \times 10 \times 100}{0.20 \times 4}} = 50$$

Determination of the inventory carrying and order or acquisition costs required for application of this basic formula will be covered in a later portion of this discussion.

This basic formula, developed in the early part of this century, is in fairly widespread use in solving today's problems of inventory control. There are, however, several points that should be made regarding use of this formula.

As we shall discuss a little later, some of the costs required for application of the formula are somewhat difficult to determine precisely. It should be remembered, however, that all factors influencing the answer are under a square-root sign, which allows some latitude in the determination of these costs and acts as a sort of "forgiveness factor." In addition, while carrying or acquisition costs may be approximated and the resulting equating of the two not completely precise, the answer should be considerably better than an out and out guess or an intuitive approach.

Another limiting factor possibly to be found in the use of the formula is that when constant carrying and acquisition costs are used across a wide range of inventory items, the answers become somewhat impractical at the extreme ends of the range. That is, use of the formula may indicate that an unworkably large amount should be ordered for a low-cost item or that too frequent orders should be placed for a high-cost item. These difficulties can be overcome by actually recognizing the variations in costs for various types of items or, in a more practical way, by limiting the answers at each end of the range.

It can also be pointed out that this basic EOQ formula does not consider all variables in the problem, an obvious example being that quantity discounts are not directly recognized. If quantity discounts are a significant factor, the difficulty may be overcome by a simple one-time computation that can be used in determining alternate order quantities from those developed by the formula.

This is done by calculating the additional cost incurred for various increased order quantities and charting these with order quantities down the side, unit cost across the top, and additional cost in the appropriate boxes. Thus, the saving by quantity discount can be compared directly with the additional cost incurred because of the larger size of the order, and an intelligent decision can be made accordingly.

Another factor that must be considered in using the formula is that the computation for each order is somewhat complicated. Probably one of the reasons for the considerably extended use of this formula in recent years is the availability of electronic data processing equipment. Such equipment has made it relatively easy to compute EOQ amounts at the time of each reorder. There are, however, other methods of applying this basic formula. One practical way is to develop a table of EOQ amounts based on various ranges of annual dollar usage. While not completely precise at the extremes of each range, this method is preferable to more arbitrary determination of order quantities. Another method of applying the formula is through the use of a nomograph. An EOQ nomograph is a sort of poor man's slide rule and utilizes three equidistant parallel lines with logarithmic scales. The simplest form uses one column for monthly usage in units, the middle scale for order quantity, and the other scale for unit cost. By connecting the appropriate monthly usage with the proper unit cost, the line crosses the middle scale at the economic order quantity. Once a nomograph has been prepared, it can be published in various formats and can even be printed on the back of the requisition form for ready reference.

Safety-Stock Quantities. It has been demonstrated that safety-stock quantities directly affect average inventory holdings. It would then follow that safety-stock levels directly affect inventory holding or carrying costs.

Since safety stock is carried to provide protection against stockouts, the determination of safety-stock quantities requires the balancing of holding costs against outage costs (as differentiated from EOQ considerations where we were balancing holding costs against acquisition costs). As we shall discuss further under the cost portion of this presentation, the cost of an outage is somewhat difficult, if not impossible, to determine precisely. Most approaches to the development of safety-stock quantities take this fact into consideration.

There is probably no widely accepted formula for safety-stock computations as there is for determining economic order quantities. Most approaches do, however, attempt to provide safety stock that will cover *reasonable maximum usage* during the *lead-time period*. Let's take a look at some of the ways this somewhat arbitrary amount may be determined.

One method is tied in with several other inventory refinements, which will be discussed later. The key point in this method is a definition of the *maximum* amount of usage fluctuations (expressed as a percentage) for which protection would be provided. Items for which usage fluctuations are greater than or equal to the maximum considered are given maximum protection. Those for which usage fluctuations are not equal to the maximum are protected for historical actual amounts. Under this method, more consistent use items are given proportionately less safety stock than those with more erratic use patterns.

Another approach—one which requires substantial data and computing facilities—to handle safety-stock computations takes into consideration that most inventory usage patterns follow some standard statistical distribution. On this basis, percentage of outage based on standard statistical factors can be determined. Then, by computing holding costs for various levels of inventory, a chart can be prepared showing cost for various percentages of inventory coverage. Such a chart can be helpful to management in determining just how far it is willing to go in providing inventory protection.

Other safety-stock formulas take into consideration such refinements as the average size of requisition quantities. The formula used by one of the major airlines combines this feature with the statistical approach mentioned above.

In summary, it should be emphasized that considerable judgment enters into safety-stock computations and that the answer should be designed and tempered to fit the situation. The definition that safety stock should provide protection for *reasonable* maximum usage during the lead-time period is a good guide. It remains then to apply some judgment to determine what is reasonable in any given situation.

We have now covered some basic methods of inventory control based on the fixed order quantity approach. Included in these techniques were consideration of certain costs and a requirement for an estimate of future usage. These two items, costs and estimate of future usage, will be discussed next.

INVENTORY COSTS

Major categories of inventory costs are:

Acquisition costs
Holding costs
Outage costs

In discussing these costs it is probably best first to define each item of cost and then to consider some practical means of quantifying these various items.

Acquisition Costs

Costs related to acquisition of purchased items would include the following categories of expense:

Requisitioning
Purchase order (including expediting)
Trucking
Receiving
Placing in storage
Accounting and auditing:
    Inventory
    Disbursements

Acquisition costs pertaining to company-manufactured pieces include several of the above mentioned items but also comprehend some different categories, notably set-up costs rather than purchase-order costs. A complete list of manufactured-item acquisition costs could include:

Requisitioning
Set-up
Receiving
Placing in storage
Accounting and auditing
    Inventory
    Product costs

In considering just how much of any of these costs should be applied to inventory-control decisions, we again must use some rule-of-thumb or arbitrary methods. To begin with, records frequently are not kept in such a way that the above mentioned categories of cost are readily accessible. Very often determination of these costs must be made by special study. Then we have the problem of deciding what degree of variability should be used when these costs are applied in the EOQ formula. (This is the only computation reviewed in this presentation where acquisition costs are used.) Welch, in his book *Scientific Inventory Control,* suggests that the effect of a 25 percent change in order rate should be used as a basis for determining acquisition costs. This is a reasonably good approach because some of these costs do not increase in a straight line but rather in a stair-step pattern. This 25 percent rule tends to give some weight to the latter condition. In any event, *all* acquisition costs should *not* be used in the standard EOQ formula, but the *variable* portion determined on some reasonable basis should be applied.

Holding or Carrying Costs

Holding or carrying costs to be considered in the solution of inventory control problems would include the following items:

Interest
Insurance
Taxes
Storage
Obsolescence

In arriving at these costs for inventory control solutions, it is probably best to consider only those items meeting the following two tests:

Out-of-pocket expenditures
Foregone opportunities for profit

An example of the application of these tests would be the consideration of warehouse space costs only to the extent that additional facilities would need to be acquired or that unused space could be rented for profit. These rules would also indicate that interest would be considered from the standpoint of foregone profit opportunity when sufficient capital existed in the business that money need not be borrowed to finance inventories.

Again, as with acquisition costs, holding costs are somewhat difficult to determine precisely because the usual records do not easily identify them. In addition, problems exist with the application of the above mentioned rules or tests. As a guide to reasonableness of holding costs that may be computed, the following table of representative cost ranges is offered:

Item	Approximate Range
Interest	4-10%
Insurance	1- 3
Taxes	1- 3
Storage	0- 3
Obsolescence	4-16
Total	10-35%

This table is a composite taken from various references and tempered with personal experience. Obviously any extreme situation may fall outside the ranges shown, but the table should be representative of the majority of situations.

Outage Costs

This category of costs is mentioned primarily because it exists and not because definitive rules can be set forth for computing outage costs. It was noted earlier that outages result in:

Decreased customer service level, which *may* result in decreased
    sales
Less efficient production operations
High costs resulting from "crash" procurements

It is probably obvious that outages affect the items named above; the unanswered question in most cases is, How much? Unless some very direct relationships exist, the cost of an outage is difficult to quantify.

The fact that answers to the determination of outage costs are approximate and arbitrary in nature does not necessarily mean, however, that their significance should be ignored. As was seen in the computation of safety stocks (where these costs apply), knowledge of the cost of alternatives enables the application of enlightened judgment to produce satisfactory answers to the problem of just how great an outage rate is acceptable.

DETERMINATION OF EXPECTED USAGE

All replenishment of inventory requires some sort of forecast for determining expected usage. This forecast can take various forms, including:

Hunches
Visual review of past history
Computation of average demand over a past period
Exponential smoothing of past demand
Tying past demand to a more reliable forecast
Relationship with other forecast items

This is obviously only a partial list, but it can serve as a basis for discussing forecasting methods as they relate to inventory control situations.

The first two of these categories have been included not because of their advantages but because of their widespread use. Whenever human judgment is the primary ingredient in inventory usage forecasts, the resulting answers tend to show the influence of overcompensation for the current situation. For example, when usage temporarily increases, much greater quantities are ordered. When usage then seeks its normal trend and declines, a large overstock results. Human reaction to temporary decreases in usage, on the other hand, often results in stockouts.

The point of this discussion is that an answer arrived at in a methodical, consistent fashion is usually much more reliable over a period of time than an answer obtained by hunch. In fact, in a particular application of some of these inventory control principles, a good portion of the benefit was obtained by replacing a usage forecast based mainly on human judgment by one based on principles *consistently* applied to past usage.

In direct computation of usage forecasts, either the averaging of past demand for a selected period of time or the exponential smoothing of past demand provides an acceptable method. The characteristics of the inventory in question and the facilities available for making the computation should influence the decision as to which method to use. Exponential smoothing gives greater weight to more recent periods and has the advantage of not requiring detailed usage history for each inventory item.

In certain production situations the last two forecasting methods outlined above can be used to advantage. The use of other forecasts can probably best be illustrated by a method that utilizes the explosion of a finished item into its component and piece parts. The demand for the finished item is

CHART 22-7

DISTRIBUTION OF INVENTORY USAGE VALUES CUMULATIVE PERCENTAGES

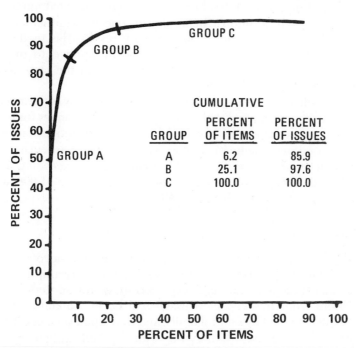

GROUP	CUMULATIVE PERCENT OF ITEMS	PERCENT OF ISSUES
A	6.2	85.9
B	25.1	97.6
C	100.0	100.0

THE FACT THAT IN ALL INVENTORIES A FEW ITEMS ACCOUNT FOR MOST OF THE DOLLAR USAGE
MAKES IT POSSIBLE TO CONCENTRATE THE CONTROL EFFORT WHERE IT IS MOST NEEDED.
THIS IS THE A-B-C APPROACH.

forecast directly, and the component and piece parts then become a logical
extension of that forecast.

OTHER REFINEMENTS

Two inventory control concepts that have been used successfully and
have fairly broad application should also be covered in a general discussion
of inventory control principles. These two are:

A-B-C approach
Use of control limits

A-B-C Approach

This concept is based on the premise that in most inventories approximately 10 percent of the items account for about 85 percent of the annual
dollar usage. At the other extreme, about 75 percent of the items account
for only about 5 percent of the annual dollar usage. Recognition of this situation and division of the inventory into three groups (A, B, and C) based on
annual dollar usage has commonly been called the A-B-C method.

These relationships appear to exist in virtually all inventories, and because of this and the advantages of being able to place emphasis on the important items, this approach has begun to be used somewhat more extensively in recent years. In addition to being able to concentrate attention on the items that make the big difference in inventory results, this method also enables several different methods of control to be applied to the same inventory. An alternative to this approach is the use of the same method but varying decision rules for each group.

In order to utilize this concept, it is first necessary to analyze the inventory to determine the approximate distribution of items so that ranges for each of the A-B-C categories can be set. Chart 22-7 shows the distribution of inventory usage values based on an actual inventory study. In this particular case, A items were determined to be those with annual usage exceeding $1,000, B items to include those with annual usage of from $100 to $1,000, and C items to have annual usage of less than $100.

Use of Control Limits

This approach, based on statistical quality control concepts, emphasizes the management by exception technique. The key assumption in this approach is that there is a "normal," expected usage for an item and that some deviations from this expected usage will occur. Significant usage deviations are determined by control limits, and only upon such occurrences need the item be reviewed. Otherwise, with the item operating within limits, decision rules can be applied mechanically to produce desired results.

This technique can also be combined with the A-B-C approach by varying the degree of control for each of the A-B-C categories. The tighter control is obviously applied to the A items, and because of the more frequent and earlier inspection of usage variances, less safety stock is required for these items. This then meets the requirement of minimizing inventory balances on the 10 percent of the items that account for 85 percent of the annual dollar usage. Also, because only 10 percent of the items are being more tightly controlled, effort required for inventory administration is minimized.

SUMMARY

We have now reviewed some of the basic principles of inventory control. This has not been a complete coverage; instead, emphasis has been placed on the order-point approach because it probably has the widest application in problems of inventory control and is well accepted today. The basic principles reviewed are just that—basic principles. As always, a specific solution must be worked out for the problem at hand. It is hoped that the points discussed will be helpful and can be applied in a practical way to the solution of some of these specific problems.

PART VII. FINANCIAL SIDE OF MERGERS AND ACQUISITIONS

The merger movement that gathered momentum in the late 1960's is likely to represent a pervasive and fundamental change in the historical scope of activities of individual business corporations. The current merger wave is the longest and largest in the history of the United States. Various studies suggest that the rate of diversification through mergers and acquisitions has probably doubled since 1950 and that this tendency has been fairly widespread throughout the economy. In 1950 only four mining and manufacturing firms with assets of $10 million or more disappeared through merger; the assets of these acquired corporations were about $150 million. In 1968 *Mergers and Acquisitions* journal counted 1,831 major transactions (transactions involving firms with assets of $700,000 or more) that involved about $23 billion in assets. Additionally, the type of merger taking place is changing from predominantly horizontal and vertical mergers to conglomerate mergers.

With the increasing popularity of business acquisitions, the financial executive's task of evaluating a potential acquisition candidate has become very significant as well as very difficult. More sophisticated methods of evaluating acquisition proposals considering future effects have been developed. In addition, more complex instruments of financing such acquisitions have been devised in recent years. The articles presented in this section provide an insight into these developments which is very useful to both acquisition candidates and to rapidly diversifying corporations.

The article by Donald J. Smalter and Roderic C. Lancey shows the importance of P/E (price-earnings ratio) analysis in acquisition strategy. Most successful growth companies can link their achievements with a mixture of three types of strategies—internal programs for new products and market development, joint ventures, and acquisitions. One aspect of the growth by acquisition strategy is maintaining and improving the acquiring company's P/E ratio. A high P/E ratio, which is essential to an acquisition strategy, depends upon a steady, high, long-term growth rate for earnings per share. Well selected acquisitions acquired on favorable terms contribute to a favorable growth rate.

Major questions covered in the article include: (1) What factors appear to control the level of the P/E ratio? (2) How can a company raise its P/E ratio? (3) How can an acquisition upgrade the company's per-share earnings results? (4) How does a candidate company's P/E ratio affect the acquiring firm's acquisition strategy? (5) Under what circumstances can both parties experience marginal gains?

Smalter and Lancey use a hypothetical case to show how the P/E ratio relates to immediate dilution or additions to per-share earnings. They demonstrate how quickly acquired earnings must grow to wash out immediate dilution during the post-merger years.

The second article in this section is an address by William G. Stott at the 36th International Conference of the Financial Executives Institute in Montreal. This article highlights the changes that have taken place in the evaluation of common stock over the last three decades. The security analyst in the 1930's was mainly concerned with book values and financial strength. However, Graham and Dodd in 1934 asserted the importance of "normal earning power" and recommended paying a variable but low historic multiple for such earning power. The concept of long-range earnings growth was emphasized in the mid-1950s. Since "growth" is the name of the game in today's business world, some financial managers play this game by acquiring other companies. Acquirers generally seem to regard the probable effect on their per-share earnings as the critical element in deciding whether to acquire another firm.

For some companies it is easy to determine the cash value of a candidate for a merger or the exchange ratio of common for common. However, neither of these two methods may be the better since ownership, dilution, and dividend yield must be considered. Modern convertible preferred stock has provided a much more versatile and flexible means of exchange than the traditional means such as a straight bond or preferred stock. In acquisition strategy, one must consider leverage and tax minimization as a means of increasing earnings. The three of these—convertible preferred stock, leverage, and tax minimization—used in unison will inevitably make possible a successful acquisition. Numerical illustrations show the essential structures of these alternative financial devices.

Stott points out that some members of the accounting profession and the SEC are becoming critical of the procedures acquirers typically use in their reports to stockholders. However, he believes (writing in 1967) that the great wave of acquisition financing will continue for several years and that its future will remain as fascinating as its past.

The article by Robert W. Ackerman and Lionel L. Fray deals with the subject of financial evaluation of a potential acquisition. The financial aspects of an acquisition are critical because a firm's survival and growth ultimately are measured in economic terms that reflect the quality of its investments. According to these authors, a firm's acquisition program should be closely related to its objectives. Regardless of the stress placed on particular objectives, the firm's economic goals are of critical importance, and the most fundamental measure of economic performance is growth in EPS (earnings per share). However, the analysis that stops at a consideration of the immediate EPS impact of an acquisition is inappropriate for the company concentrating on long-term growth.

An approach has been developed to answer the question, If we are to suffer an initial dilution in EPS, how long will it be before the earnings of the acquisition will overcome it? The question is answered by projecting the EPS of the parent company with and without the acquisition and noting the point at which dilution should be erased. The authors relate such analysis to the concept of return on investment.

An important consideration of any acquisition from a financial standpoint is the medium of exchange. The use of cash or debt raises a number of accounting and tax issues that can radically alter the effects of an acquisition upon the acquirer's EPS. An exchange of common stock creates the possibility of dilution that is not recognized explicitly in the return-on-investment technique. Convertible preferred securities, which recently have been popular as acquisition instruments, require further analysis. (Analysis related to acquisitions using convertible preferred securities has been omitted from this article since it has been covered by Anthony Meyer in Part V.) As a result of these problems, the effects of time should be considered, and future effects should be discounted to the present and measured with other alternatives.

23.   P/E ANALYSIS IN ACQUISITION STRATEGY*

DONALD J. SMALTER †
and RODERIC C. LANCEY ††

The achievements of most successful growth companies have been based on a mixture of three types of strategies: internal programs for new products and market development, joint ventures, and acquisitions. Each of these routes provides top management with a means to implement over-all corporate objectives and goals.

Use of the mergers and acquisitions route has been increasing sharply during the past several years. Continued growth in its popularity is likely because it serves numerous corporate needs and growth motivations. An acquisition can strengthen a weakness; for instance, it can help to fill a raw material need or improve a vulnerable patent position. It can buy valuable time for a company. It can help management capitalize on the strengths of each partner and utilize the synergistic possibilities which may arise in terms of geographic and product line expansion. It can provide diversification opportunities. And it can enable a company to enter growth markets and reduce its dependence on existing activities for earnings growth.

One aspect of growth by acquisition which deserves particular attention is that of maintaining and improving the acquiring company's price-earnings (P/E) ratio. The importance of this ratio in any acquisition strategy may not always be fully appreciated; yet the ratio has a decided impact on the range of purchasable companies. The relationship between the P/E ratio of the candidate and that of the prospective parent determines whether there is earnings dilution and hence whether the survivor can afford to swap stock. Also, the stock market's valuation of the negotiating companies, as reflected in their P/E ratios, is by far the most important financial factor in the negotiation of agreeable exchange terms.[1]

In this discussion we shall summarize the factors which most directly influence and control a company stock's P/E ratio. We shall attempt to develop a useful perspective on the ratio's controlling effect in stock-for-stock and stock-for-assets acquisition strategy. More specifically, these

---

*Reprinted from *Harvard Business Review* (November-December, 1966), pp. 85-95:
© 1966 by the President and Fellows of Harvard College; all rights reserved.

†Donald J. Smalter, Corporate Director of Strategic Planning, International Minerals and Chemical Corporation, Skokie, Illinois.

††Roderic C. Lancey, Corporate Planner, International Minerals and Chemical Corporation, Skokie, Illinois.

[1]See F. K. Reilly, "What Determines the Ratio of Exchange in Corporate Mergers?" *Financial Analysts Journal* (November-December, 1962), p. 47.

questions will be addressed:

> What factors appear to control the level of the P/E ratio?
> How can a company raise its P/E ratio?
> How can an acquisition upgrade the company's per-share earnings results?
> How does a candidate company's P/E ratio affect the acquiring firm's acquisition strategy?
> Under what circumstances (if any) can both parties experience "magical gains"?

A high P/E ratio brings a number of values to any company. It enables a more advantageous exchange of shares; that is, it enables "cheaper" acquisitions of other companies, a point to be developed later in this discussion. Also, it generates capital gains for shareholders and provides additional incentive for executive stock-option compensation. It enhances the possible use of stock as a substitute for dividends, thereby preserving cash for internal expansion, and provides greater net proceeds to the company for any new equity offering.

Of course, good decision rules for selecting candidates for acquisition are not by themselves the answer to management's need. As we know well from the experience of our own company, International Minerals & Chemical Corporation, and other organizations, much work must also go into making contacts with the heads of other companies, negotiating prices, revising the post-merger organization structure, and related activities. These tasks will *not* be discussed in this article, but their omission here takes nothing away from their importance.

INFLUENCES ON P/E LEVEL

The range of P/E ratios for companies varies widely. Within the process industries, for example, the ratios range from a low in the vicinity of 8 to a high of over 40. Exhibit 23-1 shows average ratios during the past three years for several components of the process industries.

Generally, a few companies in each category enjoy a P/E ratio considerably higher than the group average. To illustrate:

1. Pennsalt, a specialty chemical manufacturer, has consistently commanded a P/E ratio of at least 20 during the past several years. Two points seem to stand out: first, the company has maintained an aggressive R & D program, with emphasis on "glamour" chemicals; and second, it has *frequently* introduced new chemical specialty products which apparently impress investors.
2. In the diversified chemical category, Du Pont has enjoyed a ratio typically 20 percent to 25 percent above the group average. This highly diversified corporation has supported an innovative research program for years and regularly introduces new products which seem to convey promises of great commercial potential, such as Corfam, its new substitute for leather.

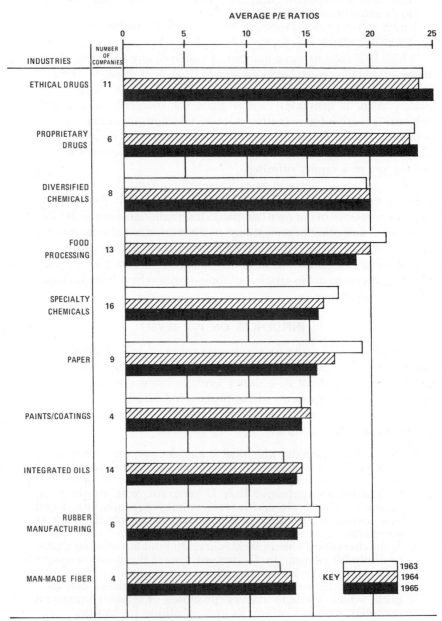

EXHIBIT 23-1
AVERAGE PRICE-EARNINGS RATIOS IN SELECTED PROCESS INDUSTRIES

SOURCE: Quarterly service of Value Line Investment Survey, Part III (New York, Arnold Bernhard & Co., Inc.).

We have conducted an extensive study of the literature to learn more about the factors affecting the P/E ratio. No great agreement was found among investment analysts on how to rate the price of a stock. In fact, the consensus of experienced investment analysts seems to be that much of the rating process is based on psychological reactions to future prospects and on subjective judgments rather than on detailed, soundly conceived quantitative analysis. Only recently have there been any serious attempts to develop formulas for determining the future market value of a stock in a systematic mathematical manner. The editorial box following this article includes some of the more revealing passages from articles which deal with aspects of P/E ratios germane to this article.

Controlling Factors

On the basis of our study, we have selected six factors controlling P/E ratios. Ranked in order of importance, they are as follows:

1. The prospect of *future per-share earnings growth* is the obvious primary influence affecting the P/E ratio.
2. Investors want *minimum fluctuation* from the anticipated earnings trend line. In other words, lower risks are associated with stocks which appear to promise lower per-share earnings volatility.
3. Investors favor companies which promise earnings growth for *long term*. They develop confidence, based on a company's historical performance, that the company's earnings growth will continue steadily for many years' duration.
4. Heavy emphasis on *research and development* is often a major component of a company's growth image. Investors are willing to pay high prices for Polaroid, Corning Glass, 3M, and IBM because they expect these firms to identify and successfully commercialize new products.
5. *Frequent introduction of new products* reinforces investors' confidence that R & D expenditures are productive. Thus, R & D results and investors' expectations become closely associated and help to sustain superior P/E ratios.
6. Companies which participate in *recognized* growth markets are apt to have bright futures. This point follows from the previous two and means that companies which expend resources in growth markets will receive recognition from investors, provided earnings benefits appear achievable.

When judging the price they are willing to pay, many investors, especially the more speculative types looking for capital gains appreciation, tend to place relatively low marks on such well known factors as:

A high rate of return on equity.
A high rate of earnings retention or plowback.
A high rate of dividend payout.
A high rate of dividend yield.
A low level of debt utilization in the capital structure.

The last point—de-emphasis of the level of debt utilization—appears significant. It can be shown that many companies with high P/E ratios possess long-term debt in excess of 30 percent of capital structure. This illustrates, perhaps, that such companies have *generated* numerous opportunities which warrant extension of their debt burden, with the benefits accruing to the stockholders through the effects of leveraging.

RAISING THE RATIO

From the previous discussion we may conclude that management must continuously strive to produce a *steady* upward trend in per-share earnings over the long term. First of all, internally generated growth opportunities should be carefully considered. Projects should be appraised both for overall profitability and for the incremental risks which would be incurred if additional debt financing were used to lever the anticipated profits for the common shareholder. Secondly, earnings growth can benefit directly from a deliberate acquisition strategy. A company can acquire other firms that (a) expand its market position in fields of high growth potential, (b) improve its technological capability and image, or (c) improve its per-share earnings because of a favorable trading position. Let us consider each of these three possibilities.

Picking Growth Prospects

In attempting to develop a rational approach for planning its growth, management should first examine growth opportunities and rates in the industries and/or business missions which it serves.[2] As illustrated in Exhibit 23-2, these rates can vary considerably, typically from 8 percent or 9 percent down to 2 percent per year. Spectacular growth in excess of 20 percent will be found in some of the newer, usually technically oriented and specialized markets until they begin to approach supply-and-demand equilibrium.

It is much more difficult to grow profitably in mature industries which demonstrate a decaying growth rate or a rate below that of the gross national product. So it is desirable to identify those businesses which have good or even outstanding growth rate potentials. This objective should dominate any searching process unless it is possible to pinpoint *bargain* candidates, i.e., sick or poorly performing companies that can be converted into healthy, contributing assets if marketing, merchandising, or other types of know-how are applied.

Buying Technology

In considering the acquisition of companies with desired technological strengths, management should ask if the *time* is right for buying. In a

---

[2]For an exposition of corporate missions, see Donald J. Smalter and Rudy L. Ruggles, Jr., "Six Business Lessons From the Pentagon," *Harvard Business Review* (March-April, 1966), pp. 65-68.

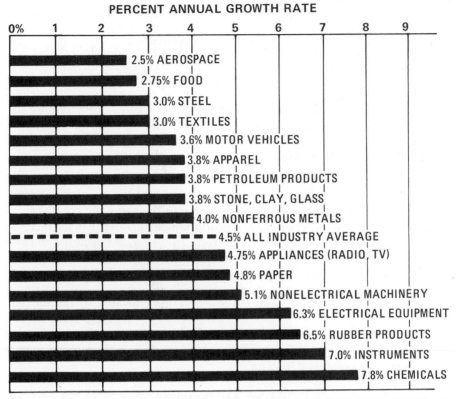

EXHIBIT 23-2
INDUSTRY GROWTH RATE PROJECTIONS THROUGH 1980

PERCENT ANNUAL GROWTH RATE

2.5% AEROSPACE	
2.75% FOOD	
3.0% STEEL	
3.0% TEXTILES	
3.6% MOTOR VEHICLES	
3.8% APPAREL	
3.8% PETROLEUM PRODUCTS	
3.8% STONE, CLAY, GLASS	
4.0% NONFERROUS METALS	
4.5% ALL INDUSTRY AVERAGE	
4.75% APPLIANCES (RADIO, TV)	
4.8% PAPER	
5.1% NONELECTRICAL MACHINERY	
6.3% ELECTRICAL EQUIPMENT	
6.5% RUBBER PRODUCTS	
7.0% INSTRUMENTS	
7.8% CHEMICALS	

SOURCE: "ECONOMISTS PAINT A BRIGHT PICTURE FOR 1980," *CHEMICAL ENGINEERING*, JANUARY 31, 1966, p. 34.

business where technology is critical, there is a well known time lag before it is possible to capitalize on scientific findings. For instance, over the years Textron has demonstrated awareness of this fact; it has acquired companies that already have expended substantial efforts in developing new technology. At the appropriate time, but not before, these companies were acquired, and additional financial resources were applied to capitalize on their know-how.

Naturally, it is preferable to acquire firms whose products are in early growth phases of the life cycle, rather than declining phases, and that possess exceptional potential for creating new products from their R & D programs. But simply to look at an industry segment and find that it is growing is not enough. Inspection must take place in depth, and analyses must be conducted which determine *where* the profits are to be made. In devising a growth strategy, questions like these must be addressed:

Should horizontal moves be undertaken for the purpose of broadening the product line?

What products, when combined with present products, could be sold profitably through common distribution channels?
Should vertical integration be pursued?
What percentage of the market will be a captive market in the future?
What are the possibilities for technical innovation?
Could any shortcuts in distribution channels be developed that would increase profits and bring a unique competitive advantage?
Are there companies available which might fulfill these needs and desires?

The answers to these questions do not come easily. They require inquisitive, perceptive, and time-consuming analysis.

Favorable Trading Position

In any acquisition involving the use of common stock or other securities exchangeable into common stock, it is essential that the acquired earnings be evaluated for their per-share contribution to the surviving company. If the increase in the number of shares is proportionally greater than the increase in annual earnings, then *dilution* is incurred. However, *the opposite can also occur*. Whether or not dilution results depends on:

1. The ratio of the buying price to the earnings of the acquired company.
2. The value assigned to the securities to be exchanged by the surviving company.

This brings us to the next major question in our discussion—determining whether an acquisition will upgrade earnings per share in the merged organization and improve its P/E ratio.

IMPACT ON EARNINGS

Here we want to propose a way of analyzing anticipated earnings. For the sake of specificity, let us consider the hypothetical case outlined in Exhibit 23-3.

> The management of a growing corporation, Company A, is considering the purchase of either of two smaller companies, B and C. Both B and C are believed to offer A some attractive opportunities to serve A's needs and growth objectives. Although B and C have the same assumed sales, earnings, and shares outstanding (an extremely unlikely occurrence, in reality, but convenient for purposes of illustration), B has a considerably greater P/E ratio. This advantage substantially differentiates the bargaining positions of B and C in merger negotiations. As a result, B negotiates a selling price of 22.5 times earnings, well above A's multiplier of 18. A's shareholders would then incur some minor and immediate dilution in their per-share earnings if B were bought.
>
> This would not be true, however, if Company C were bought. Here shareholders of Company A would benefit by obtaining an immediate boost in per-share earnings in the current year. In this case, A would utilize its higher P/E ratio to escalate per-share earnings. (Looking at the problem from the standpoint of stockholders of B and C, per-share earnings for B would rise from $5 to $5.82, and per-share earnings for C would drop from $5 to $4.37.)

Exhibit 23-3
Comparative Effect on Earnings of Two Prospective Acquisitions
(Purchase by Exchange of Stock)

Financial Data Prior To Acquisition

	Company A	Candidate B	Candidate C
Sales ($ millions)	$300	$100	$100
Earnings ($ millions)	$ 25	$ 10	$ 10
Shares (millions)	10	2	2
Earnings per share	$ 2.50	$ 5	$ 5
Stock price	$ 45	$100	$ 75
P/E multiple	18	20	15

Acquisition of B by A

Negotiated price is $225 million, or 22.5 times current estimated earnings. This is equivalent to a 12.5% premium over the current P/E ratio for B's stock. To make the purchase, therefore, A must issue 5 million shares of its common stock ($225 million divided by $45).

Earnings-per-share computations are as follows:

(a) COMPANY B—$2.00 per share ($10 million earnings divided by 5 million shares).

(b) COMPOSITE OPERATIONS—$2.33 per share (composite earnings of $25 million plus $10 million, or $35 million, divided by 10 million shares of A's stock outstanding plus 5 million shares issued to B).

(c) EFFECT ON SHAREHOLDERS OF A—6.8% dilution ($2.50 minus $2.33, or $0.17, divided by $2.50).

Acquisition of C by A

Negotiated price is $150 million, or 15 times current estimated earnings. This is the same ratio as the current one on the market for C's stock. To make the purchase, therefore, A must issue 3.333 million shares of its common stock ($150 million divided by $45).

Earnings-per-share computations are as follows:

(a) COMPANY C—$3.00 per share ($10 million divided by 3.333 million shares).

(b) COMPOSITE OPERATIONS—$2.62 per share (composite earnings of $25 million plus $10 million, or $35 million, divided by 10 million shares of A's stock outstanding plus 3.333 million shares issued to C).

(c) EFFECT ON SHAREHOLDERS OF A—4.8% gain ($2.62 minus $2.50, or $0.12, divided by $2.50).

But these numerical comparisons do not provide the answer. It is axiomatic that A carefully identify its motivations and needs in acquiring C instead of, or in addition to, B. Immediate per-share benefits may well prove illusory unless the composite company can exploit some available strengths and capabilities which will boost the acquired earnings over the longer term, at a rate *at least* equivalent to what A expects to achieve without acquiring C. Otherwise, C would gradually exert a "sea anchor" effect on Company A's overall earnings growth; i.e., C would gradually increase *future* dilution.

Company A should also attempt to estimate how investors will react to an acquisition of B or C. Exhibit 23-4 shows composite stock prices which could result from a range of P/E multiples for each merger, as well as the

EXHIBIT 23-4
RANGE OF STOCK PRICES DUE TO MERGER OF COMPANY A
WITH COMPANY B OR COMPANY C

P/E ratio	Composite stock price of A and B	Value of extinguished B stock	Composite stock price of A and C	Value of extinguished C stock
15	—	—	$39.30	$65.50
16	—	—	41.87	69.87
17	—	—	44.50	74.25
18	$42.00	$104.75	47.25	78.62
19	44.25	110.62	49.75	83.00
20	46.62	116.37	—	—
21	49.00	122.25	—	—
22	51.25	128.00	—	—

values associated with the "extinguished" shares of B or C. We see that:

1. If A acquires B, investors would have to upgrade A's multiplier to at least 19.3 to sustain its current $45 stock price; otherwise, the dilutional effect of acquiring B will immediately lower A's stock value, and B's original shareholders would not obtain the value originally anticipated.
2. If A acquires C, the multiplier could relax to 17 without reducing A's current stock price, and *any higher value would benefit both A's and C's shareholders.*

These are only the immediate effects on A's existing shareholders. Of equal, if not greater, importance are the price effects over the longer term. Management should, therefore, focus major attention on the likely P/E multipliers which investors will apply to future composite earnings.

Testing for Dilution

The reader may already have noted in these straight common-for-common swap examples that there is a sample method to test for dilution: divide the acquiring company's stock value by the negotiated P/E multiple being applied to the acquired earnings. (For instance, if A acquires B, divide $45 by 22.5 to get $2; if A acquires C, divide $45 by 15 to get $3.) The quotient should equal or exceed the acquiring company's current per-share earnings; if it does not, immediate dilution will result, as illustrated in Exhibit 23-3.

In more complicated swap arrangements involving use of securities convertible into common stock at some future date, the same technique can be used. Here the conversion price is divided by a multiplier based on the level of acquired earnings at the probable date of conversion. The quotient is then compared with per-share earnings anticipated at that future date *without* the proposed acquisition.

STRATEGIC CONSIDERATIONS

Exhibit 23-3 was designed to illustrate how the P/E ratio relates to imme-

EXHIBIT 23-5
IMMEDIATE PER-SHARE EFFECTS OF PROSPECTIVE ACQUISITIONS BY COMPANY A

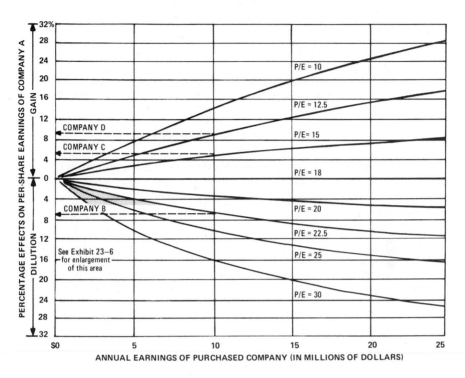

diate dilution or additions to per-share earnings. However, these two simple examples fail to provide adequate perspective on how the P/E ratio can influence selection and implementation of an acquisition strategy. To do this, the *amount* of earnings being acquired must be considered simultaneously along with the negotiated P/E multiplier being applied to them, as illustrated in Exhibit 23-5. This diagram is constructed with Company A data (10 million shares, earnings of $25 million, a stock value of $45, and a P/E of 18). It measures per-share effects on Company A's current earnings ($2.50 per share) for any combination of negotiated P/E ratios over the range of 10 to 30 for a given amount of acquired earning power.

A similar diagram could be readily constructed for any company whose management desires a tool for quick, visual reading of the effects on earnings of prospective acquisitions.

Exhibit 23-5 obviously divides into two fields of interest, with an 18 multiplier representing the boundary line between dilution of and additions to per-share earnings. Consider the field of prospective acquisitions with earnings at negotiated P/E ratios below 18:

1. Company C, which earns $10 million, would bring an immediate beneficial boost of 12 cents, or 4.8 percent, to Company

A's per-share earnings. But perhaps another candidate—call it Company D—with the same approximate earning power and attributes for A's particular needs is available at a P/E of 12.5. The benefits to A would be over 9 percent, or double those of Company C.
2. Alternatively, perhaps A should be considering a larger candidate with a somewhat lower P/E than 15, and reach for substantially greater benefits than C can offer. A candidate with $15 million in earnings and a P/E of 12.5 would generate an addition of about 32 cents (approximately 13 percent) to A's immediate per-share results.

ACCOUNTING FOR GROWTH

To refer back to the example previously described, acquisition of Company B by Company A would immediately reduce A's current per-share earnings by 17 cents, or nearly 7 percent (see Exhibit 23-3). Before proceeding to absorb this impact, A's management should consider the following kinds of questions:

Should there be a guideline or decision rule which sets a limit on dilution due to acquisitions?
If so, should this statement apply uniformly to all candidates, or should a range of limits be selected in recognition of the purpose or motive that may be served by selected types of candidates?
Even after adjusting for anticipated synergisms and savings, will the acquired earnings grow fast enough to eliminate per-share dilution over the next several years?
Is it likely that some permanent drawbacks will result which are justifiable in terms of overall corporate needs and objectives?

One area likely to be of special interest to growth-oriented companies is the acquisition of new technology. Company A, for example, may have inadequacies or even voids in its R & D skills, manufacturing technologies, or patent position in an attractive growth market. By identifying its technical needs, A could set some specific acquisition decision rules for this area, such as:

1. Up to 5 percent immediate dilution is acceptable even though there are no direct assurances that acquired earnings will grow as fast as A's projected rate.
2. The acquired company's P/E ratio should exceed 22.5.

The shaded area in Exhibit 23-6 blocks out the resulting "field of interest" for A's searching process. This delineation restricts A's candidate list to small companies—those with earnings ranging from $1 million to $7.5 million. (The lower limit of $1 million is selected arbitrarily for this discussion, since, in Company's A's case, dilution resulting from buying a company with earnings below this level would be minor.) A prime motivation would be to exploit substantially greater P/E ratios of *qualified* candidates which have already obtained recognition of technical competence from investors. Note that a candidate earning slightly over $2 million would be acceptable, even with a negotiated P/E of 30! Company A would, therefore, deliberately

EXHIBIT 23-6
FIELD OF INTEREST IN SEARCHING FOR ACQUISITIONS

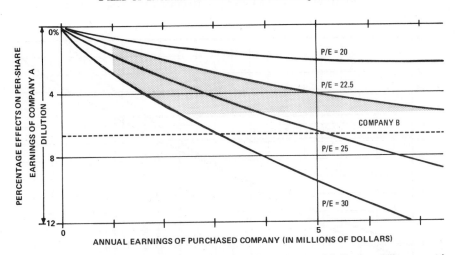

search for technology sources whose P/E ratio would "rub off" onto A's overall image to investors and either reduce or eliminate adverse stock-price effects.

Company B does not strictly satisfy these guidelines; it falls outside the colored area. Perhaps B is attractive, however, because it could save A several years in building a position in a desirable growth market. If so, this means that A is looking to B primarily for direct contributions to A's earnings growth. This in turn raises a more serious issue: How fast must acquired earnings grow to wash out immediate dilution during the next several years? Exhibit 23-7 has been prepared to illustrate the answer to this problem:

> The exhibit assumes that Company A is planning on a 10 percent per year growth in its per-share earnings for current operations. To learn how fast acquired earnings must grow to eliminate dilution completely within three or four years for a range of negotiated P/E ratios, run a line horizontally from the acquisition's P/E ratio to the time period curves; the growth rate figure directly beneath the point of intersection is the answer.

The results are somewhat unsettling, as Company B's earnings, including synergistic contributions and savings, would have to grow at 18 percent per year to eliminate dilution within three years and 16 percent per year to wash out dilution in four years. A higher priced candidate—say, Company E, priced at 25 times earnings—would demand acquired earnings growth in excess of 20 percent per year to eliminate dilution. Since these levels of earnings growth are so high, A's management is challenged to define (at least to itself) the reasons which would justify some *permanent* dilution in its per-share earnings.

It is difficult to generalize on these issues, since each company encounters a unique set of circumstances, including its own anticipated rate of earnings growth, its P/E ratio, and the P/E ratio of desirable acquisition candidates.

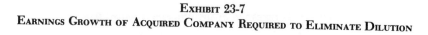

EXHIBIT 23-7
EARNINGS GROWTH OF ACQUIRED COMPANY REQUIRED TO ELIMINATE DILUTION

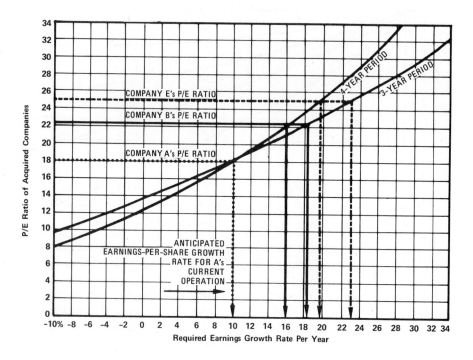

It seems clear, however, that management should deliberately define its acquisition decision rules and clearly perceive the per-share effects of each acquisition candidate. Preparation of charts similar to Exhibits 23-5 and 23-7 is particularly helpful in developing this perspective and in formulating an overall acquisition strategy.

CONCLUSION

Growth companies have been sharply increasing their use of acquisitions as a major component of their overall corporate growth strategy. At the same time, they apparently recognize that an acquisition program can be meaningful and truly successful only if it is closely keyed to corporate motives, needs, and objectives, and contributes to the company's longer term growth goals for its per-share earnings.

Per-share earnings are directly affected by any acquisition based on the exchange of common stock or securities convertible into common stock. When this is the case, management's acquisition strategy should be formulated to link earnings growth goals to the company's P/E ratio. This ratio, when compared with the most likely negotiated P/E ratio of qualified acquisition candidates, directly determines whether per-share earnings will be diluted or beneficially boosted, both immediately and during the longer term future.

In this article we have suggested that acquisition strategy can be more clearly perceived and communicated if management defines the firm's fields of interest—that is, identifies preferred zones in a diagram like Exhibit 23-5, which correlates the amount of acquired earning power, the related P/E ratios, and the resulting per-share effects. Such a diagram forces management to think through the role being assigned to acquisitions and to ascertain whether or not candidates which serve business needs and motives are also compatible with the company's basic financial goal—*sustained* growth in per-share earnings.

WHAT EXPERTS SAY ABOUT P/E RATIOS

"High price-earnings multiples typically reflect investor satisfaction with companies of high quality or with those which have experienced several years of expansion and rising earnings. In such cases, prices have often risen faster than earnings. A resultant increase in price-earnings ratios may be justified in individual instances, but under the impact of public approval or even glamour, it often runs to extremes." —S. Francis Nicholson, "Price-Earnings Ratios," *Financial Analysts Journal* (July-August, 1960), p. 45.

"Although prospective earnings frequently enter into theoretical analyses, any attempt at empirical measurement of earnings ordinarily requires heavy reliance on past data. Since stock prices are determined primarily by how people feel about the future, considerable instability has resulted in computed price-earnings ratios." —Oswald D. Bowlin, "The Price-Earnings Ratio: A Whimsical Variable," *Commercial Financial Chronicle* (September 7, 1961), p. 4.

"The extent to which he [the investor] will be willing to pay more depends upon the outlook for the earnings and dividends of the two companies and the investor's best guess as to how other investors will view the two firms sometime in the future." —Sanford L. Margoshes, "Price-Earnings Ratio in Financial Analysis," *Financial Analysts Journal* (November-December, 1960), p. 126.

"The price-earnings concept is relevant principally in analyses of growth stocks. It is fairly obvious that IBM's notoriously high P/E (currently around 50) reflects an expectation that its earnings will grow considerably. A corporation whose earnings are stable, on the other hand, is valued by investors principally for its net-asset value and/or its yield. . . . How *should* stock prices be related to earnings? Scarcely any two analysts will answer this question quite the same way; but most would probably agree that, in gauging the answer for any particular stock, there are two basic judgments the investor must make at the outset: one about the company's expected growth rate; another about the return the public will demand from stock investments in general." —"Personal Investing," *Fortune* (January, 1963), pp. 184 and 186.

24. THE CHANGING FACE OF CORPORATE FINANCE*

WILLIAM G. STOTT †

Today I am going to try to highlight for you some of the key changes that have taken place over the past 30 years in the field I think I know best—the investment field. When I went to Wall Street in the 1930's, the security analyst was concerned primarily with book values and financial strength. Bankruptcy had been the order of the day and those who had anything left were interested in the survival of the fittest. There was no talk of growth in earnings and, in fact, relatively little talk of earnings. Earnings were important only in so far as we all knew that, like stock prices, they could go down.

In 1934, the first edition of *Security Analysis* by Graham and Dodd made its appearance. This book was, and its subsequent editions remain, the bible of the security analyst. In the light of the times, it took courage in 1934 to assert that there was such a thing as a sound investment in common stocks. But by 20-20 hindsight the philosophy was cautious and conservative. The approach to investment taken by Graham and Dodd was largely statistical. While it gave considerable weight to balance-sheet strength and book values, it rested fundamentally on the determination of "normal earning power" and recommended paying a variable but low historic multiple for such earning power, depending upon the character of the company and the business. In other words, it was a guide to buying bargains in the stock market. By the middle of the 1950's, however, it was difficult to find a bargain in the market using the old guidelines of Graham and Dodd. So the investment game began to change.

The concept of long-range earnings growth began to take hold in earnest in the mid-1950's. Analysts and investors paid less and less attention to "normal" earning power or even to earnings stability. They paid more and more attention to the fundamental competitive position of industries and companies, to changing processes and technologies, and to earnings projections over an extended time horizon. By 1961 the growth concept had reached fever pitch, and price-earnings ratios of 40 or 50 and even 100 were readily justified by discounting projections of future earnings growth. But the soaring 1960's initially refused to soar, and in 1962 the investment community took its lumps. The price-earnings ratios of the growth stocks evaporated like snow in May, and the price of even such stalwart growth companies as I.B.M. fell by 50 percent. Disenchantment, however, proved exceedingly brief. When the economy started rolling again in 1963, growth

*From *The Morgan Guaranty Survey* (October, 1967), pp. 3-8. Reprinted by permission. This article was originally an address by Mr. Stott at the 36th International Conference of the Financial Executives Institute in Montreal.

†Executive Vice-President, Morgan Guaranty Trust Company of New York.

quickly reassumed its exalted status in investment thinking. Today, as I am sure you all are aware, growth is unmistakably the name of the game.

Actually, however, relatively few companies can be classified as inherently growth companies. These lucky ones generally are operating in an environment of greater than average industry growth and possess some unique attribute—such as important patent protection, exceptional marketing or manufacturing skills, unusually imaginative research, or a competitive situation which affords leeway for prices to be raised and profit margins to be maintained under almost any circumstances. The great majority of companies do not have any of these special characteristics. But since your bosses and mine know that growth is the name of the game, they are going to try to get into the game even if operating in the most pedestrian of industries.

How does today's manager play the growth game? First, of course, he tries to wring every nickel's worth of earnings out of the old dry cleaning business—even though he can't sleep for worrying about "Wash-and-Wear" and "Perma-Press." And almost invariably the pursuit of increased earnings takes the form of heavy reliance on modern and sophisticated management tools. Haphazard, rule-of-thumb procedures give way to rigorous cost control, precise accounting, and long-term budgeting and planning—with the company's financial executive inevitably emerging with greatly elevated status in the management team. The return on assets and conformance to budgets become the crucial topics of the day. Slowly, but fairly surely, the return on capital starts to improve, and it keeps going up until one fine day the boss realizes that he now has 98 percent of the really good, high-margin dry cleaning business where the return on assets is worthwhile. And it isn't long before he begins to dream of other fields to conquer. In no time at all he and his financial executive are deeply involved in the search for something to acquire and in elaborate calculations as to how an acquisition can be financed. And that is really what I came here to talk about in the first place—financing!

I think it is no exaggeration to say that the most imaginative financings of recent years have been associated with acquisitions. The more successful of these recent financings have resulted in substantially increased earnings per share, and indeed acquirers generally seem to regard the probable effect on their per-share earnings as the critical element in deciding whether or not to acquire another firm.

Let us return to our dry cleaning establishment and imagine that, as a result of impressive earnings growth produced by modern management techniques, the market now values the stock at 25 times earnings with a yield of 2 percent. For those of you who don't follow the new math any better than I do, let us say the stock sells for $25, earns $1, and pays 50 cents. Those numbers should be easy to remember. Clearly this company is in a good position to use its own common stock to acquire another dry cleaner (or any other type of business for that matter) which sells for less than 25 times earnings and pays no more than the equivalent of 50 cents—and *most importantly* to increase earnings per share by so doing.

For example, suppose our dry cleaner (Company A) finds a firm (Company B) whose stock is selling for $15 a share and which is earning $1 a share and paying 30 cents a share in dividends. It could offer Company B's stockholders 8/10ths of a share of Company A stock for each share of Company B outstanding. And this offer would in all probability be accepted, since each 8/10ths of a share of Company A common would have a market value of $20 and would carry a dividend of 40 cents—a one-third increase for Company B stockholders in both market value and dividends. Significantly, the merged company would have fewer shares outstanding than the two companies had in combination when they were separate entities, since for each 80 shares of Company A's stock that were newly issued to effect the acquisition 100 shares of Company B's stock would be retired. Therefore, earnings per share for the merged company would be higher than they were for either Company A or Company B. If for the sake of simplicity we assume that both companies had the same number of shares outstanding, earnings per share of the merged company would be $1.11, compared with the $1 per share earned in each case previously. This 11 percent increase is an obviously happy outcome.

But now let us assume that Company A is not quite so fortunate as we have just imagined. Our dry cleaner, instead, finds a company whose stock is selling for $15 a share and which is earning $1 a share but which, for reasons best known to the management, is paying a dividend of 80 cents. While Company B shareholders would in this instance also be perfectly willing to accept the equivalent of $20 a share for their $15 stock, they will not accept a reduction in the 80-cent dividend. Obviously our dry cleaner cannot use its common stock for the acquisition, for as we have already seen the 8/10ths of a share required to produce the $20 market value provides a dividend of only 40 cents.

I sense, though, that you are all ahead of me, aware that I am about to proceed to that miracle of miracles—the modern convertible preferred. The solution to the problem is easy. To acquire Company B's stock, our dry cleaner issues a low par-value preferred paying a dividend of 80 cents a share convertible into 8/10ths of a share of Company A common. This will produce the dividend required by Company B stockholders, and the preferred will certainly sell for at least $20, since it can be exchanged at any time for 8/10ths of a share of the Company A common that sells for $25.

In this instance, the merger produces even better results in terms of increased earnings per share of common stock outstanding, since Company B's common is replaced by preferred. This is so even though total earnings potentially available to the common stockholders of the merged company have to be reduced by the amount of the fixed commitment on the newly issued preferred. Again, if Company A and Company B are assumed to have had the same number of common shares outstanding, it doesn't require the new math to see that new per-share earnings will be $1.20—or an increase of 20 percent *before dilution*—that is, before conversion of the preferred into common (when earnings would revert to the $1.11 of our previous illustration). This result thus outshines the straight common-for-common exchange, or at least it would if there somehow could be assurance that the holders of the preferred wouldn't exercise their privilege of conversion.

So, the next step becomes obvious. It is simply to invent a convertible preferred that probably will not be converted—or at least not for a long time. One of the easiest solutions is to tie the payment of the preferred dividend to the common dividend. In the case of our dry cleaner, for example, it is unlikely that conversion of preferred into common will take place until the company pays a common dividend of $1 a share. At that point a dividend of 80 cents will be available either from the preferred or from the 8/10ths of a share of common available through conversion. But when the common dividend exceeds $1, conversion will take place and earnings will be diluted—that is, *reduced* on a per share basis. But suppose the dividend provision for our convertible preferreds reads as follows: "The preferred dividend will always be 80 percent of the common dividend but never less than 80 cents." The need to convert is eliminated, since the dividend on the preferred will rise in line with the dividend available on the 8/10ths of a share of common. As you know, a number of convertible preferreds have precisely this kind of flexible dividend arrangement in order to maintain a differential between the preferred yield and the common yield.

Perhaps one of the most ingenious of the modern convertible preferreds is a Participating Convertible Preference stock. To date, this kind of stock has not been issued for acquisition purposes. It has been used rather to re-structure a single company's capital accounts—specifically to reduce the number of common shares outstanding and also to replace preferred stock carrying a cash dividend commitment with preferred stock free of such a commitment.

The maiden venture in this type of financing occurred roughly two years ago when a company offered an issue of Participating Convertible Preference stock on a share-for-share exchange basis to the holders of a previously issued $3-dividend preferred stock and to holders of the company's common stock. Each share of preference stock was made convertible initially into one share of common stock, and it was specified that the preference stock was to receive the same cash dividend as that paid on the common. As it happens, though, the company has been paying no cash dividend on the common, so it was further provided that the conversion ratio for the preference stock would increase at the compound rate of 3.09 percent per year for 24 years. Thus, the stock was convertible into 1.0309 shares of common in fiscal 1967, 1.0628 shares at present, and it will be convertible into 2.0145 shares by 1989. As would be expected, those holders of the $3-dividend preferred who had a prime interest in current income were not especially attracted by the offering. But other holders of the outstanding preferred welcomed the opportunity to move from a tax situation in which dividends were being taxed as current income to one in which appreciation was subject to capital-gains taxation. And many holders of the company's common, apparently anticipating that the new preference stock would sell at an attractive premium in relation to the common, also were induced to make the exchange. As a result, the exchange offer was substantially over-subscribed.

An important feature of the offering was that the conversion ratio was *not* protected against dilution from stock dividends on the common of 2½ percent or less per annum. Since the company's common has been paying yearly stock dividends of 2½ percent and presumably will continue to do so at least until it pays a cash dividend, the *real* annual increase in the conversion rate is only 0.59 percent—or just over one half of 1 percent a year (i.e., 3.09 percent minus 2.50 percent). Thus, by 1989, if the 2½ percent stock dividend continues to be paid on the common, the preference stock will be convertible into only 1.154 *adjusted* shares of common stock. This made the new preference stock less attractive than it would have been had the conversion ratio been fully protected against dilution. But holders nevertheless could look forward to the maintenance of a premium in relation to the company's common stock, a consideration making the likelihood of conversion remote. In brief, a convertible preferred was created that is not only unlikely to be converted but which pays no cash dividends and increases in value only slowly relative to the common.

Because of their versatility, convertible preferreds have become increasingly popular. However, they are seldom employed to raise new money because they do not provide the tax shelter of debt or convertible debt, and in general their usefulness as an acquisition vehicle is pretty well limited to those acquirers whose common stocks sell at fairly high price-earnings ratios or provide low yields. Companies whose stocks sell at low price-earnings ratios or provide high yields usually must look to other means to accomplish an acquisition. Typically, low price-earnings ratio acquirers employ financing devices that stress a combination of tax minimization and leverage.

There is almost no limit to the number of illustrations I could use to point up the importance of leverage and tax minimization as a means of increasing earnings. But one of the most imaginative transactions I know of was the acquisition by a rather small construction company of a pipeline company that had been jointly owned by a number of oil companies.

The pipeline company, which had assets on its book valued at some $80 million, was purchased for $288 million in cash. The construction company prior to the acquisition had net assets of only some $30-odd million, and its average earnings had been less than $3 million a year. Because of the assured generation of cash by the pipeline operation, however, the acquirer was able to borrow the full amount of the purchase price. Almost $200 million in senior debt was issued in a private placement against the pipeline's assets. The remainder of the acquisition was financed by the retention of $60 million of subordinated debt obligations by the selling oil companies and the sale of $28 million of convertible debentures to the public.

Before the acquisition, the pipeline was generating income after taxes of $10 million. By using accelerated depreciation for tax purposes on the greatly enlarged asset base of the new company, the pipeline's $9 million annual current income tax liability was almost eliminated. And on a cash basis, this virtually offset the $10 million increase in interest expense. However, by opting to use straight-line depreciation in reporting to stockholders (thereby reducing the annual depreciation subtraction from income) and by employing a unique presentation of deferred taxes, pro forma reported net income rose by more than $5 million, without any immediate increase in common shares outstanding. The construction company came out of the deal with a highly leveraged capital structure—with only 12 percent of its capital accounted for by common equity. The heavy orientation toward debt appeared to be justified, however, because of the stability characterizing the pipeline's earnings and because cash flow was ample in relation to debt-servicing requirements.

With the use of convertibles and the use of tax-minimization and leverage techniques both so effective in increasing earnings, it was virtually inevitable that a would-be acquirer would come along who would perceive the enormous potential of employing both in concert. He did, and—not surprisingly—he added a few touches of his own in the process.

The case I'm referring to involved a highly imaginative takeover by a conglomerate of a meat packing company more than twice the conglomerate's size. Prior to the takeover, the meat packer had 2.5 million shares outstanding selling at $46 a share. The conglomerate was already a highly leveraged company. The meat packer had little debt.

During December, 1966 and January, 1967, the conglomerate purchased 53 percent of the meat packer's shares at $62. This came to roughly $80 million, all of which the conglomerate initially borrowed on a short-term basis from foreign and domestic banks at rates up to 7⅞ percent. The remaining 47 percent of the meat packer's shares was subsequently exchanged for—I am sure I don't have to tell you—a convertible preferred stock of the conglomerate.

With full ownership of the meat packer, the conglomerate has since carried out its own ingenious program for financing the acquisition. Dubbed "operation redeployment," this program has involved the creation of three separate operating subsidiaries—each of which has undertaken its own financing, including the issuance of both debt and convertible preferred. Of the $80 million in debt assumed by the conglomerate in acquiring the meat packer, $46 million was applied pro rata to these subsidiaries. Each subsidiary then created an issue of convertible preferred stock which is held by the parent. Subsequently, each subsidiary sold publicly between 25 percent and 30 percent of its new common stock which, unlike the shares held by the parent, are dividend paying. Through these public sales of stock, the three subsidiaries raised $45 million—or approximately enough to repay the short-term debt assigned them. The remaining $34 million of debt still on the books of the parent is well protected by the conglomerate's retention of equity in the subsidiaries.

What did the conglomerate accomplish? The immediate effect was sharply increased earnings per share. According to one Wall Street brokerage house, common earnings of the merged company in 1967 are expected to total $7.50 to $8 per share *before dilution*, compared with combined earnings of $4.32 on an equivalent per share basis for the conglomerate and the meat packer in 1966. And it may well be that the meat packer's very conservative balance sheet will provide further leverage opportunities *a la* "operation redeployment." Significantly, the market price of the conglomerate has tripled since the takeover occurred.

As you can see, investment analysis has come a long way from where it was in the 1930's when balance-sheet strength and book values were the order of the day. And I must acknowledge that I have by no means touched on all the ingenious financing methods that are currently being employed to enhance earnings per share. Perhaps the most conspicuous of my omissions is the family of financing procedures peculiarly appropriate to natural resource companies, including, for instance, so-called carve-outs and production-payment loans. These yield important tax advantages in acquisitions, which I would have liked to explore with you at some length if only more time were available.

I would be derelict if I left you with the impression that all is beer and skittles for the acquirer. From time to time, as I am sure you know, the monetary authorities tend to frown on the use of bank credit for takeovers. Moreover, it seems clear from some recent failures of acquisition attempts to be consummated that the going is getting tougher. In part at least, this simply reflects the fact that everyone's pencil is getting a bit sharper, so that attractive deals aren't as easy to arrange as once was the case. Finally, some members of the accounting profession and also the SEC are tending to become critical of the procedures acquirers typically use in their reports to stockholders, with the contention frequently voiced, for example, that earnings per share should be reported on a fully diluted basis in instances where convertible issues (whether equity or debt) exist and where warrants and options are outstanding.[1] I venture to guess, however, that despite such problems as these the great wave of acquisition financing that has been witnessed of late has far from run its course, and I have no hesitancy in predicting that its future will remain as fascinating as its past.

---

[1] See American Institute of Certified Public Accountants' Accounting Principles Board, Opinion No. 15, "Earnings Per Share," issued May, 1969. [Editors' Note.]

25. FINANCIAL EVALUATION OF A POTENTIAL ACQUISITION*

ROBERT W. ACKERMAN †
and LIONEL L. FRAY††

Thorough analysis of a potential acquisition is difficult to prescribe generically. One reason is the wide degree to which companies vary in the nature of their businesses and the particular problems they face. How can the purchase of an electronics firm by an automotive parts company be compared to the prospective merger of a textile company and a machine-tool maker? The variables involved are so numerous that many businessmen seem to view each transaction as a largely unrelated event. Yet if a company has decided to pursue an acquisition program to fulfill its growth and flexibility objectives, it is highly beneficial to be able to evaluate all acquisition candidates with an approach that would facilitate consistent progress toward these goals. Such an approach should include the major points of interest and concern that, in effect, determine the value of the transaction to the acquiring company.

Our purpose is to describe those elements of acquisition analysis that are generic—the financial elements. Each firm's management will need to develop the other elements which suit its particular industry or qualitative situation. This is not to say that noneconomic considerations are unimportant. Indeed, without sufficient concentration on the broader strategic issues, it is questionable whether consistent, controllable, long-term growth can be achieved at all except, perhaps, in a holding company, investment-oriented context. Yet the financial aspects of an acquisition always are critical because a corporation's survival and growth ultimately are measured in economic terms that, in turn, reflect the quality of its investments.

A firm's acquisition program should be closely related to its objectives as a corporation. Although the content of the objectives may be different for each corporation, two broad categories can be distinguished. One or more economic objectives are generally articulated expressing the desired level of profitability and possibly the desired level of sales. A second group of objectives tends to be a qualitative expression of the manner in which the corporation is to conduct its business; for instance, the image to be attained in the marketplace, the preferred sources of revenues, the importance to be placed on activities associated with the firm's place in society, and so forth.

There are several schools of thought regarding the weight to be given to particular objectives. In one view, the firm's primary purpose is economic, and other objectives are merely constraints on the methods employed by the

*From *Financial Executive* (October, 1967), pp. 35-54. Reprinted by permission.
†Robert W. Ackerman, Harbridge House, Inc., an international consulting firm, Boston, Massachusetts.
††Lionel L. Fray, a principal in the General Management Group at Harbridge House, Inc.

firm to achieve its economic objectives. A second point of view is that the firm's several objectives are of equal importance and that the job of top management is to take actions that have the effect of meeting all the firm's objectives in a balanced fashion. Regardless of the stress placed on particular objectives, the firm's economic goals are of critical importance.

In our view, however, the form of the economic objectives is not solely a matter of judgment. We believe that the most fundamental measure of economic performance is growth in earnings per share (EPS). This measure accurately reflects the chief concern of the majority of shareholders oriented to capital appreciation. It relates to the return on investment[1] as perceived by the financial community, and it indirectly relates to the most fundamental of all basic economic values: the present value of future earnings. A recent survey has shown, in fact, that of the *Fortune* list of the top 500 corporations, 75 percent stated that they had specific financial criteria. Forty-eight percent stated financial criteria in levels or growth of earnings per share. Furthermore, for those firms having multiple financial objectives, a majority stated that EPS was the most important.

The EPS growth objective provides the firm with a way of planning acquisition activities for the long term. The difference between its objective and the expectation from its current complex of business units over the planning period constitutes a diversification gap. The company can then plan to fill a portion of this gap with acquisitions. In effect, the objective helps form an overall framework for programming and evaluating acquisition activity.

The techniques currently used to judge the financial attractiveness of acquisitions often are closely related to the tactics employed to achieve growth. For example, a typical practice is to place considerable emphasis on the immediate earnings-per-share impact of an acquisition. An improvement will occur initially in an exchange of common shares if the earnings on each share issued for the acquisition are higher than the purchasing company's earnings per share, or, in other words, when the price-earnings (P/E) ratio of the purchaser is higher than the P/E ratio of the selling company. Hence, with a high P/E ratio, a "growth" company can maintain the appearance of growth by making advantageous financial deals even though many of the purchases themselves have limited growth expectations. Although such a firm may display substantial growth in jobs and earnings, its continued long-term growth of earnings per share is threatened. Such a strategy will be successful only as long as a sufficient number of properly priced acquisitions are available and the parent company's P/E ratio remains high. Should either of these conditions change, making impossible further acquisitions in the increasing quantity necessary to sustain the apparent growth while the base of operations mushrooms, the rate will fall to the weighted average of the component units, which may be quite low.

---

[1]Franco Modigliani and Merton H. Miller, "Cost of Capital, Corporation Finance, and the Theory of Investment," *American Economics Review* (June, 1958).

The analysis that stops at a consideration of the immediate EPS impact is inappropriate for the company concentrating on long-term development. Furthermore, since the exciting growth fields normally invite high P/E ratios, there has been no way to evaluate whether the growth is worth the price in dilution of earnings for these companies. A somewhat different approach, then, has been developed to answer the question, "If we are to suffer an initial dilution in EPS, how long will it be before the earnings of the acquisition will overcome it?" The question is answered simply by projecting the EPS of the parent company with and without the acquisition and noting the point at which dilution should be erased, assuming, of course, that the forecasted growth of the new company's earnings is higher than the parent's.[2] This analysis will yield a measure in terms of time; criteria can then be established to define what constitutes an acceptable period.

Although this line of reasoning represents an improvement over the approach emphasizing immediate EPS, it still retains a serious weakness: it does not relate directly to the firm's fundamental objective. There is neither a way to link the results to growth of earnings per share nor a mechanism for comparing alternatives having varying growth rates and P/E ratios. Furthermore, it is not possible to compare the impact of different financial means of accomplishing the acquisition with the magnitude of the diversification gap.

The techniques described below, which are based upon measures of return on investment, provide some tools for overcoming these deficiencies. They relate only to measurable financial considerations, however; the final decision of whether to acquire a firm must also be based upon additional considerations and noneconomic factors. We will first explain the approach in broad terms and then will indicate in more detail the ways it is applied in transactions using cash, common stock, and convertible preferred stock.

First, the approach depends upon a forecast of the future performance of the proposed acquisition under the stewardship of the parent company. The acquired organization's future earnings must be adjusted to take into account operating compatibilities that can reduce costs or increase revenues relative to what they would have been had the acquisition not taken place. Marketing expenses may be reduced by consolidating sales forces and piggybacking television advertisements, operating costs may be reduced by combining facilities, overall administrative overhead may be cut back, and so forth. More important, the future earnings growth rate may be affected favorably by changes in strategy or exploitation of new expansion areas (products or markets) in the context of the larger organization. This kind of forecasting, which is essential to *any* analysis of the desirability of a proposed acquisition, is difficult to prescribe generically. Once the forecast is made, however, the evaluation can begin.

---

[2]Donald J. Smalter and Roderic C. Lancey, "P/E Analysis in Acquisition Strategy," *Harvard Business Review* (November-December, 1966), p. 85.

ROI TECHNIQUE

For some years, return-on-investment (ROI) techniques have been applied successfully to capital budgeting problems. The ROI analysis requires an estimate of relevant cash flows and the determination of a discount rate to be used in equating future cash inflows with the initial investment. With certain modifications, this technique can be applied to the evaluation of acquisition possibilities.

From a financial standpoint, the desired return from an acquisition is normally stated in terms of the future earnings that will accrue to the acquiring company. In other words, the purchaser (P) pays a price to the seller (S) in the form of cash or securities. In return, P expects a stream of profits that will contribute to P's earnings per share. While it is true that in certain types of businesses, such as real estate, P may be more interested in cash flow, these situations are the exception. An expectation of a contribution to earnings per share is, of course, entirely consistent with a central growth and profitability objective stated in terms of EPS.

In the simplest case, S will make no financial demands on P and will, in fact, be able to support its growth through internally generated funds and still be able to cover its share of P's dividend. Such an approximation may be valid for a large number of instances, and we will accept it for the moment, neglecting the consequences of other cash flows to or from the corporate treasury. We shall also sidestep temporarily the problems caused by issuing new common stock. Under these simplified circumstances, the ROI is simply the rate that will cause the discounted future *earnings* to equal the purchase price.

We now have a means for evaluating the impact of the two critical variables describing an acquisition candidate: expected earnings growth and current P/E ratio. By calculating the present value of S's future profits using P's ROI objective as a discount rate and then dividing the result of this calculation by the number of S's shares outstanding, we can obtain the price per share that P should pay for S. This price then may be compared with the current market quotation or with the asking price.

As an aid to making these calculations, we prepared many charts which relate the growth rate of the proposed acquisition to a discount rate criterion and which tell us the P/E ratio that should be paid for the acquisition. Figure 25-1 indicates the returns available under the assumption of steady growth for ten years at the various rates listed on the horizontal axis. In all cases growth drops off to 4 percent after the tenth year for an additional 40 years (thus assuming that after its near term period of rapid growth, the firm would continue to grow at a rate approximating the gross national product), ceasing to grow thereafter but continuing to generate a constant level of earnings. For example, a company that expects to grow at 15 percent per year for the next ten years, 4 percent for the next 40 years, and to stop growing from that point on, and is for sale at 25 times earnings, represents an after-tax return on investment of about 12 percent. Alternatively, for a

Figure 25-1

Price-Earnings Ratio vs. Earnings Growth
(Semilogarithmic Graph)

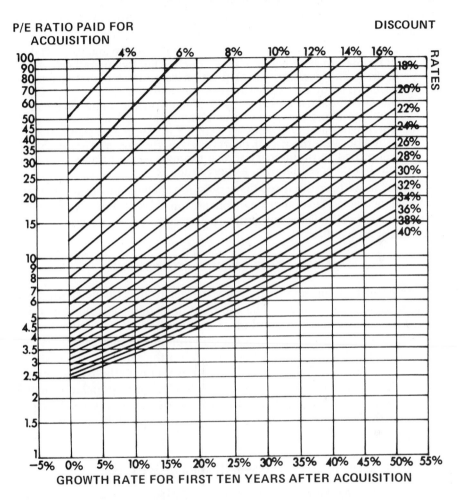

company forecasting 10 percent growth, the purchase price should be no more than 24 times earnings if the purchaser's ROI objective is 10 percent.[3]

As a method of placing a value on future earnings, this technique is not entirely new. For instance, a recent issue of *Fortune* describes how security analysts interested in portfolio selection relate stock values to expected

---

[3]Although a simple chart in this form is very useful, it does not fit all cases very well. The rapid growth period may extend beyond ten years, and it may change gradually (typically from a very high growth rate to a more moderate one). For this reason, we have developed a computer program which can generate sets of these graphs using any combination of growth rates the user desires. Thus, for example, the user could specify the proposed acquisition's growth rates for the first three years, the next five, the next ten, and the next 20.

growth rates of earnings per share.[4] For evaluating the financial attractiveness of potential acquisitions, this method has perhaps even more relevance
because the acquiring company actually includes the earnings in its financial
statements, whereas the investor participates in them only indirectly. Among
its particular advantages are the following:

1. Long-term corporate objectives are the key to the analysis. The
   ROI criterion is set with the idea of achieving the overall growth
   desired, and earnings for acquisition candidates over the long
   term are made an explicit part of the analysis.
2. Many companies now can be evaluated in the same financial
   terms, resulting in improved consistency in results.
3. The quality and efficiency of search for candidates should improve because the use of charts such as the one in Figure 25-1
   can provide a preliminary screen through which to pass a large
   number of possibilities in a short time.

Thus far, we have discussed the acquisition analysis only in general terms
and have neglected several critical concerns in the process. We now shall
turn to more specific cases and indicate how some of the unresolved problems might be handled.

ANALYSIS OF SPECIFIC ACQUISITIONS

An important consideration of any merger from a financial standpoint
is the medium of exchange. The use of cash or debt or a nonconvertible
preferred security raises a number of accounting and tax issues that can
radically alter the effects of an acquisition upon the purchaser's earnings
per share. An exchange of common stock, on the other hand, creates the
possibility of dilution that is not recognized explicitly in the ROI technique.
Convertible preferred stocks, which recently have been popular as acquisition instruments, entail further analytical problems. As a result, certain
additions to the analysis must be included to cope with these complex
variables.

Acquisitions Using Cash or Fixed-Obligation Securities

From the purchaser's standpoint, acquisitions for cash or fixed obligations may appear highly desirable. A stream of future earnings from a
going concern can be acquired without dilution of equity and with less
apparent risk than exists in attempting to develop the business internally.
In this situation, the ROI method may be used directly to evaluate the return
to the company over the long run. The future earnings from the acquired
company, however, must be converted into what they would be *in the
hands of the purchaser*. Here lies the rub. Such transactions are of a taxable
nature and are treated as a purchase on the buyer's books. If the acquisition
price far exceeds the book value, as occurs frequently in growth industries,

---

[4]Daniel Seligman, "Why the Market Acts That Way," *Fortune* (November, 1966), p. 154.

additional charges to income may be assumed by virtue of the transaction in the form of goodwill amortization and/or depreciation of assets restated at fair market value. To illustrate this point, let us consider an example of a potential acquisition involving a purchaser (P) and a seller (S) having the profiles in Table 25-1.

If P purchases S and is successful in revaluing assets with a remaining life of 20 years to the extent of the entire $12 million excess of purchase price over net book value, the additional annual charge to P would be $300,000 after taxes. This is a substantial portion of the expected earnings in the first years after the acquisition. But if goodwill is established for the full amount and P has a policy of amortizing this over 20 years, the annual after-tax profit impact would be $600,000. Stated another way, P really is paying 96 rather than 24 times current earnings for S in the latter case. As a result, the ROI drops from an apparent 11 percent to between roughly 8 percent and 6 percent, depending upon the amount of goodwill necessary.

Future earnings alone do not reflect the total financial impact of an acquisition. We stated the assumption earlier that the only further monetary transactions would be the payment to the corporate treasury each year of an amount sufficient to cover any cash dividends paid to the corporation's shareholders as a result of the acquisition. This approximation may not be sufficiently accurate in some cases. For instance, a growth company may require additional investment beyond its own internal generation capabilities; indeed, this may be its primary purpose for selling out. In effect, the parent must consider the incremental investments as a part of the transaction if the growth targets are to be achieved. The procedure in these instances is to calculate the present value of the future investments (or divestments) using the corporate ROI target as the discount rate and to adjust the initial cash outlay by this amount.

One further problem remains—that of leverage. As a part of the diversification program, a desirable debt capacity level may have been established

TABLE 25-1

ADDITIONAL CHARGES TO INCOME WHEN ACQUISITION PRICE EXCEEDS BOOK VALUE

	Purchaser	Seller
After-Tax Profits per Year	$ 10,000,000	$ 800,000
Shares Outstanding	$ 5,000,000	$ 800,000
Earnings per Share	$ 2	$ 1
Expected Growth Rate		
Next 10 Years	8%	12%
Thereafter	4%	4%
Objectives in EPS Growth, Next 10 Years	10%	Not Applicable
Price-Earnings Ratio	18:1	24:1
Stock Market/Purchase Price per Share	$ 36	$ 24
Total Market Value	$180,000,000	$19,200,000
Total Net Book Value	$100,000,000	$ 7,200,000
Goodwill	Not Applicable	$12,000,000

for the corporation. The question arises: Does not an acquisition candidate's lower level of debt represent an added resource that can, in effect, be used to pay in part for the investment? Conversely, does not a debt-equity ratio higher than the preferred figure call for an added investment to equalize it? To some degree the answer to these questions is yes. Adjustments in the initial investment certainly should be made for any balance sheet changes that would be made after the merger, including the level of debt. Thus, if the acquisition candidate is in the same general industry segment as the purchaser, the debt level should be adjusted to the purchaser's preferred rate. If the candidate is not, the adjustment should be with reference to the expected financial leverage available to the purchaser after the proposed transaction. On the other hand, probably no adjustment should be made if cash is not a scarce resource; that is, if the corporation has no prospect of utilizing the debt capacity available at the preferred rate.

In summary, the financial attractiveness of an acquisition for cash is analyzed by comparing:

1. The present value of future earnings from the acquisition in the hands of the buyer, using as a discount rate the corporate ROI target, with
2. The initial cash investment adjusted, with the qualifications noted above, for future investments or divestments and debt-level equalization.

A major cash acquisition should be scrutinized from several other financial viewpoints in addition to the ROI potential. Typically, the diversifying corporation has a limited cash pool in the form of current and future cash availabilities and borrowing capacity not needed to pursue growth in existing businesses. In a sense this also represents a contingency fund that can be tapped should unforeseen circumstances arise. Hence, a sizable depletion of this pool should be weighed carefully in light of (1) future cash investments that may be defensively critical; (2) projects generated internally or future cash acquisitions that may exhibit higher investment returns; (3) contingencies; and (4) possible miscalculations in estimated cash needs.

Acquisitions Using Common Stock

Acquisitions to be executed by an exchange of common stock involve a number of different problems. The exchange medium is now a variable unit rather than a fixed one: the common shares issued will participate in the growth of both the parent company and the acquired one. To take this situation into account, two types of analysis should be performed: (1) an ROI measure similar to the one proposed for cash acquisitions, and (2) an earnings-per-share-issued (EPSI) measure that will be outlined below. Guidelines should be formulated to judge the results of each analysis, and a potential acquisition should be measured on both counts.

An estimate of future earnings for the acquisition remains the critical input in each case. Once again, it should be forecasted as it would exist *in the hands of the buyer.* The difficulties are somewhat easier to handle now, however, because stock-for-stock transactions generally are accompanied by a pooling-of-interest accounting whereby the balance sheet items on the acquired company's books are simply added, line for line, to those of the surviving entity. In short, the problem of goodwill is avoided, though, of course, the acquiring company loses the privilege of writing up the assets to fair market value and thereby obtaining the additional depreciation income tax deduction.

Provided a pooling of interest is possible and desirable (see "A Critical Study of Accounting for Business Combinations," *Accounting Research Study No. 5,* American Institute of Certified Public Accountants, for a discussion of this question), the only major adjustments necessary to the projected-earnings stream of the selling company are those that should result from combining the activities of the two companies and possibly enlarging the scope of the seller's operations.[5] Before accepting these estimates, though, consideration might be given to the effects of any changes in accounting policies that might have to be made after the merger; for example, amortization of the investment credit, accounting for the past service cost of pension funds, and so forth.

The present value of the future earnings may then be calculated in the same manner as before. The investment value, however, provides a conceptual difficulty if an ROI measure is desired. Assuming the stock of the acquiring company is held publicly, one approach is to use the current market value of the shares issued. From the seller's standpoint, this is substantially accurate because their proceeds, if converted into cash, would have the same value, aside from the tax implications, as the cash transaction. The buyer, however, is relinquishing a share of its business. On the one hand, only a piece of paper is involved, which by itself does not deplete the physical resources of the corporation at all. But on the other hand, the certificates represent the present value of the corporation's future earnings which, if converted into a stock price, might differ from the current market value of the shares. As a practical matter, the use of market price is easier and probably desirable; a company whose stock is grossly undervalued by the market, however, would be understating the magnitude of the investment.

Additional cash investments or throw-offs resulting from the acquisition again should be treated as adjustments to the initial investment. Debt capacity adjustments, if appropriate, should also be made as before. The ROI then can be calculated and the results compared with the acquisition criteria.

The ROI method is not concerned directly with the problem of dilution.

---

[5]In August, 1970, the American Institute of Certified Public Accountants issued two new opinions relating to this subject which modified previous positions. These statements are APB Opinion No. 16, "Business Combinations" and APB Opinion No. 17, "Intangible Assets." The text of these opinions is published in the *Journal of Accountancy,* October 1970, pp. 69-89. [Editors' Note.]

In transactions involving common stock, however, this may be a critical determinant of the financial attractiveness of a merger. To take this into account, let us start by stating that *long-run dilution* occurs when, in the planning horizon year, the earnings per share issued for the acquired company are less than the earnings per share of the corporation as a whole, *assuming it achieves its growth objective*. In other words, to avoid dilution, it is not sufficient for an acquisition merely to increase the EPS of the buyer over what they otherwise would have been. The acquisition must meet instead the same earnings goals as the overall corporation, for if it does not, the diversification gap will have been increased rather than closed.

As an example, let us again consider the acquisition of S by P. Although P expects earnings growth from its current business of 8 percent over the next ten years, which indicates an EPS of $4.32 in the tenth year, it has set its objective at a 10 percent rate of $5.19 per share. Hence, there is a diversification gap of $.87 per share or, in absolute terms, $4,350,000 profit on the *current* shares outstanding.

If P acquires S at an exchange price of $24 per share, P will issue 533,333 shares of its common stock, each initially returning $1.50 earnings per share. Since S is expected to grow at 12 percent over the next ten years, it will have profits of $2,408,000 in the tenth year, and the yield to P will increase to $4.66 per share. The initial dilution of $.05 in P's EPS will have been erased and, in fact, P's earnings in the tenth year now will be $4.36 per share rather than $4.32. On this basis, the transaction, although not a bonanza, appears to be clearly acceptable from a financial standpoint.

A closer inspection, however, reveals that the size of the gap actually has been increased. It now will be necessary to close a gap of $.83 on a 5,533,333-share base, or roughly $4,425,000, an increase of $75,000, as a result of the acquisition. It follows that unless S could be purchased so that it would earn $5.19 on each of P's shares issued—that is, at a price of about $20.88 per share—dilution with respect to the growth objective will result. The price of $20.88 is determined as shown in Equation 25-1.

EQUATION 25-1

$$\frac{\text{Earnings in 10th Year}}{\text{P Shares Issued}} = \$5.19; \quad \text{P Shares} = \frac{2,408,000}{5.19} = 464,000;$$

$$\text{Price per S Share} = \frac{36 \times 464,000}{800,000} = \$20.88 \text{ per Share.}$$

In order to make this evaluation more quickly, a chart could have been constructed specifically for P that would indicate the relationship between growth rates and initial earnings per share issued for acquisitions it might consider. A sample EPSI chart is shown in Figure 25-2. The top line on the graph represents the combination of growth rates and initial earnings required to earn $5.19 per share ten years hence. Unless acquisitions fall on or below this line, the size of the diversification gap will be increased.

We have stated the minimum acceptable purchase price for acquisitions involving common stock. The objective, however, is to close the diversification gap; some criteria must be established to evaluate when a

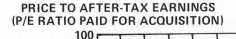

FIGURE 25-2
EARNINGS PER SHARE ISSUED (EPSI)
(SEMILOGARITHMIC GRAPH)

PRICE TO AFTER-TAX EARNINGS
(P/E RATIO PAID FOR ACQUISITION)

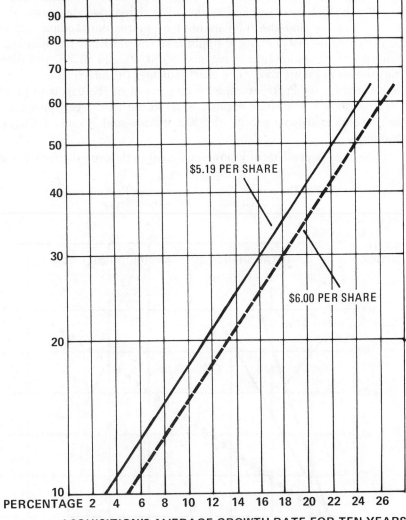

ACQUISITION'S AVERAGE GROWTH RATE FOR TEN YEARS
NOTE: P STOCK PRICE ASSUMED TO BE $36 PER SHARE.

stock transaction is making an acceptable contribution. The problem, of course, is that the overall size of the corporation can grow very quickly through the exchange of shares with the very real danger of overexpansion, multiplying integration problems, and general loss of control. It also is apparent that, as the capital base expands, the annual increments in absolute profits necessary to sustain EPS growth increase very rapidly.

To illustrate this point, let us examine the four variables that P must consider in establishing an EPSI target: (1) the percentage of the gap to be closed with stock; (2) the size of the overall company if the growth objective is met; (3) the number of shares that can be comfortably issued; and (4) the earnings per share issued. Clearly, as the percentage of the gap to be closed with stock increases and as the EPSI demanded decreases, the size of the company and the total number of shares outstanding will mushroom. To make this analysis, P might take several EPSI possibilities, each above the $5.19 minimum (for instance, $5.50, $6, and $6.50), and draw the chart shown in Figure 25-3. The chart indicates the interrelationship among these variables for P; for example, if 60 percent of the gap is to be closed with stock, each new share earning $6.50 in the tenth year, then the company overall will have profits of $36.2 million and 7 million shares outstanding.

The chief executives of P now must deal with some difficult questions.

FIGURE 25-3
EPSI OBJECTIVES, COMPANY SIZE, AND PERCENTAGE OF
GAP CLOSED WITH COMMON STOCK

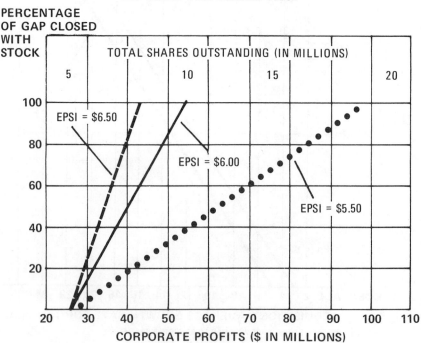

How much profit can be expected from internal developments and cash acquisitions in the future, considering the company's research strength, availability of cash deals in the marketplace, and so forth? What types of mergers for stock are possible, and how do the P/E ratios compare with P's? How many shares can be issued without losing control of the company? How big a company is desirable, and what changes might be necessary if P were $50 million in profits rather than $25 million ten years from now?

After deliberating on these questions, let us assume that P's management decided that about 50 percent of the gap would have to be closed through stock transactions. Furthermore, issuing more than 2.5 million to 3 million new shares or creating a company larger than $40 million in profits in ten years would pose problems for management in maintaining effective control over the operation. These decisions indicate that, on the average, each new share issued must earn $6 a decade from now.

A new EPSI line indicating the match between initial earnings per share issued and growth rates for the company acquired can now be placed on our EPSI chart in Figure 25-2. If the EPS growth objective is to be met under the restraints discussed above, stock acquisitions should be made on or below the $6 EPSI criteria line.

One final step is necessary: the EPSI analysis should be compared with the ROI described earlier. The acquisition price should satisfy both criteria. Care must be taken in making this comparison, however, because the assumptions behind the tests are quite different. The EPSI analysis picks a point in time to measure the impact of an acquisition, whereas the ROI represents the expectations of the buying company for, theoretically, an infinite period.

In some instances, management may feel that a cash transaction is preferable but has no way to evaluate how much of a premium could be offered while preserving the financial attractiveness of the acquisition. An approximation of the answer to this question may be obtained by comparing the EPSI chart with an ROI analysis, using in the first case the earnings expected in the target year, assuming pooling of interest accounting treatment, and in the second case the adjusted-earnings stream following a cash transaction. The difference will yield a rough indication of alternative purchase prices.

TRUER PICTURE OF FINANCIAL VALUE

Diversification planning is an integral part of the long-range planning process of many large U.S. corporations. Ideally, corporate objectives and strategies will be formulated to serve as guides for the allocation of the corporation's resources to worthwhile diversification ventures. Unfortunately, the methods employed to scan the environment for opportunities, and the techniques used to evaluate them once located, all too often bear little relationship to the corporate objectives. This situation is aggravated in decentralized organizations by the additional complexities of conforming diversification activities at the divisional level to overall goals. The result frequently appears to be a halting, uneven approach to growth through diversification very probably accompanied by less-than-desired performance.

We have outlined very briefly an approach to diversification evaluation that has been useful in coming to grips with some of these difficulties. For growth companies that have established an economic objective related to the long-term growth of earnings per share, this approach can help avoid the mistake that can occur when only the effects of short-term dilution or accretion are considered. The issuance of shares by the purchaser in such a manner as to make only minor contributions to closing the diversification gap, or, in some cases, to actually widen it, results in a diversification program running literally on a treadmill but making little progress. When the return-on-investment criteria are applied, where the return is the discounted future earnings of proposed acquisition, a somewhat truer picture of the real financial value emerges.

Several examples using various mediums of exchange demonstrated the application of this approach to determining the financial attractiveness of acquisitions. There are, of course, many more steps necessary to implement diversification strategies; we hope this may form one important and useful part of this process.[6]

---

[6]A section of the original article, dealing with acquisitions using convertible preferred stock, has been omitted from this presentation since the topic has been adequately covered by Anthony Meyer in Article 16.

PART VIII. NEW APPROACHES TO FINANCIAL ANALYSIS

In recent years several new approaches to financial analysis have been suggested by various academicians. The traditional techniques, such as ratio analysis, break-even analysis under certainty, and funds-flow analysis, do not enable the decision maker to consider explicitly the risk variable involved in a given situation. Newer approaches to financial analysis provide better conceptual frameworks within which to treat the uncertainty and risk involved in decision making. The main theme in this section is that an objective measure of risk and uncertainty should be used in order to improve the quality of a decision. These articles form a set of new approaches to financial analysis which will be used more frequently by practitioners as well as academicians in the 1970s.

The article by Professor Ralph O. Swalm explains the fundamentals of "cardinal utility theory." In the first part of his article, he describes the basic principles through simple illustrations. The author then discusses some fundamental and profound questions that elicit divided thought among scholars and should be of particular interest to those trying to evaluate current research efforts. The final section describes some results and implications of his recent study employing utility theory concepts. These findings bear on the measurement of businessmen's attitudes toward risk and should be of general interest to policy makers.

Cardinal utility theory, according to Swalm, describes very adequately man's behavior in risk situations. Each individual has a measurable preference among various choices available in risk situations, and such preference is called his utility. In any decision involving risk, a man will choose that alternative which maximizes his utility. Once we know his utility function, which is a relationship between utility and some monetary measurement such as dollars, we should be able to predict his choice in a given situation. By using the probability concept, the author describes a well-known technique to determine a person's utility function.

Swalm raises another question in his paper: How do businessmen act in situations where they recognize risks? He uses a research approach to provide an answer by conducting individual interviews with 100 business executives to determine their utility functions in making corporate decisions. One of the disturbing results found was that the executives' utility functions appear to be more influenced by the amount of money with which they are accustomed to dealing as individuals than by the financial position of the company. Swalm's research work raises many important questions for which there are as yet no definite answers. If his sample of research subjects is a representative one, United States businessmen surely are not the risk takers so often alluded to in the classical defense of the capitalistic system.

Professors Alexander A. Robichek and James C. Van Horne show how a simulation approach can be developed for incorporating the effects of abandonment into the information provided for the investment decision. Monte Carlo simulation, which is used in the article, is a technique to investigate the implications of uncertainty in a systematic manner.

The consideration of possible future abandonment is a dimension frequently omitted from capital-budgeting analysis. Abandonment value can be defined as the net disposal value of the project that would be available to the company in either cash or cash savings. This article examines the importance of abandonment value to capital budgeting, analyzes its effect on a project's expected return and risk, and proposes a framework for taking account of this neglected dimension.

What effect does the incorporation of abandonment value have on a capital-budgeting decision? The authors show that a previous "no-invest" decision can be completely reversed when abandonment value is considered. They also show that such measures of risk as the variance, the standard deviation, and the semi-variance are actually more favorable when abandonment value is incorporated in the decision-making process. Significant abandonment value for a project may result in a higher expected present value or internal rate of return and lower expected risk than would be the case if the project had no abandonment value over its economic life. The appendix to the article describes the Simulation Model as used to analyze such decisions.

Professors Robert K. Jaedicke and Alexander A. Robichek criticize the conventional cost-volume-profit (C-V-P) analysis because it does not include adjustments for risk and uncertainty. Their discussion suggests some changes which might be made in traditional C-V-P analysis in order to make it a more useful tool in analyzing decision problems under uncertainty. The authors discuss normal probability concepts and utilize them in C-V-P analysis. The degree of risk involved in a given alternative is estimated in terms of standard deviations. From this type of analysis, the probability of loss, break even, or profit can be judged. The technique used serves the traditional analysis but also adds another dimension; that is, risk is brought in as another important decision factor. Further, the establishment of probabilities with respect to various levels of profits and losses for each alternative should aid the decision maker.

26. UTILITY THEORY—INSIGHTS INTO RISK TAKING*

RALPH O. SWALM †

PREFACE. The term "cardinal utility theory" is new to most businessmen. But it is a term that will appear more and more regularly in management articles, books, meetings, and discussions in the future. It is a useful concept, may lead to surprising findings, and (just to clinch matters) is now being taught to students in business schools.

This article is the first one to explain for businessmen the rudiments of utility theory. The description of these principles comes in the first main section of the text. There follows a short discussion of some questions that elicit divided thought among scholars (this part may be of particular interest to those trying to evaluate current research efforts). In the final sections, the author describes some results and implications of a recent study employing utility theory concepts. These unusual findings bear on businessmen's attitudes toward risk and should be of quite general interest to policy makers.

— *The Editors of* HARVARD BUSINESS REVIEW

Suppose that you were lucky enough to be offered the following alternatives:

1. Accept the payment of a tax-free gift of $1 million.
2. Toss a fair coin. If heads comes up, you get nothing; if tails comes up, you get a tax-free gift of $3 million.

Which would you choose? Would it be the certain $1 million or the 50-50 chance of $3 million or nothing?

When confronted with this choice, most people say they would choose the certain $1 million, even though the gamble has what is called an expected value of $1.5 million. (The term "expected value," often used in quantitative analysis, is the product of the hoped-for gain and the probability of winning it—$3,000,000 × .50 in this case.) Said another way, the average winnings in this case, if you gamble repeatedly, are half again as large as your winnings if you take the certain $1 million.

Indeed, even when the winnings on the gamble increase to $5 million if tails comes up, many people will still prefer the certain $1 million!

This is especially perplexing when one reads some of the articles about the application of decision theory to business decisions. Many writers assume, without apparent question, that a businessman will of course want

---

†Professor of Industrial Engineering at Syracuse University; also Director of the Engineering Economy Division of the American Institute of Industrial Engineers.

to choose that alternative which maximizes his expected—or average—return.[1]

There is little or no recognition of the fact that rational people, whether they are businessmen or bartenders, sometimes prefer an alternative other than the one with the highest expected value. For these situations a different basis for the explanation and prediction of behavior needs to be found.

One theory that purports to describe man's behavior in such risk situations more adequately has been given the name *cardinal utility theory*. The formulation of cardinal utility theory was proposed by John von Neumann and Oskar Morgenstern in their monumental *Theory of Games and Economic Behavior*.[2] Oversimplifying a bit, this concept proposes that each individual attempts to optimize the expected value of something which is defined as utility and that for each individual a relationship between utility and dollars can be found.

This article is, in a sense, a progress report aimed at exploring the usefulness of cardinal utility theory in understanding how businessmen make decisions in risk situations where the stakes are large. I use the term "progress report" advisedly, for research so far has raised as many questions as it has answered, and much remains to be done in this area. After explaining cardinal utility theory, I shall raise the question of whether businessmen consider uncertainty in their decisions and, if so, how they might be expected to behave. Then I shall report some research findings on decision making in the face of risks. These findings cast serious doubts on the classical notion of the American businessman as a risk taker and on the validity of many control systems set up to monitor managers' behavior.

NATURE OF THE THEORY

To begin, what is cardinal utility theory all about? Let me try to explain the basic notions as simply as I can.

Personal Utility Functions

According to the theory, each individual has a measurable preference among various choices available in risk situations. This preference is called his "utility." Utility is measured in arbitrary units which we will call "utiles." By suitable questioning we can determine for each individual a relationship between utility and dollars which is called his utility function. This plot offers a picture of his attitude toward taking risks.

In any decision involving risk, a man will choose that alternative which maximizes his utility. Once we know his utility function, the odds he assigns

---

[1]See, for example, David B. Hertz, "Risk Analysis in Capital Expenditure Decisions," *Harvard Business Review* (January-February, 1964), p. 95; and John F. Magee, "Decision Trees for Decision Making," *Harvard Business Review* (July-August, 1964), p. 126, and "How to Use Decision Trees in Capital Investment," *Harvard Business Review* (September-October, 1964), p. 79.

[2]Princeton, N. J.: Princeton University Press, 1947.

to events in a decision-making situation, and the consequences of each possible outcome, we should be able to predict his choice in that situation, since he will attempt to maximize his utility. Perhaps an example will make this clearer:

Suppose a decision maker's utility function has been determined as shown in Exhibit 26-1. (I will explain how to determine the function later.) With such a diagram in hand, you should be able to predict the decision maker's preference for alternatives such as these:

1. Receive a certain $100,000.
2. Have an 80 percent chance of winning $200,000 and a 20 percent chance of losing $50,000.

To make the prediction, you must calculate the decision maker's expected utility for the two alternatives. First read from Exhibit 26-1 the utility for the three sums involved, as follows:

Sum	Utility
$100,000	15 utiles
$200,000	20 utiles
—$50,000	—10 utiles

Then calculate the expected utility of the two alternatives. The expected utility of the certain $100,000 is 15 utiles. The expected utility of the second alternative is 14 utiles—

$$.80 \times [20 \text{ utiles}] + .20 \times [-10 \text{ utiles}].$$

Since the first alternative has the higher expected utility, utility theory would predict that the decision maker in our example would prefer it over the second alternative.

Before showing how to determine an individual's utility function, let me mention that while relative utilities are measurable, absolute utility is not. That is, the scale on which utility is measured has no natural origin; instead, one is free to assign arbitrary utility values to any two sums of money. But, having done this, there will be for each individual a unique value for the utility that he would assign to any other sum of money. Thus, once we begin matching utiles and sums of money for the businessman in Exhibit 26-1, a curve or "profile" of his attitude toward risk is created which establishes his preferences for all stakes in the area described.

Our ordinary temperature scales are examples of this same sort of scale. We are free to define 32°F as the freezing point of water and 212°F as its boiling point and then measure all other temperatures on this scale. But having defined two arbitrary points, we cannot logically say that a temperature of 80°F is twice as hot as one of 40°F, for if we transposed to the Centigrade scale, we would describe these same temperatures as about 27°C and 4½°C.

Unlike temperature scales, however, utility scales are postulated as personal and subjective. There is, therefore, no reason to expect one man's utility function (or plot of utility versus dollars) to agree with another's.

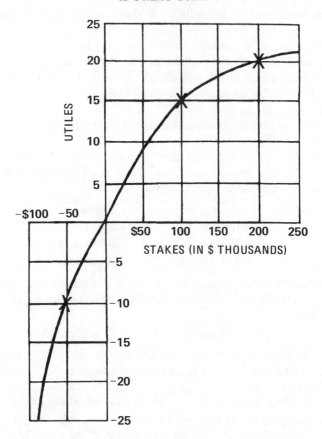

EXHIBIT 26-1
A UTILITY CURVE

Equating Alternatives

How can we determine a person's utility function? The basic principle
to use is this: if a decision maker is indifferent between two alternatives, the
expected utility of the alternatives is the same. To illustrate, suppose that
Abner McGillicuty is one of those mentioned at the outset of this article who
would choose a certain $1 million in preference to a 50-50 gamble on $3
million or nothing. The utility concept simply states that, on Abner's utility
scale, the distance corresponding to the interval from 0 to $1 million is more
than half of the distance corresponding to the interval from 0 to $3 million.

Suppose, further, that the winnings if tails comes up can be increased
until Abner becomes indifferent to taking the gamble or taking the certain
$1 million. Assume, for the sake of argument, that he becomes indifferent
when this amount reaches $5 million. In utility theory terms, the two alter-
natives then have equal utility.

Since each of the two possibilities in the coin-tossing example has a

50 percent likelihood of occurrence, the expected (or average) utility of the uncertain outcome can be calculated as:

$$.50 \times [\text{utility of } \$5,000,000] + .50 \times [\text{utility of } 0].$$

Now define the utility of any two of these points. For example, Abner's utility of $5 million might be defined as 10 utiles, and his utility of 0 as 0 utiles. Then determine the utility of the third point by simple algebra. Thus, if U represents the utility of a sum, then:

$$.5 \times U [\$5,000,000] + .5 \times U [0] = U [\$1,000,000].$$

Substituting the defined values leads to:

$$.5 [10 \text{ utiles}] = U [\$1,000,000].$$
$$5 \text{ utiles} = U [\$1,000,000].$$

Thus, it can be seen that, on Abner's utility scale, the distance corresponding to the interval from 0 to $1 million is the same as the distance corresponding to the interval from $1 million to $5 million.

Note that it is tempting but incorrect to state that his utility for $5 million (10 utiles) is twice his utility for $1 million (5 utiles). For, as in the temperature example, it would be equally logical to define the utility of $5 million as 100 utiles and the utility of 0 as 90 utiles. In this case the utility of $1 million would be 95 utiles. The *distances* in utiles between 0 and $1 million would still be the same as that between $1 million and $5 million, but 95 would hardly be described as half of 100!

Plotting Abner's assigned utilities against dollars, there are three points on his utility function, as shown in Exhibit 26-2.

Further Delineation

Clearly, Abner's "utility function" (or plot of utility versus dollars) is nonlinear, but three points can hardly be said to determine the outlines of the function. So it is necessary to seek more points.

Suppose Abner is asked the question: "You now have a contract offering a 50-50 chance of making $1 million or nothing. Would you sell it for $400,000?" If he would, this indicates his utility for $400,000 is greater than his utility for the contract. To find the certain amount that has, for Abner, the same utility as the gamble, he might be asked if he would sell the contract for $200,000. If at this price he refuses to sell, it is known that his utility for $200,000 is less than that for the contract. Now the certain sum which has the same utility as the 50-50 chance at $1 million has been fixed as being somewhere between $200,000 and $400,000. By continuing the "hunting" process, hopefully, the precise point at which he is indifferent can be determined. Assume it is found to be $300,000. This, then, is the monetary sum to which Abner would assign 2.5 utiles on a scale in which 0 equals 0 utiles and $1 million equals 5 utiles. For:

$$.5 \times U [0] + .5 \times U [\$1,000,000] = U [\$3,000,000].$$

Exhibit 26-2
THREE POINTS ON ABNER'S UTILITY FUNCTION

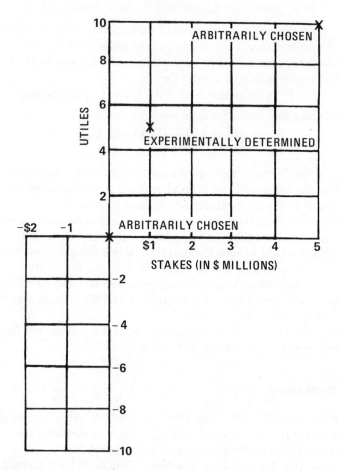

Substituting:

$$.5 \times [0 \text{ utiles}] + .5 \times [5 \text{ utiles}] = U \ [\$3,000,000]$$
$$2.5 \text{ utiles} = U \ [\$3,000,000].$$

So far Abner's behavior has been tested in situations where he can only gain. His behavior pattern in loss situations could be examined by asking questions such as: "Suppose you are asked to make a bid which, if successful, will net you $300,000 but which, if unsuccessful, will cost you $100,000. Would you choose to bid if you evaluated your chances of getting the bid as 3 to 1?" (In this case the certainty option is to do nothing and, of course, gain or lose nothing.) Again, by successive probings, varying the amount of the loss or, alternatively, the odds assigned, one could eventually arrive at an indifference situation. Suppose, for Abner, this involves a loss of $100,000 at the original odds of 3 to 1. In this situation:

Exhibit 26-3
Abner's Completed Utility Function

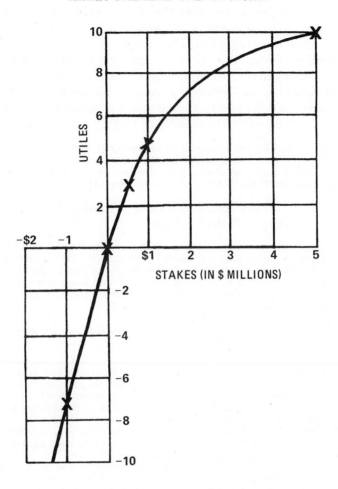

$$.75 \times U [\$300,000] + .25 \times U [-\$100,000] = U [0]$$
$$.75 \times 2.5 \text{ utiles} + .25 \ U [-\$100,000] = 0 \text{ utiles}$$
$$U [-\$100,000] = -7.5 \text{ utiles}$$

There are now five points on Abner's utility function, which can be tentatively connected by a smooth curve as shown in Exhibit 26-3.

Now some checkpoints should be tried to test the validity of the inferences made in connecting the points on Abner's utility function. If these points check out, we now, according to utility theory, should be able to predict Abner's decisions in any risk situation in which the gains do not exceed $5 million or the losses do not go below $100,000 provided we know the probabilities he attaches to the various outcomes of these situations.

PROPER ROLE

What is the proper use of utility theory? As indicated, my own belief is that it will prove to be useful in *describing* and *predicting* executive behavior. Before substantiating this belief I want to point out, however, that some authorities question this position. They insist that the theory is *prescriptive* (or "normative"), that it indicates how executives *should* behave rather than how they *do* behave. Foremost among these authorities is Howard Raiffa. In reference to Savage's theory (which combines cardinal utility theory with subjective probability),[3] Raiffa has commented:

> Savage's theory is not a descriptive or predictive theory of behavior. It is a theory which purports to advise any one of its believers how he *should* behave in complicated situations, *provided* he can make choices in a coherent manner in relatively simple, uncomplicated situations.[4]

People do not always behave in a manner consistent with maximizing their utility, according to Raiffa, and this

> ... clearly demonstrates how important it is to have a theory which can be used to aid in the making of decisions under uncertainty. If most people behaved in a manner roughly consistent with [the] theory, then the theory would gain stature as a descriptive theory but would lose a good deal of its normative importance. We do not have to teach people what comes naturally. But as it is, we need to do a lot of teaching.[5]

A similar viewpoint has been expressed as follows by a person with whom I have had correspondence:

> The utility model is *not* a good descriptive theory for risk-taking situations. When people do what comes naturally, they are as inconsistent as can be. The real question is whether they want to act inconsistently or whether they wish to employ a methodology which would allow them to resolve their inconsistencies and allow them to analyze complex problems.
>
> But, alas, most businessmen are not perfectly rational men; rather, they are as inconsistent as all mortals are. There is no need to have a prescriptive theory of utility for the perfectly rational man. Just tell him to do what comes naturally. The *raison d'être* for utility theory is that most of us are not supermen—we make errors of judgment and are inconsistent in our choices. And knowing this, some of us, when faced with an important and complex problem, might wish to employ, in a conscious manner, decision aids that will help police our inconsistencies and help guide us to an appropriate course of action. Utility theory purports to be such a decision aid.

Taking a contrary view are other authorities. Here are just a couple of samples from the literature (the emphasis on "predict" is mine):

1. The Von Neumann-Morgenstern measure of utility is a special type of cardinal measure. . . . The use of this utility measure enables us to *predict*

---

[3]See, Leonard J. Savage, *Foundations of Statistics* (New York: John Wiley & Sons, Inc., 1954).

[4]"Risk, Ambiguity, and the Savage Axioms: Comment," *Quarterly Journal of Economics* (November, 1961), p. 690.

[5]*Ibid.*

which of certain lotteries a person will prefer. . . .[6]

2. In the preceding chapters, we have discussed the rules which a rational person could be expected to observe when he has to make decisions under uncertainty. If we know these rules, we should be able to *predict* how a decision maker will behave in a given situation.[7]

More Useful Tests

The question of the degree to which businessmen *are* rational and of the extent to which utility theory *is* useful for predictive purposes should be determinable by experiment.

Indeed, experiments have been performed involving bets on drawing colored balls from several urns when varying degrees of information are available. These tests have shown that in risk situations many people do not behave in accordance with certain postulates (sometimes called Savage's Axioms) which rational people should be expected to follow. The prescriptive and descriptive schools each find the results consistent with their positions.[8]

It is my contention that results of experiments involving bets on colored balls in urns are much less relevant to industrial situations than is a direct examination of the degree to which a utility function derived from one set of reasonably realistic questions can be used to predict a businessman's answers to a different set of questions. One of the major purposes of the research reported later in this article is to make such an examination.

Utility theory, we have seen, is a refinement on methods which assume the desirability of optimizing expected dollar income in risk decisions. It suggests that a man will (or perhaps should) attempt to optimize expected *utility* rather than expected dollar gain—and that a function relating utility to dollar gain can be found for each rational individual.

Discovering such a function is not easy, and the results of hypothetical tests will always leave something to be desired. But surely we will get nearer the truth as we pose questions to businessmen which more closely approximate the day-to-day problems with which they have to deal on the job.

Theory vs. Reality

Do today's businessmen use approaches, such as those proposed by David Hertz and John Magee, which explicitly take risk into consideration in the making of day-to-day decisions?

---

[6]Harold Bierman, Jr., Charles P. Bonini, Lawrence E. Fouraker, and Robert K. Jaedicke, *Quantitative Analysis for Business Decisions* (Rev. ed.; Homewood, Ill.: Richard D. Irwin, Inc., 1965), p. 194.

[7]Karl Borsch, "The Economics of Uncertainty," working paper #70 (Los Angeles: Western Management Sciences Institute, University of California, Los Angeles, March, 1965).

[8]See, for example, Daniel Ellsberg, "Risk, Ambiguity, and the Savage Axioms," *Quarterly Journal of Economics* (November, 1961), p. 643.

The best available evidence indicates that very few do. In general, their approaches to decision making can be described, to use technical phraseology, as "models under assumed certainty." In other words, in their approaches to or "models" of decision making, probabilities seldom appear directly.

Why is this so? William T. Morris thinks that uncertainty gets suppressed in the analysis because of the fact that the human mind has limited information-handling capacities:

> The key to understanding any decision-making process is to discover the ways in which the decision maker simplifies the complex fabric of the environment into workable conceptions of his decision problems. The human mind has limited information-handling capacities; thus, both analysts and managers deal with decisions in terms of conceptual simplifications or models of reality. Perhaps the most obvious of these simplications is that of suppressing one's necessary ignorance of the future and considering a decision *as if* only one possible future could occur. This is not to pretend that one *knows* the future with certainty but is simply an act of conceptual simplification. It allows one to answer the question, "If this particular set of circumstances were to occur, what would be the reasonable course of action for management?" If a manager does undertake the course of action which results, one may think of him as *acting as if* the set of circumstances in question were sure to occur.
>
> Likewise, when an analyst suppresses risk and uncertainty in making a management decision explicit, it does not imply that he claims knowledge of the future. It is one of the many ways in which science may simplify the real world in order to study it. None of us can know the future, but it is often very useful to ask questions about how we would act if we did. . . .
>
> It is traditional to study the great majority of managerial decisions as decisions under assumed certainty. Thus, in the selection of equipment the selection of materials and designs, the choice of operating methods and policies, and so on, the assumption of certainty is widely used.[9]
>
> One should never lose sight of the fact, however, that such a model is a result of one's decision to simplify by suppressing uncertainties about the future. Its "reasonableness" is a matter of judgment at first and what sort of results it leads to ultimately. It does not mean that the future is certain, only that one studies the decision *as if* the future were certain.[10]

There may be another reason for playing down uncertainty. Often risk is introduced late in the analysis on a somewhat ad hoc basis, instead of making specific probability statements about events in the analysis. Thus, in using methods such as the justly celebrated profitability index approach described by Ray I. Reul,[11] one elects to use a model that assumes that projected cash flows will be certain to occur and later to interpret the resulting profitability index in the light of living in an uncertain world. Likewise, if a simple payback criterion is applied to test a proposed expenditure, the calculation assumes that the projected incomes and outgoes will be certain

---

[9]William T. Morris, *The Analysis of Management Decisions* (Rev. ed.; Homewood, Ill.: Richard D. Irwin, Inc., 1964), pp. 49 and 50.

[10]*Ibid.*, p. 10.

[11]See, for instance, "Profitability Index for Investments," *Harvard Business Review* (July-August, 1957), p. 116.

to occur, even though the selection of a cutoff point (such as a 2-year pay-back) may be made in an attempt to take risk into consideration.

It is unusual to find examples of explicit probability statements in actual practice; yet modern theory increasingly deals with approaches or "models" requiring such statements. Texts and articles appear in greater and greater numbers on such subjects as decision trees, statistical inference, Monte-Carlo methods, and so forth. More and more businessmen, and particularly tomorrow's businessmen in today's schools, are exhorted to use sophisticated models that recognize risk explicitly.

When businessmen behave contrary to the way theorists urge them to behave, the reason is not always that the businessmen are unwise. Sometimes the theories are inadequate; more often, perhaps, logic lies somewhere between practice and theory. We can often refine our theories by looking a bit more closely at what the businessman has learned through experience and, perhaps intuitively, put into practice.

ATTITUDES TOWARD RISK

How do businessmen act in situations where they recognize risks? In the research to be reported, utility theory was used to help answer this question. That is, we determined the utility functions (such as the ones in Exhibit 26-1 and 26-3) of a large number of executives and used these functions as the basis of interpretation. The executives were in different lines of work and had diverse backgrounds.

Despite the fact that utility theory is urged on businessmen by the textbook writers, only two serious attempts to determine the utility functions of businessmen have been reported.[12] Together, these reports attempt to find utility functions for 32 businessmen, of whom half are in a single large but unnamed chemical company and half in the oil exploration field.

It is true that there have been a number of very carefully planned experiments testing utility functions of graduate students and other suitable warm bodies faced with gambles involving, quite literally, pennies. But such experiments have limited relevance to the world of business. As Jacob Marchak says:

> Tentative explorations performed . . . on graduate students or by these students on their wives do supply some preliminary evidence that deserves to be treated in a more rigorous way. It would be worthwhile to perform such experiments on mature executives, rather than on students.[13]

Research Approach

Ideally we would have liked to have our subjects deal with real sums

---

[12]See, P. E. Green, "Risk Attitudes and Chemical Investment Decisions," *Chemical Engineering Progress* (January, 1963), p. 35; and C. Jackson Grayson, Jr., *Decisions Under Uncertainty* (Boston: Harvard Business School, Division of Research, 1960).

[13]"Actual vs. Consistent Decision Behavior," *Behavioral Science* (April, 1964), p. 104.

in real situations. However, even the wealthiest foundation could not be expected to underwrite repeated million-dollar experiments, and few businesses would allow their executives to participate in experiments whose possible outcomes might require their treasurer to pay out large sums! So, we were forced to ask a number of businessmen how they would behave in risk situations as described to them. We did our best to make the situations seem real and to get realistic replies.

We sought to find the utility functions displayed in making corporate, rather than private, decisions. We were able to question a rather wide range of decision makers (though most had an engineering background) in one company—I shall call it "Company A"—and a smaller number of decision makers in a cross section of industries. Altogether, about 100 executives were tested.

EXHIBIT 26-4

INSTRUCTIONS TO PARTICIPANTS IN TESTS

"We are about to perform a series of experiments; in each of these, you will be asked to make a decision in a situation involving risk. Although real-life risk situations often involve a continuum of possible alternatives, we shall, to simplify matters, look only at simple cases in which you are asked to choose between a choice that leads to a certain gain (or loss) of a known amount and a course of action that could lead to either of two outcomes, each of which is considered—on the basis of the best information available at the time you are required to make your decision—to have a 50-50 chance of occurring.

"In all cases we will assume that all incomes or outgoes will take place in the very near future or, alternatively, that these can be considered the present worths of all future cash flows that are affected by your decision. All amounts are considered to be net after taxes.

"You are asked to make these choices in your capacity as a corporate decision maker, not as a private individual dealing with your own funds. Try to give replies that represent the actual action you would take if presented with his choice at work TODAY. We want to know what you would actually DO, not what you feel you should do or what the speaker might expect you to do.

"Conceptually, all of the questions you will be asked are of this general form:

Suppose you are faced with choosing between one of two alternative courses of action. The first involves undertaking to bid on a new project. If the bid is successful, your company will make a net gain of, say, $100,000. If unsuccessful, you will be reimbursed for the costs of making the bid, making your net gain zero. Your best available information leads you to assign a 50-50 chance to these possible events.

Your second possible course of action is to put the manpower you might spend in making the bid into cost-reduction efforts. Based on past experience, you are certain that this would result in a net gain. How large would this certain gain have to be to make you indifferent as to which choice to make? In other words, at what certain income would you be indifferent to your company's getting that income or getting a 50-50 chance of making $100,000 or nothing?

"In all of the questions you are asked, the following will hold true. You will always be presented with two mutually exclusive choices. One will always involve a 50-50 chance between two possible outcomes; the second will always involve a certain outcome. The dollar amounts of two of your three possible final outcomes will be given; you will be asked to fix the amount of the third in such a way that you would be indifferent to the choice between the gamble and the certain outcome."

Except in a few cases, each man was interviewed individually; this consumed one to two hours per man. After first introducing the utility theory concept (in much the same way as in this article), we set the stage for the experimental evaluation of his corporate utility function with an explanation such as that shown in Exhibit 26-4 (which is a somewhat abridged version of that actually used). Sometimes the construction of the question was varied, but the reader will recognize that the approach used was very similar to that employed in deriving Exhibit 26-3.

Because of the possible confounding of utility and subjective probabilities and because there was considerable evidence that few could sense fine distinctions between one course of action that had, say, a 90 percent probability of success and another that had, say, a 95 percent probability, we limited all our risks to those involving a 50-50 chance. These were easily understood as equivalent to a flip of a coin. (Nevertheless, the 50-50 chance caused many respondents difficulty because, as they put it, "We just don't go into an investment unless the chances of success are much better than 50-50." The concept that many bids are made when the odds of success are 50-50 or less helped a bit here. Interestingly, several research administrators in the same companies as the participants objected that their odds were never this good!)

After discussing our instructions thoroughly, we then asked each man what the maximum single amount that he might recommend be spent in any one year might be. We defined his *planning horizon* as twice this amount. We did this to examine the hypothesis that a man's corporate utility function was more a function of his own corporate planning horizon than it was of the actual resources of the corporation. This also enabled us to ask each man questions regarding sums that had meaning to him.

We then started a line of questioning, similar to the questions in the instructions, involving sums of money up to the man's planning horizon. For examples of such questions, see Exhibit 26-5.

Finally, the points determined by this series of questions were plotted to yield a utility function for a man. In each case, the horizontal scale (gains and losses) was plotted in terms of the planning horizon rather than actual dollar amounts. The vertical scale was established by defining the utility of the planning horizon as 120 utiles and the utility of 0 dollars as 0 (120 was used to permit a sequence of even numbers when the figure was repeatedly halved). About half the points plotted were "checkpoints" to test the consistency of the replies.

EXHIBIT 26-5
EXAMPLES OF QUESTIONS ASKED

Suppose a man's planning horizon is $1 million. Our first question would be structured somewhat as follows (the situation was varied to some degree to fit the man's own background):

> Suppose you are faced with two choices. The first is to recommend that your company commit a certain amount of engineering manpower to making a bid. If successful, the bid will result in a net profit, after tax, of $1 million. If unsuccessful, you will be reimbused for the expenses incurred, so that your net return will be zero. Your best estimate of the odds favoring success is 50-50.
>
> Your second alternative is to recommend that the same engineering manpower be employed in developing a new plant layout. You are certain that this would result in an after-tax income of, say, $300,000. These are mutually exclusive alternatives; that is, acceptance of one precludes the possibility of accepting the other. Either opportunity will be lost if not accepted now. Which would you recommend?

If he recommended the bid, the $300,000 figure was increased; if he said he would recommend the layout, the question was repeated with a lower income (say $200,000) postulated as the income from the revised layout. This process was repeated until a value was found at which the respondent was indifferent to the choice of recommending the investment in the bid or the layout. (It was recognized, of course, that in the real world, an AREA of indifference, rather than a unique point, would be found.)

The value of the certainty option at this point of indifference was noted and used as the basis for a second question. Suppose, for the respondent, that this amount were $250,000. The next question might be:

> Suppose you planned to purchase a general-purpose machine, but a colleague proposed, instead, to buy a more efficient special-purpose machine. Both cost the same; the difficulty is that the contract for which the special-purpose machine would be required has only a 50-50 probability of being received. If it is received, the special-purpose machine will yield a profit of $250,000. If not, your net income will be zero. On the other hand, the general-purpose machine will produce a certain savings of, say, $100,000. Which would you recommend?

(In actual practice, this question would take longer to state and explain; here we offer only bare essentials.)

Again, the "certain savings" would be manipulated until a point of indifference was reached. This same sort of question would be asked repeatedly to establish a number of points which would, hopefully, define the respondent's utility curve; additional questions would be asked to establish still more points that would act as checks on the curve.

In some questions, losses were involved. For example, one question might take this form:

> Suppose your company is being sued for patent infringement. Your lawyer's best judgment is that your chances of winning the suit are 50-50; if you win, you will lose nothing, but if you lose, it will cost the company $1 million. Your opponent has offered to settle out of court for $200,000. Would you fight or settle?

If this situation could not be envisaged by the decision maker or if he indicated a special reaction to a question involving a suit, a question involving a different context but the same sum of money would be tried.

Findings and Contrasts

Some sample utility functions from the research are shown in Exhibit 26-6. The numbers refer to the designations used in the original research. All but Man #1 are from Company A.

The first observation is that in most cases the points do not lie on a smooth curve. However, although there is scatter, the points show a trend sufficiently clear for a curve to be fitted through them in much the same way that an engineer fits a curve to experimental data.

Reasonably accurate predictions can be made about answers to questions involving risk and sums of money within the range covered by the curve, as shown by the closeness of most of the points to the curve.

Now consider some of the differences in attitude which these utility functions reveal. For example, consider Group A. One could characterize Man #1 as extremely conservative, #27 as conservative, #10 as moderately conservative, #6 as linear, #34 as inclined toward risk, and #4 as a gambler.

To illustrate more specifically, contrast Man #4, a gambler, with Man #27, a conservative. Both have a planning horizon of $200,000 (to which, as earlier mentioned, we have arbitrarily assigned a utility of 120 utiles on a scale in which 0 dollars is assigned to 0 utiles). Suppose each of these men was faced with a decision of whether or not he should recommend taking a 50-50 chance of making $200,000 or nothing (this gamble is easily shown to be worth 60 utiles to either) in preference to recommending a line of action that would lead with certainty to an income of $100,000 (or 50 percent of the man's planning horizon). Man #4 would recommend the gamble, and Man #27, the certain $100,000. For the first, $100,000 has a utility of only about 25 utiles (reading from the curve); for the second, it has a utility of more than 80 utiles, well in excess of the 60 which the gamble is worth. In fact, proceeding across the 60-utile line in each case, we find that Man #4 would still want to gamble until the certainty option rose to about 75 percent ($150,000) of his planning horizon, whereas Man #27 would not gamble if the certainty option were about 30 percent ($60,000) of his planning horizon.

In short, one executive values the gamble at less than $60,000; the other, at $150,000. Yet both are employed by the same corporation and are making decisions that involve the same corporate funds! Does this raise some interesting questions? If you were their common supervisor, would you wish to know of this difference? Would you be curious as to how these utility functions compared with your own—or to those of your company president?

While Group A shows how different and how personal utility functions usually are, Group B shows how similar some can be. Note that all the men represented in Group B can be termed quite conservative.

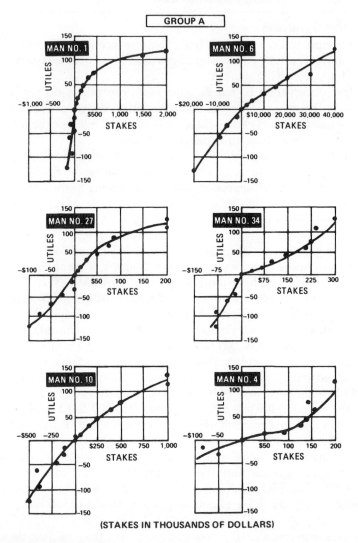

EXHIBIT 26-6
SAMPLES OF UTILITY FUNCTIONS

GROUP A

(STAKES IN THOUSANDS OF DOLLARS)

Some Disturbing Results

A finding that will disturb many businessmen is that the men's utility functions appear to be more closely related to the amounts with which they are accustomed to deal as individuals than to the financial position of the company. To see this, look at Group C, showing the utility functions of four men. Note that these men have planning horizons ranging from $50,000 to $24 million; however, their utility functions, when plotted against amounts shown in terms of their planning horizons, are roughly comparable. Plotted on an absolute scale, they clearly would not be.

EXHIBIT 26-6 (cont.)

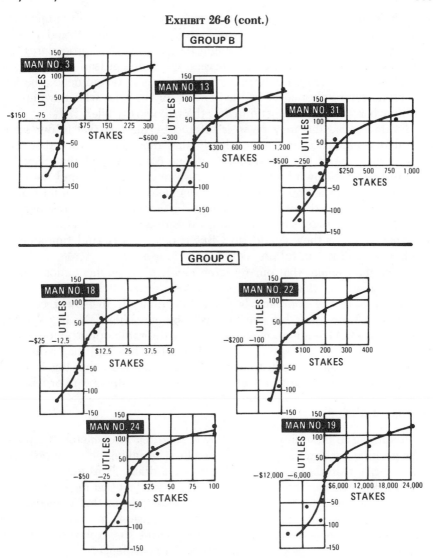

Yet another disturbing phenomenon is a fairly consistent pattern of sharp slopes found in the negative quadrants. Man #3 (Group B) is fairly typical. Note that if we assign 120 utiles to his planning horizon of $300,000, we must assign —120 utiles to a loss of only about $55,000. This means that he would recommend a proposal that had a 50-50 chance of either making his company $300,000 or losing $60,000. But it seems rather clear that Company A, being an industrial giant, would gain if its managers took such favorable gambles.

We would pay little attention if Man #3 were a maverick, but he is not. If you look over the rest of the curves, you will agree that he is not atypical. These curves certainly do not portray the risk takers of which we hear so much in industrial folklore. They portray decision makers quite unwilling to take what, for the company, would seem to be rather attractive risks. One cannot help wondering if this might be due to control procedures that bias managers against making any decision which might lead to a loss. Do our control procedures unduly reward the man who recommends the low but certain return alternative at the expense of the man who is willing to gamble when the potential gain makes the risk worthwhile?

Evidence that this may be so is offered by the fact that in our study several respondents stated quite clearly that they were aware that their choices were not in the best interests of the company but that they felt them to be in their own best interests as aspiring executives, and therefore they represented the choices they would actually make. From an experimenter's viewpoint this was encouraging, for it indicated the respondents were truly trying to give answers that represented what they *would* do and not what they felt they *should* do. But it raises a vast and fundamental question regarding control procedures now in use.

Even the thought that our research involved recommendations rather than decisions and that top decision makers would behave more in the best interests of the company is not comforting. If the lower echelons screen out all proposals but the low-risk, low-gain type, the top decision makers never get to rule on many potentially desirable opportunities. Furthermore, some of our respondents are themselves heads of major divisions of one of our country's industrial giants. We would say that this research indicates that a good hard look at existing control systems is in order.

Further Questions

Returning to the utility curves shown, note that, in general, the points in the positive quadrant appear to come closer to falling on a smooth, continuous curve than do those in the negative quadrant. This may be due to the questions asked, or it may be a reflection of the fact that the respondents simply are not accustomed to consider loss situations or that they become frustrated and less rational when faced with decisions involving potential loss. Certainly more research is required before an explanation of this phenomenon can be made with any degree of confidence.

Actually, many questions like this might be raised; a great deal more research needs to be done. For example, would the same curves have resulted if we had varied the probabilities? How stable, over time, are these results? (The limited data we have obtained thus far show surprising stability, but more research is needed.) In cases where incomes are spread over long time periods, are the appropriate utilities based on the present worth of the incomes—or should we take the present worths of the utilities of each cash flow?

Indeed, the research performed thus far raises more questions than it has given definitive answers to. But the questions it raises would seem to demand answers, and so it is confidently expected that this will be but one of a series of progress reports offered by many researchers. The alert businessman will want to keep abreast of these reports and perhaps even to support some studies, for they may help him to better understand his own and others' decisions and thus perhaps help him to make better ones.

CONCLUSION

Cardinal utility theory is not a completely satisfactory predictor of executive behavior when decisions involving risks must be made, nor is it a completely satisfactory method of describing such behavior. Authorities like Ward Edwards have pointed to various weaknesses or possible weaknesses in the theory—its assumption that man is rational, for instance, its overlooking of the possibility that people exhibit preferences for different probabilities, and the difficulties of measurement.[14]   Nevertheless, it seems to me that the study reported shows that utility theory has much to offer businessmen as a tool of prediction and description. The results for the businessmen participating in the study were reasonably consistent and useful and point to individual characteristics that were not otherwise apparent. And future studies along similar lines could be even more helpful. Moreover, since (as our experiments show) the criterion of expected value tends to be rejected by businessmen, we have no other good basis for prescribing or predicting decisions that involve risk if we reject utility theory.

What broad conclusions can be drawn from the research project? Six stand out:

1. Businessmen do *not* attempt to optimize the expected dollar outcome in risk situations involving what, to them, are large amounts. As a result, methodologies which assume they do will tend to be rejected by such businessmen. More acceptable approaches are, therefore, needed. Cardinal utility theory offers at least a step in the right direction.
2. Cardinal utility theory offers a reasonable basis for judging the internal consistency of a series of decisions made by an executive dealing with risks, and can be an aid in increasing the consistency of such decisions.
3. The theory offers a relatively simple way of classifying many types of industrial decision makers. For example, a supervisor may learn that, in decisions involving significant risks, one man tends to be quite conservative, a second tends to be a gambler, and a third tends to be moderately conservative. If he is moderately conservative himself, he will be happier delegating decisions to the third than to either of the other two. Does he need cardinal utility theory to see these differences? Not always, but much of the time it *will* reveal characteristics that are not otherwise apparent. It does this because it allows comparability (in real life, different executives usually face different problems and risks), shows a range of feeling

---

[14]See, "The Theory of Decision Making," *Psychological Bulletin* (July, 1954); reprinted as Chapter 33 in Albert H. Rubenstein and Chadwick J. Haverstroh (eds.), *Some Theories of Organization* (Homewood, Ill.: Richard D. Irwin, Inc., 1960), pp. 385-430.

about risk (in real life the boss is likely to get but one recommendation on a question), offers more objectivity (the subordinate's manner, his reputation, and other factors do not color the situation), and makes more precision possible (the risk taker's ideas are pinned to specific numbers).

4. The action a junior executive recommends in a risk situation is a function of his own planning horizon (that is, it is related to the largest single amount he would recommend to be spent) rather than to the financial condition and position of his company. If top management deems this undesirable (and to me this would almost certainly seem to be the case), then the utility theory concept offers a promising way to begin corrective action.

5. Attitudes toward risk decisions vary even more widely among various decision makers in a given company then we are inclined to think. Indeed, what one man calls white, another will swear is black. The risk one man would recommend, another would shun as the plague. Utility theory offers a means of determining the degree to which this is true among decision makers in a company.

6. If the decision makers interviewed are at all representative of U.S. executives in general, our managers are surely not the takers of risk so often alluded to in the classical defense of the capitalistic system. Rather than seeking risks, they shun them, consistently refusing to recommend risks that, from the overall company viewpoint, would almost surely be attractive.

In "The Change Seekers," Patrick H. Irwin and Frank W. Langham, Jr. observed:

> Top management must expect some changes to fail. If *all* changes succeed, it can only mean lack of imaginative, competitive striving. Some failures should be anticipated rather than penalized. . . . Above all, top management needs the courage to take carefully considered risks. Without such courage, much is lost.[15]

The executive who agrees with this statement will be concerned over the results of the research reported in this article. He may well find himself asking questions like these: Is management sufficiently aware of the degree to which, for one reason or another, company decision makers avoid situations offering good chances for large gains because of the possibility of loss? Is the risk-shunning behavior of managers a product of corporate control procedures? Should management reexamine these procedures and consider possibilities for revising them?

Cardinal utility theory offers one method of answering these questions in a factual way. Why not use it?

---

[15]*Harvard Business Review* (January-February, 1966), p. 91.

27. ABANDONMENT VALUE AND CAPITAL BUDGETING*

ALEXANDER A. ROBICHEK †
and JAMES C. VAN HORNE ††

In the appraisal of investment proposals, insufficient attention in the literature is paid to the possibility of future abandonment. Customarily, projects are analyzed as though the firm were committed to the project over its entire estimated life. However, many projects have significant abandonment value over their economic lives; and this factor must be considered in the capital-budgeting process if capital is to be allocated optimally. This paper will examine the importance of abandonment value to capital budgeting, analyze how it can affect a project's expected return and risk, and propose a framework for taking account of this seldom considered dimension. In this regard, a simulation method is developed for incorporating the effects of abandonment into the information provided for the investment decision.

THE INVESTMENT DECISION

The current literature in the field of capital budgeting favors the use of the discounted cash-flow approach to project selection. The basic decision rule given by this approach can be stated in one of two ways: 1) accept a project if the present value of all expected cash flows, discounted at the cost of capital rate, is greater than, or equal to, zero; and 2) accept a project if the internal rate of return (i.e., the discount rate which equates the present value of expected cash inflows with the present value of expected cash outflows) is greater than, or equal to, the firm's cost of capital.[1]

These two rules will lead to the same optimal selection of investment proposals if the following conditions hold:

1. A meaningful cost of capital rate does exist in the sense that the firm has access to capital at this cost.
2. There is no capital rationing. If a project meets the acceptance criterion, capital is available at the cost of capital rate to finance the project.
3. All projects, existing as well as proposed, have the same degree of risk, so that the acceptance or rejection of any project does not affect the cost of capital.
4. A meaningful, unique internal rate of return exists.

*From the *Journal of Finance* (December, 1967), pp. 577-590; and (March, 1969), pp. 96 and 97. Reprinted by permission.
†Alexander A. Robichek, Professor of Business Administration, Graduate School of Business, Stanford University.
††James C. Van Horne, Associate Professor of Finance, Graduate School of Business, Stanford University.

[1]See, for example, Solomon, reference [13]; and Bierman and Smidt, reference [1], especially Chapters 2 and 3.

In the absence of these assumptions, the capital-budgeting decision becomes considerably more complex.[2] Inasmuch as the resulting problems do not affect the central thesis of this paper, we assume initially all four of the conditions listed above.

THE ABANDONMENT OPTION

The economic rationale behind the capital-budgeting decision rule can be applied directly to the abandonment decision. We submit that a project should be abandoned at that point in time when its abandonment value exceeds the net-present value of the project's subsequent expected future cash flows discounted at the cost of capital rate.[3] Using the internal rate of return method, the decision rule would be to abandon when the rate of return on abandonment value is less than the cost of capital. In either case, funds will be removed from a project whenever their incremental return is less than the minimum acceptable standard—namely, the cost of capital.[4]

Although the abandonment concept itself is quite simple, problems of measurement exist in estimating cash flows and abandonment value. Fortunately, the measurement of these factors has been analyzed ably elsewhere;[5] consequently, in this paper we shall not be concerned with how they may be determined. "Cash flows" are assumed to be all cash revenues that would be lost by abandonment less all cash expenses avoided. Abandonment value is assumed to represent the net disposal value of the project that would be available to the company in either cash or cash savings.[6]

EFFECT OF ABANDONMENT

When the possibility of future abandonment is recognized, what effect does it have upon project selection? We suggest that the effect may be quite dramatic and that altogether different selection decisions may be reached when abandonment is considered explicitly. To illustrate, consider the following example: Project A, costing $4,800 at time 0, is expected to generate cash flows over three years, after which time, there is no expected salvage value. The cash flows and their respective probabilities are shown in Table 27-1.[7] There are 27 possible sequences (or branches) of cash flows over the 3-year period. For instance, sequence No. 11 represents a cash-flow pattern of $2,000 in year 1, $1,000 in year 2, and $1,000 in year 3. The joint probability of each sequence of cash flows is shown in the last column of the table. For

---

[2]See Lorie and Savage, reference [6]; Teichroew, Robichek, and Montalbano, reference [14]; and Weingartner, reference [16].

[3]Dean, reference [2] discusses this problem in the Appendix to this book.

[4]The existence of the abandonment possibility may affect the "riskiness" of the project. This aspect is considered in detail later in the paper.

[5]For an excellent discussion on measuring cash flows and abandonment value, see Shillinglaw's two articles, references [11] and [12]. For a somewhat related discussion involving replacement, see Moore, reference [9].

[6]See Shillinglaw, reference [11], p. 270.

[7]For additional discussion of decision trees, see Magee, reference [7].

sequence No. 11, the probability of occurrence is ($1/2 \times 1/4 \times 1/2 = 1/16 = 4/64$). The abandonment value at the end of each period is shown below the cash flows; this value is \$3,000 at the end of the first year, \$1,900 at the end of the second, and zero at the end of the third year.[8] After the third year, the project is not expected to provide any cash flow or residual value.

If we assume that the firm's cost of capital is 10 percent, then the expected net-present value of Project A can be computed.[9] The procedure involves the following steps: (1) compute the net-present value for each cash flow sequence; (2) obtain the *expected* net-present value by multiplying the computed net-present value by the probability of occurrence of that sequence;[10] and (3) add the expected net-present values for all sequences.

When we follow this procedure for Project A, we find that the expected net-present value is —\$144.23. Since this value is less than zero, the project is unacceptable under conventional standards. However, when we allow for abandonment, the results for the project are changed. Recall that the decision rule is to abandon a project if the abandonment value exceeds the expected cash flows for all subsequent periods, discounted at the cost of capital rate. Applying this rule to Project A, a revised set of relevant expected cash-flow sequences is obtained.[11] For example, if the cash flow in period 1 turned out to be \$1,000, the only relevant cash-flow sequences would be 1 through 9 in Table 27-1. The project would be abandonment at the end of period 1 because the sum of the expected net-present value of cash flows for sequences 1 through 9 for periods 2 and 3 discounted to period 1 (\$577.86) is less than the abandonment value at the end of period 1 (\$3,000). Consequently, for the "branch" encompassing sequences 1 through 9 in Table 27-1, the cash flow for period 1 becomes \$4,000 (i.e., the sum of the \$1,000 cash flow during the period plus the abandonment value of \$3,000); and there are no cash flows in the remaining two periods. Similarly, it is found that abandonment takes

---

[8]For simplicity, we assume that the abandonment values over time are known and invariant with respect to the cash-flow patterns. For many projects, these assumptions are not unreasonable. For example, general-purpose buildings and machine tools are likely to have abandonment values that are, to a great extent, invariant with the results of operations for which they are used. When the assumptions are inappropriate, the proposed approach can be modified by specifying probability distributions for the abandonment values.

The modifications would fall into two basic categories depending on whether the abandonment values: (a) vary independently of the expected cash-flow patterns; or (b) are correlated in some measure with them. In the first case, the decision rule is to abandon the project at that point in time when the *expected* abandonment value at the end of time t exceeds the present value of the project's expected subsequent cash flows. In the second case, different expected abandonment values would be projected for the different "branches" of cash flows. The decision rule would be to abandon a project at that point in time when the expected abandonment value *for the particular cash-flow branch* exceeds the present value of expected subsequent cash flows for that branch.

[9]While this example is analyzed in terms of the net-present value, it also could be analyzed in terms of the internal rate of return.

[10]For example, the expected net-present value for sequence No. 11 ($E(NPV_{11})$) is determined as follows:

$$E(NPV_{11}) = \left[-4{,}800 + \frac{2{,}000}{(1 + .10)} + \frac{1{,}000}{(1 + .10)^2} + \frac{1{,}000}{(1 + .10)^3} \right] (4/64) = -87.76.$$

[11]If the project is abandoned, the cash flows lost are those in Table 27-1.

place at the end of period 2 for the cash-flow sequences 10 through 12, 13 through 15, and 19 through 21 in Table 27-1. The expected net-present values of cash flows for the above three "branches" for period 3 discounted to period 2 ($909.09, $1,818.18, and $1,818.18 respectively) are less than the abandonment value at the end of period 2 ($1,900). For the branch encompassing cash-flow sequences 10 through 12, the cash flow for period 2 becomes $2,900; and for the two branches encompassing sequences 13 through 15 and 19 through 21, the cash flow becomes $3,900 for each branch. Taking account of these changes, the revised cash-flow sequences are shown in Table 27-2.

Based upon the cash-flow information in Table 27-2, the expected net-present value for Project A is now recalculated and found to be $535.25—a considerable improvement over the —$144.23 calculated before. Whereas the project would have been rejected previously, the consideration of the abandonment option results in the acceptance of the project.

The discussion so far serves to illustrate the importance of considering abandonment value when evaluating projects. The funds committed to

TABLE 27-1
EXPECTED FUTURE CASH FLOWS FOR PROJECT A

PERIOD 1 CASH FLOW	PROBABILITY	PERIOD 2 CASH FLOW	CONDITIONAL PROBABILITY	PERIOD 3 CASH FLOW	CONDITIONAL PROBABILITY	CASH FLOW SEQUENCE NUMBER	PROBABILITY OF SEQUENCE (IN 64ths)
		0	.25	−$1,000	.25	1	1/64
				500	.50	2	2/64
				0	.25	3	1/64
$1,000	.25	$ 500	.50	− 500	.25	4	2/64
				0	.50	5	4/64
				500	.25	6	2/64
		1,000	.25	0	.25	7	1/64
				1,000	.50	8	2/64
				2,000	.25	9	1/64
		1,000	.25	0	.25	10	2/64
				1,000	.50	11	4/64
				2,000	.25	12	2/64
2,000	.50	2,000	.50	1,000	.25	13	4/64
				2,000	.50	14	8/64
				3,000	.25	15	4/64
		3,000	.25	2,000	.25	16	2/64
				3,000	.50	17	4/64
				4,000	.25	18	2/64
		2,000	.25	1,000	.25	19	1/64
				2,000	.50	20	2/64
				3,000	.25	21	1/64
3,000	.25	3,000	.50	2,000	.25	22	2/64
				3,000	.50	23	4/64
				4,000	.25	24	2/64
		3,500	.25	3,000	.25	25	1/64
				3,500	.50	26	2/64
				4,000	.25	27	1/64
ABANDONMENT VALUE AT END OF PERIOD $3,000		$1,900		0			

TABLE 27-2

EXPECTED FUTURE CASH FLOWS FOR PROJECT A WITH THE CONSIDERATION OF ABANDONMENT VALUES

Period 1		Period 2		Period 3		Cash Flow Sequence Number	Probability of Sequence (in 64ths)
Cash Flow	Probability	Cash Flow	Conditional Probability	Cash Flow	Conditional Probability		
$4,000	.25	0		0		1	16/64
2,000	.50	2,900	.25	0		2	8/64
		3,900	.50	0		3	16/64
		3,000	.25	2,000	.25	4	2/64
				3,000	.50	5	4/64
				4,000	.25	6	2/64
3,000	.25	3,900	.25	0		7	4/64
		3,000	.50	2,000	.25	8	2/64
				3,000	.50	9	4/64
				4,000	.25	10	2/64
		3,500	.25	3,000	.25	11	1/64
				3,500	.50	12	2/64
				4,000	.25	13	1/64

some projects may be far more flexible than those committed to others. Not to take account of the possible mobility of funds and to regard all outlays as sunk overlooks an extremely important dimension. Such an omission may provide very misleading information for decision making and may result in capital-budgeting decisions that are sub-optimal.

SIMULATION AND THE ABANDONMENT OPTION

In the preceding section of this paper, the attempt was made to show how the possibility of abandonment may affect the investment decision. To illustrate the problem, a relatively simple example was used—Project A, which had a total of 27 possible cash-flow sequences. While this Project was useful for purposes of illustration, most projects under consideration are considerably more complex with respect to the possible number of cash-flow sequences. As a result, the approach illustrated above that evaluates each separate cash-flow sequence becomes unfeasible.

In practice, it is often true that management has reasonably good knowledge of the possible range of cash flows to be expected from a project.[12] If probability distributions of these cash flows over time can be specified, Monte Carlo simulation[13] may serve as a practical substitute for the "all inclusive" approach described earlier. To illustrate the application of simulation techniques to the problem at hand, consider Project B, which has an estimated life of ten years, no expected salvage value, and expected cash flows and abandonment values as shown in Table 27-3.

If no account is taken of the possibility of abandonment, the internal rate of return for this Project is 10 percent. If a discount rate of 8 percent is assumed, the Project has an expected net-present value of $565.

Assume now that the abandonment values and the cash outflow in year 0, shown in Table 27-3, are known with certainty but that the expected cash flows for years 1 through 10 are random variables distributed normally with a constant standard deviation of $100. We must specify also whether the yearly cash flows are independent of each other (i.e., the "actual" cash flows in any one period do not affect the cash flows of subsequent periods) or whether, in some measure, they are correlated over time.[14] The latter relationship is considered to be more representative of the real world; consequently, we specify in our simulation approach a provision to generate revised cash forecasts as "actual" simulated cash flows deviate from expected cash flows. The particular manner in which forecasts are revised is described fully in the Appendix.[15]

---

[12]For example, Grayson, reference [3], has been successful in obtaining probabilistic information relating to possible cash flows of oil exploration projects.

[13]Monte Carlo simulation is a technique which investigates the implications of uncertainty in a systematic manner. The readers who are unfamiliar with this approach will find it described in most basic operations research texts. For one such description, see Sasieni, Yaspan, and Friedman, reference [10], pp. 58-67.

[14]See Hillier, reference [5], especially pp. 447-449.

[15]The form of the cash-forecast revision rule was selected solely to illustrate the methodology of Monte Carlo simulation. We were not concerned particularly with the rule's realism, because in practice each project faces a distinct set of circumstances.

TABLE 27-3
EXPECTED CASH FLOWS AND ABANDONMENT VALUES FOR PROJECT B
(DOLLARS)

| | | | | | Year | | | | | |
0	1	2	3	4	5	6	7	8	9	10
Expected Cash Flow										
—6,145	1,000	1,000	1,000	1,000	1,000	1,000	1,000	1,000	1,000	1,000
Expected Abandonment Value										
	— 6,200	5,700	5,180	4,580	3,980	3,300	2,570	1,780	920	0

The net-present value and the internal rate of return for Project B are simulated 100 times with the consideration of abandonment and 100 times without the abandonment option. We specified that in simulating with the abandonment option, the decision rule to abandon was identical in form to the one described in connection with Project A—abandon the project at the end of year t if the revised expected cash flows for years t + 1 through 10, discounted at 8 percent to year t, are less than the abandonment value at year t. A detailed description of this rule is given in the Appendix. The simulation results are summarized in Table 27-4.

TABLE 27-4
RESULTS OF SIMULATION FOR PROJECT B

| | Net Present Value | | Internal Rate of Return | |
	Without Abandonment	With Abandonment	Without Abandonment	With Abandonment
Expected Value	$672	$991	9.83%	13.62%

Note that for the "without abandonment" option there are differences between the simulated expected values in Table 27-4 and the calculated expected values based upon the data in Table 27-3. For the net-present value case, the simulated mean value is $672, as compared with a calculated value of $565; for the internal rate of return, the simulated mean value is 9.83 percent, while the computed value is 10 percent. These differences are insignificant statistically,[16] and we conclude that the simulation technique described approximates fairly the actual distributions of net-present value and internal rate of return for Project B.

It is seen in Table 27-4 that explicit consideration of the abandonment

---

[16]The differences in means between simulated and calculated value is less than .08 standard deviations for the net-present value and about .03 standard deviations for the internal rate of return.

FIGURE 27-1
FREQUENCY OF ABANDONMENT OF PROJECT B BEFORE END OF ESTIMATED USEFUL LIFE

FIGURE 27-1
FREQUENCY OF ABANDONMENT OF PROJECT B BEFORE END OF ESTIMATED USEFUL LIFE

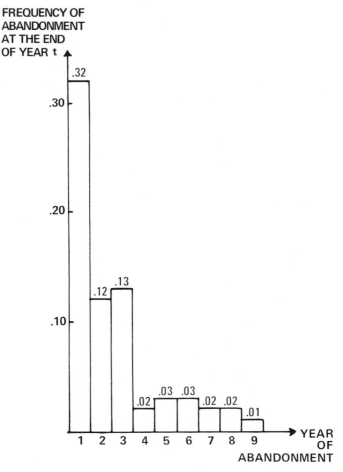

option results in a significant increase in Project B's expected value of return, whether this return is measured in terms of the net-present value or of the internal rate of return. Based upon the simulation undertaken, Figure 27-1 shows the frequency with which abandonment takes place for each year of Project B's life. For this particular simulation, the project is abandoned before the end of its originally estimated useful life in 70 percent of the cases. Clearly the abandonment results would be different under alternative assumptions as to: abandonment values; expected cash flows; distribution of cash flows; the manner in which forecasts are revised; and the discount rate.

THE ABANDONMENT OPTION AND PROJECT RISK

Our discussion thus far has been limited to capital-budgeting decisions solely based upon expected net-present value or internal rate of return.

TABLE 27-5
SELECTED VALUES FOR PROJECTS A AND B

	Without Abandonment	With Abandonment
Project A		
Net Present Value:		
Expected Value	$—144	$ 535
Standard Deviation	2,372	1,522
V/2SV	.945	1.29
Project B (Simulated Values)		
Net Present Value:		
Expected Value	$ 672	$ 991
Standard Deviation	1,422	888
V/2SV	1.01	2.96
Internal Rate of Return		
Expected Rate	9.83%	13.62%
Standard Deviation	5.31	2.25
V/2SV	.75	1.25

This limitation was in order because of our assumption that all projects are of "equal risk." Specifically, Projects A and B are assumed to be "equally risky," whether evaluated with or without the abandonment option. In this section it is demonstrated that the presence of abandonment value may reduce the "risk" of a project over that which would be present if there were no abandonment value. By a reduction in risk, we mean either or both of the following: (1) a lower variance of the probability distribution around the expected value of returns;[17] and (2) a shift in the skewness of the probability distribution toward the right, reducing both the range and the magnitude of undesirable returns, i.e., those to the left of the expected value of returns.

In order to evaluate the effect that abandonment value has upon risk, let us consider Projects A and B both with and without the abandonment option. In this regard, we can compute such measures of risk as the variance, V, the standard deviation, S, and the semi-variance, SV.[18] In addition, a

---

[17]For a discussion of expected return and variance as they relate to capital budgeting, see Hertz, reference [4], Hillier, reference [5], and Van Horne, reference [15].

[18]Semi-variance is the variance of the probability distribution to the left of expected net-present value and may be thought to represent a measure of downside risk. Mathematically, it can be expressed as

$$SV(X) = \sum_{i=1}^{m} \{[X_i - E(X)]^2 P(X_i)\}$$

where X_i is the observation, $E(X)$ is the expected net-present value, $P(X_i)$ the probability of the event X_i, and m denotes the number of observations to the left of the mean. See Markowitz, reference [8], p. 191.

measure of relative skewness can be obtained by computing the ratio V/2SV. For symmetrical probability distributions, V/2SV equals one; for distributions skewed to the right, it is greater than one; and for distributions skewed to the left, it is less than one.

In addition to the expected value of returns, S and the ratio V/2SV were computed for Projects A and B with and without the consideration of the abandonment option. The principal results are summarized in Table 27-5.

For Project A, note that when abandonment is considered not only does the expected net-present value increase from —$144 to $535 but the standard deviation decreases from $2,372 to $1,522. Also, the skewness of the probability distribution of net-present values changes from slightly negative to positive. This latter result suggests that much of the downside risk can be eliminated if the Project is abandoned when events turn unfavorable. Figure 27-2 illustrates this point graphically—it depicts the cumulative probability distribution for Project A with and without the consideration of abandonment. For example, with abandonment, there is a 48/64 probability that the Project will provide an expected net-present value of more than zero; without abandonment, the probability is only 40/64 that the net present value will be greater than zero. Moreover, with abandonment, there is no probability that the expected net-present value will be less than —$1,164; while without abandonment, there is an 18/64 probability that it will be less than this amount.[19] For a given probability, the expected net-present value is higher with abandonment value than without through probability 27/64, after which the expected net-present values are about the same for both distributions.[20]

For Project B, a comparison of the simulation results, with and without the abandonment option, yields conclusions similar to those arrived at from the analysis of data for Project A. Again, consideration of the abandonment option results in a number of desirable occurrences: the expected value of returns (either net-present value or internal rate of return) increases; the standard deviation decreases; and the skewness of the probability distributions shifts to the right. The distributions of individual simulation values for Project B follow the general pattern illustrated in Figure 27-2 for Project A, and we shall not reproduce them here.

In our analysis, the acceptance or rejection of any project was assumed not to change the discount rate, i.e., the firm's cost of capital. The effect that the acceptance of a project will have on the discount rate will depend upon the characteristics of existing investments, the manner in which the project's expected returns are related to the expected returns of other projects, and the expectations and preferences of investors and lenders. The

---

[19]Since Figure 27-2 is in terms of discrete probability distributions, this probability is denoted by the first dot to the left of the point where net-present value equals zero.

[20]For illustrative purposes, the same cost of capital rate was used to discount the subsequent cash flows for each event-tree. In practice, there may be situations when this approach is not completely appropriate.

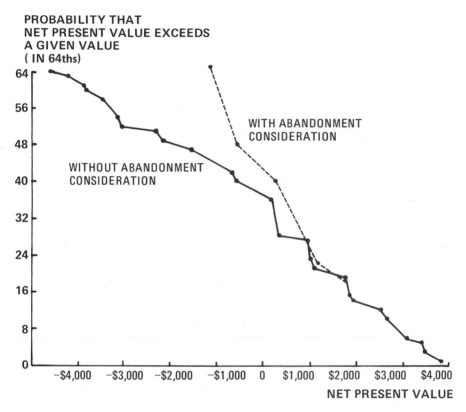

FIGURE 27-2
CUMULATIVE PROBABILITY DISTRIBUTIONS
PROJECT A

determination of this effect is extremely complex; and, inasmuch as it does not invalidate any of the basic tenets of this paper, we do not attempt to deal with it here.[21] We would suggest, however, that the acceptance of Project A (or B) with the possibility of abandonment is likely to result in a more favorable change (if a change takes place) in the discount rate than would occur from the acceptance of Project A (or B) without the abandonment option.

CONCLUSIONS

Any estimate of future cash flows implies that a particular operating strategy will be followed. All too often, however, this strategy is not stated explicitly. Specifically, the consideration of possible abandonment is a dimension frequently omitted from capital-budgeting analysis. As illustrated in our examples, significant abandonment values for a project may

---

[21]In this paper, we do not consider the portfolio problem of risk to the firm as a whole. For an analysis of this problem, see Van Horne, reference [15].

result in a higher expected net-present value or internal rate of return and lower expected risk than would be the case if the project had no abandonment value over its economic life. It is important to take account of the fact that different investment projects provide different degrees of flexibility with respect to the possible mobility of funds if the project turns bad. To ignore these differences may result in sub-optimal investment decision. Since having the option to abandon never decreases project value, the typical consequences of ignoring the option would be to underestimate the value of a project. The framework proposed in this paper allows the firm to incorporate the possibility of abandonment into its capital-budgeting procedures.

APPENDIX

Description of the Simulation Model

Let
  $EC_{t.\tau}$ = expected cash flow in year t as of year τ.
  AV_t = abandonment value in year t.
  AC_t = "actual" simulated cash flow in year t.
The values for AV_t and $EC_{t.o}$ are input as given in Table 27-3.

Rule to Generate Revised Cash Flow Forecasts

where

$$EC_{t.r} = EC_{t.r-1} [1 + X\alpha], \qquad (1)$$

$$X = \frac{AC_r - EC_{r.r-1}}{EC_{r.r-1}},$$

and α varies depending on the values of X as shown below.

$$
\begin{array}{lll}
 & \text{If} \;-.05 \leqslant X \leqslant .05 & \text{then}\; \alpha = \;\;0 \\
\text{If}-.10 \leqslant \alpha <-.05 \; \text{or} & .05 < X \leqslant .10 & \text{then}\; \alpha = \;.5 \\
\text{If}-.15 \leqslant \alpha <-.10 \; \text{or} & .10 < X \leqslant .15 & \text{then}\; \alpha = 1.0 \\
\text{If}-.20 \leqslant \alpha <-.15 \; \text{or} & .15 < X \leqslant .20 & \text{then}\; \alpha = 1.5 \\
\text{If}-.20 > X & \text{or} & X > .20 \quad \text{then}\; \alpha = 2.0
\end{array}
$$

In words, the above rule revises the expected cash flow forecasts as of year τ for subsequent years if $(X\alpha)$ differs from zero, where X represents the percentage difference between "actual" simulated cash flows and "expected" cash flows and α is a parameter dependent upon X. For example, if the "actual" cash flow in year 5 were 4 percent greater than the "expected" cash flow for year 5 as of year 4, α would be zero, and the expected cash flows for all subsequent years (as of year 5) would remain the same as of year 4. On the other hand, if the "actual" cash flows were 18 percent less than the "expected" cash flows, all subsequent cash flows would be revised downward by 27 percent.

$$[X\alpha = (-.18)(1.5) = -.27].$$

Decision Rule to Abandon

Given all $EC_{t.\tau}$ for $\tau < t \leqslant 10$, compute for all $\tau < 10$ the discounted present value of cash flows in Eq. 2:

$$PV_r = \sum_{t=r+1}^{10} \frac{EC_{t.r}}{(1+.08)^{(t-r)}} \tag{2}$$

If $PV_\tau \geqslant AV_\tau$ then continue simulation.

If $PV_\tau < AV_\tau$ abandon project; in this case AC_τ (final) $= AC_\tau + AV_\tau$ and all $EC_{t.\tau} = 0$ for $t > \tau$.

Compute Net-Present Value and Rate of Return

After all the final cash flows are determined for each run j, compute the net-present value in (Eq. 3) and rate of return from (Eq. 4):

$$NPV_j = -6145 + \sum_{t=1}^{10} \frac{AC_t}{(1+.08)^t}; \tag{3}$$

Solve for R_j in (Eq. 4)

$$6145 = \sum_{t=1}^{10} \frac{AC_t}{(1+R_j)^t}. \tag{4}$$

Complete Simulation

Go to next simulation run. Run simulation 100 times and compute mean, variance, standard deviation, and semi-variance.

REFERENCES

1. Bierman, Jr., H., and S. Smidt. *The Capital Budgeting Decision*. New York: The MacMillan Company, 1966.
2. Dean, J. *Capital Budgeting*. New York: Columbia University Press, 1951, pp. 163-168.
3. Grayson, C. J. *Decision under Uncertainty*. Cambridge, Mass.: Harvard University Press, 1960.

4. Hertz, D. B. "Risk Analysis in Capital Budgeting," *Harvard Business Review*. Vol. XLII (January-February, 1964), pp. 95-106.
5. Hillier, F. S. "The Derivation of Probabilistic Information for the Evaluation of Risky Investments," *Management Science*. Vol. IX (April, 1963), pp. 443-457.
6. Lorie, J. H., and L. J. Savage. "Three Problems in Rationing Capital," *Journal of Business*. Vol. XXVIII (October, 1955), pp. 229-239.
7. Magee, J. F. "How to Use Decision Trees in Capital Investment," *Harvard Business Review*. Vol. XLII (September-October, 1964), pp. 79-96.
8. Markowitz, H. M. *Portfolio Selection*. New York: John Wiley & Sons, Inc., 1959.
9. Moore, C. L. "The Present-Value Method and the Replacement Decision," *Accounting Review*. Vol. XXXIX (January, 1964), pp. 94-102.
10. Sasieni, M., A. Yaspan, and L. Friedman. *Operations Research—Methods and Problems*. New York: John Wiley & Sons, Inc., 1959.
11. Shillinglaw, G. "Profit Analysis for Abandonment Decisions," *The Management of Corporate Capital*, edited by E. Solomon. Glencoe, Ill.: The Free Press of Glencoe, 1959, pp. 269-281.
12. —————————. "Residual Values in Investment Analysis," *The Management of Corporate Capital*, edited by E. Solomon. Glencoe, Ill.: The Free Press of Glencoe, 1959, pp. 259-268.
13. Solomon, E. "The Arithmetic of Capital-Budgeting Decisions," *Journal of Business*. Vol. XXIX (April, 1956), pp. 124-129.
14. Teichroew, D., A. A. Robichek, and M. Montalbano. "An Analysis of Criteria for Investment and Financing Decisions under Certainty," *Management Science*, Vol. XII (November, 1965), pp. 151-179.
15. Van Horne, J. C. "The Capital-Budgeting Decision Involving Combinations of Risky Investments," *Management Science*. Vol. XIII (October, 1966), pp. B84-92.
16. Weingartner, H. M. *Mathematical Programming and the Analysis of Capital Budgeting Problems*. Englewood Cliffs, N.J.: Prentice-Hall, Inc., 1963.

ABANDONMENT VALUE AND CAPITAL BUDGETING: REPLY*

The comment by Professors Dyl and Long (DL) is, for the most part, an appropriate modification of our procedure for evaluating the abandonment of an investment project. We accept their principal point—in our original paper[1] we omitted from consideration the possibility that future abandonment may be more desirable than either "present" abandonment or continuation of the project to the end of its economic life. In certain cases, deferral of abandonment to a future date may be the optimal alternative.

DL propose the following algorithm for the optimal abandonment decision rule:

Calculate:

$$\underset{\tau+1 \leqslant a \leqslant n}{\text{Max}} \quad PV_{\tau.a}, \tag{1}$$

where τ is the "current" period, a is any period of possible future abandonment, and n represents the life of the project. In determining the maximum

---

*This article appears at the request of the authors of Article 27. It originally appeared in *Journal of Finance*, XXIV (March, 1969), pp. 96-97.

[1] Alexander A. Robichek and James C. Van Horne, "Abandonment Value and Capital Budgeting," *Journal of Finance*, XXII (December, 1967), pp. 577-89.

$PV_{\tau.a}$, the algorithm requires that present values be computed under the assumption of abandonment in every period $\tau + 1 \leqslant a \leqslant n$. In other words, n different $PV_{\tau.a}$'s are computed; $PV_{\tau.a}$ represents the abandonment value in period a plus the expected values of cash flows in the first a periods, all discounted to their present value at time τ.[2] Having calculated present values for all future a's, the largest such value is then compared with the current abandonment value. The decision rule is to abandon the project at time τ if the current abandonment value, AV_τ, exceeds the maximum $PV_{\tau.a}$. If AV_τ is less than (or equal to) the maximum $PV_{\tau.a}$, then the project should be held and abandoned at time a corresponding to the maximum $PV_{\tau.a}$.

The consideration of deferred abandonment, as proposed by DL, is important in situations where abandonment value and expected future cash flows do not decline rapidly over time. However, in cases where expected abandonment values decline significantly over time and where expected future cash flows deteriorate when a project turns bad, the possibility of deferred abandonment rarely will need be considered.

Operationally, the DL algorithm is cumbersome and, in a sense, incorrect. DL's rule (if $AV_\tau \leqslant$ max. $PV_{\tau.a}$, then the project should be held and abandoned at $\tau = a$) holds only under the condition of certainty with respect to future cash flows and abandonment values. Where uncertainty obtains, as it does in most problems affecting abandonment decisions, DL's rule is not correct. Consider the situation where $AV_\tau \leqslant$ max. $PV_{\tau.a}$. This result tells us *only* that the project should be held beyond period τ. The project may or *may not* be abandoned at time a for which $PV_{\tau.a}$ is maximum. Maximum $PV_{\tau.a}$ is computed at time τ using expected cash flows and abandonment values *estimated as of that time*. Because the project is held beyond time τ, expectations may (and probably will) change. As a result, a completely different set of values may have to be considered to reach an optimal decision at time a_{max}, or before if the project should be abandoned prior to that time.

Accordingly, we propose the following modified algorithm to be used in evaluating abandonment decisions:

(a) Compute $PV_{\tau.a}$ for a = n, where

$$PV_{T.a} = \sum_{t=T+1}^{a} \frac{EC_{t.T}}{(1+k)^{(t-T)}} + \frac{AV_{a.T}}{(1+k)^{(a-T)}}. \tag{2}$$

(b) If $PV_{\tau.n} > AV_\tau$,
continue to hold project and evaluate it again at time $\tau + 1$, based upon expectations at that time.

---

[2]This assumes that abandonment values over time are known and invariant with respect to the cash-flow patterns. As noted in *ibid*. p. 579, probability distribution of future abandonment values could be incorporated into the analysis.

(c) If $PV_{\tau.n} \leqslant AV_\tau$,

   compute $PV_{\tau.a}$ for $a = n - 1$.

(d) Compare $PV_{\tau.n-1}$ with AV_τ as in (b) and (c) above. Continue procedure until either the decision to hold is reached or $a = \tau + 1$.

(e) If $PV_{\tau.a} \leqslant AV_\tau$ for all $\tau + 1 \leqslant a \leqslant n$, then abandon project at time τ.

   The algorithm described above will provide the optimal decision with respect to abandonment. It is also considerably less costly and time consuming than DL's procedure. In conclusion, we wish to thank Dyl and Long for pointing out an important omission in our previous paper.

28. COST-VOLUME-PROFIT ANALYSIS UNDER CONDITIONS OF UNCERTAINTY*

ROBERT K. JAEDICKE †
and ALEXANDER A. ROBICHEK ††

Cost-volume-profit analysis is frequently used by management as a basis for choosing among alternatives. Such decisions as: (1) the sales volume required to attain a given level of profits, and (2) the most profitable combination of products to produce and sell are examples of decision problems where C-V-P analysis is useful. However, the fact that traditional C-V-P analysis does not include adjustments for risk and uncertainty may, in any given instance, severely limit its usefulness. Some of the limitations can be seen from the following example.

Assume that the firm is considering the introduction of two new products, either of which can be produced by using present facilities. Both products require an increase in annual fixed cost of the same amount, say $400,000. Each product has the same selling price and variable cost per unit, say $10 and $8 respectively, and each requires the same amount of capacity. Using these data, the breakeven point of either product is 200,000 units. C-V-P analysis helps to establish the breakeven volume of each product, but this analysis does not distinguish the relative desirability of the two products for at least two reasons.

The first piece of missing information is the *expected* sales volume of each product. Obviously, if the annual sales of A are expected to be 30,000 units and of B are expected to be 350,000 units, then B is clearly preferred to A so far as the sales expectation is concerned.

However, assume that the expected annual sales of each product is the same—say 300,000 units. Is it right to conclude that management should be indifferent as far as a choice between A and B is concerned? The answer is "no," *unless* each sales expectation is certain. If both sales estimates are subject to uncertainty, the decision process will be improved if the relative risk associated with each product can somehow be brought into the analysis. The discussion which follows suggests some changes which might be made in traditional C-V-P analysis so as to make it a more useful tool in analyzing decision problems under uncertainty.

SOME PROBABILITY CONCEPTS RELATED TO C-V-P ANALYSIS

In the previous section, it was pointed out that the *expected* volume of the annual sales is an important decision variable. Some concepts of proba-

---

*From *The Accounting Review* (October, 1964), pp. 917-926. Reprinted by permission.
†Robert K. Jaedicke, Professor of Accounting, Graduate School of Business, Stanford University.
††Alexander A. Robichek, Professor of Business Administration, Graduate School of Business, Stanford University.

TABLE 28-1
PROBABILITY DISTRIBUTION FOR PRODUCTS A AND B

Events (Units Demanded)	Probability Distribution— (Product A)	Probability Distribution— (Product B)
50,000	—	.1
100,000	.1	.1
200,000	.2	.1
300,000	.4	.2
400,000	.2	.4
500,000	.1	.1
	1.00	1.00

bility will be discussed using the example posed earlier.

The four fundamental relationships used in the example were: (1) the selling price per unit; (2) the variable cost per unit; (3) the total fixed cost; and (4) the expected sales volume of each product. In any given decision problem, all four of these factors can be uncertain. However, it may be that, *relative to* the expected sales quantity, the costs and selling prices are quite certain. That is, for analytical purposes, the decision maker may be justified in treating several factors as certainty equivalents. Such a procedure simplifies the analysis and will be followed here as a first approximation. In this section of the paper, sales volume will be treated as the only uncertain quantity. Later, all decision factors in the above example will be treated under conditions of uncertainty.

In the example, sales volume is treated as a *random variable*. A random variable can be thought of as an *unknown quantity*. In this case, the best decision hinges on the value of the random variable, sales volume of each product. One decision approach which allows for uncertainty is to estimate, for each random variable, the likelihood that the random variable will take on various possible values. Such an estimate is called a subjective probability distribution. The decision would then be made by choosing that course of action which has the highest *expected monetary value*. This approach is illustrated in Table 28-1.

The expected value of the random variables, sales demand for each product, is calculated by weighting the possible conditional values by their respective probabilities. In other words, the expected value is a weighted average. The calculation is given in Table 28-2.

Based on an expected value approach, the firm should select product B rather than A. The expected profits of each possible action are as follows:

Product A:
$2(300,000 \text{ units}) - \$400,000 = \$200,000$

Product B:
$2(305,000 \text{ units}) - \$400,000 = \$210,000$

Several observations are appropriate at this point. First, the respective probabilities for each product, used in Table 28-1, add to 1.00. Furthermore,

TABLE 28-2
EXPECTED VALUE OF SALES DEMAND FOR PRODUCTS A AND B

(1) Event	(2) P(A)	(1 × 2)	(3) P(B)	(1 × 3)
50,000	—	—	.1	5,000
100,000	.1	10,000	.1	10,000
200,000	.2	40,000	.1	20,000
300,000	.4	120,000	.2	60,000
400,000	.2	80,000	.4	160,000
500,000	.1	50,000	.1	50,000
	1.00		1.00	
Expected Value		300,000 units		305,000 units

the possible demand levels (events) are assumed to be mutually exclusive and also exhaustive. That is, the listing is done in such a way that no two events can happen simultaneously and any events *not* listed are assumed to have a zero probability of occurring. Herein are three important (basic) concepts of probability analyses.

Secondly, the probability distributions may have been assigned by using historical demand data on similar products, or the weights may be purely subjective in the sense that there is no historical data available. Even if the probability distributions are entirely subjective, this approach still has merit. It allows the estimator to express his uncertainty about the sales estimate. An estimate of sales is necessary to make a decision. Hence, the question is *not* whether an estimate must be made, but simply a question of the best way to make and express the estimate.

Now suppose that the expected value of sales for each product is 300,000, as shown in Table 28-3. In this example, it is easy to see that the firm would *not* be indifferent between products A and B, even though the expected value of sales is 300,000 units in both cases. In the case of product A, for example, there is a .1 chance that sales will be only 100,000 units, and in that case, a loss of $200,000 would be incurred (i.e., $2 × 100,000 units − $400,000). On the other hand, there is a .3 chance that sales will be above 300,000 units, and if this is the case, higher profits are possible with product A than with product

TABLE 28-3

Demand	P(A)	E.V.(A)	P(B)	E.V.(B)
100,000 units	.1	10,000	—	—
200,000 units	.2	40,000	—	—
300,000 units	.4	120,000	1.00	300,000
400,000 units	.2	80,000	—	—
500,000 units	.1	50,000	—	—
	1.00		1.00	
Expected Sales Demand		300,000		300,000

B. Hence, the firm's attitude toward risk becomes important. The expected value (or the mean of the distribution) is important but so is the "spread" in the distribution. Typically, the greater the spread, the greater the risk involved. A quantitative measure of the spread is available in the form of the standard deviation of the distribution, and this concept and its application will be refined later in the paper.

THE NORMAL PROBABILITY DISTRIBUTION

The preceding examples were highly simplified, and yet the calculations are relatively long and cumbersome. The possible sales volumes were few in number, and the probability distribution was discrete, that is, a sales volume of 205,762 units was considered an impossible event. The use of a continuous probability distribution is desirable not only because the calculation will usually be simplified but because the distribution may also be a more realistic description of the uncertainty aspects of the situation. The normal probability distribution will be introduced and used in the following analysis which illustrates the methodology involved. This distribution, although widely used, is not appropriate in all situations. The appropriate distribution depends on the decision problem and should, of course, be selected accordingly.

The normal probability distribution is a smooth, symmetric, continuous, bell-shaped curve as shown in Figure 28-1. The area under the curve sums to 1. The curve reaches a maximum at the mean of the distribution, and one half the area lies on either side of the mean.

On the horizontal axis are plotted the values of the appropriate unknown quantity or random variable; in the examples used here, the unknown quantity is the sales for the coming periods.

FIGURE 28-1

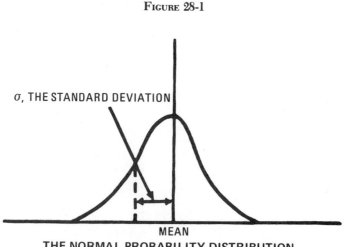

σ, THE STANDARD DEVIATION

MEAN

THE NORMAL PROBABILITY DISTRIBUTION

FIGURE 28-2

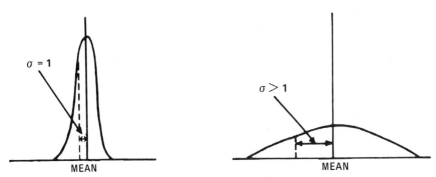

$\sigma = 1$

$\sigma > 1$

MEAN   MEAN

NORMAL PROBABILITY DISTRIBUTIONS WITH DIFFERENT STANDARD DEVIATIONS

A particular normal probability distribution can be completely determined if its mean and its standard deviation, σ, are known. The standard deviation is a measure of the dispersion of the distribution about its mean. The area under any normal distribution is 1, but one distribution may be "spread out" more than another distribution. For example, in Figure 28-2, both normal distributions have the same area and the same mean. However, in one case the σ is 1, and in the other case the σ is greater than 1. The larger the σ, the more spread out is the distribution. It should be noted that the standard deviation is not an area but is a measure of the dispersion of the individual observations about the mean of all the observations—it is a distance.

Since the normal probability distribution is continuous rather than discrete, the probability of an event cannot be read directly from the graph. The unknown quantity must be thought of as being in an interval. Assume, for example, that the mean sales for the coming period are estimated to be 10,000 units and the normal distribution appears as in Figure 28-3. Given Figure 28-3, certain probability statements can be made. For example:

FIGURE 28-3

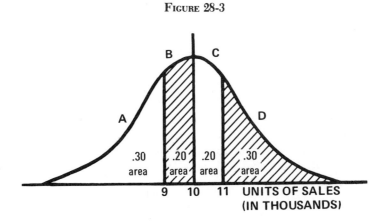

B   C

A   D

.30   .20   .20   .30
area   area   area   area

9   10   11   UNITS OF SALES
                    (IN THOUSANDS)

1. The probability of the actual sales being between 10,000 and 11,000 units is .20. This is shown by area C. Because of the symmetry of the curve, the probability of the sales being between 9,000 and 10,000 is also .20. This is shown by shaded area B. These probabilities can be given a frequency interpretation. That is, area C indicates that the actual sales will be between 10,000 and 11,000 units in about 20 percent of the cases.

2. The probability of the actual sales being greater than 11,000 units is .30 as shown by area D.

3. The probability of the sales being greater than 9,000 units is .70, the sum of areas B, C, and D.

Given a specific normal distribution, it is possible to read probabilities of the type described above directly from a normal probability table.

Another important characteristic of any normal distribution is that approximately .50 of the area lies within $\pm$ .67 standard deviations of the mean; about .68 of the area lies within $\pm$ 1.0 standard deviations of the mean; .95 of the area lies within $\pm$ 1.96 standard deviations of the mean.

As was mentioned above, normal probabilities can be read from a normal probability table. A partial table of normal probabilities is given in Table 28-4. This table is the "right tail" of the distribution; that is, probabilities of the unknown quantity being greater than X standard deviations

TABLE 28-4

AREA UNDER THE NORMAL PROBABILITY FUNCTION

X	0.00	0.05
.1	.4602	.4404
.3	.3821	.3632
.5	.3085	.2912
.6	.2743	.2578
.7	.2420	.2266
.8	.2119	.1977
.9	.1841	.1711
1.0	.1587	.1469
1.1	.1357	.1251
1.5	.0668	.0606
2.0	.0228	.0202

from the mean are given in the table. For example, the probability of the unknown quantity being greater than the mean plus .35σ is .3632. The distribution tabulated is a normal distribution with mean zero and standard deviation of 1. Such a distribution is known as a standard normal distribution. However, any normal distribution can be standardized, and hence, with proper adjustment, Table 28-4 will serve for any normal distribution.

For example, consider the earlier case where the mean of the distribution is 10,000 units. The distribution was constructed so that the standard deviation is about 2,000 units.[1] To standardize the distribution, use the following formula, where X is the number of standard deviations from the mean:

$$X = \frac{\text{Actual Sales} - \text{Mean Sales}}{\text{Standard deviation of the distribution}}$$

To calculate the probability of the sales being greater than 11,000 units, first standardize the distribution and then use the table.

$$X = \frac{11,000 - 10,000}{2,000}$$

$$= .50 \text{ standard deviations.}$$

The probability of being greater than .50 standard deviations from the mean, according to Table 28-4, is .3085. This same approximate result is shown by Figure 28-3; that is, area D is .30.

THE NORMAL DISTRIBUTION USED IN C-V-P ANALYSIS

The normal distribution will now be used in a C-V-P analysis problem, assuming that sales quantity is a random variable. Assume that the per-unit selling price is $3,000, the fixed cost is $5,800,000, and the variable cost per unit is $1,750. Breakeven sales (in units) is calculated as follows.

$$S_B = \frac{\$5,800,000}{\$3,000 - \$1,750} = 4,640 \text{ units.}$$

Furthermore, suppose that the sales manager estimates that the mean expected sales volume is 5,000 units and that it is equally likely that actual sales will be greater or less than the mean of 5,000 units. Furthermore, assume that the sales manager feels that there is roughly a 2/3 (i.e., .667) chance that the actual sales will be within 400 units of the mean. These subjective estimates can be expressed by using a normal distribution with mean $E(Q) = 5,000$ units and standard deviation $\sigma_q = 400$ units. The reason that σ_q is about 400 units is that, as mentioned earlier, about 2/3 of the area under the normal curve (actually .68) lies within 1 standard deviation of the mean. The probability distribution is shown in Figure 28-4.

The horizontal axis of Figure 28-4 denotes sales quantity. The probability of an actual sales event taking place is given by the area under the probability distribution. For example, the probability that the sales quantity will exceed 4,640 units (the breakeven point) is the shaded area under the probability distribution (the probability of actual sales exceeding 4,640 units).

---

[1] To see why this normal distribution has a standard deviation of 2,000 units, remember that the probability of sales being greater than 11,000 units is .30. Now examine Table 28-4, and it can be seen that the probability of a random variable being greater than .5 standard deviations from the mean is .3085. Hence, 1,000 units is about the same as one-half standard deviations. So, 2,000 units is about 1 standard deviation.

FIGURE 28-4

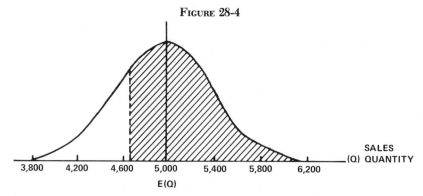

The probability distribution of Figure 28-4 can be superimposed on the profit portion of the traditional C-V-P; this is done in Figure 28-5. The values for price, fixed costs, and variable costs are presumed to be known with certainty. Expected profit is given by:

$$E(Z) = E(Q)(P\text{-}V) - F = \$450,000,$$

where

$$E(Z) = \text{Expected Profit}$$

$$E(Q) = \text{Expected Sales}$$

$$P = \text{Price}$$

$$V = \text{Variable Cost}$$

$$F = \text{Fixed Cost.}$$

FIGURE 28-5

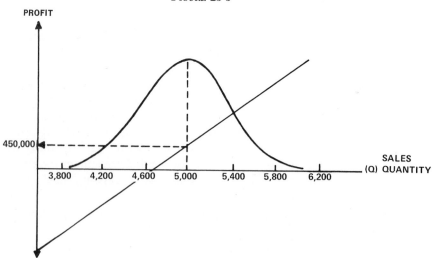

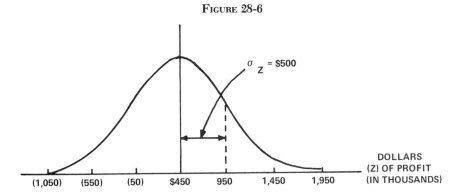

FIGURE 28-6

The standard deviation of the profit (σ_Z) is:
$$\sigma_Z = \sigma_Q \times \$1,250 \text{ contribution per unit}^{\ *}$$

$$= \ 400 \text{ units} \times \$1,250 = \$500,000.$$

Since profits are directly related to the volume of sales and since it is the level of profits which is often the concern of management, it may be desirable to separate the information in Figure 28-5 which relates to profit. Figure 28-6 is a graphical illustration of the relationship between profit level and the probability distribution of the profit level. A number of important relationships can now be obtained in probabilistic terms. Since the probability distribution of sales quantity is normal with a mean of 5,000 units and a standard deviation of 400 units, the probability distribution of profits will also be normal with a mean, as shown earlier, of \$450,000 and a standard deviation of \$500,000.

Using the probability distribution shown in Figure 28-6, the following probabilities can be calculated (using Table 28-4).

1. The probability of at least breaking even. This is the probability of profits being greater than zero and can be calculated by summing the area under the distribution to the right of zero profits. This probability can be calculated as 1—(the probability of profits being less than zero). Since the distribution is symmetric, Table 28-4 can be used to read left tail as well as right tail probabilities. Zero profits fall .9 standard deviations to the left of the mean
$$\left(\text{i.e., } \frac{\$450,000 - 0}{\$500,000} = .9 \right).$$
Hence, the probability of profits being less than zero is:
$$P \text{ (Profits} < .9\,\sigma \text{ from the mean)} = .184.$$
Therefore,
$$P \text{ (Profits} > 0) = 1 - .184 = .816.$$

---

*Editors' note: \$3,000 selling price per unit—\$1,750 variable cost per unit = \$1,250 contribution per unit.

2. The probability of profits being greater than $200,000.
   P (Profits > $200,000)

$$= 1 - P\left(\text{Profits} < \frac{450{,}000 - 200{,}000}{500{,}000} \, \sigma \right.$$

$$\left. \text{from the mean}\right)$$

$$= 1 - P \ (\text{Profits} < .5\,\sigma \ \text{from the mean})$$

$$= 1 - .3085 = .692.$$

3. The probability of the loss being greater than $300,000.
   P (Loss > $300,000)

$$= P\left(\text{Loss} > \frac{450{,}000 - (-300{,}000)}{500{,}000},\right.$$

$$\left. \text{or } 1.5\,\sigma \ \text{from the mean}\right).$$

$$P = .067.$$

The question of how the above information can be used now arises. The manager, in choosing between this product and other products or other lines of activity, can probably improve his decision by considering the risk involved. He knows that the breakeven sales level is at 4,640 units. He knows that the expected sales are 5,000 units, which would yield a profit of $450,000. Surely, he would benefit from knowing that:

1. The probability of at least reaching breakeven sales is .816,
2. The probability of making at least $200,000 profit is .692,
3. The probability of making at least $450,000 profit is .50,
4. The probability of incurring losses, i.e., not achieving the break-even sales volume, is (1—.816=.184),
5. The probability of incurring a $300,000 or greater loss is .067,

etc.

If the manager is comparing this product with other products, probability analysis combined with C-V-P allows a comparison of the risk involved in each product, as well as a comparison of relative breakeven points and expected profits. Given the firm's attitude toward and willingness to assume risk (of losses as well as high profits), the decision of choosing among alternatives should be facilitated by the above analysis.

SEVERAL RELEVANT FACTORS PROBABILISTIC

It is evident from the above discussion that profit, Z, is a function of the quantity of sales in units (Q), the unit selling price (P), the fixed cost (F), and the variable cost (V). Up to this point P, F, and V were considered only as given constants, so that profit was variable only as a function of changes in sales quantity. In the following discussion, P, F, and V will be treated in a manner similar to Q, i.e., as random variables whose probability distribution is known. Continuing the example from the preceding section, let

Variable	Expectation (Mean)	Standard Deviation
Sales Quantity (Q)	$E(Q') = 5{,}000$ units	$\sigma_{Q'} = 400$ units
Selling Price (P)	$E(P') = \$3{,}000^2$	$\sigma_{P'} = \$50^2$
Fixed Costs (F)	$E(F') = \$5{,}800{,}000^2$	$\sigma_{F'} = \$100{,}000^2$
Variable Costs (V)	$E(V') = \$1{,}750^2$	$\sigma_{V'} = \$75^2$

For purposes of illustration, the random variables will be assumed to be independent, so that no correlation exists between events of the different random variables.[3] In this case, the expected profit $E(Z')$ and the related standard deviation $\sigma_{Z'}$ can be calculated as follows:

$$E(Z') = E(Q') \left[E(P') - E(V') \right] - E(F')$$
$$= \$450{,}000.$$
$$\sigma_{Z'}{}^4 = \$681{,}500.$$

Note that when factors other than sales are treated as random variables, the expected profit is still $450,000 as in the previous cases. However, the profit's risk as measured by the standard deviation is increased from $500,000 to $681,500. The reason for this is that the variability in all of the components (i.e., sales price, cost, etc.) will add to the variability in the profit. Is this change in the standard deviation significant? The significance of the change is a value judgment based on a comparison of various probabilistic measures and on the firm's attitude toward risk. Using a normal distribution, Table 28-5 compares expected profits, standard deviations of profits, and select probabilistic measures for three hypothetical products.

In all three situations, the proposed products have the same breakeven quantity—4,640 units. The first case is the first example discussed where sales quantity is the only random variable. The second case is the one just discussed; that is, all factors are probabilistic. In the third case, the assumed product has the same expected values for selling price, variable cost, fixed cost, and sales volume, but the standard deviations on each of these random variables have been increased to $\sigma_{Q''} = 600$ (instead of 400 units);

---

[2]The mean and standard deviation for P, F, and V can be established by using the same method described earlier. That is, the sales manager may estimate a mean selling price of $3,000 per unit, and, given the above information, he should feel that there is roughly a two-thirds probability that the actual sales price per unit will be within $50 of this mean estimate.

[3]This assumption is made to facilitate computation in the example. Where correlation among variables is present, the computational procedure must take into account the values of the respective covariances.

[4]For the case of independent variables given here, $\sigma_{Z'}$ is the solution value in the equation:

$$\sigma_Z = \sqrt{\left[\sigma_Q{}^2 (\sigma_P{}^2 + \sigma_V{}^2) + E(Q')^2 (\sigma_V{}^2 + \sigma_V{}^2) \right.}$$
$$\left. + \left[E(P') - E(V') \right]^2 \sigma_Q{}^2 + \sigma_F{}^2 \right]$$

TABLE 28-5
COMPARISON OF EXPECTED PROFITS, STANDARD DEVIATIONS OF PROFITS,
AND SELECT PROBABILISTIC MEASURES°

	Products		
	(1)	(2)	(3)
Expected profit	$450,000	$450,000	$ 450,000
Standard deviation of profit	$500,000	$681,500	$1,253,000
The probability of:			
(a) at least breaking even	.816	.745	.641
(b) profit at least + $250,000	.655	.615	.564
(c) profit at least + $600,000	.382	.413	.456
(d) loss greater than $300,000	.067	.136	.274

°Note: The above probabilities, in some cases, cannot be read from Table 28-4. However, all probabilities come from a more complete version of Table 28-4.

$\sigma_{P''}$= $125 (instead of $50); $\sigma_{F''}$= $200,000 (instead of $100,000); and $\sigma_{V''}$= $150 (instead of $75).

Table 28-5 shows the relative "risk" involved in the three new products which have been proposed. The chances of at least breaking even are greatest with product 1. However, even though the standard deviation of the profit on product 3 is over twice that of product 1, the probability of breaking even on product 3 is only .17 lower than product 1. Likewise, the probability of earning at least $250,000 profit is higher for product 1 (which has the lowest σ) than for the other two products.

However, note that the probability of earning profits above the expected value of $450,000 (for each product) is *greater* for products 2 and 3 than for 1. If the firm is willing to assume some risk, the chances of high profits are improved with product 3, rather than with 2 and 1. To offset this, however, the chance of loss is also greatest with product 3. This is to be expected, since product 3, has the highest standard deviation (variability) as far as profit is concerned.

The best alternative cannot be chosen without some statement of the firm's attitude toward risk. However, given a certain attitude, the proper choice should be facilitated by using probability information of the type given in Table 28-5. As an example, suppose that the firm's position is such that any loss at all may have an adverse effect on its ability to stay in business. Some probability criteria can, perhaps, be established in order to screen proposals for new products. If, for example, the top management feels that any project which is acceptable must have no greater than a .30 probability of incurring a loss, then projects 1 or 2 would be acceptable, but project 3 would not.

On the other hand, the firm's attitude toward risk may be such that the possibility of high profit is attractive, provided the probability of losses can be reasonably controlled. In this case, it may be possible to set a range within which acceptable projects must fall. For example, suppose that the firm is willing to accept projects where the probability of profits being greater than $600,000 is at least .40, provided that the probability of a loss being greater than $300,000 does not exceed .15. In this case, project 2 would be acceptable, but project 3 would not . Given statements of attitude toward risk of this nature, it seems that a probability dimension added to C-V-P analysis would be useful.

SUMMARY AND CONCLUSION

In many cases, the choice among alternatives is facilitated greatly by C-V-P analysis. However, traditional C-V-P analysis does not take account of the relative risk of various alternatives. The interaction of costs, selling prices, and volume are important in summarizing the effect of various alternatives on the profits of the firm. The techniques discussed in this paper preserve the traditional analysis but also add another dimension—that is, risk is brought in as another important decision factor. The statement of probabilities with respect to various levels of profits and losses for each alternative should aid the decision maker once his attitude toward risk has been defined.

PART IX. FINANCIAL IMPACT OF ACCOUNTING PRACTICES, PRINCIPLES, AND DISCLOSURE

One of the major problems in a free enterprise system is the lack of adequate, accurate, and timely disclosure of financial information flowing from the corporate management to the investing public. Investors can make intelligent and independent decisions only if they have reasonably full and fair information about the corporation in which they want to invest. Consequently, the less adequate, accurate, and timely information available to the investing world, the less the market price will be representative of the security's fair or intrinsic value, and the greater will be the inefficient allocation of resources and the opportunity for mismanagement. This section deals with several aspects of corporate financial disclosure which are of great importance to the financial executive as well as to the investing public.

The first paper, by Harold Burson, provides very useful guidelines for corporate financial disclosure. Observations resulting from recent court decisions and the SEC pronouncement on matters affecting disclosure are reviewed. Cases involving Texas Gulf Sulphur and Merrill Lynch, Pierce, Fenner and Smith are discussed.

There has been no change in the philosophy of accurate and timely disclosure of appropriate corporate news, but corporate executives are no longer sure of the ground rules. Consequently, they tend to adopt a safe approach of not disclosing anything to anyone except what is legally required. Such an approach, according to Burson, is neither safe nor sound from a business or investor relations point of view. Burson further speaks out positively for the public interest which brought about timely disclosure in the first place. A major aspect of the public interest relates to the corporate executive's basic responsibility to present and prospective stockholders. Most corporate executives would agree that a consistent flow of company news is both desirable and necessary in the present-day world.

The author believes that more information is not the same as greater disclosure; more information frequently leads to confusion. The corporate executive should provide timely and significant information to the investing public. However, the definition of "significant" remains a matter of individual judgment. According to guidelines provided and discussed by Burson, any information is significant if investors' decisions could be affected by the news. A corporation has an obligation to see that the insiders refrain from taking advantage of the information for purposes of personal gain.

Burson suggests that only a minute percentage of the entire investing public have the capability of deciding whether to buy, sell, or hold a corporate security. The security analyst is the one who has some influence on the investment decisions of millions of investors, and, therefore, he plays an important role in the allocation of resources within the economy. Security analysts are classified in two groups. One group represents the retail brokerage firm, and the other group is employed directly by institutional investors. Guidelines and alternative methods for communicating with security analysts are discussed.

The article from *Forbes* deals with the growing credibility gap with respect to corporate earnings reports. The CPA certification on financial reports has been the "Good Housekeeping Seal" of fiscal approval. However, the fact that there are more than 50 major lawsuits pending against the "Big Eight" public accounting firms, which handle about 80 percent of the U.S. auditing business of listed companies, causes alarm as to the worth of such certification. The issue is not the integrity of the accountants but accounting itself. The article provides realistic illustrations of the impact of generally acceptable alternative accounting procedures on earnings per share.

Shrewd corporate managements can push the flexible accounting principles to the breaking point in order to keep earnings and the price of their stocks as high as possible. Although there are many instances in which CPA's have disagreed with management, in the close day-to-day association of auditor and client there is bound to be some give and take, especially since the accounting rules permit it.

The accountants recognize the problem and are working on it, but they are the men in the middle. They concede that accounting has many deficiencies. The Accounting Principles Board of the American Institute of Certified Public Accountants has recommended several new uniform practices and others are currently under consideration, but the progress is very slow.

The article by Professor Robert K. Mautz deals with financial reporting by conglomerate companies. The article summarizes the findings and recommendations of a study by the Research Foundation of the Financial Executives Institute. The objective of the study was to determine the usefulness, practicability, and desirability of publishing corporate operating results on a more detailed basis than company totals. Based on separate questionnaires—answered by (1) financial analysts and investment advisors and by (2) corporate executives—the study found that management sees a number of hazards in disclosing financial data by divisions or products.

In the last part of his article, Professor Mautz presents five recommendations for reporting by conglomerate companies. First, companies which are unitary in nature should not be expected to fractionalize themselves for reporting purposes. Second, companies which to a material degree have activity in more than one broadly defined industry should meet the extended disclosure requirements. Third, management, because of its familiarity with company structure, is in the most informed position to separate the company into realistic components for reporting purposes. Fourth, disclosures recommended may be included in parts of the annual report other than the formal financial statements at the discretion of management. Last, the complexities of reporting diversified activities are so great that recommendations should be applied with judgment and flexibility by all concerned. Within this framework, diversified companies should report sales and the relative contribution to profits of each major broad industry group.

The area of disclosure requires many judgmental determinations. Therefore, guidelines covering substance will always be difficult to implement. The financial executive will be torn between what is safe and what is best for the company and its stockholders. If the initiative for the fuller disclosure does not come from the corporate management and the accounting profession, it will come from regulatory agencies such as the SEC.

29. GUIDELINES FOR FINANCIAL DISCLOSURE*

HAROLD BURSON †

The opinion of the U.S. Circuit Court of Appeals in the case brought by the Securities and Exchange Commission against Texas Gulf Sulphur has had a significant effect on corporate management's attitude toward the disclosure of corporate news.

Up to that point—the opinion was handed down August 14, 1968—most of the listed and/or larger corporations were making a conscious effort to provide a flow of substantive information. Their reasons, of course, were varied. And some were more active in this area than others. But, in general, management was committed to free and easy disclosure. The motivation was: "It's good for the business and good for the stockholder."

SAY NOTHING

Since the Texas Gulf Sulphur opinion, however, the policy for many has changed to: "Say nothing to nobody."

This policy looked even better to management two weeks after the Gulf Sulphur opinion when the SEC charged Merrill Lynch, Pierce, Fenner & Smith with improper use of corporate information to favor a group of large investors, allegedly at the expense of smaller ones.

NEED FOR GROUND RULES

The SEC has emphasized that recent court cases "should not be interpreted as inhibiting companies from talking to analysts about business trends, industry developments, capital spending, new products, or other matters." Yet even the more venturesome corporate managers have been less than eager to pursue contacts with the press and particularly with security analysts. Some of them, in the words of one analyst, have "clammed up completely."

There has been no change in the principle of full as well as timely release of appropriate corporate news. But corporate executives are no longer sure of the ground rules. They tend to adopt what they think is a "safe" approach: "If I don't say anything I can't get into trouble; therefore, I won't say anything." The fact is, this approach is neither safe (there are bound to be information leaks) nor sound from a business or investor-relations point of view.

One consequence of this attitude would be a breakdown, or at least a disruption, in communications. Obviously this could become an unsettling

---

*From *Financial Executive* (November, 1968), pp. 21-32. Reprinted by permission.
†President of Burson Marsteller Associates; director and executive committee member of Marsteller, Inc.; and President of Marsteller International S.A., New York City.

factor in the marketplace. And this result is certainly not in the best interests of the investing public, shareholders, or the corporations themselves.

RESPONSIBILITY TO STOCKHOLDERS

It is time, therefore, to speak out positively for the investor—the public interest which brought about timely disclosure in the first place.

The channels of communication for timely disclosure are well established. The corporate officer, speaking for his company, is the source of basic data. He transmits it to either a security analyst or a news writer who, in turn, transmits it to a broader audience that encompasses the general investing public.

The legal problems, up to this point, have not been in the simple communication or transmission of the news, no matter how sensitive. The problems have occurred when parties to the news transmission process are said to have used the news improperly.

A major aspect of the public interest relates to the corporate executive's basic responsibility to stockholders and prospective stockholders. He is obliged to provide sufficient and proper data on which realistic investment decisions can be made. In this way, he helps to foster a broad and active market for the company's securities at fair price levels.

The recognition and assumption of this responsibility to the stockholder —present and future—is what financial public relations is all about. It is the basic charter for the free flow of "full and timely disclosure" *over and above* the legal requirements of the SEC or the exchanges. It is first-line evidence of the corporation's good faith with the investing public—to do more than required by law or regulation to keep the public informed of a company's operations, good or bad.

Most corporate officers would agree that a consistent flow of company news is both desirable and necessary. They've come a long way since "the public be damned" was uttered in response to a reporter's inquiry in 1879. Their thinking has changed, too, since their predecessors way back in the 1930s condemned securities legislation calling for disclosure that by today's standards seems almost primitive. The 1968 corporate chief executive not only wants to talk about his company, he enjoys it.

However, it is not unusual today for some corporate officer to say no to every opportunity to meet with financial reporters or security analysts. They're actually afraid that talking will get them or their companies into trouble. Ironically the heads of companies least likely to get into trouble are among the most cautious.

SENSITIVE INDUSTRIES

It should be recognized that some companies and some industries are more sensitive than others to the disclosure of information. Their securities, therefore, are likely to respond in a more direct manner to the release of information. Such companies include those in the extractive industries (where a major discovery may have significant influence on the company's future), the electronics industry, and the high technology or other "hot" issue industries. It would seem that the stable, mature industrial company listed on a major exchange is not nearly as sensitive to market gyrations.

Perspective is called for as well in evaluating the function of the security analyst. (It appears that he, rather than the news reporter, is "most feared" as a result of recent events.)

The security analyst's function is, in some ways, comparable to that of a drama or movie critic. But one big difference (overlooking the dollars) is that while the playgoer knows soon after buying his ticket whether the critic's evaluation is sound, the investor does not. Not only do stocks have less visceral appeal, their performance must be judged over a longer term.

QUANTITY vs. QUALITY

Of the entire investing public, only a minute percentage have the capability of deciding whether to invest in one company (or even one industry) over another. Nor is the potential stockholder likely to get all the information he needs from an annual report, which may be factual but is not necessarily without bias. The comment has been made that the indiscriminate distribution of prospectuses to potential investors has done more to confuse the average investor than any other single SEC requirement. In fact, even the sophisticated (as opposed to the professional) investor is likely to be incapable of making an independent evaluation of an underwriting without the assistance of a competent analyst. More information is not the same as greater disclosure; more information frequently leads to confusion. The function of the security analyst is to put quantities of information in perspective for the investor.

It would, therefore, be of some value to recognize the positive function of the security analyst and his role vis-à-vis the public interest. True, the security analyst is in a position to benefit (or detract from) a company's objectives depending on his specific analysis and recommendations. But, in either case, he very likely is representing the public interest that is the basis of long-term investor confidence.

Given the present method of operation in the securities marketplace, the investment function requires a security analyst or his equivalent—an informed professional critic—motivated to gather as much information about a company as he can and able to make sense of it. If the function had not evolved (its evolution as a function parallels the growth in broadly based stock ownership), it would have to be invented now. It's also true that if the function is worthwhile, if it performs a service to the investor—large or small—it merits support. It must have factual input. And this input can originate only with corporate management.

Establishing the fact that the security analyst function is vital to the public interest is simple when compared to trying to define "news which might bear on the thinking of the investor," or any other definition of significant or material information. Some kinds of news are *prima facie* in their significance: changes in sales and earnings forecasts, dividend changes, labor unrest, technological breakthroughs, and major discoveries in the extractive industries. From the standpoint of the guidelines (SEC and major stock exchanges), this kind of news item is easy to deal with. All that is required is to broadcast the news immediately and impartially on the widest possible basis.

DEFINING "SIGNIFICANT"

The definition of "significant" or "material" remains, however, a matter of individual judgment by the corporate officer. The guidelines say it is material information if investment decisions could be affected by the news. This is a subtlety that can hardly be pinpointed more precisely by guidelines or other legislative compulsion. It is a judgment governed largely by the good faith of corporate management to keep the investing community informed.

But the mechanical rules on dissemination are clear enough: prompt distribution to Dow Jones, the major press associations, to one or more major newspapers, etc., and to the Stock List Department of the New York Stock Exchange, where applicable. Much has been made of the possibility that the news may never appear in print and that no one can force Dow Jones or any other independent publication to carry a news item either immediately or ever. It also has been pointed out that the news goes through many hands between the originator and the receiver. Presumably, it might be used improperly (one of the intermediaries may buy or sell on the basis of what is still regarded as inside information). But these are situations that cloud the true issue.

A company has two basic obligations. The first is to disseminate the news according to stated guidelines. The second is to see that its employees (legal insiders and others not clearly defined by the statutes) refrain from taking advantage of the information for purposes of personal gain. If "outside" insiders act improperly, the corporation is not the liable party (assuming it has lived up to its obligations). The liable parties are those who have acted in an improper manner.

When is disclosure accomplished? The SEC has said that disclosure occurs when the story is published, not when it is released. In more recent pronouncements, the thought has been introduced that disclosure has not been accomplished until some time after publication, when the investing community has had time to digest or evaluate the news. But what is publication? Is it appearance on the Dow Jones broad tape, or must it be circulated by a newspaper? Or is it a market letter from a retail brokerage firm? This admittedly is a grey area, although up to now the question itself has not been material to specific actions.

It's simple enough for the corporate executive to order a news release issued when he makes a forecast for a security analyst. (Although forecasting appears to be diminishing, there's nothing in the guidelines that discourages this practice.) But there are many reasons why some subjects that could be significant or material may not lend themselves to news releases. One is that the significance may be more readily appreciated by the analyst than by the specific corporate executive.

For example, let us assume that an analyst is told that the widget market has been soft for two months but that the executive believes it is only a temporary lull. The analyst has already learned that two competitors have had similar results going back four months or more. Further, one large widget user has intimated he may be switching to a better material. The analyst returns to his office and recommends that two funds unload their widget stock, resulting in a price drop of 10 percent or more. Question: Was there any wrongdoing? And, if so, by whom?

ANALYSTS vs. REPORTERS

It is not coincidental that this article deals mainly with security analysts and makes only passing reference to financial reporters representing newspapers or magazines. This is not to deny the importance of these news disseminators or to minimize their service to the investing community. Their function, however, is not only better defined but also better understood by the corporate executive. Where the reporter has the single purpose of disseminating news, the security analyst has the overlapping functions of disseminating news and stimulating trading. The security analyst, by virtue of the organizational structure of which he is a part, can, in fact, influence the price of a security through buys or sells; the newspaperman cannot.

TWO KINDS OF ANALYST

Generally speaking, security analysts fall into two broad categories—although to consider the two principal categories as totally separate is an oversimplification. In one instance, the security analyst represents a retail brokerage firm whose customers are large and small investors across the United States and perhaps abroad. These customers are both individuals and institutions. The analyst's employers generally do not trade for their own accounts. They make a recommendation to an individual or an institution; the individual or institution makes an arm's length decision (the arm is longer in some cases than in others) to buy, sell, or hold.

In the other instance, the security analyst is employed directly by an institution—a bank trust department, a pension fund, a mutual fund, an insurance company. He is a member of the management team that makes the buy-or-sell decision for its own account. He is in a position to act directly on information he receives. There is no incentive for him to broadcast his findings; in fact, it may be detrimental to his own interests to do so.

The security analyst representing the retail brokerage firm may be regarded as one of the "media" through which news is disseminated. But the institutional analyst is in a somewhat different position. He may be an actual or potential shareholder. The best guide for dealing with both is to treat them like any shareholder who might call. They should be given no more information than anyone else and certainly nothing of a confidential nature. The relationship between corporate management and the security analyst has taken one of three forms:

1. The man-to-man interview, wherein a security analyst speaks to one or more corporate officers in a single company;
2. An address to one of the 41 security analyst societies in major cities across the U.S. or to one of the many splinter groups that cover a single industry or segment of the economy;
3. A meeting with a handpicked group of analysts — ranging in size from perhaps half a dozen up to 50 — all thought to have a special interest in a company or vice versa.

EXCHANGING CONFIDENCES

The Man-to-Man Interview

Almost every company develops a coterie of security analysts who follow its stock. The number—ranging from half a dozen up to 50 or so—depends largely on the the company itself, its field of business, and its size. These are the security analysts who know a company or an industry intimately. They are men (and women) who become first-name friends with the upper echelon of a company's management. Frequently they know as much about a company (and particularly its competition) as all except the best informed corporate officers. Their friendships within a company mature over a period of years. Confidences are shared on both sides of the desk. It is only natural to believe that these security analysts learn more about a company than other analysts and certainly more than the average investor. And much of what they know about a company is a result of an accumulation of data from many sources rather than from a specific pronouncement in a single meeting with a corporate officer.

The free and easy relationship between corporate executive and security analyst has been the first casualty of the indecision resulting from the Texas Gulf and Merrill Lynch cases. Company presidents are having to tell long-time friends not only that they will no longer share industry confidences with them but, more dramatically, that they cannot talk to them at all.

Going to this extreme, the company president is overreacting. No one has said he cannot talk with security analysts. Chances are he has never said anything in previous meetings that he would not want to say in a future meeting. The only new caution is that a press release should be issued if significant information is disclosed for the first time. To facilitate this, the corporate officer might prepare a subject agenda to guide his responses. If significant new disclosures are made, a press release is in order. Otherwise the interview should move along accustomed lines.

Security Analyst Society Presentation

Corporate officers do not seem to be challenging the major security analyst society presentations. These are open to a wide range of analysts and usually to the press as well. Disclosure is on an impartial basis. Some local societies specify that news releases quoting the text of the speaker be held back until the program begins. The New York Society, for example, recently moved up its release time from 2:00 to 1:00 o'clock. As soon as the speaker begins, the full text may be made available to the press. The Boston Society recently decided to invite the press to its meetings for the first time after a corporate executive stated he would not speak before an analysts' group that banned the press.

At these meetings, the corporation rather than the analyst society is responsible for what is said. It seems reasonable, therefore, for the company to operate under its own ground rules. It should insist on having the press present and should be prepared to release the text of the speech at an appropriate time. If a local society specifically excludes the press, the company should accept an invitation to appear only if it can release the text of its presentation to the press simultaneously.

SPECIALIZED GROUPS

Special consideration should be given to some of the "splinter" or specialized groups that have formed in various localities. The composition and admission requirements of these groups vary. Some are "closed," with membership by invitation only. Others admit nonmember analysts and the press to their meetings. It is possible that the closed groups could be regarded as "privileged" and that disclosure to them is not full and impartial.

From a practical standpoint, the company cannot overlook the specialized group as an outlet for its message. Its membership usually brings to such meetings a greater in-depth knowledge of a company and its industry than can be found at a full society meeting. Questioning is more specific and in better perspective. If the company's objective is to gain the broadest understanding from the investing community, the meeting of the specialized group of analysts is an important vehicle.

The Small Select Security Analyst Meeting

In recent years, corporate managements have learned to identify those analysts most interested in their companies or industries. They also have identified the likely major investors, i.e., the institutions with large purchasing power (and, conversely, selling power, too). It is understandable that managements wish to bring together those security analysts who have more than a passing interest in a particular company or industry. The objective is no longer simply to convey special or even updated information. Such a meeting provides an occasion for analysts to "know management better" or observe for themselves the company's "management in depth."

At a time when much is made of judging companies on management rather than on performance over a short-term period, the small informal meeting is an understandable activity. But the composition of the group can present problems. There are two possibilities. One is the group consisting of representatives of both broadly based brokerage firms and large institutional investors; the other is the group composed entirely of large institutional investors, sometimes brought together under the auspices of a brokerage firm serving the institutional market. Generally such gatherings have excluded the press (and the press has sometimes expressed its dismay at the omission). In light of recent commentary by the courts, the SEC, and others, it would seem prudent to make such gatherings broad enough to include the large retail brokerage firms and the press, as well as major institutional investors.

There seems little doubt that corporate executives are uncertain about how they should handle their relations with security analysts. They have turned to their legal staffs and to their public relations advisers for guidance. The posture of the legal staffs has understandably been one of "go slow until the law is spelled out." The public relations counsels generally have urged a less inhibited approach: meet with the analyst but issue a news release immediately on significant new disclosures.

There have been reports of security analysts arriving for an appointment with a chief executive officer (sometimes a friend of many years' standing) only to find themselves flanked by a lawyer on one side and a public relations man on the other. This kind of "protection" is hardly conducive to the kind of easy give-and-take that is most worthwhile to corporate officer and security analyst alike.

One point not denied by the corporate executive who restricts his meetings with analysts is that the corporation itself has much to gain from the interest of the security analyst. Nor does he deny the legitimacy of the analyst's search for information. But he seems to have overlooked the interest of the public—that amorphous "average investor" who is the ultimate recipient of the fallout from these meetings.

REAFFIRMING DISCLOSURE

Only through contacts with security analysts seriously interested in his company or industry can the corporate chief executive fulfill his responsibility to stockholders to see that there is a ready market at a fair price. Without disclosure on a continuing basis—and in depth—this objective is difficult to attain.

The New York Stock Exchange has reported that more than 26 million

Americans own securities. The problem—and it is not a simple one—is not to deprive those 26 million of what they should rightfully have because of selfish actions by limited groups or individuals. The objective is not to ferment further an atmosphere in which disclosure already has been materially reduced but to reaffirm the principle of full and timely disclosure and to provide comprehensible guidelines. This, it seems to me, is the job of the SEC and the major stock exchanges in fulfilling a basic responsibility to the investing community, which today is a substantial segment of our total population.

BURSON-MARSTELLER RELEASE TO CORPORATE CLIENTS . . .

How to Achieve Successful Relationships with the Financial Community

WHY DISCLOSURE? The easy answer is to say the law requires certain disclosure and so do the major exchanges. But every chief executive has an added obligation to stockholders. In protecting their interest, he is obliged to provide sufficient corporate and financial data on which the investing public can base intelligent decisions. In this way he helps foster a broad and active market for the company's securities at fair price levels.

"FULL AND TIMELY" DISCLOSURE. As a principle of the SEC and the major exchanges, full and timely disclosure still stands. Nothing in the recent pronouncements, opinions, and discussions—official or unofficial—should be construed to mean that the SEC or the major exchanges are seeking to inhibit the flow of information on which the public can make investment decisions. The present requirement, it would appear, is for public companies to disclose more rather than less and to do so on an impartial and nondiscriminatory basis.

WHAT MUST BE DISCLOSED? As a general rule, a company must disclose anything that would materially affect an investment decision. Legislation and rules of the major exchanges identify certain kinds of financial data that must be disclosed. The problem is not in this area. The disclosure problem, if any, involves news that requires a judgment factor in determining whether it might affect stock prices or trading.

A company can release any news it wants to release provided it is factually based. The only prohibition is against news that is false or misleading.

Conversely, a company does not have to release news that it needs to keep confidential for sound business reasons, competitive or otherwise. As long as such news remains "secret," there is no problem. But once the news leaks, the company is required to make full public disclosure (even though wide knowledge of the news may be disadvantageous to a particular action —as in the case of a prospective merger). The guideline on disclosing this kind of news is its likely influence on stock prices or trading, and this is a gray area indeed.

INSIDERS ARE CRITICAL. Each instance cited thus far by the SEC has involved actions based on information in the hands of parties the SEC has chosen to regard as insiders (even though not necessarily so defined by legislation). The problem, therefore, is to avoid creating insiders, especially insiders over whom the corporation can exercise no control (i.e., newsmen and security analysts). The safe course may very well be to avoid any situation likely to create an "outside" insider. But it is not very practical to believe such a policy can or should be followed, even temporarily. The approach more likely to contribute to overall corporate objectives is prompt and broad disclosure of any material data provided to an individual or a small group of individuals. Generally, trouble has resulted not from the act of releasing information but from what the SEC has charged to be the improper use of information by individuals with preferential access to that information. In the case of Texas Gulf, the additional charge was made that the information released was false and misleading.

WHAT CONSTITUTES PUBLIC DISCLOSURE? The *Company Manual* of the New York Stock Exchange prescribes a generally accepted method for disseminating important news. Although the SEC has raised questions on when disclosure is actually accomplished, these questions are in the context of when insiders can trade safely in their own stock. For general purposes, it seems to us that public disclosure occurs after material has appeared on the Dow Jones wire, or has been made available to a significant number of retail brokerage firms, or has appeared in print in a publication with substantial circulation. The requirement also may be satisfied by a letter to all stockholders. This is a general assumption; it does not cover trading activities by insiders.

TIMING. All important corporate news must be released on an "immediate" basis. However, there is no way in which a corporation can control the timing by which its news will be carried by the Dow Jones and other news services.

When news of major significance is to be released, the soundest procedure is for the company to call the stock list department of the exchange on which it is listed to alert them that important news is about to be released. The exchange can then consider the advisability of stopping trading in the company's stock while the news is being disseminated. The company itself may, in some instances, be well advised to request the exchange to stop trading.

WHO ARE INSIDERS? For all intents and purposes, everyone with significant, confidential information about a company should be regarded as an insider. This certainly includes top or middle management. It should also include the company's legal counsel, public relations counsel, CPA's, and other consultants inside and out.

DEALING WITH OUTSIDERS.   A company normally addresses four principal audiences with news that could affect stock prices and trading: the press, security analysts, stockholders, and employees.

THE PRESS

RELEASE CORPORATE NEWS PROMPTLY. This applies especially to stories on earnings (most listed companies already seem to be handling dividend announcements properly). The approval process should be shortened. The number of people who see earnings before public release should be minimized. Release should not be held up until a report to shareholders can be printed. If it's important for the board to know operating results first, board members should get the information before a scheduled meeting so as to avoid delay in the general distribution.

Other significant corporate news should be treated similarly. This runs the range of major new discoveries—new products or new processes—to acquisitions, unexpected changes in top management, and labor problems. It does not mean that all corporate news must be released on a truly immediate basis—only that which is significant.

RELEASE CORPORATE NEWS BROADLY. Distribution lists should include a broad selection of media reaching the investing public. The fastest available means of transmitting news should be employed. For purposes of corporate news disclosure, the retail brokerage firms should be regarded as publications or a press association. Distribution lists should be tailored to concentrations of stockholders.

INTERVIEWS. There is no restriction against them. But disclosure of news that could affect securities prices should be followed up with a covering press release. The reporter should be told that a release will be made. The interview should not be inhibited by the presence of a lawyer. But if having a representative of the public relations department present has been an established practice (it is in many companies), it should be continued. He should prepare an agenda of subjects to be introduced and try to anticipate questions from the reporter. If new and significant information is included, a release should be ready to go at the end of the interview. This applies particularly if earnings prospects, either revising or confirming a previous estimate, are to be discussed. (No one says earnings shouldn't be forecast, but if they are, two things should be kept in mind: 1. the extreme importance of basing the forecast on "sound business judgment"; and 2. the necessity of releasing the forecast broadly.)

PRESS CONFERENCES. This vehicle for distributing news presents some problems and, in years gone by, has been a troublesome area for corporations. The problem is that staging a press conference requires advance preparation. Guaranteeing a good turnout requires notice (for all except the largest corporations); it also requires advance notice of the subject that will be discussed. Speculation on what will be revealed at a press conference has sometimes been responsible for unusual stock market activity in a company's stock. On those occasions when a company has a major announcement (one that could affect the price of its securities), it should consider releasing the news by the fastest possible means and following up with a press conference to provide any further detail the press may require. Only a small percentage of company press conferences are likely to be affected, since most deal with subjects of little significance to the company as a whole.

Each press conference should be followed with a broadly distributed release as soon as the meeting is concluded.

SECURITY ANALYSTS

INDIVIDUAL MEETINGS.   The cautious corporate officer can easily take the position that the safe course is to grant no interviews with individual security analysts. Such a posture has two principal pitfalls:

1. Sooner or later an analyst asking for an interview will be one of the company's long standing supporters who is difficult to refuse, or he will represent a major stockholder (a fund or a trust department), and neither is likely to be ignored:
2. It may likely be in the company's best interests to maintain the interest of its most avid supporters.

Not to take advantage of such opportunities is to default an important aspect of the communications function.

But to say that the corporate officer should act as he has always acted with security analysts is to be insensitive to changing attitudes on the part of the sec and perhaps the major exchanges. The important difference is that a corporate officer can no longer afford to pass on information to one analyst (even the analyst of a major shareholder) which he is unwilling to disclose to other analysts, the press, shareholders, and the investing public at large.

MEETINGS OF SECURITY ANALYST SOCIETIES. Because of the number of analysts usually present, representing a broad segment of the investment community, and the press, the formal security analyst society presentation is the least sensitive of the communications vehicles involving analysts. Generally speaking, the only restriction is that the corporate officer say nothing that can be construed as false or misleading. Good practice dictates that a press release be issued to coincide with the presentation. It would also seem prudent to distribute the record of the meeting (prepared text plus questions) to all shareholders. The same thinking should apply to organized splinter groups. (The company should insist on the admission of the press.)

INFORMAL MEETINGS OF ANALYSTS IN SMALL GROUPS. This technique has been effective in bringing about greater rapport between management and the investment community. Its use has been growing. It would be a mistake to deprive the corporation and the analyst community of this vehicle because of doubts and fears of acting improperly. Ultimately, it is the shareholder and general investing public that gains most from these exchanges. The principal pitfall to avoid is bringing together a group that could in any way be construed as being discriminatory to other segments of the investment community or to other stockholders. For example, it would not be prudent to call a meeting made up entirely of major stockholders or even major funds and disclose information not available to others. Such meetings should be broadly based with representation from the national retail brokerage firms as well as the press. The issuance of a press release should be accepted practice in connection with such meetings.

MAILINGS TO SECURITY ANALYSTS. The press should be included on the mailing list and the same data be made available to stockholders, either by direct mailing or by notice that such material is available.

STOCKHOLDERS

GENERAL. The stockholder is assumed to be a part of the general investing community entitled to access to the same sources of information as the non-stockholder. However, none of the regulatory bodies prescribes preferential treatment in disclosure to stockholders. In fact, it is inferred that they should not have preferential treatment. But good investor relations calls for providing the stockholder with at least as much information as provided to the general investing community.

MAILINGS. When significant information is furnished to stockholders, it should be made available also to the press and security analysts. If an important announcement is not published by the press or Dow Jones, a mailing to stockholders is required.

EMPLOYEES

Middle and upper management employees should be treated as insiders. It is difficult to make exceptions. (Research department personnel have access to information that may make them insiders.) A reporting system should be established for purchases and sales in company stock, even though not specifically required by existing legislation.

Procedures should be designed to keep company secrets secret. Highly sensitive information should be disseminated on the basis of "need to know." When it becomes apparent that sensitive information is no longer secret, there should be a procedure to effect prompt disclosure to the public.

PRUDENCE AND CAUTION. Many corporate executives are asking how they can protect themselves in the disclosures process. Both legal and public relations counsel are more frequent visitors to the executive suite than ever before. Clearly this is an area where the advice of specialists can be helpful. Calling on knowledgeable counsel for guidance is one of the requisites of avoiding trouble.

Some company presidents are asking lawyers and/or public relations men to accompany them in meetings with individual newsmen or analysts. But this is not necessarily a satisfactory procedure when it impedes the normal discussion interchange. A protective technique that may be in order is to tape record such interviews (always telling the other parties that a tape is being made). The reason is more for reviewing the discussion to determine if significant undisclosed information has been disclosed than for protecting against misquotation. (One financial magazine now tapes all its interviews.)

SUMMARY

The area of disclosure requires many judgmental determinations. Therefore, guidelines covering substance will always be difficult to come by. (Guidelines covering mechanics can be and are more precise.) The corporate executive always will be torn between, What is safe? and, What is best for the company and its stockholders? Nor are all companies alike in their vulnerability, even to news improperly disclosed. In a real sense, the issue becomes intensely personal; its resolution will be at the highest level of the corporate structure. A good starting point to achieving an answer is to "position" the company, to put the company in perspective as a factor in the securities marketplace. Once that is accomplished, a program of specific do's and don'ts may be developed.

30. WHAT <u>ARE</u> EARNINGS?   THE GROWING CREDIBILITY GAP*

For decades the accounting profession basked in the highest kind of public confidence. If they certified an earnings statement, it meant what it said: that the company did so much better—or so much worse—than the year before and so much better or worse than its competitors. The same was true of balance sheets. People tended to believe what they read in annual reports. It was there in hard figures. And figures don't lie. Not CPA-certified ones.

After all, weren't the CPAs independent and impartial?   Hadn't the Securities Act of 1933 set them up as the public's protectors against wrong and misleading financial statements? People bought and sold stocks—and bought companies—on the basis of what the CPAs certified. Theirs was the "Good Housekeeping Seal" of fiscal approval.

Now all at once there are more than 50 major lawsuits pending against the Big Eight[1] public accounting firms, which handle about 80 percent of the U.S. auditing business of listed companies, charging irregularities and negligence in preparing earnings reports and other financial statements. Not the least of these is the suit against Peat, Marwick, Mitchell & Co. in the celebrated Yale Express bankruptcy case. In 1965 it was suddenly discovered that the company's very healthy profits for 1963 and 1964 were in fact losses.

With equal suddenness a barrage of public criticism has landed on the profession for its highly flexible "generally accepted accounting principles," the rules under which earnings figures are determined.   Sophisticated investors and businessmen have long understood that there is more to earnings and assets than meets the eye. Now the ranks of the skeptics are swelling. More and more people are wondering whether some well publicized corporate "turnarounds" are quite as dramatic as the CPA-audited statements say they are.

Perhaps most worrisome of all to the CPAs and to the managements that employ them, the Securities and Exchange Commission has been issuing thinly disguised threats to take unilateral action if the accountants themselves do not quickly tighten up their rules. In response, the Accounting Principles Board, the profession's rule-making body, has finally swung into high gear with a batch of new opinions during the past six months, after years of dragging its heels.

"We have the gun at our back today," says Joseph P. Cummings, a member of the APB and a partner of Peat, Marwick.

---

*Reprinted by permission of *Forbes Magazine* (May 15, 1967), pp. 28 ff.
[1]Arthur Andersen & Co.; Ernst & Ernst; Haskins & Sells; Lybrand, Ross Bros. & Montgomery; Peat, Marwick, Mitchell & Co.; Price Waterhouse & Co.; Touche, Ross, and Co., and Arthur Young & Co.

WHO WAGS WHOM?

Amid all the furor, it has been easy to miss the main point. The accountants' honesty and integrity are not essentially at issue. The overwhelming majority are sincere men whose last thought is to try deliberately to pull the wool over the public's eyes. They are painfully aware that their only stock in trade is a good reputation.

The main issue is accounting itself. And the question that needs to be asked is: Just what *are* earnings, anyway? For it has become clear that there is a considerable gap between what CPAs think earnings ought to be and what the public, the user of earnings reports, thinks they are.

In our complicated, changing world, it is not really possible to distill a whole year's operations of a vast business enterprise into a single, absolute figure. The public, however, doesn't always appreciate this. Thus, the annual net earnings figure tends to have a magical significance—not only for the ordinary investor but for security analysts and even for acquisition-minded managements. It becomes, in effect, what grades are for the student —a measure of excellence or lack of excellence, of progress or lack of progress.

People tend to demand this kind of simplicity, and the single, conveniently packaged net earnings figure has always seemed to fill the bill perfectly. Companies report them frequently—annually, quarterly, and sometimes even monthly—and they carry the blessing of certified public accountants. So it is that reported earnings have become the common denominator of the stock market. On their reliability, billions of investment dollars are wagered.

What people are now beginning to understand is that these earnings figures, as determined under the so-called generally accepted accounting principles, are far from precise. Nor are they exactly comparable with those of other companies. What's more, they never have been. The accountants have never said they were. They have insisted all along, even when they pleaded for their congressional mandate back in 1933, that accounting principles must of necessity be flexible. Since companies can be managed differently, the CPAs reason they should be able to account differently, too. They argue that enough options should be built into accounting so that managements are not straitjacketed by purely accounting considerations in formulating their operating strategies.

In short, today's highly flexible accounting practices have grown up over the years to accommodate the needs of company managements. If this flexibility also happens to help stockholders and others, so much the better. But this, to the accountants, is not the main goal of accounting. "The accounting tail should not wag the management dog," the accountants are fond of saying.

"There can never be one set of inflexible rules in the name of uniformity," contends John W. Queenan, managing partner of Haskins & Sells. "Companies that appear on the surface to be the same may actually operate much differently. One company may use the newest equipment; its competitor may get by with heavy maintenance of old equipment. It should be the job of accounting to reflect these differences in operating conditions."

An oft-cited example to back up the argument for flexibility is that of the company which elects not to include the results of a money-losing subsidiary in its reported earnings. Management is pouring money into the subsidiary, which promises eventually to be highly profitable. But the accountants argue that if management were forced to include it in current earnings, showing a heavy investment with no return, it might decide to forego a very beneficial enterprise.

There is a good logic in the accountants' position. But the trouble is that it ignores the plight of investors who must somehow attempt to evaluate companies on the basis of highly variable information. It tends to ignore, too, the congressional mandate to serve the public under which the accounting profession has prospered. For in actual practice, the approach of maximum management choice has tended to be carried to extremes. Corporate earnings figures have become little more than a composite of a great many accounting estimates and judgments. At worst, this opens possibilities for the baldest of manipulation. At best, it can make seemingly comparable companies report quite uncomparable statements.

Sun Oil, for example, elects to charge off its drilling costs for new wells right away, while competitor Continental Oil capitalizes the costs of successful wells and writes them off gradually. U.S. Steel takes the 7 percent investment tax credit on its capital expenditures into income over a period of years, while Lukens Steel takes all of its tax credits immediately. Litton Industries and other acquisition-minded companies have the option of treating an acquisition as either an outright purchase or a pooling of interests. Delta Air Lines depreciates its planes over ten years, while United Air Lines, at the other end of the spectrum, writes off its 727 jets over as long as 16 years. Douglas Aircraft elects to record some of its aircraft development costs as assets, while competitors may charge similar expenditures against current income.

Industry is shot through with such accounting variations. They are all perfectly acceptable under present accounting rules, and they allow managements the kind of freedom the CPAs believe they ought to have. But the effect on reported earnings can run into millions of dollars. They make it almost impossible, if not dangerous, to compare the performances of companies with their competitors.

FALSE ISSUE?

Conservative accountants, however, insist that the issue of comparability is a false one. Says Herman W. Bevis, head partner at Price Waterhouse & Co., "A single accounting treatment applied to differing facts and circumstances can produce a lack of comparability just as surely as diverse accounting treatments applied to similar facts and circumstances."

What Bevis says may in some cases be true, but it doesn't much help investors make sense of financial statements. And while more CPAs are coming to realize that some concessions must be made for the needs of investors, Bevis' argument is the prevailing one in the profession. The leading dissenter is Chairman Leonard Spacek of Arthur Andersen & Co., an outspoken critic of his own profession. More standpat accountants regard him as a boat-rocker. He argues for more standardization to aid investors. "If you look at the opinions of the Accounting Principles Board, you will rarely ever see the investor's point of view established," he charges. Says another concerned CPA, Jacob S. Seidman, senior partner in the firm of Seidman & Seidman: "Watchdogs can't afford to be accommodating."

But the fact is that businessmen know that, by and large, accountants are accommodating and flexible about "certified" earnings and assets. Chairman Ernest Henderson of Sheraton Corp. puts it bluntly. "My earnings, sir, are what you say they are," he told a *Forbes* reporter not long ago. An upright man, Henderson has never been accused of manipulating earnings; he was merely giving voice to the knowledgeable cynicism many businessmen display when they talk about financial figures which the public regards as sacrosanct—but aren't.

Another hard-bitten old tycoon, a veteran of dozens of acquisitions, says, "When they come to me with a company and say, 'Look at that earnings growth, up X percent every year,' I say to myself, 'And I know why your company is for sale; it's on the brink; you've used up all the credits you had.'"

Says the head of a leading Wall Street investment firm: "You don't have to be in our end of the securities business very long before you realize that what companies call their earnings can be almost anything they want them to be." A partner of one of the Big Eight firms says frankly: "Give me the books of almost any company and within a year's time I can double the earnings."

GUILTY OR NOT GUILTY?

Under the present accounting rules, there is a very fine line between "maximizing" and plain, old fashioned manipulation. Take the well publicized Westec scandal that broke last summer [1966]. When the facts were known, it was quite clear that Westec Corp.'s acquisition-minded management had been pushing the flexible accounting principles to the breaking point in order to keep earnings and the price of its stock as high as possible. Westec took directly into income nonrecurring profits on sales of oil properties; it treated oil production payments sold to an insurance company as current income rather than deferring them until oil was actually produced; it included in its earnings for a given year the profits of companies not acquired until the following year. Just nine months after reporting 1965 earnings of $4.9 million and assets of $56 million, Westec was in bankruptcy, its stock down 33 percent before trading was suspended. In spite of all this, Leonard Spacek points out that Westec had not exceeded the rules. "I just wish they were guilty of something," he said, "but from what I can see they aren't."

The motives are certainly purer on the part of Honeywell Inc.'s highly respectable management, which spaces out the depreciation on its leased computers over longer periods than its competitors in order to show earnings in the best light. The accountants insist on its right to do so, within the bounds of "fairness" and "consistency" with past accounting treatment. But where does this leave the investor who is trying to compare Honeywell's profits against those of other computer makers?

Nor is R.J. Reynolds deliberately trying to mislead investors by valuing its inventories of leaf tobacco by the last-in, first-out method while other major tobacco companies use different methods. It is merely taking what it considers the best advantage of the choices available. The net result in a period of generally rising prices—higher manufacturing costs but lower income taxes—is to make it very difficult for the average investor to compare Reynolds against its competitors.

And what is the average investor to make of the 1966 earnings statement of the vast and venerable Pennsylvania Railroad? Pennsy reported net consolidated earnings of $90.3 million, $6.49 a share. Only in the footnotes, however, did it specify that nearly $10 million, more than 70 cents a share of this, was a capital gain on the exchange of some Norfolk & Western stock that it had owned for many years. In short, more than 10 percent of the year's "earnings" were from an item that more conservative accounting would have set off and identified as extraordinary income. But under the prevailing rules it was allowed to lump the capital gain unnoticed into "dividends, interest, and *other income*." One could hardly accuse the Pennsy of "rigging" its earnings, but the results were clearly misleading.

YOU CAN LOOK IT UP

In these and hundreds of other cases, neither management nor the CPAs are wholly to blame. What is at fault, if fault there be, are accounting rules which, under the guise of affording management legitimate choices, result in distorted earnings figures. In all too many cases the question is not whether a given accounting treatment fits, but whether the companies' accountants can be convinced to accept it.

Toward this end companies and their auditors, too, will go to great lengths to seek out precedents. In many cases it is simply a matter of leafing through the pages of a thick, red book entitled *Accounting Trends & Techniques*, which the American Institute of Certified Public Accountants (AICPA) prepares each year, after combing through hundreds of annual reports. A single precedent, perhaps backed by the threat of the company "to take our auditing business elsewhere," can be enough to make a questionable accounting treatment "generally accepted."

The accountants maintain that they are not the pawns of management. "We had over a hundred cases last year where we had to say 'no' to management," says Richard T. Baker, managing partner of Ernst & Ernst. Even the SEC's Chief Accountant, Andrew Barr, backs them up on this contention. "Believe me," he says, "we see plenty of cases where the accountants have stood up to management. These cases never hit the newspapers." Adds Queenan of Haskins & Sells: "No single client makes up more than a tiny portion of our total billings. We can afford to lose a big client if it comes to that."

ALWAYS ROOM FOR GIVE

But in the close day-to-day association of auditor and client, there is bound to be some give and take, especially since the accounting rules permit it. After all, management hires the auditors in the first place. The accountants work on a daily basis in management's offices, plants, and board rooms. Scores of CPAs each year take jobs with clients, a situation that accounting firms cite as a built-in advantage to their profession in their college recruiting. More and more, CPAs are also being given consulting jobs that extend beyond accounting into marketing, production, and even the hiring and firing of key management personnel.

There is a real question, too, whether a firm *could* afford to lose a prestigious client like Ford Motor or Union Carbide over an accounting dispute that is within the broad boundaries of "generally accepted" accounting practices. In fact, there are cynics who believe the need to keep big clients happy is the true reason why the CPAs have permitted the excessive flexibility of accounting principles to develop.

Sometimes the instances of compromise between management and auditors are not too difficult to spot. A well-known industrial company that is in financial trouble recently made a change in its accounting procedures that resulted in adding several million dollars to earnings. The convenient timing was too obvious to overlook. So was the lack of consistency with the company's past practices, one test of accounting that most CPAs do religiously insist upon. When asked about it, the company's auditors shrugged. "Well, you should have seen all the proposals they trotted out that we didn't approve."

Perhaps the classic case in which the auditors were talked into stretching accounting methods was the Ethyl Corporation sale of nearly five years ago. The implications of this case still worry thoughtful accountants.

Late in 1962 the tiny Albemarle Paper Manufacturing Co. had put together a fancy financial deal to acquire far larger Ethyl from its two joint owners, General Motors and Standard Oil of New Jersey. The deal was virtually the same for both giant sellers: Each owned 50 percent of Ethyl's shares; each had held them for 38 years; each would net about $40 million on the sale. But when Jersey and GM stockholders opened their annual reports a few months later, the deal could not have looked more different.

GM recorded the proceeds as *income* for the year, even before a penny of operating expenses was deducted. All the way down its income statement, to the net earnings figure at the bottom, the subtotals were inflated. Jersey went to the other extreme. It never showed the Ethyl profit on its earnings statement at all, not even under "nonrecurring income" below the net income figure. Instead, it buried its profit on Ethyl back in the "statement of stockholders' equity," a section of an annual report few people bother to read.

The contrast was spectacular. Here were the two largest industrial corporations in the world, with over 2 million stockholders and most of the financial community looking on. Yet each came up with a radically different treatment of earnings from the identical transaction. What's more, the treatments had been duly certified by two of the nation's most respected accounting firms, Haskins & Sells for GM and Price Waterhouse for Jersey.

The accountants have never made any claims that theirs is an exact trade. In fact, until the recent uproar developed, they never said anything at all, and that may have been an even greater sin. By silently hiding behind their congressionally ordained image of independence, they caused, perhaps unintentionally, many people to believe that accounting and earnings figures were something they were not. Admits Walter Hanson, the managing partner of Peat, Marwick, Mitchell: "Quite frankly, we found that it was to our advantage not to destroy people's illusions about us."

But the illusions have been shattered anyway, what with the scandals and the generally increasing air of skepticism. Under the changed circumstances, a continued policy of silence and no comment would only have made things worse. So today, the Big Eight firms are cooperating with the press in a way they never did before. In most cases, they are discussing their problems with reporters and editors in a fairly frank way.

At such meetings the refrain is much the same. The accountants recognize the problem and are working on it, but they are the men in the middle. As one CPA puts it: "We just provide the investor with a diving board. We say, here is management's diving board. It looks good to us, but how you dive is up to you."

Here is where Arthur Andersen's Spacek takes his fellow accountants to task. "My brethren say, just tell the investors what the facts are and let them be on their guard," he says. "I say 'booby trap.' We cannot just present statements to investors and say, 'You ought to be able to find the booby traps.' "

BUILT-IN PROBLEMS

The accountants, though, are not burying their heads in the sand. They concede that accounting has many deficiencies, some of which do not submit to easy remedy. For example, the public demands annual, quarterly, and in some industries even monthly earnings reports. But, the CPAs point out, the operations of most companies simply do not fit into these neat time spans.

While it was writing off heavy development expense for its DC-8 jets in 1960 and 1961, Douglas Aircraft reported miserable earnings even though the company was in relatively good shape. In the three years that followed when most of these expenses had been charged off, the company's reported profits were sharply higher on lower sales. In both periods investors were misled as to Douglas' true health by the necessity of reporting earnings for arbitrary time periods.

Much the same was true at Xerox in the late Fifties. The company was reporting almost no profits at all as it spent heavily to ready its 914 copier for market. No one but those inside Xerox had any hint of the tremendous profit surge that followed the 914's introduction in 1960.

The CPAs also point out that it is impossible to boil down all the efforts of multidivisioned, billion-dollar companies like Textron, FMC Corp., and International Telephone & Telegraph into a single meaningful figure.

They readily concede that adequate procedures to account for inflation have not yet been developed by the profession. A company like Weyerhaeuser carries 2 million acres of timberland on its books at their 1913 value. Certainly that timber is worth a good deal more today, but there are no methods to account for the appreciation. Its certified book value figure is almost meaningless as a result. Also, increases in companies' sales totals over the years surely owe something to price increases, above and beyond increases in the number of product units sold. But, again, there is no way to account for it.

Economists say there should be some way for a company like Texas Gulf Sulphur to account for the value of its famous Timmins mine in Canada, which could eventually net the company $550 million. The accountants hasten to agree. But how, they ask? By introducing even more estimates to the accounting process?

PAINFUL PROGRESS

Even in the most critical area of all, the extreme flexibility of existing procedures, the accountants do not deny that at least some tightening up is in order. "We want flexibility but not undesirable flexibility," says Baker of Ernst & Ernst. With fortuitous timing, the Accounting Principles Board of the AICPA has come up with several new rulings during the past six months. Companies must adhere to these rulings under pain of having their accountants write an "exception" into their certification of the financial statements.

Under new APB rulings, companies no longer have the option, as U.S. Steel has done, of sharply varying their contributions to employee pension funds from year to year and thus giving earnings a tremendous boost.

Under these new rules, companies with majority-owned U.S. subsidiaries that are not consolidated in their income statements must show the full amount of the subsidiaries' earnings rather than just the dividends (if any) they remit. Companies must also disclose more data when they elect to treat an acquisition as a pooling of interests rather than as a purchase. Now, too, nonrecurring income, like that of General Motors in the Ethyl sale, must be reported as such in the earnings statement.

Other rulings are currently in the works. One deals with narrowing the choices oil companies have in writing off their drilling expenses on new wells. Another involves accounting for the value of intangible assets, such as well-known brand names, trademarks, and patents. Certainly Xerox' copier patents, one key to the company's fabulous success, are worth far more than the $44 million of measurable cost assigned to them on the books. Still another future ruling may provide research-oriented companies with definite procedures on accounting for their heavy R & D expenses. Even the question of price-level adjustments is being investigated.

But the progress is discouragingly slow. It can take years of study, review, and seeking outsiders' comments before an APB opinion is actually put in force. Some, like the price-level opinion, may never see the light of day. Inevitably there is compromise. The recent pension fund opinion, which the CPAs understandably hail as a sign of great progress, took three years to produce and then still left companies with the choice of two different accounting treatments.

"We all want more uniformity," explains Haskins & Sells' Queenan, "but the question is *whose* uniformity?"

So, the sudden burst of APB activity is commendable, but the accountants are still begging the question in several important areas. For example, the SEC has been talking for over a year about requiring so-called conglomerate companies to break down their earnings by major product lines. It is basically an accounting problem. Yet it is a group called the Financial Executives Institute, an organization composed mainly of corporate financial officers and Wall Streeters, not practicing accountants, that took the initiative in setting up a study team. The CPAs contend that it is none of their business, that it is a matter for the companies themselves to work out. They also take a pessimistic view of its feasibility, saying, as Peat, Marwick's Walter Hanson does, "that it would involve making even more estimates and judgments, thus compounding the present complaints against earnings reports."

Indications are clear that the SEC will not buy this refusal of conglomerates to break down results. Last month it was reported that by the end of the summer the Commission hopes to amend its rules to require companies issuing new securities to provide earnings breakdowns by major product groups. To the SEC and to the investing public, such information is better than none at all, even if it does involve making more estimates.

Another case where the CPAs have fumbled the ball has been spotlighted recently as Congress wrangles over restoring the 7 percent investment tax credit on new plant and equipment purchases. When the credit was first made law in 1962, the accountants, no doubt under pressure from their clients, were divided over laying down a hard-and-fast rule for handling it. The result: If the tax credit is restored, companies will have the choice of taking all the tax credits right away or spacing them out over the lives of the plant and equipment purchased, even though the tax credit is no different for one company than another. This will provide yet another opportunity to produce widely varying earnings by strictly bookkeeping means.

FOREWARNED IS FOREARMED

Despite the CPAs' good intentions, the APB's recent awakening, and increased pressure from the SEC, the present flexibility of accounting principles seems certain to be around for some time to come.

What, then, can the ordinary investor, who lacks the accounting background to see through distorted earnings reports, do? First, investors should not place so much naive credence in earnings reports. Second, they should at least be aware of the important danger areas.

Merger-happy companies, both buyers and sellers, must be watched with particular care. Few carry their rigging of earnings to the extreme that Westec did, but their policy of seeking acquisitions makes it inevitable that they will attempt to keep their earnings and the price of their stock as high as they can. Stretched-out depreciation is one of the most common techniques. Another is the capitalizing as assets of expenditures for items that might normally be classified as charges against current income, such as product-development costs and start-up costs on new plants. One CPA recalls a small midwestern trucking company that went so far as to capitalize the cost of the tires on its trucks. Another tells of the tiny New England manufacturing concern that was so anxious to impress potential suitors that it capitalized the cost of a new paint job on its plant.

Corporate conglomerates, with their constant acquisitions, are a complex case. Two of today's more active acquisitors are Gulf & Western Industries and White Consolidated Industries. Both know their way around when it comes to accounting. White Consolidated, in acquiring two companies during 1966, paid $8.2 million less than their book value. Of this excess, some $1.3 million was used to write down inventories; another $2.2 million was applied against "various assets, liabilities, and turn-around expenses;" and $600,000 more was taken directly into income. The result of these and other accounting treatments, says one CPA, was to add around $5.5 million to the company's 1966 reported net income of $14.3 million.

When Gulf & Western acquired New Jersey Zinc Co. last year, G&W switched that company's method of accounting exploration and development costs. The result: an increase of $1.6 million in earnings over the years 1965 and 1966.

Gulf & Western uses the pooling-of-interests technique in accounting for acquired companies. Under the so-called purchase method, a buyer can put the acquired company's assets on its books at the purchase price. But under the pooling method, it can elect to put the company on its books at the company's own book value.

The pooling method can benefit reported earnings when the book value is *lower* than the acquisition price; it will produce a lower depreciation base, thus enabling the acquiring company to report lower depreciation expenses and higher profits. The pooling method has become increasingly popular in recent years, having been used by such giant companies as Litton Industries, Textron, Raytheon and RCA.

Acquisition-hungry companies will sometimes come up with complex new kinds of securities whose effects on earnings must be examined. The recent rash of convertible debentures and convertible preferred stocks is an example. Litton Industries is a master at this. The company now has three issues of convertible debentures and two issues of convertible preferred stock outstanding. In its most recent annual report, Litton went part of the way toward allowing for their conversion into common shares: its $2.25-per-share earnings were based on the present common shares, plus those that would be outstanding if one of the convertible preferred issues were entirely converted. But no mention was made of the additional dilution of earnings if the other convertible securities were converted.

TROUBLESOME

Companies that are in trouble bear especially close watching, too. When Control Data hit rough going three years ago, it changed some of its accounting methods. In mid-1964 it began deferring some of its development expenses rather than writing them off immediately. A few months later it also lowered its depreciation charges by switching from an accelerated method to the straight-line method. As a result, CD's fiscal 1965 reported earnings were $3.4 million higher than they would have been under its older accounting policies.

The asset values of troubled companies can sometimes shrink without warning. Stockholders of Sperry Rand found this out in 1965 when the company suddenly wrote off $14 million of the value of its rental computers. And what about the assets of a company like American Motors, whose survival in the auto business is in doubt? Says one CPA: "Their balance sheet wouldn't be worth much if they went out of the auto business."

A company that is having a bad year may write off a number of losses in that period. This, too, can pose a threat to the unwary, innocent investor; he may decide the company is going to the dogs and sell just at a time when the stock, having discounted the bad developments, is ready to bottom out. Take the example of Monsanto last year. Sharp price declines in synthetic fibers clipped 55 cents off the company's earnings per share. During the year Monsanto also wrote off its money-losing Spandex fiber operation, penalizing earnings by another 19 cents. But Monsanto's future earnings should benefit as a result; it has already swallowed the losses rather than capitalizing them. But who has warned investors not to take the reported decline too literally?

Care must also be taken in assessing the earnings reports of companies where a new management has recently taken over. "There is a tendency for the new management suddenly to become very pessimistic about the future of a product line or about the value of the inventories," explains one CPA diplomatically. The new management trims out all the excess expenses it can find during its first year in office, blaming the low earnings that result on the old bunch. Meantime, the stage has been set for a stirring recovery of earnings the following year. There is nothing illegal about it. It is just highly misleading to unwary readers of financial statements.

The tremendous rise of consumer credit has led to another area of fuzzy accounting. A company like Sears, Roebuck records installment sales as current income even though the payments may be spread out over a period of years. In Sears' case this may be—and probably is—sound. But it was this accounting procedure that got Brunswick Corp. into hot water during the great bowling boom of the early Sixties. When the boom collapsed, customers who had purchased equipment from Brunswick on the installment plan began defaulting on their payments in droves. Brunswick, which had taken the full amounts of installment contracts as current income, suddenly found itself coming up short. General Development Corp., the Florida land company, had the same trouble. It was crediting the full amount of mortgages on properties it sold as current income, even though the mortgages ran as long as 30 years. When defaults on the loans soared in 1962, GD's earnings plummeted.

The government has not made the investor's lot any less complicated by permitting for tax [purposes] accelerated depreciation [and] variable depreciation lives on plant and equipment, and then throwing in the investment tax credit for good measure. Companies end up keeping two sets of books, one for the stockholders and one for the tax collector. Even where footnotes in their statements try to explain the tax intricacies, the average reader is rarely equipped to understand them.

THE WHOLE STORY

Footnotes, in fact, are yet another area where the accountants seem bent on accommodating management ahead of the stockholders. They could be a big help in enabling stockholders to ferret out the truth behind various accounting treatments. But the accountants do not require them to be inserted unless a given accounting procedure makes a "material" difference. What is "material"? This is one of the great unresolved debates within the profession. As a result, the amount of footnote disclosure depends on which firm is auditing a company's books and often on which partner within a firm is heading up the job.

The accountants also will not require a footnote if the information, in the words of one CPA, "might injure the interests of the client." What worries them is their legal liability, which the courts have held to be stronger to the company itself than to stockholders and other third parties. But critics may rightly ask: Is this not precisely the kind of information that stockholders, the owners of the company, have a right to know?

Even when included, footnotes usually provide only the barest details. They may tell the reader that a company values its inventories on the last-in, first-out method. This is confusing enough. But what is never disclosed is the dollar effect on earnings and how these treatments compare with what competitors are doing. As a result, footnotes, as now handled, are almost useless to the average reader of financial statements.

Some companies, on their own, do provide useful supplementary information outside of their audited financial statements. Almost every company nowadays includes a ten-year summary of key financial figures. A few, like International Harvester, give a breakdown of sales by product line, and some, like Koppers, have even begun to do the same with earnings per share. Monsanto included in its 1966 annual report a detailed account in cents per share of the major items that increased and decreased its reported earnings. Whether this breakdown was precise accounting or not, stockholders had a good idea of what happened to earnings.

PROFESSIONAL SKEPTICS

Professional investors, the men who manage large portfolios of stocks, regard published earnings with the utmost skepticism. One Wall Streeter who specializes in arranging mergers and acquisitions says: "The only reason we look at a company's competition is to get an idea of what phase a company is in vis-à-vis its industry and subjectively analyze its management."

What he is saying is that officially reported earnings and assets, no matter how illustriously certified, do not play a major role in his decision making. And yet most investors must depend on information this sophisticated investor regards as almost useless.

The ordinary investor can well take a cue from this professional. He can accept the fact that a company's greatest asset will never appear on any audited statement: the quality of the company's management and the validity of its corporate philosophy. If these are sound, the long earnings swings and asset trend will be upward. If they are not, year-to-year or quarter-to-quarter "gains" are meaningless.

This is not to say that the accountants can't improve on reporting or that management couldn't be more cautious about what it officially reports. Both sides certainly can and almost certainly will improve their standards. Even then, however, the smart investor will do well to remember that it's the intangibles that really count—and no accounting system can ever measure them.

TAKE A NUMBER . . .

Here's an actual case—modified to mask company identity—of how different bookkeeping methods can greatly change the bottom line of the income statement. Same company, same sales volume, same operating policies, but very different net earnings.

GOLDEN FLEECE MANUFACTURING CO.

CONSOLIDATED INCOME STATEMENT	Method A (Conservative)	Method B (Liberal)
Net Sales	$240,809,200	$243,924,600
Cost of Goods Sold	201,287,300	199,248,200
Gross Profit	39,521,900	44,676,400
Other Operating Income		1,191,000
	39,521,900	45,867,400
Selling, General & Administrative Expenses	24,210,700	26,468,300
	15,311,200	19,399,100
Other Income (Expenses):		
Interest Expense	(1,810,900)	(1,873,400)
Net Income—Subsidiaries	538,900	
Amortization of Goodwill	(170,000)	
Miscellaneous	(269,000)	(229,200)
	(1,711,900)	(2,102,600)
Net Income Before Taxes	13,599,300	17,296,500
State Income Taxes	638,000	812,900
Federal Income Taxes—Deferred		348,900
Federal Income Taxes—Current	5,238,000	6,440,000
Charges Equivalent to Tax Reductions from:		
Investment Tax Credits	775,000	
Tax Loss Carryovers	990,000	297,000
	7,641,000	7,898,800
Net Income	**5,958,300**	**9,397,700**
Earnings Per Share	**$1.99**	**$3.14**

Source: Practicing Law Institute, December, 1966. Conference on Corporate Accounting Problems.

INVENTORIES:

A uses last-in, first-out;
B uses first-in, first-out.

Difference—$1,196,500

DEPRECIATION:

A uses sum-of-the-years' digits;
B uses straight-line.

Difference—$253,100

RESEARCH EXPENSES:

A charges as incurred;
B amortizes over 3 years.

Difference—$191,500

ACQUISITION:

A treats as purchase;
B treats partly as purchase, partly as pooling of interests.

Difference
(See next 3 items)

GOODWILL FROM ACQUISITION:

A amortizes over 10 years;
B does not amortize.

Difference—$170,000

ACQUISITION DEPRECIATION:

A uses "larger" base in purchase;
B uses "smaller" base in purchase and pooling of interests.

Difference—$63,800

ACQUISITION LOSS CARRYOVERS:

B applies against federal income taxes to extent of pooling of interests.

Difference—$693,000

TAXES ON SUBSIDIARY PROFITS:

A makes provision as income earned;
B makes no provision until dividends received.

Difference—$45,000

INVESTMENT TAX CREDITS:

A amortizes over useful lives of equipment;
B credits against current taxes.

Difference—$656,000

UNFUNDED PENSION COSTS:

A amortizes over 18 years;
B does not amortize.

Difference—$50,500

RETIREMENT ALLOWANCES:

A accrues and expenses prior to retirement;
B does not accrue or expense until allowances paid.

Difference—$120,000

Total Difference: $3,439,400

FAIRCHILD HILLER CORP.

9 mos Sept 30:	b-1966	1965
Share earns	a-$.88	$.69
Sales, etc.	146,902,000	c-62,111,000
Net income	a-3,910,000	2,064,000

a-Excludes net gain of $1,630,000, equal to 37 cents a share, from partial liquidation of investment in stock of RAC Corp. b-Includes operations of Republic Aviation division. c-Restated by company.

FAIRCHILD HILLER CORP.

9 mos. to Sept. 30	1966	1965
Net income	*$5,540,000	$2,064,000
Shr. earns.	1.25	69c

*After a special gain of $1,630,000 from a partial liquidation of stock in the RAC Corporation.

Teleprompter Corp. nine months to Sept. 30 net $236,761 or 29 cents a share vs $210,430 or 28 cents a share.

TELEPROMPTER CORP.

9 mos. to Sept. 30	1966	1965
Revenues	R$14,803,628	$4,006,091
Net income	663,211	*210,430
Shr. earns.	81c	28c

*No provisions were made for Federal income taxes due to tax-loss carryforwards.

88 CENTS OR $1.25?

Did Fairchild Hiller earn 88 cents or $1.25 per share during the first nine months of 1966? Did Teleprompter earn 29 cents or 81 cents?

It depended on which newspaper you read Nov. 2, 1966. Quite clearly, three of the nation's largest dailies could not get together on the reports.

These clippings from the *New York Times*, the *Wall Street Journal* and the *World Journal Tribune* are not isolated examples; they have occurred with disturbing frequency. The main problem has been the so-called "extraordinary" or "nonrecurring" gains and losses—items like a profit on the sale of a plant or a write-off of a discontinued product line. It was not necessarily the fault of the newspapers; the accountants themselves could not agree on whether or not to include them in net income. So the public, through the press, was left to figure it out.

Since 1967 the CPAs are requiring companies to *include* extraordinary items in their "net income" figures, and to identify that part of it that is "extraordinary." Under the new setup, Fairchild's earnings were $1.25 per share, with 37 cents of extraordinary income; Teleprompter's were 81 cents with 52 cents of extraordinary income.

31. FINANCIAL REPORTING BY CONGLOMERATE COMPANIES*

ROBERT K. MAUTZ †

Diversified companies with certain characteristics should report sales and the relative contribution to profits of each major broad industry group, according to the recommendations in the study conducted by the Research Foundation of Financial Executives Institute.

The report is the result of a year of intensive research by the Foundation to determine the usefulness, practicability, and desirability of publishing corporate results of operations on a more detailed basis than total company results. Its findings place stress on the necessity for management of a corporation, working within recommended guidelines, to make the determination of the information and group breakdowns which would be meaningful to investors.

"Management, because of its familiarity with company structure," states the study, "is in the most informed position to separate the company into realistic components for reporting purposes. To require reporting on some rigid basis might fractionalize a company into unnatural parts which could not fairly reflect the results of its operations."

The report suggests that companies which are unitary in nature, that is, which operate almost completely within a single broadly defined industry, or which are highly integrated, should not be expected to fractionalize themselves for reporting purposes, but companies which to a material degree have activity in more than one broadly defined industry should meet the extended disclosure requirements.

According to the study, a "material degree" means 15 percent or more of a company's gross revenue. No present system of industry or product classification appears ideally suited to the identification of broad industry groups, so considerable discretion to management in defining broad industry groupings is essential.

The study recommends that disclosures may be included in parts of the annual report other than the formal financial statements. Whether in narrative or tabular form, they should be grouped and should carry a clear indication of the limitation of their usefulness.

The findings have been released in summary form. The full report, including voluminous statistical data, will be released in late spring of this year.

The Financial Executives Research Foundation enlisted the assistance of representatives of the American Bar Association, the New York Stock Exchange, the Securities and Exchange Commission, the Investment Bankers

---

*From *Financial Executive* (February, 1968), pp. 46-63. Reprinted by permission.

†Professor of Accounting, College of Commerce and Business Administration, University of Illinois.

Association, the Financial Analysts Federation, the National Association of Accountants, and the American Institute of Certified Public Accountants in providing information in the course of the study.

The study takes a financial or business point of view, reflecting the concern of financial executives for both the informational needs of investors and the welfare of present shareholders.

The summary report, including conclusions and recommendations, is as follows.

SCOPE OF THE RESEARCH

The purpose of this research, as stated at the inception of the project, ". . . is to complete an investigation of the usefulness, practicability, and desirability of corporate disclosure in published and other generally available reports, of the scope, nature, and results of operations on some basis more detailed than total company figures, for the purpose of making recommendations to interested parties respecting whether disclosure is desirable and, if so, the kinds and extent of such disclosure." This led to an early emphasis on diversification in general rather than to a study of conglomerate diversification in particular.

Efforts were necessary to determine:
1. The information needs of those who make investment decisions;
2. The extent of present internal reporting on a less than total company basis;
3. Any limitations on the usefulness of such internally reported data as conceived by:
   a. those who produce and use such data internally
   b. by those who would use them externally if made available,
4. The disadvantages to corporate shareholders if increased disclosures were to be made.

Two lengthy questionnaires were developed, tested, and mailed. The investors' questionnaire was answered by 218 financial analysts and investment advisors from widely scattered geographic locations and filling a variety of roles in the investment market. Of these, 77 percent were Chartered Financial Analysts.

The corporate questionnaire brought useful responses from 412 companies of varying sizes representative of all major, nonregulated industries. These included 66 of the 100 largest industrial corporations listed in the "Fortune 500" and 212 or 42.4 percent of the entire "500." Also included were 26 of Fortune's 46 "most diversified companies."

A number of meetings were held in various parts of the country to provide the research staff with opportunities to seek information from, and exchange views with, financial executives, financial analysts, fund managers, and industrial and public accountants. Studies were made of published annual reports, and relevant writings on the subject were examined.

Both the conceptual and the pragmatic aspects of the subject received attention in the study. At the same time that questionnaires were developed and distributed to secure information about internal reporting practices and the opinions of financial executives and financial analysts, efforts to identify and clarify concepts essential to the research were also undertaken.

Financial analysts were selected as the group to represent the views of all those who read and rely on reported corporate financial data. They seem to be satisfactory representatives of this point of view because, as a group, they include a diversity of positions and interests and because they include in their ranks some of the most sophisticated of all users of published financial statements.

Neither the importance nor the problems of the individual investor was overlooked. To the extent that the individual investor desires to make informed investment decisions, he needs the same information as the financial analyst serving an institutional investor. Hence, if the needs of the most sophisticated users are met, other investors should be supplied with at least as much information as they can use effectively.

Financial analysts have become an important factor in the investment market because that market has changed significantly in recent years. The amounts of available investment funds have increased dramatically with increased levels of affluence and as new methods of wealth accumulation have been discovered and developed. At the same time, industry has become more complex technically, financially, and organizationally. With great sums to invest in a highly complex market, fund managers have sought the most expert advice obtainable. Analytical methods developed to supply investment advice to major investors are soon adapted and made available to other portfolio managers and investors of all kinds. One result has been an institutionalization of the investment procedure involving careful research, recommendations based upon such research, and review of such recommendations for reasonableness and conformity with the decision maker's investment policy.

Using the term "conglomerate company" in the broadest sense, an attempt was made to conceptualize the common characteristics which establish a group of companies appropriately designated by that term as distinct from all other companies. Given the point of view of the study, attention was directed to those variables of interest to investors which would be influenced by various aspects of diversification. Thus the tentative definition adopted was essentially a definition of diversified companies. As proposed, the definition was conceptual and was accompanied by a caveat that modification might be necessary before it would be practicably applicable.

Other aspects given conceptual attention were the separation of a diversified company into reportable components, the nature and influence of costs common to two or more reportable components of a diversified company, and the effect of the pricing of transactions between such components. Tentative conclusions resulting from this portion of the study were:

1. No one basis of segmentation of diversified companies for reporting purposes appears to apply to all companies. This argues strongly for a flexible approach, perhaps even freedom, for management to select a basis appropriate to the specific company.
2. Because of common cost allocations and intra-company pricing, data prepared for management purposes could be misleading if supplied to others who are less well acquainted with the company and who may not know the purpose for which the information was prepared.
3. The relative importance of common costs in segment reporting tends to decrease as the breadth of the reporting segments is increased.
4. Disparate components may have so few intra-company transactions and such a small portion of common costs that these present no serious deterrent to the presentation of operating data for such components.

RESULTS OF THE CORPORATE QUESTIONNAIRE

Perhaps the overriding impression one received from the corporate questionnaires is the variety of responses to almost all questions and the lack of unanimity or even near unanimity on any important point. To those familiar with business, this comes as no surprise; to those not so familiar, it warrants considerable thought. The impact of this variety in business structure and practice is a strong argument for the flexibility which is incorporated in the final recommendations.

Most of the responding companies provide operating data for internal company purposes on the basis of organizational units, although this is done in a wide variety of ways and for a variety of internal control purposes. Organizational units were defined in the questionnaire as components of the company identifiable in terms of the company's organization chart, reporting operating data to some top management group, and accounting for 2 percent or more of the company's sales or gross revenue. The number of such units reported was generally less than ten, and only a very few companies listed more than 15. For some companies, a close relationship existed between organizational units and their major product lines, leading to the conclusion that in a broad sense they are organized on a product-line basis. For almost as many other companies, there was very little relationship between organizational units and products.

More than half the responding companies prepare complete income statements by organizational units, and most of the remainder provide substantial operating data, although somewhat short of a complete income statement. Fewer companies, although still a significant proportion, supply some operating information by products. Generally the amount of information supplied is less than that available by organizational units. Yet when queried as to the most suitable basis for reporting operating data on some basis more detailed than total company figures, almost as many chose a

TABLE 31-1

Percent of Assets Identified with Units Specified	Total Companies Responding on an Organizational Unit Basis		Total Companies Responding on a Product-Line Basis	
	Number	Per-cent	Number	Per-cent
Under 50%	48	11.9	158	41.0
50-59%	6	1.5	11	2.9
60-69%	20	4.9	23	6.0
70-79%	28	6.9	28	7.3
80-89%	51	12.5	46	11.9
90% and over	253	62.3	119	30.9
Totals	406	100.0%	385	100.0%

product basis as chose organizational units. (For use in answering the questionnaire, product or product line categories were defined by each respondent, the only requirement being that a product or product line account for 5 percent or more of a company's gross revenue.)

Common costs were reported to exceed 10 percent of sales by 38 percent of these companies which provide internal operating data on an organizational unit basis and by 57 percent of the companies which report operating data internally on a product-line basis. (Common costs were defined in these questions by specifically listing certain items of expense, all of which would be shown in an income statement after the determination of gross margin on sales or gross profit. Thus, common costs of production were excluded from consideration.)

Practices with respect to the extent of allocation of common costs and the number and variety of allocation bases used vary widely.

The impact of intra-company pricing does not appear to be as material as that of common costs. For 24 percent (92 of 382) of the companies which provide internal operating data on an organizational unit basis, internal sales amounted to 10 percent or more of total sales. For 37 percent (63 of 169) of the companies which report operating data internally on a product-line basis, internally used product amounted to more than 10 percent of total production.

A variety of pricing methods for intra-company transfers is used, often by the same company.

Responses to the corporate questionnaire indicate that a significant number of companies cannot identify a large proportion of their assets with either organization units or product lines (see Table 31-1). The word "identified" may have been misinterpreted by some respondents. It was intended to convey the idea of direct attribution without allocation or pro-rating. Some apparently read it to mean that the assets could be allocated on a reasonable basis. These results may, therefore, imply a greater ability to supply information about assets committed to individual organizational units and product lines than actually exists.

The corporate questionnaire results support the tentative conclusion reached in the conceptual study that if diversified companies are to be separated into parts for financial reporting purposes, a flexible approach is essential. This follows both from preferences expressed by respondents and because of practical problems in reporting.

Some questions asked for opinions about disclosure preferences under the assumption that disclosure would be required even if the respondent disapproved of such reporting in general. Preferences are shown below, but it should be noted that preferences of some companies are impracticabilities for others. A number of companies include more than 50 separate corporations, thus making corporate entities an unlikely basis for effective reporting. A number of those reporting on an organizational unit basis also indicated numbers of units too large to constitute a practicable reporting base. Some companies stated they do not now report internally on the basis of product lines and indicated serious problems if they attempted to do so (see Table 31-2).

TABLE 31-2

Preferred Bases to Be Used for Reporting	Responses	
	Number	Percent
Legal corporate entities	55	14.2
Organizational units	153	39.5
Products or services	132	34.1
Other	47	12.2
Total	387	100.0%

Different methods for reporting the results of operations on a less than total company basis (assuming that such reporting were required) were also found "most satisfactory" by significant numbers of the corporate respondents:

	Companies Responding	
In the statement of income	100	25.8%
In a footnote to the financial statements	33	8.5
In the text of the annual report	189	48.7
In some other way	66	17.0
	388	100.0%

While not covered in the questionnaires, a matter implied or discussed specifically in many conversations with management representatives and analysts is the importance of so segmenting the company that the reporting segments represent the company as an operative entity. Companies organize in various ways to achieve like results. Personnel available at critical moments, the sequence in which essential decisions are made, commitments made by previous managements, management judgment as to operating policies, and a host of other factors exert varying influences upon the way in which a given company is structured. Arbitrary segmentation might divide integrated and coherent activities in ways that would make reports about them so unrepresentative as to be misleading. Thoughtful segmentation into a company's natural components, with full awareness of the intimacy of coherent activities, can be accomplished only by those well acquainted with the organization and inner workings of the company.

Managements see a number of hazards in disclosing operating and other data for the segments of a diversified company. These include the possibility that:

1. Confidential information would be revealed to competitors about profitable or unprofitable products, plans for new products or entries into new markets, apparent weaknesses which might induce competitors to increase their own efforts to take advantage of the weakness, and the existence of advantages not otherwise indicated.

2. Information thus made available would cause customers to challenge prices to the disadvantage of the company.

3. Operating data by segments might be misleading to those who read it. Segment data prepared for internal management purposes often includes arbitrary judgments which are known to those using the data and taken into account in making evaluations. The difficulty of making such background information available and understandable to outside users is considered by many to be insurmountable.

4. The cost of providing segment data where it is not now prepared could be significant.

5. Uniform reporting categories would be established which might call for additional expense in recording and reporting and which, because arbitrarily defined, might not fairly represent the operations of the enterprise as a going concern. Some fear that establishment of arbitrary reporting requirements might in turn lead to arbitrary rules for business activity to make the required reporting possible.

These are the more important reasons why some managements expressed themselves as generally opposed to disclosing any operating information on some basis more detailed than total company figures. Many expressed a willingness to disclose sales data but nothing more, while a significant number indicated at least qualified approval of increased disclosure generally.

RESULTS OF THE INVESTORS' QUESTIONNAIRES

The investors' questionnaires indicate that analysts rate "maximum return in the long run from a combination of dividends and capital appreciation" as the most important investment objective with "maximum capital appreciation in the long run" as next. These two are by far the most important objectives for those responding to the questionnaire.

The most important company characteristics in attaining these objectives are indicated as growth potential, managerial ability, and profitability, in that order.

The return on common stock equity, return on total assets, and ratio of net income to sales were rated as the most useful indicators of profitability.

The preferred indicators of growth potential are growth of major markets, rate of growth in earnings per share, and research and development expenditures.

Managerial ability is best indicated by the growth of the company, the return on common stock equity, and the personal reputation of key personnel.

In summary, these responses stress the importance of information (A) descriptive of a company's activities, (B) indicative of its share of markets, and (C) showing its success in terms of net income and return on equity data.

Diversified companies constitute a special problem to investors because of their activity in different industries. To judge the future prospects of such a company, one must examine the company's activities industry by industry before they can be considered in combination. Responses indicate that a substantial number of analysts now attempt to analyze diversified companies on a segmented basis, including estimates of cost of goods sold and allocation of operating expenses to arrive at net income by segments.

Although analysts state that financial statements and other material in the annual report provide the leading sources of information in the analysis of conglomerate companies by segments, a substantial majority indicate that annual reports do not provide satisfactory clues to appropriate segmentation. This leads to a conclusion that investment decisions are based on calculations which may not fairly reflect the facts.

Analysts are aware that common costs present significant allocation problems, and a majority agree that the allocation of such costs to organizational units or to products may be misleading. Most of those responding indicated that the point at which segment profit figures lose their significance because of the influence of common costs is 10 percent of sales or less, and relatively few felt results were reliable which included common cost allocations in excess of 20 percent of sales. Similar questions concerning intracompany sales brought similar answers.

In those cases in which common costs or intra-company pricing are sufficient to destroy the significance of segment net income figures for analytical purposes, a substantial number of analysts indicated they would find useful a "defined profit" which is computed by subtracting direct expenses of the segment from segment sales.

No clear preference for one basis of common cost allocation versus other possibilities was indicated.

The items of information about the segments of a conglomerate company considered most important by analysts are sales or other gross revenue, net income, and operating income (sales less cost of goods sold, selling expenses, and general and administrative expenses). Some analysts indicated that total assets and net assets committed to the activities of the segments were also important.

For comparisons of segments of one company with similar segments of other companies or with other segments of the same company, net income, sales, and assets invested were considered the most important items of information, and in that order.

The bases most often mentioned as appropriate in determining the minimum point at which an organizational unit becomes significant enough to require separate reporting were sales, net income, assets employed, net income before allocation of common costs, and total costs and expenses. Regardless of the base selected, a substantial majority indicated that the measure should be under 20 percent, with the largest grouping at the 10 to 14 percent range. In answer to another question, most respondents indicated that the maximum number of segments to be reported for a typical company should be 11 or less.

Analysts indicated that audit by independent CPAs would add satisfactory objectivity to common cost allocations, to definition of segments for reporting purposes, and to the results of operations including intracompany transactions.

Based on the following summary, the conclusion appears that most analysts would prefer but not insist upon audited data for the segments of diversified companies.

COVERAGE OF SEGMENT REPORTS BY INDEPENDENT CPAS OPINION

	Total Responses	Percent of Responses
Essential	59	27.2%
Desirable	122	56.2
Immaterial	36	16.6
Total	217	100.0%

In contradiction to their preference for a relatively small number of reporting units, a substantial number expressed a preference for uniform definition of reporting segments on some product basis such as the Standard Industrial Classification. This reveals a basic unfamiliarity with the Standard Industrial Classification and with the disadvantages of reporting a functioning, viable organization in terms of arbitrary and, therefore, probably artificial subdivisions.

CONCLUSIONS

Sufficient examples were cited in the corporate questionnaire responses to add substantial weight to the contention that disclosure of profit on individual products might be advantageous to competitors and/or customers to the detriment of shareholders in the disclosing company. Assertions that inordinate amounts of management time might be required to respond to questions encouraged by additional disclosures also appeared to reflect valid fears based upon experience. Unquestionably, excessively detailed disclosures could provide aid and comfort to those whose interests are opposed to the interests of the shareholders. Illustrations cited, however, relate to disclosures about specific products or specific decisions, a degree of detail well beyond that suggested by responses to the investors' questionnaire or incorporated in the accompanying recommendations.

The difference in point of view between the most reluctant corporate representative and the most demanding financial analyst was an extreme one. The views of more moderate financial executives and financial analysts appear reconcilable. For diversified companies, the majority of the financial analysts seek reliable data as a basis for predicting the prospects of the company in the near and long-term future. Such data should reflect the operations of the company's components separately and in total as viable parts of a complete enterprise, not as minute, arbitrarily segmented pieces bearing little resemblance to the operating organization. No great extent of detail is desired; indeed, reasonable summarization is essential. At the same time, information indicating the major industries in which a single enterprise is active is necessary and data showing the extent of involvement and success in each are considered essential.

A careful review of the specific objections to additional disclosure cited by corporate executives finds few, if any, concerned with disclosures of this nature. If presented in appropriate terms, disclosures useful to investors ordinarily need not be harmful to the disclosing enterprise. In recognition of the possibility of harm to shareholders in unusual cases, consideration needs to be given to recognition of possible hardship cases where the disadvantages of disclosure exceed the benefits to investors. Also, because companies vary, reasonable freedom for the management of each company to seek and identify appropriate terms of disclosure appears essential.

The conceptual definition of a conglomerate company requires modification in two respects if it is to be adapted to practical problems of financial reporting. First, common usage requires recognition that the class of companies described in the definition is more appropriately referred to as diversified companies than as conglomerate companies. In general usage, the term conglomerate company is used more and more in a restricted sense to describe diversified companies containing disparate components typically obtained through business acquisitions.

Second, for all practical purposes, the type of diversification of significance for financial reporting purposes can be viewed as industry diversification. The tentative conceptual definition noted the possibility of internal diversification resulting from either management decentralization or nonintegrated operations and of external or market diversification because of differences in customers or products or because of geographical distribution of its assets. Conceptually, these are all possible; practically, with the exception of industry diversification, they are either unlikely to exist or extremely difficult to identify.

Managerial decentralization sufficient to permit a company to experience rates of profitability, degrees of risk, and opportunities for growth that vary within the company to any material extent are theoretically possible but highly improbable. Common ownership of the company's components is itself enough to forbid such a degree of decentralization to influence profits, risk, or growth opportunities for any significant period of time.

Diversified markets might influence the investment variables actually as well as theoretically, but the practical definition of markets presents untold difficulties. Pragmatic distinctions among customers or geographic area are elusive indeed, except for the domestic versus international classification which already is provided for by generally accepted accounting principles applicable to conglomerate and nonconglomerate companies alike.

Activity in different industries remains as the only practicable basis for identifying diversified companies. Even here difficulties appear. No single, inclusive industry classification appears to provide the well-defined, mutually exclusive categories needed. And if one were established, its application to all companies might well be undesirable. The operations of different businesses do not necessarily fall into the same well-defined, mutually exclusive categories. There are certain clearly disparate and separable activities such as newspaper publishing and steel making, for example, that might be combined under one corporate roof. But newspaper publishing and radio or television broadcasting may be joined harmoniously and become virtually inseparable for meaningful reporting purposes. Steel making may have a close tie to bridge building which, in turn, may find heavy construction of other kinds a natural direction for expansion. If such coherent activities were required to report separately from one another in order to fit some uniform system of industry categories, the reported results might ill reflect operational entities within a company.

Industry diversification may thus fall into disparate or coherent patterns, depending less on the specific industries involved and more on the organization and operation of the specific company. To require reporting on some strict industry basis might fractionalize a company into unnatural parts which could not fairly reflect the results of its operations.

Both analysts and companies found gross revenue, net income, and assets invested to be satisfactory bases for determining the point at which a segment of the company should be reported separately. Gross revenue, which was the basis favored by both groups, appears to have advantages over the others. Net income is certainly the most volatile measure of the three and, during periods of low net income for the total company, might be reduced to a point where almost any segment reporting a profit would constitute a material portion of total net income. Its use would also raise interesting questions about net losses, either for the total company or for the segments, as indicators of materiality. Assets committed to reporting segments provide a satisfactory measure only if a high percentage of assets can be identified with segment operations. Responses to the corporate questionnaire suggest that some companies find difficulty in so identifying any substantial portion of total assets.

This leaves gross revenue as the most reliable and easiest measure to apply. Disadvantages exist here also. There is no assurance that gross revenues will vary proportionately with assets invested. Conceivably, a segment which utilized as much as one half of the company's total assets might produce only a small portion of the total revenue and thus not be marked for separate reporting by a test based solely on gross revenue. This suggests the need for a supporting test. The guide might be an appropriate percent of gross revenue unless gross revenue is not proportional to net income or assets invested, in which case a more representative measure should be sought. Where assets invested cannot be determined with accuracy, approximations may be required for this purpose.

General agreement is indicated by both analysts and corporate managements with respect to the point at which a given segment becomes sufficiently material to merit separate reporting and the total number of segments to be so reported. The financial analysts indicated that materiality fell in the 10 to 20 percent range and indicated that gross revenue, net income, and assets employed were the preferred bases to which such measures should be applied. Responses to a similar question in the corporate questionnaire picked the same three bases and approximately the same percentage measure. A guide set at 15 percent of gross revenue (already accepted by the Securities and Exchange Commission as a significance test for certain purposes) with recourse to an equivalent portion of net income or total assets when revenue is an unsatisfactory indicator, appears reasonable.

In reply to a question directed at ascertaining the maximum number of segment reports for a typical company which can be utilized effectively for analytical purposes, analysts stated a preference for a relatively small number rather than a large number of reporting components. A substantial number indicated they could not use more than about a dozen, while 56 percent of those responding stated they would prefer to deal with only eight or fewer. Generally, the numbers of organizational units and product lines reported in the corporate questionnaire fell within this range. 85 percent of those responding listed less than ten organizational units. The numbers of products listed did not differ materially from the numbers of organizational units, indicating that whichever base is selected, results fall within the range preferred by analysts.

Both analysts and corporate executives indicated an awareness of the significance of common costs and the possibility that their allocation might produce results subject to misinterpretation. This might lead one to consider defined profit as the natural solution. The corporate questionnaire, however, reveals that many management representatives are not enthusiastic about a defined profit figure. Their objections question the desirability of describing any figure as "profit" before all costs and expenses have been deducted. They fear that readers will misinterpret such a figure and may conclude the company is far more profitable than it really is. Thus, although some accept the notion of defined profit for segment reporting, others prefer a net income figure either before or after taxes. To require either one of these for all companies would force some into a position they could justifiably protest as a hardship. A reasonable solution appears to be to leave the choice to the individual company management. Thus, a company would be permitted to report either a defined profit before the allocation of common costs or an income figure after the allocation of common costs providing (A) that there is full disclosure of the nature of the "profit" figure reported, and (B) that if income is chosen and the method of allocating common costs or pricing intra-company transactions significantly influences the reported income, the method for allocating any significant amounts of common cost and for determining any significant intra-company pricing is disclosed.

A combination of factors leads to the conclusion that the extended disclosures may be made acceptably elsewhere in the annual report than in the audited financial statements. Financial analysts do not feel the application of the independent CPA's opinion to this information is essential. Responses show a majority of company representatives prefer to report it elsewhere than in the financial statements, yet the results of the corporate questionnaire also suggest that a number of companies will submit the extended disclosures to their auditors for review, and, as experience accumulates, more companies will probably choose to do so. For the present, however, this can scarcely be viewed as a requirement.

The importance of freedom to experiment with a variety of methods of presentation is apparent. Individual companies will seek ways to present their diversified activities as effectively as possible and may employ a number of presentations before settling on the one they find most useful. Because the disclosure of the results of diversified activities on a less than total company basis will represent an innovation in the reports of many companies, there exists the possibility that some readers will utilize the data in ways for which they were never intended. To reduce this possibility as much as possible, the grouping of such disclosures with a warning note to those who read them should be beneficial.

RECOMMENDATIONS

A. Companies which are unitary in nature, that is, which operate almost completely within a single broadly defined industry, or which are highly integrated, should not be expected to fractionalize themselves for reporting purposes.

1. Unless a company has components which (a) operate in different industries, broadly defined, and (b) experience rates of profitability, degrees of risk, or opportunities for growth independent of other components, and (c) meet the test of materiality (as stated in B-2 below), the company should be considered unitary in nature.

2. Companies, or parts of companies, whose segments transfer substantial amounts of products to or receive substantial amounts of products from, or render substantial services to, other segments with which they are integrated in a product sense, should be considered unitary in nature rather than diversified.

B. Companies which to a material degree have activity in more than one broadly defined industry should meet the extended disclosure requirements in C following.

1. Activity in more than one broadly defined industry exists when a company either (a) receives gross revenue from, (b) derives income from, or (c) utilizes assets in industries subject to significantly different rates of profitability, diverse degrees of risk, or varying opportunities for growth.

   No present system of industry or product classification appears ideally suited to the identification of broad industry groups for reporting purposes. If any of the existing systems (including the Standard Industrial Classification at the 2-digit level) is applied without consideration of a company's historical development and the interrelated nature of its established activities, the disadvantages to shareholders may be substantial. Considerable discretion to management in defining broad industry groupings for the purpose of meeting the disclosure requirements in C is essential.

2. Ordinarily, a "material degree," as the term is used here, means 15 percent or more of a company's gross revenue. If the amounts of gross revenue are significantly disproportionate to the amounts of income from, or the assets employed in, diversified components, as compared to other components of the company, a more representative test of the materiality of the diversification should be used.

C. Management, because of its familiarity with company structure, is in the most informed position to separate the company into realistic components for reporting purposes. Therefore, management should determine the number and scope of a diversified company's reporting components and report the activities of those components within the following guidelines:

1. Identify and describe the components which are subject to separate reporting.
2. Disclose any significant changes from the previous period in the composition of the reporting components.
3. For each reporting component:
   a. Disclose sales or other gross revenue.
   b. Disclose the relative contribution made by each component to the income of the enterprise. The contribution to income made by each component may be calculated before or after the allocation of common or corporate costs but in any case should be clearly described. In the event of a change in the method of computing or reporting either gross revenue or the relative contribution to income of the reporting components, the change should be clearly described.
4. If the method of pricing intra-company transfers or allocating common or corporate costs significantly affects the reported contribution to income of the reporting components, the method used should be disclosed in general terms similar to the following:
   a. "Corporate expenses were allocated to the reporting components on the basis of a formula giving approximately equal weight to assets employed, sales, and number of employees."
   b. "Intra-company transactions are priced at close approximations of open market prices for similar products and services."

D. Disclosures recommended under C may be included in parts of the annual report other than the formal financial statements at the discretion of management. Whether in narrative or tabular form, they should be grouped and should carry a clear indication of the limitations of their usefulness. Words similar to the following may prove useful: "The data supplied in (specify pages, paragraphs, or schedules) presents certain information relative to the nature, principal types, and results of the company's diversified activities. No assurance can be or is given that they have been prepared on a basis comparable with similar data for other companies."

E. Because of the innovative nature of these recommendations and the innate complexities of reporting diversified activities, the recommendations should be applied with judgment and flexibility by all concerned. In those cases where management sincerely believes the recommended disclosures, if followed, would have a significantly adverse effect upon the interests of shareholders, a statement to this effect should be made in lieu of extended disclosures.

PART X. INTERNATIONAL FINANCIAL MANAGEMENT

An increasing commitment to international business is one of the most significant changes occurring in the American economy. For several years, the rate of increase in direct overseas investment has outstripped the rate of increase in domestic investment. As foreign operations grow in relative importance, a stage is reached at which they can no longer be treated as isolated parts of the parent company's business.

The articles in this section recognize the growing importance of the international business finance brought about largely by United States direct investment abroad. All articles examine the various phases of international finance at the micro-level.

In his article, Professor Merwin H. Waterman argues that the problems of financial management of multinational corporations are not different from those of domestic corporations, but the answers to these problems are different. He classifies all universal business problems into two categories: first, inside problems such as investment justification, working capital management, and funds management; second, outside problems such as raising funds, relations with securities markets, lending institutions, stockholders, and environmental conditions. However, the dominant factor is environmental conditions. The problems of financial management that are unique to multinational corporations derive from the fact that their operations take place in two or more environments. Waterman suggests that "any study of financial problems of overseas business operations must be largely a study of facts, conditions, instruments, and institutions bearing on financial management in a still segmented world."

Are there any theoretical peculiarities in foreign investment theory that require special justification? The answer is no, according to Waterman. However, the potential profit rate must be determined after including factors such as political stability, currency convertibility, marketing vagaries, nationalistic labor, and fund-raising restrictions.

Waterman further deals with the factors in a multinational business environment that affect the management of working capital and considers those tools, instruments, and schemes which are necessary to increase the efficiency of such management.

The second part of the article deals with income administration and dividend policy which are complicated by many impediments such as taxes, exchange controls, and restrictions by the host country of managerial choice with respect to income administration in international business operations.

In the field of finance, the separate nationalistic legal patterns and political philosophies influence the relations of business to the financial institutions and the use by business of the instruments and tools of finance. Based on his experience, he sums up, "It is not possible to generalize about financial markets and institutions or financial instruments and their use." For most multinational companies, the answer to banking problems would seem to lie in the establishment of relationships with both host country and international bankers. Gradually, American banking methods, systems, and philosophies are moving into other parts of the world, influencing the banking practices in foreign countries. As these changes take place, many nations are moving toward a united world economy as characterized by the European Economic Community, the European Free Trade Association, and the expanding participation by United States corporations.

While Waterman's article is based on his experience, the articles by Professors Surendra S. Singhvi and David B. Zenoff are based on empirical research. Singhvi's paper studies overseas reinvestment decisions of United States international corporations. The first part of the paper deals with the importance of overseas operations, in general, and the overseas reinvestment decisions, in particular. Some of the major reasons for the growing importance of overseas operations are: (1) increased domestic competition, which has squeezed domestic profit margins relatively to foreign operations; (2) favorable investment climate abroad for American corporations; and (3) better institutional structure of world commerce, which provides incentives for foreign investments. An outstanding characteristic of international companies is that they tend to begin with a small investment in a given country and expand these operations out of retained earnings. Since these companies generally rely heavily on internal cash flow as a source of financing, the overseas reinvestment decisions are very important for them.

In the second part of his paper, Singhvi explains why different standards are used for domestic and overseas reinvestment decisions. The reason for this difference is the involvement of a greater risk in overseas operations due to the presence of several unique factors in the foreign environment.

The third part of Professor Singhvi's paper presents the results of his research based on interviews with 12 United States firms engaged in overseas operations. He concludes that in order to succeed in the complex world of business, one must establish both quantitative and qualitative standards for making overseas reinvestment decisions.

Professor David B. Zenoff summarizes a study of the dividend remittance practices of the wholly-owned European and Canadian subsidiaries of 30 of the largest American manufacturing firms. The main focus of the study was on two of the many unanswered questions pertaining to the direction and size of capital flows associated with United States direct investment abroad: (1) what factors influence the dividend remittance practices of wholly-owned foreign subsidiaries; and (2) what kinds of remittance decisions have the large multinational firms been making?

One of the general conclusions is that transferring funds from foreign affiliates is an aspect of the international finance function which can and should be managed. In comparison with domestic operations, the international financial executive may expect to have less freedom of action in directing the financing and funds remittances of affiliates abroad. Zenoff points out that even in less developed countries, many investors have begun to find that through careful planning it has been possible to manage at least a good portion of the international funds flow. However, it has been found that one cannot quickly and significantly alter the amount of funds remitted to the owner firm without drawing too much attention from local tax authorities and receiving unfavorable tax treatment for the transaction.

Zenoff also suggests that accessibility to foreign-generated funds can be a key area. He raises several questions such as, Could presently blocked funds be made more available to the rest of the company if different forms of remittance were attempted? The important point for management and the student of finance to realize is that control of international funds deserves the same consideration as is given to domestic finance.

32. FINANCIAL MANAGEMENT IN MULTINATIONAL CORPORATIONS*

MERWIN H. WATERMAN †

I.

Basically, the problems of financial management of multinational business are not different from those of domestic corporations; by "domestic" I mean those domiciled and operating in any single country of the world that I have so far encountered. After extended experiences in a variety of European countries and a brief visit to oriental ones, I have concluded that search for fundamental differences has been in vain. The problems are the same; it is only the answers that are different. It is true that my experiences have been confined to those countries that are generally labelled "capitalistic," where there is at least a semblance of free enterprise and where a substantial portion of the whole economy is characterized by a profit motivated private sector.

A simple classification of these universal business financial problems would be but 2-fold—the inside problems and the outside problems; there can be no others. Even the subclassifications under these two main heads are not many; let us say, for instance:

Inside problems such as,

1. Investment justification, by projects or business activities;
2. Control and efficient use of capital resources, particularly in terms of working capital management; and
3. Fund management, involving income administration and control, dividend policy; and

Outside problems such as,

1. Capital raising and relations with securities markets;
2. Relations with lending institutions, long and short term,
3. Owner-stockholder relations; and
4. Environmental conditions.

Obviously business problems do not fit only into any such watertight compartments, and if any one of the suggested subclasses tends to dominate all of the others in the international arena, it is environmental conditions—especially those in terms of the legal, political, institutional, macro-economic, traditional, and, yes, even moral factors.

ENVIRONMENTAL PROBLEMS

Really the problems of financial management unique to multinational corporations derive from the fact that their operations take place in two or

---

*Reprinted by permission from the January and March 1968 issues of the *Michigan Business Review*, published by the Graduate School of Business Administration, The University of Michigan.

†Professor of Finance, Graduate School of Business Administration, University of Michigan.

more environments. Even this characteristic is not solely one of the multinational units; so-called domestic business need not be very large before it begins to have to adapt itself to a variety of financial, legal, and economic conditions. So, it may be concluded that any study or analysis of financial problems under the "international" or "multinational" head must be largely a study of facts, conditions, instruments, and institutions bearing on financial management in a still segmented world. Any study of these phenomena would be dated before the pages could be numbered; the winds of change are scattering the facts like chaff. Perhaps, however, we can identify the general direction of the winds in some instances, even though observations may be hazardous as predictions of the future.

What may be helpful and what this analysis will try to accomplish by example and experience is to indicate to the financial manager or student some of the kinds of variables he may expect to encounter in foreign business. Wherever possible comparisons between countries or environments will be used to alert the reader and to help him to interpret the conditions as he finds them on the day when his own problems arise. It is certain the answer to a single actual problem encountered during 1968 or subsequently will be of little practical application to solutions of future problems. To the extent possible the discussion will be kept multinational; i.e., applicable to the financial manager of any international business located anywhere. The fact that the author is an American with a special interest in American business in Europe will undoubtedly intrude and color the presentation, but we hope it will not be miscolored by this interest.

INVESTMENT JUSTIFICATION

Modern, efficient financial management has learned to emphasize the importance of the allocation of capital resources by some kind of rate of return or valuation process as applied to decisions on capital commitments. Here is not the place to present the variety of methods of comparing various investment alternatives nor the occasion for trying to set standards of investment goals in terms of cost of capital or otherwise. It is sufficient to say that in most acceptable approaches to these problems the element of risk plays a significant role. Profit and profit potential are closely related to and dependent upon the risk of an enterprise or projects in our capitalistic system, and the amount of this profit (or potential) is necessarily related to the amount of capital resources put out at risk. It is then the problem of the decision maker to judge whether the rate of return (potential) on the investment is sufficient to compensate for the risk entailed—in light of alternative opportunities.

Are there any theoretical pecularities in foreign investment theory that require special justification? I would say, "No," because I think that adequate consideration of the risks involved will result in an intelligently determined potential profit rate (or discount rate) which, when applied to estimated profits or payout, can provide the basis for judgment, just as in case of decisions with respect to home-side investments. Actually some currently existing worldwide companies don't know which investments to call "home-side;" in a sense they are all "foreign," and there is no reason why any of the acceptable techniques of investment justification could not be used to sort out or rank the alternative opportunities according to the risk rate investment relationships.

The solutions are not made simpler by saying that these are the same old problems; when we say that the rate of return or discount rate can be made to reflect the risk, keep in mind how difficult that expression is even in the simplest one-country situation. Then compare it with a multi-country decision where each environment has its own variables and unknowns in such areas as political stability, currency convertibility and exchange control, marketing vagaries, nationalistic labor and investment ideas, and capital raising restrictions. All that management needs to do is equate all these things and express them in a rate of return (or discount) on what they think will be the investment commitment, and the office boy can give the answer on the calculator! That's all!

SPECIAL EXCHANGE RISKS

Perhaps some special and practical words of warning might be added to the theoretical considerations with respect to the application of "payout period" or "discounted cash flow" methods of investment analysis and justification as applied to multinational situations. Generally within our own country it can be assumed that the results of a business investment can be "paid out" and that "cash" will "flow." These assumptions make sense of the mathematical logic of discounting and give some credence to the element of timing of the investment return. But as an owner or shareholder in a business that is earning or generating cash beyond the borders of our country, you may take a dim view of all this going on behind a wall of nationalistic restrictions—economic or political. The mathematical logic of discounting reduces to minuscule the dollars, the pounds, the francs (Belgian, French, or Swiss), the deutschmarks, the lire, or the yen that you may never get, or whose receipt for your benefit may be indefinitely postponed. Just try discounting $1 million of annual potential that you might get for an indefinite period beginning in 15 years. In perpetuity and beginning right now the annual million would be worth $10 million, if discounted at 10 percent; but, all of that coming after 15 years until foreverafter [sic] would be worth only roughly one quarter of the total, or $2.5 million. So, you would have to project a substantially higher ultimate return on undistributed earnings to reach the value justification of $10 million at 10 percent.

It has been said to me that only the very large, diversified corporation can afford to take the risks of foreign investment, particularly in those countries where inflation risks so readily turn to actualities. Such large companies may be better able to take risks. Perhaps they may be more skilled at evaluation, or have taxable income from other sources that help them to absorb losses, or know better how to cope with problems of expropriation, devaluation of currency, and other problems of foreign management. But isn't it a matter of degree? A capital-intensive industry perhaps would require such large unit investments as to overextend a small concern, but even such a business may have the possibility of hedging the risk with funds borrowed in host country currencies (and payable in same) which might so minimize that particular risk of inflation as to reduce the investment exposure.

Thus, may we leave this investment justification problem with the comment that there is very little new under the sun, but also with a recognition of the extreme difficulty of evaluating risks of foreign investment. This has real meaning in terms of financial management, because it demands skill, knowledge, and experience that come neither from studying books nor discussing cases. It's a "know how" requirement coupled with a "know what" that must go with the essential "know why." As the number of countries and environments increases, somewhere it becomes impossible for one person or staff to handle foreign affairs with one hand while handling domestic with the other; specialization or a series of specializations becomes necessary to keep abreast of the facts and environmental changes. The essentials of the coordinating and decision-making functions will not change; the principles can remain firmly established, but the implementation of financial policy with respect to investment justification in foreign lands must rest on an even wider range and variety of facts than many of us are accustomed to assembling and assimilating.

FINANCIAL CONTROLS IN MULTINATIONAL BUSINESS

More frequent, though perhaps less romantic than decisions to build a new plant in a foreign country, are those daily decisions affecting the management of a company's working capital. This pertains to all of its forms—inventory, receivables, and cash. What are the factors in a multinational business environment that affect the management of working capital, and what tools, instruments, and schemes need to be considered to the end of increasing the efficiency of that management? What reasonably can be done either to increase the numerator of the profit/investment fraction or to decrease the denominator, since either will move to maximize the utilization of capital resources and increase the rate of return thereon.

Generally speaking, it would seem that decisions regarding inventory management would be most closely related to rationalization of production in a multinational company; material would be stored in the place and form and processed where the costs of processing and carrying would be minimized. However, one offsetting factor will be the tariff, and it may prove to be more economical to ship bits and pieces in export for assembly elsewhere, thus changing the locale of the financing problem if not its magnitude. In England and on the European continent it seems often to be easier and cheaper to finance working capital than plants and equipment. During the 1966 period of credit restriction in England, there was for a time a priority indicated by government policy in favor of loans for "working capital" purposes. If it is possible to relate working capital requirement to the export potential of a national unit of a multinational concern, loans may become cheaper or easier to get within the framework of credit policy guidelines or the more complete credit controls such as have existed in France— at least until very recently. It is doubtful, therefore, whether the financial problems of inventory can be isolated within the international picture; certainly they do not exist in a vacuum, but the controller or financial manager can do some thinking in terms of inventory management—both with respect to ways of keeping the amount down and in minimizing the costs of carrying.

WORKING CAPITAL PROBLEMS

With respect to this whole matter of working capital finance, the internal control and mobility possibilities of the components seem worth mentioning in some detail. Inventories have their possibilities as mentioned above. Receivables perhaps even more so can be, shall we say, juggled? Particularly are intra-company, inter-country receivables sources of interesting potentials for management. Receivables are generated when company X in country A ships to its sister company Y in country B, both X and Y subsidiaries of company Z. Eventually there will probably be a transfer of funds in payment in the opposite direction, but when? It depends on whether, at least for the time being, it is easier or cheaper to get capital in country A or B; if in A, then company X can hang on to its receivables in either open book form or in the form of notes or bills until management directs payment. So-called receivable financing may be especially a cheap source of finance, because in European countries there is a predilection for discountable bills. Particularly for those bills originating from an export transaction, as implied here, favorably low or subsidized rates of interest are often available. (Of course, this latter facility applies both to export to outsiders and to sister companies.) Relations of company A shipping to another sister C in country W may be such that C has or can get all the money it needs cheaply, so prompt payment of the bill is called for and the company C carries the load as an inventory financing problem.

Beyond this matter of relative cost that can be affected by judicious receivable-payable financing, there are matters of exchange restrictions in some areas; even France with its 1967 liberalization of controls has seemingly changed only from a "no, but" situation to a "yes, but" one. Transfers of substantial amounts of funds must still be explained. There are still definite limits and restrictions on foreign exchange in so many non-European areas that special long term commitments may become involved, and this is a problem not of working capital but of permanent (more or less) finance.

The difficulties of Krupp in Germany came from inadequate solution to these problems. The degree of flexibility and maneuverability that can be achieved by a multinational corporation dealing among countries with monetary restrictions is very great; literally, by anticipation or postponement of payments among units, the methods and locale of financing can be directed so as to take fullest advantage of markets and to avoid the effects of many restrictions. It would seem that the greater the number of intra-company, inter-country transactions, the greater the opportunities. A smaller company with only one foreign branch or subsidiary, for instance, would not have the same benefits of diversification and choice of movement available to it.

MANAGEMENT OF CASH

Cash, as such, is generally considered the most useless and sterile asset on a company's balance sheet—necessary as a lubricant to operation but containing no motive power. Particularly since World War II, the management of cash funds by most business corporations has received much greater attention in order to minimize these sterile amounts and to direct these amounts into some earning form while retaining them in reasonably liquid form readily available for management use. In the multinational business the opportunities and risks of fund management assume new proportions. Within the category that we usually see on a balance sheet labelled "cash and marketable securities" can now be counted:

1. Cash, in various currencies
2. Bank deposits
   a. in various currencies
   b. with various maturities (or withdrawal restrictions)
3. Certificates of deposit
   a. in various currencies
   b. with various maturities (or withdrawal restrictions)
4. Marketable securities
   a. in various currencies
   b. with various maturities (or withdrawal restrictions)
   c. secondary market liquidity.

Almost daily the conditions pertaining to the world's security and money markets are changing. In the United States within the last few years, the "uneconomy" of demand deposits in noninterest paying commercial bank accounts has been overcome by the purchase of "Certificates of Deposit" (CD's) carrying varying rates of interest for maturities from one month to 12; these are now also available in European centers through U.S. bank branches. There is even talk of sterling CD's in England as a British Prices and Incomes Board report suggests a range of deposits of varying size and maturity with varying interest rates. ("Bank Charges," Cmnd. 3292, HMSO.) Thus even within the category of bank deposits, the fund manager has numerous alternatives involving risks and profits.

In most currencies the exchange risks can be hedged by buying forward cover—at a cost—i.e., deposits in pounds sterling can be hedged by selling pounds for future delivery; or if it is deutschmarks you want, buy them now and take them later, getting less or more as your pounds go up or down in value related to the marks. The technicalities of these forward transactions are not within the scope of this presentation. Suffice to say that there are costs of brokerage, the risk costs reflected in the differential price of currency for future delivery, and the carrying costs of the deposit. Against these costs can be balanced the benefit of the hedge plus any interest received on the deposit and, of course, the less quantifiable need to maintain funds in more or less liquid form in various markets and currencies. Again, we may conclude that this area of fund management on an international basis is a very complicated one requiring very special skill and knowledge of market institutions and instruments.

These considerations of working capital management are really only suggestive—suggestive of the many directions in which the financial manager must turn to survey the whole of the opportunities to make the most efficient use of the capital resources under his control. The complications involved rightly suggest the need for specialists in money markets by countries, in tax implications of various moves, in legal and political problems of fund movements, and in the economics of foreign exchange transactions. Unless a firm is large enough itself to afford such specialists, it could better depend on the services of institutions such as commercial, merchant, or investment bankers.

Another interesting dimension of financial operations of this type is their market effect. As more and more multinational corporations react to their own needs and to the costs of meeting them, the increasing number and scope of transactions should sharpen the international money markets and tend to bring them closer together. Certainly it could be expected that businesses themselves will become an influence through their exchange and fund operations. When a company such as Dow Chemical opens its own bank (Dow Banking Corporation) in Switzerland and buys an interest in another in the Netherlands, you have a further example of direct participation of business in the financial markets.

II.

In the January issue of the *Review*, a bit was said about the solutions of financial management problems that are more or less unique to multinational corporations. It was emphasized—particularly in problems of working capital management—that environmental conditions affect the answers to the problems, although the financial theories and principles are the same as at home. In this article, I have tried to set down some things to watch for in other areas of financial management and control; again, this is not an all-inclusive study of events and institutions. Rather, the items are suggestive of the types of considerations that must be included in any management's decision-making process.

INCOME ADMINISTRATION AND DIVIDEND POLICY

By tradition (and taxation) there seem to be separate problems of income or profit administration in multinational corporations, although we all recognize that it is only "funds" that can be administered or their flow directed. If this fact of life is accepted, then we must agree that it is really impossible to distinguish between capital funds and profit funds. When one sees the pounds, francs, deutsche marks, lira, or yen that he may have in the bank or cash drawer, those that may have come from the issue of securities look surprisingly like the ones that resulted from profitable (or not) commercial transactions, such as the sale of goods or services. In all countries it is true that funds available for administration are affected by income taxes, and thus income administration or determination becomes an important matter. In some countries what is done with the actual funds, paid out or kept in the business, also affects available funds via the corporate tax or personal tax withholding route. Even in our simplest domestic enterprise, one scarcely orders lunch without considering the tax implications. When the movement of funds across country boundaries between jurisdictions that have different tax laws begins to take place, the implications and complications increase in more than geometric proportion. It will not be possible to discuss these tax impacts in detail here. I can only emphasize their importance and the need to consider them in each and every individual decision involving income or fund administration. Some general examples will be cited but nothing inclusive.

The object of business, be it domestic, foreign, or multinational, is ultimately to bring through to the owner or shareholder funds representing return on or of his investment. The timing of the receipt of those funds by the owner introduces the discounting process and develops values both for funds that will be taken out and those that may be left in the business to generate future profits (and funds). In the multinational corporation funds for distribution to the shareowners must come through to the treasury of the corporation, either the parent of foreign subsidiaries or the home office of branches abroad. Here the complications begin again.

Within many countries there are impediments to managerial choice with respect to fund administration in purely national businesses as well as in the local units of multinational concerns. Germany's tax law is such that a rate of only 15 percent[1] is paid on the annual income equivalent of dividends paid out, whereas 51 percent is paid on the balance of taxable income. (Remember when the United States had a discriminatory federal income tax on "undistributed profits" in 1937?) The reports of Ford-Werke Aktiengesellschaft show that they have been paying out in common dividends an amount equal to 100 percent of the previous year's profits. Then these amounts have been loaned back to Ford-Werke by parent Ford, and

---

[1]Equivalent, actually, to 23.44 percent, because the tax on distributed profits is not treated as a deductible expense but as undistributed income (taxed at 51 percent).

lately (1964-1965) these loans have been capitalized by allocation to "legal reserve." In this case the company had to balance the costs (in U.S. income tax) of taking the money home and sending it back as loan capital subject to a German capital issue tax, against the differential tax impact of a so-called reinvestment of earnings program. So, round Robin Hood's barn they went to accomplish an increase in Ford-Werke equity in tune with the company's capital expansion.

Another choice sometimes to be made is that between moving funds from the foreign subsidiary to the ultimate dividend paying parent by means of royalty payments, management fees, or franchise fees—rather than by dividends. Insofar as such fee payments are expensable (for tax purposes) in the host country of the subsidiary, the decision will rest on a comparison of the income tax rates applicable in the subsidiary host country and the parent host country, respectively. Maneuvering of intra-company, inter-country pricing becomes a means of tax minimization and has led even to the establishment of pure sales companies in so-called tax haven countries in order to concentrate profits in the lowest tax area. Obviously when any of these movements of funds or "income" reach a sufficient magnitude, some jurisdictions will consider them as tax evasion rather than just a tax minimization move and react accordingly. Within the confines of The European Economic Community, at least, there are hopes and some expectations that standardization and uniformity in tax statutes and procedures will ultimately change these possibilities of maneuvering profits, or at least remove the tax motivation.[2]

As a matter of contrast, consider some such complicated U.S. domestic situation as the American Telephone and Telegraph Company with its dozens of subsidiaries scattered throughout the country, operating in 48 states and the District of Columbia. Within the entire A.T.&T. system it is possible to rationalize the management of funds on an overall basis. For one thing, there are no tax implications of fund transfers as far as federal income taxes are concerned; they are assessed and paid on the basis of a consolidated tax return. Funds are moved from subsidiaries to parent as dividends on shares owned or interest on loans and advances. Generally, share ownership is at or near 100 percent of each subsidiary, so only nominal amounts are syphoned out of the system to minority interests where dividends are distributed. Decisions for such moves then can be made on the basis of an overall, national system policy and on fund requirements for expansion and debt payments of the several subsidiaries, debt payments of the parent, and dividends to ultimate parent company shareowners.

Among multinational corporations freedom of fund movement in some instances may be restricted by exchange controls or direct control

---

[2]A good summary of European (EEC) country tax characteristics is contained in *The Development of the European Capital Market*, Chap. 14, Annex, European Economic Community Commission, Brussels, November 1966.

on capital movements with no distinction between funds as profit or capital. All these factors create problems for the financial manager; he must be aware of them and have his tax and corporate counsel at hand to participate in decisions. It is not difficult to find, in addition to the outright governmental restrictions or directives on the movement of funds from country to country, political pressures all the way up to guidelines designed to achieve the same ends. Even the United States is limiting capital movements abroad by taxes and by trying to encourage homeward movements of profits by counting earnings left abroad as a "capital movement" in that direction.[3] The use of private business as an instrument of public policy by government fiat may not be palatable, but it's an old game and becoming ever more popular when a government itself can not effectuate its own policies. This may be another example of what is known as the modern "political economy" with which we must live, which we must interpret and to which we must react to the best of our ability. Late in 1966 U.S. corporations in Germany had to borrow very expensive D-Marks (at rates as high as 8 percent) because Europe-dollars were not available, because the U.S. branch banks were sending the dollars home to help on the government-created credit squeeze, whereas Germany had a tax on new foreign money coming in which was designed to stave off an inflationary condition caused in large part by their own lack of control over German state security issues for financing expansion programs. (That's a good German sentence; read it again, because it expresses the complex interrelations.) And so it goes; irrationalities introduced by government economic controls and balance of payment manipulations are everyday facts of life that are continually shifting the scene in which financial operations must be carried on.

The problems of budgeting and financial control as we know them in a domestic business become more than usually insoluble in the multinational corporation. There must be budgets for country-by-country operations; these must reflect company pricing and payment policies—intrasystem. Tax considerations and government fund movement restrictions must be counted in, and somehow all of these must be coordinated with the company's expansion policy at home and abroad, its dividend hopes and expectations, and its alternative sources of funds, at home and abroad. It is this last item of interest to which I now turn: sources of funds, at home and abroad.

FINANCIAL MANAGEMENT—INSTITUTIONS AND INSTRUMENTS

The business environment of the world is just about as segmented as the political environment; in some respects even more so. The variety and divergency of political entities bring with them their institutions and instruments

---

[3]The new 1968 U.S. regulations applicable to Europe call for a program limiting the annual investment of earnings of such overseas operations to 35 percent of each company's average *total* investment during the years 1965 and 1966. The permissive percentage is 65 percent for Britain, Canada, Japan, Australia, and oil-producing nations. No funds at all can be sent to continental Europe from the United States.

applicable to their commercial activities. In the field of finance, the separate nationalistic legal patterns and political philosophies and goals definitely influence the relations of business to the financial institutions and the use by business of the instruments and tools of finance. Based on my only brief forays into the Far East—Hong Kong, Taiwan, and Japan—this presentation cannot reflect any great depth of understanding of financing in those areas. Longer professional exposure to southern Italy was now eight years ago, and this has not been followed up. The Scandinavian countries have never yet been included, nor have Latin American ones, in any visit—even for sightseeing. However, on the basis of experience limited primarily to England and Central Europe, it is possible to come up with one generalization, namely, *it is not possible to generalize about financial markets and institutions or financial instruments and their uses!* Tendencies and contrasts perhaps we can talk about, but again they are only things for the financial manager to watch out for, pointing the way for him to plot his course in handling the affairs of the multinational corporation.

Banks and Bank Loans

In the United States the financial manager is more or less accustomed to thinking of his banker(s) first when he needs funds—almost regardless of purpose. Bank borrowing may shortly or ultimately be refinanced in the form of a security issue—bond or equity—if the capital need is sufficiently permanent. But such is the nature of bank/business relationships that short, medium, and even fairly long term bank loans are things to be considered in financial planning. This is not quite so true in Europe, at least as far as the so-called commercial banks are concerned. They are more tuned to the short-term advances for commercial transactions (domestic or foreign), and they just love security, either in the form of a wide balance sheet margin in current assets or an actual pledge of assets. A Sf.50,000 gold bar would undoubtedly get you a Sf.40,000 loan from a Swiss bank if pledged as security, and the loan might even be renewed at the end of a year! Of course, this is exaggerated, but it does exemplify the extreme in contrast to the frequent habit in the U.S. for banks to negotiate a loan to a concern, not ignoring security but depending heavily on the basis of a budgeted payout period that would meet a schedule of maturities. A Swiss bank might extend itself to two or three years for a native Swiss concern, but not for a loan across its borders—where many of them go.

Loans to finance exports will usually be unquestioned, but other loans might be interpreted as contributing to undesirable expansion and internal inflationary influences and thus be subject to restraint. One multinational concern arranged for very satisfactory bank credits (in some instances at subsidized rates) in a number of European countries on the basis of the export of components hither and yon. One can easily sense the possibility of using a bank to finance an export deal so that the company can import! After all, it is the financial manager's job to match the overall fund disbursements of his company with receipts from all sources.

The Europe overdraft scheme for making bank advances to customers is, in many respects, a handy gadget. Arrangements for overdrafts can be made as long as they are within bank or government policy limits in England and on the Continent; borrowers pay interest only on the amounts and for the time that funds are actually borrowed. This is in contrast to the formality of the promissory note which is the typical instrument for borrowing from U.S. banks and which requires not only payment of interest for the period of the note(s) but also usually involves the requirement that some percentage of the loan be left on deposit with the lending bank—5, 10 or 20 percent, depending on the tightness of the market. Yet this latter instrument is a contract in definite terms. On the other hand, overdraft privileges may be subject to change almost without notice, there being no specific maturity on which the borrower may depend. The budget plans of a multinational corporation could be substantially upset by vagaries of call by lending banks, if it had this exposure in several different countries. Overdraft privileges may run for years, although they are considered "short term" loans, but then one day they may be reduced as the result perhaps of bank policy or government fiat. The latter was the case in England in the summer of 1966 when the government asked the banks to impose credit restrictions.

Another variant, while not exclusive to the overdraft, is the tied interest rate that is characteristic of it; interest is usually x percent above the bank rate or discount rate. (This type of deal also exists in the U.S. when interest on a formal loan may be expressed as x percent above the prime rate in New York.) A borrower may find it an advantage to use the overdraft scheme which does not relate his borrowings so much to his ability to pay from generated funds but just to his balance sheet position. He may also be willing to take the risks implied in the looser overdraft arrangements.

Generally speaking, it makes sense for a foreign concern or subsidiary thereof to use some banking facilities in host countries. U.S. branch banks sometimes find resistance to their efforts to get accounts even from subsidiaries of U.S. companies with which they have homeside relations. Relationships developed with host country bankers may have been well-established before the appearance of the U.S. branch or they may have existed for long when the subsidiary was acquired. In some environments it is customary for a company to include on its letterhead the name of its bank affiliation. It is considered good business to have local (or host country) banking relationships where a business lives and operates. The desirability of such a relationship seems obvious, but the problem may be one of adequacy of facilities. In England one of the "big five" could probably handle most situations, or one of the "big three" in Germany; but in the Netherlands one of the reasons for bank mergers has been to create sufficiently large institutions to carry the requirements of large, multinational firms. In France, likewise, there have been recent mergers which may improve the competitive position of the banks there vis-à-vis multinational banks.

But it isn't always size; it's sometimes the service concept. Otherwise why would Bache and Co. think it could successfully open a bank (not a large one) in Frankfurt, Germany, right under the noses of the Deutsche and Dresdner banks? (Mostly, at the moment, because it can be a member of the Stock Exchange.) Or how could Dow Chemical Company be able to show a good year operating a brand new bank in Zurich, supposedly the "bankingest city" in the world? For most multinational companies or even just international ones, the answer to banking problems would seem to lie in the establishment of relationships with both host country and international bankers. In some instances these may be one and the same. Some English banks are opening in the U.S. and have old establishments in other parts of the world. At least one Dutch bank is again moving out across borders after a lengthy hiatus in the foreign and colonial activities of the Netherlands. The top six or seven U.S. banks may have the most branches throughout the world, but others are developing, so the choice is not limited. The origin and flow of transactions by a multinational company would seem to indicate an important test of U.S. banking choice; do the banks have branches where the business is, and are their facilities modern and adequate?

Term Loans

Mention was made of the fact or tendency of English and European banks not to go in for term loans. Perhaps one reason why the opposite has been true in the U.S. is that the latter environment does not always include so-called merchant banks. Merchant banking in Europe and in England is probably older even than commercial banking as we think of it today. Longer term credits and advances were needed in the old days to finance transactions through slower trade channels and to carry risky trade ventures. That type of lending became the province of merchant bankers who are still doing business at the old stand. In America, investment bankers tended to cater to the long-term needs by acting as middlemen for sale of securities to the general public; there is some of this in Europe, yes, but there is still more left for institutional and merchant bank financing. The commercial banking function has remained more or less separate from that of merchant banking. On the Continent the two are often combined in a single firm but with the functions separate. In Holland and Germany, more than elsewhere, the bankers tend to be all things to all people—commercial, savings, investment, and merchant bankers.

Facilities for furnishing intermediate-term capital in Europe are presently in a further stage of development. In England the major banks own the equity in Industrial and Commercial Finance Corporation (I.C.F.C.) which is now quite well established in the business of furnishing capital—both debt and equity—to smaller- and medium-size enterprises. Further institutionalization of this market is occurring on the Continent; in

France the Bank of America and the Banque de Paris et des Pays-Bas have joined to form a medium-term lending unit. A more than Common Market move is indicated by the recent establishment of an international institution under joint ownership of Barclays Bank of England, Banque National de Paris, Algemene Bank Nederland, and the Dresdner Bank of Germany. It is presumed that this investment type operation will cater to and serve multinational concerns. It is probable that some of these modernization moves would have taken place anyway, but some credit must be given to the aggressive competition of the U.S. banks that have moved abroad in all directions with a special emphasis on the European situation and with their concept of the term loan. They have moved not only by way of branches, the number of which has multiplied 7-fold since 1958, but they have also bought varying proportions of ownership in native banking establishments. The number of U.S. banks with branches overseas reached 14 in 1966 (from seven in 1958), and the number of branches rose from 119 to 244 in this 8-year period.[4] Seventeen other banks have established overseas subsidiaries under the Edge Act sections of the Federal Reserve Act.

Influence of American Methods

One way or another, what may be called American banking methods, systems, and philosophies are moving and will continue to move into other parts of the world. Local and multinational businesses will find new banking concepts based more and more on service to business with less emphasis on banking for banking's sake. In the fall of 1967, banks in the Netherlands started a bank checking system. The Prices and Incomes Board in England suggested that British use competitive deposit rates and service facilities. Belgian bankers are learning the hows and wherefores of term lending. There are German bankers who will privately admit that it might be a good idea to separate out from their institutions the functions of brokerage, underwriting, and industrial stock ownership which have for so long characterized their commercial banks. In Switzerland a banker says, "No, we are not interested in extending our services; we are quite happy and doing well enough as we are," but one wonders how long the banks in this little country, whose chief attraction to world capital is shelter, will continue to do well if the Common Market really develops and becomes stabilized. With more or less worldwide competition becoming the order of the day, a market orientation of management in the field of banking may leave the self-satisfied at the post.

Any conclusion regarding banks and their contributions to the solution of the financial problems of the multinational business must await developments. Either native country banks will grow and offer services compatible

---

[4]Robin Pringle, "Why American Banks Go Overseas," *The Banker* (November, 1966), p. 722.

with internationalization of business, or foreign banks that do respond to the needs of their customers (capital users) will make the greater share of loans and profits. The financial manager who expects these changes to take place overnight is wrong; the banking habits, customs, and laws are slow to change. It will be some time, for instance, before open book credit in commercial or consumer transactions in Europe will replace bills and cash. The banks will need to educate their respective customers in the use of the services they can offer, just as some multinational businesses may need to educate the banks with respect to the kind of service they need and expect. The next few years should be interesting and dynamic. A view of changes that have actually taken place between two visits—1958 and 1967—promises that more will be forthcoming in the banking field as well as in other phases of finance. The EEC's special study of "The Development of the European Capital Market" (the so-called Segré Report) points out that shortcomings of the European capital markets "are due not so much to insufficient savings as to the impossibility of adjusting correctly supply and demand on markets that are too narrow."

FACTORS IN INTERNATIONAL FINANCE

Now the recent and more stringent restrictions on foreign loans by U.S. banks, particularly to finance operations in Europe, will upset further the development of anything that can be called international finance. These regulations will tend to force European financing of European operations whether to be accomplished by European banks or by U.S. bank branches from their foreign dollar or foreign currency deposits.

The need within the banking systems to provide these adjustments is emphasized by the fact that one new medium for so doing has entered the scene—the Euro-dollar deposits. U.S. dollars owned and deposited in Europe (including England) are loaned hither and yon, even having been sent to America to help relieve the credit storage there in late 1966. These funds are loaned from bank to bank and from bank to industrial user. This whole operation represents a money market over and above the existing and fragmented national ones. Another start at an attempted European solution to the financing of intercountry projects may be the newly formed Societe Financiere d'Europ, which was mentioned above, even though it may operate more in the area of term loans rather than in the servicing of commercial transactions. Anyway, it is an international organization there to accomplish whatever jobs its management may find or imagine, and imagination in such a spot will be a big asset. As multi- and international businesses develop on the new scales characterized by such as the EEC, the EFTA, and the greatly expanding participation by U.S. corporations, it is as if there were a vacuum being created in the money and banking system. This vacuum will be filled by something; in our day it will probably not be an international monetary system or unit, but with advent of full convertibility, it can as well be done by multinationally recognized institutions.

33. OVERSEAS REINVESTMENT DECISIONS*

SURENDRA S. SINGHVI †

An increasing commitment to international business is one of the most significant changes in the American economy that has occurred during recent years. Growth-minded corporations are plowing dollars into international operations as never before. For the past seven years, the rate of increase in direct investment abroad has outstripped the rate of increase in domestic investment. A 1963 study by McKinsey and Company showed that 100 major United States corporations increased their foreign investments almost five times as fast as their domestic assets in 1961 and 1962.[1] As shown in Exhibit 33-1, the rate of increase in direct foreign investments has outstripped the rate of increase in gross private domestic investment.

The major reasons for this rapid expansion of foreign operations are:

1. Increasing domestic competition has squeezed domestic profit margins relatively to foreign operations.
2. Some corporations seek to participate in the more rapidly expanding foreign markets.
3. American corporations now operate in a generally favorable business climate abroad; substantial American economic aid has influenced this climate.
4. Institutional structure of the world commerce, i.e., commercial treaties, E.E.C., E.F.T.A., L.A.F.T.A., etc., provides incentives for foreign operations.

As foreign operations grow in relative importance, a stage is reached at which they can no longer be treated as a separate, isolated part of the

EXHIBIT 33-1

DIRECT FOREIGN INVESTMENTS AND GROSS PRIVATE DOMESTIC INVESTMENTS
(1958 = 100)

Year	Direct Investment Abroad	Gross Private Domestic Investment
1958	100.00	100.00
1959	116.17	128.45
1960	143.44	126.86
1961	135.39	121.55
1962	140.05	139.75
1963	159.86	144.88
1964	194.50	154.95

Source: *Economic Indicators* (February, 1965), pp. 1 and 25. (Prepared for Joint Economic Committee); *Survey of Current Business* (March, 1965), p. 12 (U.S. Department of Commerce).

---

*From *The Business Quarterly* (Spring, 1967), pp. 35-39. Reprinted by permission.

†General Supervisor, Financial Planning and Analysis, Armco Steel Corporation, Middletown, Ohio. Also Adjunct Associate Professor of Finance, Miami University, Oxford, Ohio.

[1]"Overseas Market," *Business Management* (January, 1965), p. 71.

parent company's business. President Eisenhower, in an address, pointed out that there were no longer foreign affairs and foreign policy—the proper term today is world affairs—and concluded, "We have discovered that we can't separate what we do abroad from what we do at home."[2] If an international corporation is to prosper during the 1960s and 1970s, its traditional domestic orientation must give way to a broad international outlook. While considering a company's long-term interests, an executive must ask: "Where in the world should I invest my company's time, manpower, and funds for the best long-term interests of the stockholder?"[3] It is a development of the greatest interest to executives who are personally involved in this process of internationalization and find themselves dealing with unfamiliar problems in unfamiliar settings.

An outstanding characteristic of companies engaged in foreign investment is that they tend to begin with a small investment in a particular country and expand out of retained earnings. During the last six years, nearly 15 percent of the funds used to finance foreign activities of manufacturing concerns[4] was obtained from parent companies and others in the United States, while approximately 60 percent of the finances was provided from internal sources of the foreign enterprises. The remaining 25 percent came from foreign creditors and investors.[5] This reveals the increasing importance of reinvestments of internal cash flow as a major source of financing foreign subsidiaries.

The decision to reinvest earnings is of a recurring nature. It is becoming a more important type of decision in international corporations because:

1. Reinvested earnings provide substantial impetus to further international business activity;
2. Some corporations realize the long-run advantages to themselves in contributing to a country's development. Reinvestment of earnings can make possible a contribution to a country's development. Once their contribution has been made, the subsidiary can earn large amounts of profits in the years to follow.[6]

In order to arrive at a reinvestment decision with respect to overseas operations it may be necessary to have some predetermined *standards*. If a standard used in investment decision is the extent of contribution to the economic growth of the country, the objective of maximizing dividend payout may not be achieved. If no standard is used for such decisions, it is quite possible that a firm may forego an attractive reinvestment oppor-

---

[2]Address given at St. John's College, Annapolis, May 22, 1959; reported in *The New York Times*, May 23, 1959, p. 14.

[3]McKinsey and Company, *International Enterprises: A New Dimension of American Business* (New York, 1962), p. 21.

[4]Foreign activities of manufacturing concerns are referred to here since investments in such concerns represent the largest single item of total United States direct investments abroad.

[5]Balance of Payments: 1963 Supplement, p. 218; *Survey of Current Business* (Washington: U.S. Department of Commerce, October, 1964), p. 12.

[6]This was revealed in an interview with one of the officers of Arthur D. Little, Inc. of Boston in December, 1964.

tunity by overemphasizing one type of risk. The use of rate of return as the important criterion for reinvestment decisions and ignoring other criteria may put a firm in an untenable situation similar to the firms in Cuba during the political crisis a few years ago.

The development and maintenance of effective standards for managerial performance is a difficult as well as an important task. Many executives, especially in international divisions, prefer to keep on doing the same old things in the same old way. This is usually the path of least resistance but not the path of progress in a competitive world. Such people usually oppose standards programs. It is sufficient to note here that a sound standards program promotes progress and the quality of management is limited to a considerable degree by the quality of its standards.

GREATER RISK IN OVERSEAS OPERATION DEMANDS HIGHER RETURN

Standards for reinvestment decisions in international operations are different from those used in domestic operations. If a 20 percent after-tax rate of return, for example, is satisfactory for domestic operations, a higher rate of return is usually expected in the case of overseas operations. The reason for this difference is the involvement of a greater risk in overseas operations. This risk is due to the presence of the following unique factors in the foreign environment.

Anticipated Currency Blockage

Anticipated currency blockage, where earnings have to be plowed back in the foreign subsidiary, is a matter of great concern to international corporations. The main objective of having overseas operations, like domestic operations, is to earn profits in order to declare higher dividends to stockholders. A bank account constantly increasing in size is hardly a satisfactory investment if one can never draw a check on it. Similarly, an overseas operation is hardly justifiable if its earnings can't be remitted to the parent for an uncertain period of time.[7] A higher rate of return on investments is expected if the local government's restrictions on the repatriation of profits are anticipated. In the case of Brazil, for example, a higher rate of return is expected because of the Brazilian government's restrictions on the repatriation of profits.

Expropriation and Nationalization

Expropriation and nationalization of business and industry by local governments create a great concern for foreign investors. A local government may not nationalize all industries, but a few precedents create risk and unsuitable climate for foreign investments. For example, the nationalization of life insurance companies, railroad companies, and the Imperial

---

[7]Edward J. Mock, "Financing Overseas Subsidiaries and Evaluating Their Earnings," *Business Topics* (Summer, 1964), p. 32.

Bank of India by the Indian government created an unsuitable climate for foreign investors in 1950s.

Hyper-inflation in a Local Country

Hyper-inflation in a local country brings down the exchange value of the local currency, and consequently a higher profit in local currency may not be higher in terms of the currency of the parent company.

Concessions and Restraints by a Local Government

Concessions and restraints by a local government may increase or decrease the risk involved in an investment proposal. A wide variety of incentives range from tax holidays to tariff protection, anti-dumping legislation, duty-relief, and development loans. A tax holiday of 15 years by the Nigerian government or an investment credit by the Indian government may require a relatively lower rate of return on an investment proposal. Southern Italy now offers tax exemption for several years as a means of attracting manufacturers to that part of the country. In many countries it is possible to carry forward losses from year to year, for deduction from later profits, before taxation. In England, these losses can be carried forward for six years and, in Germany, for five years; while in the U.S., it can be done to a limited extent and for a maximum of only three years. On the other hand, exchange controls and restrictions about personnel recruitment may require a higher rate of return.

Geographical Distance, Foreign Currency, and Foreign Language

Geographical distance, foreign currency, and foreign language are barriers in gathering information rapidly. Operating environments differ from the U.S. in terms of culture, politics, and economics. Inadequate information or lack of rapid communication creates difficulty with respect to decisions.

Minority Ownership

Sometimes minority ownership is required by the company law of the foreign country. This may create a problem of keeping trade secrets, and, therefore, some corporations don't consider a foreign investment at all if minority ownership is required. In such cases of minority ownership, the standards for reinvestment decisions are set up in view of the local partner's interest.

Superior Knowledge and Capability to Contribute to Economic Development

A sense of obligation to demonstrate the power of superior knowledge and capability to contribute to economic development is necessary sometimes in overseas operations. The responsibility for protecting the public interest borne by the foreign government must be shared by investors asking public support. It is charged by the people of the local country that public interest is being exploited to achieve unnecessarily high profit by foreign investors. Foreign investments are expected by them to yield a net gain to the entire economy, not just profit to the firm.[8] A foreign company must work in the spotlight of the foreign nation's public opinion and governmental attention. It must be especially concerned with the establishment of precedents and with public, government, and labor relations, since it is a guest whose freedom, resources, and continued existence depend on the sanction of the host and acceptance by the public.[9]

The standards used for new or initial overseas investments are different from the standards used for overseas reinvestment decisions. The executives of U.S. international corporations give thorough consideration to new dollar investments, but they regard their foreign earnings much as a man does his winnings at the race track, in that they are much more willing to utilize them than fresh dollar capital for additional foreign investment.[10] Their viewpoint is, "The earnings from our foreign operations represent extra funds. If we should lose them it will be unpleasant, but after all, it won't affect our overall operations. Let's take a chance with them, and to the extent that we can finance an investment with local earnings, let's go ahead and do so.[11] The managements of some corporations, according to Professor Robinson, seem to possess an unconscious feeling that foreign earnings held abroad differ somehow from domestic dollar resources.[12] The local management is more inclined to retain earnings in order to meet any emergency as well as to expand local operations. Furthermore, it is much easier for a local management to obtain approval for an expenditure of funds if the funds are locally available from earnings than if additonal investment from the U.S. is required. The reason for such a situation may be explained as follows: A firm which has earned profits is considered promising, and, therefore, the approval to reinvest earnings in the subsidiary is given with ease.

It appears that some standards may be useful guides for overseas reinvestment and that these standards may be different from the standards used for new investments as well as reinvestment of earnings in a domestic subsidiary. If the foreign environment is similar to the environment in the United States, the important standard for reinvestments may be a *cut-off rate*.[13] But in reality the foreign environment involves many risk elements,

---

[8]Simon Williams, "Negotiating Investment in Emerging Countries," *Harvard Business Review* (January-February, 1965), pp. 95-96.

[9]C. Wickham Skinner, "Management of International Production," *Harvard Business Review* (September-October, 1964), p. 127.

[10]E. R. Barlow and Ira T. Wender, *Foreign Investment and Taxation* (Englewood Cliffs, N.J.: Prentice Hall, Inc., 1955), p. 161.

[11]*Ibid.*, p. 24.

[12]Richard D. Robinson, *International Business Policy* (New York: Holt, Rinehart & Winston, Inc., 1964), p. 188.

[13]A cut-off rate is the minimum rate of return expected from an investment proposal. The United Fruit Company refers to their rate as "bogey" or target rate of return.

and the standards used for reinvestment decisions should be adjusted accordingly.

RESULTS OF LIMITED RESEARCH REVEALING

Research was undertaken by the author to seek insight into the overseas reinvestment decisions. Executives of ten U.S. international corporations and two consulting firms were interviewed.[14] Although the sample size is very small, the research reveals some significant aspects of the overseas reinvestment decisions.

In some cases, such decisions are not significant, since these firms are new in the field of international business. Many international firms of long standing make such decisions every year, but they have not developed ground rules for such decisions. Executives of these firms are not aware of the standards used by them for such decisions, or the standards used by them are not very specific. Most of the executives have mentioned the following standards or criteria being used by them for overseas reinvestment decisions:

A. Quantitative standards, which are relatively objective:
   1. Cut-off rate, based on discounted cash-flow method
   2. Payback period
   3. Degree of success, measured by the discrepancy between the planned activities and the actual performance in the previous year
B. Qualitative standards, which are relatively subjective:
   4. Risk of expropriation
   5. Risk of inconvertibility
   6. Risk of war
   7. Risk of devaluation
   8. Extent of competition in the foreign country
   9. Recommendations of the local management
   10. Incentives provided by the foreign country

In order to overcome the risks of expropriation, inconvertibility, and war, some of the firms interviewed have bought the investment guarantee insurance from the Agency for International Development. Some of the executives did not know whether this insurance program is applicable to reinvested earnings. Others think that the premium[15] is relatively high.

It was expressed by two firms that the decision to reinvest earnings is contingent upon the firm's decision to stay and/or to expand operations in the foreign country. Sometimes such decisions are dependent to a great extent upon the available investment alternatives in the foreign country. In most of these firms, reinvestment decisions are group decisions. Most of

[14]U.S. international corporations: (1) United Shoe Machinery Corporation; (2) United Fruit Company; (3) Ludlow Corporation; (4) Raytheon Corporation; (5) Gillette Company; (6) Kendall Company; (7) Hitchiner Manufacturing Company; (8) First National Bank of Boston; (9) Polaroid Company; and (10) Richardson Merill, Inc.
Consulting firms: (1) Arthur D. Little, Inc. and (2) Ebasco, Inc.

[15]The present premium rate is one half percent for each type of the risks covered; i.e., risks of expropriation, inconvertibility, and war.

them don't have ground rules in black and white, and, therefore, such decisions are based on the intuition and subjective judgment of those who are involved in decision making.

A greater need for more objective standards for overseas reinvestment decisions was expressed to the interviewers. A cut-off rate or pay-off period method is frequently used as a crude guideline for such decisions. Subjective standards are reflected in a cut-off rate or a pay-back period, but the procedure is very unsystematic. Consequently, attractive opportunities are overlooked sometimes while other times too much risk is accepted.

REINVESTMENT DECISIONS AT CRUCIAL LEVELS
FOR INTERNATIONAL FIRMS

The expansion of overseas operations out of earnings over the last decade has elevated reinvestment decisions to crucial levels for international firms. As these operations expand and competition increases, one cannot depend upon intuition and subjective judgment only. Some objective standards are desirable in order to improve the quality of reinvestment decisions and to become as systematic as possible. One should keep in mind that there cannot be one standard for such decisions, but the unique factors present in foreign environment require a set of standards or criteria.

It is not possible here to make any generalization on the basis of this research, but some observations can be made. The reinvestment decisions are not given as much attention by many firms as the initial investment decisions. Several firms don't have written ground rules for reinvestment decisions. Reinvested earnings are covered under the investment guarantee insurance, if these earnings are invested to expand the overseas operations. Many executives of the firms interviewed didn't know this fact and, therefore, didn't buy insurance for reinvested earnings. The present status of such decision making is certainly not systematic, and most of the interviewees expressed need for objective criteria to improve such decisions.

Very few studies have been done in connection with reinvestments in overseas operations at the micro-level. This research suggests the following questions for further research to improve overseas reinvestment decisions:

1. What standards should be used to make rational overseas reinvestment decisions, and how should these standards be developed?
2. To what extent is decentralization practiced with respect to reinvestment decisions in international corporations?
3. Does the rate of reinvestment differ from country to country? If yes, what factors do explain these differences?

34. REMITTING FUNDS FROM FOREIGN AFFILIATES *

DAVID B. ZENOFF†

As part of the current efforts to understand the investment behavior and overseas operation experiences of large internationally oriented American business corporations, as well as the balance of payments effects of the actions which they take, a study was recently made of the dividend remittance practices of the wholly-owned European and Canadian subsidiaries of 30 of the largest American manufacturing corporations.

The main focus of study was on two of the many unanswered questions pertaining to the direction and size of capital flows associated with United States direct investment abroad: What factors influence the dividend remittance practices of wholly-owned foreign subsidiaries, and what kinds of remittance decisions have the large so-called multinational companies been making? This article will discuss the major findings in these areas, based upon interviews with corporate treasurers and financial managers and on companies' financial records.

The questions of what proportion of overseas earnings should be reinvested and what amount should be remitted to the parent company are of prime importance in the increasingly complex responsibilities of the international financial manager. With the increased restrictiveness of the United States voluntary balance of payments program, these questions have taken on added complexity.

The present study focused on United States manufacturing companies' wholly-owned affiliates in Europe and Canada. The intent was to concentrate on the industrial sector, form of ownership, and geographical areas in which there has been the greatest concentration of foreign direct investment.[1]

For purposes of the study, a "multinational business corporation" was defined as an American corporation which was ranked by *Fortune* magazine as one of the largest 500 in 1965, had operating subsidiaries in at least six foreign countries, and owned no less than one quarter of the equity of each subsidiary. The study concentrated on large companies because of the great impact which they have had on the balance of international payments for both the United States and foreign countries. In one recent year, for example, several of these giant corporations each received from their over-

---

*From *Financial Executive* (March, 1968), pp. 46-63. Reprinted by permission.

†Assistant Professor of International Business, Graduate School of Business, Columbia University.

[1]Approximately 60 percent of the total book value of United States direct investment abroad is in the countries of Europe and Canada; since 1960, about 65 percent of all new American establishments abroad were in manufacturing, and somewhat more than one half of the number of manufacturing affiliates abroad are wholly owned by the United States parent companies. Sources: *Survey of Current Business*, various issues; Booz, Allen, and Hamilton, *66 Months of New Foreign Business Activity of United States Firms* (New York, 1965); Judd Polk, Irene Meister, and Lawrence Veit, *U. S. Production Abroad and the Balance of Payments: A Survey of Corporate Investment Experience* (New York: National Industrial Conference Board, 1966).

seas subsidiaries more than $20 million in dividends. And it is estimated that the 160 firms which fit the description of a multinational company account for at least one half of the total book value of United States direct investment abroad in manufacturing.

For each of the 30 companies studied, information was sought from both the company officer who was interviewed (treasurers or comptrollers of the parent corporation or international division) and from the company record of dividends actually remitted from overseas subsidiaries. The queries focused on the period from 1960 to 1965 because data for this period was readily available and managers could more easily recall the immediately preceding period than any earlier one.

DECISION-MAKING PROCESS

The following discussion will concentrate on the effects which environmental and internal considerations were found to have on the foreign remittance decisions of the 30 companies studied.

Uncertainty About the Foreign Environment

The greater uncertainty American corporate officers had about the foreign business environment when compared to the domestic scene was usually attributed to three principal factors:

1. Being in international business added to the number of economic, political, and business variables which management needed to review.
2. The difficulties in obtaining and evaluating timely reliable information on conditions abroad were greater.
3. The relative lack of personal familiarity [was combined with the lack of] a businessman's feel for the foreign operating climate in which their company had investments.

It is not surprising that in response to the higher level of riskiness which they perceived in the foreign environment, most managers have developed both a strong aversion to holding corporate-controlled funds overseas and an acute awareness of the extent to which their equity funds abroad were exposed. Equity, from the parent company's viewpoint, was normally considered to include a subsidiary's net worth and its long- and short-term debt to the parent. Being exposed seemed to be roughly synonymous with vulnerability to partial or total loss in dollar value.

To avoid being overly exposed abroad, a wide variety of practices was followed. Many firms severely limited the amount of their initial dollar commitment by keeping the capitalization of the subsidiaries small; some subsequently refused to provide additional company funds other than through reinvestment of local earnings; many companies pressed subsidiaries to maximize their use of local debt sources as the primary means of adding to working capital or for capital expansion purposes; and the majority of the firms did not permit their foreign subsidiaries to hold on to funds generated locally which were in excess of agreed-upon working capital requirements. The foregoing was a commonly used dividend decision rule for most of the companies.

From the field research it was possible to identify a range of these attitudes about foreign riskiness and the use of corporate-controlled funds overseas. At one extreme were about 15 percent of the firms which directed their subsidiaries to remit 90 to 100 percent of their earnings each year in order to "minimize the possibilities of exchange loss and any uncertainty about how much control we have over these funds." These companies operated to the greatest extent possible on local (foreign) capital, and subsidiaries were allowed to cut the size of their payout ratios only if they had urgent unsupplied requirements for funds.

A somewhat more moderate position was taken by the majority (about 70 percent) of the American companies which, as indicated above, directed their subsidiaries to remit all excess funds; i.e., those funds not required for working capital purposes or for planned capital expansion within the forthcoming 12 months. Many of these much preferred to operate on local borrowings rather than on reinvested earnings, but they were less dogmatic than the extreme group and would usually compare the costs of borrowing abroad with reinvesting the earnings. A few of the companies refused to borrow from an outside source to meet their subsidiaries' requirements. In spite of their aversion to holding excess funds abroad, these firms preferred to rely on the available foreign cash flow for local reinvestment rather than remitting a dividend.

At the other end of the spectrum was a group comprising about 15 percent of the sample population whose preference for fund remittances was subservient to their goal of making each foreign subsidiary financially self-reliant. To this end, the parent companies decided to pass up opportunities to receive dividends from the subsidiaries, permitting the affiliates to reinvest their earnings to "strengthen their balance sheets and enhance their position with foreign bankers."

Largely in response to what might be termed a long-run apprehension about the possibility of foreign governments imposing exchange controls, about one quarter of the companies made it mandatory that each of their subsidiaries "develop a pattern of continuity and consistency in their dividend payout." In essence they believed that the imposition of exchange controls was not a farfetched possibility, even in Europe or Canada. If restrictions were placed on capital outflows, these managers believe their subsidiaries would have a much better chance for approval to remit their annual dividends to the parent company than would subsidiaries which had an irregular payout record. Their affiliates could point to a history of such outflows, identifiable in terms of regularity in timing and relationship to earnings.

Risk of Currency Value Change

Officers of approximately 60 percent of the companies indicated that if they believed there was an increased likelihood of a devaluation within the "foreseeable future" (i.e., forthcoming eight months), they would seriously consider using the subsidiary dividend as a method of minimizing its exposure overseas, if they were actually to take any special defensive actions. The majority doubted that they would do much ("It is kind of difficult to out-guess the devaluation; the experts don't agree, and we would just be guessing"). If they did take action, most doubted that their strategy would include a change in the timing or the amount of the dividend. Instead, they said that they preferred to use the intercompany loan account or the forward purchase of exchange to guard against exchange losses; these methods were thought to be less open to public reporting and, therefore, not as likely to be known outside the firm.

Approximately 40 percent of the companies studied responded that they did not consider the threat of devaluation during the process of deciding upon the foreign dividend. There were two fundamental explanations for this exclusion:

1. Devaluation threats were of real concern to management and a stimulus for action, but where they were anticipated, the form of hedging was other than adjusting the timing or size of a subsidiary's dividend.
2. The threat of devaluation was not of sufficient concern to trigger a specific management response to it. Companies either took a general stance against loss from devaluation ("We are not in the currency exchange business; we try to keep our foreign exposure down always, but we don't try to make windfalls"), or they somehow ignored it ("Devaluation fears are not part of management operating decisions" or "We have been overseas so long that every time someone expects a devaluation we can't afford the time to play around").

Tax Costs and Considerations

Field interviews confirmed the researcher's expectation that almost every multinational business corporation takes taxation into account—to some degree—when the foreign dividend decision is being made. The degree of influence which taxation exerted on the final decision and the nature of the analysis to the tax variable were found to differ considerably among the companies. The range of these differences is illustrated by the quotes from two interviews:

> Our goal for each subsidiary is for it to become financially independent . . . it should build up and maintain a solid current position . . . a dividend will be paid only if the subsidiary has met this objective and has no foreseeable capital requirements . . . taxes are *not* very important relative to the other criteria. We do not calculate the tax effects of paying a dividend. . . . As an example, we won't pay a dividend in light of the change in the English tax law.

There are two bases for our dividend decision: the cash position of the subsidiary . . . and taxation. . . . We try to juggle to get the best overall tax credit. We calculate the tax effect of various levels of dividends from subsidiaries; in fact we just hired a new tax man to calculate optimum dividends from a tax point of view. . . .

The fact that more than two thirds of the firms shared the latter company's attitude toward taxes was indicative of the significant importance of the taxation influence on the foreign dividend decision. Foreign and United States taxation legislation is very complicated and detailed, and tax matters of large corporations are normally handled by trained tax accountants on the comptrollers' or treasurers' staffs.

The attitudes which companies took toward the taxation variable in the foreign dividend decision can be categorized according to the firms' tax objectives:

1. About one quarter of the firms, which were the most tax-conscious, made every attempt to minimize the corporation's total tax burden and normally gave this consideration higher priority than any others in the dividend decision.
2. For 35 percent of the companies, taxes assumed considerable importance, and the objective of minimizing the corporation's total tax burdens was of about equal importance to one or two other factors, such as the risk of leaving funds abroad or the subsidiary's requirements for funds.
3. For a little more than one fifth of the companies, paying taxes to the United States on dividends received from overseas was considered a fact of doing business, and no effort was made to delay or avoid this obligation. Their main interest in taxes was to avoid penalty taxes—those which were designed to induce or retard income distribution in particular countries. This approach is illustrated by the excerpt from an interview with an executive of one multinational company:

There are two angles to this tax rate which we should not confuse. One is tax penalties—for paying too high or too low a dividend. That we try to avoid at all costs. But merely having to pay a tax on income—and whether we pay it this year or next—this doesn't bother us. There is no substantial loss (in paying U.S. taxes on foreign dividends) unless one considers the loss the use of the tax money that may have been paid . . . but for a company like ours that has a substantial amount of ready cash, there is no real loss involved. . . . What I referred to earlier (i.e., penalties) was failure to pay a required dividend and incurring a tax that would not otherwise be paid at all, such as Germany. . . . In general, then, we do not compute in detail in advance what the tax situation is when we try to estimate future dividends.

4. A few multinational corporations assigned a general low level of importance to any kind of tax consideration (i.e., which may have had relevance to the foreign dividend) and rarely based their decisions on analysis of the tax variable.

Exhibit 34-1 provides a demonstration of the differences in subsidiaries' payouts that resulted when parent companies differed in their tax objectives. The companies in the sample which owned subsidiaries in Germany were divided into two groups: those that could be termed "tax conscious" and those that were not. Because the German tax law is designed

Exhibit 34-1

Average Dividend Payout Ratios

	Parent Companies Tax Conscious	Parent Companies Not Tax Conscious
Mean payout ratio for wholly-owned German subsidiaries	.73	.70
Mean payout ratio for all other wholly-owned subsidiaries located in Canada and Europe other than in Germany	.47	.81

to encourage a high level of corporate earnings distribution, one would expect to find evidence that the law had a greater impact on the tax-conscious group of companies than on the other, non-tax-conscious firms.

As summarized in Exhibit 34-1, the data from a small sample of companies appears to be consistent with the foregoing expectation.

The influence which taxation could have on the foreign dividend decision was also recognized in a recent National Industrial Conference Board report:

> Local tax laws may be conducive to maintaining a higher rate of dividends than would be maintained if only the financial needs of the subsidiary were considered. Until recently, Germany was a good example of such a situation. . . . Even though the parent company had to pay an additional 15 percent withholding tax on dividends considered to be leaving the country, it was advantageous for most interviewed companies to declare a maximum dividend and then to provide funds . . . needed by the subsidiaries.[2]

Where tax analysis was of some importance, the comptroller usually had the responsibility for advising the decision maker on the tax effects of various payout decisions which they were considering. Depending upon the composition of the overseas operations (i.e., number of affiliates and their legal forms) and the tax objectives of the firm, the design of the analysis might include the total tax burden to the corporation (foreign plus United States taxes minus United States tax credits) which would result from different payout possibilities for each of the foreign subsidiaries. Companies which extended calculations to this level usually went on to compute the optimum foreign dividend—the payout ratio for each of the overseas operations which would minimize the overall corporate tax liability.

The Method by Which the Parent Company Retained Control of the Dividend Decision

In all cases studied, the final decision on the exact amount of foreign earnings to be remitted to the parent company was made by the parent

---

[2]Polk, Meister, and Veit, *op. cit.*, p. 91.

rather than by the subsidiary. The headquarters staff concluded that where the ideas of the parent company were not the same as those of the affiliates the parent should have the final say-so because it had a clearer view of how to serve the best interests of the company as a whole. This appeared to be especially true when it came to guarding the firm's equity funds against being overly exposed to the multitude of risks in the foreign environment. It was also valid for a number of companies which held that one of the values in making subsidiaries remit dividends was to impress upon their managers ("remind" and "discipline" were the words used by the various corporate officers) that the capital on which they were operating was the risk capital of the parent company. The few companies that referred to this particular consideration in their dividend decisions used it to justify either a basic reason for requiring subsidiaries to pay *any* dividend to the parent or one of the bases for believing that each subsidiary should strive to pay out a "regular and consistent pattern" of its earnings.

In about one half of the companies studied, the initial recommendation for the level of a dividend to be paid by a foreign subsidiary came from the manager of that operation. In most firms where this procedure was followed, the dividend was included in the subsidiary's budgets or similar pro-forma statements which it was required to submit periodically to the parent company. In the other half of the sample, the initiative in dividend planning was from a member of the parent company management responsible for making recommendations (and, in some cases, the decisions) as to whether or not each of the foreign subsidiaries should pay a dividend and its amount. In about two thirds of the firms, the officer of the parent corporation was the one to either review the recommendation from the subsidiaries or to prepare the plans on behalf of the foreign affiliates. In the remainder of the companies, an officer of the international division had this responsibility.

To assist the financial vice-president or treasurer in making the final decision or, in a few corporations, to act in their stead, the comptroller, who usually advised on taxes, or corporate vice-president in charge of the international division was normally involved. In approximately two thirds of the companies, this decision was reached in the beginning of the fiscal period and incorporated into the respective budgets of the subsidiaries and the parent company. If the subsidiary's operating results subsequently proved to be in line with the initial expectations, the budgeted dividend would normally be treated as irrevocably binding upon the subsidiary, to be altered only in the case of an unforeseen contingency. In those firms which decided upon the foreign dividend after actual operating results had been analyzed, the decision was transmitted as a recommendation to the board of directors of each subsidiary.

Other Forms of Funds Transfer From the Overseas Subsidiaries

One of the areas of inquiry in the field research was to try to determine if the use of other forms of remittance from foreign subsidiaries had any direct influence on the foreign dividend decision. While it is not within the scope of this article to present a comprehensive examination of the rationale, opportunities for, and actual utilization of management fees, royalties, interest expenses and repayment of intercompany loans, etc., it is appropriate to discuss the more limited question of the effect of the use of other remittance forms on the foreign dividend decision.

There are probably two primary reasons why American multinational corporations would decide to use these other forms of remittance: to get around restrictions on dividend remittances by foreign host countries and to try to minimize the overall corporate tax liability on the complex intercompany flow of funds. It was not surprising to find that firms had decided to employ these techniques for both reasons. In this discussion, however, attention will be restricted to the tax motive.

European and Canadian governments will, within rather ill-defined limits, permit companies incorporated within their borders to deduct from their taxable incomes as expenses of conducting their business, certain "reasonable" fees, royalties, interest payments, and export commissions which are paid to the American parent for services and resources rendered. Many of these remittances are, however, subject to a 5 to 15 percent foreign withholding tax. A different situation occurs when the subsidiary makes a repayment of loan principal to the parent company: as long as the foreign corporation is not deemed to be too thinly capitalized, the payment is neither deductible as a business expense nor subject to a withholding tax at the time of remittance.

The United States Internal Revenue Code requires the recipient parent corporations to treat royalties, management fees, interest payments, etc. as ordinary income for taxation purposes, allowing them to apply the foreign withholding taxes as foreign tax credits. Repayment of an intercompany loan by the subsidiary is not counted as income to the parent for domestic tax purposes.

From an overall corporate tax point of view, the relative attractiveness of using any one or combination of these remittance forms in lieu of, or complementary to, a dividend appears to depend on the individual circumstances. The use of debt repayment may be extremely desirable if the foreign host governments do not levy their taxes on the capital of the subsidiary. The use of royalties, fees, etc., which provide *low* foreign tax credits, may be timely if the United States parent company has excess tax credits. And, as reported by some firms, within the past few years the United States Internal Revenue Service has strongly urged some American companies to charge their subsidiaries for certain transfers of technology, management services, and overall support which hitherto had been "gifts" by the parent firm.

It was found that, in addition to dividends, just about all of the companies used some form of remittance to transfer funds from subsidiaries to the parent. These took on a variety of forms and names: royalties, management fees, repayment of loans, interest on loans, administrative and technical assistance fees, trademark licenses, and commissions on exports made by the subsidiary to third countries. Approximately 60 percent of the firms used the so-called management fees, 40 percent used royalties, 30 percent used repayment of loans made by the parent company, and a few firms utilized the other types of remittances.

The aggregate data on remittances made by United States owned manufacturing operations abroad indicate that royalties and fees have become an increasingly important form of remittance from Canada and Europe. In fact, during the past five to seven years, the total amount of royalties and fees remitted from these areas by manufacturing companies increased by about 100 percent, while total remittances (dividends, interest, and royalties and fees) increased by 43 percent. At the present time, royalties and fees account for approximately one third of the total remittances from Canada and Europe.

The amount of funds which companies transferred via each of these methods was said to be determined by four main factors:

1. The value of the services and benefits provided the foreign subsidiary;
2. The amount allowed by foreign taxing authorities as deductible business expenses;
3. The total amount of contribution to the overhead of the international division desired from overseas operations pro-rated to each subsidiary; and
4. The overall corporate tax picture, including the availability of foreign tax credits and the possibilities of remitting funds in the form of dividends.

One third of the companies indicated that their analysis of the foreign dividend decision was either tempered by or made in conjunction with the decision on the volume of funds to transfer by management fees, royalties, etc. The remainder stated that their dividend decision was "wholly apart from any consideration of other forms of remittance." The following excerpt from an interview with the assistant treasurer of the international division of a multinational corporation with extensive foreign operations is representative of the latter type of management approach:
Question:
    Does anyone sit down and say, "We would like to receive the following amount of funds from, say, our German subsidiary this year in each of the following forms: dividends, management fees, loan repayments, etc."?
Answer:
    This has not been done yet. We are looking forward to this with a better cash management and a better financial management of our operations in the future when we will have more, let's say, "financial budgeting" coming from each subsidiary telling us in advance what we can expect from them in the forthcoming year. Then we would see what would be the best way of bringing it out. We really have not reached a point yet in which the distribution of excess cash flow is a problem for us. We either have substantial intercompany accounts, or we have substantial local financing which has built up

and continued through the years because of our expansion. We would first wish to use that excess cash to start paying back the outside bank borrowing. So far, then, we have not reached a point where a cash accumulation is a problem for us—and how to remit it out might be a problem for us.

Among those companies that were to some degree influenced by the use of other forms of remittance in deciding upon the foreign dividend, there were two general approaches. In one of these, the dividend decision was primarily the result of having considered a small number of factors (threat of devaluation, taxes, etc.) which the management believed to be the most relevant criteria. Once the dividend was tentatively decided upon, they considered the inflow of funds which were expected in the forms of management fees, royalties, etc., and determined if these expected streams would in any way alter the tentative decision on dividends.

In the second group of companies, the foreign dividend resulted from the "selection of the best ways to remit funds from among dividends, fees, royalties. . . ." The firms which followed this approach either decided upon the total amount or percentage of foreign earnings that should be remitted back to the parent and then decided upon the best method to obtain them from a tax point of view; or they did not predesignate how much should be remitted from abroad and made individual decisions for each subsidiary, based upon whatever criteria they considered important and the tax effects of various forms of remittance that might be used.

The Nature of the Capital-Budgeting Approach to Overseas Operations

To some degree, every company tailored its foreign dividend to suit the individual fund requirements of its overseas subsidiaries. The extent to which these companies were influenced by the overseas requirements must be viewed in light of their attitudes toward investing equity dollars in overseas ventures, using local (foreign) debt sources, temporarily foregoing dividends from abroad, developing financially self-reliant subsidiaries, retaining foreign earnings overseas, and guaranteeing the debt of their subsidiaries. These attitudes or operating policies determined, of course, the range of financing alternatives that a particular company might be expected to consider when planning for the fund requirements of a subsidiary and its pro forma dividend declarations.

The general reluctance of American manufacturing companies to invest ample funds in each of their foreign operations or to accumulate funds abroad for long-term requirements has been discussed in this article and elsewhere. The attitudes of these firms toward borrowing abroad and the particulars (forms and sources of the debt) of the borrowing that has taken place are less well documented. However, the present study and the macro data on the sources of funds for United States owned manufacturing enterprises in Europe and Canada suggest that, even before the advent of the U.S.

balance of payments programs, the majority of the companies preferred to supplement the subsidiaries' internally generated funds with foreign borrowings rather than to supply funds from the United States by means of equity, and even debt, and that they frequently used locally obtained debt funds as a supplement to or in lieu of reinvested earnings.

Due to the cost of debt, the mix of retained earnings and local borrowings may have varied among firms and even between subsidiaries of the same company. But, with very few exceptions, the fund requirements of the subsidiary was one of the most heavily weighed considerations in the foreign dividend decision process. Some firms carefully compared the costs of using borrowed funds versus retained earnings to finance overseas expansion and working capital needs. Many began their analysis with the expectation that a particular percentage of current earnings ought to be reinvested in each subsidiary:

> Since the War we have reinvested between 33 and 40 percent of the subsidiaries' earnings each year and have found that amount to be appropriate to maintain their growth and provide us with a regular dividend.

A small minority of the companies appeared to overlook the fund requirements of the subsidiaries by automatically directing them to remit between 90 to 100 percent of their earnings every year. These firms permitted deviations only if the subsidiary could convincingly demonstrate that its fund requirements vis-à-vis the costs of locally obtained debt made the reinvestment of earnings the more attractive source of financing.

The uses for which the foreign subsidiary might require funds would be either working capital or capital expansion. It was learned that the companies usually transferred abroad the United States techniques and approaches for controlling as well as estimating the working capital needs of each foreign subsidiary. However, the criteria which many firms used for evaluating proposed capital expansion and their methods of capital budgeting differed at times from those in the United States. Companies which normally evaluated the relative attractiveness of domestic investment opportunities in terms of their rate of return on invested capital used the following approaches to make decisions on foreign investment opportunities:

1. Many companies did not place much weight on rate of return or a quantitative measure of the "goodness" of a proposal. They felt that the difficulties in forecasting future flows of funds in foreign environments were such that it was impossible to place much confidence in the figures which were generated. Consequently, they tended to rely much more heavily on strictly qualitative judgments on how well the proposal fitted into the overall strategy of the subsidiary and how much of a need for it the operation appeared to have.

2. Those firms that did use rate of return or payback calculations as the basis for evaluating investments were fairly well split between their reliance on a worldwide minimum acceptable

rate and the use of an *ad hoc* reasonable cutoff figure for a particular subsidiary.

3. Once a plan for expansion of fixed assets in an overseas subsidiary had been judged acceptable, by whatever standards, funds were allocated to it in different ways by different companies. The majority of the companies did not evaluate the relative desirability of the proposal by comparing it to other acceptable projects which had been proposed by sister subsidiaries or the parent company. Essentially three reasons were given for not making a comparison:

> We don't *need* to make these comparisons because there is an abundance of capital and/or credit available to finance whatever investments we wish to undertake.
>
> We haven't needed to compare alternatives because there usually aren't many worthwhile opportunities competing for funds at any given time; we are in a liquid position.
>
> We don't wish to invest more of the parent's funds in a going subsidiary, and, at the present time, none of the subsidiaries has a surplus; therefore, we can't shift funds between subsidiaries and there is no need to make a comparison of proposals.

The Parent Corporation's Policy of Paying Dividends to Its Own Shareholders

About one third of the companies indicated that they were strongly influenced in the foreign dividend decision by the proportion of their own earnings which were paid in dividends to the corporate shareholders. In most of these instances, they were referring to the publicly owned American corporation. In a few cases, however, the reference was to the domestic holding company which legally owned the overseas subsidiaries and which itself was a wholly-owned (management) subsidiary of the publicly owned multinational corporation. Under both organizational forms, the essential point was the same: the dividend payout ratio of the parent company provided a significantly important guide to what the foreign dividends should be.

The guide was utilized by the companies in one or two ways. A few of the firms used the parent payout figure as the payout goal for the overall foreign operations: that particular percentage of the total foreign earnings must be remitted to the parent company, even though for an individual subsidiary the amount declared will not necessarily be identical or even close to that target. As a matter of fact, these companies set the overall target and then proceeded on the basis: "Where should we get the money?" There was no systematic attempt made to receive a certain percentage of each subsidiary's earnings.

Most of the companies using parent payout ratios as a guide approached the foreign dividend decision in a somewhat different manner. They set a payout target for each subsidiary identical to the payout ratio of the parent. An attempt was made to adhere to the target rate, although deviations were permitted if they believed certain conditions warranted them (e.g., tax effects, devaluation threat). From the available evidence, it appears that in the great majority of cases the dividend payouts of overseas subsidiaries were not exactly the same as the parent company's.

The companies gave four somewhat related reasons for placing so much importance on the parent payout ratio:

1. Cash was required by the parent company to meet its own obligations to stockholders, and the subsidiaries must meet their portion of the obligation by providing their share of the cash.

2. By paying to the parent company the same percentage of its earnings that the latter pays to its owners, the subsidiary was demonstrating its value and perhaps worthiness to the ultimate shareholder. This was reflected in the following quotes from discussions at two companies about their dividend policy guidelines: "The parent company gives its shareholders an annual return on their investment; the subsidiaries also have this responsibility." "Every corporation must recognize its obligations to reimburse its shareholders for the use of their funds."

3. For the many companies that have had difficulties in obtaining dividend payments from a portion of their subsidiaries in less developed countries, the establishment of a uniform dividend payout rate throughout the corporate system, justified by the obligation to the stockholders, was hoped to be persuasive enough to gain official approval for these subsidiaries to make the remittance to the parent company. The excerpt below is from an interview held with a member of the holding company which manages the international operations of a large multinational corporation:

> International as such is expected to contribute 55 percent of its earnings to the parent company, and in order to do that it is necessary for us to maintain the policy that the subsidiary companies must also supply 55 percent of their earnings. The policy also came about on the basis that this could not be criticized in the field. In other words, it would not be unrealistic in the minds of any local interested foreign agency—the ministries, the government, or whatever organization there might be—to expect at least a 55 percent distribution of the profits of the company in that year. . . .

4. In a few companies the interviewee said that the parent payout ratio provided a useful rule of thumb for foreign dividend remittances; the amount reinvested in the subsidiary seemed to them to have fulfilled the affiliate's requirements, while concurrently providing a satisfactory amount of funds to the parent company.

The Desire of the Parent Company to Present the Strongest Possible Financial Statements to the Public

Subject to the regulations of the Securities and Exchange Commission Act summarized below, it appears that publicly owned American corporations may exercise choice in the matter of whether they will include the status of their overseas investments in their reports to stockholders on operations and net worth. The relevant legislation requires that "the annual report must contain the consolidated financial statements if they are necessary to reflect adequately the financial position and results of operations of the issuer and its subsidiaries."[3] In practice, the company's choice is really dual in nature: What information does the corporation wish to include, and in what form does it desire to present it?

With respect to the task of deciding upon a dividend rate for overseas subsidiaries, a company's consolidation practices present certain constraints and opportunities for management's consideration. If the parent company consolidates its financial statements to include all or a large segment of its overseas subsidiaries, the dividends actually remitted by the consolidated subsidiaries will not have any effect on the reported income of the corporation. Hence, the firm cannot manage its foreign dividends in such a way as to affect favorably the overall profits reported to the shareholders. On the other hand, to the extent that the parent corporation's dividend policy is anchored to its earnings, the inclusion of positive foreign earnings in the consolidated statements can be expected to increase the amount paid out in the form of dividends and, concomitantly, to increase the parent's requirements for cash to make the distribution.

The fact that only the remittances received from the affiliates are recorded in the company's income when a corporation does not consolidate the results of foreign operations gives management certain latitude in deciding to what extent overseas operating results will increase the reported corporate earnings.

Approximately 30 percent of the firms studied did not consolidate the results of foreign operations in their reports to stockholders. In the main, their overseas earnings were a smaller percentage of total worldwide profits (18 percent on the average) than the mean for the entire sample (25 percent), and the number of foreign subsidiaries which each company owned (ten on the average) was one half of the average number owned by companies in the sample. It follows that companies could be expected to consolidate their public reports only after the overseas operations accounted for a sizeable or profitable portion of the total corporate picture, in accord with the intent of the SEC Act.

Among the firms that did not consolidate their foreign results, there were no noticeable patterns in their approach to the foreign dividend decision or in the criteria they used, except that all of them disclaimed being interested in or influenced by the dividend policy of the parent company. In a few of the interviews, the corporate officers stated that the unconsolidated status of foreign subsidiaries provided them with both constraint and flexibility in making the foreign subsidiaries' dividend analyses. They were relatively free to decide how foreign earnings would affect the stockholders' earnings per share, but they said that they were under self-imposed pressure to set a floor below which the total dollar value of foreign dividends should not go. The floor was informally established at the amount

---

[3]Quoted from the recent amendments to Rule 14a-3 under the Securities and Exchange Commission Act of 1934.

of the previous year's foreign dividend receipts, which was also found to be true for the dividend policies of the publicly owned American corporations.

METHODS FOR REMITTANCE DECISIONS

It was evident in the study that multinational business corporations were distinctive by their differences. The nature of their differences included the attitude of top management vis-à-vis international operations, the financial and managerial resources which a firm was able to devote to its international commitments, and its competitive position in foreign markets.

As a means of identifying the differences and similarities between firms so that an analysis can be made of factors that influenced particular companies, four distinguishing company characteristics will be used. These are the number of foreign subsidiaries owned by the firm, the length of its experience in foreign operations, the importance of the earnings of overseas subsidiaries, and the policies of the parent company toward consolidating the operating results of the overseas operations in its reports to the stockholders.

A brief review follows to orient the reader to the relevance of each of these characteristics to the decision on foreign dividends.

The Number of Foreign Subsidiaries Owned by the Company

When a multinational company owns a large number of foreign subsidiaries (say 35) whose aggregate income is considered to be of significant importance to the worldwide corporation, the foreign dividend decision-making becomes complex and difficult. If the firm is prone to base its decisions on its feel for the foreign environment as well as on the immediate needs and future plans of both the individual subsidiaries and the corporation as a whole, it is apparent that it will either have to invest a sizeable amount of its resources in the analysis of these variables or it will have already developed a problem-solving program for cutting through the maze of government regulations, external information, and internal strategies which impinge upon the decision.

The Length of Experience Which a Firm Has Had in Foreign Business

The relationship between a company's experience in performing a task and the approach which it is likely to take each time the task must be accomplished is summarized in this excerpt from Simon and March:

> Problem-solving activities can generally be identified by the extent to which they involve search: search aimed at discovering alternatives of action or consequences of action. . . . An environmental stimulus [that] immediately evokes a highly complex and organized set of responses . . . is called a performance program. In this case, search has been eliminated from the

problem, but choice—of a very routinized kind—remains . . . in general, we would anticipate that programs will be generated by past experience and in expectation of future experience in a given situation.[4]

It may be expected that the longer the international experience of a company or its managers is, the more likely it would be that the firm had developed an organizational capacity for readily answering the recurring question of how much of a dividend should be remitted by overseas subsidiaries, so that each year's decision would not require a special search for alternatives or consequences of actions. This is in contrast to companies relatively new in the international business field; they would have to take a more exploratory approach to the dividend analysis. Their policies and objectives were most likely not clearly defined and/or in a state of flux, typical of an organization which was maturing and becoming knowledgeable.

The Importance of Overseas Subsidiaries' Earnings to the Company

A high degree of correlation between the importance of the decision to the firm and the amount of thought and preparation given to the decision could be anticipated. Depending on the firm, "importance" could be measured in terms of absolute dollar value of the foreign dividends or how sizeable the dividends were relative to the worldwide corporate income. However defined, since a final decision on the dividend was a matter of management's judgment, the essential difference between companies with important foreign earnings and those for which it was not as important could be expected to be in the amount and comprehensiveness of the information provided to managers to assist them in exercising judgment.

The Consolidation Practices of the Parent Company

This characteristic of both company policy and the size of overseas operations has been discussed at length previously. All that needs to be reiterated is that when the parent company does not consolidate the results of foreign operations, its management is provided the opportunity to manage reported earnings to the extent of being able to decide how large the dividends from overseas should be. When the parent company does consolidate the foreign results, it is very possible that the parent company will require the subsidiaries to declare the same proportion of their earnings as dividends as the parent had, so that the foreign affiliates provide their share of the funds required to meet stockholder obligations.

Two fairly distinctive classes of multinational firms evolve from the study. In one class are the companies which have years of experience in international business and relatively large numbers of foreign subsidiaries and

---

[4]James G. March and Herbert A. Simon, *Organizations* (New York: John Wiley & Sons, Inc., 1958), pp. 139-143.

which consolidate the results of overseas operations—a relatively large percentage of the total corporate earnings. For identification purposes, these will be called Group I. In the other class the companies had relatively small foreign earnings, relatively few foreign subsidiaries, and fairly limited experience in international business. These will be called Group II companies.

The decision variables which appeared to be the most influential for members of each are listed below:

Group I

Parent payout ratio
Patterns of regularity
Other forms of remittance
Threat of devaluation

Group II

Taxation
Threat of devaluation
Other forms of remittance

Group II companies appear to take an exploratory, cautious, and flexible approach to the foreign dividend decision. Each of the decision variables for this class of firms requires analysis by the management, and decisions based on the informational content of these factors could differ largely from one year to the next and from one subsidiary to another.

Group I firms—those which appear to be more truly international in their overall posture—were most influenced by the payout ratio of the parent companies and by the need to produce patterns of regularity in subsidiaries' dividend payouts. The importance given to these particular factors suggests that the decision-making process among Group I firms is in effect a problem-solving program wherein historically developed rules of thumb are used (e.g., the parent's payout ratio), or standards are employed to approximate reasonably satisfying outcomes in normal periods. Both the parent payout ratio and patterns of regularity could be considered examples of these standards.

It is also noteworthy that in both of these classes of multinational companies there were companies which considered the threat of devaluation and other forms of remittance to be of importance in the foreign dividend decision. It may be surmised that for the Group I firms considerations of this nature were prompted by the importance and complexities of their foreign operations. To protect the value of their equity and to try to rationalize the flows of funds between the multitude of overseas affiliates and the parent, the large internationally oriented companies considered as important the analysis of these variables.

The Group II companies looked at devaluation threats and other forms of remittance probably because the small size of their international operations allowed them to evaluate the environment of each foreign country in which they owned a subsidiary, as well as to analyze the pros and cons of remitting funds in the forms of royalties, fees, repayment of loan principal, etc. Because they were new in international operations, these companies very likely were unable to approach the foreign dividend decision with any rules of thumb or standards of performance which could greatly simplify the decision-making process.

FOREIGN DIVIDEND PAYOUT POLICIES

In the preceding sections the discussion focused on how companies approached the decision on foreign dividends and on those factors that exerted an important influence on the corporate officers responsible for making the decisions. It was shown that particular types of multinational companies tended to follow similar practices and that they frequently considered the same factors to be of prime importance in the process of determining which course of action to take. The discussion will be continued here with a description and analysis of the foreign dividend decisions which were made in these companies and the patterns of payout policies which were observed among similar types of firms. The discussion will be divided into two main parts: (A) the range of payout practices which was observed and illustrations of the various types and (B) analysis and some conclusions which can be drawn from the evidence about the kind of payout practices which were adhered to by particular types of multinational companies.

The Range of Foreign Dividend Payout Practices

Approximately one quarter of the companies in the sample had adopted the policy of establishing a target payout ratio for all of their foreign subsidiaries and expected each of them to abide by it unless unusual circumstances warranted deviation. While the companies differed in their respective thinking about what constituted unusual circumstances, the reference was generally to either (1) a tax regulation which would in effect penalize the company if it remitted the target rate of dividends or (2) a dire need for funds by one of the subsidiaries which could not be satisfied by local borrowing.

Following are illustrations of the reasons why certain companies have selected this kind of policy and the differences in their implementation of it:

> Our European subsidiaries must each remit 60 to 66 percent of their after-tax earnings. This policy has been used historically and found to be appropriate for the entire postwar period. The earnings which are reinvested in the foreign operations have been enough to maintain their growth, while at the same time providing a record of regular dividend payments from each of these foreign countries. . . . When local taxes warrant an increase or decrease in the payout rate (as in Germany), we do change the

dividend from the normal 60 to 66 percent. But, subsequently the parent company will reinvest the difference. The English subsidiary paid an abnormally high dividend in early 1966 because of that country's new tax law. . . . In the next three years we'll be undertaking sizeable expansion in Europe, but the normal dividend will be retained. If local borrowing is not enough, the parent will supply more dollars. We are primarily concerned with having a long-standing, regular dividend in each country so the host governments will respect it.

The policy is for a subsidiary to pay out 50 percent of the prior year's earnings when the organization is in a position to do so and it has the resources to accomplish it. Once a subsidiary has reached financial maturity and is committed to being a dividend payer, there is very, very little that can happen to change that. In other words, even if we go through an expansion program, we expect that they will continue to make a 50 percent distribution of their profits. If that expansion requires additional financial resources, then the subsidiary must provide them through other means, perhaps borrowing. . . . The local tax rate would not for the most part be any reason for changing the 50 percent distribution. The fact that the U.K. rate might be 48 to 50 percent, whereas the German rate might be 30 percent, for example, would not change the policy; we would expect 50 percent to come out of each location regardless of the local tax structure. . . . We never did wish our foreign operations to sit around with cash, either in their bank account or reinvested by them locally. We would much prefer that they send all of their cash accumulation not only to meet our requirements in the United States but also give us the resources to finance other operations that are in the development stage.

From the policy manual of the international division of a multinational corporation:

The overall dividend target is 60 percent of the total International Division profits after tax. This can be established as the goal for each individual subsidiary abroad. Where foreseeable financial requirements for retained earnings do not exist, higher payments will be expected . . . wherever financial requirements for capital investment programs cannot be met by internally generated funds and by local borrowing, the corporation management should be asked to give consideration to a temporary reduction of dividends.

About 20 percent of the companies studied followed the practice of using a target payout ratio as a guide to what the parent company wanted to receive from each of its wholly-owned affiliates. With the target as a starting point for analysis, the specific percentage to be paid out was based on the evaluation of those internal and environmental factors which the parent company considered to be critical. The variations in this approach are illustrated below with excerpts from interviews with two companies.

We start with 60 percent as a flexible, rule-of-thumb target for the foreign dividends. It's based on the 60 percent which the parent company tries to distribute to its own shareholders. For each subsidiary, we adjust this figure for the exchange risk, the subsidiary's cash position vis-à-vis its needs, the tax credit situation, the desire to make our dividends look regular to the host governments, and any restrictive covenants which may exist on the affiliate's long-term debt. The final payout could vary from 5 to 95 percent of earnings.

The parent company wants to get some dividend each year from all of its overseas subsidiaries. Therefore, it established a minimum distribution percentage—a level below which no dividend can go. The parent also

Exhibit 34-2

Characteristics	Groups			
	Policy 1 Adherents	Policy 2 Adherents	Sample of 30 Firms	Universe
Average number subsidiaries owned by each company	12	32	20	20
Length of experience in international business	57% Old 43% New	91% Old 9% New	77% Old 23% New	75% Old 25% New
Consolidation practices: do or do not	57% Do 43% Do Not	91% Do 9% Do Not	70% Do 30% Do Not	75% Do 25% Do Not
Earnings of foreign subsidiaries as percentage of total company net profits	15%	40%	25%	22%

established a 50 percent payout target, which is very flexible and is used as a guide. The actual payout is based on the working capital needs of the affiliates, their capital expansion plans, and the threat of devaluation. Last year [1965] for instance, we were afraid that there'd be a devaluation of the pound, so we increased the size of our dividend from the English subsidiary and also had it paid earlier than the usual date.

The majority of the companies in the sample (60 percent) pursued a .somewhat different practice. They started with the objective of having each subsidiary remit all excess funds in its possession. The exact amount was determined by a flexible approach; they evaluated all of those factors which they considered to be critical—excluding any target payout percentage —and made their decision entirely apart from what that subsidiary had paid the previous year, what other subsidiaries expected to declare in the current fiscal period, or what percentage of its earnings the parent company was distributing to its owners. This policy is illustrated below.

In general, we want to have subsidiaries remit as much as they can. We base our final decision on the amount on two factors: taxation and the subsidiary's cash position. First we calculate the tax effects of various levels of dividends from various subsidiaries, attempting to juggle remittances to get the best possible overall tax credit. Then we look at the subsidiaries' cash requirements and current position. (We want each subsidiary to have both equity and debt so that we can select the best forms of remittance from a worldwide tax point of view.) Based on its cash position and how remittances from that subsidiary would fit into the company-wide tax credit situation, we make our decision on its dividend distribution.

The Payout Practices of Particular Types of Companies

From the range of payout practices which was described above, it is useful for the purpose of analysis to categorize the practices into two main groups. One group—which will be called "payout policy 1"—is based on the desire of the parent companies to have all excess funds remitted from overseas, with the exact percentage of earnings distribution determined by an appraisal of whatever factors management considers critical for this decision. The decision itself is in no way constrained by the payout histories of the parent company or the foreign subsidiary, and in fact the amount of variability in the subsidiaries' dividend payouts has been demonstrated to exceed that for subsidiaries owned by companies following payout policy 2, which is described below.

The second policy is designed around a target payout ratio. The targets themselves were found to vary from as high as 100 percent of earnings to as low as 25 to 30 percent. They were used by some firms as a strict guide for dividend declarations and as a point of departure for others. In the majority of cases, however, the total amount of dividends remitted by overseas subsidiaries was reasonably close to the target which a company used.

The proportion of companies which followed payout policy 1 (e.g., the flexible approach) was slightly larger than those pursuing payout policy 2 (e.g., the target payout ratio): 54 percent to 46 percent of the total number. Using the four characteristics already discussed to provide a profile of the adherents to each of these policies, certain important conclusions may be deduced. For perspective, the profiles are compared with those of the sample and of the universe.[5]

The profiles of these two policy groups are distinctive in several important ways. The companies which adhered to payout policy 1 had, on the average, 40 percent fewer foreign subsidiaries than the sample or universe populations; foreign earnings which, as a percentage of total company profits, were only about seven tenths of the size of the average for the sample; and considerably less experience in international business than did any of the other reference groups. And fewer numbers of these firms consolidated foreign operating results, compared to the others.

At the other extreme, the companies which followed payout policy 2 had on the average significantly larger foreign earnings, as a percentage of total company profits, more international experience, and more numerous overseas subsidiaries than did the companies in the universe, the sample, or the group which adopted payout policy 1. These firms also consolidated foreign operating results in almost all cases (91 percent), whereas only 57 percent of the companies consolidated in the first group.

Relative to each other and to the averages for the universe, these two groups of companies represent the two general "types" of multinational companies which were identified and discussed earlier: one class of company which had an international posture and the other class which had considerably less involvement with international business. Considering

---

[5]The universe was composed of 160 United States companies which fit the description of "multinational" discussed earlier.

the findings of the preceding section of this article on factors which influence the foreign dividend decision, and the topic presently discussed, the payout practices of these companies, it is not surprising to find that the same companies which rely wholly on a current analysis of taxation, threat of devaluation, etc., are those that have adopted the policy with the highest amount of variability. And, similarly, one might expect that the firms which placed much weight on historical payout rates and proven standards of distribution would also be those which would gear their present distribution of foreign earnings to a target payout ratio.

CONCLUSIONS

The primary purpose of this article has been to describe financial practices of United States multinational companies. One of the general conclusions, however, is essentially normative in character: Transferring funds from foreign affiliates is an aspect of the international finance function which can and should be managed.

Compared to purely domestic operations, the financial planner for foreign operations may be expected to have less freedom of action in directing the financing and funds remittances of affiliates abroad. Exchange controls, niggardly treasury or tax authorities, tight credit conditions in a foreign economy, or the U.S. balance of payments restrictions may severely limit the choice of actions for the international headquarters. However, in 15 to 20 countries—mostly the so-called developed ones—these environmental restrictions are becoming more rare, and the way is open for decisive management of affiliates' affairs. And, even in the more cautious and suspicious less developed nations, many investors have begun to find that through careful planning it has been possible to manage at least a good portion of the international fund flows which emanate from them.

In a recent visit to a large internationally oriented consumer goods company, the writer was told by the vice president for international finance:

> It is impossible for us to *significantly* alter, from one period to the next, the amount of funds to be remitted by a foreign subsidiary in dividend or royalty form. The *change* itself would draw too much attention from the local tax authorities, and they would probably decide that the increased royalty would *not* be allowed as a tax deductible expense or that the dividend was "unjustifiably" large, and, therefore, our request for foreign exchange would be denied. . . . For U.S. tax credit purposes, it is in our best interests to increase the inflow of royalty and fee income from our foreign affiliates. Therefore, I am making plans now to *slowly* but *steadily* increase the amount remitted in these forms over the next four or five years. We are carefully *documenting* the amount and type of management service and industrial property rights which headquarters provides the affiliates, just in case a foreign government questions us on the increase in royalties and fees. By 1972 I expect that we will have the "right" mix of remittances coming in from our 47 overseas operations.

It is this type of planning and foresight in foreign remittance and financing matters that must be stressed. A company's policy on international funds transfer is one which readily lends itself to management review and redoing. Consider as examples: The taxation effects of a particular decision can be calculated and compared to alternative approaches. The key, of course, is to try to minimize the worldwide tax liability by including in the analysis the foreign tax rate, the United States rate, and the company's United States foreign tax credit position.

Accessibility to foreign-generated funds can be a key area. Could presently blocked funds be made more available to the rest of the company if different forms of remittance were attempted? Would not the local government feel more understanding toward a foreign exchange request which was based on the requirement to repay an intercompany loan or to compensate the parent company for the use of its industrial property rights?

Another critical question: How do present approaches to affiliate financing and fund remittances endanger or otherwise affect the acceptability of the foreign subsidiary vis-à-vis the local government or public opinion? In the medium or long term is the affiliate likely to be permitted to remit funds, or borrow funds, or even to continue to be foreign-owned, if its present policies are viewed as "subverting local monetary policies" or "drying up the foreign money markets" or "effecting a continual drain on the balance of payments"? Could management today alter the financing pattern and remittance mix in order to buy insurance for another 5- or 10-years' operations?

The list of potential areas for management review could be readily extended; however, a detailed discussion of this area is beyond the scope of the article. The important point is to recognize that management control of international funds deserves the same consideration as is provided domestic finance. Company-owned Swiss francs or pound sterling or Mexican pesos no longer deserve a second-class status. The treasurer or controller who subscribes to a thoughtful and creative approach to managing funds in the United States must recognize the opportunity and obligation to do so internationally.

ALPHABETICAL INDEX OF AUTHORS